Rick

ENGLAND

2011

England

LEGEND

══ A24 ══	Freeway/Motorway
────────	Major Rail Line
✈	Airport
♣	National Park/ Natural Wonder
■	Ruin, Museum, Other Point of Interest
⌂	Castle/Monument/Palace

0 km   50 km   100 km

0 miles   50 miles

Berwick-upon-Tweed
Holy Island
BAMBURGH CASTLE
Alnwick
Newcastle-upon-Tyne
BEAMISH MUSEUM • Durham
A1
Middlesbrough
Staithes
Grosmont
NORTH YORK MOORS • Whitby
Goathland
Robin Hood's Bay
YORKSHIRE DALES
RIEVAULX ABBEY
Thirsk • Hutton-le-Hole
CASTLE HOWARD • EDEN CAMP • Pickering
Scarborough
York
Bridlington
eeds
Doncaster
M62
Sheffield
M1
Kingston-upon-Hull
Grimsby

North Sea

G L A N D
MIDLANDS
Lincoln
Newark
Derby
Nottingham
M1
Leicester
Coventry
Warwick
Stratford
OLDS Moreton
Oxford
LENHEIM ALACE
Didcot
M40
Reading
Thames

Boston
The Wash
Skegness
Cromer
King's Lynn
Stamford
Peterborough
Northampton
Ely
Norwich
Great Yarmouth
EAST ANGLIA
Cambridge
Ipswich
Harwich
Colchester

To Esbjerg (Denmark)
To Amsterdam (Netherlands)
To Hoek van Holland (Netherlands)

M1
Luton
Hertford
Stansted
M11
London
City
Windsor
Heathrow
Greenwich
M3
Southend-on-Sea
Whitstable
Ramsgate
Winchester
Gatwick
M23
M20 M2
Canterbury
WHITE CLIFFS OF DOVER
Ostende Bruges
Southampton
Portsmouth
ARUNDEL
SIBSINGHURST GARDENS
Ashford
Folkestone
Dover
Channel Tunnel
Dunkerque
E40
KENT
Battle
Rye
Calais
BELGIUM
ewport
FISHBOURNE ROMAN PALACE
Brighton
Hastings
Pevensey
Isle of Wight
Newhaven
Alfriston
Beachy Head
Eastbourne
Boulogne
FRANCE
E17
Lille
E42

Channel

To Cherbourg (France)
To Ouistreham (France)
To Dieppe (France)
A16
To Paris
A26
To Paris
To Brussels

West London

To British Library

BLOOMSBURY

13 National Portrait Gallery
14 Natural History & Science Museums
15 Piccadilly Circus
16 Royal Albert Hall
17 Royal Mews
18 Speakers' Corner
19 St. Martin-in-the-Fields
20 Tate Britain
21 Trafalgar Square
22 Victoria & Albert Mus.
23 Westminster Abbey
24 Britain & London Visitors Centre

BRITISH MUSEUM

CARTOON MUSEUM

Tottenham Court Road

NEW OXFORD ST.
HIGH HOLBORN

Bond Street
OXFORD ST.
Oxford Circus

HANOVER SQUARE

SOHO

ST. GILES
DENMARK ST.

Soho Square

CHINATOWN

Leicester Square

COVENT GARDEN

SOTHEBY'S AUCTION HOUSE

Berkeley Square

PICCADILLY CIRCUS
Piccadilly Circus

Leicester Square

NATIONAL GALLERY

ROYAL ACADEMY OF ARTS

MAYFAIR

PICCADILLY
ST. JAMES

Trafalgar Square

FORTNUM & MASON

Charing Cross Station

Green Park

RITZ HOTEL

ST. JAMES'S SQUARE

CHRISTIE'S

ADMIRALTY ARCH

NORTHUMBERLAND

CHARLES ST.
CURZON ST.

Green Park

ST. JAMES'S PALACE

THE MALL

St. James's Park

HORSE GUARDS PARADE

HORSEGUARDS

PICCADILLY

CONSTITUTION HILL

QUEEN VICTORIA MEMORIAL

DOWNING ST.

KING CHARLES ST.

Westminster

BUCKINGHAM PALACE

Buckingham Palace Gardens (private)

WELLINGTON BARRACKS

BIRDCAGE WALK

GREAT GEORGE ST.
BRIDGE ST.
BIG BEN

Parliament Square

St. James's Park

ST. MARGARET'S

HOUSES OF PARLIAMENT

ROYAL MEWS

PETTY FRANCE

WESTMINSTER ABBEY

JEWEL TOWER

WESTMINSTER

Dean's Yard

GREAT PETER ST.

Smith Square

ST. JOHN'S

WESTMINSTER CATHEDRAL

Victoria Station

Westminster School Playing Fields

HORSEFERRY RD.

PAGE ST.

VINCENT ST.

Victoria Coach Station

To Gatwick Airport

PIMLICO

Eccleston Square

Warwick Square

WARWICK WAY

TATE BRITAIN

MILLBANK PIER

LAMBETH BRIDGE

Thames River

East London

Barbican ⊖
BEECH ST.
CHISWELL ST.
SUN ST.
BANGLATOWN
SPITALFIELDS MARKET
LONG LN.
ALDERSGATE
SILK ST.
BARBICAN CENTRE
MOOR LN.
MOORGATE
ELDON ST.
BRUSHFIELD
COMMERCIAL ST.
BRICK LN.
BARBICAN
MUSEUM OF LONDON
20
MOORFIELDS
FINSBURY CIRCUS
Liverpool Street Station
EAST END
Moorgate ⊖
LONDON WALL
LIVERPOOL ST.
Liverpool St. ⊖
MIDDLESEX ST.
WENTWORTH ST.
Aldgate East ⊖
ANGEL ST.
WOOD ST.
GRESHAM ST.
LONDON WALL
PETTICOAT LANE MARKET
CUTLER ST.
HOUNDSDITCH
GOULSTONE ST.
ABRAHAM ST.
WHITECHAPEL RD.
St. Paul's ⊖
ST. PAUL'S ⊕
28
THE CITY
CHEAPSIDE
NEW CHANGE
ST. MARY-LE-BOW
BANK OF ENGLAND
OLD BROAD ST.
TOWER 42
BISHOPSGATE
ST. MARY AXE
DUKE ST.
30 ST. MARY AXE (THE GHERKIN)
Aldgate ⊖
ALIE ST.
WHITE-CHAPEL
PETER'S HILL
WATLING ST.
THREADNEEDLE ST.
Bank ⊖
CORNHILL
LEADENHALL ST.
MINORIES
MANSELL ST.
VICTORIA ST.
THAMES ST.
18
MILLENNIUM BRIDGE
KING WILLIAM ST.
LOMBARD ST.
GRACECHURCH ST.
FENCHURCH ST.
LLOYD'S OF LONDON
14
LEADENHALL MARKET
JEWRY ST.
COOPERS ROW
Mansion House ⊖
CANNON ST.
MANSION HOUSE
Tower Hill ⊖
Tower Hill
BANKSIDE PIER
SOUTHWARK BRIDGE
Cannon Street Station
Monument ⊖
THE MONUMENT
19
LOWER THAMES ST.
BYWARD ST.
TOWER HILL
ALL HALLOWS
TOWER OF LONDON
32
ST. KATHARINE DOCK
TATE MODERN
29
SHAKESPEARE'S GLOBE
24
PARK ST.
34
8
4
LONDON BRIDGE
LONDON BRIDGE PIER
TOOLEY ST.
TOWER PIER
TOWER OF LONDON
ST. KATHARINE'S PIER
BANKSIDE
SUMNER ST.
26
9
HMS BELFAST
TOWER BRIDGE
31
SOUTHWARK ST.
London Bridge ⊖
London Bridge Station
BATTLE BRIDGE LN.
THE SCOOP
CITY HALL
3
UNION ST.
1
BOROUGH MARKET
22
OLD OPERATING THEATRE MUSEUM
ST. THOMAS ST.
33
TOOLEY ST.
SOUTHWARK
BOROUGH HIGH ST.
NEWCOMEN ST.
SNOWSFIELDS
BERMONDSEY
MARSHALSEA RD.
REDCROSS WAY
Borough ⊖
Borough
TABARD ST.
GREAT DOVER ST.
SOUTHWARK BRIDGE RD.
TRINITY ST.
RD.
HARPER RD.
NEW KENT RD.
HEYGATE ST.
RODNEY RD.
WALWORTH RD.
BROWNING ST.

SIGHTS

1. Borough Market
2. BFI Southbank (Cinema)
3. City Hall
4. The Clink Prison Museum
5. Courtauld Gallery
6. Covent Garden
7. To Geffrye Museum
8. Golden Hinde Replica
9. HMS Belfast
10. Houses of Parliament & Big Ben
11. Imperial War Museum
12. The Inns of Court
13. Jubilee Walkway
14. Leadenhall Market
15. London Duck Tours
16. London Eye
17. London Transport Museum
18. Millennium Bridge
19. The Monument
20. Museum of London
21. Old Bailey
22. Old Operating Theatre Museum & Herb Garret
23. Royal Courts of Justice
24. Shakespeare's Globe
25. Sir John Soane's Museum
26. Southwark Cathedral
27. St. Bride's Church
28. St. Paul's Cathedral
29. Tate Modern
30. Temple Church
31. Tower Bridge
32. Tower of London
33. Unicorn Theatre (for kids)
34. Vinopolis: City of Wine

Rick Steves'

ENGLAND

2011

AVALON
TRAVEL

CONTENTS

Top Destinations in England

INTRODUCTION

From the grandeur and bustle of London, to a pastoral countryside that inspired Shakespeare, to some of the quaintest towns you'll ever experience, England delights. Stand in a desolate field and ponder an ancient stone circle. Strike up a conversation just to hear the Queen's English. Bite into a scone smothered with clotted cream, sip a cup of tea, and wave your pinky as if it's a Union Jack.

This book breaks England into its top big-city, small-town, and rural destinations. It gives you all the information and opinions necessary to wring the maximum value out of your limited time and money in each of these locations.

Note that this book covers only England, which occupies the southern two-thirds of the island of Great Britain. If you want to visit Wales and Scotland too, pick up a copy of *Rick Steves' Great Britain* instead.

Experiencing English culture, people, and natural wonders economically and hassle-free has been my goal for more than three decades of traveling, tour guiding, and travel writing. With this new edition, I pass on to you the lessons I've learned, updated for your trip in 2011.

While including the predictable biggies (such as Big Ben, Stratford-upon-Avon, and Stonehenge), the book also mixes in a healthy dose of Back Door intimacy (windswept Roman lookouts, angelic boys' choirs, and nearly edible Cotswold villages). This book is selective. For example, there are plenty of great countryside palaces; I recommend just the best—Blenheim.

The best is, of course, only my opinion. But after spending half my adult life researching Europe, I've developed a sixth sense for what travelers enjoy. The places featured in this book will knock your spots off.

About This Book

Rick Steves' England 2011 is a personal tour guide in your pocket. The book is organized by destination. Each destination is a mini-vacation on its own, filled with exciting sights, strollable neighborhoods, homey and affordable places to stay, and memorable places to eat. In the following chapters, you'll find these sections:

Planning Your Time suggests a schedule with thoughts on how best to use your limited time.

Orientation includes specifics on public transportation, helpful hints, local tour options, easy-to-read maps, and tourist information.

Sights describes the top attractions and includes their cost and hours.

Self-Guided Walks take you through interesting neighborhoods, with a personal tour guide in hand.

Sleeping describes my favorite hotels, from good-value deals to cushy splurges.

Eating serves up a range of options, from inexpensive pubs to fancy restaurants.

Connections outlines your options for traveling to destinations by train, bus, and plane, plus route tips for drivers.

British History and Culture is a quick overview of Britain, past and present.

The **appendix** is a traveler's tool kit, with telephone tips, useful phone numbers, transportation basics (on trains, buses, car rentals, driving, and flights), recommended books and films, a festival list, climate chart, handy packing checklist, a hotel reservation form, and a fun British–Yankee dictionary.

Browse through this book and select your favorite sights. Then have a brilliant trip! Traveling like a temporary local, you'll get the absolute most out of every mile, minute, and dollar. I'm happy that you'll be visiting places I know and love, and meeting my favorite English people.

Planning

This section will help you get started on planning your trip—with advice on trip costs, when to go, and what you should know before you take off.

Travel Smart

Your trip to England is like a complex play—easier to follow and to really appreciate on a second viewing. While no one does the same trip twice to gain that advantage, reading this book in its entirety before your trip accomplishes much the same thing.

Design an itinerary that enables you to visit sights at the best

Key to This Book

Updates

This book is updated every year, but things change. For the latest, visit www.ricksteves.com/update, and for a valuable list of reports and experiences—good and bad—from fellow travelers, check www.ricksteves.com/feedback.

Abbreviations and Times

I use the following symbols and abbreviations in this book:
Sights are rated:

▲▲▲	**Don't miss**
▲▲	**Try hard to see**
▲	**Worthwhile if you can make it**
No rating	**Worth knowing about**

Tourist information offices are abbreviated as **TI,** and bathrooms are **WC**s. To categorize accommodations, I use a **Sleep Code** (described on page 23).

Like England, this book uses the **24-hour clock** for schedules. It's the same through 12:00 noon, then keep going: 13:00, 14:00, and so on. For anything over 12, subtract 12 and add p.m. (14:00 is 2:00 p.m.).

When giving **opening times,** I include both peak season and off-season hours if they differ. So, if a museum is listed as "May–Oct daily 9:00–16:00," it should be open from 9 a.m. until 4 p.m. from the first day of May until the last day of October (but expect exceptions).

For **transit** or **tour departures,** I first list the frequency, then the duration. So, a train connection listed as "2/hour, 1.5 hours" departs twice each hour, and the journey lasts an hour and a half.

possible times. Note holidays, specifics on sights, and days when sights are closed. If you're using public transportation, read up on the tips for trains and buses (see pages 696 and 703 of the appendix). If you're renting a car, study my driving tips and the examples of road signs (see page 706).

Mix intense and relaxed periods in your itinerary. To maximize rootedness, minimize one-night stands. It's worth a long drive after dinner to be settled into a town for two nights. B&Bs are also more likely to give a better price to someone staying more than one night. Every trip (and every traveler) needs at least a few slack days (for picnics, laundry, people-watching, and so on). Pace yourself. Assume you will return.

Reread this book as you travel, and visit local TIs. Upon arrival in a new town, lay the groundwork for a smooth departure; write down (or print out from an online source) the schedule for the train or bus that you'll take when you depart. Drivers can study

England at a Glance

▲▲▲**London** Thriving metropolis packed with world-class museums, monuments, churches, parks, palaces, theaters, pubs, Beefeaters, telephone boxes, double-decker buses, and all things British.

▲▲**Greenwich, Windsor, and Cambridge** Easy side-trips from London: famous observatory at the maritime center of Greenwich, the Queen's palace at Windsor, and England's best university town, Cambridge.

▲**Canterbury** Pleasant pilgrimage town with England's top church.

▲**Dover and Southeast England** The imposing Dover Castle, famous White Cliffs, lush Sissinghurst Gardens, hill town of Rye, and historic site of the Battle of Hastings.

▲**Brighton** Flamboyant beach resort on England's south coast, near the rolling hills of South Downs Way and the chalky cliffs at Beachy Head.

▲**Portsmouth** Newly rejuvenated shipbuilding city with top nautical sights at the Historic Dockyard, plus Roman ruins and stately Arundel Castle nearby.

▲**Dartmoor** Mysterious, desolate, moor-cloaked national park with wild ponies, hiking paths, and an ancient stone circle.

▲**Cornwall** Feisty peninsula littered with prehistoric ruins, plus the seaside resort towns of Penzance and St. Ives, King Arthur's supposed Tintagel Castle, the tip of England at Land's End, and other offbeat sights.

▲▲▲**Bath** Genteel Georgian showcase city, built around the remains of an ancient Roman bath.

▲▲**Near Bath** England's mysterious heart, including the prehistoric-meets–New Age hill at Glastonbury, spine-tingling stone circles at Stonehenge and Avebury, enjoyable cathedral towns of

Wells and Salisbury, and delightful Dorset countryside.

▲**Oxford** Stately university town with Blenheim Palace—one of England's best—on its doorstep.

▲▲**The Cotswolds** Remarkably quaint villages—including the cozy market town Chipping Campden, popular hamlet Stow-on-the-Wold, and handy transit hub Moreton-in-Marsh—scattered over a hilly countryside.

▲**Stratford-upon-Avon** Shakespeare's hometown and top venue for seeing his plays performed, plus the medieval Warwick Castle and Coventry's inspiring cathedral nearby.

▲**Ironbridge Gorge** Birthplace of the Industrial Revolution, with sights and museums that tell the earth-changing story.

▲**Blackpool and Liverpool** England's tackiest, most fun-loving beach resort at Blackpool, and the increasingly rejuvenated port city (and Beatles hometown) of Liverpool.

▲▲**The Lake District** Idyllic lakes-and-hills landscape, with enjoyable hikes and joyrides, time-passed valleys, William Wordsworth and Beatrix Potter sights, and the charming home-base town of Keswick.

▲▲▲**York** Walled medieval town with grand Gothic cathedral, excellent museums (Viking, Victorian, Railway), and atmospheric old center.

▲**North Yorkshire** Smattering of ruined abbeys, desolate moors, seaside towns (including bustling Whitby and tiny Staithes), and other sights near York.

▲**Durham and Northeast England** Youthful working-class town with magnificent cathedral, plus (nearby) an open-air museum, the Roman remains of Hadrian's Wall, Holy Island, and Bamburgh Castle.

the best route to their next destination.

Get online at Internet cafés or at your hotel, and buy a phone card or carry a mobile phone: You can get tourist information, learn the latest on sights (special events, tour schedules, etc.), book tickets and tours, make reservations, reconfirm hotels, research transportation connections, check weather, and keep in touch with your loved ones.

Connect with the culture. Set up your own quest for the best pub, cathedral, or chocolate bar. Be open to unexpected experiences. Slow down and enjoy the friendliness of your English hosts. You speak the language—use it! Ask questions; most locals are eager to point you in their idea of the right direction. Keep a notepad in your pocket for organizing your thoughts. Wear your money belt, and figure out how to estimate prices in dollars. Those who expect to travel smart, do.

Trip Costs

Five components make up your trip costs: airfare, surface transportation, room and board, sightseeing and entertainment, and shopping and miscellany. Note that the global economic crisis—and the UK's own budget woes—have prompted the government to increase the VAT (Value-Added Tax, like a national sales tax) from 17.5 percent to 20 percent, effective January 1, 2011. Because prices already include VAT, don't be surprised if things cost more than what I've listed in this book.

Airfare: A basic round-trip US-to-London flight costs $700–1,200, depending on where you fly from and when (cheaper in winter). If your trip extends beyond England, consider saving time and money by flying "open jaw" (into one city and out of another; for instance, into London and out of Amsterdam).

Surface Transportation: For a three-week whirlwind trip of all my recommended English destinations, allow $550 per person for public transportation (train pass, key buses, and Tube fare in London) or $900 per person (based on two people sharing) for a three-week car rental, parking, gas, and insurance. Leasing is worth considering for trips of two and a half weeks or more. Car rental and leases are cheapest when arranged from the US. Train passes are normally available only outside of Europe (although you can buy a bus pass in England). You may save money by simply buying tickets as you go. For more on public transportation and car rental, see "Transportation" in the appendix.

Room and Board: You can thrive in England on $115 per day per person for room and board (less in villages). A $115-per-day budget allows an average of $15 for lunch, $30 for dinner, $5 for snacks, and $65 for lodging (based on two people splitting a $130 double room that includes breakfast). Students and tightwads can do it on $60 ($35 for hostel bed, $25 for groceries).

Sightseeing and Entertainment: Figure on paying roughly $10–30 apiece for the major sights that charge admission (Stonehenge-$11, Shakespeare's Birthplace in Stratford-$20, Westminster Abbey-$24, Tower of London-$27), $7 for minor ones (climbing church towers), $12 for guided walks, and $20–40 for bus tours and splurge experiences. For information on various sightseeing passes, see page 20.

Fortunately, many of the best sights in London are free, including the British Museum, National Gallery, National Portrait Gallery, Tate Britain, Tate Modern, Victoria & Albert Museum, and the British Library (though most request donations). An overall average of $30 a day works in most cities (allow $50 for London). Don't skimp here. After all, this category is the driving force behind your trip—you came to sightsee, enjoy, and experience England.

Shopping and Miscellany: Figure roughly $2 per postcard, $3 for tea or an ice-cream cone, and $5 per pint of beer. Shopping can vary in cost from nearly nothing to a small fortune. Good budget travelers find that this category has little to do with assembling a trip full of lifelong and wonderful memories.

Sightseeing Priorities

Depending on the length of your trip, and taking geographic proximity into account, here are my recommended priorities.

3 days:	London
5 days, add:	Bath and nearby sights (take a minibus tour or choose some combination of Stonehenge, Avebury, Wells, Glastonbury, and Salisbury)
7 days, add:	Cotswolds
9 days, add:	York
11 days, add:	Lake District
14 days, add:	Durham, Stratford, Warwick
17 days, add:	Ironbridge Gorge, Blackpool
21 days, add:	Cornwall, Dartmoor
24 days, add:	Choose two of the following—Cambridge, Oxford, Portsmouth, Brighton, Canterbury, and Dover

This list includes virtually everything on "England's Best Three-Week Trip by Car" itinerary and map (see next page).

Your itinerary will depend on your interests. Nature-lovers will likely put the lovely Lake District and the more remote Dartmoor nearer the top of their list, while engineers are drawn like a magnet to Ironbridge Gorge. Coastal Blackpool offers amusement-park fun, refreshing for families and those who've had enough of

England's Best Three-Week Trip by Car

Day	Plan	Sleep in
1	Arrive in London, bus to Bath	Bath
2	Bath	Bath
3	Pick up car, Avebury, Wells, Glastonbury	Bath
4	Early drive to Cornwall	Penzance
5	Cornwall	Penzance
6	Dartmoor	Salisbury
7	Salisbury, Portsmouth	Salisbury
8	Oxford, Blenheim	Chipping Campden
9	Explore the Cotswolds	Chipping Campden
10	Stratford, Warwick, Coventry	Ironbridge Gorge
11	Ironbridge Gorge	Blackpool
12	Liverpool, Blackpool	Blackpool
13	South Lake District	Keswick area
14	North Lake District	Keswick area
15	Hadrian's Wall and Durham, to York, turn in car	York
16	York	York
17	Early train to London	London
18	London	London
19	London	London
20	Canterbury, Dover	London
21	Greenwich, Windsor, Cambridge, Brighton (choose one)	London
22	Whew!	

While this three-week itinerary is designed to be done by car, it can be done by train and bus or, better yet, with a BritRail & Drive Pass (best car days: Cornwall/Dartmoor, Cotswolds, and Lake District); for more on the pass, see page 700. For three weeks without a car, I'd cut back on the recommended sights with the

museums. Literary fans like Cambridge, Oxford, Stratford, Bath, and the South Lake District.

When to Go

In England, July and August are peak season—my favorite time—with very long days, the best weather, and the busiest schedule of tourist fun.

Prices and crowds don't go up during peak times as dramatically in England as they do in much of Europe, except for holidays and festivals (see "Holidays and Weekends" sidebar, later). Still, travel during "shoulder season" (May, early June, Sept, and early most frustrating public transportation (Cornwall, Dartmoor, and Ironbridge Gorge). Lacing together the cities by train is very slick, and buses get you where the trains don't go. With more time, everything is workable without a car.

Oct) is easier and can be a bit less expensive. Shoulder-season travelers usually enjoy smaller crowds, decent weather, the full range of sights and tourist fun spots, and the ability to grab a room almost whenever and wherever they like—often at a flexible price. Winter travelers find absolutely no crowds and soft room prices, but shorter sightseeing hours and reliably bad weather. Some attractions are open only on weekends or are closed entirely in the winter (Nov–Feb). The weather can be cold and dreary, and nightfall draws the shades on sightseeing well before dinnertime. While rural charm falls with the leaves, city sightseeing is fine in the winter.

Plan for rain no matter when you go. Just keep traveling and take full advantage of bright spells. The weather can change several times in a day, but rarely is it extreme. As the locals say, "There is no bad weather, only inappropriate clothing." Bring a jacket and dress in layers. Temperatures below 32°F cause headlines, and days that break 80°F—while increasingly frequent in recent years—are still rare in England. July and August are not much better than shoulder months. May and June can be lovely anywhere in England. (For more information, see the climate chart in the appendix.) While sunshine may be rare, summer days are very long. The midsummer sun is up from 6:30 until 22:30. It's not uncommon to have a gray day, eat dinner, and enjoy hours of sunshine afterward.

Know Before You Go

Your trip is more likely to go smoothly if you plan ahead. Check this list of things to arrange while you're still at home.

You need a **passport**—but no visa or shots—to travel in Great Britain. You may be denied entry into certain European countries if your passport is due to expire within three to six months of your ticketed date of return. Get it renewed if you'll be cutting it close. It can take up to six weeks to get or renew a passport (for more on passports, see www.travel.state.gov). Pack a photocopy of your passport in your luggage in case the original is lost or stolen.

Book rooms well in advance if you'll be traveling during peak season and any major **holidays.**

Most people fly into London and remain there for a few days. Instead, consider a gentler **small-town start** in Bath (the ideal jet-lag pillow), and let London be the finale at the end of your trip. You'll be more rested and ready to tackle England's greatest city. Heathrow Airport has direct bus connections to Bath and other cities. (Bristol Airport is also near Bath.)

If you'll be in London or Stratford and want to **see a play,** check theater schedules ahead of time. For simplicity, I book plays while in England, but if there's something you just have to see, consider buying tickets before you go. For the current schedule of London plays and musicals, visit www.officiallondontheatre.co.uk. Because Stratford's main theater recently reopened after a long renovation, tickets to Shakespeare performances there are likely to sell out even earlier than usual (see www.rsc.org.uk for details). Note that if it's just Shakespeare you're after—with or without Stratford—you can see his plays in London, too.

At **Stonehenge,** anyone can see the stones from behind the rope line, but if you want to go inside the stone circle, you'll need advance reservations (see page 404).

Call your **debit- and credit-card companies** to let them know

Holidays and Weekends

Popular places are even busier on weekends—especially sunny weekends, which are sufficient cause for an impromptu holiday in this soggy corner of Europe. Three-day weekends can make towns, trains, buses, roads, and hotels even more crowded. Book your accommodations well in advance if you'll be traveling during busy times.

A few national holidays jam things up, especially Bank Holiday Mondays. Mark these dates in red on your travel calendar: New Year's Day, Good Friday through Easter Monday (April 22–25 in 2011), the Bank Holidays that occur on the first and last Mondays in May (May 2 and 30 in 2011) and the last Monday in August (Aug 29), Christmas, and December 26 (Boxing Day). For more information, check the list of holidays and festivals on page 717.

Many businesses, as well as many museums, close on Good Friday, Easter, and New Year's Day. On Christmas, virtually everything closes down, even the Tube in London (taxi rates are high). Museums are also generally closed December 24 and 26; smaller shops are usually closed December 26.

the countries you'll be visiting, to ask about fees, and more (see page 15).

Do your homework if you want to buy **travel insurance.** Compare the cost of the insurance to the likelihood of your using it and your potential loss if something goes wrong. For more information, see www.ricksteves.com/audioeurope.

If you're bringing an MP3 player, you can download free information from **Rick Steves Audio Europe,** featuring hours of travel interviews on Great Britain, audio tours of major sights in London, and more (at www.ricksteves.com and on iTunes; for details, see page 713).

If you're planning on **renting a car** in Great Britain, you'll need your driver's license. An International Driving Permit is recommended (see page 704).

If traveling to continental Europe on the **Eurostar** train, consider ordering a ticket in advance (or buy it in Britain); for details, see page 191.

Because **airline carry-on restrictions** are always changing, visit the Transportation Security Administration's website (www.tsa.gov/travelers) for an up-to-date list of what you can bring on the plane with you...and what you have to check. Some airlines may restrict you to only one carry-on (no extras like a purse or daypack); check with your airline or at the British transportation website (www.dft.gov.uk).

INTRODUCTION

Practicalities

Emergency and Medical Help: Dial 999 for police or medical emergencies. If you get sick, do as the Brits do and go to a pharmacist for advice. Or ask at your B&B or hotel for help—they'll know the nearest medical and emergency services.

Lost or Stolen Passport: To replace a passport, you'll need to go in person to a US embassy or consulate (see page 693). While not required, having a backup form of ID—ideally a photocopy of your passport and driver's license—speeds up a replacement. For more info, see www.ricksteves.com/help.

Time Zones: Britain is one hour earlier than most of continental Europe and five/eight hours ahead of the East/West coasts of the US. The exceptions are the beginning and end of Daylight Saving Time: Britain and Europe "spring forward" the last Sunday in March (two weeks after most of North America), and "fall back" the last Sunday in October (one week before North America). For a handy online time converter, try www.timeanddate.com/world clock.

Business Hours: In England, most stores are open Monday through Saturday from roughly 10:00 to 17:00. In London, stores stay open later on Wednesday or Thursday (until 19:00 or 20:00), depending on the neighborhood. Sundays have the same pros and cons as they do for travelers in the US (special events, limited hours, banks and many shops closed, limited public transportation, no rush hours, street markets lively with shoppers). Saturdays are virtually weekdays with earlier closing hours and no rush hour (though transportation connections can be less frequent than on weekdays).

Watt's Up? Britain's electrical system is different from North America's in two ways: the shape of the plug (three square prongs—not the two round prongs used in continental Europe) and the voltage of the current (220 volts instead of 110 volts). For your North American plug to work in Britain, you'll need a three-prong adapter plug, sold inexpensively at travel stores in the US, and in British airports and drugstores. As for the voltage, most newer electronics or travel appliances (such as hair dryers, laptops, and battery chargers) automatically convert the voltage—if you see a range of voltages printed on the item or its plug (such as "110–220"), it'll work in Great Britain and Europe. Otherwise, you can buy a converter separately in the US (about $20), though these tend to be heavy and unreliable, and get really hot when in use. For small appliances that don't automatically convert voltage, I suggest going without or buying a cheap replacement in England. Low-cost hairdryers and other small appliances are sold at Superdrug, Boots, or Argos stores (ask your hotelier for the closest branch).

Discounts: Discounts (called "concessions" or "concs" in Britain) aren't listed in this book. However, many English sights offer discounts for seniors (loosely defined as those who are retired or willing to call themselves a senior), youths (ages 8–18), groups of 10 or more, families, and students or teachers with proper identification cards (www.isic.org). Always ask. Some discounts are available only for EU citizens.

News: British papers cover global events, and Americans can also keep in touch via the *International Herald Tribune* (published almost daily throughout Europe and online at www.iht .com). Other newsy sites are http://news.bbc.co.uk and www .europeantimes.com. Every Tuesday, the European editions of *Time* and *Newsweek* hit the stands with articles of particular interest to travelers in Europe. Sports addicts can get their daily fix online at www.espn.com or from *USA Today*. Many hotels have BBC News (of course) and CNN television channels.

Money

This section offers advice on how to pay for purchases on your trip (including getting cash from ATMs and paying with plastic), dealing with lost or stolen cards, VAT (sales tax) refunds, and tipping.

What to Bring

Bring both a credit card and a debit card. You'll use the debit card at cash machines (ATMs) to withdraw pounds for most purchases, and the credit card to pay for larger items. Some travelers carry a third card as a backup, in case one gets demagnetized or eaten by a temperamental machine.

As an emergency backup, bring several hundred dollars in hard cash (in easy-to-exchange $20 bills). Avoid using currency exchange booths (lousy rates and/or outrageous fees); if you have foreign currency to exchange, take it to a bank. Don't use traveler's checks—they're a waste of time (long waits at slow banks) and a waste of money in fees.

Cash

Cash is just as desirable in Britain as it is at home. Small businesses (hotels, restaurants, and shops) prefer that you pay your bills with cash. Some vendors will charge you extra for using a credit card, and some won't take credit cards at all.

Throughout Britain, ATMs (which locals call "cashpoints")

Exchange Rate

I list prices in pounds (£) throughout this book.

1 British pound (£1) = about $1.60

While the euro (€) is now the currency of most of Europe, Britain is sticking with its pound sterling. The British pound (£), also called a "quid," is broken into 100 pence (p). Pence means "cents." You'll find coins ranging from 1p to £2, and bills from £5 to £50. Counterfeit pound coins are easy to spot (real coins have an inscription on their outside rims; the fakes look like tree bark).

London is so expensive that some travelers try to kid themselves that pounds are dollars. But when they get home, that £1,000 Visa bill isn't asking for $1,000...it wants $1,600. (To get the latest rate and print a cheat sheet, see www .oanda.com.)

---

are the standard way for travelers to get cash. To withdraw money from an ATM, you'll need a debit card (ideally with a Visa or MasterCard logo for maximum usability), plus a PIN code. Know your PIN code in numbers because there are no letters on European keypads. You could use a credit card for ATM transactions, but it's generally more expensive (since it's considered a "cash advance" rather than a "withdrawal"). For security, it's best to shield the keypad when entering your PIN at the ATM.

When using an ATM, taking out large sums of money can reduce the number of per-transaction bank fees you'll pay. If the machine refuses your request, try again and select a smaller amount (some cash machines limit the amount you can withdraw—don't take it personally). If that doesn't work, try a different machine.

Most ATMs in Britain are located outside of a bank. Try to use the ATM when the branch is open; if your card is eaten by a machine, you can immediately go inside for help. If the ATM dispenses big bills, try to break them at a bank or larger store, since it's easier to pay for purchases at small businesses using smaller bills.

Even in jolly olde England, you'll need to keep your cash safe. Use a money belt—a pouch with a strap that you buckle around your waist like a belt and wear under your clothes. Pickpockets target tourists. A money belt provides peace of mind, allowing you to carry lots of cash safely. Don't waste time every few days tracking down a cash machine—withdraw a week's worth of money, stuff it in your money belt, and travel!

Credit and Debit Cards

Visa and MasterCard are more commonly accepted than American Express. While you can use either a credit or a debit card for most transactions, using a credit card offers a greater degree of fraud protection (since debit cards draw funds directly from your account).

Just like at home, credit and debit cards are accepted by larger hotels, restaurants, and shops. I typically use my debit card for withdrawing cash from ATMs, and I use my credit card only in a few specific situations: to book hotel reservations by phone, to make major purchases (such as car rentals, plane tickets, and long hotel stays), and to pay for things near the end of my trip (to avoid another visit to the ATM).

Ask Your Credit- or Debit-Card Company: Before your trip, contact the company that issued your debit or credit cards.

• Confirm your card will work overseas, and alert them that you'll be using it in Europe; otherwise, they may deny transactions if they perceive unusual spending patterns.

• Ask for the specifics on transaction **fees.** When you use your credit or debit card—either for purchases or ATM withdrawals—you'll often be charged additional "international transaction" fees of up to 3 percent (1 percent is normal) plus $5 per transaction. If your fees are too high, consider getting a card just for your trip: Capital One (www.capitalone.com) and most credit unions have low-to-no international fees.

• If you plan to withdraw cash from ATMs, confirm your daily **withdrawal limit** (£300 is usually about the maximum). Some travelers prefer a high limit that allows them to take out more cash at each ATM stop, while others prefer to set a lower limit in case their card is stolen.

• Ask for your credit card's **PIN** in case you encounter Europe's chip-and-PIN system. For security reasons, most banks will only mail a PIN, so give yourself plenty of time to get the code if you don't already know it.

Chip and PIN: If your card is declined for a purchase in Europe, it may be because of chip and PIN, which requires cardholders to punch in a PIN instead of signing a receipt. Much of Europe, including Great Britain, Ireland, France, the Netherlands, and Scandinavia, is adopting this system. Chip and PIN is used by some merchants and also at automated payment machines—such as those at train stations, parking garages, luggage lockers, and self-serve pumps at gas stations. If you're prompted to enter your PIN (but don't know it), ask if the cashier can print a receipt for you to sign instead, or just pay cash. If you're dealing with an automated machine that won't take your card, look for a cashier nearby who can make your card work. The easiest solution is to carry sufficient cash.

INTRODUCTION

Dynamic Currency Conversion: If merchants offer to convert your purchase price into dollars (called dynamic currency conversion, or DCC), refuse this "service." You'll pay even more in fees for the expensive convenience of seeing your charge in dollars.

Damage Control for Lost Cards

If you lose your credit, debit, or ATM card, you can stop people from using it by reporting the loss immediately to the respective global customer-assistance centers. Call these 24-hour US numbers collect: Visa (410/581-9994), MasterCard (636/722-7111), and American Express (623/492-8427). Diner's Club has offices in Britain (0870-1900-011) and the US (702/797-5532, call collect).

At a minimum, you'll need to know the name of the financial institution that issued you the card, along with the type of card (classic, platinum, or whatever). Providing the following information will allow for a quicker cancellation of your missing card: full card number, whether you are the primary or secondary cardholder, the name exactly as printed on the card, billing address, home phone number, circumstances of the loss or theft, and identification verification (your birth date, your mother's maiden name, or your Social Security number—memorize this, don't carry a copy). If you are the secondary cardholder, you'll also need to provide the primary cardholder's identification-verification details. You can generally receive a temporary card within two or three business days.

If you promptly report your card lost or stolen, you typically won't be responsible for any unauthorized transactions on your account, although many banks charge a liability fee of $50.

Tipping

Tipping in Britain isn't as automatic and generous as it is in the US, but for special service, tips are appreciated, if not expected. As in the US, the proper amount depends on your resources, tipping philosophy, and the circumstances, but some general guidelines apply.

Restaurants: At a pub or restaurant with waitstaff, check the menu or your bill to see if the service is included; if not, tip about 10 percent. Many restaurants in London now add a 12 percent "optional" tip onto the bill—read your bill carefully, and tip only what you think the service warrants. At pubs where you order at the counter, you don't have to tip. (Regular customers ordering a round sometimes say, "Add one for yourself" as a tip for drinks ordered at the bar—but this isn't expected.)

Taxis: To tip the cabbie, round up. For a typical ride, round up to a maximum of 10 percent (to pay a £4.50 fare, give £5; for a £28 fare, give £30). If the cabbie hauls your bags and zips you to the airport to help you catch your flight, you might want to toss in a little more. But if you feel like you're being driven in circles or otherwise ripped off, skip the tip.

Special Services: Tour guides at public sights sometimes hold out their hands for tips after they give their spiel. If I've already paid for the tour, I don't tip extra unless they've really impressed me. At hotels, if you let porters carry your luggage, it's polite to give them 50p for each bag (another reason to pack light). I don't tip the maid, but if you do, you can leave 50p per overnight at the end of your stay.

In general, if someone in the service industry does a super job for you, a small tip of a pound or two is appropriate, but not required.

When in doubt, ask. If you're not sure whether (or how much) to tip for a service, ask your hotelier or the TI; they'll fill you in on how it's done on their turf.

Getting a VAT Refund

Wrapped into the purchase price of your British souvenirs is a Value-Added Tax (VAT) of 20 percent (as of January 1, 2011). If you purchase more than £20 (about $32) worth of goods at a store that participates in the VAT-refund scheme, you're entitled to get most of that tax back. Getting your refund is usually straightforward and, if you buy a substantial amount of souvenirs, well worth the hassle. If you're lucky, the merchant will subtract the tax when you make your purchase. (This is more likely to occur if the store ships the goods to your home.) Otherwise, you'll need to:

Get the paperwork. Have the merchant completely fill out the necessary refund document, called a "Tax-Free Shopping Cheque." You'll have to present your passport at the store.

Get your stamp at the border or airport. Process your cheque(s) at your last stop in the EU (e.g., at the airport) with the customs agent who deals with VAT refunds. It's best to keep your purchases in your carry-on for viewing, but if they're too large or dangerous (such as knives) to carry on, track down the proper customs agent to inspect them before you check your bag. You're not supposed to use your purchased goods before you leave. If you show up at customs wearing your new Wellingtons, officials might look the other way—or deny you a refund.

Collect your refund. You'll need to return your stamped document to the retailer or its representative. Many merchants work with a service, such as Global Refund (www.globalrefund.com) or Premier Tax Free (www.premiertaxfree.com), which have offices at major airports, ports, or border crossings. These services, which extract a 4 percent fee, can refund your money immediately in your currency of choice or credit your card (within two billing cycles). If the retailer handles VAT refunds directly, it's up to you to contact the merchant for your refund. Or you can mail the documents from your point of departure (using a stamped, addressed envelope you've prepared or one that's been provided by the merchant). You'll then have to wait—it can take months.

Customs for American Shoppers

You are allowed to take home $800 worth of items per person duty-free, once every 30 days. The next $1,000 is taxed at a flat 3 percent. After that, you pay the individual item's duty rate. You can also bring in duty-free a liter of alcohol (slightly more than a standard-size bottle of wine; you must be at least 21), 200 cigarettes, and up to 100 non-Cuban cigars.

As for food, you can take home vacuum-packed cheeses; dried herbs, spices, or mushrooms; and canned fruits or vegetables, including jams and vegetable spreads. Baked goods, candy, chocolate, oil, vinegar, mustard, and honey are OK. Fresh fruits or vegetables (even that banana from your airplane breakfast) are not permitted. Meats are generally not allowed. Just because a duty-free shop in an airport sells a food product doesn't mean it will automatically pass US customs. Be prepared to lose your investment.

Note that you'll need to carefully pack any bottles of wine, jam, honey, oil, and other liquid-containing items in your checked luggage, due to the three-ounce limit on liquids in carry-on baggage. To check customs rules and duty rates before you go, visit www.cbp.gov, and click on "Travel," then "Know Before You Go."

Sightseeing

Sightseeing can be hard work. Use these tips to make your visits to England's finest sights meaningful, fun, efficient, and painless.

Plan Ahead

Set up an itinerary that allows you to fit in all your must-see sights. For a one-stop look at opening hours in the bigger cities, see the "At a Glance" sidebars throughout this book. Most sights keep stable hours, but you can easily confirm the latest by checking their website or asking at the local TI.

Don't put off visiting a must-see sight—you never know when a place will close unexpectedly for a holiday, strike, or restoration. On holidays (see list on page 718), expect shorter hours or closures.

When possible, visit major sights in the morning (when your energy is best) and save other activities for the afternoon. Hit the museum highlights first, then see the rest if you have the stamina and time.

Going at the right time helps avoid crowds. This book offers tips on specific sights. Try visiting very early, at lunch, or very late. Evening visits are usually peaceful, with fewer crowds. For specif-

Get It Right

Americans tend to use "England," "Britain," and "UK" inter-changeably, but they're not the same:
- **England** is in the southeast part of Britain. All of the places in this book are part of England.
- **Britain** is the name of the island.
- **Great Britain** is the political union of England, Scotland, and Wales.
- The **United Kingdom** adds Northern Ireland.
- The **British Isles** (not a political entity) also includes the independent Republic of Ireland.
- The **British Commonwealth** is a loose association of possessions and former colonies (including Canada, Australia, and India) that profess at least symbolic loyalty to the Crown.

ics on London at night, see the sidebar on page 90.

Study up. To get the most out of the self-guided walks and sight descriptions in this book, read them before you visit.

At Sights

Here's what you can typically expect:

Some important sights may have metal detectors or conduct bag searches that will slow your entry, while others may require you to check daypacks and coats. They'll be kept safely. If you have something you can't bear to part with, stash it in a pocket or purse. To avoid checking a small backpack, carry it under your arm like a purse as you enter. From a guard's point of view, a backpack is generally a problem while a purse is not.

At churches—which often offer interesting art (usually free) and a cool, welcome seat—a modest dress code (no bare shoulders or shorts) is encouraged.

Flash photography is sometimes banned, but taking photos without a flash is usually OK. Look for signs or ask. Flashes damage oil paintings and distract others in the room. Even without a flash, a handheld camera will take a decent picture (or buy postcards or posters at the museum bookstore). If photos are permitted, video cameras are generally OK, too.

Museums have special exhibits in addition to their permanent collection. Some exhibits are included in the entry price; others come at an extra cost (which you may have to pay even if you don't want to see the exhibit).

Many sights rent audioguides, which generally offer excellent recorded descriptions (about £3.50; sometimes included with admission). If you bring along your own pair of headphones and a

Y-jack, you can sometimes share one audioguide with your travel partner and save money. Or download my free London audio tours—covering the British Museum, British Library, St. Paul's Cathedral, and the City of London and Westminster walks—onto your MP3 player and bring them along (see page 712). Guided tours, which usually cost around £3–8 and vary widely in quality, are most likely to occur during peak season.

Some sights run short films featuring their highlights and history. These are generally well worth your time. I make it standard operating procedure to ask when I arrive at a sight if there is a film.

Expect changes—artwork can be on tour, on loan, out sick, or shifted at the whim of the curator. To adapt, pick up any available free floor plans as you enter. Ask the museum staff if you can't find a particular piece.

Important sights often have an on-site café or cafeteria (usually a good place to rest and have a snack or light meal). The WCs are usually free and nearly always clean (it's smart to carry tissues in case a WC runs out of TP).

Many places sell postcards that highlight their attractions. Before you leave, scan the postcards and thumb through the biggest guidebook (or skim its index) to be sure you haven't overlooked something that you'd like to see.

Most sights stop admitting people 30–60 minutes before closing time, and some rooms close early (often 45 minutes before the actual closing time). Guards usher people out, so don't save the best for last.

Every sight or museum offers more than what is covered in this book. Use the information in this book as an introduction—not the final word.

Sightseeing Passes and Memberships

Many sights in England are covered by the Great British Heritage Pass or these memberships: English Heritage or National Trust. If you're a whirlwind sightseer, seriously consider the Great British Heritage Pass, which covers the most sights.

Great British Heritage Pass: The best deal for busy travelers, this pass covers all of the major English Heritage and National Trust sights, plus many others (including several major attractions in Scotland, Wales, and Northern Ireland). Covering about 600 historic sights, this pass is good for a certain number of consecutive days (£45/4 days, £65/7 days, £85/15 days, £115/30 days; £99/£143/£187/£253 family pass also available for up to 2 adults and 3 kids ages 5–15—though note that kids already get discounts at sights; tel. 0870-242-9988, www.britishheritagepass.com). You can buy this pass online (£6.50 extra for shipping) or at various tourist information centers in Britain; for example, in London, this pass is sold by the Britain and London Visitors Centre on Lower Regent Street.

Memberships: Many sights in England are managed by either the English Heritage or the National Trust (the sights don't overlap). Both organizations sell annual memberships that allow free or discounted entry to the sights they supervise; the English Heritage also sells passes. You can join the National Trust or English Heritage online or at just about any of their sights.

Membership in **English Heritage** includes free entry to more than 400 sights in England and half-price admission to about 100 more sights in Scotland and Wales. For most travelers, the **Overseas Visitor Pass** is a better choice than the pricier one-year membership (Visitor Pass: £20/7 days, £24.50/14 days, discounts for couples and families; Membership: £44 for one person, £77 for two, discounts for seniors and students, children under 19 free; toll tel. 0870-333-1182, www.english-heritage.org.uk).

Membership in the **National Trust** is best suited for garden-and-estate enthusiasts, ideally those traveling by car. It covers more than 300 historic houses, manors, and gardens throughout Great Britain (£48.50 for one year, student and family discounts, children under 5 free, www.nationaltrust.org.uk).

Things to Consider: If you have children and you're all avid sightseers, consider the Great British Heritage family pass; otherwise don't get a pass or membership for them, because they get in free or cheap at most sights. Similarly, people over 60 get "concessions" (discounted prices) at many English sights (and can get a senior discount on an English Heritage membership). If you're traveling by car and can get to the more remote sights, you're more likely to get your money's worth out of a pass or membership, especially during peak season (Easter–Oct). If you're traveling off-season (Nov–Easter) when many of the sights are closed, the deals are a lesser value.

The Bottom Line: These various deals can save a busy sight-seer money...but only if you choose carefully. Make a list of the sights you plan to see, check which sights are covered (visit the websites listed above), and then add up the total if you were to pay individual admissions to the covered sights. Compare the total to the cost of the pass or membership. Keep in mind that an advantage to any of these deals is that you'll feel free to dip into lesser sights that normally aren't worth the cost of their admission.

Sleeping

I favor accommodations (and restaurants) handy to your sight-seeing activities. In England, small bed-and-breakfast places (B&Bs) generally provide the best value, though I also include some bigger hotels. Rather than list lodgings scattered throughout a city, I choose two or three favorite neighborhoods and recommend the best accommodations values in each, from $30 bunk beds to fancy-for-my-book $300 doubles. Outside of pricey London, you can expect to find good doubles for $80–160, including cooked breakfasts and tax. (For specifics on London, see page 144.)

I look for places that are friendly; clean; a good value; located in a central, safe, quiet neighborhood; and not mentioned in other guidebooks. I'm more impressed by a handy location and a fun-loving philosophy than flat-screen TVs and shoeshine machines. For tips on making reservations, see page 29.

Rates and Deals

I've described my recommended accommodations using a Sleep Code (see sidebar). Prices listed are for one-night stays in peak season, usually include a hearty breakfast, and assume you're booking directly (not through a TI or online hotel-booking engine).

You should find prices listed in this book to be good through 2011 (except during major holidays and festivals—see page 717)—though some might increase slightly due to the January 2011 VAT tax hike. B&B rates tend to be pretty straightforward, but can be soft in slow times. However, at hotels, the official "rack rates" (the highest rates a hotel charges) can be misleading, since they omit lower promotional rates, cheaper oddball rooms, and special clearance deals. (Some fancy £120 rooms can rent for a third off if you arrive late on a slow day and ask for a deal.) Given the economic downturn, hoteliers are willing and eager to make a deal. I'd suggest emailing several hotels to ask for their best price. Comparison-shop and make your choice.

As you look over the listings, you'll notice that some accommodations promise special prices to my readers who book direct (without using a room-finding service or hotel-booking website, which take a commission). To get these rates, mention this book when you reserve, then show the book upon arrival.

In general, prices can soften if you do any of the following: offer to pay cash, stay at least three nights, or mention this book. You can also try asking for a cheaper room or a discount, or offer to skip breakfast. To save money off-season, consider arriving without a reservation and dropping in at the last minute.

When establishing prices, confirm if the charge is per person or per room (if a price is too good to be true, it's probably per

Sleep Code

(£1 = about $1.60, country code: 44)

To help you easily sort through these listings, I've divided the rooms into three categories, based on the price for a double room with bath:

$$$ **Higher Priced**
$$ **Moderately Priced**
$ **Lower Priced**

To give maximum information in a minimum of space, I use the following code to describe accommodations. Prices in this book are listed per room, not per person. When a price range is given for a type of room (such as "Db-£80–120"), it means the price fluctuates with the season, size of room, or length of stay.

S = Single room, or price for one person in a double.

D = Double or twin room. (I specify double- and twin-bed rooms only if they are priced differently, or if a place has only one or the other. When reserving, you should specify.)

T = Three-person room (often a double bed with a single).

Q = Four-person room (adding an extra child's bed to a T is usually cheaper).

b = Private bathroom with toilet and shower or tub.

s = Private shower or tub only. (The toilet is down the hall.)

According to this code, a couple staying at a "Db-£80" hotel would pay a total of £80 (about $130) per night for a room with a private toilet and shower (or tub). Unless otherwise noted, credit cards are accepted and breakfast is included.

If I mention "Internet access" in a listing, there's a public terminal in the lobby for guests to use. If I include "Wi-Fi," you can generally access it in your room (usually for free), but only if you have your own laptop.

person). Because many places in England charge per person, small groups often pay the same for a single and a double as they would for a triple. In this book, however, room prices are listed per room, not per person.

Helpful Hints

Many places listed have three floors of rooms and steep stairs; expect good exercise and be happy you packed light. You'll generally find an elevator (called a "lift" here) only at larger hotels. If you're concerned about stairs, call and ask about ground-floor rooms or pay for a hotel with a lift. Air-conditioning is rare (I've noted which of my listings have it), but most places have fans. On hot summer nights, you'll want your window open—though in big cities, you may have to put up with street noise.

Learn the terminology: An "en suite" room has a bathroom (toilet and shower/tub) actually inside the room; a room with a "private bathroom" can mean that the bathroom is all yours, but it's across the hall; and a "standard" room has access to a bathroom down the hall that's shared with other rooms. (Confusingly, pricey hotels might call an en suite room "standard" to differentiate it from a fancier "superior" or "deluxe" room—if you're not sure, ask for clarification.)

Figuring there's little difference between "en suite" and "private" rooms, some places charge the same for both. If you want your own bathroom inside the room, request "en suite."

If money's tight, ask for a standard room. You'll almost always have a sink in your room. And, as more rooms go "en suite," the hallway bathroom is shared with fewer standard rooms.

"Twin" means two single beds, and "double" means one double bed (in my listings, I list all two-person rooms as "doubles"). If you will take either one, let them know, or you might be needlessly turned away. Most hotels offer family deals, which means that parents with young children can easily get a room with an extra child's bed or a discount for larger rooms. Call to negotiate the price. Teenage kids are generally charged as adults. Kids under five almost always sleep free.

Note that to be called a "hotel," a place technically must have certain amenities, including a 24-hour reception (though this rule is loosely applied). A place called "townhouse" or "house" (such as "London House") is like a big B&B or a small family-run hotel—with fewer amenities but more character than a "hotel."

England has a rating system for hotels and B&Bs. These diamonds and stars are supposed to imply quality, but I find that they mean only that the place sporting these symbols is paying dues to the tourist board. Rating systems often have little to do with value.

Hoteliers and B&B hosts can be a great help and source of advice. Most know their city well and can assist you with everything from public transit and airport connections to finding a good restaurant, the nearest Internet café, or launderette.

Even at the best places, mechanical breakdowns occur: Air-conditioning malfunctions, sinks leak, hot water turns cold, and toilets gurgle and smell. Report your concerns clearly and calmly at the front desk. For more complicated problems, don't expect instant results.

If you suspect night noise will be a problem, ask for a quiet room in the back or on an upper floor. To guard against theft in your room, keep valuables out of sight. Some rooms come with a safe, and others have safes at the front desk. Use them if you're concerned.

Checkout can pose problems if surprise charges pop up on your bill. If you settle up your bill the day before you leave, you'll have time to discuss and address any points of contention (before 19:00, when the night shift usually arrives).

If you're traveling beyond my recommended destinations, you'll find accommodations where you need them. Any town with tourists has a TI that books rooms or can give you a list and point you in the right direction. In the absence of a TI, ask people on the street or in pubs or restaurants for help. Online, visit www.smoothhound.co.uk, which offers a range of accommodations for towns throughout the UK (searchable by town, airport, hotel name, or price range).

Types of Accommodations

B&Bs

Compared to hotels, bed-and-breakfast places give you double the cultural intimacy for half the price. While you may lose some of the conveniences of a hotel—such as lounges, in-room phones, frequent bed-sheet changes, and being able to pay with a credit card—I happily make the trade-off for the lower rates and personal touches. If you have a reasonable but limited budget, skip hotels and go the B&B way.

You'll generally pay £25-50 (about $40-80) per person for a double room in a B&B in England. Lately the big, impersonal chain hotels are offering rooms cheaper than the mom-and-pop places (but without breakfast); see "Big, Cheap, Modern Hotels," later. When considering the price of a B&B or small hotel, remember you're getting two breakfasts (up to a £25 value) for each double room.

B&Bs range from large guest houses with 15-20 rooms to small homes renting out a spare bedroom, but they typically have six rooms or fewer. The philosophy of the management determines the character of a place more than its size and facilities offered. I avoid places run as a business by absentee owners. My top listings are run by people who enjoy welcoming the world to their breakfast table.

B&B proprietors are selective as to whom they invite in for the night. At some B&Bs, children are not welcome. Risky-looking people (two or more single men are often assumed to be potential troublemakers) find many places suddenly full. If you'll be staying for more than one night, you are a "desirable." In popular weekend-getaway spots, you're unlikely to find a place to take you

Smoke-Free Great Britain

Great Britain's public places are now smoke-free. Hotels, B&Bs, and restaurants are required to be non-smoking (though hoteliers are permitted to designate specific rooms for smokers). In the "Sleeping" sections of each chapter, I've listed the rare instance where a hotel has smoking rooms—but for the most part, the smoke truly has cleared in Britain.

for Saturday night only. If my listings are full, ask for guidance. Mentioning this book can help. Owners usually work together and can call up an ally to land you a bed.

B&Bs come with their own etiquette and quirks. Owners are at the whim of their guests—if you're getting up early, so are they; and if you check in late, they'll wait up for you. Be considerate. It's polite to call ahead to confirm your reservation the day before and give them a rough estimate of your arrival time. This allows them to plan their day and run errands before or after you arrive...and it also allows them to give you specific directions for driving or walking to their place.

B&Bs serve a hearty fried breakfast of eggs and much more (for details on breakfast, see page 34). Because your B&B owner is also the cook, there's usually a limited time span when breakfast is served (typically about an hour—make sure you know when it is). Sometimes they'll even designate a specific time when all guests are expected to gather to eat. It's an unwritten rule that guests shouldn't show up at the very end of the breakfast period and expect a full cooked breakfast. If you do arrive late (or need to leave before breakfast is served), most B&B hosts are happy to let you help yourself to cereal, fruit, and coffee; ask politely if it's possible.

B&Bs are not hotels. Think of your host as a friendly acquaintance who's invited you to stay in her home, rather than someone you're paying to wait on you.

Americans sometimes assume they'll get new towels each day. The English don't, and neither should you. Hang towels up to dry and reuse.

Be aware of luggage etiquette. A large bag in a compact older building can easily turn even the most graceful of us into a bull in an English china shop. If you've got a backpack, don't wear it indoors. If your host offers to carry your bag upstairs, accept—they're adept at maneuvering luggage up tiny staircases without damaging their walls and banisters. Finally, use your room's luggage racks—putting bags on empty beds can dirty and scuff nice comforters. Treat these lovingly maintained homes as you would a friend's house.

In almost every B&B, you'll encounter unusual bathroom fixtures. The "pump toilet" has a flushing handle that doesn't kick in unless you push it just right: too hard or too soft, and it won't go. Be decisive but not ruthless. There's also the "dial-a-shower," an electronic box under the shower head where you'll turn a dial to select the heat of the water and (sometimes with a separate dial or button) turn on or shut off the flow of water. If you can't find the switch to turn on the shower, it may be just outside the bathroom.

Most rooms in most B&Bs come with a hot-water pot, cups, tea bags, and coffee packets (if you prefer decaf, buy a jar at a grocery before leaving home, and dump into a baggie for easy packing). Electrical outlets have switches that turn the current on or off; if your electrical appliance isn't working, flip the switch at the outlet.

Most B&Bs come with thin walls and doors. This can make for a noisy night, especially with people walking down the hall to use the bathroom. If you're a light sleeper, bring earplugs. And please be quiet in the halls and in your rooms (talk softly, and keep the TV volume low). Those of us getting up early will thank you for it.

Your B&B bedroom probably won't include a phone. In this mobile-phone age, street phone booths can be few and far between. Some B&B owners will allow you to use their phone (with an international phone card), but many are disinclined to let you ring up charges. That's because most British people pay for each local call (whether from a fixed line or a mobile phone), and rates are expensive. Therefore, to be polite, ask to use their phone only in an emergency—and offer to use an international calling card or to pay for the call. If you plan to be staying in B&Bs and making frequent calls, consider buying a British mobile phone (see page 692). And if you're bringing your laptop, look for places with Wi-Fi (noted in my hotel listings).

Many B&B owners are also pet owners. And, while pets are rarely allowed into guest rooms, and B&B proprietors are typically very tidy, those with pet allergies might be bothered. I've tried to list which B&Bs have pets, but if you're allergic, ask about pets when you reserve.

Remember that you'll likely need to pay cash for your room. Plan ahead so you have enough cash to pay up when you check out.

Big, Cheap, Modern Hotels

American-style hotel chains—popular with budget tour groups— offer all the predictable comforts in a no-frills, practical package. While most travelers prefer the classic British B&B experience, chain hotels—which are popping up in bigger cities all over Britain—can be a great value. They offer simple, clean, and modern rooms for up to four people (two adults/two children) for £60–100, depending on the location. Some are located near the train station, on major highways, or outside the city center. What you lose in charm, you gain in savings.

These hotels are especially worth considering for families, as kids generally stay for free (but check details on the websites). Most rooms have a double bed, single bed, five-foot trundle bed, private shower, WC, and TV. There's usually an attached restaurant, good security, an elevator, and a 24-hour staffed reception desk. Breakfast is always extra. Of course, they're as cozy as a Motel 6, but many travelers love them...or, at least, the value they provide.

Here are some tips for getting the best deal:

Book through their websites, as they are often the easiest way to make reservations, and will generally net you a discount. Midweek prices are generally higher than weekend rates, and Sunday nights can be shockingly cheap. The price ranges I list tend to be wide, as the specific rates vary dramatically with demand. In fact, the rates for a particular room for a specific date can change from day to day or week to week (like airline tickets), making it difficult to know when to book. On the hotel's online reservation form, punch in the dates you're considering to see what the going rate is. Also on the websites, look for special offers. For the best deals, book at least three weeks in advance, prepay in full...and hope you don't have to change your plans (since these promotional rates are nonrefundable).

The biggest chains are **Premier Travel Inn** (www.premier inn.com, reservations tel. 0870-242-8000) and **Travelodge** (www.travelodge.co.uk, reservations tel. 0870-085-0950). Premier Inn has a "Premier Offer" non-flexible booking option on certain dates, but you have to book at least three weeks in advance and prepay for your room in its entirety (not changeable or refundable). Travelodge has a similar, nonrefundable "Saver" rate, where you prepay for your stay at least three weeks in advance (changes possible for a small fee until up to a week ahead).

Other chains with locations in Britain include the Irish chain **Jurys Inn** (www.jurysinns.com) and the French-owned **Ibis** (www.ibishotel.com). Couples could also consider **Holiday Inn Express,** which are spreading throughout England. These are like a Holiday Inn Lite, with cheaper prices and no restaurant. Many of their hotels allow only two per room, but some take up to four (doubles cost about £60–100, make sure Express is part of the name or you'll pay more for a regular Holiday Inn, www.hiexpress.co.uk, reservations tel. 0871-423-4896).

Meanwhile, **easyHotel** is a different animal—an extremely

basic, pay-as-you-go bargain chain with several branches in London (see page 160 for details).

For recommendations for online hotel deals in London, as well as using auction-type sites, see page 144.

Hostels

England has hundreds of hostels of all shapes and sizes. Choose your hostel selectively. Hostels can be historic castles or depressing tenements, serene and comfy or overrun by noisy school groups.

You'll pay about £20–25 for a bed. People of any age are welcome, if you don't mind dorm-style accommodations (usually in rooms of four to eight beds) and meeting other travelers. Cheap meals are sometimes offered, and kitchen facilities may be available.

There are two basic types of hostels: official and independent. Unfortunately, many of the official hostels (overseen by Hostelling International) have become overpriced and, in general, I no longer recommend them. Many of the independent hostels are more fun, easygoing, and cheaper. Hostels of Europe (www.hostelseurope .com) and Hostels.com have good listings. You can also book online for many hostels (for London: www.hostellondon.com; for England: www.yha.org.uk).

Phoning

To call England from the US or Canada, you'll need to know England's country code: 44. To call from the US or Canada, dial 011-44-local number (drop the initial 0 from the local number). If calling England from another European country, dial 00-44-local number (without its initial zero). For more tips on calling, see page 688.

Making Reservations

Given the quality of the places I've found for this book, I'd recommend that you reserve your rooms in advance, particularly if you'll be traveling during peak season. Book several weeks ahead or as soon as you've pinned down your travel dates. Note that some national holidays jam things up and merit your making reservations far in advance (see "Holidays and Weekends" sidebar on page 11). Just like at home, holidays that fall on a Monday, Thursday, or Friday can turn the weekend into a long holiday, so book the entire weekend well in advance.

Requesting a Reservation: To make a reservation, contact hotels directly by email, phone, or fax. Email is the clearest and most economical way to make a reservation. Or you can go straight to the hotel website; many have secure online reservation forms and can instantly inform you of availability and any special deals.

But be sure you use the hotel's official site and not a booking agency's site—otherwise you may pay higher rates than you should. If phoning from the US, be mindful of time zones (see page 12).

The hotelier wants to know these key pieces of information (also included in the sample request form in the appendix):
- number and type of rooms
- number of nights
- date of arrival
- date of departure
- any special needs (e.g., bathroom in the room or down the hall, twin beds vs. double bed, air-conditioning, quiet, view, ground floor, etc.)

When you request a room, use the European style for writing dates: day/month/year. For example, a two-night stay in July would be "2 nights, 16/07/11 to 18/07/11." Consider in advance how long you'll stay; don't just assume you can tack on extra days once you arrive. Mention any discounts offered—for Rick Steves readers or otherwise—when you make the reservation.

If you don't get a reply to your email or fax, it usually means the hotel is already fully booked (but you can try sending the message again, or call to follow up).

Confirming a Reservation: If the hotel's response includes its room availability and rates, it's not a confirmation. You must tell them that you want that room at the given rate. Most hoteliers will request your credit-card number for a one-night deposit to hold the room. While you can email your credit-card information (I do), it's safer to share that confidential info via phone call, fax, two successive emails, or secure online reservation form (if the hotel has one on its website).

Canceling a Reservation: If you must cancel your reservation, it's courteous to do so with as much advance notice as possible—at least three days. Simply make a quick phone call or send an email. Family-run hotels and B&Bs lose money if they turn away customers while holding a room for someone who doesn't show up. Understandably, many places bill no-shows for one night.

Hotels in larger cities such as London sometimes have strict cancellation policies. For example, you might lose a deposit if you cancel within two weeks of your reserved stay, or you might be billed for the entire visit if you leave early. Internet deals may require prepayment, with no refunds for cancellations. If concerned, ask about cancellation policies before you book.

If canceling via email, request confirmation that your cancellation was received to avoid being billed accidentally.

Reconfirming Your Reservation: Always call to reconfirm your room reservation a day or two in advance from the road. Smaller hotels and B&Bs appreciate knowing your time of arrival.

If you'll be arriving after 17:00, be sure to let your hotelier know. On the small chance that a hotel loses track of your reservation, bring along a hard copy of their emailed or faxed confirmation. Don't have the TI reconfirm rooms for you; they'll take a commission.

Reserving Rooms as You Travel: You can make reservations as you travel, calling hotels or B&Bs a few days to a week before your arrival. If everything's full, don't despair. Call a day or two in advance and fill in a cancellation. If you'd rather travel without any reservations at all, you'll have greater success snaring rooms if you arrive at your destination early in the day. When you anticipate crowds (weekends are worst), call hotels at about 9:00 or 10:00 on the day you plan to arrive, when the hotel clerk knows who'll be checking out and just which rooms will be available.

Most TIs in Britain can book you a room in their town, and also often in nearby towns. They generally charge a £4 fee, and you'll pay a 10 percent "deposit" at the TI and the rest at the B&B (meaning that you pay extra and the B&B loses money, as the TI keeps the "deposit"). While this can be useful in a pinch, it's a better deal for everyone (except the TIs) to book direct, using the listings in this book.

Eating

England's reputation for miserable food, while once well-deserved, is now dated. The British cuisine scene is lively, trendy, and pleasantly surprising. (Unfortunately, it's also expensive.) Even the basic, traditional pub grub has gone "upmarket," with gastropubs that serve fresh vegetables rather than soggy fries and mushy peas.

All English eateries are now smoke-free. Restaurants and pubs that sell food are non-smoking indoors; establishments keep their smokers contented by allowing them to light up in doorways and on outdoor patios.

Budget Eating Tips

You have plenty of inexpensive choices: pub grub, daily lunch and early-bird specials, ethnic restaurants, cafeterias, fast food, picnics, fish-and-chips, greasy-spoon cafés, pizza, and more.

I've found that portions are huge and, with locals feeling the pinch of their recession, **sharing plates** is generally just fine. Ordering two drinks, a soup or side salad, and splitting a £10 meat pie can make a good, filling meal. If you are on a limited budget, share a main course in a more expensive place for a nicer eating experience.

Pub grub is the most atmospheric budget option. You'll usually get fresh, tasty buffets under ancient timbers, with hearty lunches and dinners priced reasonably at £6–10 (see "Pubs," later).

Classier restaurants have some affordable deals. Lunch is usually cheaper than dinner; a top-end, £25-for-dinner-type restaurant often serves the same quality two-course lunch deals for £10. Look for early-bird dinner specials, allowing you to eat well and affordably (generally two courses-£17, three courses-£20), but early (about 17:30–19:00, last order by 19:00).

Ethnic restaurants from all over the world add spice to England's cuisine scene. Eating Indian, Bangladeshi, Chinese, or Thai is cheap (even cheaper if you do take-out). Middle Eastern stands sell gyro sandwiches, falafel, and *shwarmas* (lamb in pita bread). An Indian samosa (greasy, flaky meat-and-vegetable pie) costs £2, can be microwaved, and makes a very cheap, if small, meal. (For more, see "Indian Food," later.) You'll find all-you-can-eat Chinese and Thai places serving £6 meals and offering £3.50 take-away boxes. While you can't "split" a buffet, you can split a take-away box. Stuff the box full, and you and your partner can eat in a park for less than £2 each—making this England's cheapest hot meal.

Most large **museums** (and some historic **churches**) have handy, moderately priced cafeterias.

Fast food places, both American and British, are everywhere.

Cheap chain restaurants, such as steak houses and pizza places, serve no-nonsense food in a family-friendly setting (steak-house meals about £10; all-you-can-stomach pizza about £5). For specific chains to keep an eye out for, see "Good Chain Restaurants," on the next page.

Bakeries sell yogurt, cartons of "semi-skimmed" milk, pastries, and pasties (PASS-teez). Pasties are heavy, savory meat pies that originated in the Cornish mining country; they had big crust handles so miners with filthy hands could eat them and toss the crust. The most traditional filling is beef stew, but you'll also find them with chicken, vegetable, lamb and mint, and even Indian flavors inside (see sidebar on page 327).

Picnicking saves time and money. You can easily get prepared food to go. Munch a relaxed "meal on wheels" picnic during your open-top bus tour or river cruise to save 30 precious minutes for sightseeing.

Good **sandwich shops** and corner **grocery stores** are a hit with local workers eating on the run. Try boxes of orange juice (pure, by the liter), fresh bread, tasty English cheese, meat, a tube of Colman's English mustard, local eatin' apples, bananas, small

---

Sounds Bad, Tastes Good

The English have a knack for making food sound funny. Here are a few examples:

Toad in the Hole: Sausage dipped in batter and fried

Bubble and Squeak: Leftovers, usually potatoes, veggies, and meat, all fried up together

Bap: Small roll

Treacle: Golden syrup, similar to light molasses

---

tomatoes, a small tub of yogurt (drinkable), trail mix, nuts, plain or chocolate-covered digestive biscuits, and any local specialties. At **open-air markets** and **supermarkets,** you can get produce in small quantities (3 tomatoes and 2 bananas cost about £1). Supermarkets often have good deli sections, even offering Indian dishes, and sometimes salad bars. Decent packaged sandwiches (£3-4) are sold everywhere (for a few options, see "Carry-Out Chains," later).

Good Chain Restaurants

I know—you're going to Britain to enjoy characteristic little hole-in-the-wall pubs, so mass-produced food is the furthest thing from your mind. But several excellent chains with branches across the UK can be a nice break from pub grub. I've recommended these restaurants throughout this book, but if you see a location that I haven't listed...go for it.

Sit-Down Chains

Wagamama Noodle Bar, serving up fresh and reliably delicious pan-Asian cuisine, is stylish, youthful, and mod. There's one in almost every midsize city in the UK, and after you've sampled their udon noodles, fried rice, or curry dishes, you'll know why. They're usually in a sprawling, loud, and modern hall filled with long shared tables and busy servers who scrawl your order on the placemat. Portions are huge enough for light eaters on a tight budget to share (typically £7-10 entrées, good vegetarian options).

At **Yo! Sushi,** freshly prepared sushi dishes trundle past on a conveyor belt. Color-coded plates tell you how much each dish costs (£1.75–5), and a picture-filled menu explains what you're eating. Just help yourself.

Gourmet Burger Company (GBK) offers burgers that are, if not quite gourmet, very good. Choices range from a simple cheeseburger to more elaborate options, such as Jamaican (£7-8 burgers). Choose a table and order at the counter—they'll bring the food to you.

Loch Fyne Fish Restaurant, a Scottish chain, serves up fish, oysters, and mussels in a lively, upscale-but-unpretentious setting (£10–15 entrées, early-bird deals).

Ask and **Pizza Express** serve quality pasta and pizza in a pleasant, sit-down atmosphere that's family-friendly. **Jamie's Italian** (from celebrity chef Jamie Oliver) is hipper and pricier, and feels more upmarket.

Carry-Out Chains

While the following places might have some seating, they're an easy place to grab some prepackaged food on the go.

Major supermarket chains have smaller, offshoot branches that specialize in sandwiches, salads, and other prepared foods "to go." These can be a picnicker's dream come true. Some shops are stand-alone, while others are located inside a larger store. The most prevalent—and best—is **M&S Simply Food** (an offshoot of the Marks & Spencer department-store chain; no seating but plasticware is provided). **Sainsbury's Local** grocery stores also offer some decent prepared food; **Tesco Express** and **Tesco Metro** are a distant third.

Other "cheap and cheery" chains, such as **Pret à Manger** and **Eat,** provide office workers with good, healthful sandwiches, salads, and pastries to go.

West Cornwall Pasty Company sells a variety of these traditional savory pies for around £3—as do many smaller, independent bakeries.

The Great English Breakfast

The traditional "fry," or "full English breakfast"—generally included in the cost of your room—is famous as a hearty way to start the day. Also known as a "heart attack on a plate," the breakfast is especially feast-like if you've just come from the land of the skimpy continental breakfast across the Channel.

The standard fry gets off to a healthy start with juice and cereal or porridge. (Try Weetabix, a soggy English cousin of shredded wheat and perhaps the most absorbent material known to humankind.) Next, with tea or coffee, you get a heated plate with a fried egg, Canadian-style bacon or sausage, a grilled tomato, sautéed mushrooms, and baked beans. Toast comes in a rack (to cool quickly and crisply) with butter and marmalade. This protein-stuffed meal is great for stamina and tides many travelers over until dinner.

You'll figure out quickly which parts of the "fry" you like and don't like. Your host appreciates knowing this up front, rather than serving you the whole shebang and having to throw out uneaten food. There's nothing wrong with skipping some or all of the fry—few Brits actually start their day with this heavy breakfast. Many progressive B&B owners offer vegetarian, organic, or other creative variations on the traditional breakfast.

These days, the best coffee is served in a *cafetière* (also called a "French press"). When your coffee has steeped as long as you like, plunge down the filter and pour.

Afternoon Tea

People of leisure punctuate their day with an "afternoon tea" at a tearoom. You'll get a pot of tea, small finger foods (like cucumber sandwiches), homemade scones, jam, and thick clotted cream. A lighter "cream tea" gets you tea and a scone or two. Tearooms, which often serve appealing light meals, are usually open for lunch and close at about 17:00, just before dinner. For more on this most English of traditions, see page 178.

Pubs

Pubs are a basic part of the British social scene, and, whether you're a teetotaler or a beer-guzzler, they should be a part of your travel

here. "Pub" is short for "public house." It's an extended living room where, if you don't mind the stickiness, you can feel the pulse of England.

Smart travelers use the pubs to eat, drink, get out of the rain, watch sporting events, and make new friends. Unfortunately, many city pubs have been afflicted with an excess of brass, ferns, and video games. Most traditional atmospheric pubs are in the countryside and in smaller towns.

Pub Grub

Pub grub gets better each year. In London, it offers the best indoor eating value. For £6–10, you'll get a basic budget hot lunch or dinner in friendly surroundings. (For something more refined, try a gastropub, which serves higher-quality meals for £12–18.) The *Good Pub Guide* is excellent (www.thegoodpubguide.co.uk). Pubs that are attached to restaurants, advertise their food, and are crowded with locals are more likely to have fresh food and a chef—and less likely to be the kind of pub that sells only lousy microwaved snacks.

Pubs generally serve traditional dishes, such as fish-and-chips, vegetables, "bangers and mash" (sausages and mashed potatoes), roast beef with Yorkshire pudding (batter-baked in the oven), and assorted meat pies, such as steak-and-kidney pie or shepherd's pie (stewed lamb topped with mashed potatoes). Side dishes include salads (sometimes even a nice self-serve salad bar), vegetables, and—invariably—"chips" (French fries). "Crisps" are potato chips. A "jacket potato" (baked potato stuffed with fillings of your choice) can almost be a meal in itself. A "ploughman's lunch" is a "traditional English meal" of bread, cheese, and sweet pickles that nearly every tourist tries...once. These days, you'll likely find more Italian pasta, curried dishes, and quiche on the menu than traditional fare.

Meals are usually served 12:00–14:00 and 18:00–20:00—generally not throughout the day. Since they make more money selling beer, many pubs stop serving meals early in the evening. There's often no table service. Order at the bar, then take a seat and they'll bring the food when it's ready (or sometimes you pick it up at the bar). Pay at the bar (sometimes when you order, sometimes after you eat). Don't tip unless it's a place with full table service. Servings are hearty, service is quick, and you'll rarely spend more than £10. (If you're on a tight budget, consider sharing a meal—note the size of portions around you before ordering.) A beer or cider adds another couple of pounds. (Free tap water is always available.)

Beer

The British take great pride in their beer. Many Brits think that drinking beer cold and carbonated, as Americans do, ruins the taste. Most pubs will have **lagers** (cold, refreshing, American-style beer), **ales** (amber-colored, cellar-temperature beer), **bitters** (hop-flavored ale, perhaps the most typical British beer), and **stouts** (dark and somewhat bitter, like Guinness). At pubs, long-handled pulls are used to pull the traditional, rich-flavored "real ales" up from the cellar. These are the connoisseur's favorites: fermented naturally, varying from sweet to bitter, often with a hoppy or nutty flavor. Notice the fun names. Short-hand pulls at the bar mean colder, fizzier, mass-produced, and less interesting keg beers. Mild beers are sweeter, with a creamy malt flavoring. Irish cream ale is a smooth, sweet experience. Try the draft cider (sweet or dry)... carefully.

Order your beer at the bar and pay as you go, with no need to tip. An average beer costs £3. Part of the experience is standing before a line of "hand pulls," or taps, and wondering which beer to choose.

Drinks are served by the pint (20-ounce imperial size) or the half-pint. (It's almost feminine for a man to order just a half; I order mine with quiche.) Proper English ladies like a half beer and half 7-Up **shandy.**

Besides beer, many pubs actually have a good selection of wines by the glass, a fully stocked bar for the gentleman's "G and T" (gin and tonic), and the increasingly popular bottles of alcohol-plus-sugar (such as Bacardi Breezers) for the younger, working-class set. **Pimm's** is a refreshing and fruity summer cocktail, traditionally popular during Wimbledon. It's an upper-class drink—a rough bloke might insult a pub by claiming it sells more Pimm's than beer. Teetotalers can order from a wide variety of soft drinks. Children are served food and soft drinks in pubs, but you must be 18 to order a beer.

Pub hours vary. Pubs generally serve beer Monday–Saturday 11:00–23:00 and Sunday 12:00–22:30, though many are open later, particularly on Friday and Saturday. As it nears closing time, you'll hear shouts of "Last orders." Then comes the 10-minute warning bell. Finally, they'll call "Time!" to pick up your glass, finished or not, when the pub closes.

A cup of darts is free for the asking. People go to a public house to be social. They want to talk. Get vocal with a local. This is easiest at the bar, where people assume you're in the mood to talk (rather than at a table, where you're allowed a bit of privacy). The pub is the next best thing to having relatives in town. Cheers!

Indian Food

Eating Indian food is "going local" in cosmopolitan, multiethnic England. You'll find recommended Indian restaurants in most English cities, and even in small towns. Take the opportunity to sample food from Britain's former colony. Indian cuisine is as varied as the country itself. In general, they use more exotic spices than British or American cuisine—some hot, some sweet. Indian food is very vegetarian-friendly, offering many meatless dishes to choose from on any given menu.

For a simple meal that costs about £10–12, order one dish with rice and *naan* (Indian flatbread that can be served plain, with garlic, or other ways). You'll generally pay separately for the rice (it's not included in the entrée price, as it often is at Indian restaurants in the US). Many restaurants have a fixed-price combination meal that offers more variety, and is simpler and cheaper than ordering à la carte. For about £20, you can make a mix-and-match platter out of several sharable dishes, including *dal* (lentil soup) as a starter; one or two meat or vegetable dishes with sauce (for example, chicken curry, chicken *tikka masala* in a creamy tomato sauce, grilled fish tandoori, chickpea *chana masala*, or the spicy *vindaloo* dish); *raita* (a cooling yogurt that's added to spicy dishes); rice; *naan;* and an Indian beer (wine and Indian food don't really mix)

British Chocolate

My chocoholic readers are enthusiastic about British choco-
lates. As with other dairy products, chocolate seems richer
and creamier here than it does in the US, so even the basics
like Kit Kat and Twix have a different taste. Some favorites include Cadbury Gold bars (filled with liquid caramel),
Cadbury Crunchie bars, Nestlé's Lion bars (layered wafers
covered in caramel and chocolate), Cadbury's Boost bars (a
shortcake biscuit with caramel in milk chocolate), Cadbury
Flake (crumbly folds of melt-in-your-mouth chocolate), Galaxy
chocolate bars (especially the ones with hazelnuts), and Aero
(a light-as-air chocolate bar filled with little bubbles). Thornton
shops (in larger train stations) sell a box of sweets called the
Continental Assortment, which comes with a tasting guide.
The highlight is the mocha white-chocolate truffle. British
M&Ms, called Smarties, are better than American ones. At ice-
cream vans, look for the beloved traditional "99p"—a vanilla
soft-serve cone with a small Flake bar stuck right into the
middle. For a break from chocolate, buy a roll of wine gums—
similar to Jujubes, but tangier and less sweet (Maynards is the
biggest brand).

or chai (a cardamom- and cinnamon-spiced tea, usually served
with milk). An easy way to taste a variety of dishes (especially for
a single diner) is to order a *thali*—a sort of sampler plate, generally
served on a metal tray, with small servings of various specialties.

Desserts (Sweets)

To the British, the traditional word for dessert is "pudding,"
although it's also referred to as "sweets" these days. Sponge cake,
cream, fruitcake, and meringue are key players.

Trifle is the best-known British concoction, consisting of
sponge cake soaked in brandy or sherry (or orange juice for children), then covered with jam and/or fruit and custard cream.
Whipped cream can sometimes put the final touch on this "light"
treat.

Castle puddings are sponge puddings cooked in small molds
and topped with Golden Syrup (a popular brand and a cross
between honey and maple syrup). Bread-and-butter pudding consists of slices of French bread baked with milk, cream, eggs, and
raisins (similar to the American preparation), served warm with
cold cream. Hasty pudding, supposedly the invention of people
in a hurry to avoid the bailiff, is made from stale bread with dried
fruit and milk. Queen of puddings is a breadcrumb pudding
topped with warm jam, meringue, and cream. Treacle pudding

INTRODUCTION

How Was Your Trip?

Were your travels fun, smooth, and meaningful? If you'd like to share your tips, concerns, and discoveries, please fill out the survey at www.ricksteves.com/feedback. I value your feedback. Thanks in advance—it helps a lot.

---

is a popular steamed pudding whose "sponge" mixture combines flour, suet (animal fat), butter, sugar, and milk. Christmas pudding (also called plum pudding) is a dense mixture with dried and candied fruit served with brandy butter or hard sauce. Sticky toffee pudding is a moist cake made with dates, heated and drizzled with toffee sauce, and served with ice cream or cream. Banoffee pie is the delicious British answer to banana cream pie.

The English version of custard is a smooth, yellow liquid. Cream tops most everything custard does not. There's single cream for coffee. Double cream is really thick. Whipped cream is familiar, and clotted cream is the consistency of whipped butter.

Fool is a dessert with sweetened pureed fruit (such as rhubarb, gooseberries, or black currants) mixed with cream or custard and chilled. Elderflower is a popular flavoring for sorbet.

Scones are tops, and many inns and restaurants have their secret recipes. Whether made with fruit or topped with clotted cream, scones take the cake.

Traveling as a Temporary Local

We travel all the way to Europe to enjoy differences—to become temporary locals. You'll experience frustrations. Certain truths that we find "God-given" or "self-evident," such as cold beer, ice in drinks, bottomless cups of coffee, hot showers, and bigger being better, are suddenly not so true. One of the benefits of travel is the eye-opening realization that there are logical, civil, and even better alternatives.

Europeans generally like Americans. But if there is a negative aspect to their image of us, it's that we are loud, aggressive, impolite, rich, superficially friendly, and a bit naive.

The English (and Europeans in general) place a high value on speaking quietly in restaurants and on trains. Listen while on the bus or in a restaurant—the place can be packed, but the decibel level is low. Try to adjust your volume accordingly to show respect for their culture.

While the English look bemusedly at some of our Yankee excesses—and worriedly at others—they nearly always afford us individual travelers all the warmth we deserve. Judging from all the happy feedback I receive from travelers who have used this book, it's safe to assume you'll enjoy a great, affordable vacation—with the finesse of an independent, experienced traveler.

Thanks, and have a brilliant holiday!

Back Door Travel Philosophy
From *Rick Steves' Europe Through the Back Door*

Travel is intensified living—maximum thrills per minute and one of the last great sources of legal adventure. Travel is freedom. It's recess, and we need it.

Experiencing the real Europe requires catching it by surprise, going casual..."Through the Back Door."

Affording travel is a matter of priorities. (Make do with the old car.) You can travel—simply, safely, and comfortably—anywhere in Europe for $120 a day plus transportation costs (allow more for bigger cities). In many ways, spending more money only builds a thicker wall between you and what you came to see. Europe is a cultural carnival, and, time after time, you'll find that its best acts are free and the best seats are the cheap ones.

A tight budget forces you to travel close to the ground, meeting and communicating with the people, not relying on service with a purchased smile. Never sacrifice sleep, nutrition, safety, or cleanliness in the name of budget. Simply enjoy the local-style alternatives to expensive hotels and restaurants.

Connecting with people carbonates your experience. Extroverts have more fun. If your trip is low on magic moments, kick yourself and make things happen. If you don't enjoy a place, maybe you don't know enough about it. Seek the truth. Recognize tourist traps. Give a culture the benefit of your open mind. See things as different but not better or worse. Any culture has much to share.

Of course, travel, like the world, is a series of hills and valleys. Be fanatically positive and militantly optimistic. If something's not to your liking, change your liking.

Travel can make you a happier American as well as a citizen of the world. Our Earth is home to six and a half billion equally important people. It's humbling to travel and find that people don't have the "American Dream"—they have their own dreams. Europeans like us, but, with all due respect, they wouldn't trade passports.

Thoughtful travel engages us with the world. In tough economic times, it reminds us what is truly important. By broadening perspectives, travel teaches new ways to measure quality of life.

Globetrotting destroys ethnocentricity, helping you understand and appreciate different cultures. Rather than fear the diversity on this planet, celebrate it. Among your prized souvenirs will be the strands of different cultures you choose to knit into your own character. The world is a cultural yarn shop, and Back Door travelers are weaving the ultimate tapestry. Join in!

ENGLAND

ENGLAND

England (pop. 50 million) is a hilly country the size of Louisiana (50,346 square miles) and located in the lower two-thirds of the isle of Britain. Scotland is to the north and the English Channel to the south, with the North Sea to the east and Wales (and the Irish Sea) to the west. Fed by ocean air from the southwest, the climate is mild, with a chance of cloudy, rainy weather almost any day of the year.

England has an economy that can stand alongside many much larger nations. It boasts high-tech industries (software, chemicals, aviation), international banking, and textile manufacturing, and is a major exporter of beef. While farms and villages remain, England is now an urban, industrial, and post-industrial colossus.

England traditionally has been very class-conscious, with the wealthy landed aristocracy, the middle-class tradesmen, and the lower-class farmers and factory workers. While social stratification is fading with the new global economy, regional differences remain strong. Locals can often identify where someone is from by their dialect or local accent—Geordie, Cockney, or Queen's English.

One thing that sets England apart from its fellow UK countries (Scotland, Wales, and Northern Ireland) is its ethnic makeup. Traditionally, those countries had Celtic roots, while the English mixed in Saxon and Norman blood. In the 20th century, England welcomed many Scots, Welsh, and Irish as low-wage workers. More recently, it's become home to immigrants from former colonies of its worldwide empire—

particularly from India/Pakistan/Bangladesh, the Caribbean, and Africa—and to many workers from poorer Eastern European countries. These days it's not a given that every "English" person speaks English. Nearly one in three citizens does not profess the Christian faith. As the world becomes interconnected by communications technology, it's possible for many immigrants to physically inhabit the country while remaining closely linked to their home culture—rather than truly assimilating into England.

This is the current English paradox. England—the birthplace and center of the extended worldwide family of English-speakers—is losing its traditional Englishness. Where Scotland, Wales, and Northern Ireland have cultural movements to preserve their local languages and customs, England does not. Politically, there is no "English" party in the UK Parliament. While Scotland, Wales, and Northern Ireland have their own parliaments to decide local issues, England must depend on the decisions of the UK government at large. Except for the occasional display of an English flag at a soccer match (the red St. George's cross on a white background), many English people don't really think of themselves as "English"—more as "Brits," a part of the wider UK.

Today, England tries to preserve its rich past as it races forward as a leading global player. There are still hints of its legacy

of farms, villages, Victorian lamplighters, and upper-crust dandies. But it's also a jostling world of unemployed factory workers, investment bankers, soccer matches, rowdy "stag" parties, and faux-Tudor suburbs. Modern England is a culturally diverse land in transition. Catch it while you can.

LONDON

London is more than 600 square miles of urban jungle. With eight million people, it's a world in itself and a barrage on all the senses. On my first visit, I felt extremely small.

London is more than its museums and landmarks. It's a living, breathing, thriving organism...a coral reef of humanity. The city has changed dramatically in recent years, and many visitors are surprised to find how "un-English" it is. ESL (English as a second language) seems like the city's first language, as white people are now a minority in major parts of the city that once symbolized white imperialism. Arabs have nearly bought out the area north of Hyde Park. Chinese takeouts outnumber fish-and-chips shops. Eastern Europeans pull pints in British pubs. Many hotels are run by people with foreign accents (who hire English chambermaids), while outlying suburbs are home to huge communities of Indians and Pakistanis. London is a city of eight million separate dreams, inhabiting a place that tolerates and encourages them. With the English Channel Tunnel and discount airlines making travel between Britain and the Continent easier than ever, London is learning—sometimes fitfully—to live as a microcosm of its formerly vast empire. The city, which has long attracted tourists, seems perpetually at your service, with an impressive slate of sights, entertainment, and eateries, linked by a great transit system. In anticipation of the 2012 Olympic Games and a greater onslaught of tourists than usual, London is busy spiffing up the place, especially its rapidly developing Olympic Park in East London.

With just a few days here, you'll get no more than a quick splash in this teeming human tidal pool. But with a good orientation, you'll find London manageable and fun. You'll get a sampling of the city's top sights, history, and cultural entertainment, and a good look at its ever-changing human face.

Blow through the city on the open deck of a double-decker orientation tour bus, and take a pinch-me-I'm-in-London walk through the West End. Ogle the crown jewels at the Tower of London, hear the chimes of Big Ben, and see the Houses of Parliament in action. Cruise the Thames River, and take a spin on the London Eye. Hobnob with the tombstones in Westminster Abbey, and visit with Leonardo, Botticelli, and Rembrandt in the National Gallery. Enjoy Shakespeare in a replica of the Globe Theatre and marvel at a glitzy, fun musical at a modern-day theater. Whisper across the dome of St. Paul's Cathedral, then rummage through our civilization's attic at the British Museum. And sip your tea with pinky raised and clotted cream dribbling down your scone.

Planning Your Time

The sights of London alone could easily fill a trip to England. It's a great one-week getaway. But on a three-week tour of England, I'd give London three busy days. You won't be able to see everything, so don't try. You'll keep coming back to London. After dozens of visits myself, I still enjoy a healthy list of excuses to return. If you're flying in, consider starting your trip in Bath and making London your English finale. Especially if you hope to enjoy a play or concert, a night or two of jet lag is bad news.

Here's a suggested three-day schedule:

Day 1

9:00	Tower of London (crown jewels first, then Beefeater tour, then White Tower).
13:00	Grab a picnic, catch a boat at Tower Pier, and relax with lunch on the Thames while cruising to Westminster Pier.
14:30	Tour Westminster Abbey, and consider their evensong service (at 15:00 Sat–Sun, at 17:00 Mon–Fri).
17:00	(or after evensong) Follow my self-guided Westminster Walk. When you're finished, if it's a Monday or Tuesday, you could return to the Houses of Parliament and pop in to see the House of Commons in action (until 22:30).

no ceremony in rain

Day 2

8:30 Take a double-decker hop-on, hop-off London sightseeing bus tour (from Green Park or Victoria) and hop off for the Changing of the Guard.

11:00 Buckingham Palace (guards change most days May–July at 11:30, alternate days Aug–April—confirm).

12:00 Walk through St. James' Park to enjoy London's delightful park scene.

13:00 Covent Garden for lunch, shopping, and people-watching.

14:30 Tour the British Museum.

Evening Have a pub dinner before a play, concert, or evening walking tour.

Day 3 (or More)

Choose among these remaining London highlights: National Gallery, British Library, Cabinet War Rooms and Churchill Museum, Imperial War Museum, the two Tates (Tate Modern on the south bank for modern art, Tate Britain on the north bank for British art), St. Paul's Cathedral, or the Museum of London; take a spin on the London Eye or a cruise to Kew or Greenwich; enjoy a Shakespearean play at Shakespeare's Globe; do some serious shopping at one of London's elegant department stores or open-air markets; or take another historic walking tour.

No matter how long your visit, take advantage of the free, self-guided **Rick Steves Audio Tours** of major London sights and neighborhoods (download them from www.ricksteves.com or search for "Rick Steves Audio Tours" on iTunes); these are available for the British Museum, the British Library, St. Paul's Cathedral, the Westminster neighborhood, and The City.

Orientation to London

(area code: 020)

To grasp London more comfortably, see it as the old town in the city center without the modern, congested sprawl. (Even at that, it's still huge.)

The Thames River (pronounced "tems") runs roughly west to east through the city, with most of the visitor's sights on the north bank. Mentally, maybe even physically, with scissors, trim down your map to include only the area between the Tower of London (to the east), Hyde Park (west), Regent's Park (north), and the South Bank (south). This is roughly the area bordered by the Tube's Circle Line. This four-mile stretch between the Tower and Hyde Park (about a 1.5-hour walk) looks like a milk bottle on its side (see map on next page), and holds 80 percent of the sights mentioned in this chapter.

Sprawling London becomes much more manageable if you think of it as a collection of neighborhoods:

Central London: This area contains Westminster and what Londoners call the West End. The **Westminster** district includes Big Ben, Parliament, Westminster Abbey, and Buckingham Palace—the grand government buildings from which Britain is ruled. Trafalgar Square, London's gathering place, has many major museums. The **West End** is the center of London's cultural life, with bustling squares: Piccadilly Circus and Leicester Square (pronounced "LESS-ter") host cinemas, tourist traps, and nighttime glitz. Soho and Covent Garden are thriving people-zones with theaters, restaurants, pubs, and boutiques. And Regent and Oxford streets are the city's main shopping zones.

North London: Neighborhoods in this part of town—including Bloomsbury, Fitzrovia, and Marylebone—contain such major sights as the British Museum and the overhyped Madame Tussauds Waxworks. Nearby, along busy Euston Road, is the British Library plus a trio of train stations (one of them, St. Pancras International Station, is linked to Paris and Brussels by the Eurostar "Chunnel" train).

The City: Today's modern financial district, called simply "The City," was a walled town in Roman times. Gleaming skyscrapers are interspersed with historical landmarks such as St. Paul's Cathedral, legal sights (Old Bailey), and the Museum of London. The Tower of London and Tower Bridge lie at The City's eastern border.

The South Bank: The South Bank of the Thames River

ers major sights (Tate Modern, Shakespeare's Globe, London Eye) linked by a riverside walkway. Within this area, **Southwark** (SUTH-uck) stretches from the Tate Modern to London Bridge. Pedestrian bridges connect the South Bank with The City and Trafalgar Square.

West London: This huge area contains neighborhoods such as Mayfair, Belgravia, Chelsea, South Kensington, and Notting Hill. It's home to London's wealthy, and has many trendy shops and enticing restaurants. Here you'll find a range of museums (Victoria and Albert Museum, Tate Britain, and more), my top hotel recommendations, lively Victoria Station, and the vast green expanses of Hyde Park and Kensington Gardens.

East London: Just east of The City is the **East End**—the increasingly gentrified former stomping ground of Cockney ragamuffins and Jack the Ripper. Even farther to the east, London's version of Manhattan—the **Docklands**—has sprung up around Canary Wharf. Energized by big businesses, the Docklands show you London at its most modern. Historic **Greenwich** lies just south of the Docklands/Canary Wharf area, across the Thames. And the **2012 Olympic Park** is being built in the once-dreary Stratford district, a short train ride to the north.

Tourist Information

The **Britain and London Visitors Centre,** just a block off Piccadilly Circus, is the best tourist information service in town (June–Sept Mon–Fri 9:30–18:30, Sat 9:00–17:00, Sun 10:00–16:00; Oct–May Mon–Fri 9:30–18:00, Sat–Sun 10:00–16:00; 1 Lower Regent Street, tel. 020/8846-9000, toll tel. 0870-156-6366, www.visitbritain .com, www.visitlondon.com). If you visit only one TI, make it this one. Unfortunately, London's many "Tourist Information Centres" (which represent themselves as TIs at major train and bus stations and airports) are now simply businesses, selling advertising space to companies with fliers to distribute.

The Britain and London Visitors Centre has many different departments. It's a great one-stop shopping place to get tourist information, buy advance tickets to big sights, buy sightseeing passes, arrange coach tours, buy theater tickets, plan travel beyond London, and even book trains to the Continent. Bring your itinerary and a checklist of questions.

Entering the lobby, check out the various departments and get in the right line for what you need. At the Tourist Information desk handling both London and Britain inquiries, pick up various free publications: the *London Planner* (a free monthly that lists all the sights, events, and hours), walking tours info, a theater guide, London bus map, and the *Guide to River Thames Boat Services.* The staff sells a good £1 map and all the various sightseeing passes (both the nationwide passes described on page 20, and the London Pass described below).

The Entertainment and Tickets desk sells tickets to plays (steep 20 percent booking fee). The Hotels and Travel desk sells long-distance bus tickets and passes, train tickets (convenient for reservations), and Fast Track tickets to some of London's attractions. These tickets, which allow you to skip the queue at the sights at no extra cost, are worthwhile for places that can have long ticket lines, such as the Tower of London, the London Eye, and Madame Tussauds Waxworks. (If you're going to the Waxworks, buy tickets here, since—at £22.50—they're cheaper than at the sight itself.)

The Visitors Centre reserves hotel rooms, but you can avoid their £5 booking fee by contacting hotels on your own. A Rail Europe section books the Eurostar and train travel or train passes on the Continent.

Upstairs, you'll find more brochures, Internet access (£1/20 minutes), and comfy chairs where you can read or get organized.

The **London Pass** is pricey, and only worth considering for the most rabid sightseer (£40/1 day, £55/2 days, £63/3 days, £90/6 days; days are calendar days rather than 24-hour periods; includes 160-page guidebook, toll tel. 0870-242-9988, www.londonpass .com). It lets you skip the lines and covers plenty of sights that cost £11–17, including the Tower of London, St. Paul's Cathedral, Shakespeare's Globe, Cabinet War Rooms, Windsor Castle, and Kew Gardens. If you saw just these sights without the pass, you'd pay about £90, the cost of a six-day London Pass. Busy sightseers can make a short pass work for a longer trip by seeing only covered sights during the validity of the pass, and touring London's many free sights (listed on page 52) before or after the pass' validity period. Note that the pass doesn't include Westminster Abbey, the London Eye, or Madame Tussauds Waxworks. Think through your sightseeing plans carefully, and do the math before you buy.

Arrival in London

By Train: London has nine major train stations, all connected by the Tube (subway). All have ATMs, and many of the larger stations also have shops, fast food, exchange offices, and luggage storage. From any station, you can ride the Tube or taxi to your hotel. For more info on train travel, see www.nationalrail.co.uk.

By Bus: The main intercity bus station is Victoria Coach Station, one block southwest of Victoria train station (and the Victoria Tube station). For more on bus travel, see www.national express.com.

By Plane: London has five airports. Most tourists arrive at Heathrow or Gatwick airports, although flights from elsewhere in Europe may land at Stansted, Luton, or London City airports. For

Affording London's Sights

London is one of Europe's most expensive cities, with the dubious distinction of having some of the world's most expensive admission prices. Fortunately, many of its best sights are free.

Free Museums: Many of the city's biggest and best museums won't cost you a dime. Free sights include the British Museum, British Library, National Gallery, National Portrait Gallery, Tate Britain, Tate Modern, Wallace Collection, Imperial War Museum, Victoria and Albert Museum, Natural History Museum, Science Museum, National Army Museum, Sir John Soane's Museum, the Museum of London, the Geffrye, and on the outskirts of town, the Royal Air Force Museum London.

About half of these museums request a donation of a few pounds, but whether you contribute or not is up to you. If I spend money for an audioguide, I feel fine about not otherwise donating. If that makes you uncomfortable, donate.

Free Churches: Smaller churches let worshippers (and tourists) in free, although they may ask for a donation. The big sightseeing churches—Westminster Abbey and St. Paul's—charge steep admission fees, but offer free evensong services daily. Westminster Abbey also offers free organ recitals most Sundays at 17:45.

Other Freebies: There are plenty of free performances, such as lunch concerts at St. Martin-in-the-Fields (see page 89) and summertime movies at The Scoop amphitheater near City Hall (Tube: London Bridge, schedule at www.morelondon.com—click on "The Scoop"). For other freebies, check out www.freelondonlistings.co.uk. There's no charge to enjoy the pageantry of the Changing of the Guard, rants at Speaker's Corner in Hyde Park, displays at Harrods, the people-watching scene at Covent Garden, and the colorful streets of the East End. It's free to view the legal action at the Old Bailey and the legislature at work in the Houses of Parliament. And you can get into a bit of the Tower of London by attending Sunday services in the Tower's chapel (chapel access only).

Greenwich makes for a very cheap day out (see next chapter). Its many good museums are all free, and the journey there is covered by a cheap Zones 1–2 Tube ticket.

Sightseeing Deals: If you buy a paper One-Day Travelcard or rail ticket at a National Rail station (such as Paddington or Victoria), you may be eligible for two-for-one discounts at many popular sights, such as the London Eye, Tower of London, Tate Modern, and Madame Tussauds Waxworks. Get details and print vouchers at www.daysoutguide.co.uk, or look for brochures with coupons at major train stations.

Good-Value Tours: The £5-8 city walking tours with professional guides are one of the best deals going. (Note that the guides for the "free" walking tours are unpaid and expect tips—I'd pay for a professionally-guided tour instead.) Hop-on, hop-off big-bus tours (£22–26), while expensive, provide a great overview, and include free boat tours as well as city walks. A one-hour Thames ride to Greenwich costs £9.50 one-way, but most boats come with an entertaining commentary. A three-hour bicycle tour is about £16–19.

Pricey...But Worth It? Big-ticket sights worth their hefty admission fees are Kew Gardens (£13.50), Shakespeare's Globe (£10.50), and the Cabinet War Rooms, with its fine Churchill Museum (£14.95).

The London Eye has become a London must-see—though if you're on a tight budget, it's difficult to justify its very high cost (£18). While Hampton Court Palace (£14) is expensive, it is well-presented and a reasonable value if you have an interest in royal history. The Queen charges big time to open her palace to the public: Buckingham Palace (£16.50, Aug–Sept only) and her art gallery and carriage museum (adjacent to the palace, £8.75 and £7.75, £15 for both) are expensive but interesting. Madame Tussauds Waxworks is pricey but still fun and popular (£28, £22.50 if purchased at TI, drops to £14 after 17:00 if booked online). The Vinopolis wine museum provides a way to get a buzz and call it museum-going (from £20, entry includes tastes of wine).

Many smaller museums cost only around £5. My favorites include the Courtauld Gallery (free on Mon until 14:00) and the Wellington Museum at Apsley House (£6, www.english-heritage.org.uk).

Not Worth It: The London Dungeon, at £22.50, is gimmicky, overpriced, and a terrible value...despite the long line at the door.

Theater: Compared with Broadway's prices, London theater is a bargain. Seek out the freestanding "tkts" booth at Leicester

Square to get discounts from 25 to 50 percent on good seats (though not necessarily for the hottest shows; see page 139). If you're willing to settle for the cheapest seats (possibly with obstructed views), ask the theater's box office for their best deal (even the hottest shows generally have some £10–20 tickets). A £5 "groundling" ticket for a play at Shakespeare's Globe is the best theater deal in town (see page 140). Tickets to the Open Air Theatre at north London's Regent's Park start at £12 (see page 141).

London doesn't come cheap. But with its many free museums and affordable plays, this cosmopolitan, cultured city offers days of sightseeing thrills without requiring you to pinch your pennies (or your pounds).

specifics on getting from London's airports to downtown London, see "London Connections" on page 181; for hotels near Heathrow and Gatwick, see page 162.

Helpful Hints

Theft Alert: Wear your money belt. The Artful Dodger is alive and well in London. Be on guard, particularly on public transportation and in places crowded with tourists, who, considered naive and rich, are targeted. The Changing of the Guard scene is a favorite for thieves. And more than 7,500 purses are stolen annually at Covent Garden alone.

Pedestrian Safety: Cars drive on the left side of the road—which can be as confusing for foreign pedestrians as for foreign drivers. Before crossing a street, I always look right, look left, then look right again just to be sure. Most crosswalks are even painted with instructions, reminding foreign guests to "Look right" or "Look left."

Medical Problems: Local hospitals have good-quality 24-hour-a-day emergency care centers where any tourist who needs help can drop in and, after a wait, be seen by a doctor. Your hotel has details. St. Thomas' Hospital, immediately across the river from Big Ben, has a fine reputation.

Getting Your Bearings: London is well-signed for visitors. A new initiative called Legible London is erecting thoughtfully designed, pedestrian-focused maps around town. In this sprawling city—where predictable grid-planned streets are relatively rare—it's also smart to buy and use a good map. The *Benson's London Street Map* (£2.75), sold at many newsstands and bookstores, is my favorite for efficient sightseeing.

Festivals: For one week in February and another in September, fashionistas descend on the city for **London Fashion Week** (www.londonfashionweek.co.uk). The famous **Chelsea Flower Show** blossoms in late May (book ahead for this popular event at www.rhs.org.uk/chelsea). During the annual **Trooping the Colour** in June, there are military bands and pageantry, and the Queen's birthday parade (www.trooping-the-colour.co.uk). Tennis fans pack the stands at the **Wimbledon Tennis Championship** on June 20–July 3 in 2011 (www.wimbledon.org), and partygoers head for the **Notting Hill Carnival** in late August.

Winter: London dazzles year-round, so consider visiting in winter, when airfares and hotel rates are generally cheaper and there are fewer tourists. For ideas on what to do, see the "Winter Activities in London" article at www.ricksteves.com/winteracts.

Internet Access: As nearly all hotels offer Internet access and cafés all over town have free Wi-Fi, there are fewer actual Internet cafés. If you need to get online, you'll find Internet cafés near Trafalgar Square (456 Strand), on Oxford Street (at #358, opposite Bond Street Tube station), and near Victoria Station (at 164 Victoria Street).

Travel Bookstores: Located between Covent Garden and Leicester Square, the very good **Stanfords Travel Bookstore** stocks current editions of many of my books (Mon–Fri 9:00–19:30, Thu 9:00–20:00, Sat 10:00–20:00, Sun 12:00–18:00, 12–14 Long Acre, Tube: Leicester Square, tel. 020/7836-1321, www.stanfords.co.uk).

Two impressive **Waterstone's** bookstores have the biggest collection of travel guides in town: on Piccadilly (Mon–Sat 9:00–22:00, Sun 12:00–18:00, Costa Café, 203 Piccadilly, tel. 020/7851-2400) and on Trafalgar Square (Mon–Sat 9:30–21:00, Sun 12:00–18:00, Costa Café on second floor, tel. 020/7839-4411).

Baggage Storage: Train stations have replaced their lockers with more secure baggage storage counters, known locally as "left luggage." Each bag must go through a scanner (just like at the airport), so lines can be slow. Expect long waits in the morning to check in (up to 45 minutes) and in the afternoon to pick up (each item-£8/24 hours, most stations daily 7:00–23:00). You can also store bags at the airports (similar rates and hours, www.excess-baggage.com). If leaving London and returning later, you may be able to leave a box or bag at your hotel for free—assuming you'll be staying there again.

Bike Rental: Barclays Cycle Hire rents bikes from self-service docking stations (most likely won't work with US credit or debit cards, www.tfl.gov.uk).

Getting Around London

To travel smart in a city this size, you must get comfortable with public transportation. London's excellent taxis, buses, and subway (Tube) system make a private car unnecessary.

If you do have a car, stow it—you don't want to drive in London. If you need convincing, here's one more reason: An £8 **congestion charge** is levied on any private car entering the city center during peak hours (Mon–Fri 7:00–18:00, no charge Sat–Sun and holidays, fee payable at gas stations, convenience stores, and self-service machines at public parking lots, or online at www.cclondon.com). Traffic cameras photograph and identify every vehicle that enters the fee zone; if you get spotted and don't pay up by midnight that day (or pay £10 until midnight of the following day), you'll get socked with at least a £60 penalty. The system has been effective in cutting down traffic jam delays and bolstering

London's public transit. The revenue that's raised subsidizes the buses, which are now cheaper, more frequent, and even more user-friendly than before. Today, the vast majority of vehicles in the city center are buses, taxis, and service trucks. (Drivers—or American city planners—can find out more information on the congestion charge at www.cclondon.com.)

Public-Transit Passes

London has the most expensive public transit in the world—save money on your Tube and bus rides using a multi-ride pass. You have three options: pay double by buying individual tickets as you go; buy a £3 Oyster card and top it up as needed to travel like a local for about £1–2 per ride; or get a Travelcard for unlimited travel on one or seven days.

The transit system has six zones. Since almost all of my recommended accommodations, restaurants, and sights are within Zones 1 and 2, those are the prices I've listed here—but you'll pay more to go farther afield. Specific fares and other details change constantly; for a complete and updated list of prices, check www.tfl.gov.uk.

Individual Transit Tickets

These days in London, individual paper tickets are dinosaurs; there's no point buying one unless you're literally taking just one ride your entire time in the city. Because individual fares (£4 per Tube ride, £2 per bus ride) are about double the cost of using a pay-as-you-go Oyster card (explained below), in just two or three rides you'll recoup the £3 added deposit for the Oyster. If you do buy a single ticket, avoid ticket-window lines in Tube stations by using the coin-op machines; practice on the punchboard to see how the system works (hit "Adult Single" and your destination). These tickets are valid only on the day of purchase.

Oyster Cards

A pay-as-you-go Oyster card (a plastic card embedded with a computer chip) is the standard, smart way to economically ride the Tube, buses, Docklands Light Railway (DLR), and Overground. On each type of transport, you simply lay the card flat against the yellow card reader at the turnstile or entrance, it flashes green, and the fare is automatically deducted. (You'll also touch your card again to exit the Tube and DLR turnstiles, but not to exit buses.)

With an Oyster card, rides cost about half the price of individual paper tickets (£1.80 or £2.30 per Tube ride—depending on time of day, £1.20 per bus ride). You buy the card itself at any Tube station ticket window for a £3 deposit, then load it up with as much credit as you want. (For extra peace of mind, ask about registering your card against theft or loss.) When your balance gets low, you simply add credit—or "top up"—at a ticket window or machine. A price cap on the pay-as-you-go Oyster card guarantees you'll never pay more than the One-Day Travelcard price within a 24-hour period.

You can see how much credit remains on your card or review the trips you've taken so far by swiping it at any automatic ticket machine. Oyster card balances never expire (though they need reactivating at a ticket window every two years), so you can use the card whenever you're in London, or lend it to someone else. If you're done with the card (and don't mind a short wait), you can turn it in to reclaim your £3 deposit at any ticket window.

Travelcards

Like the Oyster card, Travelcards are valid on the Tube, buses, Docklands Light Railway (DLR), and Overground. The difference is that Travelcards let you ride as many times as you want within a one- or seven-day period for one fixed price.

Before you buy a card, estimate where you'll be going; there's a card for Zones 1 and 2, and another for Zones 1–6 (which includes Heathrow Airport). If Heathrow is the only ride you're taking outside Zones 1–2 (which is likely), you can pay a small supplement to make the Zones 1–2 Travelcard stretch to cover that one ride.

The **One-Day Travelcard** gives you unlimited travel for a day (Zones 1–2: £7.20, off-peak version £5.60; Zones 1–6: £15, off-peak version £7.50; cheaper off-peak versions are good for travel after 9:30 on weekdays and anytime on weekends). This Travelcard works like a traditional paper ticket: You buy it at any Tube station ticket window or machine, then feed it into a turnstile (and retrieve it) to enter and exit the Tube. On a bus, just show it to the driver when you get on.

The **Seven-Day Travelcard** is a great option if you're staying four or more days and plan to use the buses and Tube a lot. It's actually issued on a plastic Oyster card, but gives you unlimited travel anytime, anywhere in Zones 1 and 2 for a week (£25.80 plus the refundable £3 deposit for the Oyster card). As with an Oyster card, you'll touch it to the yellow pad when entering or exiting a Tube turnstile, or when boarding a bus.

Discounts

Groups: A gang of 10 or more adults can travel all day on the Tube for £3.70 each (but not on buses). Kids ages 11–17 pay £1 when part of a group of 10.

Families: A paying adult can take up to four kids (aged 10 and under) for free on the Tube, Docklands Light Railway (DLR), and Overground all day, every day (kids 10 and under are always free on buses). At the Tube station, use the manual gate, rather than the turnstiles, to be waved in. Other child and student discounts are explained at www.tfl.gov.uk/tickets.

River Cruises: A Travelcard gives you a 33 percent discount on most Thames cruises (see "Cruises" on page 72). If you pay for Thames Clippers (including the Tate-to-Tate museum boat) with your pay-as-you go Oyster card, you'll get a 10 percent discount.

Sightseeing Deal: Buy a paper One-Day Travelcard or rail ticket at a National Rail station, and you may qualify for two-for-one discounts at many popular sights (look for brochures with coupons at major train stations, or print vouchers at www.daysout guide.co.uk).

Passes: The Bottom Line

Struggling to choose which pass works best for your trip? First of all, skip the individual tickets. On a short visit (three days or fewer), if you think you'll be zipping around a lot, consider a One-Day Travelcard for each day you're here (or at least for your busiest days); if you'll be taking fewer, more focused rides, get an Oyster card and pay as you go. If you're in London four days or longer, the Seven-Day Travelcard will likely pay for itself.

By Tube

London's subway system (called the Tube or Underground—but never "subway," which refers to a pedestrian underpass) is one of this planet's great people-movers and often the fastest long-distance transport in town (runs Mon–Sat about 5:00–24:00, Sun about 7:00–23:00). While technically not part of the Tube, two other commuter rail lines are tied into the network: The Docklands Light Railway (called DLR, runs to the Docklands, 2012 Olympics site, and Greenwich) and the Overground.

Get your bearings by studying a map of the system (free at any station). Each line has a name (such as Circle, Northern, or Bakerloo) and two directions (indicated by the end-of-the-line stops). Find the line that will take you to your destination, and figure out roughly what direction (north, south, east, or west) you'll need to go to get there.

You can use an Oyster card, Travelcard, or individual tickets (all explained earlier) to pay for your journey. At the Tube station, touch your Oyster card flat against the turnstile's yellow card reader, both when you enter and exit the station. If you have a regular paper ticket or a One-Day Travelcard, feed it into the turnstile, reclaim it, and hang on to it—you'll need it later.

Find your train by following signs to your line and the (general) direction it's headed (such as Central Line: east). Since some

tracks are shared by several lines, double-check before boarding a train: First, make sure your destination is one of the stops listed on the sign at the platform. Also, check the electronic signboards that announce which train is next, and make sure the destination (the end-of-the-line stop) is the direction you want. Some trains, particularly on the Circle and District lines, split off for other directions, but each train has its final destination marked above its windshield.

Trains run roughly every 3–10 minutes. If one train is absolutely packed and you notice another to the same destination is coming in three minutes, wait to avoid the sardine routine. Rush hours (8:00–10:00 and 16:00–19:00) can be packed and sweaty. Bring something to do to make your waiting time productive. If you get confused, ask for advice from a local, a blue-vested staff person, or at the information window located before the turnstile entry.

You can't leave the system without touching your Oyster card to an electronic reader, or feeding your ticket or One-Day Travelcard into the turnstile. (If you have a single-trip paper ticket, the turnstile will eat your now-expired ticket; if it's a One-Day Travelcard, it will spit out your still-valid card.) Save walking time by choosing the best street exit—check

the maps on the walls or ask any station personnel.

The system can be fraught with construction delays and breakdowns (the Circle Line is notorious for problems). This will be especially noticeable in 2011, as London gears up for the 2012 Olympics. Most construction is scheduled for weekends. Closures are known and publicized in advance (online at www .tfl.gov.uk and with posters in the Tube). Pay attention to signs and announcements explaining necessary detours. Closed Tube lines are often replaced by temporary bus service, but it can be faster to figure out alternate routes on the Tube; since the lines

LONDON

LONDON

Handy Bus Routes

Since London instituted a congestion charge for cars, the bus system has gotten faster, easier, and cheaper than ever. Tube-oriented travelers need to get over their tunnel vision, learn the bus system, and get around fast and easy. The best views are upstairs on a double-decker.

Here are some of the most useful routes:

Route #9: Knightsbridge (Harrods) to Hyde Park Corner to Piccadilly Circus to Trafalgar Square. This is one of two "Heritage Routes," using old-style double-decker buses.

Routes #11 and #24: Victoria Station to Westminster Abbey to Trafalgar Square

N

REGENT'S PARK

BRITISH LIBRARY •

BRITISH MUSEUM

#15
PADDINGTON STATION

MARBLE ARCH

OXFORD CIRCUS

TRAFALGAR SQUARE
#9 + #24

KENS. GDNS.

HYDE PARK

PICCADILLY CIRCUS

WEST- MINSTER ABBEY

HIGH STREET KENSINGTON
#9

HARRODS

HYDE PARK CORNER

THAMES RIVER

VICTORIA STATION
#11 + 24

VICTORIA COACH STATION #11

#24

DCH

(#11 continues to St. Paul's and Liverpool Street Station).

Route #RV1 (a scenic South Bank joyride): Tower of London to Tower Bridge to Southwark Street (five-minute walk behind Tate Modern/Shakespeare's Globe) to London Eye/Waterloo Station/County Hall, then over Waterloo Bridge to Aldwych and Covent Garden.

Route #15: Paddington Station to Oxford Circus to Regent Street/TI to Piccadilly Circus to Trafalgar Square to Fleet Street to St. Paul's to Tower of London. This is the other "Heritage Route," using old-style double-decker buses.

In addition, several buses (including #6, #13, #15, #23, #139, and #159) make the corridor run from Trafalgar, Piccadilly Circus, and Oxford Circus to Marble Arch. Check the bus stop closest to your hotel—it might be convenient to your sightseeing plans.

LONDON

LEGEND

`--- #9`

`..... #11 + #24`

`--- #RV1`

`— #15`

LIVERPOOL STREET STATION
#11

COVENT GARDEN
#RV1

← ST. PAUL'S

TOWER OF LONDON
#15 + #RV1

TATE MODERN & SHAKESPEARE'S GLOBE

#RV1

TOWER BRIDGE

WATERLOO STATION, LONDON EYE & COUNTY HALL

NOT TO SCALE

cross each other constantly, there are several ways to make any journey. For help, check out the "Journey Planner" at www.tfl .gov.uk.

Tube Etiquette

- When your train arrives, stand off to the side and let riders exit the train before you try to board.
- Avoid using the hinged seats near the doors of some trains when the car is jammed; they take up valuable standing space.
- If you're blocking the door when the train stops, step out of the car and off to the side, let others off, then get back on.
- Talk softly in the cars. Listen to how quietly Londoners communicate and follow their lead.
- On escalators, stand on the right and pass on the left. But note that in some passageways or stairways, you might be directed to walk on the left (the direction Brits go behind the wheel).
- When leaving a station, it's polite to hold the door for the person behind you.
- Discreet eating and drinking are fine (nothing smelly); drinking alcohol and smoking are not.

By Bus

If you figure out the bus system, you'll swing like Tarzan through the urban jungle of London. Pick up a free bus map at a TI, transport office, or some major museums; it will list the bus routes best for sightseeing. Also see the "Handy Bus Routes" sidebar.

Buses are covered by Travelcards and Oyster cards (previous page). Or you can buy individual tickets from a machine at bus stops (no change given). Any bus ride in downtown London costs £2 for those paying cash, or £1.20 if using an Oyster card (with a cap of £3.90 maximum per day). If you're staying longer, consider the £16.60 Seven-Day bus pass.

The first step in mastering London's bus system is learning how to decipher the bus stop signs (see photo). In the first column, find your destination on the list—e.g., Paddington. In the next column, find a bus that goes there—the #23. The final

O		
Oakwood ⊖	N91	🅞 ⊗
Old Coulsdon	N68	Aldwych
Old Ford	N8	Oxford Circus
Old Kent Road Canal Bridge	53, N381	🅞
	453	🅞 🅞
	N21	🅞
Old Street ⊖ ≷	243	Aldwych
Orpington ≷	N47	🅞
Oxford Circus ⊖	Any bus	🅞
	N18	🅞

P		
Paddington ⊖ ≷	23, N15	🅞 🅞 🅞
Palmers Green ≷	N29	🅞
Park Langley	N3	🅞 🅞
Peckham	12	🅞 🅞
	N89, N343	🅞
	N136	🅞 🅝
	N381	🅞
Penge Pawleyne Arms	176	🅞
	N3	🅞 🅝
Petts Wood ≷	N47	🅞
Pimlico Grosvenor Road	24	🅞 🅝
Plaistow Greengate	N15	🅞 🅞
Plumstead ≷	53	🅞
Plumstead Common	53	🅞

column has a letter within a circle (e.g., "M") that tells you exactly which bus stop you need to stand at to catch your bus. (You'll find the same letter marked on a neighborhood map nearby.) Make your way to that stop—you'll know it's yours because it will have the same letter on its pole—and wait for the bus with your number on it to arrive. Hop on, and you're good to go.

As you board, touch your Oyster card to the electronic card reader, or, if you have a paper ticket or a One-Day Travelcard, show it to the driver. On "Heritage Routes" #9 and #15 (which use older double-decker buses), you may still pay a conductor; take a seat, and he or she will come around to collect your fare or verify your pass. There's no need to tap your card or show your ticket when you hop off.

If you have an Oyster card or Travelcard, save your feet and get in the habit of hopping buses for quick little straight shots, even just to get to a Tube stop. During bump-and-grind rush hours (8:00–10:00 and 16:00–19:00), you'll usually go faster by Tube.

By Taxi

London is the best taxi town in Europe. Big, black, carefully regulated cabs are everywhere. (While historically known as "black cabs," some of London's official taxis are now covered with wildly colored ads.) Some cabs are switching to biofuels—a good use for frying oil used for all those fish-and-chips.

I've never met a crabby cabbie in London. They love to talk, and they know every nook and cranny in town. I ride in a taxi each day just to get my London questions answered (drivers must pass a rigorous test on "The Knowledge" of London geography to earn their license).

If a cab's top light is on, just wave it down. Drivers flash lights when they see you wave. They have a tight turning radius (on new cabs, the back tires actually pivot), so you can hail cabs going in either direction. If waving doesn't work, ask someone where you can find a taxi stand. Telephoning a cab will get you one in a few minutes, but costs a little more (toll tel. 0871-871-8710; £2 surcharge, plus extra fee to book ahead by credit card).

Rides start at £2.20. The regular tariff #1 covers most of the day (Mon–Fri 6:00–20:00), tariff #2 is during "unsociable hours" (Mon–Fri 20:00–22:00 and Sat–Sun 6:00–22:00), and tariff #3 is at night (nightly 22:00–6:00) and on holidays. Rates go up about 15–20 percent with each higher tariff. All extra charges are explained in writing on the cab wall. Tip a cabbie by rounding up (maximum 10 percent).

Connecting downtown sights is quick and easy, and will cost you about £6–8 (for example, St. Paul's to the Tower of London). For a short ride, three adults in a cab generally travel at close to Tube prices—and groups of four or five adults should taxi everywhere. All cabs can carry five passengers, and some take six, for the same cost as a single traveler.

Don't worry about meter cheating. Licensed British cab meters come with a sealed computer chip and clock that ensures you'll get the correct tariff. The only way a cabbie can cheat you is by taking a needlessly long route. Another pitfall is taking a cab when traffic is bad to a destination efficiently served by the Tube. On one trip to London, I hopped in a taxi at South Kensington for Waterloo Station and hit bad traffic. Rather than spending 20 minutes and £2 on the Tube, I spent 40 minutes and £16 in a taxi.

If you overdrink and ride in a taxi, be warned: Taxis charge £40 for "soiling" (a.k.a., pub puke). If you forget this book in a taxi, call the Lost Property office and hope for the best (toll tel. 0845-330-9882).

Tours in London

▲▲▲Hop-on, Hop-off Double-Decker Bus Tours

Two competitive companies (Original and Big Bus) offer essentially the same two tours of the city's sightseeing highlights, with nearly 30 stops on each route. Big Bus tours are a little more expensive (£26), while Original tours are cheaper (£22 with this book) and nearly as good.

These 2–3-hour, once-over-lightly bus tours drive by all the famous sights, providing a stress-free way to get your bearings and see the biggies. They stop at a core group of sights regardless of which overview tour you're on: Piccadilly Circus, Trafalgar Square, Big Ben, St. Paul's, the Tower of London, Marble Arch, Victoria Station, and elsewhere. With a good guide and nice weather, I'd sit back and enjoy the entire tour. (If you don't like your guide, you can hop off and try your luck with the next departure.)

Each company offers at least one route with live (English-only) guides, and a second (sometimes slightly different route) comes with recorded, dial-a-language narration. In addition to the overview tours, both Original and Big Bus include the Thames River boat trip by City Cruises (similar to the £13 "River Red Rover" ticket explained on page 73) and three 1.5-hour walking tours.

Pick up a map from any flier rack or from one of the countless

> ## Combining a London Bus Tour the Changing of the Guard
>
> For a grand and efficient intro to London, consider catching either of the bus companies' overview tours at 8:30, riding 90 percent of the loop (which takes just over two hours, depending on traffic), and hopping off at Buckingham Palace in time to catch the Changing of the Guard ceremony. Both tours depart at 8:30 every morning—choose between the Big Bus Tour (live guide, catch it at the Green Park Tube station) or the Original Bus Tour (recorded narration, catch it at Grosvenor Gardens a block from Victoria Station). If you miss the 8:30 bus, there's generally another departure in 20 minutes that might get you to the ceremony a bit late (confirm with the driver).

salespeople, and study the complex system. Sunday morning—when the traffic is light and many museums are closed—is a fine time for a tour. Unless you're using the bus tour mainly for hop-on, hop-off transportation, consider saving time and money by taking a night tour (described later).

Buses run about every 10–15 minutes in summer, every 20 minutes in winter, and operate daily. They start at about 8:30 and run until early evening in summer, or until late afternoon in winter. The last full loop usually leaves Victoria Station about 17:00 (confirm by checking the schedule or asking the driver).

You can buy tickets from drivers or from staff at street kiosks (credit cards accepted at kiosks at major stops such as Victoria, ticket good for 24 hours).

Original London Sightseeing Bus Tour—There are two versions of their basic highlights loop: **The Original Tour** (live guide,

marked with a yellow triangle on the front of the bus) and the **City Sightseeing Tour** (essentially the same route but with recorded narration, a kids' soundtrack option, and a stop at Madame Tussauds; bus marked with a red triangle). Other routes include the blue-triangle **Museum Tour** (connecting far-flung museums and major shopping stops), and green, black, and purple triangle routes (linking major train stations to the central route). All routes are covered by the same ticket. Keep it simple and just take one of the city highlights tours (£25, £22 after £3 discount with this book, limit two discounts per book, they'll rip off the corner of this page—raise bloody hell if the staff or driver won't honor this discount; also online deals, info center at 17 Cockspur Street, tel. 020/8877-1722, www.theoriginaltour.com).

Big Bus London Tours—For £26 (up to 30 percent discount if you book low-use times online—requires printer), you get the same basic overview tours: Red buses come with a live guide, while the blue route has a recorded narration and a longer path (one hour longer) around Hyde Park. These pricier Big Bus tours tend to have better, more dynamic guides than the Original tours, and more departures as well—meaning shorter waits for those hopping on and off (daily 8:30–18:00, winter until 16:30, info center at 48 Buckingham Palace Road, tel. 020/7233-9533, www.bigbus tours.com).

London by Night Sightseeing Tour—This tour offers a two-hour circuit, but after hours, with no extras (e.g., walks, river cruises), and at a lower price. While the narration can be pretty lame, the views at twilight are grand—though note that it stays light until late on summer nights, and London just doesn't do floodlighting as well as Paris (£16, £11 online, drivers take cash only). From May through late September, there are nightly departures at 19:30 (open top), 20:00 (open top), 20:30 (closed top), and 21:30 (open top) from Victoria Station (Jan–April and late Sept–late Dec departs at 19:30 only with closed-top bus, no tours between Christmas and New Year). Buses leave from the curb immediately in front of Victoria Station (closest to building at muster point C; or you can board at any stop, such as Paddington Station, Marble Arch, Trafalgar Square, London Eye, or Tower of London; tel. 020/8545-6109, www.london-by-night.net). For a memorable and economical evening, munch a scenic picnic dinner on the top deck. (There are plenty of take-away options within the train stations and near the various stops.)

▲▲Walking Tours

Several times a day, top-notch local guides lead (sometimes big) groups through specific slices of London's past. Look for brochures at TIs or ask at hotels, although the latter usually push higher-priced bus tours. *Time Out*, the weekly entertainment guide (£3 at newsstands), lists some, but not all, scheduled walks. Check with the various tour companies by phone or online to get their full picture.

To take a walking tour, you simply show up at the announced location and pay the guide. Then enjoy two chatty hours of Dickens, Harry Potter, the Plague, Shakespeare, Legal London, the Beatles, Jack the Ripper, or whatever is on the agenda.

The Essential London Walk—Blue Badge Tourist Guides offer a basic two-hour walk for £5, 365 days a year at 10:00 (from the

Eros statue on Piccadilly Circus—look for the guide with the Blue Badge umbrella, www.touristguides.org.uk). Tours go rain or shine, and there's no need to pre-book—just show up. This is the best deal going, as you know you'll get a well-trained guide leading you through the historic core of London (from Piccadilly, you walk to Trafalgar Square, Whitehall, Westminster Abbey, the Houses of Parliament, and the Thames, and end at Buckingham Palace—just in time for the last part of the Changing of the Guard).

London Walks—This leading company lists its extensive and creative daily schedule in a beefy, plain *London Walks* brochure. Pick it up at TIs, hotels, or St. Martin-in-the-Fields' Café in the Crypt on Trafalgar Square, or access it on their website. Just perusing their fascinating lineup of tours inspires me to stay longer in London. Their two-hour walks, led by professional guides and actors, cost £8 (cash only, walks offered year-round, private tours for groups-£120, tel. 020/7624-3978 for a live person, tel. 020/7624-9255 for a recording of today's or tomorrow's walks and the Tube station they depart from, www.walks.com).

London Walks also offers "Explorer Days" tours into the countryside, a good option for those with limited time and transportation (£14 plus £10–46 for transportation and any admission costs, cash only: Stonehenge/Salisbury, Oxford/Cotswolds, Cambridge, Bath, and so on). These are economical in part because everyone gets group discounts for transportation and admissions.

Sandemans New London "Free Royal London Tour"—This company employs English-speaking students (rather than licensed guides) who recite three-hour spiels covering the basic London sights. While the fast-moving, youthful tours are light and irreverent, and can be both entertaining and fun, it's misleading to call the tours "free," as tips are expected (the guides are unpaid). With the Essential London Walk (listed earlier) offered daily at a reasonable price by professional Blue Badge guides, taking this "free" tour makes no sense to me (daily at 11:00 and 13:00, meet at Wellington Arch, Tube: Hyde Park Corner, Exit 2). Sandemans also has other guided tours for a charge, including a Pub Crawl (£12, Tue–Sat at 19:30, meet at Belushi's at 9 Russell Street, Tube: Covent Garden, www .newlondon-tours.com).

Beatles Walks—Fans of the still–Fab Four can take one of three Beatles walks (London Walks, listed earlier, has two that run 5 days/week; Big Bus, above, includes a daily walk with their bus tour). For more on the Beatles, see page 104.

Daily Reminder

Sunday: The Tower of London and British Museum are both especially crowded today. The Speakers' Corner in Hyde Park rants from early afternoon until early evening. These places are closed: Banqueting House, Sir John Soane's Museum, and legal sights (Houses of Parliament, City Hall, and Old Bailey; the neighborhood called The City is dead). Westminster Abbey and St. Paul's are open during the day for worship but closed to sightseers. With all these closures, this morning is a good time to take a bus tour. Most big stores are open 12:00–18:00. Street markets are flourishing at Camden Lock, Spitalfields, Petticoat Lane, Brick Lane, and Greenwich, but Portobello Road and Brixton markets are closed (though the Brixton farmers' market is open 10:00–14:00). Theaters are quiet, as most actors take today off. (There are a few exceptions, such as *The Lion King* and Shakespeare's Globe, which offer Sunday performances in summer.)

Monday: Virtually all sights are open except for Apsley House, Sir John Soane's Museum, Vinopolis, and a few others. The Courtauld Gallery is free until 14:00. The Houses of Parliament are usually open until 22:30.

Tuesday: Virtually all sights are open, except for Vinopolis and Apsley House. The British Library is open until 20:00. On the first Tuesday of the month, Sir John Soane's Museum is also open 18:00–21:00. The Houses of Parliament are usually open until 22:30.

Wednesday: Virtually all sights are open, except for Vinopolis.

Jack the Ripper Walks—Each walking tour company seems to make most of its money with "haunted" and Jack the Ripper tours. Many guides are historians and would rather not lead these lightweight tours—but, in tourism as in journalism, "if it bleeds, it leads" (which is why the juvenile London Dungeon is one of London's busiest sights).

Two reliably good two-hour tours start every night at the Tower Hill Tube station exit. **Ripping Yarns** is guided by off-duty Yeoman Warders—the Tower of London "Beefeaters" (£7, pay at end, nightly at 18:45, no tours between Christmas and New Years, mobile 07813-559-301, www.jack-the-ripper-tours.com). **London Walks'** guides leave from the same spot later each night (£7, pay at the start, nightly at 19:30, tel. 020/7624-3978, recorded info tel. 020/7624-9255, www.jacktheripperwalk.com). After taking both, I found the London Walks more entertaining, informative, and with a better route (along quieter, once-hooker-friendly lanes, with less traffic), starting at Tower Hill and ending at Liverpool Street Station rather than returning to Tower Hill. Groups can be huge

Thursday: All sights are open, plus evening hours at the British Museum (selected galleries until 20:30), National Portrait Gallery (until 21:00), and Vinopolis (until 22:00).

Friday: All sights are open, except the Houses of Parliament. Sights open late include the British Museum (selected galleries until 20:30), National Gallery (until 21:00), National Portrait Gallery (until 21:00), Vinopolis (until 22:00), Victoria and Albert Museum (until 22:00), and Tate Modern (until 22:00). Best street market today: Spitalfields.

Saturday: Most sights are open except legal ones (Old Bailey, City Hall, Houses of Parliament; skip The City). Vinopolis is open until 22:00, the Tate Modern is open until 22:00. Today's the day to hit the Portobello Road street market; the Camden Lock and Greenwich markets are also good.

Notes: The St. Martin-in-the-Fields church offers concerts at lunchtime (Mon, Tue, and Fri at 13:00) and in the evening (jazz Wed at 20:00; classical at 19:30 Thu–Sat, sometimes Tue). Evensong occurs daily at St. Paul's (Mon–Sat at 17:00 and Sun at 15:15), Westminster Abbey (Mon–Fri at 17:00—may be spoken on Wed, Sat–Sun at 15:00), and Southwark Cathedral (weekdays at 17:30, Sat at 16:00, Sun at 15:00, no service on Wed or alternate Mon). London by Night Sightseeing Tour buses leave from Victoria Station every evening (19:30–21:30, only at 19:30 in winter). The London Eye spins nightly (last departure between 20:00 and 21:30, depending on the season).

LONDON

for both, but there's always room—just show up.

Private Walks with Local Guides—Standard rates for London's registered Blue Badge guides are about £125 for four hours, and £200 or more for nine hours (tel. 020/7780-4060, www.tourist guides.org.uk or www.blue-badge.org.uk). I know and like four fine local guides: **Sean Kelleher** (tel. 020/8673-1624, mobile 07764-612-770, seankelleher@btinternet.com), **Britt Lonsdale** (£150/half-day, £250/day, great with families, tel. 020/7386-9907, mobile 07813-278-077, brittl@btinternet.com), and two others who work in London when they're not on the road leading my Britain tours, **Tom Hooper** (mobile 07986-048-047, tomh@ricksteves.net) and **Gillian Chadwick** (mobile 07889-976-598, gillianc@ricksteves.net).

Driver-Guides—These two guides have cars or a minibus (particularly helpful for travelers with limited mobility) and charge around £290/half-day and £420/day for London tours (see websites and contact them for details): **Robina Brown** (tel. 020/7228-2238, www.driverguidetours.com, robina@driverguidetours.com) and

London

Janine Barton (tel. 020/7402-4600, http://seeitinstyle.synthasite.com, jbsiis@aol.com).

London Duck Tours

A bright-yellow amphibious WWII-vintage vehicle (the model that landed troops on Normandy's beaches on D-Day) takes a gang of 30 tourists past some famous sights on land—Big Ben, Trafalgar Square, Piccadilly Circus—then splashes into the Thames for a cruise. All in all, it's good fun at a rather steep price. The live guide works hard, and it's kid-friendly to the point of goofiness (£20, April–Sept daily 10:30–18:00, shorter hours Oct–March, 1–4/hr, 1.25 hours—45 minutes on land and 30 minutes in the river, £3 booking fee online, these book up in advance, departs from Chicheley Street—you'll see the big, ugly vehicle parked 100 yards behind the London Eye, Tube: Waterloo or Westminster, tel. 020/7928-3132, www.londonducktours.co.uk).

Bike Tours

London, like Paris, is committed to creating more bike paths, and many of its best sights can be laced together with a pleasant pedal through its parks. A bike tour is a fun way to see the sights and enjoy the city on two wheels.

London Bicycle Tour Company—Three tours covering London are offered daily from their base at Gabriel's Wharf on the south bank of the Thames. Sunday is the best, as there is less car traffic (**Central Tour**—£15.95, April–Oct daily at 10:30, Nov–March only on Mon–Fri, 6 miles, 2.5 hours, includes Westminster, Covent Garden, and St. Paul's; **Royal West Tour**—£18.95, April–Oct Sat–Sun at 12:00, Nov–March only on Sun, 9 miles, 3.5 hours, includes Westminster, Hyde Park, Buckingham Palace, and Covent Garden; **East Tour**—£18.95, April–Oct Sat–Sun at 14:00, Nov–March only on Sat at 12:00, 9 miles, 3.5 hours, includes south side of the river to Tower Bridge, then The City to the East End;

book ahead for off-season tours). They also rent bikes (£3.50/hour, £20/day; office open daily 10:00–18:00, west of Blackfriars Bridge on the South Bank, 1a Gabriel's Wharf, tel. 020/7928-6838, www .londonbicycle.com).

Fat Tire Bike Tours—Daily bike tours cover the highlights of downtown London on two different itineraries (£2 discount with this book): Royal London (£20, daily March–Nov at 11:00, June–Aug also at 15:30, 7 miles, 4 hours, meet at Queensway Tube station; includes Parliament, Buckingham Palace, Hyde Park, and Trafalgar Square) and River Thames (£30, mid-March–Nov Thu–Sat at 10:30, 5 hours, meet at Waterloo Tube station—exit 2; includes London Eye, St. Paul's, Tower of London, Trafalgar Square, Covent Garden, and boat trip on the Thames). The spiel is light and irreverent rather than scholarly, but the price is right. Reservations are easy online and required for River Thames tours and kids' bikes (off-season tours by arrangement, mobile 078-8233-8779, www.fattirebiketourslondon.com). The schedule changes often—confirm online or by phone.

▲▲Cruises

Boat tours with entertaining commentaries sail regularly from many points along the Thames. The options are confusing, since several companies offer essentially the same trip. Your basic options are to use the boats either for a scenic joyride cruise within central London, or for transportation to an outlying sight (such as Greenwich or Kew Gardens).

Boats come and go from several docks in central London (see sidebar). The most popular places to embark are Westminster Pier (at the base of Westminster Bridge across the street from Big Ben) and Waterloo Pier (at the London Eye, across the river).

Buy boat tickets at the kiosks on the docks. While individual Tube and bus tickets don't work on the boats, a Travelcard can snare you a 33 percent discount on most cruises (just show the card when you pay for the cruise; no discount with the pay-as-you-go Oyster card except on Thames Clippers). Because different companies vary in the discounts they offer, always ask. Children and seniors generally get discounts. You can purchase drinks and scant, pricey snacks on board. Clever budget travelers pack a picnic and munch while they cruise.

Round-trip fares are only a bit more than one-way. Still, for pleasure and efficiency, consider combining a one-way cruise (to Kew, Greenwich, or wherever) with a Tube or train ride back.

Tourist-Oriented Cruises in Central London

London offers many made-for-tourist cruises on slow-moving, open-top boats accompanied by commentary about passing sights.

Thames Boat Piers

While Westminster Pier is the most popular, it's not the only dock in town. Consider all the options (listed from west to east, as the Thames flows):

Millbank Pier (north bank), at the Tate Britain Museum, is used primarily by the "Tate to Tate" service (express connection to Tate Modern at Bankside Pier).

Westminster Pier (north bank), near the base of Big Ben, offers round-trip sightseeing cruises and lots of departures in both directions (though Thames Clippers don't stop here). Nearby sights include Parliament and Westminster Abbey.

Waterloo Pier (a.k.a. **London Eye Pier,** south bank), right at the base of the London Eye, is a good, less-crowded alternative to Westminster, with many of the same cruise options (Waterloo Station is nearby).

Embankment Pier (north bank) is near Covent Garden, Trafalgar Square, and Cleopatra's Needle (the obelisk on the Thames). This pier is used mostly for special boat trips (such as some RIB trips, and lunch and dinner cruises).

Festival Pier (south bank) is next to the Royal Festival Hall, just downstream from the London Eye.

Blackfriars Pier (north bank) is in The City, not far from St. Paul's.

Bankside Pier (south bank) is directly in front of the Tate Modern and Shakespeare's Globe.

London Bridge Pier (a.k.a. **London Bridge City Pier,** south bank) is near the HMS *Belfast* and the start of my Bankside Walk.

Tower Pier (north bank) is at the Tower of London, at the east edge of The City and near the East End.

St. Katharine's Pier (north bank) is just downstream from the Tower of London.

Canary Wharf Pier (north bank) is at the Docklands, London's new "downtown."

In outer London, you might also use the piers at **Greenwich, Kew Gardens,** and **Hampton Court.**

City Cruises runs boats from Westminster Pier across the river to Waterloo Pier, then downriver to Tower Pier and on to Greenwich (tel. 020/7740-0400, www.citycruises.com). If you want just a sample, hop on their 30-minute cruise only as far as Tower Pier (£8 one-way, £10.50 round-trip, daily April–Oct roughly 10:00–19:00, until 18:00 in winter, 2/hr). City Cruises also offers a £13 "River Red Rover" ticket good for all-day hop-on, hop-off travel (also included with the bus tours described on page 64)—though the line's limited stops in central London make this a lesser deal than it might seem.

Thames River Services runs a similar service with even fewer stops: Westminster to St. Katharine's Pier to Greenwich (tel. 020/7930-4097, www.thamesriverservices.co.uk). They have classic boats and feel a little friendlier and more old-fashioned. For more details, see "Cruising Downstream, to Greenwich and the Docklands," later.

The **Circular Cruise** offered by Crown River Services is a handy hop-on, hop-off route with stops at the Westminster, Festival, Embankment, Bankside, London Bridge, and St. Katharine's piers (£3 to go one stop, £8 one-way for a longer trip, £10.50 for an all-day ticket, daily 11:00–18:30, every 30 minutes late May–early Sept, fewer stops and less frequent off-season, tel. 020/7936-2033, www.crownriver.com).

The **London Eye** operates its own river cruise, offering a 40-minute live-guided circular tour from Waterloo Pier. As it's much pricier than the alternatives for just a short loop, it's a poor value (£12, reservations recommended, 10 percent discount if you pre-book online, no Travelcard discounts, departures daily generally at :45 past the hour, April–Oct 10:45–18:45, Nov–March 11:45–16:45, closed mid-Jan–mid-Feb, toll tel. 0870-500-0600, www.londoneye.com).

Careening at Top Speed Along the Thames: Two competing companies invite you aboard a small, 12-person, high-speed rigid inflatable boat (RIB—similar to a Zodiac) for an adrenaline-fueled tour of the city (London RIB Voyages: stand-up comedian guides, £32.50/50 minutes, £45/1.25 hours, tel. 020/7928-8933, www .londonribvoyages.com; Thames RIB Experience: £29/50 minutes, £45/1.5 hours, toll tel. 0870-224-4200, www.thamesribexperience .com).

Away from the Thames, on Regent's Canal: Consider exploring London's canals by taking a cruise on historic Regent's Canal in north London. The good ship *Jenny Wren* offers 1.5-hour guided canal boat cruises from Walker's Quay in Camden Town through scenic Regent's Park to Little Venice (£9; Aug daily at 10:30, 12:30, 14:30, and 16:30; April–July and Sept–Oct daily at 12:30 and 14:30, Sat–Sun also at 16:30; Walker's Quay, 250 Camden High Street, 3-minute walk from Tube: Camden Town; tel. 020/7485-4433, www.walkersquay.com). While in Camden Town, stop by the popular, punky Camden Lock Market to browse through trendy arts and crafts (daily 10:00–18:00, busiest on weekends, a block from Walker's Quay, www.camdenlockmarket.com).

Commuting by Clipper

Thames Clippers, with their fast, sleek, 220-seat catamarans, are designed for commuters rather than sightseers. Think of the clippers as express buses in the river—they zip no-nonsense through London every 20 minutes, stopping at most of the major docks en route: Embankment, Waterloo, Blackfriars or Bankside, London Bridge, Tower, Canary Wharf (Docklands), and Greenwich (roughly 20 minutes from Embankment to Tower, 10 more minutes to Docklands, 10 more minutes to Greenwich). However, the clippers are less pleasant for joyriding than the cruises described earlier. There's no commentary, and no open deck up top (the only outside access is on a crowded deck at the exhaust-choked back of the boat, where you're jostling for photos). Any one-way ride costs £5.30, and a River Roamer all-day ticket costs £12 (33 percent discount with Travelcard, 10 percent off with a pay-as-you-go Oyster card, tel. 020/7001-2222, www.thamesclippers.com).

The company also offers two express trips. The **"Tate to Tate"** boat service, which directly connects Tate Britain (Millbank Pier) and the Tate Modern (Bankside Pier), is made for art-lovers (£5 one-way, covered by £12 River Roamer day ticket; buy ticket at gallery desk, at kiosk by the dock, or onboard; daily 10:00–17:00, runs every 40 minutes, 18-minute trip, www.tate.org.uk/tatetotate). The O_2 **Express** runs only on nights when there are events going on at the O_2 Arena (formerly the Millennium Dome; from Waterloo Pier, £6 one-way, £12 round-trip, 30 minutes).

Cruising Downstream, to Greenwich and the Docklands

Greenwich: Both of the big tour companies (City Cruises and Thames River Services, described earlier) head to Greenwich from Westminster Pier. The cruises are usually narrated by the captain, with most commentary given on the way to Greenwich. The companies' prices are the same (£9.50 one-way, £12.50 round-trip), though their itineraries are slightly different: **City Cruises** stops at Waterloo/London Eye Pier and Tower Pier on the way to Greenwich (if you buy their £13 River Red Rover ticket, you can hop on and off all day long; daily April–Oct generally 10:00–17:00, less off-season, 2/hour, 1.25 hours from Westminster to Greenwich; cheaper to go from Tower Pier to Greenwich—£8 one-way, £10.50 round-trip, only 30 minutes to Greenwich—but you miss all the scenery in central London). **Thames River Services** stops only at St. Katharine's Pier on the way to Greenwich, making the trip a little faster (April–Oct 10:00–16:00, July–Aug until 17:00, daily 2/hour; Nov–March shorter hours and runs every 40 minutes; 1 hour from Westminster to Greenwich).

The **Thames Clippers,** described earlier, are cheaper, faster, and make more stops downtown, but have no commentary and no seating up top (£5.30 one-way, £12 for an all-day pass, 3/hour, about 45 minutes from Westminster to Greenwich).

To maximize both efficiency and sightseeing, I'd take a boat to Greenwich one way, and go the other way on the DLR (Docklands Light Railway), with a stop in the Docklands (Canary Wharf station).

The Docklands: Thames Clippers connect the Docklands' Canary Wharf Pier to both central London and Greenwich (£5.30 one-way, £12 for an all-day pass, no commentary, 3/hour, roughly 10 minutes to Tower, 30 minutes to Waterloo, 15 minutes to Greenwich).

Cruising Upstream, to Kew Gardens and Hampton Court Palace

Boats operated by the Westminster Passenger Services Association leave for Kew Gardens from Westminster Pier (£12 one-way, £18 round-trip, cash only; 4/day, April–Oct daily at 10:30, 11:15, 12:00, and 14:00; 1.5 hours, about half the trip is narrated, tel. 020/7930-2062, www.wpsa.co.uk). Most boats continue on to Hampton Court Palace for an additional £3 (and another 1.5 hours). Because of the river current, you'll sometimes save 30 minutes cruising from Hampton Court back into town (depends on the tide—ask before you commit to the boat). Romantic as these rides sound, it can be a long trip...especially upstream.

Self-Guided Walk

Westminster Walk

Just about every visitor to London strolls along historic Whitehall from Big Ben to Trafalgar Square. This quick, nine-stop walk gives meaning to that touristy ramble. Under London's modern traffic and big-city bustle lie 2,000 fascinating years of history. You'll get a whirlwind tour as well as a practical orientation to London. (Those traveling with an iPod or other MP3 player can download a free **Rick Steves Audio Tour** of this walk at www.ricksteves.com, or search for "Rick Steves' Audio Tours" on iTunes).

Start halfway across **Westminster Bridge** (❶) for that "Wow, I'm really in London!" feeling. Get a close-up view of the **Houses of Parliament** and **Big Ben** (floodlit at night). Downstream you'll see the **London Eye.** Down the stairs to Westminster Pier are boats to the Tower of London and Greenwich (downstream) or Kew Gardens (upstream).

En route to Parliament Square, you'll pass a **statue of Boadicea** (❷), the Celtic queen defeated by Roman invaders in A.D. 60.

Westminster Walk

TO COURTAULD GALLERY & "THE CITY"

LEICESTER SQUARE

NAT'L PORTRAIT GALLERY

tkts

ST. MARTIN-IN-THE-FIELDS

CHAR. CROSS

THE STRAND

CHARING CROSS STATION

GORDON'S WINE BAR

VILLIERS ST.

NATIONAL GALLERY

CHARING CROSS

S. HOLMES PUB

EMBANKMENT

EMBANK. PIER

JUBILEE PED. BRIDGE

TRAFALGAR SQUARE

END

NORTHUMBERLAND

WHITEHALL

OLD ADMIRALTY

SITE OF OLD SCOTLAND YARD

THE MALL

GUARDS ROAD

ST. JAMES'S PARK

HORSE GUARDS

HAIG STATUE

HORSE GUARDS AVE.

BANQUETING HOUSE

MIN. OF DEF.

THAMES

EMBANKMENT

VICTORIA

WATERLOO PIER

WESTMINSTER PIER

LONDON EYE

COUNTY HALL

WALKWAY

CHURCHILL MUSEUM & CABINET WAR ROOMS

CENOTAPH

KING CHARLES

*10 DOWNING

PARL. ST.

Westminster

CHURCHILL STATUE

GREAT GEORGE

BIRDCAGE WALK

WESTMINSTER ARMS PUB

PARL. SQ.

WESTMINSTER BRIDGE

START

BIG BEN

TO BUCKINGHAM PALACE

TOTHILL ST.

St James's Park

VICTORIA ST.

TO VICTORIA STATION

WESTMINSTER ABBEY

HOUSES OF PARLIAMENT

JUBILEE

BURGHERS OF CALAIS

200 YARDS

200 METERS

⊖ TUBE STATION

← BLDG. ENTRANCES

↗ VIEW

DCH

① Westminster Bridge
② Statue of Boadicea
③ View of Parliament Square
④ Walking Along Whitehall
⑤ Cenotaph
⑥ #10 Downing Street & Ministry of Defense
⑦ Banqueting House
⑧ Horse Guards
⑨ Trafalgar Square

LONDON

For fun, call home from a pay phone near Big Ben at about three minutes before the hour, to let your loved ones hear the bell ring. You'll find four red phone booths lining the north side of **Parliament Square** (❸) along Great George Street.

Wave hello to Churchill in Parliament Square. To his right is **Westminster Abbey** with its two stubby, elegant towers.

Head north up Parliament Street, which turns into **Whitehall** (❹), and walk toward Trafalgar Square. You'll see the thought-provoking **Cenotaph** (❺) in the middle of the street, reminding passersby of Britain's many war dead. To visit the Churchill Museum and Cabinet War Rooms (see page 83), take a left before the Cenotaph, on King Charles Street.

Continuing on Whitehall, stop at the barricaded and guarded **#10 Downing Street** (❻) to see the British "White House," home of the prime minister. Break the bobby's boredom and ask him a question. The huge building across Whitehall from Downing Street is the **Ministry of Defense** (MOD), the "British Pentagon."

Nearing Trafalgar Square, look for the 17th-century **Banqueting House** across the street (❼) and the **Horse Guards** (❽) behind the gated fence (Changing of the Horse Guards Mon–Sat at 11:00, Sun at 10:00, dismounting ceremony daily at 16:00).

The column topped by Lord Nelson marks **Trafalgar Square** (❾). The stately domed building on the far side of the square is the **National Gallery** (free), which has a classy café upstairs in the Sainsbury wing. To the right of the National Gallery is **St. Martin-in-the-Fields Church** and its Café in the Crypt.

To get to Piccadilly from Trafalgar Square, walk up Cockspur Street to Haymarket, then take a short left on Coventry Street to colorful **Piccadilly Circus.**

Near Piccadilly, you'll find the **Britain and London Visitors Centre** (on Lower Regent Street) and piles of theaters. **Leicester Square** (with its half-price "tkts" booth for plays—see page 139) thrives just a few blocks away. Walk through seedy **Soho** (north of Shaftesbury Avenue) for its fun pubs (consider my recommended Soho "Food Is Fun" Three-Course Dinner Crawl on page 172). From Piccadilly or Oxford Circus, you can take a taxi, bus, or the Tube home.

Sights in London

Central London

Westminster

▲▲▲**Westminster Abbey**—The greatest church in the English-speaking world, Westminster Abbey is the place where England's kings and queens have been crowned and buried since 1066. Like a stony refugee camp huddled outside St. Peter's Pearly Gates,

Westminster Abbey has many stories to tell. The steep admission includes an excellent audioguide—worthwhile if you have the time and interest. To experience the church more vividly, take a live tour, or attend evensong or an organ concert (see below).

Two tiny **museums** ring the cloisters. The Chapter House, where the monks had daily meetings, features fine architecture and stained glass with faded but well-described medieval art. The Abbey Museum has exhibits on royal coronations, funerals, Abbey history, a close-up look at medieval stained glass, and replicas of the crown jewels used for coronation practice. Look into the impressively realistic eyes of Elizabeth I, Charles II, Admiral Nelson, and a dozen others, part of a compelling series of wax-and-wood statues that, for three centuries, graced coffins during funeral processions.

Cost: £15, £30 family ticket (covers 2 adults and 1 child), cash only, includes cloisters, audioguide, and Abbey Museum.

Hours: Abbey open Mon–Fri 9:30–16:30, Wed until 19:00 (main church only), Sat 9:30–14:30, last entry one hour before closing, closed Sun to sightseers but open for services; Abbey Museum open daily 10:30–16:00; cloisters open daily 8:00–18:00; 1.5-hour guided tour-£3, up to 5/day in summer; Tube: Westminster or St. James's Park. Info desk tel. 020/7222-5152 or 020/7654-4834, www.westminster-abbey.org.

Crowd-Beating Tips: The main entrance, on the Parliament Square side, often has a sizable line; visit early, during lunch, or late to avoid tourist hordes. Sat and Mon are worst. Midmornings are also crowded, while weekdays after 14:30 are less congested; come then and stay for the 17:00 evensong.

Music: The church hosts evensong performances daily, sung every night but Wednesday, when it may be spoken (Mon–Fri at 17:00; Sat–Sun at 15:00). A free 30-minute organ recital is often held on Sunday at 17:45.

▲▲Houses of Parliament (Palace of Westminster)—This Neo-Gothic icon of London, the royal residence from 1042 to 1547, is now the meeting place of the legislative branch of government. The Houses of Parliament are located in what was once the Palace of Westminster—long the palace of England's medieval kings—until it was largely destroyed by fire in 1834. The palace was rebuilt in the Victorian Gothic style (a move away from Neoclassicism back to England's Christian and medieval heritage, true to the Romantic Age) and completed in 1860.

London at a Glance

▲▲▲**Westminster Abbey** Britain's finest church and the site of royal coronations and burials since 1066. **Hours:** Mon–Fri 9:30–16:30, Wed until 19:00, Sat 9:30–14:30, closed Sun to sightseers except for worship. See page 78.

▲▲▲**Churchill Museum and Cabinet War Rooms** Underground WWII headquarters of Churchill's war effort. **Hours:** Daily 9:30–18:00. See page 83.

▲▲▲**National Gallery** Remarkable collection of European paintings (1250–1900), including Leonardo, Botticelli, Velázquez, Rembrandt, Turner, Van Gogh, and the Impressionists. **Hours:** Daily 10:00–18:00, Fri until 21:00. See page 85.

▲▲▲**British Museum** The world's greatest collection of artifacts of Western civilization, including the Rosetta Stone and the Parthenon's Elgin Marbles. **Hours:** Daily 10:00–17:30, Thu–Fri until 20:30, but only a few galleries open after 17:30. See page 98.

▲▲▲**British Library** Impressive collection of the most important literary treasures of the Western world. **Hours:** Mon–Fri 9:30–18:00, Tue until 20:00, Sat 9:30–17:00, Sun 11:00–17:00. See page 100.

▲▲▲**St. Paul's Cathedral** The main cathedral of the Anglican Church, designed by Christopher Wren, with a climbable dome and daily evensong services. **Hours:** Mon–Sat 8:30–16:30, closed Sun except for worship. See page 106.

▲▲▲**Tower of London** Historic castle, palace, and prison housing the crown jewels and a witty band of Beefeaters. **Hours:** March–Oct Tue–Sat 9:00–17:30, Sun–Mon 10:00–17:30; Nov–Feb Tue–Sat 9:00–16:30, Sun–Mon 10:00–16:30. See page 107.

▲▲▲**Victoria and Albert Museum** The best collection of decorative arts anywhere. **Hours:** Daily 10:00–17:45, Fri until 22:00. See page 121.

▲▲**Houses of Parliament** London's famous Neo-Gothic landmark, topped by Big Ben and occupied by the Houses of Lords and Commons. **Hours** (both Houses): Generally Mon–Tue 14:30–22:30, Wed–Thu 11:30–17:50, closed Fri–Sun and most of Aug–Sept. See page 79.

▲▲**National Portrait Gallery** A *Who's Who* of British history, featuring portraits of this nation's most important historical figures. **Hours:** Daily 10:00–18:00, Thu–Fri until 21:00, first and second floors open Mon at 11:00. See page 88.

▲▲**London Eye** Enormous observation wheel, dominating—and offering commanding views over—London's skyline. **Hours:** Daily July–Aug 10:00–21:30, June and Sept 10:00–21:00, Oct–May 10:00–20:00. See page 112.

▲▲**Imperial War Museum** Examines the military history of the bloody 20th century. **Hours:** Daily 10:00–18:00. See page 113.

▲▲**Tate Modern** Works by Monet, Matisse, Dalí, Picasso, and Warhol displayed in a converted powerhouse. **Hours:** Daily 10:00–18:00, Fri–Sat until 22:00. See page 114.

▲▲**Shakespeare's Globe** Timbered, thatched-roofed reconstruction of the Bard's original wooden "O." **Hours:** Theater complex, museum, and actor-led tours generally daily 9:00–17:00; in summer, morning theater tours only. Plays are also held here. See page 115.

▲▲**Tate Britain** Collection of British paintings from the 16th century through modern times, including works by William Blake, the Pre-Raphaelites, and J. M. W. Turner. **Hours:** Daily 10:00–18:00, first Fri of the month until 22:00. See page 119.

▲▲**Natural History Museum** Packed with stuffed creatures, engaging exhibits, and enthralled kids. **Hours:** Daily 10:00–17:50. See page 123.

▲▲**The Docklands** London's emerging new "Manhattan," with a forest of skyscrapers. **Hours:** Always open, but most interesting at the end of the workday. See page 127.

▲**Courtauld Gallery** Fine collection of paintings filling one wing of the Somerset House, a grand 18th-century palace. **Hours:** Daily 10:00–18:00. See page 94.

▲**Buckingham Palace** Britain's royal residence with the famous Changing of the Guard. **Hours:** Palace—Aug–Sept only, daily 9:45–18:00; Guard—generally May–July daily at 11:30, Aug–April every other day. See page 95.

▲**Old Operating Theatre Museum** 19th-century hall where surgeons performed amputations for an audience of aspiring med students. **Hours:** Daily 10:30–16:45. See page 118.

Tourists are welcome to view debates in either the bickering House of Commons or the genteel House of Lords. You're only allowed inside when Parliament is in session, indicated by a flag flying atop the Victoria Tower at the south end of the building (generally Mondays through Thursdays). During the summer recess, when Parliament is not in session, visitors can still take a guided tour. While the actual debates are generally quite dull, it is a thrill to be inside and see the British government in action.

Cost and Hours: Free, both Houses usually open Mon–Tue 14:30–22:30, Wed–Thu 11:30–17:50, closed Fri–Sun and most of Aug–Sept, generally less action and no lines after 18:00, Tube: Westminster. Tel. 020/7219-4272, see www.parliament.uk for schedule. The House of Lords has more pageantry, shorter lines, and less interesting debates (tel. 020/7219-3107 for schedule, visit www.parliamentlive.tv for a preview).

Visiting the Houses of Parliament (HOP): Enter the venerable HOP midway along the west side of the building (across the street from Westminster Abbey) through the Visitor Entrance (with the tourist ramp, next to the St. Stephen's Entrance—if lost, ask a guard). As you enter, you'll be asked if you want to visit the House of Commons or the House of Lords. Inquire about the wait—an hour or two is not unusual. If there's a long line for the House of Commons and you just want a quick look inside the grand halls of this majestic building, start with the House of Lords. Once inside, you can switch if you like.

Just past security (where you'll be photographed and given a badge to wear around your neck), you enter the vast and historic

Westminster Hall, which survived the 1834 fire. The cavernous hall was built in the 11th century, and its famous self-supporting hammer-beam roof was added in 1397. Racks of brochures here explain how the British government works, and plaques describe the hall. The Jubilee Café, open to the public, has

live video feeds showing exactly what's going on in each house. Just seeing the café video is a fun experience (and can help you decide which house—if either—you'd like to see). Walking through the hall and up the stairs, you'll enter the busy world of government with all its high-powered goings-on.

Houses of Parliament Tours: Though Parliament is in recess during much of August and September, you can get a behind-the-scenes peek at the royal chambers of both houses during these months with a tour (£14, 1.25 hours, generally Mon–Fri, times vary, so confirm in advance; book ahead through www.ticket

master.co.uk). The same tours are offered Saturdays year-round.

Jewel Tower: Across the street from the Parliament building's St. Stephen's Gate, the Jewel Tower is a rare remnant of the old Palace of Westminster used by kings until Henry VIII. The crude stone tower (1365–1366) was a guard tower in the palace wall, overlooking a moat. It contains a fine little exhibit on Parliament and the tower (£3, daily March–Oct 10:00–17:00, Nov–Feb 10:00–16:00, tel. 020/7222-2219). Next to the tower (and free) is a quiet courtyard with picnic-friendly benches.

Big Ben: The clock tower (315 feet high) is named for its 13-ton bell, Ben. The light above the clock is lit when the House of Commons is sitting. The face of the clock is huge—you can actually see the minute hand moving. For a good view of it, walk halfway over Westminster Bridge.

▲▲▲Churchill Museum and Cabinet War Rooms

—This is a fascinating walk through the underground headquarters of the British government's fight against the Nazis in the darkest days of the Battle for Britain. The attraction includes two parts: the war rooms themselves, and a top-notch museum dedicated to the man who steered the war from here, Winston Churchill. For details on all the blood, sweat, toil, and tears, pick up the excellent, essential, and included audioguide at the entry, and dive in.

Cabinet War Rooms: The 27-room, heavily fortified nerve center of the British war effort was used from 1939 to 1945.

 Churchill's room, the map room, and other rooms are just as they were in 1945. As you follow the one-way route, be sure to take advantage of the audioguide, which explains each room and offers first-person accounts of wartime happenings here (it takes about 45 minutes, not counting the Churchill Museum). Be patient— it's well worth it. While the rooms are spartan, you'll see how British gentility survived even as the city was bombarded—posted signs informed those working underground what the weather was like outside, and a cheery notice reminds you to turn off the light switch to conserve electricity.

Churchill Museum: Don't bypass this museum, which occupies a large hall about a half-dozen rooms into the war rooms. It dissects every aspect of the man behind the famous cigar, bowler hat, and V-for-victory sign. It's extremely well-presented and engaging, using artifacts, quotes, political cartoons, clear explanations, and high-tech interactive exhibits to bring the colorful statesman to life; this museum alone deserves an hour. You'll get a taste of Winston's wit, irascibility, work ethic, passion for painting, American ties, writing talents, and drinking habits. The exhibit shows Winston's warts as well: It questions whether his party-switching was just political opportunism, examines the basis for his opposition to Indian self-rule, and reveals him to be an intense taskmaster who worked 18-hour days and was brutal to his staffers (who deeply respected him nevertheless).

A long touch-the-screen timeline lets you zero in on events in his life from birth (November 30, 1874) to his first appointment as prime minister in 1940. Many of the items on display—such as a European map divvied up in permanent marker, which Churchill brought home from the postwar Potsdam Conference—drive home the remarkable span of history this man lived through. Imagine: Churchill began his military career riding horses in the cavalry, and ended it speaking out against the proliferation of nuclear armaments. It's all the more amazing considering that, in the 1930s, the man who would become my vote for greatest states-man of the 20th century was once considered a washed-up loony ranting about the growing threat of fascism.

Cost and Hours: £14.95, daily 9:30–18:00, last entry one hour before closing; on King Charles Street, 200 yards off White-hall, follow the signs, Tube: Westminster. Tel. 020/7930-6961, www.iwm.org.uk. The museum's gift shop is great for anyone nos-talgic for the 1940s. Note that this wonderful museum is far supe-rior to the Winston Churchill's Britain at War Experience (next to the London Dungeon on the South Bank); give that one—and the London Dungeon—a miss.

Eating: If you're hungry, get your rations at the Switch Room café (in the museum) or, for a nearby pub lunch, try the Westminster Arms (food served downstairs, on Storey's Gate, a couple of blocks south of Cabinet War Rooms).

Horse Guards—The Horse Guards change daily at 11:00 (10:00 on Sun), and there's a colorful dismounting ceremony daily at 16:00. The rest of the day, they just stand there—terrible for video cameras (on Whitehall, between Trafalgar Square and #10 Downing Street, Tube: Westminster, www.changing-the-guard.com). Bucking-ham Palace pageantry is canceled when it rains, but the horse guards change regard-less of the weather.

▲Banqueting House—England's first Renaissance building (1619–1622) was designed by Inigo Jones. Built by King James I and decorated by his son Charles I, the Banqueting House came to symbolize the

Stuart kings' "divine right" management style—the belief that God himself had anointed them to rule. The house is one of the few London landmarks spared by the 1698 fire, and the only surviving part of the original Palace of Whitehall. Today it opens its doors to visitors, who enjoy a restful 20-minute audiovisual history, a 30-minute audio tour, and a look at the exquisite banqueting hall itself. As a tourist attraction, it's basically one big room—but what a grand room it is, with sumptuous ceiling paintings by Peter Paul Rubens. At Charles I's request, these paintings drove home the doctrine of the legitimacy of the divine right of kings. Ironically, in 1649—divine right ignored—King Charles I was famously executed right here.

Cost and Hours: £4.80, includes audioguide, Mon–Sat 10:00–17:00, closed Sun, last entry at 16:30, subject to closure for government functions, aristocratic WC, immediately across Whitehall from the Horse Guards, Tube: Westminster. Tel. 020/3166-6154 or 020/3166-6155, www.hrp.org.uk.

On Trafalgar Square

▲▲**Trafalgar Square**—London's recently renovated central square, the climax of most marches and demonstrations, is a thrilling place to simply hang out. Lord Nelson stands atop his

185-foot-tall fluted granite column, gazing out toward Trafalgar, where he lost his life but defeated the French fleet. Part of this 1842 memorial is made from his victims' melted-down cannons. He's surrounded by spraying fountains, giant lions, hordes of people, and—until recently—even more pigeons. A former London mayor decided that London's "flying rats" were a public nuisance and evicted Trafalgar Square's venerable seed salesmen (Tube: Charing Cross).

▲▲▲**National Gallery**—Displaying Britain's top collection of European paintings from 1250 to 1900—including works by Leonardo, Botticelli, Velázquez, Rembrandt, Turner, Van Gogh, and the Impressionists—this is one of Europe's great galleries. You'll peruse 700 years of art—from gold-backed Madonnas to Cubist bathers. The newly remodeled museum is surprisingly family-friendly (especially on Sunday mornings), with a variety of

National Gallery Highlights

☒ ELEVATOR / LIFT
☰ STAIRS

30 YARDS
30 METERS

SAINSBURY WING
ENTRANCE ON LEVEL 0
SELF-GUIDED TOUR
STARTS ON LEVEL 2

SAINSBURY
ENTRANCE

MEDIEVAL & EARLY RENAISSANCE
① ANONYMOUS – The Wilton Diptych
② UCCELLO – Battle of San Romano
③ VAN EYCK – The Arnolfini Marriage

ITALIAN RENAISSANCE
④ BOTTICELLI – Venus and Mars
⑤ CRIVELLI – The Annunciation, with Saint Emidius

HIGH RENAISSANCE
⑥ MICHELANGELO – Entombment
⑦ RAPHAEL – Pope Julius II
⑧ HOLBEIN – The Ambassadors
⑨ DA VINCI – The Virgin of the Rocks; Virgin and Child with St. Anne and St. John the Baptist

VENETIAN RENAISSANCE
⑩ TINTORETTO – The Origin of the Milky Way
⑪ TITIAN – Bacchus and Ariadne

NORTHERN PROTESTANT ART
⑫ VERMEER – A Young Woman
⑬ "A Peepshow"
⑭ REMBRANDT – Belshazzar's Feast
⑮ REMBRANDT – Self-Portrait

TRAFALGAR ⚓ SQUARE

BAROQUE & ROCOCO

16 RUBENS –
The Judgment of Paris

17 VAN DYCK –
Equestrian Portrait of Charles I

18 VELÁZQUEZ –
The Rokeby Venus

19 CARAVAGGIO –
The Supper at Emmaus

20 BOUCHER –
Pan and Syrinx

BRITISH

21 CONSTABLE – The Hay Wain

22 TURNER –
The Fighting Téméraire

23 DELAROCHE –
The Execution of Lady Jane Grey

IMPRESSIONISM & BEYOND

24 MONET –
Gare St. Lazare

25 MONET –
The Water-Lily Pond

26 MANET –
Corner of a Café-Concert
(a.k.a. The Waitress)

27 RENOIR –
Boating on the Seine

28 SEURAT –
Bathers at Asnières

29 VAN GOGH –
Sunflowers

30 CÉZANNE – Bathers

Trafalgar Square

- ⊖ TUBE STATION
- ← BLDG. ENTRANCES

TO COVENT GARDEN

CHARING CROSS

⊖ Leicester Square

LEICESTER SQUARE
tkts

NAT'L. PORTRAIT GALLERY

ST. MARTIN-IN-THE-FIELDS

TO COURTAULD GALLERY & THE CITY

THE STRAND

CHARING CROSS STATION

VILLIERS

TO THAMES RIVER

NATIONAL GALLERY

GEO. WASH.

FOURTH PLINTH

NELSON'S COLUMN

CHARING CROSS

CANADA HOUSE

TO PICCADILLY

PALL MALL

CHAS. I

NORTHUMBERLAND

Charing Cross

TRAFALGAR SQUARE
PEDESTRIAN AREA

TO ST. JAMES'S PALACE

THE MALL

ADMIRALTY ARCH

WHITEHALL

TO GOLDEN JUBILEE (PEDESTRIAN) BRIDGE & SOUTH BANK

TO BUCKINGHAM PALACE

TO BIG BEN

200 YARDS

200 METERS

---

kids' activities. While the collection is huge, following the route suggested on my "National Gallery Highlights" map will give you my best quick visit. For a more thorough tour, the £3.50 audio-guide is excellent.

Cost and Hours: Free, but suggested donation of £2–3; daily 10:00–18:00, Fri until 21:00; last entry to special exhibits 45 minutes before closing, free one-hour overview tours daily at 11:30 and 14:30, plus Fri at 19:00; no photography, on Trafalgar Square, Tube: Charing Cross or Leicester Square. Recorded info tel. 020/7747-2885, switchboard tel. 020/7839-3321, www.nationalgallery.org.uk.

Eating: The excellent-but-pricey museum restaurant called the National Dining Rooms is a good spot to split afternoon tea (see page 179). Two cheaper eateries, also in the museum, are located near the Getty Entrance: the National Café (with both a table-service restaurant and an easier-on-the-budget sandwich/soup/salad/pastry buffet) and the Espresso Bar (sandwiches, soft couches, and ArtStart computers).

▲▲**National Portrait Gallery**—Put off by halls of 19th-century characters who meant nothing to me, I used to call this "as interesting as someone else's yearbook." But a selective walk through this

500-year-long *Who's Who* of British history is quick and free, and puts faces on the story of England. The collection is well-described, not huge, and in historical sequence, from the 16th century on the second floor to today's royal family on the ground floor.

Some highlights: Henry VIII and wives; portraits of the "Virgin Queen" Elizabeth I, Sir Francis Drake, and Sir Walter Raleigh; the only real-life portrait of William Shakespeare; Oliver Cromwell and Charles I with his head on; portraits by Gainsborough and Reynolds; the Romantics (William Blake, Lord Byron, William Wordsworth, and company); Queen Victoria and her era; and the present royal family, including the late Princess Diana.

Cost and Hours: Free, but suggested donation of £5, temporary exhibits extra; daily 10:00–18:00, Thu–Fri until 21:00, first and second floors open Mon at 11:00, last entry to special exhibits 45 minutes before closing, excellent themed audioguides-£3; entry 100 yards off Trafalgar Square, around corner from National Gallery, opposite Church of St. Martin-in-the-Fields; Tube: Charing Cross or Leicester Square. Tel. 020/7306-0055, recorded info tel. 020/7312-2463, www.npg.org.uk.

Eating: The elegant Portrait Restaurant on the top floor is pricey but has a fine view of Trafalgar Square (£15–20 entrées, reservations smart, tel. 020/7312-2490). The Portrait Café in the basement (take the lift down) is cheaper and offers sandwiches, salads, and pastries.

▲**St. Martin-in-the-Fields**—The church, built in the 1720s with a Gothic spire atop a Greek-type temple, is an oasis of peace on the wild and noisy Trafalgar Square. St. Martin cared for the poor. "In the fields" was where the first church stood on this spot (in the 13th century), between Westminster and The City. Stepping inside, you still feel a compassion for the needs of the people in this neighborhood—the church serves the homeless and houses a Chinese community center. The modern east window—with grillwork bent into the shape of a warped cross—was installed in 2008 to replace one damaged in World War II.

A new freestanding glass pavilion to the left of the church serves as the entrance to the church's underground areas. There you'll find the concert ticket office, a gift shop, brass-rubbing center, and the recommended support-the-church Café in the Crypt.

Cost and Hours: Church entry free, donations welcome, £3.50

n for Early Birds and Night Owls

Most sightseeing in London is restricted to the hours between 10:00 and 18:00. Here are a few exceptions:

Sights Open Early

Every day, several sights open at 9:45 or earlier.

Westminster Cathedral: Daily at 7:00.

St. Paul's Cathedral: Mon–Sat at 8:30.

Shakespeare's Globe: Daily at 9:00.

Madame Tussauds Waxworks: Daily mid-July–Aug at 9:00, Sept–mid-July Mon–Fri at 9:30, Sat–Sun at 9:00.

Tower of London: Tue–Sat at 9:00.

Churchill Museum and Cabinet War Rooms: Daily at 9:30.

Kew Gardens: Daily at 9:30.

Westminster Abbey: Mon–Sat at 9:30.

British Library: Mon–Sat at 9:30.

Buckingham Palace: Aug–Sept daily at 9:45.

Sights Open Late

Every night in London, at least one sight is open late (in addition to the London Eye and Madame Tussauds which are open late daily). Here's the scoop from Monday through Sunday:

London Eye: Last ascent July–Aug daily until 21:30, June and Sept until 21:00, otherwise until 20:00.

Madame Tussauds: Mid-July–Aug daily until 21:00; Sept–mid-July Mon–Fri until 19:30, Sat–Sun until 20:00.

Clink Prison Museum: July–Sept daily until 21:00, Oct–June Sat–Sun until 19:30.

Houses of Parliament (when in session, roughly Oct–July): Mon–Tue until 22:30.

British Library: Tue until 20:00.

Sir John Soane's Museum: First Tue of month until 21:00.

British Museum (some galleries): Thu–Fri until 20:30.

National Portrait Gallery: Thu–Fri until 21:00.

Vinopolis: Thu–Sat until 22:00, Sun until 18:00.

National Gallery: Fri until 21:00.

Victoria and Albert Museum: Fri until 22:00.

London Transport Museum: Some Fri until 22:00.

Tate Modern: Fri–Sat until 22:00.

Tate Britain: First Fri of the month until 22:00.

audioguide at shop downstairs; hours vary but generally Mon–Fri 8:30–13:00 & 14:00–18:00, Sat 9:30–13:00 & 14:00–18:00, Sun 15:30–17:00; Tube: Charing Cross. Tel. 020/7766-1100, www2 .stmartin-in-the-fields.org.

Music: The church is famous for its concerts. Consider a free lunchtime concert (Mon, Tue, and Fri at 13:00), an evening concert (£6–25, several nights a week at 19:30), or Wednesday night jazz in the church's café (£5–10, at 20:00). See the website for the concert schedule.

The West End and Nearby

To explore this area during dinner, see my recommended Soho "Food Is Fun" Three-Course Dinner Crawl, and munch your way from Covent Garden to Soho (see sidebar on page 172).

▲**Piccadilly Circus**—Although this square is slathered with neon billboards and tacky attractions, the surrounding streets are packed

with great shopping opportunities and swimming with youth on the rampage. For overstimulation in a grimy mall that smells like teen spirit, drop by the extremely trashy Trocadero Center for its Funland arcade games, multiplex cinema, and 10-lane bowling alley (admission to Trocadero is free; individual attractions have separate admissions; located between Piccadilly and Leicester squares on Coventry Street). Nearby Shaftesbury Avenue and Leicester Square teem with fun-seekers, theaters, Chinese restaurants, and street singers. To the northeast is London's Chinatown and, beyond that, the funky Soho neighborhood (described next). And curling to the northwest from Piccadilly Circus is genteel Regent Street, lined with the city's most exclusive shops.

▲**Soho**—North of Piccadilly, seedy Soho has become seriously trendy and is well worth a gawk. It's the epicenter of London's thriving and colorful youth, a fun and funky *Sesame Street* scene populated by people of every color of the racial rainbow...straight, gay, and everything in between.

Soho is also London's red light district (especially near Brewer and Berwick Streets), where "friendly models" wait in tiny rooms up dreary stairways, and voluptuous con artists sell strip shows. Though venturing up a stairway to check out a model is interesting, anyone who goes into any one of the shows will be ripped off. Every time. Even a £5 show in a "licensed bar" comes with a £100

West End & Nearby

LONDON

TUBE STATION
BLDG. ENTRANCES
VIEW

cover or minimum (as it's printed on the drink menu) and a "security man." You may accidentally buy a £200 bottle of bubbly. And suddenly, the door has no handle. While this all sounds creepy, it's easy to avoid trouble if you're not looking for it. In fact, the sleazy joints share the block with respectable pubs and restaurants, and elderly couples out for a stroll pass neon signs that flash *Licensed Sex Shop in Basement.*

▲▲Covent Garden—The centerpiece of this boutique-ish shopping district is an iron-and-glass arcade. The "Actors' Church" of St. Paul, the Royal Opera House, and the London Transport Museum (described next) all border the square, and venerable theaters are nearby. The area is a people-watcher's delight, with cigarette eaters, Punch-and-Judy acts, food that's good for you (but not your wallet), trendy crafts, sweet whiffs of marijuana, two-tone hair (neither natural), and faces that could set off a metal detector (Tube: Covent Garden). For better Covent Garden lunch deals, walk a block or two away from the eye of this touristic hurricane (check out the places north of the Tube station, along Endell and Neal Streets).

▲London Transport Museum—This modern, well-presented museum, located right at Covent Garden, is fun for kids and thought-provoking for adults (if a bit overpriced). Whether you're cursing or marveling at the buses and Tube, the growth of Europe's third-biggest city (after Moscow and Istanbul) has been made possible by its public transit system.

Cost and Hours: £10, includes optional £2 donation, Sat–Thu 10:00–18:00, Fri 11:00–18:00, open some Fri until 22:00 for special events, last entry 45 minutes before closing, pleasant upstairs café with Covent Garden view, in southeast corner of Covent Garden courtyard, Tube: Covent Garden. Switchboard tel. 020/7379-6344 or recorded info tel. 020/7565-7298, www.ltmuseum.co.uk.

▲Courtauld Gallery—While less impressive than the National Gallery, this wonderful collection of paintings is still a joy. The gallery is part of the Courtauld Institute of Art, and the thoughtful description of each piece of art reminds visitors that the gallery is still used for teaching. You'll see medieval European paintings and works by Rubens, the Impressionists (Manet, Monet, and Degas), Post-Impressionists (such as Cézanne), and more. Besides the permanent collection, a quality selection of loaners and temporary exhibits are often included in the entry fee.

Cost and Hours: £5, free Mon until 14:00; open daily 10:00–18:00, last entry at 17:30; downstairs cafeteria, lockers, and WC; bus #6, #9, #11, #13, #15, or #23 from Trafalgar Square; Tube: Temple or Covent Garden. Shop tel. 020/7848-2579, recorded info tel. 020/7848-2526, www.courtauld.ac.uk.

Somerset House: The Courtauld Gallery is located at Somerset House, a grand 18th-century civic palace that offers a marvelous public space (housing temporary exhibits) and a riverside terrace with several eateries (between the Strand and the Thames). The palace once held the national registry that recorded Britain's births, marriages, and deaths: "...where they hatch 'em, match 'em, and dispatch 'em." Step into the courtyard to enjoy the fountain. Go ahead...walk through it. The 55 jets get playful twice an hour. In the winter, this becomes a popular ice-skating rink with a toasty café for viewing the scene (www.somerset-house.org.uk).

Buckingham Palace

There are three palace sights that require admission: the State Rooms (Aug–Sept only), Queen's Gallery, and Royal Mews. You can pay for each separately, or buy a combo-ticket. The combo-

ticket for £30.50 admits you to all three sights; a cheaper version for £15 covers the Queen's Gallery and Royal Mews. Many tourists are more interested in the Changing of the Guard, which costs nothing at all to view.

▲**State Rooms at Buckingham Palace**—This lavish home has been Britain's royal residence since 1837. When the Queen's at home, the royal standard flies (a red, yellow, and blue flag); otherwise, the Union Jack flaps in the wind. The Queen opens her palace to the public—but only in August and September, when she's out of town.

Cost and Hours: £17 for lavish State Rooms and throne room, includes audioguide; Aug–Sept only, daily 9:45–18:00, last admission 15:45; only 8,000 visitors a day by timed entry; come early to the palace's Visitor Entrance (opens 9:15) or book ahead in person or by phone or online (£1.25 extra); Tube: Victoria. Tel. 020/7766-7300, www.royalcollection.org.uk.

▲**Queen's Gallery at Buckingham Palace**—Queen Elizabeth's personal collection of art is on display in a wing adjoining the palace. Her 7,000 paintings make up the finest private art collection in the world, rivaling Europe's biggest national art galleries. It's actually a collection of collections, built on by each successive monarch since the 16th century. She rotates her paintings, enjoying some privately in her many palatial residences while sharing others with her subjects in public galleries in Edinburgh and London. Small, thoughtfully presented, and always exquisite displays fill the five rooms open to the public. As you're in "the most important building in London," security is tight.

In addition to the permanent collection, you'll see temporary exhibits and a small room glittering with the Queen's personal jewelry. Compared to the crown jewels at the Tower, it may be Her Majesty's bottom drawer—but it's still a dazzling pile of diamonds. Temporary exhibits change about twice a year, and are lovingly described by the included audioguide. While admission tickets come with an entry time, this is only enforced during rare days when crowds are a problem.

The gallery is scheduled to close from early 2011 until mid-April, when it reopens with an all-new exhibit (possibly "Dutch Landscapes").

Buckingham Palace Area

100 YARDS
100 METERS

ST JAMES'S PALACE

TO TRAFALGAR SQUARE

GREEN PARK

N

THE MALL

ST. JAMES'S

BUCKINGHAM PALACE

PARK LAKE

PARK

PRIVATE PARK

SPUR RD

WALK

TO BIG BEN

BIRDCAGE

ROYAL MEWS

BUCK. GATE

WELLINGTON BARRACKS

BUCKINGHAM

GUARDS' MUSEUM

GUARDS' CHAPEL

FRANCE

QUEEN'S GALLERY

GATE

PETTY

St. James's Park

TO VICTORIA STATION

DCH

GUARDS' ROUTE   VIEW
PATHWAYS IN   TUBE STN.
THE PARK

❶ Changing of the Guard   ❸ Wellington Barracks
❷ Victoria Memorial   ❹ St. James's Palace
   (Best Views)   ❺ Spur Road

Cost and Hours: £8.75, daily 10:00–17:30, last entry one hour before closing, Tube: Victoria. Tel. 020/7766-7301, but Her Majesty rarely answers. Men shouldn't miss the mahogany-trimmed urinals.

Royal Mews—Located to the left of Buckingham Palace, the Queen's working stables, or "mews," are open to visitors. The visit is likely to be disappointing unless you follow the included audioguide or the hourly guided tour, in which case it's thoroughly entertaining—especially if you're interested in horses and/or royalty. The 40-minute tours show off a few of the Queen's 30 horses, a fancy car, and a bunch of old carriages, finishing with the Gold State Coach (c. 1760, 4 tons, 4 mph). Queen Victoria said absolutely no cars. When she died, in 1901, the mews got its first Daimler. Today, along with the hay-eating transport, the stable is home to five Bentleys and Rolls-Royce Phantoms, with one on display.

Cost and Hours: £7.75, April–July and Oct Sat–Thu 11:00–16:00, Aug–Sept 10:00–17:00, last entry 45 minutes before closing, closed Fri and Nov–March, guided tours on the hour, Buckingham Palace Road, Tube: Victoria. Tel. 020/7766-7302.

▲▲**Changing of the Guard at Buckingham Palace**—This is the spectacle every visitor to London has to see at least once: stone-

faced, red-coated, bearskin-hatted guards changing posts with much fanfare, in an hour-long ceremony accompanied by a brass band.

It's 11:00 at Buckingham Palace, and the on-duty guards are ready to finish their shift. Nearby at St. James's Palace (a half-mile northwest), a second set of guards

is also ready for a break. At a third location, fresh replacement guards gather for a review and inspection at Wellington Barracks, 500 yards east of the palace (on Birdcage Walk).

At 11:15, the tired St. James's guards head out to the Mall, and then take a right turn for Buckingham Palace. At 11:30, the replacement troops, led by the band, also head for Buckingham Palace. Meanwhile, a fourth group—the Horse Guard—passes by along the Mall on their way back to Hyde Park Corner from their own changing-of-the-guard ceremony on Whitehall (which just took place at Horse Guards Parade at 11:00, or 10:00 on Sun).

At 11:45, the tired and fresh guards converge on Buckingham Palace in a perfect storm of Red Coat pageantry. Everyone parades around, the guard changes (passing the regimental flag, or "color") with much shouting, the band plays a happy little concert, and then they march out. At noon, two bands escort two detachments of guards away: the tired guards to Wellington Barracks and the fresh guards to St. James's Palace. As the fresh guards set up at St. James's Palace and the tired ones dress down at the barracks, the tourists disperse.

Cost and Hours: Free, daily May–July at 11:30, every other day Aug–April, no ceremony in very wet weather; exact schedule subject to change—call 020/7766-7300 for the day's plan, or check www.changing-the-guard.com or www.royalcollection.org.uk (click "Visit," then "Changing the Guard"); Buckingham Palace, Tube: Victoria, St. James's Park, or Green Park. Or hop into a big black taxi and say, "Buck House, please" (a.k.a. Buckingham Palace).

Sightseeing Strategies: Most tourists just show up and get lost in the crowds, but those who know the drill will enjoy the event more. The action takes place in stages over the course of an hour, at several different locations. The main event is in the forecourt right in front of Buckingham Palace (between Buckingham Palace and the fence) from 11:30 to 12:00. To see it close up, you'll need to get here no later than 10:30 to get a place right next to the fence.

But there's plenty of pageantry elsewhere. Get out your map and strategize. You could see the guards mobilizing at Wellington Barracks or St. James's Palace (11:00–11:15). Or watch them parade with bands down The Mall and Spur Road (11:15–11:30). After the ceremony at Buckingham Palace is over (and many tourists have gotten bored and gone home), the parades march back along those same streets (12:10).

Pick one event and find a good, unobstructed place from which to view it. The key is to either get right up front along the road or fence, or find some raised elevation to stand or sit on—a balustrade or a curb—so you can see over people's heads.

For the best overall view, stake out the high ground on the circular Victoria Memorial (come before 11:00 to get a place). From the Memorial, you have good views of the palace as well as the arriving and departing parades along The Mall and Spur Road. The actual changing of the guard in front of the palace is a nonevent. It is interesting, however, to see nearly every tourist in London gathered in one place at the same time. Afterward, stroll through nearby St. James's Park.

North London

▲▲▲British Museum—Simply put, this is the greatest chronicle of civilization...anywhere. A visit here is like taking a long hike through *Encyclopedia Britannica* National Park. While the vast British Museum wraps around its Great Court (the huge entrance hall), the most popular sections of the museum fill the ground floor: Egyptian, Assyrian, and ancient Greek, with the famous Elgin Marbles from the Athenian Parthenon. The museum's stately Reading Room—famous as the place where Karl Marx hung out while formulating his ideas on communism and writing *Das Kapital*—sometimes hosts special exhibits.

From the Great Court, doorways lead to all wings. Huge winged lions (which guarded an Assyrian palace 800 years before Christ) guard these great galleries. For a brief tour, connect these ancient dots:

Start with the **Egyptian** section. Wander from the Rosetta Stone past the many statues. At the end of the hall, climb the stairs

British Museum Overview

MONTAGUE PLACE RUSSELL SQUARE

ENTRANCE

BLOOMSBURY STREET

GREECE ASSYRIA EGYPT

CAFÉ

ROSETTA STONE

READING ROOM

THE GREAT COURT

THE KING'S GALLERY

INFO INFO

WINGED LIONS

SHOP

COATS

CAFÉ

COLUMNS

MAIN ENTRANCE

MONTAGUE ST.

DCH

TO TOTTENHAM COURT ROAD
(10 MIN. WALK)

GREAT RUSSELL ST.

TO HOLBORN
(10 MIN. WALK)

LONDON

to mummy land.

Back at the winged lions, explore the dark, violent, and mysterious **Assyrian** rooms. The Nimrud Gallery is lined with royal propaganda reliefs and wounded lions (from the ninth century B.C.).

The most modern of the ancient art fills the **Greek** section. Find Room 11, behind the winged lions, and start your walk through Greek art history with the simple and primitive Cycladic fertility figures. Later, painted vases show a culture really into partying. The finale is the Elgin Marbles. The much-wrangled-over bits of the Athenian Parthenon (from about 450 B.C.) are even more impressive than they look. To best appreciate these ancient carvings, take the audioguide tour (described later).

Be sure to venture upstairs to see artifacts from **Roman Britain** (Room 50) that surpass anything you'll see at Hadrian's Wall or elsewhere in Britain. Nearby, the Dark Age Britain exhibits offer a worthwhile peek at that bleak era; look for the Sutton Hoo Burial Ship artifacts from a seventh-century royal burial on the east coast of England (Room 41). A rare Michelangelo cartoon (preliminary sketch) is in Room 90.

Cost and Hours: Free but a £4, $6, or €5 donation requested; temporary exhibits extra, daily 10:00–17:30, Thu–Fri until 20:30—

North London

but not all galleries open after 17:30, least crowded weekday late afternoons, Great Russell Street, Tube: Tottenham Court Road. Switchboard tel. 020/7323-8000, general info tel. 020/7323-8299, collection questions tel. 020/7323-8838, www.britishmuseum.org.

Tours: The 1.5-hour Highlights tours, led by licensed guides, are expensive but meaty, giving an introduction to the museum's masterpieces (£8, daily at 10:30, 13:00, and 15:00). The free 30- to 40-minute eyeOpener tours are led by volunteers, who focus on select rooms (daily 11:00–15:30, generally every half-hour, plus Thu at 18:15 and 19:15).

The £4.50 **audioguide** (called a "Multimedia Guide") offers dial-up audio commentary and video on 200 objects, as well as several theme tours (for example, 1.5-hour Highlights tour or Parthenon Sculptures tour). They're substantial and cerebral (must leave photo ID). There's also a fun children's audioguide (£3).

Those traveling with an iPod or other MP3 player can download a free **Rick Steves audio tour** of the British Museum at www.ricksteves.com (or search for "Rick Steves' Audio Tours" on iTunes).

▲▲▲**British Library**—Here, in just two rooms, called "The Treasures of the British Library," are the literary treasures of Western civilization, from early Bibles to the Magna Carta to Shakespeare's *Hamlet* to Lewis Carroll's *Alice's Adventures in Wonderland*. You'll see the Lindisfarne Gospels transcribed on an

British Library Highlights

MAGNA CARTA

SACRED TEXTS

Codex Sinaiticus

PRINTING

Printed Prayer Sheet

Gutenberg Bible

Illum. Manuscripts

SCIENCE

↑ To Café

BIBLES

Lindisfarne Gospels

King James Bible

First Folio

Beowulf

Chaucer

Temporary Exhibits

Shakespeare

Historical Documents

LITERATURE

MAPS

Beatles

MUSIC

Main Stairs Up

Elev.

Handel

Pearson Gallery (Temp. Exhibits)

Stairs Down

Stairs Up to Ritblat Gallery

Info Desk

Shop

Main Entrance

Newton Statue

PIAZZA

DCH

To Euston Road Entrance

LONDON

illuminated manuscript, as well as Beatles lyrics scrawled on the back of a greeting card. The British Empire built its greatest monuments out of paper, and it's with literature that England made her lasting contribution to civilization and the arts.

Cost and Hours: Free but £2 suggested donation, temporary exhibits extra, Mon–Fri 9:30–18:00, Tue until 20:00, Sat 9:30–17:00, Sun 11:00–17:00, helpful free computers give you extra info, ground-floor café, self-service cafeteria upstairs, Tube: King's Cross St. Pancras—walk a block west to 96 Euston Road, Euston Tube station is also nearby; bus #10, #30, #73, #91, #205, or #390. Tel. 019/3754-6060 or 020/7412-7676, www.bl.uk.

Tours: Those traveling with an iPod or other MP3 player can download a free **Rick Steves audio tour** of the British Library at www.ricksteves.com (or search for "Rick Steves' Audio Tours" on iTunes).

▲**Wallace Collection**—Sir Richard Wallace's fine collection of 17th-century Dutch Masters, 18th-century French Rococo, medieval armor, and assorted aristocratic fancies fills the sumptuously furnished Hertford House on Manchester Square. From the rough and intimate Dutch lifescapes of Jan Steen to the pink-cheeked Rococo fantasies of François Boucher, a wander through this little-visited

mansion makes you nostalgic for the days of the empire. While this collection would be a big deal in a mid-sized city, it's small potatoes here in London...but enjoyable nevertheless.

Cost and Hours: Free, daily 10:00–17:00, £4 audioguide, free guided tours or lectures almost daily—call to confirm times, just north of Oxford Street on Manchester Square, Tube: Bond Street. Tel. 020/7563-9500, www.wallacecollection.org.

▲**Madame Tussauds Waxworks**—This is gimmicky and expensive, but dang good...a hit with the kind of travelers who skip the British Museum. The original Madame Tussaud did wax casts of heads lopped off during the French Revolution (such as Marie-Antoinette's). She took her show on the road and ended up in London in 1835. Now it's all about squeezing Tom Cruise's bum, gambling with George Clooney, and partying with Beyoncé,

Britney, and Brangelina. In addition to posing with all the eerily realistic wax dummies—from Johnny Depp to Barack Obama to the Beatles—you'll have the chance to tour a hokey haunted-house exhibit; learn how they create this waxy army; hop on a people-mover and cruise through a kid-pleasing "Spirit of London" time trip; and meet your favorite Marvel super heroes before heading into an auditorium for a nine-minute "4-D" show—a 3-D movie heightened by wind, "back ticklers," and other special effects.

Cost and Hours: £28, no waiting in line if you buy ticket on their website (10 percent discount), or TI (£22.50), £41 combo-ticket with London Eye, cheaper for kids. From 17:00 to closing, it's £14 if you buy in advance online. Children under 5 are always free. Open Mon–Fri 9:30–19:30, Sat–Sun 9:00–20:00, mid-July–

Aug and school holidays daily 9:00–21:00, last entry two hours before closing; Marylebone Road, Tube: Baker Street. Toll tel. 0871-894-3000, www.madametussauds.com. Check the website for discounts on this pricey waxtravaganza.

Crowd-Beating Tips: This popular attraction can be swamped by crowds. To avoid the hassle, buy your tickets and reserve an entry time in advance, either online (10 percent discount) or by phone (same price as box office). If you wait to buy tickets at the attraction, you'll discover that the ticket-buying line twists endlessly once inside the door (believe the posted signs warning you how long the wait will be—an hour or more is not unusual at busy times). If you buy your tickets at the door, try to arrive after 15:00.

▲**Sir John Soane's Museum**—Architects love this quirky place, as do fans of interior decor, eclectic knickknacks, and Back Door

sights. Tour this furnished home on a bird-chirping square and see 19th-century chairs, lamps, and carpets, wood-paneled nooks and crannies, and stained-glass skylights. The townhouse is cluttered with Soane's (and his wife's) collection of ancient relics, curios, and famous paintings, including Hogarth's series on *The Rake's Progress* (read the fun plot) and several excellent Canalettos. In 1833, just before his death, Soane established his house as a museum, stipulating that it be kept as nearly as possible in the state he left it. If he visited today, he'd be entirely satisfied. You'll leave wishing you'd known the man.

Cost and Hours: Free but donations much appreciated, Tue–Sat 10:00–17:00, first Tue of the month also 18:00–21:00, closed Sun–Mon, last entry 30 minutes before closing, long entry lines on Sat and first Tue, good £1 brochure, £5 guided tour Sat at 11:00, 13 Lincoln's Inn Fields, quarter-mile southeast of British Museum, Tube: Holborn. Tel. 020/7405-2107, www.soane.org.

Cartoon Museum—This humble but interesting museum is located in the shadow of the British Museum. While its three rooms are filled with British cartoons unknown to most Americans, the satire of famous bigwigs and politicians—from Napoleon to Margaret Thatcher, the Queen, and Tony Blair—shows the power of parody to deliver social commentary. Upstairs, you'll see pages spanning from *Tarzan* to *Tank Girl*, and *Andy Capp* to the British *Dennis the Menace*—interesting only to comic-book diehards.

Cost and Hours: £5.50, Tue–Sat 10:30–17:30, Sun 12:00–17:30, closed Mon, 35 Little Russell Street—go one block south of the British Museum on Museum Street and turn right, Tube:

Tottenham Court Road. Tel. 020/7580-8155, www.cartoonmuseum.org.

Pollock's Toy Museum—This rickety old house, with glass cases filled with toys and games lining its walls and halls, is a time-warp experience that brings back childhood memories to people who grew up without batteries or computer chips. Though the museum is small, you could spend a lot of time here, squinting at the fascinating toys and dolls that entertained the children of 19th- and early 20th-century England. The included information is great. The story of Theodore Roosevelt refusing to shoot a bear cub while on a hunting trip was celebrated in 1902 cartoons, resulting in a new, huggable toy: the Teddy Bear. It was popular for good reason: it could be manufactured during World War I without rationed products; it coincided with the new belief that soft toys were good for a child's development; it was an acceptable "doll for boys"; and it's *the* toy children keep long after they've grown up.

Cost and Hours: £5, kids-£2, generally Mon–Sat 10:00–17:00, closed Sun, last entry 30 minutes before closing, 1 Scala Street, Tube: Goodge Street. Tel. 020/7636-3452, www.pollockstoymuseum.com.

Beatles and Beyond—Central London is surprisingly devoid of sights associated with the famous '60s rock band. To see much of anything, consider taking a guided walk (described on page 67).

For a photo op, go to **Abbey Road** and walk the famous crosswalk pictured on the *Abbey Road* album cover (Tube: St. John's Wood, get information and buy Beatles memorabilia at the small kiosk in the station). From the Tube station, it's a five-minute walk west down Grove End Road to the intersection with Abbey Road. The Abbey Road recording studio is the low-key, white building to the right of Abbey House (it's still a working studio, so you can't go inside). Ponder the graffiti on the low wall outside, and...imagine. To re-create the famous cover photo, shoot the crosswalk from the roundabout as you face north up Abbey Road. Shoes are optional.

Nearby is **Paul McCartney's current home** (7 Cavendish Avenue): Continue down Grove End Road, turn left on Circus Road, and then right on Cavendish. Please be discreet.

The **Beatles Store** is at 231 Baker Street (Tube: Baker Street). It's small—some Beatles-logo T-shirts, mugs, pins, and old vinyls like you might have in your closet—and has nothing of historic value (open eight days a week, 10:00–18:30, tel. 020/7935-4464, www.beatlesstorelondon.co.uk; another rock memorabilia store is

The City

across the street).

A few doors down is the **Sherlock Holmes Museum,** a meticulous recreation of the (fictional) apartment of the (fictional) detective at the (real) address of 221b Baker Street. Fans will like it. Others might enjoy the Victorian-era furniture, clothes, pipes, paintings, and chamber pots, which give a glimpse at daily life from the time (£6, daily 9:30–18:30, large gift shop for Holmes connoisseurs, Tube: Baker Street, tel. 020/7935-8866, www.sherlock-holmes.co.uk).

The City

When Londoners say "The City," they mean the one-square-mile business center in East London that 2,000 years ago was Roman Londinium. The outline of the Roman city walls can still be seen in the arc of roads from Blackfriars Bridge to Tower Bridge. Within The City are 23 churches designed by Sir Christopher Wren, mostly just ornamentation around St. Paul's Cathedral. Today, while home to only 5,000 residents, The City thrives with nearly

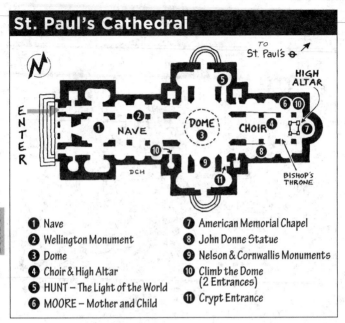

St. Paul's Cathedral

TO
St. Paul's ↗

HIGH ALTAR

ENTER

NAVE

DOME

CHOIR

BISHOP'S THRONE

DCH

1. Nave
2. Wellington Monument
3. Dome
4. Choir & High Altar
5. HUNT – The Light of the World
6. MOORE – Mother and Child
7. American Memorial Chapel
8. John Donne Statue
9. Nelson & Cornwallis Monuments
10. Climb the Dome (2 Entrances)
11. Crypt Entrance

500,000 office workers coming and going daily. It's a fascinating district to wander on weekdays, but since almost nobody actually lives there, it's dull in the evenings and on Saturday and Sunday.

St. Paul's Cathedral and Nearby

▲▲▲St. Paul's Cathedral—Wren's most famous church is the great St. Paul's, its elaborate interior capped by a 365-foot dome. Since World War II, St. Paul's has been Britain's symbol of resistance. Despite 57 nights of bombing, the Nazis failed to destroy the cathedral, thanks to the St. Paul's volunteer fire watchmen, who stayed on the dome. During your visit, you can climb the dome for a great city view. The crypt (included with admission) is a

world of historic bones and memorials (including Admiral Nelson's tomb) and interesting cathedral models.

Cost and Hours: £12.50, includes church entry and dome climb; Mon–Sat 8:30–16:30, last church entry for sightseeing 16:00, last dome entry 16:15, closed Sun except for worship, £3 tours and £4 audioguides; download free Rick Steves audio tour for your iPod/MP3 player at www.ricksteves.com or on iTunes; no

photography allowed, cheery café and pricier restaura
Tube: St. Paul's; bus #4, #11, #15, #23, or #26. Recorde
020/7236-4128, reception tel. 020/7246-8350, www.stpau...co.uk.

Music: The evensong services are free, but nonpaying visitors are not allowed to linger afterward (Mon–Sat at 17:00, Sun at 15:15, 40 minutes).

▲**Old Bailey**—To view the British legal system in action—lawyers in little blond wigs speaking legalese with a British accent—spend a few minutes in the visitors' gallery at the Old Bailey, called the "Central Criminal Court." Don't enter under the dome; signs point you to the two visitors' entrances.

Cost and Hours: Free, generally Mon–Fri 10:00–13:00 & 14:00–16:30 depending on caseload, closed Sat–Sun, reduced hours in Aug; no kids under 14; no bags, mobile phones, cameras, iPods, or food, but small purses OK; Eddie at Bailey's Café across the street at #27 stores bags for £2; 2 blocks northwest of St. Paul's on Old Bailey Street, follow signs to public entrance, Tube: St. Paul's. Tel. 020/7248-3277.

▲**Museum of London**—This museum tells the fascinating story of London, taking you on a walk from its pre-Roman beginnings to the present. It features London's distinguished citizens through history—from Neanderthals to Romans to Elizabethans to Victorians to Mods to today. The museum's displays are chronological, spacious, and informative without being overwhelming. Scale models and costumes help you visualize everyday life in the city at different periods. There are enough whiz-bang multimedia displays (including the Plague and the Great Fire) to spice up otherwise humdrum artifacts. This regular stop for the local school kids gives the best overview of London history in town.

Cost and Hours: Free, daily 10:00–18:00, last entry 30 minutes before closing, see the day's events board for special talks and tours, Tube: Barbican or St. Paul's plus a five-minute walk. Tel. 020/7814-5530, recorded info tel. 020/7001-9844, www.museum oflondon.org.uk.

The Monument—Wren's 202-foot-tall tribute to London's Great Fire was recently restored. Climb the 331 steps inside the column for a view of The City that is still monumental (£3, daily 9:30–17:30, last entry at 17:00, junction of Monument Street and Fish Street Hill, Tube: Monument, tel. 020/7626-2717, www.the monument.info).

Tower of London and Nearby

▲▲▲**Tower of London**—The Tower has served as a castle in wartime, a king's residence in peacetime, and, most notoriously, as the prison and execution site of rebels. You can see the crown jewels, take a witty Beefeater tour, and ponder the executioner's

Tower of London

- **TUBE STATION**
- **BLDG. ENTRANCES**
- **VIEW**

100 YARDS
100 METERS

TO EAST END

Tower Hill

TRINITY HOUSE GARDENS

ROMAN WALL

TO THE CITY

BYWARD ST. TOWER HILL

TO TOWER BRIDGE VIA ROAD

PEDESTRIAN WALKWAY

DRY MOAT

TICKET KIOSKS

GROUP TICKET SALES

PLAZA

LOWER THAMES ST.

ENTER

TOWER GREEN

WHITE TOWER

DRY MOAT

WC

WC

TOWER PIER

BEEFEATER TOURS START HERE

MOAT

EXIT

MOAT

VIEW OF TOWER BRIDGE

THAMES RIVER

DCH

TO TOWER BRIDGE & ST. KATH. PIER

❶ Entrance Gate
❷ Traitor's Gate
❸ White Tower
❹ Beauchamp Tower
❺ Crown Jewels
❻ Bloody Tower
❼ Medieval Palace
❽ Walk the Wall
❾ Chapel Royal of St. Peter ad Vincula
❿ Café
⓫ Trader's Gate Gift Shop (Tower Tickets)

LONDON

block that dispensed with troublesome heirs to the throne and a couple of Henry VIII's wives.

William I, still getting used to his new title of "the Conqueror," built the stone "White Tower" (1077–1097) to keep the Londoners in line. The Tower also served as an effective lookout for seeing invaders coming up the Thames. His successors enlarged it to its present 18-acre size. Because of the security it provided, the Tower served over the centuries as a royal residence, the Royal Mint, the Royal Jewel House, and, most famously, as the prison and execution site of those who dared oppose the Crown.

The Tower's hard stone and glittering jewels represent the ultimate power of the monarch. So does the executioner's block. You'll find more bloody history per square inch in this original tower of power than anywhere else in Britain. Today, though its military purpose is history, it's still home to the Yeoman Warders, a.k.a. the "Beefeaters," who host three million visitors a year.

Cost and Hours: £17, family-£47; audioguide-£4; March–Oct Tue–Sat 9:00–17:30, Sun–Mon 10:00–17:30; Nov–Feb Tue–Sat 9:00–16:30, Sun–Mon 10:00–16:30; last entry 30 minutes before closing; no photography allowed of jewels or in chapels; Tube: Tower Hill. Switchboard toll tel. 0844-482-7777.

Getting Tickets: The long but fast-moving ticket lines are worst on Sundays. Avoid lines anytime by buying your ticket online (www.hrp.org.uk), at the Trader's Gate gift shop down the steps from the Tower Hill Tube stop, at the Tower Welcome Centre to the left of the normal ticket line (credit card only), in advance at any London TI (no extra charge), or by phone (£2 extra fee, tel. 0844-482-7799 within UK, tel. 011-44-20-3166-6000 from the US). After your visit, consider taking the boat to Greenwich from here (see "Cruises" on page 72).

More Sights near the Tower—The best remaining bit of London's **Roman Wall** is just north of the Tower (at the Tower Hill Tube station).

The iconic **Tower Bridge** (often mistakenly called London Bridge) has been freshly painted and is undergoing restoration. The hydraulically powered drawbridge was built in 1894 to accommodate the growing East End. While fully modern, its design was a retro Neo-Gothic look.

You can tour the bridge at the **Tower Bridge Experience,** with a history exhibit and a peek at the Victorian engine room that lifts the span (£7, daily 10:00–18:00 in summer, 9:30–17:30 in winter, last entry 30 minutes before closing, good view, poor value, enter at the northwest tower, tel. 020/7403-3761, Tube: Tower Hill, www.towerbridge.org.uk). The visit is most interesting when the drawbridge lifts to let ships pass, as it does a thousand times a year; for the bridge-lifting schedule, see the website or call 020/7940-3984.

The chic **St. Katharine Dock,** just east of Tower Bridge, has private yachts, mod shops, and the classic Dickens Inn, fun for a drink or pub lunch. Across the bridge is the South Bank, with the

The South Bank

upscale Butlers Wharf area, City Hall, museums, and the Jubilee Walkway.

Northeast of The City

▲**Geffrye Museum**—This low-key but well-organized museum—housed in an 18th-century almshouse—is located north of Liverpool Street Station in the trendy Shoreditch area. Walk past 11 English living rooms, furnished and decorated in styles from 1600 to 2000, then descend the circular stairs to see changing exhibits on home decor. In summer, explore the fragrant herb garden.

Cost and Hours: Free, Tue–Sat 10:00–17:00, Sun 12:00–17:00, closed Mon, garden open April–Oct, 136 Kingsland Road. Tel. 020/7739-9893, www.geffrye -museum.org.uk. To get here, take the

THE CITY

TO ST. PAUL'S

MILLENNIUM BRIDGE

Tower Hill

TOWER PIER

TOWER OF LONDON

BANK-SIDE PIER

SOUTH WARK

CANNON

LONDON BRIDGE

SOUTHWARK CATHEDRAL

St. KATHARINE'S PIER

SHAKE-SPEARE'S GLOBE

CLINK

VIN-OPOLIS

"GOLDEN HINDE"

LONDON BRIDGE PIER

H.M.S. BELFAST

TOWER BRIDGE

WARK ST.

WARK

MARSHALSEA

LONDON DUNGEON

THE SCOOP

CITY HALL

HIGH ST.

OLD OPERATING THEATRE MUSEUM

LONDON BRIDGE STATION

TOOLEY

UNICORN THEATRE

Borough

BOROUGH

⊖ TUBE STN.   ]----[PEDESTRIAN BRIDGE

½ MILE

800 METERS

LONDON

Tube to Liverpool Street, then it's a 10-minute ride north on bus #149 or #242. Or take the East London line on the Overground to the Hoxton stop, which is right next to the museum.

South Bank

▲**Jubilee Walkway**—The South Bank is a thriving arts and cultural center tied together by this riverside path, a popular, pub-crawling pedestrian promenade called the Jubilee Walkway. Stretching from Tower Bridge past Westminster Bridge, it offers

grand views of the Houses of Parliament and St. Paul's. On a sunny day, this is the place to see London out strolling. The Walkway hugs the river except just east of London Bridge, where it cuts inland for a couple of blocks. Plans are underway to expand the path into a 60-mile "Greenway" encircling the city, scheduled to open in 2012 for the Olympic Games and Elizabeth's 60th year as queen (www.jubileewalkway.org.uk).

▲▲**London Eye**—This giant Ferris wheel, towering above London opposite Big Ben, is the world's highest observational wheel and London's answer to the Eiffel Tower. While the experience is memorable, London doesn't have much of a skyline, and the price is borderline outrageous. But whether you ride or not, the wheel is a sight to behold.

Designed like a giant bicycle wheel, it's a pan-European undertaking: British steel and Dutch engineering, with Czech, German, French, and Italian mechanical parts. It's also very "green," running extremely efficiently and virtually silently. Twenty-five people ride in each of its 32 air-conditioned capsules for the 30-minute rotation (you go around only once). Each capsule has a bench, but most people stand. From the top of this 443-foot-high wheel—the highest public viewpoint in the city—even Big Ben looks small. Built to celebrate the new millennium, the Eye's original five-year lease has been extended, and it's becoming a permanent fixture on the London skyline.

After buying your ticket inside, you'll be aggressively ushered into *The London Eye 4-D Experience,* a brief (four-minute) and engaging show combining a 3-D movie with wind and water effects. It basically feels like a bombastic ad for the attraction you already bought a ticket for, and in some ways is more exciting than riding the Eye itself. You can politely skip the show if you want to just get on the wheel, and have the option of coming back later to see the movie.

Cost and Hours: £18, or £41 combo-ticket with Madame Tussauds Waxworks—see page 102, other packages available. Buy tickets at the box office (in the corner of the County Hall building nearest the Eye), in advance by calling 0870-500-0600, or save 10 percent by booking online at www.londoneye.com. Open daily July–Aug 10:00–21:30, June and Sept 10:00–21:00, Oct–May 10:00–20:00, these are last-ascent times, closed Dec 25 and a few days in Jan for annual maintenance, Tube: Waterloo or Westminster. Thames boats come and go from here using the Waterloo Pier at the foot of the wheel.

Crowd-Beating Tips: While not as popular as when it opened, the London Eye can still be crowded at certain times (busiest between 11:00 and 17:00, especially on weekends year-round and every day July–Aug). At the busiest times, you might have to wait up to 30 minutes to buy your ticket, then another

30–45 minutes to board your capsule. If you plan to visit during one of those times, call ahead or go online to pre-book your ticket, then punch your confirmation code into the automated machine in the ticket office (no wait to get the ticket, but you'll still wait to board the wheel). You can pay an extra £10 for a Fast Track ticket that lets you jump the queue, but the time savings are probably not worth the expense.

By the Eye: The area next to the London Eye has developed a cotton-candy ambience of kitschy, kid-friendly attractions. There's an aquarium, game arcade, and "Movieum" dedicated to movies filmed in London, from *Harry Potter* to *Star Wars*.

▲▲Imperial War Museum—This impressive museum covers the wars of the last century—from World War I biplanes to the rise

of fascism to Montgomery's Africa campaign tank to the Cold War, the Cuban Missile Crisis, the Troubles in Northern Ireland, the wars in Iraq, and terrorism.

Allow plenty of time, as this powerful museum—with lots of artifacts and video clips—can be engrossing. The core of the permanent collection, located downstairs, takes you step by step through World Wars I and II. A special exhibit called "Monty: Master of the Battlefield" celebrates Field Marshal Bernard Montgomery. Then you move on to conflicts since 1945. Most of the displays are low-tech—glass cases hold dummies in uniforms, weapons, newspaper clippings, ordinary objects from daily life—but have excellent explanations and video clips. The Trench Experience lets you walk through a dark, chaotic, smelly WWI trench. The Blitz Experience film assaults the senses with the noise and intensity of a WWII air raid on London. Also, the cinema shows a rotating selection of films.

In the entry hall are the large exhibits—including Monty's tank, several field guns, and, dangling overhead, vintage planes.

Imagine the awesome power of the 50-foot V-2 rocket, the kind the Nazis rained down on London, which could arrive silently and destroy a city block. Its direct descendant is the Polaris missile, capable of traveling nearly 3,000 miles in 20 minutes and obliterating an entire city.

Two other sections are not to

be missed: The "Secret War" peeks into the intrigues of espionage in World Wars I and II and in conflicts since. The section on the Holocaust, one of the best on the subject anywhere, tells the story with powerful videos, artifacts, and fine explanations.

War wonks will love the place, as will general history buffs who enjoy patiently reading displays. For the rest, there are enough multimedia exhibits and submarines for the kids to climb in to keep it interesting.

Rather than glorify war, the museum does its best to shine a light on the 100 million deaths of the 20th century. It shows everyday life for people back home and never neglects the powerful human side of one of humankind's most persistent traits.

The museum (which sits in an inviting park equipped with an equally inviting café) is housed in what was the Royal Bethlam Hospital. Also known as "the Bedlam asylum," the place was so wild that it gave the world a new word for chaos. Back in Victorian times, locals—without reality shows and YouTube—paid admission to visit the asylum on weekends for entertainment.

Cost and Hours: Free, daily 10:00–18:00, temporary exhibits extra, often guided tours on weekends—ask at info desk, £4 audioguide, Tube: Lambeth North or bus #12 or bus #159. Tel. 020/7416-5000, www.iwm.org.uk.

▲▲**Tate Modern**—Dedicated in the spring of 2000, the striking museum across the river from St. Paul's opened the new century

with art from the previous one. Its powerhouse collection of Monet, Matisse, Dalí, Picasso, Warhol, and much more is displayed in a converted powerhouse. Of equal interest are the many temporary exhibits featuring cutting-edge art. Each year, the main hall features a different monumental installation by a prominent artist.

Cost and Hours: Free but £3 donations appreciated, fee for special exhibitions, daily 10:00–18:00, Fri–Sat until 22:00—good times to visit, last entry to temporary exhibitions 45 minutes before closing, audioguide-£3.50; free 45-minute guided tours at 11:00, 12:00, 14:00, and 15:00—confirm at info desk; view restaurant on top floor, cross the Millennium Bridge from St. Paul's; Tube: Southwark, London Bridge or Mansion House plus a 10–15-minute walk; or connect by "Tate to Tate" boat from Tate Britain for £5 one-way or £12 for day ticket, 33 percent discount with Travelcard or Oyster card, buy ticket on board. Tel. 020/7887-8888, www.tate.org.uk.

Crossing the Thames on Foot

You can cross the Thames on any of the bridges that carry car traffic over the river, but London's two pedestrian bridges are more fun. The Millennium Bridge (see photo) connects the sedate St. Paul's Cathedral with the great Tate Modern. The Golden Jubilee Bridge, well-lit with a sleek, futuristic look, links bustling Trafalgar Square on the North Bank with the London Eye and Waterloo Station on the South Bank.

▲**Millennium Bridge**—The pedestrian bridge links St. Paul's Cathedral and the Tate Modern across the Thames. This is London's first new bridge in a century. When it first opened, the $25 million bridge wiggled when people walked on it, so it promptly closed for an $8 million, 20-month stabilization; now it's stable and open again. Nicknamed the "blade of light" for its sleek minimalist design (370 yards long, four yards wide, stainless steel with teak planks), its clever aerodynamic handrails deflect wind over the heads of pedestrians.

▲▲**Shakespeare's Globe**—This replica of the original Globe Theatre was built, half-timbered and thatched, as it was in Shakespeare's time. (This is the first thatched roof constructed in London since they were outlawed after the Great Fire of 1666.) The Globe originally accommodated 2,200 seated and another 1,000 standing. Today, slightly smaller and

leaving space for reasonable aisles, the theater holds 800 seated and 600 groundlings. Its promoters brag that the theater melds "the three A's"—actors, audience, and architecture—with each contributing to the play. The working theater hosts authentic performances of Shakespeare's plays with actors in period costumes, modern interpretations of his works, and some works by other playwrights (generally all summer at 14:00 and 19:30—but confirm). For details on seeing a play, see page 140.

The complex has three parts: the theater itself, the box office, and a museum. The Globe Exhibition ticket (£10.50) includes both a tour of the theater and the museum. First, you browse on your own through the **museum's** displays of Elizabethan-era costumes, music, script-printing, and special effects. There are early folios and objects that were dug up on site. A video and scale models help put Shakespearean theater within the context of the times. (The Globe opened one year after England mastered the seas by defeating the Spanish Armada. The debut play was Shakespeare's *Julius Caesar*.)

Next comes the tour of the **theater**—you must take the tour at the time stamped on your ticket, but you can come back to the museum afterward; tickets are good all day. The guide (usually an actor) leads you into the theater to see the stage and the different seating areas for the different classes of people. You take a seat and learn how the new Globe is similar to the old Globe (open-air performances, standing-room by the stage, no curtain) and how it's different (female actors today, lights for night performances, concrete floor). It's not a backstage tour—you don't see dressing rooms or costume shops or sit in on rehearsals, though you may see workers building sets for a new production. You mostly sit and listen. The guides are energetic, theatrical, and knowledgeable, bringing the Elizabethan period to life.

When matinee performances are going on, you can't tour the theater. But you can see the museum, then tour the nearby (and less interesting) Rose Theatre instead.

Cost and Hours: £10.50 includes museum and 40-minute tour, £7.50 when only the Rose Theatre is available for touring, tickets good all day; complex open daily 9:00–17:00; exhibition and tours: May–Sept—Globe tours offered mornings only with Rose Theatre tours in afternoon; Oct–April—Globe tours run all day, tours start every 15–30 minutes; on the South Bank directly across Thames over Southwark Bridge from St. Paul's, Tube: Mansion House or London Bridge plus a 10-minute walk. Tel. 020/7902-1400 or 020/7902-1500, www.shakespeares-globe.org.

Eating: The Swan at the Globe café offers a sit-down restaurant (for lunch and dinner, reservations recommended, tel. 020/7928-9444), a drinks-and-plates bar, and a sandwich-and-coffee cart (daily 9:00–closing, depending on performance times).

Vinopolis: City of Wine—While it seems illogical to have a huge wine museum in beer-loving London, Vinopolis makes a good case. Built over a Roman wine store and filling the massive vaults of an old wine warehouse, the museum offers an excellent audioguide with a light yet earnest history of wine to accompany your sips of various mediocre reds and whites, ports, and champagnes. Allow some time, as the audioguide takes 1.5 hours—and the sipping can slow things down pleasantly. This place is popular. Booking ahead for Friday and Saturday nights is a must.

Cost and Hours: Self-guided tour options range from £20 to £65—each includes about five wine tastes and an audioguide. Other options are available for guided tours. Some packages also include whiskey (the new wine), other spirits, or a meal. Thu–Sat 12:00–22:00, Sun 12:00–18:00, closed Mon–Wed, last entry 2.5 hours before closing, between the Globe and Southwark Cathedral at 1 Bank End, Tube: London Bridge. Tel. 020/7940-8300, www .vinopolis.co.uk.

Southwark

These sights are in Southwark, on the South Bank. The area stretching from the Tate Modern to London Bridge, known as Southwark (SUTH-uck), was for centuries the place Londoners would go to escape the rules and decency of the city and let their hair down. Bearbaiting, brothels, rollicking pubs, and theater—you name the dream, and it could be fulfilled just across the Thames. A run-down warehouse district through the 20th century, it's been gentrified with classy restaurants, office parks, pedestrian promenades, major sights (such as the Tate Modern and Shakespeare's Globe), and this colorful collection of lesser sights. The area is easy on foot and a scenic—though circuitous—way to connect the Tower of London with St. Paul's.

The Clink Prison Museum—Proudly the "original clink," this was, until 1780, where law-abiding citizens threw Southwark troublemakers. Today, it's a low-tech torture museum filling grotty old rooms with papier-mâché gore. Unfortunately, there's little that seriously deals with the fascinating problem of law and order in Southwark, where 18th-century Londoners went for a good time.

Cost and Hours: Overpriced at £5; July–Sept daily 10:00–21:00; Oct–June Mon–Fri 10:00–18:00, Sat–Sun until 19:30; 1 Clink Street, Tube: London Bridge. Tel. 020/7403-0900, www .clink.co.uk.

Golden Hinde Replica—This is a full-size replica of the 16th-century warship in which Sir Francis Drake circumnavigated the globe from 1577 to 1580. Commanding this ship, Drake earned the reputation as history's most successful pirate. The original is long gone, but this boat has logged more than 100,000 miles, including a voyage around the world. While the ship is fun to see, its interior is not worth touring.

Cost and Hours: £6, daily 10:00–17:00; may be closed if rented out for pirate birthday parties, school groups, or weddings; Tube: London Bridge. Tel. 020/7403-0123, www.goldenhinde .com.

Southwark Cathedral—While made a cathedral only in 1905, it's been the neighborhood church since the 13th century, and comes with some interesting history. The enthusiastic docents give impromptu tours if you ask.

Cost and Hours: Free but £4 suggested donation, daily 8:00–18:00, last entry 30 minutes before closing, £2.50 guidebook, no photos without permission, Tube: London Bridge. Tel. 020/7367-6700, http://cathedral.southwark.anglican.org.

Music: The cathedral hosts evensong services (weekdays at 17:30, Sat at 16:00, Sun at 15:00, no service on Wed or alternate Mon).

▲Old Operating Theatre Museum and Herb Garret—Climb a tight and creaky wooden spiral staircase to a church attic where you'll find a garret used to dry medicinal herbs, a fascinating exhibit on Victorian surgery, cases of well-described 19th-century medical paraphernalia, and a special look at "anesthesia, the defeat of pain." Then you stumble upon Britain's oldest operating theater, where limbs were sawed off way back in 1821.

Cost and Hours: £5.80, cash only, daily 10:30–16:45, 9a St. Thomas Street, Tube: London Bridge. Tel. 020/7188-2679, www .thegarret.org.uk.

HMS *Belfast*—"The last big-gun armored warship of World War II" clogs the Thames just upstream from the Tower Bridge. This huge vessel—now manned with wax sailors—thrills kids who always dreamed of sitting in a turret shooting off their imaginary guns. If you're into WWII warships, this is the ultimate. Otherwise, it's just lots of exercise with a nice view of the Tower Bridge.

Cost and Hours: £12.95, includes audioguide, daily March–Oct 10:00–18:00, Nov–Feb 10:00–17:00, last entry one hour before closing, Tube: London Bridge. Tel. 020/7940-6300, www.hmsbelfast.iwm.org .uk.

City Hall—The glassy, egg-shaped building near the south end of Tower Bridge is London's City Hall, designed by Sir Norman Foster, the architect who worked on London's Millennium Bridge and Berlin's Reichstag. City Hall houses the office of

London's mayor—the blond, flamboyant, conservative former journalist and author Boris Johnson. He consults here with the Assembly representatives of the city's 25 districts. An interior spiral ramp allows visitors to watch and hear the action below in the Assembly Chamber—ride the lift to the second floor (the highest visitors can go) and spiral down. On the lower ground floor is a large aerial photograph of London, an information desk, and a handy cafeteria. Next to City Hall is the outdoor amphitheater called The Scoop.

Cost and Hours: City Hall is free and open to visitors Mon–Thu 8:00–18:00, Fri 8:00–17:30, closed Sat–Sun; Tube: London Bridge station plus 10-minute walk, or Tower Hill station plus 15-minute walk. Tel. 020/7983-4000.

West London

▲▲Tate Britain—One of Europe's great art houses, Tate Britain specializes in British painting from the 16th century through

modern times. The museum has a good representation of William Blake's religious sketches, the Pre-Raphaelites' realistic art, and J. M. W. Turner's swirling works. This is people's art, with realistic paintings rooted in the people, landscape, and stories of the British Isles. You'll see Hogarth's stage sets, Gainsborough's ladies, Blake's angels, Constable's clouds, Turner's tempests, the swooning realism of the Pre-Raphaelites, and the camera-eye portraits of Hockney and Freud. What you won't see here are the fleshy goddesses, naked baby angels, and Madonna-and-child altarpieces so popular elsewhere in Europe. The largely Protestant English abhorred the "graven images" of the wealthy Catholic world.

The collection is constantly in motion but the basic layout stays the same: a roughly chronological walk through British paintings from 1500 to 1901 in the west half of the building, the 20th century in the east, and the works of J. M. W. Turner in the adjoining Clore Gallery.

Cost and Hours: Free, £2 donation requested, temporary exhibits extra; daily 10:00–18:00, last entry to special exhibitions at 17:15, first Fri of the month until 22:00, last entry to special exhibitions at 20:30; no photography allowed without advance permission, café and restaurant; Tube: Pimlico, then 7-minute walk; take the "Tate to Tate" boat directly to the museum from Tate Modern; or take bus #87 from National Gallery or bus #88 from Oxford Circus. Switchboard tel. 020/7887-8888, recorded info tel.

West London

020/7887-8008, www.tate.org.uk.

Tours: Free tours are offered Mon–Fri at 11:00 (art from 1500 to 1800), 12:00 (art from 1800 to 1900), 14:00 (Turner), and 15:00 (art from the 20th century). Weekend tours cover the collection's highlights (Sat–Sun 12:00 and 15:00); call to confirm schedule. The £3.50 audioguide (with photos and video clips) is useful.

▲**Apsley House (Wellington Museum)**—Having beaten Napoleon at Waterloo, Arthur Wellesley, the First Duke of Wellington, was once the most famous man in Europe. He was given a huge fortune with which he purchased London's ultimate address, #1 London. His refurbished mansion offers a nice interior, a handful of world-class paintings, and a glimpse at the life of the great soldier and two-time prime minister. Those who

know something about Wellington ahead of time will appreciate the place much more than those who don't, as there's scarce biographical background. The place is well-described by the included audioguide, which has sound bites from the current Duke of Wellington (who still lives at Apsley).

Cost and Hours: £6, free on June 18—Waterloo Day, April–Oct Wed–Sun 11:00–17:00, Nov–March until 16:00, closed

Mon–Tue, 20 yards from Hyde Park Corner Tube st
020/7499-5676, www.english-heritage.org.uk. Hyde Par
ant and picnic-friendly rose garden is nearby.

Note that the **Wellington Arch,** which stands just across the
street, is open to the public but not worth the £4 charge (elevator
up, lousy views and boring exhibits).

▲**Hyde Park and Speakers' Corner**—London's "Central Park,"
originally Henry VIII's hunting grounds, has more than 600 acres
of lush greenery, the huge man-made Serpentine Lake, the royal
Kensington Palace and Orangery (described later), and the ornate
Neo-Gothic Albert Memorial across from the Royal Albert Hall.
The western half of the park is known as Kensington Gardens.

On Sundays, from just after noon until early evening,
Speakers' Corner offers soapbox oratory at its best (northeast

corner of the park, Tube: Marble
Arch). Characters climb their
stepladders, wave their flags,
pound emphatically on their
sandwich boards, and share
what they are convinced is their
wisdom. Regulars have resident hecklers who know their
lines and are always ready with
a verbal jab or barb. "The grass
roots of democracy" is actually a holdover from when the gallows
stood here and the criminal was allowed to say just about anything
he wanted to before he swung. I dare you to raise your voice and
gather a crowd—it's easy to do.

The **Princess Diana Memorial
Fountain** honors the "People's
Princess," who once lived in nearby
Kensington Palace. The low-key
circular stream, great for cooling
off your feet on a hot day, is in the
south central part of the park, near
the Albert Memorial and Serpentine
Gallery. (Don't be confused by signs
to the Diana, Princess of Wales
Memorial Playground, in the northwest corner of the park.)

▲▲▲**Victoria and Albert Museum**—The world's top collection
of decorative arts (vases, stained glass, fine furniture, clothing,
jewelry, carpets, and more) is a surprisingly interesting assortment
of crafts from the West, as well as Asian and Islamic cultures. The
British Galleries are grand, but there's much more to see, including Raphael's tapestry cartoons and a cast of Trajan's Column that

depicts the emperor's conquests.

The V&A grew out of the Great Exhibition of 1851, that ultimate celebration of the Industrial Revolution. Now "art" could be brought to the masses through modern technology and mass production. The museum was founded on the idealistic Victorian notion that anyone can be continually improved by education and example. After much support from Queen Victoria and Prince Albert, the museum was renamed for the royal couple, and its present building was opened in 1909.

The V&A is in the midst of a 10-year update and expansion. Changes so far include a new café, sculpture gallery, Islamic room, and refurbished Medieval and Renaissance galleries. During this chaotic time, exhibits may be rearranged, so check with the information desk for current room closures, carry a copy of the museum's detailed map, and ask a nearby guard if you can't find one of the objects I mention below.

You could spend days in this place. The museum is large and gangly, with 150 rooms and more than 12 miles of corridors. Pick up the much-needed museum map (£1 suggested donation). While just wandering works well here, consider catching one of the free one-hour orientation tours or buying the fine £5 *V&A Guide Book*.

Here are a few highlights:

The **British Galleries** sweeps chronologically through 400 years of British high-class living (1500–1900)—all laid out over two floors, and beautifully described.

In Room 46A are the plaster casts of **Trajan's Column**—a copy of Rome's 140-foot spiral relief telling the story of the conquest of Dacia (modern-day Romania).

Room 46B has plaster casts of **Renaissance sculptures** by Michelangelo and others, which allowed 19th-century art students who couldn't afford a railpass to go study the classics. Compare Michelangelo's monumental *David* with Donatello's girlish *David* (at the other end of the room), and see Ghiberti's bronze Baptistery doors that inspired the Florentine Renaissance.

In Room 48A are **Raphael's "cartoons,"** seven of the full-size designs by Raphael that were used to produce tapestries for the Sistine Chapel (approximately 13 feet by 17 feet, done in tempera on paper, now mounted on canvas). The cartoons were sent to factories in Brussels, cut into strips (see the lines), and placed on the looms. The scenes are the reverse of the final product—lots of left-handed saints.

Cost and Hours: Free, £3 donation requested, possible pricey fee for special exhibits, daily 10:00–17:45, Fri until 22:00, free one-hour tours daily on the half-hour 10:30–15:30, Tube: South Kensington, from the Tube station a long tunnel leads directly to museum. Tel. 020/7942-2000, www.vam.ac.uk.

▲▲Natural History Museum—Across the street from Victoria and Albert, this mammoth museum is housed in a giant and wonderful Victorian, Neo-Romanesque building. In the main hall,

 above a big dinosaur skeleton and under a massive slice of sequoia tree, Charles Darwin sits as if upon a throne overseeing it all. Built in the 1870s specifically for the huge collection (50 million specimens), the building has two halves: the Life Galleries (creepy-crawlies, human biology, "our place in evolution," and awe-inspiring dinosaurs) and the Earth Galleries (meteors, volcanoes, earthquakes, and so on).

Exhibits are wonderfully explained, with lots of creative, interactive displays. Pop in, if only for the wild collection of dinosaurs and to hear English children exclaim, "Oh my goodness!" Get oriented by talking with one of the many "visit planners" (helpful guides scattered throughout the museum), review the "What's on Today" board for special events and tours, and note which sections are closed (rather than "renovating," they say "we are evolving"). While the dinosaur hall often has a long line, everything else is wide open. Don't miss the vault in the mineralogy section (top floor of the green zone), with rare and precious stones (including a meteorite from Mars and the Aurora Pyramid of Hope, displaying 296 diamonds showing their full range of natural colors).

Cost and Hours: Free, fees for special exhibits, daily 10:00–17:50, last entry at 17:30, occasional tours, long tunnel leads directly from South Kensington Tube station to museum. Tel. 020/7942-5000, exhibit info and reservations tel. 020/7942-5011, www.nhm.ac.uk.

▲Science Museum—Next door to the Natural History Museum, this sprawling wonderland for curious minds is kid-perfect, with themes such as measuring time, exploring space, and the evolution of modern medicine. It offers hands-on fun, from moonwalks to deep-sea exploration, with trendy technology exhibits, an IMAX theater (£8, kids-£6.25), and cool rotating themed exhibits, including "Climate Science—The Science behind Climate Change," on display through 2011.

Cost and Hours: Free, daily 10:00–18:00, Exhibition Road, Tube: South Kensington. Toll tel. 0870-870-4868, www.sciencemuseum.org.uk.

Kensington Palace—In 1689, King William and Queen Mary moved from Whitehall in central London to the more pristine and peaceful village of Kensington (now engulfed by London). Sir Christopher Wren renovated an existing house into Kensington

Palace, which became the center of English court life until 1760, when the royal family moved into Buckingham Palace. Since then, lesser royals have bedded down in Kensington Palace. Princess Diana lived here from her 1981 marriage to Prince Charles until her death in 1997. Today it's home to three of Charles' cousins. The palace, while still functioning as a royal residence, also welcomes visitors with an impressive string of royal apartments and a few rooms of royal dresses.

While generally a ▲▲ attraction, the palace is currently being renovated, and until June 2012 it's not worth your time or money. Rather than close it during restoration, they've created a silly "Enchanted Palace" theatrical show replacing the historic artifacts of the palace (such as the wonderful royal dress collection, splendid 17th-century furniture of the William and Mary apartments, and the bed where Queen Victoria was born—fully clothed, it is said) with cheesy modern props. The only good thing about the Enchanted Palace is that it enables unwitting tourists to help pay for the £12 million renovation.

Cost and Hours: £12.50, daily 10:00–18:00, until 17:00 in winter, last entry one hour before closing, a 10-minute hike through Kensington Gardens from either Queensway or High Street Kensington Tube station. Toll tel. 0870-751-5170 or 0844-482-7777, www.hrp.org.uk.

Eating: Garden enthusiasts enjoy popping into the secluded Sunken Garden, 50 yards from the exit. Consider afternoon tea at the nearby Orangery (see page 179), built as a greenhouse for Queen Anne in 1704.

Victoria Station—From underneath this station's iron-and-glass canopy, trains depart for the south of England and Gatwick Airport. While Victoria Station is famous and a major Tube stop, few tourists actually take trains from here—most just come to take in the exciting bustle. It's a fun place to just be a "rock in a river" teeming with commuters and services. The station is surrounded by big red buses, taxis, travel agencies, and lousy eateries. It's next to the main intercity bus station (Victoria Coach Station) and the best inexpensive lodgings in town.

Westminster Cathedral—This cathedral, the largest Catholic church in England and just a block from Victoria Station, is striking, but not very historic or important to visit. Opened in 1903, it has a brick Neo-Byzantine flavor (surrounded by glassy office blocks). While it's definitely not Westminster Abbey, half the tourists wandering around inside seem to think it is. The highlight is the lift to the viewing gallery atop its 273-foot bell tower (£5 for the lift, tower open daily 9:30–12:30 & 13:00–17:00).

Cost and Hours: Free entry, daily 7:00–19:00; 5-minute walk from Victoria Station or take bus #11, #24, #148, #211, or #507 to museum's door; just off Victoria Street, Tube: Victoria; www.westminstercathedral.org.uk.

National Army Museum—This museum is not as awe-inspiring as the Imperial War Museum, but it's still fun, especially for kids into soldiers, armor, and guns. And while the Imperial War Museum is limited to wars of the 20th century, the National Army Museum tells the story of the British army from 1415 through the Bosnian conflict and Iraq, with lots of Redcoat lore and a good look at Waterloo. Kids enjoy trying on a Cromwellian helmet, seeing the skeleton of Napoleon's horse, and peering out from a World War I trench through a working periscope.

Cost and Hours: Free, daily 10:00–17:30, Royal Hospital Road, Chelsea, Tube: Sloane Square. Tel. 020/7730-0717 or 020/7881-2455, www.national-army-museum.ac.uk.

Greater London
West of Central London
▲▲**Kew Gardens**—For a fine riverside park and a palatial greenhouse jungle to swing through, take the Tube or the boat to every

botanist's favorite escape, Kew Gardens. While to most visitors the Royal Botanic Gardens of Kew are simply a delightful opportunity to wander among 33,000 different types of plants, to the hardworking organization that runs the gardens, it's a way to promote understanding and preservation of the botanical diversity of our planet. The Kew Tube station drops you in an herbal little business community, a two-block walk from Victoria Gate (the main garden entrance). Pick up a map brochure and check at the gate for a monthly listing of best blooms.

Garden-lovers could spend days exploring Kew's 300 acres. For a quick visit, spend a fragrant hour wandering through three buildings: the **Palm House**, a humid Victorian world of iron, glass, and tropical plants built in 1844; a **Waterlily House** that Monet would swim for; and the **Princess of Wales**

Greater London

RAF MUSEUM LONDON
CAMDEN LOCK MARKET
2012 OLYMPIC PARK
HYDE PARK
TRAFALGAR SQUARE
ST. PAUL'S
DOCKLANDS
LONDON CITY AIRPORT
TO HEATHROW AIRPORT
LONDON
THAMES
WESTMINSTER PIER
CANARY WHARF ON ISLE OF DOGS
O2 ARENA
GREENWICH
KEW GARDENS
BRIXTON MARKET
N
WIMBLEDON
= CENTRAL LONDON
HAMPTON COURT PALACE
DCH
5 MILES
5 KM

Conservatory, a modern greenhouse with many different climate zones growing countless cacti, bug-munching carnivorous plants, and more. The latest addition to the gardens is the **Rhizotron and Xstrata Treetop Walkway**, a 200-yard-long scenic steel walkway that puts you high in the canopy 60 feet above the ground.

Cost and Hours: £13.50, discounted to £11.50 45 minutes before closing, kids under 17 free, £5 for Kew Palace only; April–Aug Mon–Fri 9:30–18:30, Sat–Sun 9:30–19:30; closes earlier Sept–March, last entry to gardens 30 minutes before closing, galleries and conservatories close at 17:30 in high season—earlier off-season; free one-hour walking tours daily at 11:00 and 14:00; £4 narrated 40-minute hop-on, hop-off joyride on Kew Explorer tram departs on the hour from 11:00 from near Victoria Gate; Tube: Kew Gardens, boats run April–Oct between Kew Gardens and Westminster Pier—see page 76. Switchboard tel. 020/8332-5000, recorded info tel. 020/8332-5655, www.kew.org.

Eating: For a sun-dappled lunch or afternoon tea, walk 10 minutes from the Palm House to the Orangery (£8–12 lunches, £15–18 afternoon tea, daily 10:00–18:00, until 17:00 in winter, closes early for events, tel. 0844-482-7777 www.hrp.org.uk).

▲Hampton Court Palace—Fifteen miles up the Thames from downtown (a £15 taxi ride from Kew Gardens), and worth ▲▲ for palace aficionados, is the 500-year-old palace of Henry VIII. Actually, it was originally the palace of his minister, Cardinal Wolsey. When Wolsey, a clever man, realized Henry VIII was experiencing a little palace envy, he gave the mansion to his king.

The Tudor palace was also home to Elizabeth I and Charles I. Sections were updated by Christopher Wren for William and Mary. The stately palace stands overlooking the Thames and includes some impressive Tudor rooms, including a Great Hall with a magnificent hammer-beam ceiling. The industrial-strength Tudor kitchen was capable of keeping 600 schmoozing courtiers thoroughly—if not well—fed. The sculpted garden features a rare Tudor tennis court and a popular maze.

The palace, fully restored after a 1986 fire, tries hard to please, but it doesn't quite sparkle. From the information center in the main courtyard, pick up audioguides for self-guided tours of various wings of the palace (free). The Tudor kitchens, Henry VIII's apartments, and the King's apartments are most interesting; the Georgian rooms are pretty dull. The maze in the nearby garden is a curiosity some find fun (maze free with palace ticket, otherwise £3.50).

Cost and Hours: The palace costs £14, or £38 for families, online discounts, daily April–Oct 10:00–18:00, Nov–March 10:00–16:30, last entry one hour before closing, café. Toll tel. 0844-482-7777, www.hrp.org.uk.

Getting There: The train (2/hour, 35 minutes) from London's Waterloo Station drops you across the river from the palace (just walk across the bridge). Consider arriving at or departing from the palace by boat (connections with London's Westminster Pier, see page 76); it's a relaxing and scenic three- to four-hour cruise past two locks and a fun new/old riverside mix.

Royal Air Force Museum London—A hit with aviation enthusiasts, this huge aerodrome and airfield contain planes from World War II's Battle of Britain up through the Gulf War. You can climb inside some of the planes, try your luck in a cockpit, and fly with the Red Arrows in a flight simulator.

Cost and Hours: Free, daily 10:00–18:00, last entry 30 minutes before closing, café, shop, parking-£2.50, Grahame Park Way, 30-minute ride from central London, Tube: Colindale—top of Northern Line Edgware branch. Tel. 020/8205-2266, www.raf museum.org.uk.

▲▲The Docklands

London is growing east. The Docklands, at a bend in the Thames dubbed the Isle of Dogs, were once the primary harbor for the Port of London—the world's largest, with direct connections to the

North Sea. But in the 20th century, World War II damage and the transition to container shipping left the Docklands a derelict and deserted no-man's-land...the most miserable place in London. However, over the last couple of decades, things have changed dramatically, and the Docklands have been transformed into a vibrant business center. Shipping canals and a few old brick warehouses survive, but everything has been spiffed up and gentrified. Some of the UK's tallest skyscrapers tower overhead, and underfoot are sprawling subterranean supermalls.

While not full of the touristy sights that many are seeking in London, the Docklands offer a refreshing look at the British version of a 21st-century city. You can see the highlights in a short visit. It's best at the end of the workday, when it's lively with office workers (it's ideal on the way back from Greenwich—covered in the next chapter—since Greenwich and The Docklands line up on the same train tracks). Ride the Tube or the Docklands Light Railway (DLR) to the Canary Wharf stop, and go for a stroll. Explore the ultra-modern malls and delightfully peaceful parks with pedestrian bridges looping over the now-tranquil canals. Though you can't get up in the skyscrapers, the ground-floor levels are welcoming with fun art. Photographers can't help but capture jumbo jets gliding past gleaming towers, goofy pose-with-me statues, and trendy pubs filled with trendier young professionals. Then head over to West India Quay to visit the Museum of London Docklands (see below). If you're at the Docklands, it's a relatively straightforward detour to see the Olympics 2012 sights in Stratford (see next section).

▲**Museum of London Docklands**—Illuminating the gritty and fascinating history of this site, this museum traces the story of what was London's primary harbor (free, daily 10:00–18:00, West India Quay, Tube: West India Quay or Canary Wharf, tel. 020/7001-9844, www.museumindocklands.org.uk).

2012 London Olympic Park, in Stratford

From July 27 to August 12, 2012, all eyes will be on London as it hosts athletes from 205 nations in the 30th Olympiad. Though events will take place throughout the city, festivities will center around Olympic Park, filling the Lea Valley, about seven miles northeast of central London. Once voted the worst place to live in London, Lea Valley was the site of derelict factories, mountains of discarded tires, and Europe's biggest refrigerator dump. Now it's Europe's biggest construction site, with a veritable

2012 Olympics Venues

Although most of the Olympic Games will be held in London's East End, there will be sports and activities all over London and Britain. These are the main venues:

Olympic Park, in the Stratford district of East London, is the heart of the games. Here you'll find the 80,000-seat Olympic Stadium (for opening and closing ceremonies) and the Olympic Village, where the athletes will stay. A 12,000-seat basketball arena is under construction—and will be completely dismantled when the games are over. The Aquatics Centre, with its swooping wave-like roofline, may become the architectural "face" of the games.

Central London will be the site of—really?—beach volleyball. Tons of sand will be spread across the parking lot behind #10 Downing Street and Horse Guards, creating an urban beach ringed with bleachers. Triathletes will compete in **Hyde Park,** swimming in the Serpentine lake, then biking and running around the park. **Greenwich Park** (near the *Cutty Sark,* see page 200) will hold equestrian events, while the nearby **O_2 Arena** (formerly the "Millennium Dome") will host gymnastics and more basketball.

Farther afield, you'll find tennis at **Wimbledon** (of course), volleyball at **Earl's Court,** and football/soccer at **Wembley Stadium.** The Olympic torch will wend its way through various communities. And anywhere you go, you can't avoid the universally ridiculed Olympic mascots—those alien/Gumby/Cyclops-like creatures named Wenlock and Mandeville.

Tickets go on sale spring 2011 by lottery for British and EU residents only (US residents can check www.tickets .london2012.com for up-to-date info).

army of workers, fleets of trucks, clusters of concrete-mixing towers, and forests of cranes working furiously to get everything ready on time. Work is scheduled to be complete in July of 2011, when a rigorous 12-month testing process will begin. (For now, you can either view the site on your own, or go on a guided tour—both explained later.)

London is the first city to host the modern games three times—first in 1908, and then in 1948 (the first post-World-War-II Olympics, known as the "Austerity Games"). The city won the 2012 bid for its grand and green vision, including a promise to permanently improve the least desirable part of the city. The site's connection to the broader world will be extraordinary: It will take just two hours to go from Paris to Olympic Park (ride the Eurostar to St. Pancras International Station in downtown London, and connect via a seven-minute bullet train to Stratford Station).

These will be the greenest games ever. There will be no public parking at the site—event tickets will include an all-day London Tube pass. About 90 percent of demolition material has been recycled. More than half of the deliveries will be by train or boat rather than by truck. Half a million trees are being planted, and 1.4 million tons of dirt have been cleansed of arsenic, lead, and other toxic chemicals—a reminder of this site's dirty industrial past. Locals whine about the cost—as locals have whined about big public building projects, I imagine, since the days when great cities built great Gothic churches. But the $14 billion project is a stimulus plan, with 90 percent local investment and employment.

About 75 percent of the construction will be "legacy building," giving these structures a practical life in a reinvigorated community after the games. Many of the buildings will be converted to housing (enough for 16,000 residents), with half of these units designated for low-income people. Bridges leading to the site, built double-wide for huge crowds, will be scaled back. The commercial zone, Stratford City, will become the biggest shopping center in Europe. Between the bullet trains, Tube, regional rail services, and DLR, residents of post-Olympics Stratford will enjoy the best public transit in town, with multiple connections to central London. (Don't confuse it with Stratford-upon-Avon, the famous Warwickshire town where Shakespeare was born. That's two hours northwest of London.)

Suddenly, Stratford is a place with a future (and poor little Grandmas who've called it home are now worth something to their relatives and developers...and chocolate and flowers appear on Sundays). It seems fitting that this most multiethnic part of London will host these famously multiethnic games.

Visiting the Olympic Park Site

On Your Own: A viewpoint on the greenway (called "The View Tube") comes with information boards, a lookout tower, a café (already well-known for its coffee and brownies), and a WC. It's free and a short walk from the Pudding Mill Lane DLR station. Along the way, you'll see some of the legion of Nepali Gurkhas employed here for security.

Getting There: Ride the Tube (Jubilee Line) from central London to Stratford, where you can change to the DLR to Pudding Mill Lane. To go direct on the DLR, take a Stratford-bound train from Bank (in central London, also accessible from the Monument Tube station) or from Canary Wharf (in the Docklands), and get off at Pudding Mill Lane.

On a Tour: Blue Badge guides lead 1.5-hour guided walks of the area, weaving background about its Industrial Age heritage into the excitement of today's building project and impressive vision (£8, pay guide directly in cash, online reservations recommended but not required, daily at 11:00, www.toursof2012sites.com). Meet at Bromley-by-Bow Tube station (District or Hammersmith Line).

Note that the Stratford, Pudding Mill Lane, and Bromley-by-Bow stations are (barely) inside Zone 2, which means the trip is covered by any Tube ticket or pass covering Zones 1–2.

Shopping in London

Department Stores

Harrods—Harrods is London's most famous and touristy department store. With more than four acres of retail space covering seven floors, it's a place where some shoppers could spend all day. (To me, it's still just a department store.) Big yet classy, Harrods has everything from elephants to toothbrushes (Mon–Sat 10:00–20:00, Sun 12:00–18:00, mandatory storage for big backpacks-£3, no shorts or flip-flops, on Brompton Road, Tube: Knightsbridge, tel. 020/7730-1234, www.harrods.com).

While the store is famous partly for its Egyptian theme and its memorials to Princess Diana and her boyfriend, Dodi Fayed, those were the pet projects of Harrods' former owner, Mohamed Al Fayed (Dodi's Egyptian father). Al Fayed sold the store in May of 2010 to a Qatari investment group, so it's possible some of these features (especially the Di and Dodi stuff) could change.

Sightseers should pick up the free *Store Guide* at any info post. Here's what I enjoy: On the ground floor, find the Food Halls, with their Edwardian tiled walls, creative and exuberant displays, and staff in period costumes—not quite like your local supermarket back home.

Descend to the lower ground floor and follow signs to the Egyptian Escalator (in the center of the store), where you'll likely find a memorial to Dodi Fayed and Princess Diana. Photos and flowers honor the late Princess and her lover, who both died in a car crash in Paris in 1997. Inside a small, clear pyramid, you can see a wine glass still dirty from their last dinner and the engagement ring that Dodi purchased the day before they died. True Di-hards can go back up one level to the ground floor and follow signs to Door #3 in Menswear (near Men's Designer and Men's Tailoring, at the escalator). A huge (and more than a little creepy) bronze statue shows Di and Dodi releasing a symbolic albatross.

Back in the center of the store, ride the Egyptian Escalator—lined with pharaoh-headed sconces, papyrus-plant lamps, and hieroglyphic balconies—to the fourth floor. From the escalator, make a U-turn left and head to the far corner of the store (toys) to find child-size luxury cars that actually work. If you have £10,000 to spare, these are the perfect gift for the child who has everything.

LONDON

Also on the fourth floor is **The Georgian Restaurant,** where you can enjoy a fancy afternoon tea (see page 180). For non-tea drinkers, 27 other eateries are scattered throughout the store, including a sushi bar, kosher deli, pizzeria, classic pub, and—for the truly homesick—a Krispy Kreme.

Many of my readers report that Harrods is overpriced, snooty, and teeming with American and Japanese tourists. It's the only shopping mall I've seen with its own gift store. Still, it's the palace of department stores. The nearby Beauchamp Place is lined with classy and fascinating shops.

Harvey Nichols—Once Princess Diana's favorite, "Harvey Nick's" remains the department store *du jour* (Mon–Sat 10:00–20:00, Sun 12:00–18:00, near Harrods, 109–125 Knightsbridge, Tube: Knightsbridge, tel. 020/7235-5000, www.harveynichols.com). Want to pick up a little £20 scarf for the wife? You won't do it here, where they're more like £200. The store's fifth floor is a veritable food fest, with a gourmet grocery store, a fancy restaurant, a Yo! Sushi bar, and a lively café. Consider a take-away tray of sushi to eat on a bench in the Hyde Park rose garden two blocks away.

Street Markets

Antique buffs, people-watchers, and folks who brake for garage sales love London's street markets. There's good early-morning market activity somewhere any day of the week. The best—which combine lively stalls and a colorful neighborhood with cute and characteristic shops of its own—are Portobello Road and Camden Market. Any London TI has a complete, up-to-date list. If you like to haggle, there are no holds barred in London's street markets. Warning: Markets attract two kinds of people: tourists and pickpockets.

In Notting Hill

Portobello Road Market—Arguably London's best street market, Portobello Road stretches for several blocks through the delightful, colorful, funky-yet-quaint Notting Hill neighborhood (immortalized by the Hugh Grant/Julia Roberts film of the same name). Already charming streets lined with pastel-painted houses and offbeat antiques shops are enlivened on Saturdays with 2,000 additional stalls (5:30–17:00), plus food, live music, and more. (It's also extremely crowded.) If you start at Notting Hill Gate and work your way north, you'll find these general sections: antiques, new goods, produce, more new goods, and a flea market. While Portobello Road is best on Saturdays, it's enjoyable to stroll this street on most other days as well, since the characteristic shops are fun to explore—but skip it on Sundays, when virtually everything is closed (Tube: Notting Hill Gate, near recommended accommodations, tel. 020/7229-8354, www.portobelloroad.co.uk).

In the East End

All three of these East End markets are busiest and most interesting on Sundays.

Spitalfields Market—This huge, mod-feeling market hall (pronounced "spittle-fields") combines a shopping mall with old brick buildings and sleek modern ones, all covered by a giant glass roof. While the shops and a rainbow of restaurant options are open every day, the open space between them is filled with stalls during the week. It's best on Sundays (9:00–17:00), when all stalls and shops are open; you'll find a lively organic food market, many ethnic eateries, crafts, trendy clothes, bags, and an antique-and-junk market. Thursdays are for antiques, Fridays specialize in cutting-edge fashion and art, and the first and third Wednesday of every month feature a record and book fair (all 10:00–16:00). It's quietest on Saturdays, Mondays, and Tuesdays, when only the shops are open—no stalls (shops open daily 11:00–19:00, Tube: Liverpool Street; from the Tube stop, take Bishopsgate East exit, turn left, walk 2 blocks, and turn right on Brushfield Street; tel. 020/7375-2963, www.visitspitalfields.com).

Petticoat Lane Market—Just a block from Spitalfields Market, this is a line of stalls on an otherwise dull, glass-skyscraper-lined Middlesex Street; adjoining Wentworth Street is grungier and more characteristic. Expect budget clothing, leather, shoes, watches, jewelry, and crowds (Sun 9:00–14:00, sometimes later; smaller market Mon–Fri 10:00–16:30 on Wentworth Street only; closed Sat; Middlesex Street and Wentworth Street, Tube: Liverpool Street). The Columbia Road flower market is nearby (Sun 8:00–15:00, http://columbiaroad.info).

Brick Lane Market—Housed in the former Truman Brewery, this market is in the heart of the "Banglatown" Bangladeshi community (Sun 10:00–17:00, tel. 020/7770-6028, www.bricklane market.com).

Other Markets

Camden Lock Market—This huge, trendy arts-and-crafts festival has become quite punky to many travelers. Still, it's London's fourth-most-popular tourist attraction (daily 10:00–18:00, busiest on weekends, Tube: Camden Town, tel. 020/7284-2084, www .camdenlockmarket.com).

Covent Garden Market—Originally the convent garden for Westminster Abbey, the iron-and-glass market hall hosted a produce market until the 1970s (earning it the name "Apple Market"). Yesteryear's produce stalls are now open 10:00–18:00 daily with antiques (Mon); clothes, gifts, and foods (Tue–Fri); and hand-made crafts (Sun; tel. 020-7836-9136, www.coventgardenlife.com /shopping/markets). The **Jubilee Hall Market** to the south follows a similar schedule (antiques Mon 5:00–18:00, general market Tue–Fri 9:30–18:00, handcrafts Sat–Sun 9:00–18:00, tel. 020/7379-4242, www.jubileemarket.co.uk).

Brixton Market—Here the food, clothing, records, and hair-braiding throb with an Afro-Caribbean beat (stalls open Mon–Tue and Thu–Sat 8:00–18:00, Wed 8:00–15:00, closed Sun; farmers' market Sun 10:00–14:00 but otherwise dead on Sundays; Tube: Brixton, www.brixtonmarket.net).

Greenwich—With several sightseeing treats just a quick DLR ride from central London, Greenwich has its share of great markets. They're especially lively on weekends. For details, see page 198.

Famous Auctions

London's famous auctioneers welcome the curious public for viewing and bidding. You can preview estate catalogs or browse auction calendars online. To ask questions or set up an appointment, contact **Sotheby's** (Mon–Fri 9:00–16:30, closed Sat–Sun, café, 34–35 New Bond Street, Tube: Oxford Circus, tel. 020/7293-5000, www .sothebys.com) or **Christie's** (Mon–Fri 9:00–17:00, Sat–Sun usually 12:00–17:00 but weekend hours vary—call ahead, 8 King Street, Tube: Green Park, tel. 020/7839-9060, www.christies.com). See map on page v for locations of both.

Entertainment in London

Theater (a.k.a. "Theatre")

London's theater rivals Broadway's in quality and usually beats it in price. Choose from 200 offerings—Shakespeare, musicals, comedies, thrillers, sex farces, cutting-edge fringe, revivals starring movie celebs, and more. London does it all well. I prefer big, glitzy—even bombastic—musicals over serious chamber dramas, simply because London can deliver the lights, sound, dancers, and multimedia spectacle I rarely get back home. (If you're a regular visitor to Broadway or Las Vegas—where you have access to similar spectacles—you might prefer some of London's more low-key offerings.)

There are also plenty of enticing plays to choose from, ranging from revivals of classics to cutting-edge works by the hottest young playwrights. Many star huge-name celebrities (you'll see the latest offerings advertised all over the Tube and elsewhere). London is a magnet for movie stars who want to stretch their acting chops. For example, since 2003, Kevin Spacey has been the artistic director of the Old Vic theatre. He has directed and appeared in several productions, and has enlisted many big-name film directors and actors for others (www.oldvictheatre.com).

Most theaters, marked on tourist maps, are found in the West End between Piccadilly and Covent Garden. Box offices, hotels, and TIs offer a handy free *London Theatre Guide* and *Entertainment Guide*. From home, it's easy to check www.officiallondontheatre .co.uk for the latest on what's currently playing in London.

Performances are nightly except Sunday, usually with one or two matinees a week (Shakespeare's Globe is the rare theater that does offer performances on Sun, May–Sept). Tickets range from about £15 to £60. Matinees are generally cheaper and rarely sell out.

To book a seat, simply call the theater box office (which may ring through to a central ticketing office), ask about seats and available dates, and buy a ticket with your credit card. You can call from the US as easily as from England. Arrive about 30 minutes before the show starts to pick up your ticket and avoid lines.

For a booking fee, you can reserve online. Most theater websites link you to a preferred ticket vendor, usually www .ticketmaster.co.uk or www.seetickets.com. In the US, Keith Prowse Ticketing is also handy by phone or online (US tel. 212/398-4175, www.keithprowse.com).

Although booking through an agency is quick and easy, prices are inflated by a standard 25 percent fee. Ticket agencies (whether in the US, at London's TIs, or scattered throughout the city) are scalpers with an address. If you're buying from an agency, look at the ticket carefully (your price should be no more than 30 percent over the printed face value; the 20 percent VAT is already included in the face value), and understand where you're sitting according to the floor plan (if your view is restricted, it will state this on the ticket; for floor plans of the various theaters, see www.theatre monkey.com).

Agencies are worthwhile only if a show you've just got to see is sold out at the box office. They scarf up hot tickets, planning to make a killing after the show is sold out. US booking agencies get their tickets from another agency, adding even more to your expense by involving yet another middleman. Many tickets sold on the street are forgeries. Although some theaters use booking agencies to handle their advance sales, you'll stand a good chance of saving money by avoiding the middleman and simply calling the box office directly to purchase your tickets (international phone calls are cheap, and credit cards make booking a snap).

Theater Lingo: stalls (ground floor), dress circle (first balcony), upper circle (second balcony), balcony (sky-high third balcony), slips (cheap seats on the fringes). Many cheap seats have a restricted view (behind a pillar).

London's Major Theaters

LONDON

Oxford Circus

OXFORD

LIBERTY DEP'T. STORE

GREAT MARLBOROUGH

POLAND

BERWICK

S O

MADDOX ST.

NEW

BOND

CONDUIT

ST.

REGENT

ST.

CARNABY ST.

BROADWICK

LEXINGTON

BERWICK

CLIFFORD

SAVILE ROW

BEAK

ST.

JAMES

ST.

BROADWICK

MAYFAIR

ST.

VIGO

SACKVILLE

GOLDEN SQ.

STREET

SHERWOOD

DEN.

BREWER

TISBURY CT.

BURLING-TON ARCADE

SHAFTES

PICCADILLY CIRCUS

Green Park

PICCADILLY   STREET

Piccadilly Circus

EROS STATUE

COVEN

RITZ HOTEL

JERMYN

ST. JAMES

STREET

LWR. REGENT

HAYMARKET

PAN

ORA

FORTNUM + MASON

BRITAIN & LONDON VISITORS CENTRE

PALL MALL

COCK

1 To Apollo Victoria & Victoria Palace

2 Cambridge

3 Dominion

4 Her Majesty's

5 Lyceum

6 Prince Edward

7 Prince of Wales

8 Queen's

9 Wyndham's

LONDON

What's On in the West End

Here are some of the perennial favorites and new hits that you're likely to find among the West End's evening offerings. If spending the time and money for a London play, I like a full-fledged, high-energy musical (which all of these are). Generally you can book tickets for free at the box office or for a £2–3 fee by telephone or online. See the map on page 136 for locations.

Avenue Q—A foul-mouthed but hilarious send-up of *Sesame Street,* this show uses actor/puppeteers to tell the story of recent college graduates making their way in the big city (£10–55, nightly 20:00, matinees Fri 17:00 and Sat 16:30, Wyndham's Theatre, Charing Cross Road, Tube: Leicester Square, toll tel. 0844-482-5141, www.avenueqthemusical.co.uk).

Billy Elliot—This adaptation of the popular British film is part family drama, part story of a boy who just has to dance set to a score by Elton John (£20–65, Mon–Sat 19:30, matinees Thu and Sat 14:30, Victoria Palace Theatre, Victoria Street, Tube: Victoria, toll tel. 0844-811-0055, www.billyelliotthemusical.com).

Chicago—A chorus-girl-gone-bad forms a nightclub act with another murderess to bring in the bucks (£25–59, Mon–Thu 20:00, Fri 17:30 and 20:30, Sat 15:00 and 20:00, Cambridge Theatre, Earlham Street, Tube: Covent Garden, booking toll tel. 0844-412-4652, www.chicagothemusical.com).

Jersey Boys—This fast-moving, easy-to-follow show tracks the rough start and rise to stardom of Frankie Valli and The Four Seasons. It's light, but the music is so catchy that everyone leaves whistling the group's classics (£20–65, Mon–Sat 19:30, matinees Tue and Sat 14:30, Prince Edward Theatre, Old Compton Street, Tube: Leicester Square, toll tel. 0844-482-5138, www.jersey boyslondon.com).

Les Misérables—Claude-Michel Schönberg's musical adaptation of Victor Hugo's epic follows the life of Jean Valjean as he struggles with the social and political realities of 19th-century France. This inspiring mega-hit takes you back to the days of France's struggle for a just and modern society (£15–59, Mon–Sat 19:30, matinees Wed and Sat 14:30, Queen's Theatre, Shaftesbury

Cheap Theater Tricks: Most theaters offer cheap returned tickets, standing-room, matinee, and senior or student standby deals. These "concessions" (discounted tickets) are indicated with a "conc" or "s" in the listings. Picking up a late return can get you a great seat at a cheap-seat price. Even if a show is "sold out," there's usually a way to get a seat. Call the theater box office and ask how.

If you don't care where you sit, you can often buy the absolutely cheapest seats—those with an obstructed view or in the nosebleed section—at the box office; these tickets generally cost less than £20. Many theaters are so small that there's hardly a bad

Avenue, Tube: Piccadilly Circus, box office toll tel. 0844-482-5138, www.lesmis.com).

The Lion King—In this Disney extravaganza, Simba the lion learns about the delicately balanced circle of life on the savanna (£20-62.50, Tue–Sat 19:30, matinees Wed and Sat 14:00, Sun 15:00, Lyceum Theatre, Wellington Street, Tube: Charing Cross or Covent Garden, booking toll tel. 0844-844-0005, theater info tel. 020/7420-8100, www.thelionking.co.uk).

Mamma Mia!—This energetic, spandex-and-platform-boots musical weaves together a slew of ABBA hits to tell the story of a bride in search of her real dad as her promiscuous mom plans her Greek Isle wedding. The production has the audience dancing by the time it reaches its happy ending (£20-85, Mon–Thu and Sat 19:30, Fri 20:30, matinees Fri 17:00 and Sat 15:00, Prince of Wales Theatre, Coventry Street, Tube: Piccadilly Circus, box office toll tel. 0844-482-5115, www.mamma-mia.com).

Phantom of the Opera—A mysterious masked man falls in love with a singer in this haunting Andrew Lloyd Webber musical about life beneath the stage of the Paris Opera (£20-59, Mon–Sat 19:30, matinees Tue and Sat 14:30, Her Majesty's Theatre, Haymarket, Tube: Piccadilly Circus or Leicester Square, US toll-free tel. 800-334-8457, London booking toll tel. 0844-412-2707, www.thephantomoftheopera.com).

We Will Rock You—Whether or not you're a Queen fan, this musical tribute (more to the band than to Freddie Mercury) is an understandably popular celebration of their work (£28-60, Mon–Sat 19:30, matinee Sat 14:30, Dominion Theatre, Tottenham Court Road, Tube: Tottenham Court Road, Ticketmaster toll tel. 0844-847-1775, www.queenonline.com/wewillrockyou).

Wicked—This lively prequel to *The Wizard of Oz* examines how the Witch of the West met Glinda the Good Witch, and later became so, you know...(£15-62.50, Mon–Sat 19:30, matinee Wed and Sat 14:30, Apollo Victoria Theatre, just east of Victoria Station, Tube: Victoria, Ticketmaster toll tel. 0844-826-8000, www.wickedthemusical.co.uk).

seat. After the lights go down, scooting up is less than a capital offense. Shakespeare did it.

Half-Price "tkts" Booth: This famous ticket booth at Leicester Square sells discounted tickets for top-price seats to shows on the push list—but only on the day of the performance (generally £3 service charge per ticket, Mon–Sat 10:00–19:00, Sun 11:00–16:00, lines often form early, list of shows available online at www.tkts.co.uk). Most tickets are half-price; other shows are discounted 25 percent. Note that the real half-price booth (with its "tkts" name) is a freestanding kiosk at the edge of the garden in

Leicester Square. Several dishonest outfits nearby advertise "official half-price tickets"—avoid these.

Here are sample prices: A top-notch seat to *Chicago* costs £59 if you buy directly from the theater; the same seat costs £32.50 at Leicester Square. The cheapest balcony seat is £25 through the theater. Half-price tickets can be a good deal, unless you want the cheapest seats or the hottest shows. But check the board; occasionally they sell cheap tickets to good shows.

West End Theaters: The commercial (nonsubsidized) theaters cluster around Soho (especially along Shaftesbury Avenue) and Covent Garden. With a centuries-old tradition of pleasing the masses, these present London theater at its glitziest. See the "What's On in the West End" sidebar.

Royal Shakespeare Company: If you'll ever enjoy Shakespeare, it'll be in Britain. The RSC performs at various theaters around London and in Stratford-upon-Avon year-round. To get a schedule, contact the RSC (Royal Shakespeare Theatre, Stratford-upon-Avon, toll tel. 0844-800-1110, www.rsc.org.uk).

Shakespeare's Globe: To see Shakespeare in a replica of the theater for which he wrote his plays, attend a play at the Globe. In this round, thatch-roofed, open-air theater the plays are performed much as Shakespeare intended—under the sky with no amplification.

The play's the thing from late April through early October (usually Mon 19:30, Tue–Sat 14:00 and 19:30, Sun either 13:00 and/or 18:30, tickets can be sold out months in advance). You'll pay £5 to stand and £15–35 to sit, usually on a backless bench. Because only a few rows and the pricier Gentlemen's Rooms have seats with backs, £1 cushions and £3 add-on back rests are considered a good investment by many. Dress for the weather. The £5 "groundling" tickets—which are open to rain—are most fun. Scurry in early to stake out a spot on the stage's edge, where the most interaction with the actors occurs. You're a crude peasant. You can lean your elbows on the stage, munch a picnic dinner (yes, you can bring in food), or walk around. I've never enjoyed Shakespeare as much as here, performed as it was meant to be in the "wooden O." If you can't get a ticket, consider waiting around. Plays can be long, and many groundlings leave before the end. Hang around outside and beg or buy a ticket from someone leaving early (groundlings are allowed to come and go). A few non-Shakespeare plays are also presented each year.

To reserve tickets for plays, call or drop by the theater box office (Mon–Sat 10:00–18:00, Sun 10:00–17:00, open one hour later on performance days, New Globe Walk entrance, no extra charge to book by phone, tel. 020/7401-9919). You can also reserve online (www.shakespeares-globe.org, £2 booking fee). If the tickets are sold out, don't despair; a few often free up at the last minute. Try calling around noon the day of the performance to see if the box office expects any returned tickets. If so, they'll advise you to show up a little more than an hour before the show, when these tickets are sold (first-come, first-served).

The theater is on the South Bank, directly across the Thames over the Millennium Bridge from St. Paul's Cathedral (Tube: Mansion House or London Bridge). The Globe is inconvenient for public transport, but the courtesy phone in the lobby lets you get a minicab in minutes. (These minicabs have set fees—e.g., £8 to South Kensington—but generally cost less than a metered cab and provide fine and honest service.) During theater season, there's a regular supply of black cabs outside the main foyer on New Globe Walk.

Outdoor Theater in Summer: Enjoy Shakespearean drama and other plays under the stars at the Open Air Theatre, in leafy Regent's Park in north London. Food is allowed: You can bring your own picnic; order à la carte from the theater menu; or pre-order a £22.50 picnic supper from the theater at least 36 hours in advance (tickets £12–50; season runs late May–mid-Sept, box office open April–late May Mon–Sat 10:00–18:00, closed Sun; late May–mid-Sept Mon–Sat 10:00–20:00, Sun 10:00–until start of play on performance days only; order tickets online after mid-Jan or by phone Mon–Sun 9:00–21:00; £1 booking fee by phone, no fee if ordering online or in person; toll tel. 0844-826-4242, www.openairtheatre.org; grounds open 1.5 hours prior to evening performances, one hour prior to 14:30 matinee, and 30 minutes prior to earlier matinees; 10-minute walk north of Baker Street Tube, near Queen Mary's Gardens within Regent's Park; detailed directions and more info at www.openairtheatre.org).

Fringe Theater: London's rougher evening-entertainment scene is thriving, filling pages in *Time Out*. Choose from a wide range of fringe theater and comedy acts (generally £5).

Classical Music

Concerts at Churches—For easy, cheap, or free concerts in historic churches, ask the TI (or check *Time Out*) about **lunch concerts,** especially:

- St. Bride's Church, with free lunch concerts twice a week at 13:15 (generally Tue, Wed, or Fri—confirm by phone or online, church tel. 020/7427-0133, www.stbrides.com).
- St. James's at Piccadilly, with 50-minute concerts on Monday, Wednesday, and Friday at 13:10 (suggested £3.50 donation, info tel. 020/7381-0441, www.st-james-piccadilly.org).
- St. Martin-in-the-Fields, offering free concerts on Monday, Tuesday, and Friday at 13:00 (suggested £3.50 donation,

church tel. 020/7766-1100, www.smitf.org).

St. Martin-in-the-Fields also hosts fine **evening concerts** by candlelight (£6–26, several nights a week at 19:30,) and live jazz in its underground Café in the Crypt (£5.50–9 tickets, Wed at 20:00).

Evensong and Organ Recitals at Churches—Evensong services are held at several churches, including:

- St. Paul's Cathedral (Mon–Sat at 17:00, Sun at 15:15).
- Westminster Abbey (Mon–Tue and Thu–Fri at 17:00, Sat–Sun at 15:00; there's a service on Wed, but it may be spoken, not sung).
- Southwark Cathedral (Mon–Tue and Thu–Fri at 17:30, Sat at 16:00, Sun at 15:00, no service on Wed or alternate Mon, tel. 020/7367-6700, www.southwark.anglican.org/cathedral).
- St. Bride's Church (Sun at 17:30, tel. 020/7427-0133, www .stbrides.com).

Free **organ recitals** are often held on Sunday at 17:45 in Westminster Abbey (30 minutes, tel. 020/7222-5152). Many other churches have free concerts; ask for the *London Organ Concerts Guide* at the TI.

Prom Concerts, Opera, and Dance—For a fun classical event (mid-July–mid-Sept), attend a **Prom Concert** (shortened from "Promenade Concert") during the annual festival at the Royal Albert Hall. Nightly concerts are offered at give-a-peasant-some-culture prices to "Promenaders"—those willing to stand throughout the performance (£5 standing-room spots sold at the door, £7 restricted-view seats, most £20–54 but depends on performance, Tube: South Kensington, toll tel. 0845-401-5045, www.bbc.co.uk /proms).

Some of the world's best **opera** is belted out at the prestigious Royal Opera House, near Covent Garden (box office tel. 020/7304-4000, www.roh.org.uk), and at the London Coliseum (English National Opera, St. Martin's Lane, Tube: Leicester Square, box office toll tel. 0871-911-0200, www.eno.org).

For **dance,** try Sadler's Wells Theatre (Rosebery Avenue, Islington, Tube: Angel, info tel. 020/7863-8198, box office toll tel. 0844-412-4300, www.sadlerswells.com).

Other Nightlife

Evening Museum Visits—Many museums are open an evening or two during the week, offering fewer crowds. See a list on page 90.

Tours—Guided walks are offered several times a day. **London Walks** is the most established company. Daytime walks vary by theme: ancient London, museums, legal London, Dickens, Beatles, Jewish quarter, Christopher Wren, and so on. In the evening, expect a more limited choice: ghosts, Jack the Ripper, pubs, or literary-themed. Get the latest from their brochure or website, or call for a recorded listing of that day's walks. Show up at the listed time and place, pay the guide, and enjoy the two-hour tour (£8, cash only, tel. 020/7624-3978, recorded info tel. 020/7624-9255, www.walks.com).

To see the city illuminated at night, consider a bus tour. A two-hour **London by Night Sightseeing Tour** leaves every evening from Victoria Station and other points (see page 66).

Summer Evenings Along the South Bank—If you're visiting London in summer, consider the South Bank.

Take a trip around the **London Eye** while the sun sets over the city (the wheel spins until late—last ascent at 21:30 July–Aug, 21:00 in June and Sept). Then cap your night with an evening walk along the pedestrian-only **Jubilee Walkway,** which runs east-west along the river. It's where Londoners go to escape the heat. This pleasant stretch of the walkway—lined with pubs and casual eateries—goes from the London Eye past Shakespeare's Globe to Tower Bridge (you can walk in either direction).

If you're in the mood for a movie, take in a flick at the **BFI Southbank,** located just across the river, alongside Waterloo Bridge. Run by the British Film Institute, the state-of-the-art theater shows mostly classic films, as well as art cinema (£9, £5 on Tue and weekday matinees, Tube: Waterloo or Embankment, box office tel. 020/7928-3232, check www.bfi.org.uk for schedules).

Farther east along the South Bank is **The Scoop**—an outdoor amphitheater next to City Hall. It's a good spot for outdoor movies, concerts, dance, and theater productions throughout the summer—with Tower Bridge as a scenic backdrop. These events are free, nearly nightly, and family-friendly. For the latest event schedule, see www.morelondon.com and click on "The Scoop" (next to City Hall, Riverside, The Queen's Walkway, Tube: London Bridge).

Cruises—During the summer, boats sail as late as 19:00 between Westminster Pier (near Big Ben) and the Tower of London. (For details, see page 72.)

A handful of outfits run Thames River evening cruises with four-course meals and dancing. **London Showboat** offers the best value (£75, April–Oct Wed–Sun, March and Nov–Dec Thu–Sat, Jan–Feb Fri–Sat, 3.5 hours, departs at 19:30 from Westminster Pier and returns by 23:00, reservations necessary, tel. 020/7740-0400, www.citycruises.com). Dinner cruises are also offered by **Bateaux London** (£75–125, tel. 020/7695-1800, www.bateauxlondon.com). For more on cruising, get the *River Thames Boat Services* brochure from a London TI.

Sleeping in London

London is an expensive city for rooms. Cheaper rooms are relatively dumpy. Don't expect £130 cheeriness in an £80 room. For £70, you'll get a double with breakfast in a safe, cramped, and dreary place with minimal service and the bathroom down the hall. For £90, you'll get a basic, clean, reasonably cheery double in a usually cramped, cracked-plaster building with a private bath, or a soulless but comfortable room without breakfast in a huge Motel 6–type place. My London splurges, at £160–260, are spacious, thoughtfully appointed places good for entertaining or romancing. Off-season, it's possible to save money by arriving late without a reservation and looking around. Competition softens prices, especially for multinight stays. Check hotel websites for special deals. Remember, all of Britain's accommodations are now non-smoking.

Looking for Hotel Deals Online

Given London's high hotel prices, consider using the Internet to help score a hotel deal. Various websites list rooms in high-rise, three- and four-star business hotels. You'll give up the charm and warmth of a family-run establishment, and breakfast will probably not be included, but you might find that the price is right.

Start by checking the websites of several chains to get an idea of typical rates and to check for online-only deals. Big London hotel chains include the following: Millennium/Copthorne (www.millenniumhotels.com), Thistle (www.thistle.com), Intercontinental/Holiday Inn (www.ichotelsgroup.com), Radisson

---

Sleep Code

(£1 = about $1.60, country code: 44, area code: 020)
S = Single, **D** = Double/Twin, **T** = Triple, **Q** = Quad, **b** = bathroom, **s** = shower only. Unless otherwise noted, credit cards are accepted and prices include breakfast.

To help you sort through these listings easily, I've divided the rooms into three categories, based on the price for a double room with bath:

$$$ Higher Priced—Most rooms £115 or more.
$$ Moderately Priced—Most rooms between £70-115.
$ Lower Priced—Most rooms £70 or less.

Prices can change without notice; verify the hotel's current rates online or by email. For other updates, see www.ricksteves.com/update.

London's Hotel Neighborhoods

THE TUBE'S CIRCLE LINE

REGENT'S PARK

NORTH LONDON

BRITISH MUSEUM

EAST END

NOTTING HILL

PADDINGTON

BLOOMSBURY

To DOCKLANDS

HYDE PARK

SOHO

WEST END

MAYFAIR

TRAF. SQ.

CENTRAL LONDON

ST. PAULS

THE CITY

TOWER OF LONDON

WEST LONDON

BELGRAVIA

VICTORIA STATION

WEST-MINSTER

SOUTH KENSINGTON

RIVER

BIG BEN

SOUTH BANK

CHELSEA

LONDON EYE

N

THAMES

DCH

HOTEL NEIGHBORHOODS

(www.radisson.com), Hilton (www.hilton.com), and Red Carnation (www.redcarnationhotels.com). For information on no-frills, Motel 6–type chains, see "Big, Good-Value, Modern Hotels," later.

Auction-type sites (such as www.priceline.com or www.hotwire.com) can be great for matching flexible travelers with empty hotel rooms, often at prices well below the hotel's normal rates.

Other favorite accommodation discount sites mentioned by my readers include www.londontown.com (an informative site with a discount booking service), http://athomeinlondon.co.uk and www.londonbb.com (both list central B&Bs), www.lastminute.com, www.visitlondon.com, http://roomsnet.com, and www.eurocheapo.com. Read candid reviews of London hotels at www.tripadvisor.com. And check the "Graffiti Wall" at www.ricksteves.com for the latest tips and discoveries.

For a good overview on finding London hotel deals, go to www.smartertravel.com and click on "Travel Guides," then "London."

Victoria Station Neighborhood (Belgravia)

The streets behind Victoria Station teem with little, moderately-priced-for-London B&Bs. It's a safe, surprisingly tidy, and decent area without a hint of the trashy, touristy glitz of the streets in front of the station. I've divided these accommodations into two broad categories: west or east of the station. Decent eateries abound in both areas (see page 173). All the recommended hotels are within a five-minute walk of the Victoria Tube, bus, and train stations. On hot summer nights, request a quiet back room.

Victoria Station Neighborhood

LONDON

❶ Lime Tree Hotel

❷ B+B Belgravia

❸ Cartref House &
   Lynton Hotel B&Bs

❹ Morgan House

❺ Luna Simone Hotel

❻ New England Hotel

❼ Best Western
   Victoria Palace

❽ Cherry Court Hotel

❾ Jubilee Hotel

❿ Bakers Hotel

⓫ easyHotel Victoria

⓬ To Vandon House Hotel

⓭ Ebury Wine Bar

⓮ Jenny Lo's Tea House

⓯ La Bottega Deli

⓰ To The Duke of
   Wellington Pub

⓱ The Thomas Cubitt Pub

⓲ Grumbles Restaurant

⓳ Seafresh Fish Restaurant

⓴ The Jugged Hare Pub

㉑ St. George's Tavern

㉒ Grocery Stores (4)

㉓ Launderettes (2)

㉔ Bus Tours – Day (2)

㉕ Bus Tours – Night

㉖ Tube, Taxis, City Buses

㉗ Green Line Coach Terminal

㉘ Buses to Luton &
   Stansted Airports

㉙ Apollo Victoria Theatre

㉚ Victoria Palace Theatre

100 YARDS
100 METERS

COACH
(BUS)
STN.

FOUNTAIN
SQUARE

🅿 PARKING

⊖ TUBE STATION

LONDON

Near the hotels on the west side is the 400-space Semley Place NCP **parking garage** (£32/day, possible discounts with hotel voucher, just west of the Victoria Coach Station at Buckingham Palace Road and Semley Place, toll tel. 0845-050-7080, www.ncp .co.uk). The best laundry options are on the east side: The handy **Pimlico Launderette** is about five blocks southwest of Warwick Square (daily 8:00–19:00, self- or full service, south of Sutherland Street at 3 Westmoreland Terrace, tel. 020/7821-8692), and **Launderette Centre** is a block northeast of Warwick Square (Mon–Fri 8:00–22:00, Sat 8:00–20:00, Sun 9:00–20:00, last wash 2 hours before closing, about £7 wash and dry, £9 full-service, 31 Churton Street, tel. 020/7828-6039).

West of Victoria Station

Here in Belgravia, the prices are a bit higher and your neighbors include Andrew Lloyd Webber and Margaret Thatcher (her policeman stands outside 73 Chester Square). All of these places line up along tranquil Ebury Street, two blocks over from Victoria Station.

$$$ Lime Tree Hotel, enthusiastically run by Charlotte and Matt, comes with 25 spacious, stylish, comfortable, thoughtfully decorated rooms and a fun-loving breakfast room (Sb-£85–95, Db-£120–140, larger superior Db-£140–160, Tb-£150–185, family room-£170–200, free Internet access and Wi-Fi, small lounge opens onto quiet garden, 135 Ebury Street, tel. 020/7730-8191, www.limetreehotel.co.uk, info@limetreehotel.co.uk, trusty Alan covers the night shift).

$$$ B+B Belgravia has done its best to make a tight-and-tangled old guesthouse sleek and mod. While the 17 rooms are small, the young, can-do staff takes good care of guests, the coffee is always on in the lobby, and the location is unbeatable (Sb-£99, Db-£125, Db twin-£135, Tb-£155, Qb-£165, free Internet access and Wi-Fi, DVD library, loaner bikes, 64–66 Ebury Street—enter at #66, tel. 020/7259-8570, www.bb-belgravia.com, info@bb -belgravia.com). A few doors down, at #82, they rent eight larger "apartments" with basic kitchenettes and a do-it-yourself continental breakfast in the fridge (Db-£120–160 depending on size, reception at main building).

$$ Cartref House B&B offers rare charm on Ebury Street, with 10 delightful rooms and a warm welcome (Sb-£73, Db-£102, Tb-£133, Qb-£164, fans, free Wi-Fi, 129 Ebury Street, tel. 020/7730-6176, www.cartrefhouse.co.uk, info@cartrefhouse.co.uk, Sharon and Derek).

$$ Morgan House rents 11 good rooms and is entertainingly run, with lots of travel tips and friendly chat from owner Rachel Joplin and her staff, Danilo and Fernanda (S-£58, D-£78, Db-£98, T-£98, family suites-£138–148 for 3–4 people, Wi-Fi, 120 Ebury Street, tel. 020/7730-2384, www.morganhouse.co.uk, morgan house@btclick.com).

$$ Lynton Hotel B&B is a well-worn place renting 13 inexpensive rooms with small prefab WCs. It's a fine value run by brothers Mark and Simon Connor (D-£80, Db-£95, these prices promised with this book in 2011, free Wi-Fi, 113 Ebury Street, tel. 020/7730-4032, www.lyntonhotel.co.uk, mark-and-simon @lyntonhotel.co.uk).

East of Victoria Station

This area is a bit less genteel-feeling than the neighborhood west of the station, but still plenty inviting. Most of these are on or near Warwick Way, the main drag through this area.

$$ Luna Simone Hotel rents 36 fresh, spacious, well-maintained rooms with modern bathrooms. It's a smartly managed place, run for more than 40 years by twins Peter and Bernard and son Mark, and they still seem to enjoy their work (Sb-£70, Db-£100, Tb-£120, Qb-£150, these prices with cash and this book in 2011, free Internet access and Wi-Fi, near the corner of Charlwood Street and Belgrave Road at 47 Belgrave Road, handy bus #24 to Victoria Station and Trafalgar Square stops out front, tel. 020/7834-5897, www.lunasimonehotel.com, stay@lunasimone hotel.com).

$$ New England Hotel, run by Jay and the Patel family, has slightly worn but well-priced rooms in a tight old corner building (small Sb-£59, Db-£89, Tb-£109, Qb-£119, pay Internet access and Wi-Fi, 20 Saint George's Drive, tel. 020/7834-1595, fax 020/7834-9000, www.newenglandhotel.com, stay@newenglandhotel.com).

$$ Best Western Victoria Palace offers modern business-class comfort compared to the other creaky old hotels listed here. Choose between the 43 rooms in the main building (Db-£120, includes breakfast, elevator, 60–64 Warwick Way), or 22 rooms in the annex a half-block away (Db-£89, breakfast-£8.50, no elevator, 17 Belgrave Road, reception at main building); both have been recently renovated (air-con, free Wi-Fi, tel. 020/7821-7113, fax 020/7630-0806, www.bestwesternvictoriapalace.co.uk, info @bestwesternvictoriapalace.co.uk).

$ Cherry Court Hotel, run by the friendly and industrious Patel family, rents 12 very small but bright and well-designed rooms in a central location (Sb-£50, Db-£55, Tb-£80, Qb-£95, Quint/b-£110, these prices are promised with this book through 2011, 5 percent fee to pay with credit card, fruit-basket breakfast in room, air-con, free Internet access and Wi-Fi, laundry, peaceful garden patio, 23 Hugh Street, tel. 020/7828-2840, fax 020/7828-0393, www.cherrycourthotel.co.uk, info@cherrycourthotel.co.uk).

$ Jubilee Hotel is a well-run slumbermill with 24 tiny rooms and many tiny beds. It's a bit musty and its windows only open a few inches, but the price is right (S-£39–45, Sb-£59–65, tiny D-£55–59, Db-£69–79, Tb-£79–95, Qb-£99–109, higher prices are for Fri–Sun, ask for the 5 percent Rick Steves discount when booking, pay Internet access and Wi-Fi, 31 Eccleston Square, tel. 020/7834-0845, www.jubileehotel.co.uk, stay@jubileehotel.co.uk, Bob Patel).

$ Bakers Hotel is a well-worn cheapie, with 11 tight rooms, but it's conveniently located and offers near-youth-hostel prices and a small breakfast (S-£40, D-£55, Db-£65, T-£65, Tb-£75, family room-£85, less for longer stays and on weeknights, pay Wi-Fi, 126 Warwick Way, tel. 020/7834-0729, www.bakershotel.co.uk, reservations@bakershotel.co.uk, Amin Jamani).

$ easyHotel Victoria, at 36 Belgrave Road, is part of the budget chain described on page 160.

"South Kensington," She Said, Loosening His Cummerbund

To stay on a quiet street so classy it doesn't allow hotel signs, surrounded by trendy shops and colorful restaurants, call "South Ken" your London home. Shoppers like being a short walk from Harrods and the designer shops of King's Road and Chelsea. When I splurge, I splurge here. Sumner Place is just off Old Brompton Road, 200 yards from the handy South Kensington Tube station (on Circle Line, two stops from Victoria Station; and on Piccadilly Line, direct from Heathrow). There's a handy **launderette** on the corner of Queensberry Place and Harrington Road (Mon–Fri 7:30–21:00, Sat 9:00–20:00, Sun 10:00–19:00, bring 50p and £1 coins).

$$$ Number Sixteen, for well-heeled travelers, packs over-the-top formality and class into its 42 rooms, plush lounges, and tranquil garden. It's in a labyrinthine building, with modern decor—perfect for an urban honeymoon (Db-from £200—but soft, ask for discounted "seasonal rates," especially on weekends and in Aug—subject to availability, does not include 20 percent VAT, breakfast buffet in the garden-£17, elevator, 16 Sumner Place, tel. 020/7589-5232, fax 020/7584-8615, US tel. 800-553-6674, www.firmdalehotels.com, sixteen@firmdale.com).

$$$ The Pelham Hotel, a 52-room business-class hotel with a pricey mix of pretense and style, is not quite sure which investment company owns it. It's genteel, with low lighting and a pleasant drawing room among the many perks (Db-£180–260, breakfast extra, does not include 20 percent VAT, lower prices Aug

South Kensington Neighborhood

KENSINGTON GARDENS

HYDE PARK

ALBERT MEMORIAL

HARVEY NICHOLS

SOUTH CARRIAGE DRIVE

KENSINGTON ROAD

KNIGHTSBRIDGE

ROYAL ALBERT HALL

Knightsbridge

PRINCE CONSORT RD.

PRINCE'S GARDENS

HARRODS

SCIENCE & NATURAL HISTORY MUSEUMS

VICTORIA & ALBERT MUSEUM

HANS RD.

BEAUFORT GDNS.

CROMWELL ROAD

THURLOE SQUARE

WALTON STREET

PONT ST.

CADOGAN

HARRINGTON

South Kens.

PELHAM

DRAYCOTT

CADOGAN ST.

Post

SLOANE AVE.

OLD BROMPTON ROAD

FULHAM

SYDNEY

KING'S ROAD

200 YARDS
200 METERS
← TO ⑩

⊕ TUBE STATION
✈ BLDG. ENTRANCES

① Number Sixteen Hotel
② The Pelham Hotel
③ Aster House
④ Brompton Hotel
⑤ La Bouchée Bistro Café & Tesco Express Grocery
⑥ Daquise Restaurant
⑦ Moti Mahal Indian Rest.
⑧ Beirut Express & Bosphorus Kebabs
⑨ Rocca di Papa
⑩ To Anglesea Arms Pub
⑪ The Capital Hotel (Afternoon Tea)
⑫ Launderette

and weekends, Web specials can include free breakfast, air-con, elevator, free Internet access, pay Wi-Fi, gym, 15 Cromwell Place, tel. 020/7589-8288, fax 020/7584-8444, US tel. 1-888-757-5587, www.pelhamhotel.co.uk, reservations@pelhamhotel.co.uk).

$$$ Aster House, run by friendly and accommodating Simon and Leonie Tan, has a cheerful lobby, lounge, and breakfast room. Its rooms are comfy and quiet, with TV, phone, and air-conditioning. Enjoy breakfast or just lounging in the whisper-elegant Orangery, a Victorian greenhouse. Simon and Leonie offer free loaner mobile phones to their guests (Sb-£120, Db-£180, bigger Db-£225, rates do not include 20 percent VAT, 20 percent discount with this book through 2011 if you book three or more nights, 25 percent off for five or more nights, additional 5 percent off with cash, check website for specials, free Wi-Fi, 3 Sumner Place, tel. 020/7581-5888, fax 020/7584-4925, www.asterhouse .com, asterhouse@btinternet.com).

$$ Brompton Hotel is a humble, borderline-dreary place with 17 rooms above a jumble of cafés and clubs. There's a noisy bar and some street noise, so ask for a room in the back if you want quiet. It has old carpets and no public spaces, and they serve breakfast in your room. In spite of all this, it's cheap for London and very well-located (Sb-£85, Db-£90, Tb-£130, "deluxe" rooms are just like the others but with a tub, save a little by booking via their website, includes continental breakfast, Wi-Fi, across from the South Kensington Tube station at 30 Brompton Road, tel. 020/7584-4517, fax 020/7823-9936, www.bromhotel.com, book @bromhotel.com).

Notting Hill and Bayswater Neighborhoods

Residential Notting Hill has quick bus and Tube access to downtown, and, for London, is very "homely" (Brit-speak for cozy). It's also peppered with trendy bars and restaurants, and is home to the famous Portobello Road Market (see page 132).

Popular with young international travelers, Bayswater's Queensway street is a multicultural festival of commerce and eateries. The neighborhood does its dirty clothes at **Galaxy Launderette** (£6 self-service, £8–10 full-service, daily 8:00–20:00, staff on hand with soap and coins, 65 Moscow Road, at corner of St. Petersburgh Place and Moscow Road, tel. 020/7229-7771). For **Internet access,** you'll find several stops along busy Queensway, and a self-serve bank of computer terminals on the food circus level—third floor—of Whiteleys Shopping Centre (daily 8:30–24:00, corner of Queensway and Porchester Gardens).

Near Kensington Gardens Square

Several big, old hotels line the quiet Kensington Gardens Square (not to be confused with the much bigger Kensington Gardens adjacent to Hyde Park), a block west of bustling Queensway, north of Bayswater Tube station. These hotels are quiet for central London, but the area feels a bit sterile, and (aside from Vancouver Studios) the hotels here tend to be quite impersonal.

$$$ Vancouver Studios offers 45 modern rooms with fully equipped kitchenettes (utensils, stove, microwave, and fridge)

Notting Hill & Bayswater Neighborhoods

⊖ TUBE STN.

1/4 MILE

400 METERS

KENSINGTON GARDENS SQUARE

SATURDAY MARKET

PORTOBELLO

KENS. PK. RD.

HEREFORD RD.

PRINCE'S SQ.

DAWSON PL.

PORCHESTER GDNS.

To PADDINGTON STATION

Bayswater

MOSCOW RD.

OSSINGTON ST.

PALACE CT.

PETE PL.

BAYSWATER ROAD

Queensway

Notting Hill Gate

LADBROKE ROAD

HILLSLEIGH RD.

NOTTING HILL GATE

FARM ST.

LUX

CAMPDEN HILL ROAD

KENS. PLACE

CAMPDEN ST.

AUBREY RD.

TO

PALACE GARDEN TERR.

KENSINGTON CHURCH STREET

KENSINGTON PALACE GDNS.

PLAY-GROUND

KENSINGTON GARDENS

BROAD WALK

To MARBLE ARCH

VIC. GATE

PALACE GREEN

KENS-INGTON PALACE

WALK

HOLLAND PARK WALK

HOLLAND PARK

DCH

KENSINGTON HIGH STREET

High Street Kensington

LONDON

1 Phoenix Hotel
2 Vancouver Studios
3 Kensington Gardens Hotel
4 Princes Square Guest Accommodation
5 Westland Hotel
6 London Vicarage Hotel
7 The Gate Hotel
8 To Norwegian YWCA
9 Maggie Jones Restaurant

10 The Churchill Arms Pub & Thai Kitchens
11 The Prince Edward Pub
12 Café Diana
13 Royal China Restaurant
14 Whiteleys Mall (Food Court, Grocery, Internet)
15 Tesco Grocery
16 Spar Market
17 The Orangery (Afternoon Tea)
18 Launderette

rather than breakfast (Sb-£89, Db-£130, Tb-£170, extra bed-£20, can be more at busy times, 10 percent discount for week-long stay or more, pay Internet access, free Wi-Fi, welcoming lounge and wonderful garden, near Kensington Gardens Square at 30 Prince's Square, tel. 020/7243-1270, fax 020/7221-8678, www.vancouver studios.co.uk, info@vancouverstudios.co.uk).

$$ Phoenix Hotel, a Best Western modernization of a 125-room hotel, offers American business-class comforts; spacious, plush public spaces; and big, fresh, modern-feeling rooms. Its prices—which range from fine value to rip-off—are determined by a greedy computer program, with huge variations according to expected demand. Book online to save money (flexible prices, but usually Sb-£65, Db-£90, elevator, free Wi-Fi, 1–8 Kensington Gardens Square, tel. 020/7229-2494, fax 020/7727-1419, US tel. 800-528-1234, www.phoenixhotel.co.uk, info@phoenixhotel .co.uk).

$$ Kensington Gardens Hotel, an annex of Phoenix Hotel down the street (see above), laces 17 pleasant rooms together in a tall, skinny building with lots of stairs and no elevator (Ss-£57, Sb-£64, Db-£86, Tb-£105; book by phone or email for these special Rick Steves prices, rather than through the pricier website; continental breakfast served at Phoenix Hotel, free Wi-Fi, 9 Kensington Gardens Square, tel. 020/7243-7600, fax 020/7792-8612, www.kensingtongardenshotel.co.uk, info@kensington gardenshotel.co.uk, Rowshanak).

$$ Princes Square Guest Accommodation is a big 50-room place that's well-located, practical, and a good value, especially with its online discounts (Sb-£50–60, Db-£60–80, Tb-£80–100, elevator, pay Wi-Fi, 23–25 Princes Square, tel. 020/7229-9876, www.princessquarehotel.co.uk, info@princessquarehotel.co.uk).

Near Kensington Gardens

$$$ Westland Hotel, conveniently located on a busy street a five-minute walk from the Notting Hill neighborhood, feels like a wood-paneled hunting lodge with a fine lounge. The 32 spacious rooms are comfortable, with old-fashioned charm. Their £130 doubles are the best value, but check their website for specials. It's been run by the Isseyegh family for three generations (Sb-£110, deluxe Sb-£124, Db-£130, deluxe Db-£152, cavernous premier Db-£172, sprawling Tb-£165–193, gargantuan Qb-£186–220, Quint/b-£234, 10 percent discount on your first-time stay in 2011 if you book direct and show the current edition of this book on arrival, discount not valid for e-books, elevator, pay Wi-Fi, garage-£12/day, between Notting Hill Gate and Queensway Tube stations at 154 Bayswater Road, tel. 020/7229-9191, fax 020/7727-1054, www.westlandhotel .co.uk, reservations@westlandhotel.co.uk, Shirley and Bertie).

$$$ London Vicarage Hotel is family-run, understandably popular, and elegantly British in a quiet, classy neighborhood. It has 17 rooms furnished with taste and quality, a TV lounge, a grand staircase, and facilities on each floor. Mandy and Monika maintain a homey atmosphere (S-£56, Sb-£95, D-£95, Db-£125, T-£120, Tb-£160, Q-£130, Qb-£176, 20 percent less in winter—check website, free Wi-Fi; 8-minute walk from Notting Hill Gate and High Street Kensington Tube stations, near Kensington Palace at 10 Vicarage Gate; tel. 020/7229-4030, fax 020/7792-5989, www.londonvicaragehotel.com, vicaragehotel@btconnect.com).

$$ The Gate Hotel has seven cramped, tired rooms on a delightful curved street near the start of the Portobello Road Market, in the heart of the characteristic Notting Hill neighborhood. While the lodgings are basic, the location is wonderful (Sb-£60, Db-£85, bigger "luxury" Db-£95, Tb-£115, each room £10 more Fri–Sat, 5 percent more if paying with credit card, continental breakfast in room, no elevator, pay Wi-Fi, 6 Portobello Road, Tube: Noting Hill Gate, tel. 020/7221-0707, fax 020/7221-9128, www.gatehotel.co.uk, bookings@gatehotel.co.uk, Jasmine).

Near Holland Park

$ Norwegian YWCA (Norsk K.F.U.K.)—where English is definitely a second language—is open to any Norwegian woman, and to non-Norwegian women under 30. (Men must be under 30 with a Norwegian passport.) Located on a quiet, stately street, it offers a study, TV room, piano lounge, and an open-face Norwegian ambience (goat cheese on Sundays!). They have mostly quads, so those willing to share with strangers are most likely to get a bed (July–Aug: Ss-£37.50, shared double-£36.50/bed, shared triple-£31.50/bed, shared quad-£28/bed, includes breakfast year-round plus sack lunch and dinner Sept–June, £20 key deposit and £2 membership fee required, pay Wi-Fi, 52 Holland Park, Tube: Holland Park, tel. 020/7727-9346 or 020/7727-9897, www.kfukhjemmet.org.uk, kontor@kfukhjemmet.org.uk). With each visit, I wonder which is easier to get—a sex change or a Norwegian passport?

Paddington Station Neighborhood

The neighborhood near Paddington Station—while a bit less charming than the other areas I've recommended—is pleasant enough, and very convenient to the Heathrow Express airport train. The area is flanked by the Paddington and Lancaster Gate Tube stops. Most of my recommendations circle Norfolk Square, just two blocks in front of Paddington Station, yet still quiet and comfortable. Its main drag, London Street, is lined with handy eateries—pubs, Indian, Italian, Greek, Lebanese, and more—plus convenience stores and an Internet café. To reach this area, exit the station toward Praed Street (with your back to the tracks, it's to the left). Once outside, continue straight across Praed Street and down London Street; Norfolk Square is a block ahead on the left.

On Norfolk Square

These places (and many more on the same street) are essentially interchangeable; all offer small rooms at a reasonable price, in tall buildings with lots of stairs and no elevator. I've chosen the ones that offer the most reasonable prices and the warmest welcome.

$$ St. David's Hotels, run by the hospitable Neokleous family, has 60 tight rooms in several adjacent buildings (S-£60, Sb-£70, D-£70, Db-£90, Tb-£100, free Wi-Fi, 14–20 Norfolk Square, tel. 020/7723-3856, fax 020/7402-9061, www.stdavids hotels.com, info@stdavidshotels.com).

$$ Tudor Court Hotel has 38 rooms run by the Gupta family (S-£39, Sb-£82, Db-£89, Tb-£108, family room-£132, 10–12 Norfolk Square, tel. 020/7723-5157, fax 020/7723-0727, www .tudorcourtpaddington.co.uk, reservations@tudorcourtpaddington .co.uk).

$$ Falcon Hotel has 19 small rooms wrapped around a tight staircase (S-£50, Sb-£55, D-£69, Db-£75, pay Wi-Fi, 11 Norfolk Square, tel. 020/7723-8603, fax 020/7402-7009, www.falcon-hotel .com, info@falcon-hotel.com).

$$ Ashley Hotel, next door, is a classic old place with 54 rooms (S-£35–40, Sb-£50–60, Db-£70–80, pay Wi-Fi, 15–17 Norfolk Square, tel. 020/7723-3375, fax 020/7723-0173, www .ashleyhotellondon.com, info@ashleyhotellondon.com).

$ easyHotel, the budget chain described on page 160, has a branch at 10 Norfolk Place.

Elsewhere near Paddington Station

To reach these hotels, follow the earlier Paddington Station directions, but continue past Norfolk Square to the big intersection with Sussex Gardens; the Royal Park is to the right, and Springfield Hotel is immediately to the left.

$$$ The Royal Park is the neighborhood's classy splurge, with 48 plush rooms, polished service, a genteel lounge (free champagne for guests nightly 19:00–20:00), and all the little extras (standard Db-£139–149, bigger "executive" Db-£169–179, prices vary with demand and do not include 20 percent VAT or breakfast, free Internet access and Wi-Fi, 3 Westbourne Terrace, tel. 020/7479-6600, fax 020/7479-6601, www.theroyalpark.com, info@theroyalpark.com).

$$ Springfield Hotel is efficiently run and old-school simple, with 17 well-worn rooms. It sits on the wide, busy street called Sussex Gardens (request a quieter back room), with several other

North London Accommodations

1. The 22 York Street B&B
2. The Sumner Hotel
3. Methodist Intl. Center
4. Hotel Ibis Euston St. Pancras & Drummond Street Eateries
5. Premier Inn Kings Cross St. Pancras
6. Premier Inn Euston
7. Travelodge London Kings Cross
8. To Jurys Inn Islington
9. London Central Youth Hostel

similar hotels nearby if you're in a pinch (Sb-£60, Db-£80–90, Tb-£100, check online for deals, extra fee for paying with credit card, 154 Sussex Gardens, tel. 020/7723-9898, fax 020/7723-0874, www.springfieldhotellondon.co.uk, info@springfieldhotellondon .co.uk).

Other Neighborhoods

North of Marble Arch: **$$$ The 22 York Street B&B** offers a casual alternative in the city center, renting 10 traditional, hardwood, comfortable rooms (Sb-£89, Db-£120, free Internet access and Wi-Fi, inviting lounge; from Baker Street Tube station, walk 2 blocks down Baker Street and take a right to 22 York Street—since there's no sign, just look for #22; tel. 020/7224-2990, www.22yorkstreet.co.uk, mc@22yorkstreet.co.uk, energetically run by Liz and Michael Callis).

$$$ The Sumner Hotel, renting 19 rooms in a 19th-century Georgian townhouse, is located a few blocks north of Hyde Park and Oxford Street, a busy shopping destination. Decorated with fancy modern Italian furniture, this swanky place packs in all the extras (Db-£160–190 depending on size, 20 percent discount with this book in 2011, extra bed-£30, air-con, elevator, free Wi-Fi, 54 Upper Berkeley Street just off Edgware Road, Tube: Marble Arch, tel. 020/7723-2244, fax 0870-705-8767, www.thesumner.com, hotel@thesumner.com, manager Peter).

Near Buckingham Palace: **$$ Vandon House Hotel,** run by Central College in Iowa, is packed with students most of the year, but rents its 32 rooms to travelers from late May through August at great prices. The rooms, while institutional, are comfy, and the location is excellent (S-£46, D-£70, Db-£90, Tb-£99, Qb-£119, only twin beds, elevator, pay Internet access and Wi-Fi; 3-minute walk west of St. James's Park Tube station or 7-minute walk from Victoria Station, near west end of Petty France Street on a tiny road, 1 Vandon Street; tel. 020/7799-6780, www.vandonhouse .com, info@vandonhouse.com).

Near Euston Station and the British Library: The **$$$ Methodist International Centre (MIC),** a modern, youthful Christian hotel and conference center, fills its lower floors with international students and its top floor with travelers. The 28 rooms are modern and sleek yet comfortable, with fine bathrooms, phones, and desks. The atmosphere is friendly, safe, clean, and controlled; it also has a spacious lounge and game room (Sb-£117 on Fri–Sun, £137 on Mon–Thu; Db-£130 on Fri–Sun, £149 on Mon–Thu; pricier "deluxe" rooms also available, buying a £100 annual membership saves you £30–40 per night—do the math to see if it's worth paying for, check website for specials, elevator, pay Wi-Fi, on a quiet street a block west of Euston Station, 81–103 Euston Street—not Euston Road, Tube: Euston, tel. 020/7380-0001, www.micentre.com, reservations@micentre.com). In addition to the rooms in the main building, they have several "annex" rooms—three rooms in one house that share a single bathroom; this could work well for families (S-£85, D-£95). In June through August, when the students are gone, they also rent simpler twin rooms in the main building (S or D-£75, includes one breakfast, extra breakfast-£13).

Big, Good-Value, Modern Hotels

London has an abundance of modern, impersonal, American-style chain hotels. While they lack the friendliness and funkiness of a memorable B&B, the value they provide is undeniable; doubles generaly go for around £90–100 (or less—often possible with promotional rates). For a more complete description of this type of accommodation—including amenities, caveats, and tips for getting the best rates—see page 27 in the Introduction. As these hotels are often located on busy streets in dreary train-station neighborhoods, use common sense after dark and wear your money belt.

Premier Inn

For any of these, call their reservations toll line at 0870-242-8000 or—the best option—book online at www.premierinn.com.

$$ Premier Inn London County Hall, literally down the hall from a $400-a-night Marriott Hotel, fills one end of London's massive former County Hall building. This family-friendly place is wonderfully located near the base of the London Eye and across the Thames from Big Ben. Its 313 efficient rooms come with all the necessary comforts, though it's quite anonymous—rather than a real reception desk, you'll find self-service check-in kiosks with a couple of clerks standing by to help (Db-£109–150 for 2 adults and up to 2 kids under age 16, elevator, pay Wi-Fi, some easy-access rooms, 500 yards from Westminster Tube stop and Waterloo Station, Belvedere Road, central reservations toll tel. 0870-242-8000, reception desk toll tel. 0870-238-3300, easiest to book online at www.premierinn.com).

$$ Premier Inn London Southwark, with 59 rooms, is near Shakespeare's Globe on the South Bank (Db for up to 2 adults and 2 kids-£91–150, elevator, pay Wi-Fi, Bankside, 34 Park Street, Tube: London Bridge, toll tel. 0870-990-6402, www.premierinn.com).

$$ Premier Inn Kings Cross St. Pancras, with 276 rooms, is across the street from the east end of King's Cross Station and near the Eurostar terminus at St. Pancras Station (Db-£96–150, air-con, elevator, pay Wi-Fi, 26–30 York Way, Tube: King's Cross St. Pancras, toll tel. 0870-990-6414, www.premierinn.com).

Other **$$ Premier Inns** charging £90–150 per room include **London Euston** (big, blue Lego-type building packed with vacationing families, on handy but noisy street at corner of Euston Road and Dukes Road, Tube: Euston, toll tel. 0870-238-3301), **London Kensington Earl's Court** (11 Knaresborough Place, Tube: Earl's Court or Gloucester Road, toll tel. 0870-238-3304), **London Victoria** (82–83 Eccleston Square, Tube: Victoria, toll tel. 0870-423-6494), and **London Putney Bridge** (farther out, 3 Putney Bridge Approach, Tube: Putney Bridge, toll tel. 0870-238-3302). Avoid the **Tower Bridge** location, which is an inconvenient 15-minute walk from the nearest Tube stop.

Other Chains

Travelodge: **$$ Travelodge London Kings Cross** is another typical chain hotel with 140 cookie-cutter rooms, just 200 yards south (in front) of King's Cross Station (Db-usually £85, family rooms, can be noisy, elevator, pay Wi-Fi, Grays Inn Road, Tube: King's Cross St. Pancras, tel. 020/7278-5179). Other convenient Travelodge London locations are nearby **Kings Cross Royal Scot, Euston, Marylebone, Covent Garden, Liverpool Street,** and **Farringdon.** For details on all Travelodge hotels, see www .travelodge.co.uk.

Ibis: **$$ Hotel Ibis London Euston St. Pancras** rents 380 rooms on a quiet street a block west of Euston Station (Db-£89–149, usually £129, no family rooms, elevator, pay Internet access and Wi-Fi, 3 Cardington Street, Tube: Euston, tel. 020/7388-7777 or 020/7304-7712, fax 020/7388-0001, www.ibishotel.com, h0921 @accor.com). There's also an **Ibis London City** (5 Commercial Street, Tube: Aldgate East, tel. 020/7422-8400), but the other Ibis locations are far from the center.

Jurys Inn: **$$ Jurys Inn Islington** rents 200-plus compact, comfy rooms near King's Cross Station (Db/Tb-£109–169, some discounted rooms available online, 2 adults and 2 kids under age 12 can share one room, 60 Pentonville Road, Tube: Angel, tel. 020/7282-5500, fax 020/7282-5511, www.jurysinns.com). You'll also find Jurys Inns at **Chelsea** (Imperial Road, Tube: Imperial Wharf, tel. 020/7411-2200) and near **Heathrow Airport** (see "Heathrow and Gatwick Airports," later).

easyHotel

With several hotels in good neighborhoods around London, easyHotel is a radical concept—offering what you need to sleep well and safe, and nothing more. Most of them are fitted into old buildings, so the rooms are all odd shapes, from tiny windowless closets to others that are quite spacious. All rooms are well-ventilated and come with an efficient "bathroom pod" that looks like it was popped out of a plastic mold—just big enough to take care of business. While they do have a 24-hour reception, everything else is spartan: you get two towels, liquid soap, and a clean bed—no breakfast, no fresh towels, and no daily cleaning. The base rate ranges from £21 to £65, depending on the room size and when you book—"The earlier you book, the less you pay." Prices are the same for one person or two, but then you're nickel-and-dimed with optional charges for the TV, Wi-Fi, luggage storage, and so on.

If you go with the basic package, it's like hosteling with privacy—a hard-to-beat value. But you get what you pay for; in my experience, easyHotels are cheap in every sense of the word (no elevator, thin walls, noisy halls filled with loud travelers seeking bargain beds, flimsy construction that often results in broken things in the room). And they're only a good deal if you book far enough ahead to get a good price, and skip the many extras...which can add up fast. Regardless of the location, reserve through their website (www.easyhotel.com).

$ easyHotel Victoria is well-located in an old building near Victoria Station (77 rooms, 36 Belgrave Road—for location, see map on page 146, Tube: Victoria, tel. 020/7834-1379, enquiries @victoria.easyhotel.com). They also have branches at **South Kensington** (34 rooms, 14 Lexham Gardens, Tube: Earl's Court or Gloucester Road, tel. 020/7136-2870, enquiries@southken.easy hotel.com), **Earl's Court** (80 rooms, 44–48 West Cromwell Road, Tube: Earl's Court, tel. 020/7373-4546, enquiries@earlscourt .easyhotel.com), **Paddington** (47 rooms, 10 Norfolk Place, Tube: Paddington, tel. 020/7706-9911, enquiries@paddington.easy hotel.com), and **Heathrow** and **Luton** airports (Heathrow location described on page 162).

Hostels

$ London Central Youth Hostel is the flagship of London's hostels, with 300 beds and all the latest in security and comfortable efficiency. Families and travelers of any age will feel welcome in this wonderful facility. You'll pay the same price for any bed in a 4- to 8-bed single-sex dorm—with or without private bathroom—so try to grab one with a bathroom (£20–30 per bunk bed—fluctuates with demand, £3/night extra for nonmembers, breakfast-£4; includes sheets, towel, and locker; families welcome to book an entire room, free Wi-Fi, members' kitchen, laundry, book long in advance, between Oxford Street and Great Portland Street Tube stations at 104 Bolsover Street, toll tel. 0870-770-6144 or 0845-371-9154, www.yha.org.uk, londoncentral@yha.org.uk).

$ St. Paul's Youth Hostel, near St. Paul's, is clean, modern, friendly, and well-run. Most of the 190 beds are in shared, single-sex 3- to 11-bunk rooms (bed-around £20 depending on demand, twin D-£60, includes locker and sheets but not breakfast, non-members pay £3 extra, cheap meals, open 24 hours, 36 Carter Lane, Tube: St. Paul's, tel. 020/7236-4965 or toll tel. 0845-371-9012, www.yha.org.uk, stpauls@yha.org.uk).

$ A cluster of three **St. Christopher's Inn** hostels, south of the Thames near London Bridge, have cheap dorm beds; one branch is for women only (£22–32, 161–165 Borough High Street, Tube: Borough or London Bridge, reservations tel. 020/8600-7500, www.st-christophers.co.uk).

Dorms

$ The **University of Westminster** opens its dorm rooms to travelers during summer break, from mid-June through late September. Located in several high-rise buildings scattered around central

London, the rooms—some with private bathrooms, others with shared bathrooms nearby—come with access to well-equipped kitchens and big lounges (S-£25–35, Sb-£35–54, D-£40–60, Db-£50–95, apartment Sb-£43–71, apartment Db-£56–82, weekly rates, tel. 020/7911-5181, www.wmin.ac.uk/comserv, unilet vacations@westminster.ac.uk).

$ **University College London** also has rooms for travelers, from mid-June until mid-September (S-£30–32, D-£55–65, breakfast extra, pay Internet access, tel. 020/7278-3895, www.ucl.ac.uk /residences).

$ **Ace Hotel,** a budget hotel within four townhouses set in a residential neighborhood, has contemporary decor (£21–32 per bed in 3- to 8-bed dorms, bunk-bed D-£53–58, bunk-bed Db-£57–68, Db with patio-£105, pay Internet access, lounge and garden, 16–22 Gunterstone Road, Tube: Baron's Court or West Kensington, tel. 020/7602-6600, www.ace-hotel.co.uk, reception@ace-hotel .co.uk).

$ The **London School of Economics** has openings in its dorms from late July through September (S-£33–43, Sb-£59–65, D-£52–60, Db-£76–94, tel. 020/7955-7575, www.lsevacations .co.uk, vacations@lse.ac.uk).

Heathrow and Gatwick Airports
At or near Heathrow Airport

It's so easy to get to Heathrow from central London, I see no reason to sleep there. But if you do, here are some options. The Yotel is actually inside the airport, while the rest are a short bus or taxi ride away. In addition to public buses, the cleverly named £4 "Hotel Hoppa" shuttle bus connects the airport to many nearby hotels (different routes serve the various hotels and terminals).

$$ **Yotel,** at the airport, has small sleep dens that offer a place to catch a quick nap (£37–64/4 hours), or to stay overnight (tiny "standard cabin"—£60/8 hours, "premium cabin"—£82/8 hours; cabins sleep 1–2 people; price is per cabin not person, reserve online for free or by phone for small fee). Prices vary by day, week, and time of year, so check their website. All rooms are only slightly larger than a double bed, and have private bathrooms and free Internet access and Wi-Fi. These windowless rooms have oddly purplish lighting (Heathrow Terminal 4, tel. 020/7100-1100, www.yotel.com, customer@yotel.com).

$ **easyHotel,** your cheapest bet, is in a low-rent residential neighborhood a £5 taxi ride from the airport. Its 53 no-frills, pod-like rooms are on two floors. Before booking at this very basic place, read the explanation on page 160 (Db-£25–45, no breakfast, no elevator, pay Internet access and Wi-Fi, Brick Field Lane; take local bus #140 from airport's Central Bus Station or the "Hotel Hoppa" #H8 from Terminals 1 or 3, or the hotel can arrange a £5 taxi to the airport; tel. 020/8897-9237, www.easyhotel.com, enquiries@heathrow.easyhotel.com).

$$ Hotel Ibis London Heathrow is a chain hotel offering predictable value (Db-£77, Db-£52 on Fri–Sun, check website for specials as low as £45, breakfast-£7, pay Internet access and Wi-Fi; 112–114 Bath Road, take local bus #105, #111, #140, #285, #423, or #555 from airport's Central Bus Station or #555 direct from Terminal 4, or the "Hotel Hoppa" #H6 from Terminals 1 or 3, or #H56 from Terminals 4 or 5; tel. 020/8759-4888, fax 020/8564-7894, www.ibishotel.com, h0794@accor.com).

$$ Jurys Inn, another hotel chain, tempts tired travelers with 300-plus cookie-cutter rooms (Db-£89–105, check website for deals, breakfast extra; on Eastern Perimeter Road, Tube: Hatton Cross plus 5-minute walk; take the Tube one stop from Terminals 1, 2, or 3; or two stops from Terminals 4 or 5; or the "Hotel Hoppa" #H9 from Terminals 1 or 3, or #H53 from Terminals 4 or 5; or buses #285, #482, #490, or #555; tel. 020/8266-4664, fax 020/8266-4665, www.jurysinns.com).

At or near Gatwick Airport

$$ Yotel, with small rooms, has a branch right at the airport (Gatwick South Terminal; see prices and contact info in Heathrow listing, earlier).

$$ Gatwick Airport Central Premier Inn rents cheap rooms 350 yards from the airport (Db-£40–75, breakfast-£8, £2 shuttle bus from airport—must reserve in advance, Longbridge Way, North Terminal, toll tel. 0871-527-8406, frustrating phone tree, www.premierinn.com). Four more Premier Inns are within a five-mile radius from the airport.

$$ Barn Cottage, a converted 16th-century barn flanked by a tennis court and swimming pool, sits in the peaceful countryside, with a good pub just two blocks away. Its two wood-beamed rooms, antique furniture, and large garden makes you forget Gatwick is 10 minutes away (S-£55, D-£75, cash only, Church Road, Leigh, Reigate, Surrey, tel. 01306/611-347, www.a1tourism.com/uk /barncott.html, warmly run by Pat and Mike Comer). Don't confuse this place with others of the same name. A taxi from Gatwick to here runs about £15; the Comers can take you back to the airport or train station for about £10.

$ Gatwick Airport Travelodge has budget rooms about two miles from the airport (Db-£39–57, breakfast extra, pay Wi-Fi, Church Road, Lowfield Heath, Crawley, £3 shuttle bus from airport, toll tel. 0871-984-6031, www.travelodge.co.uk).

Eating in London

In London, the sheer variety of foods—from every corner of its former empire and beyond—is astonishing. You'll be amazed at the number of hopping, happening new restaurants of all kinds.

If you want to dine (as opposed to eat), drop by a London newsstand to get a weekly entertainment guide or an annual restaurant guide (both have extensive restaurant listings). Visit www.london-eating.co.uk or www.squaremeal.co.uk for more options.

The thought of a £50 meal in Britain generally ruins my appetite, so my London dining is limited mostly to easygoing, fun, moderately priced alternatives. I've listed places by neighborhood—handy to your sightseeing or hotel. Considering how expensive London can be, if there's any good place to cut corners to stretch your budget, it's by eating cheaply. Pub grub (at one of London's 7,000 pubs) and ethnic restaurants (especially Indian and Chinese) are good low-cost options. Of course, picnicking is the fastest and cheapest way to go. Good grocery stores and sandwich shops, fine park benches, and polite pigeons abound in Britain's most expensive city.

Remember, London (and all of Britain) is smoke-free. Expect restaurants and pubs that sell food to be non-smoking indoors, with smokers occupying patios and doorways outside.

Central London
Near Trafalgar Square
These places are within about 100 yards of Trafalgar Square.

St. Martin-in-the-Fields Café in the Crypt is just right for a tasty meal on a monk's budget—maybe even on a monk's tomb. You'll dine sitting on somebody's gravestone in an ancient crypt. Their enticing buffet line is kept stocked all day, serving breakfast, lunch, and dinner (£6–10 cafeteria plates, hearty traditional desserts, free jugs of water). They also serve a restful cream tea (£6, daily 14:00–17:00). You'll find it directly under the St. Martin-in-the-Fields Church, facing Trafalgar Square (Mon–Wed 8:00–20:00, Thu–Sat 8:00–21:00, Sun 11:00–18:00, profits go to the church, Tube: Charing Cross, tel. 020/7766-1158 or 020/7766-1100). Wednesday evenings at 20:00 come with a live jazz band (£6-9 tickets). While here, check out the concert schedule for the busy church upstairs (or visit www.smitf.org).

The Chandos Pub's Opera Room floats amazingly apart from the tacky crush of tourism around Trafalgar Square. Look for it opposite the National Portrait Gallery (corner of William IV Street and St. Martin's Lane) and climb the stairs (to the right of the pub entrance) to the Opera Room. This is a fine Trafalgar rendezvous point and wonderfully local pub. They serve traditional, plain-tasting £6–7 pub meals—meat pies and fish-and-chips are their specialty. The ground-floor pub is stuffed with regulars and offers snugs (private booths), the same menu, and more serious beer drinking. Chandos proudly serves the local Samuel Smith beer at £2 a pint (kitchen open daily 11:00–19:00, order and pay at the bar, 29 St. Martin's Lane, Tube: Leicester Square, tel. 020/7836-1401).

Gordon's Wine Bar, with a simple, steep staircase leading into a candlelit 15th-century wine cellar, is filled with dusty old bottles, faded British memorabilia, and nine-to-fivers. At the "English rustic" buffet, choose a hot meal or cold meat dish with a salad, or a hearty (and splittable) plate of cheeses, bread, and pickles (£7.75)—or share four plates for £12. Then step up to the wine bar and consider the many varieties of wine and port available by the glass. This place is passionate about port. The low carbon-crusted vaulting deeper in the back seems to intensify the Hogarth-painting atmosphere. Although it's crowded, you can normally corral two chairs and grab the corner of a table. On hot days, the crowd spills out onto a leafy back patio, where a barbecue cooks for a long line of tables (arrive before 17:00 to get a seat, Mon–Sat 11:00–23:00, Sun 12:00–22:00, 2 blocks from Trafalgar Square, bottom of Villiers Street at #47, Tube: Embankment, tel. 020/7930-1408, www.gordonswinebar.com, manager Gerard Menan).

The Lord Moon of the Mall pub, with real ales on tap and cheap pub grub such as fish-and-chips, is a good place to experience retro English cuisine from the days when it had a horrible reputation. The pub fills a great old former Barclays Bank building a block down Whitehall from Trafalgar Square (daily 9:00–22:00, kid-friendly menu but no kids after 20:00, 16–18 Whitehall, Tube: Charing Cross or Embankment, tel. 020/7839-7701).

Near Piccadilly

Hungry and broke in the theater district? Head for Panton Street (off Haymarket, two blocks southeast of Piccadilly Circus), where several hardworking little places compete, all seeming to offer a three-course meal for about £8.50. Peruse the entire block (vegetarian, Pizza Express, Moroccan, Thai, Chinese, and two famous diners) before making your choice.

Stockpot is a meat, potatoes, gravy, and mushy-peas kind of place, famous and rightly popular for its edible, cheap English meals (Mon–Sat 7:00–23:30, Sun 7:00–22:00, 38–40 Panton Street, cash only). The **West End Kitchen** (across the street at #5, same hours and menu) is a direct competitor that's also well-known and just as good. Vegetarians may prefer the **Woodlands South Indian Vegetarian Restaurant,** which serves an impressive £18 *thali* (37 Panton Street).

Central London Eateries

1. St. Martin-in-the-Fields
Café in the Crypt
2. The Chandos Pub's Opera Room
3. Gordon's Wine Bar
4. The Lord Moon of the Mall Pub
5. Stockpot & Woodlands South
Indian Vegetarian Restaurant
6. West End Kitchen
7. Criterion Restaurant
8. The Wolseley

9. Joe Allen
10. Loch Fyne Fish Restaurant
11. Sofra Turkish Restaurant
12. Sitar Indian Restaurant
13. Belgo Centraal
14. Neal's Yard Eateries
15. Food for Thought Café

TUBE STATION
BLDG. ENTRANCES
VIEW

⑯ Yo! Sushi (3)
⑰ Wagamama Noodle Bar (4)
⑱ Busaba Eathai Thai Rest. &
   Côte Restaurant
⑲ Y Ming Chinese Rest.

⑳ New World Chinese Rest.
㉑ Jen Café
㉒ Andrew Edmunds Rest.
㉓ Mildred's Vegetarian Rest. &
   Fernandez & Wells
㉔ The Princess Louise Pub

The palatial **Criterion** offers grand-piano ambience beneath gilded tiles and chandeliers in a dreamy Byzantine church setting from 1880. It's right on Piccadilly Circus but a world away from the punk junk. It's a deal for the visual experience during lunch and before 19:00—but after 19:00, the menu becomes really expensive...and, at any hour, the service could care less. Anyone can drop in for coffee or a drink (£17–20 fixed-price meals, daily 12:00–14:30 & 17:30–19:00 & 22:00–23:30, 224 Piccadilly, tel. 020/7930-0488).

The Wolseley is the grand 1920s showroom of a long-defunct British car. The last Wolseley drove out with the Great Depression, but today this old-time bistro bustles with formal waiters serving traditional Austrian and French dishes in an elegant black-marble-and-chandeliers setting fit for its location next to the Ritz. Although the food can be unexceptional, prices are reasonable, and the presentation and setting are grand. Reservations are a must (£16.50 plates; cheaper soup, salad, and sandwich menu available; Mon–Fri 7:00–24:00, Sat 8:00–24:00, Sun 8:00–23:00, 160 Piccadilly—for exact location see map on page 166, tel. 020/7499-6996). They're popular for their fancy cream or afternoon tea (for details, see page 179).

Near Covent Garden

Covent Garden bustles with people and touristy eateries. The area feels overrun, but if you must eat around here, there are some good options.

Joe Allen, tucked in a basement a block away, serves modern international and American cuisine with both style and hubbub. Downstairs off a quiet street with candles and white tablecloths, it's comfortably spacious and popular with the theater crowd (meals for about £30, £16 two-course specials and £18 three-course specials 17:00–18:45, open daily 11:30–23:00, piano music after 21:00, 13 Exeter Street, tel. 020/7836-0651).

Loch Fyne Fish Restaurant is part of a Scottish chain that grows its own oysters and mussels. It offers an inviting atmosphere with a fine fishy energy and no pretense (£10–15 entrées, £12.50 two-course early dinner served until 18:30, open daily, a couple of blocks behind Covent Garden at 2 Catherine Street, tel. 020/7240-4999).

Sofra Turkish Restaurant is good for quality Turkish with a touch of class. They have several menus: *meze* (Turkish tapas), vegetarian, and set (£8 before 18:00, £10 after 18:00, open long hours daily, 36 Tavistock Street, tel. 020/7240-3773).

Sitar Indian Restaurant is a well-respected Indian/Bangladeshi place serving dishes from many regions, fine fish, and a tasty £17 vegetarian *thali*. It's small and dressy, with snappy service (£15 entrées, daily 12:00–24:00, next to Somerset House at 149 Strand—see map on page 166, tel. 020/7836-3730).

Belgo Centraal serves hearty Belgian specialties in a vast 400-seat underground lair. It's a mussels, chips, and beer emporium dressed up as a mod-monastic refectory—with noisy acoustics and waiters garbed as Trappist monks. The classy restaurant section is more comfortable and less rowdy, but usually requires reservations. It's often more fun just to grab a spot in the boisterous beer hall, with its tight, communal benches (no reservations accepted). Both sides have the same menu and specials. Belgians claim they eat as well as the French and as heartily as the Germans. Belgo, which offers a stunning array of dark, blond, and fruity Belgian beers, actually makes Belgian things trendy—a formidable feat (£10–14 meals, open daily 12:00–23:00; Mon–Fri £5–6.30 "beat the clock" meal specials 17:00–18:30—the time you order is the price you pay—including main dishes and fries; no meal-splitting after 18:30, and you must buy food with beer; daily £8 lunch special 12:00–17:00; 1 kid eats free for each parent ordering a regular entrée; 1 block north of Covent Garden Tube station at 50 Earlham Street, tel. 020/7813-2233).

Neal's Yard is *the* place for cheap, hip, and healthy eateries near Covent Garden. The neighborhood is a tabouli of fun, hippie-type cafés. One of the best is the venerable and ferociously vegetarian **Food for Thought,** packed with local health nuts (good £5 vegetarian meals, £7.50 dinner plates, Mon–Sat 12:00–20:30, Sun 12:00–17:00, 2 blocks north of Covent Garden Tube station, 31 Neal Street, near Neal's Yard, tel. 020/7836-0239).

Near Soho and Chinatown

London has a trendy scene that most Beefeater-seekers miss entirely. These restaurants are scattered throughout the hipster, gay, and strip-club district, teeming each evening with fun-seekers and theater-goers. Even if you plan to have dinner elsewhere, it's a treat just to wander around this lively area.

Beware of the extremely welcoming women standing outside the strip clubs (especially on Great Windmill Street). Enjoy the sales pitch—but only fools fall for the "£5 drink and show" lure. They don't get back out without emptying their wallet...literally.

Yo! Sushi is a futuristic-Japanese-food-extravaganza experience, complete with thumping rock, Japanese cable TV, and a 195-foot-long conveyor belt. For £1.25, you get unlimited green tea or water. Snag a bar stool and grab dishes as they rattle by (priced by color of dish; check the chart: £1.75–5 per dish, daily 12:00–23:00, 2 blocks south of Oxford Street, where Lexington Street becomes Poland Street, 52 Poland Street, tel. 020/7287-0443). If you like Yo!, there are about 40 other locations around town, including a

Pub Appreciation

The pub is the heart of the people's England, where all manner of folks have, for generations, found their respite from work and a home-away-from-home. England's classic pubs are national treasures, with great cultural value and rich history, not to mention good beer and grub.

The Golden Age for pub-building was in the late Victorian era (c. 1880–1905), when pubs were independently owned and land prices were high enough to make it worthwhile to invest in fixing up pubs. The politics were pro-pub as well: Conservatives, backed by Big Beer, were in, and temperance-minded Liberals were out.

Especially in class-conscious Victorian times, traditional pubs were divided into sections by elaborate screens (now mostly gone), allowing the wealthy to drink in a more refined setting, while commoners congregated on the pub's rougher side. These were really "public houses," featuring nooks (snugs) for groups and clubs to meet, friends and lovers to rendezvous, and families to get out of the house at night. Because many pub-goers were illiterate, pubs were simply named for the picture hung outside (e.g., The Crooked Stick, The Queen's Arms—meaning her coat of arms).

Historic pubs still dot the London cityscape. The only place to see the very oldest-style tavern in the "domestic tradition" is at **Ye Olde Cheshire Cheese,** which was rebuilt in 1667 (after the Great Fire) from a 16th-century tavern (£6–7 pub grub, £9–12 meals in the restaurant, open daily, 145 Fleet Street; Tube: Temple or St. Paul's, Blackfriars station is nearest but is closed until late 2011; tel. 020/7353-6170). Imagine this place in the pre-Victorian era: With no bar, drinkers gathered around the fireplaces, while tap boys shuttled tankards up from the cellar. (This was long before barroom taps were connected to casks in the cellar. Oh, and don't say "keg"—that's a gassy modern thing.)

Late-Victorian pubs, such as the lovingly restored 1897 **Princess Louise** (Mon–Fri 11:30–23:00, Sat 12:00–23:00, Sun 12:00–22:30, 208 High Holborn, Tube: Holborn, tel. 020/7405-8816), are more common. These places are fancy, often with heavy embossed wallpaper ceilings, decorative tile work, fine-etched glass, ornate carved stillions (the big central hutch for storing bottles and glass), and even urinals equipped with a place to set your glass.

London's best Art Nouveau pub is **The Black Friar** (c. 1900–1915), with fine carved capitals, lamp holders, and quirky phrases worked into the decor (£7–10 meals, open daily, Tube: Temple or St. Paul's, across from the Blackfriars Tube station—closed until late 2011—at 174 Queen Victoria Street, tel. 020/7236-5474).

Historic Pubs

Historic Pubs

1. Ye Olde Cheshire Cheese
2. The Black Friar
3. The Old Bank of England
4. The Counting House

Other Eatery

5. De Gustibus Sandwiches

The "former-bank pubs" represent a more modern trend in pub building. As banks increasingly go electronic, they're

moving out of lavish, high-rent old buildings. Many of these former banks are being refitted as pubs with elegant bars and free-standing stillions, providing a fine centerpiece. Three such pubs are **The Old Bank of England** (Mon–Fri 11:00–23:00, closed Sat-Sun, 194 Fleet Street, Tube: Temple, tel. 020/7430-2255), **The Jugged Hare** (open daily, 172 Vauxhall Bridge Road—see map on page 146, Tube: Victoria, tel. 020/7828-1543, also see listing on page 175), and **The Counting House** (Mon–Fri 11:00–23:00, closed Sat-Sun, 50 Cornhill, Tube: Bank, tel. 020/7283-7123, also see listing on page 178).

Go pubbing in the evening for a lively time, or drop by during the quiet late morning (from 11:00), when the pub is empty and filled with memories. For a guided tour, check out Bob Steel's London Heritage pub walks (about £50/group for a leisurely half-day private walk, www.aletrails.com, bsteel@blueyonder.co.uk).

The Soho "Food Is Fun" Three-Course Dinner Crawl

For a multicultural, movable feast, consider enjoying a drink and eating (or splitting) one course at each of these places. Start around 17:30 to avoid lines, get in on early-bird specials, and find waiters willing to let you split a meal. Prices, though reasonable by London standards, add up. Servings are large enough to share. All are open nightly. Arrive at 17:30 at **Belgo Centraal** and split the early-bird dinner special: a kilo of mussels, fries, and dark Belgian beer. At **Yo! Sushi,** have beer or sake and a few dishes, then slurp your last course at **Wagamama Noodle Bar.** For dessert, people-watch at Leicester Square.

handy branch a block from the London Eye on Belvedere Road, as well as outlets within Selfridges, Harvey Nichols department stores, Victoria train station, and Whiteleys Mall on Queensway.

Wagamama Noodle Bar is a noisy, pan-Asian, organic slur-pathon. As you enter, check out the kitchen and listen to the roar of the basement, where benches rock with happy eaters. Everybody sucks. Portions are huge and splitting is allowed (£7–10 meals, Mon–Sat 11:30–23:00, Sun 12:00–22:00, crowded after 19:00, 10A Lexington Street, tel. 020/7292-0990 but no reservations taken). If you like this place, handy branches are all over town, including one near the British Museum (4 Streatham Street), Kensington (26 High Street), in Harvey Nichols (109 Knightsbridge), Covent Garden (1 Tavistock Street), Leicester Square (14 Irving Street), Piccadilly Circus (8 Norris Street), Fleet Street (#109), and next to the Tower of London (Tower Place).

Busaba Eathai Thai Restaurant is a hit with locals for its snappy service, casual-yet-high-energy ambience, and good, inexpensive Thai cuisine. You'll sit communally around big, square 16-person hardwood tables or in two-person tables by the window—with everyone in the queue staring at your noodles. They don't take reservations, so arrive by 19:00 or line up (£7–10 meals, Mon–Thu 12:00–23:00, Fri–Sat 12:00–23:30, Sun 12:00–22:00, 106 Wardour Street, tel. 020/7255-8686). They have three other handy locations: on nearby Panton Street, just below Piccadilly Circus; at 22 Store Street, near the British Museum and Goodge Street Tube; and at 8–13 Bird Street, just off Oxford Street and across from the Bond Street Tube.

Côte Restaurant is a contemporary French bistro chain, serving good-value French cuisine with no pretense at the right prices (£9–13 mains, £12 three-course early dinner specials if you order by 19:00, open Mon–Wed 8:00–23:00, Thu–Fri 8:00–24:00, Sat 10:00–24:00, Sun 10:00–22:30, 124–126 Wardour Street, tel. 020/7287-9280).

Y Ming Chinese Restaurant—across Shaftesbury Avenue from the ornate gates, clatter, and dim sum of Chinatown—has dressy European decor, serious but helpful service, and authentic Northern Chinese cooking (good £10 meal deal offered 12:00–18:00, £7–10 plates, open Mon–Sat 12:00–23:45, closed Sun, 35–36 Greek Street, tel. 020/7734-2721).

New World Chinese Restaurant is a sprawling old-fashioned Chinese diner that just feels real. It's a fixture in Chinatown, serving cheap Cantonese food, including dim sum lunch and a similar dinner menu with an array of little £3 dishes (daily 11:00–24:00, 1 Gerrard Place, tel. 020/7734-0677).

Jen Café, across the street, is a humble Chinese corner eatery much loved for its homemade dumplings (£3–5 plates, long hours daily, 4 Newport Place, tel. 020/7287-9708).

On Lexington Street, in the Heart of Soho

Andrew Edmunds Restaurant is a tiny, candlelit place where you'll want to hide your camera and guidebook and not act like a tourist. This little place—with a jealous and loyal clientele—is the closest I've found to Parisian quality in a cozy restaurant in London. The modern European cooking and creative seasonal menu are worth the splurge (£6–8 starters, £11–18 entrées, Mon–Sat 12:30–15:00 & 18:00–22:45, Sun 13:00–15:30 & 18:00–22:30, come early or call ahead, request ground floor rather than basement, 46 Lexington Street, tel. 020/7437-5708).

Mildred's Vegetarian Restaurant, across from Andrew Edmunds, has cheap prices, an enjoyable menu, and a pleasant interior filled with happy eaters (£7–9 meals, Mon–Sat 12:00–23:00, closed Sun, vegan options, 45 Lexington Street, tel. 020/7494-1634).

Fernandez & Wells is a delightfully simple little wine, cheese, and ham bar. Drop in and grab a stool as you belly up to the big wooden bar. Share a plate of top-quality cheeses and/or Spanish or French hams with fine bread and oil, while sipping a nice glass of wine and talking with Dean or his staff (Mon–Sat 11:00–22:00, Sun 12:00–19:00, quality sandwiches at lunch, wine/cheese/ham bar after 16:00, 43 Lexington Street, tel. 020/7734-1546).

West London

Near Victoria Station Accommodations

These restaurants are within a few blocks of Victoria Station—and all are places I've enjoyed eating at. As with the accommodations in this area, I've grouped them by location: east or west of the station (see the map on page 146).

Cheap Eats: For groceries, a handy **M&S Simply Food** is inside Victoria Station (Mon–Sat 7:00–24:00, Sun 8:00–22:00), along with a **Sainsbury's Market** (daily 6:00–23:00, at rear entrance, on Eccleston Street). A second Sainsbury's is just north of the station on Victoria Street, and a larger Sainsbury's is on Wilton Road near Warwick Way, a couple of blocks southeast of the station (Mon–Fri 7:00–23:00, Sat 7:00–22:00, Sun 11:00–17:00). A string of good ethnic restaurants lines Wilton Road (near the recommended Seafresh Fish Restaurant). For affordable if forgettable meals, try the row of cheap little eateries on Elizabeth Street.

West of Victoria Station

Ebury Wine Bar, filled with young professionals, provides a cut-above atmosphere, delicious £13–18 entrées, and a £21 three-course and £16 two-course special anytime (it includes a glass of champagne, but you're welcome to swap it for wine). In the delightful back room, the fancy menu features modern European cuisine with a French accent; at the wine bar, find a cheaper bar menu that's better than your average pub grub. This is emphatically a "traditional wine bar," with no beers on tap (daily 11:00–23:00, reserve after 20:00, at intersection of Ebury and Elizabeth Streets, 139 Ebury Street, tel. 020/7730-5447).

Jenny Lo's Tea House is a simple budget place serving up reliably tasty £7–9 eclectic Chinese-style meals to locals in the know. While the menu is small, everything is high quality. Jenny clearly learned from her father, Ken Lo, one of the most famous Cantonese chefs in Britain, whose fancy place is just around the corner (Mon–Fri 11:30–15:00 & 18:00–22:00, closed Sat–Sun, cash only, 14 Eccleston Street, tel. 020/7259-0399).

La Bottega is an Italian delicatessen that fits its upscale Belgravia neighborhood. It offers tasty, freshly cooked pastas (£6), lasagnas, and salads (lasagna and salad meal-£8), along with great sandwiches (£3) and a good coffee bar with pastries. While not cheap, it's fast (order at the counter), and the ingredients would please an Italian chef. Grab your meal to go, or enjoy the Belgravia good life with locals, either sitting inside or on the sidewalk (Mon–Fri 8:00–19:00, Sat 9:00–18:00, Sun 10:00–17:00, on corner of Ebury and Eccleston Streets, tel. 020/7730-2730).

The Duke of Wellington Pub is a classic neighborhood place with forgettable grub, woodsy sidewalk seating, and an inviting interior (dinner served Mon–Sat 18:00–21:00, 63 Eaton Terrace, tel. 020/7730-1782).

The Thomas Cubitt Pub, packed with young professionals, is a trendy neighborhood gastropub, great for a drink or pricey meal (44 Elizabeth Street, tel. 020/7730-6060).

East of Victoria Station

Grumbles brags it's been serving "good food and wine at nonscary prices since 1964." Offering a delicious mix of "modern eclectic French and traditional English," this unpretentious little place with cozy booths inside (on two levels, including a cellar) and four nice sidewalk tables is *the* spot to eat well in this otherwise workaday neighborhood. Their traditional dishes are their forte (£9–18 plates, £10 early-bird specials 18:00–19:00, open daily 12:00–14:30 & 18:00–23:00, reservations wise, half a block north of Belgrave Road at 35 Churton Street, tel. 020/7834-0149, Alex).

Seafresh Fish Restaurant is the neighborhood place for plaice—and classic and creative fish-and-chips cuisine. You can either take out on the cheap or eat in, enjoying a white fish ambience. Though Mario's father started this place in 1965, it feels like the chippie of the 21st century (meals-£5 to go, £10–14 to sit, Mon–Sat 12:00–15:00 & 17:00–22:30, closed Sun, 80–81 Wilton Road, tel. 020/7828-0747).

The Jugged Hare pub, a 10-minute walk from Victoria Station, sits in a lavish old bank building, with vaults replaced by tankards of beer and a fine kitchen. They have a fun, traditional menu with more fresh veggies than fries, and a plush, vivid pub scene good for a meal or just a drink (£6.25 sandwiches, £8–10 meals, food served daily 12:00–21:30, drinks served daily 11:00–23:00, 172 Vauxhall Bridge Road, tel. 020/7828-1543).

St. George's Tavern is *the* pub for a meal in this neighborhood. They serve dinner from the same fun menu in three zones: on the sidewalk to catch the sun and enjoy some people-watching, in the sloppy pub, and in a classier back dining room. They're proud of their sausages and "toad in the hole." The scene is inviting for just a beer, too (£7–10 meals, Mon–Sat 10:00–22:00, Sun until 21:00, corner of Hugh Street and Belgrave Road, tel. 020/7630-1116).

Near Notting Hill and Bayswater Accommodations

For locations, see the map on page 153.

Maggie Jones, a Charles Dickens-meets-Ella Fitzgerald splurge, is exuberantly rustic and very English, with a 1940s-jazz soundtrack. You'll get solid English cuisine, including huge plates of crunchy vegetables, served by a young and casual staff. It's pricey, but the portions are huge (especially the meat-and-fish pies, their specialty). You're welcome to save lots by splitting your main course. The candlelit upstairs is the most romantic, while the basement is kept lively with the kitchen, tight seating, and lots of action. If you eat well once in London, eat here—and do it quick, before it burns down (lunch—£5 starters, £7 entrées; dinner—£6–9 starters, £13–19 entrées; Mon–Sat 12:30–14:30 & 18:30–23:00, Sun 12:30–16:00 & 18:30–22:30, reservations recommended, 6 Old

Court Place, just east of Kensington Church Street, near High Street Kensington Tube stop, tel. 020/7937-6462).

The Churchill Arms pub and **Thai Kitchens** (same location) are local hangouts, with good beer and a thriving old-English ambience in front, and hearty £6.50 Thai plates in an enclosed patio in the back. You can eat the Thai food in the tropical hideaway (table service) or in the atmospheric pub section (order at the counter and they'll bring it to you). They also serve basic English pub food (£3 sandwiches, £6 meals). The place is festooned with Churchill memorabilia and chamber pots (including one with Hitler's mug on it—hanging from the ceiling farthest from Thai Kitchen—sure to cure the constipation of any Brit during World War II). Arrive by 18:00 or after 21:00 to avoid a line. During busy times, diners are limited to an hour at the table (daily 12:00–22:00, 119 Kensington Church Street, tel. 020/7792-1246).

The Prince Edward serves good grub in a quintessential pub setting (£7–12 meals, Mon–Wed 10:00–23:00, Thu–Sat 10:00–23:30, Sun 10:00–22:30, plush-pubby indoor seating or sidewalk tables, family-friendly, pay Wi-Fi, 2 blocks north of Bayswater Road at the corner of Dawson Place and Hereford Road, 73 Prince's Square, tel. 020/7727-2221).

Café Diana is a healthy little eatery serving sandwiches, salads, and Middle Eastern food. It's decorated—almost shrinelike—with photos of Princess Diana, who used to drop by for pita sandwiches. You can dine in the simple interior, or order some food from the counter to go (£3–4 sandwiches, £6–8 meat dishes, daily 8:00–23:00, 5 Wellington Terrace, on Bayswater Road, opposite Kensington Palace Garden Gates, where Di once lived, tel. 020/7792-9606, Abdul).

On Queensway: The road called Queensway is a multiethnic food circus, lined with lively and inexpensive eateries—browse the options along here and choose your favorite. For a cut above, head for **Royal China Restaurant**—filled with London's Chinese, who consider this one of the city's best eateries. It's dressed up in black, white, and gold, with candles and brisk waiters. While it's pricier than most neighborhood Chinese restaurants, the food is noticeably better (£9–13 dishes, Mon–Thu 12:00–23:00, Fri–Sat 12:00–23:30, Sun 11:00–22:00, dim sum until 17:00, 13 Queensway, tel. 020/7221-2535). For a lowbrow alternative, **Whiteleys Mall Food Court**—at the top end of Queensway—offers a fun selection of ethnic and fast-food chain eateries among Corinthian columns, and a multiscreen theater in a delightful mall (daily 9:00–23:00; options include Yo! Sushi, good salads at Café Rouge, pizza, Starbucks, and a coin-op Internet place; third floor, corner of Porchester Gardens and Queensway).

Supermarkets: **Tesco** is a half-block from the Notting Hill

Gate Tube stop (Mon–Sat 7:00–23:00, Sun 12:00–18:00, near intersection with Pembridge Road, 114–120 Notting Hill Gate). The smaller **Spar Market** is at 18 Queensway (Mon–Sat 7:00–24:00, Sun 9:00–24:00), and **Marks & Spencer** can be found in Whiteleys Mall (Mon–Sat 10:00–20:00, Sun 12:00–18:00).

Near South Kensington Accommodations

Popular eateries line Old Brompton Road and Thurloe Street (Tube: South Kensington), and a good selection of cheap eateries are clumped around the Tube station. For locations, see the map on page 151.

La Bouchée Bistro Café is a classy hole-in-the-wall touch of France. This candlelit and woody bistro, with very tight seating, serves a two-course, £11.50 special on weekdays during lunch and from 17:30–18:30, and £17 *plats du jour* all *jour*. Reservations are smart in the evening (daily 12:00–15:00 & 17:30–23:30, 56 Old Brompton Road, tel. 020/7589-1929).

Daquise, run by a well-established Warsaw restaurateur, is ideal if you're in the mood for kielbasa and kraut (£12 meals, weekday lunch special, daily 12:00–23:00, 20 Thurloe Street, tel. 020/7589-6117).

Moti Mahal Indian Restaurant, with minimalist-yet-classy mod ambience and attentive service, serves mostly Bangladeshi cuisine that's delicious. Consider chicken *jalfrezi* if you like spicy food, and buttery chicken if you don't (£10 dinners, daily 12:00–14:30 & 17:30–23:00, 3 Glendower Place, tel. 020/7584-8428).

Beirut Express has fresh, well-prepared Lebanese cuisine. In the front, you'll find take-away service as well as barstools for quick service (£4 sandwiches). In the back is a sit-down restaurant with £14 plates (daily 12:00–23:00, 65 Old Brompton Road, tel. 020/7591-0123).

Bosphorus Kebabs is the student favorite for a quick, fast, and hearty Turkish dinner. While mostly for take-away, they have a few tight tables indoors and on the sidewalk (£5 meals, Turkish kebabs, daily until 24:00, 59 Old Brompton Road, tel. 020/7584-4048).

Rocca di Papa is a bright and dressy Italian place with a heated terrace (£8 pizza, pasta, and salads; open daily, 73 Old Brompton Road, tel. 020/7225-3413).

The Anglesea Arms, with a great terrace surrounded by classy South Kensington buildings, is a destination pub that feels like the classic neighborhood favorite. It's a thriving and happy place, with a woody ambience and a mellow back dining room a world away from any tourism. Chef Julian Legge freshens up traditional English cuisine and prints up a daily menu listing his creative meals. While it'd be a shame to miss his cooking, this is also a fine place for simply a beer (£6 starters, £13 entrées, meals served daily 12:00–15:00 & 18:00–22:00, a couple of blocks off Old Brompton Road at 15 Selwood Terrace, tel. 020/7373-7960).

Supermarket: **Tesco Express** is handy for picnics (daily 7:00–24:00, 50–52 Old Brompton Road).

Elsewhere in London

Between St. Paul's and the Tower: **The Counting House,** formerly an elegant old bank, offers great £8–10 meals, nice homemade meat pies, fish, and fresh vegetables. The fun "nibbles menu" is available starting in the early evening until 22:00 (or until 21:00 on Mon–Tue; open Mon–Fri 11:00–23:00, closed Sat–Sun, gets really busy with the buttoned-down 9-to-5 crowd after 12:15, near Mansion House in The City, 50 Cornhill—see map on page 171, tel. 020/7283-7123).

Near St. Paul's: **De Gustibus Sandwiches** is where a top-notch artisan bakery meets the public, offering fresh, you-design-it sandwiches, salads, and soups. Just one block below St. Paul's, it has simple seating or take-out picnic sacks for lugging to one of the great nearby parks (Mon–Fri 7:00–17:00, closed Sat–Sun, from church steps follow signs to youth hostel a block downhill—see map on page 171, 53–55 Carter Lane, tel. 020/7236-0056; another outlet is inside the Borough Market in Southwark).

Near the British Library: Drummond Street (running just west of Euston Station) is famous in London for cheap and good Indian vegetarian food (£5–10 dishes). Consider **Chutneys** (124 Drummond, tel. 020/7388-0604) and **Ravi Shankar** (133–135 Drummond, tel. 020/7388-6458) for a good *thali* (both open long hours daily).

Taking Tea in London

Once the sole province of genteel ladies in fancy hats, afternoon tea has become more democratic in the 21st century. While some tearooms—such as the £37-a-head tea service at the Ritz and the finicky Fortnum & Mason—still require a jacket and tie (and a bigger bank account), most happily welcome tourists in jeans and sneakers.

Tea Terms

The cheapest "tea" on the menu is generally a "cream tea"; the most expensive is the "champagne tea." **Cream tea** is simply a pot of tea and a homemade scone or two with jam and thick clotted cream. For maximum pinkie-waving taste per calorie, slice your scone thin like a miniature loaf of bread. **Afternoon tea** generally is a cream tea, plus a tier of three plates holding small finger foods (such as cucumber sandwiches) and an assortment of small pastries. **Champagne tea** includes all of the goodies, plus a glass of champagne. **High tea** generally means a more substantial late-afternoon or early-evening meal, often served with meat or eggs.

Tearooms, which often also serve appealing light meals, are usually open for lunch and close about 17:00, just before dinner. At all the places listed below, it's perfectly acceptable to order one afternoon tea and one cream tea (at about £5) and split the afternoon tea goodies.

Places to Sip Tea

The Wolseley serves a good afternoon tea in between their meal service (£10 cream teas, £20 afternoon tea, served Sun–Fri 15:30–18:30, Sat 15:30–17:30, see full listing on page 168). If you split their afternoon tea, you can actually enjoy two light meals at a great price in classic elegance.

The Orangery at Kensington Palace serves four different varieties of tea meals, from the £15 "Orangery tea" to the £35 "Tregothnan tea" in its bright white hall near Princess Di's former residence. You can also order treats à la carte. The portions aren't huge, but who can argue with eating at a princess' orangery or on its deck? (Tea served 12:00–18:00, no reservations taken; a 10-minute walk through Kensington Gardens from either Queensway or High Street Kensington Tube stations to the orange brick building, about 100 yards from Kensington Palace—see map on page 153; tel. 020/3166-6113, www.hrp.org.uk.)

The National Dining Rooms, a restaurant/café within the National Gallery on Trafalgar Square, is convenient and has a nondescript modern ambience. Although the restaurant can book up in advance, you can generally waltz in for afternoon tea at the café. To play it safe, arrive in the early afternoon to reserve a tea time, then take the self-guided National Gallery Tour (page 85) before or after your appointed time (£4 cakes and tarts, £5.50 cream tea, £16.50 afternoon tea, tea served 15:00–17:30, located in Sainsbury Wing of National Gallery, Tube: Charing Cross or Leicester Square, tel. 020/7747-2525, www.thenationaldiningrooms.co.uk).

The National Café, at the other end of the building (across the street from St. Martin-in-the-Fields), also serves tea in a more appealing, old-fashioned atmosphere—and their afternoon tea is a bit cheaper (£5.50 cream tea, £14.50 afternoon tea, tea served 15:00–17:30).

The Café at Sotheby's, located on the ground floor of the auction giant's headquarters, is manna for shoppers taking a break from fashionable New Bond Street. There are no windows—just a long leather bench, plenty of mirrors, and a dark-wood room where waiters serve sweet treats and the £6.50 mix-and-match

Neal's Yard cheese plate to locals in the know (£3 cakes and creams, £6.50 "small tea," £11 afternoon tea, £18.75 champagne tea, café open Mon–Fri only 9:30–11:30 & 12:00–16:45, afternoon tea served 15:00–16:45, reservations recommended, 34–35 New Bond Street—see map on page v, Tube: Bond Street or Oxford Circus, tel. 020/7293-5077, www.sothebys.com/cafe/restaurant.html).

The Capital Hotel, a luxury hotel a half-block from Harrods, caters to weary shoppers with its intimate five-table, linen-tablecloth tearoom. It's where the ladies-who-lunch meet to decide whether to buy that Versace gown they've had their eye on. Even so, casual clothes, kids, and sharing plates are all OK (£18.50 afternoon tea, daily 14:30–17:30, call to book ahead—especially on weekends, see map on page 151, 22 Basil Street, Tube: Knightsbridge, tel. 020/7589-5171, www.capitalhotel.co.uk).

Fortnum & Mason's St. James's Restaurant, on the fourth floor, offers plush seats under the elegant tearoom's chandeliers. You'll get the standard three-tiered silver tea tray: finger sandwiches on the bottom, fresh scones with jam and clotted cream on the first floor, and decadent pastries and "tartlets" on the top floor, with unlimited tea. Consider it dinner (about £30–38, Mon–Sat 14:00–18:30, Sun 12:00–16:30, dress up a bit for this—no shorts, "children must be behaved," see map on page 151, 181 Piccadilly, reserve in advance online or at toll tel. 0845-602-5694, www.fortnumandmason.com).

Harrods' Georgian Restaurant is where you (along with 200 of your closest friends) can enjoy a fancy tea under a skylight as a pianist tickles the keys of a Bösendorfer, the world's most expensive piano (£24 afternoon tea, includes finger sandwiches and pastries with free refills, tea served Mon–Fri from 15:00, Sat–Sun from 15:45, last order at 17:15, on Brompton Road, Tube: Knightsbridge, reservations tel. 020/7225-6800, www.harrods.com).

Cheaper Options: Taking tea is not just for tourists and the wealthy—it's a true English tradition. If you want the teatime experience but are put off by the price, most department stores on Oxford Street (including those between Oxford Circus and Bond Street Tube stations) offer an afternoon tea (some more affordable than others). For example, **John Lewis** has a mod third-floor brasserie that serves a nice £10 afternoon tea platter from 15:00 (on Oxford Street one block west of the Bond Street Tube station, tel. 020/3073-0626, www.johnlewis.com). Many museums and bookstores have cafés serving afternoon tea goodies à la carte, where you can put together a spread for less than £10—**Waterstone's** fifth-floor café and the **Victoria and Albert Museum** café are two of the best. **Teapod,** a modern option near the Tower Bridge, advertises the "best-value afternoon tea in London," serving cream tea for £5 and afternoon tea for £10, along with sandwiches, soups, salads, and pastries (Mon–Fri 8:30–18:00, Sat 9:00–19:00, Sun 10:00–19:00, 31 Shad Thames, 200 yards from the Tower Bridge on the South Bank, tel. 020/7407-0000).

In Bath: **The Pump Room** is reason enough to put off tea in London—assuming you're visiting the city of Bath. This historic, elegant Georgian hall with live music lets anyone enjoy the ritual of tea in grand style (see page 354).

London Connections

Airports

Phone numbers and websites for London's airports and major airlines are listed in the appendix. For accommodations at or near the major airports, see page 162.

Heathrow Airport

Heathrow Airport is one of the world's busiest airports. Think about it: 68 million passengers a year on 470,000 flights from 180 destinations riding 90 airlines, like some kind of global maypole dance. Read signs and ask questions. For Heathrow's airport, flight, and transfer information, call the switchboard at toll tel. 0844-335-1801, or visit the helpful website at www.heathrow airport.com.

Heathrow has five terminals: T-1 (mostly domestic and Irish flights, with some service to Europe and the US); T-2 (closed for renovation, should reopen in 2013); T-3 (North and South American, Asian, and some European flights); T-4 (European and US flights); and T-5 (British Airways flights only). You can walk between T-1 and T-3. To travel between the other terminals, you can take the Heathrow Express trains (free), buses (free), or the Tube (requires a ticket). Unlike most American airports, there is no train that links all the terminals together on one line, so you may have to transfer if you're going to T-4 or T-5.

If you're flying out of Heathrow, it's critical to confirm which terminal your flight will use (check the Web or call your airline in advance)—because if it's T-4 or T-5, you'll need to allow extra time. Taxi drivers generally know which terminal you'll need, but bus drivers may not.

Each terminal has an airport information desk (generally daily 6:00–22:00), car-rental agencies, exchange bureaus, ATMs, a pharmacy, a **VAT refund desk** (tel. 020/8910-3682; you must

London's Airports

AIRPORTS
ENGLAND
50 MILES
50 KM
LUTON
CAMBRIDGE
N
LONDON
STANSTED
BATH
LONDON CITY
WINDSOR
GREENWICH
NORTH
HEATHROW
SEA
GATWICK
CHANNEL TUNNEL
DCH
ENGLISH
CHANNEL
TO PARIS & BRUSSELS

present the VAT claim form from the retailer here to get your tax rebate on items purchased in Britain—see page 17 for details), and **baggage storage** (£8/item for 24 hours, hours vary by terminal but generally daily 5:30–23:00, www.left-baggage.co.uk). Get online 24 hours a day at Heathrow's **Internet access points** (at each terminal—T-4's is up on the mezzanine level) or with your laptop (pay Wi-Fi provided by Boingo, www.boingo.com). There's a **post office** on the first floor of T-3. Each terminal has cheap **eateries.**

Heathrow's small **"TI"** (tourist info shop), even though it's a for-profit business, is worth a visit to pick up free information: a simple map, the *London Planner,* and brochures (daily 6:30–22:00, 5-minute walk from T-3 in Tube station, follow signs to Underground; bypass queue for transit info to reach window for London questions).

Getting to London from Heathrow Airport

You have five basic options for traveling the 14 miles between Heathrow Airport and downtown London: Tube (£4.50/person), bus (£5/person), direct shuttle bus (£21.50/person), express train with connecting Tube or taxi (about £20/person), or taxi (about £55 per group).

By Tube (Subway): For £4.50, the Tube takes you from any Heathrow terminal to downtown London in 50–60 minutes on the Piccadilly Line (6/hour; depending on your destination, may require a transfer, buy ticket at the Tube station ticket window). If you plan to use the Tube for transport in London, it may make sense to buy a Travelcard or pay-as-you-go Oyster card at the Tube station ticket window at the airport. (For information on these passes, see page 56.) If your Travelcard covers only Zones 1–2, it does not include Heathrow (Zone 6); however, you can pay a small supplement for the initial trip from Heathrow to downtown.

If you're taking the Tube from downtown London *to* the airport, note that the Piccadilly Line trains don't stop at every terminal. Trains either stop at T-4, then T-1/T-3 (also called Heathrow Central), in that order; or T-1/T-3 and T-5. When leaving central London on the Tube, allow extra time if going to T-4 or T-5, since you have to be sure you get on a train going to your terminal; carefully check the destination information before you board.

By Bus: Most buses depart from the outdoor common area in the heart of the Heathrow complex called the Central Bus Station. It serves T-1 and T-3, and is a 5-minute walk from these terminals. To get to T-4 or T-5 from the Central Bus Station, go inside, downstairs, and follow signs to take Heathrow Express trains to your terminal (free, but only runs every 15–20 minutes to those terminals); or catch one of the free buses that circulate between terminals.

National Express has regular service from Heathrow's Central Bus Station to Victoria Coach Station in downtown London, near several of my recommended hotels. While slow, the bus is affordable and convenient for those staying near Victoria Station (£5, 1–2/hour, less frequent from Victoria Station to Heathrow, 45–60 minutes depending on time of day, toll tel. 0871-781-8181, www.nationalexpress.com).

By Shuttle: SkyShuttle operates buses about every half hour between all Heathrow terminals and hotels in central London (£21.50/person one-way, £34.40/person round-trip; reservations toll tel. 0845-481-0960, call between 6:00–22:00; www.skyshuttle.co.uk).

By Train: Two different trains (slow for £8, fast for £18) run between Heathrow Airport and London's Paddington Station. At Paddington Station, you're in the thick of the Tube system, with easy access to any of my recommended neighborhoods—my Paddington hotels are just outside the front door, and Notting Hill Gate is just two Tube stops away. The **Heathrow Connect** train is the slightly slower, much cheaper option, serving T-1 and T-3 at one station called Heathrow Central; use free transfers if you're coming from either T-4 or T-5 (£8 one-way, 2/hour, 30 minutes, toll tel. 0845-678-6975, www.heathrowconnect.com). The **Heathrow Express** train is fast (15 minutes to downtown from T-1 and T-3; 21 minutes from T-5; transfer required from T-4) and runs more frequently (4/hour), but it's pricey (£18 "express class" one-way, £32 round-trip, ask about discount promos at ticket desk, buy ticket before you board or pay a £3 surcharge to buy it on the train, covered by BritRail pass, daily 5:10–23:25, toll tel. 0845-600-1515, www.heathrowexpress.co.uk). At the airport, you can use Heathrow Express as a free transfer between terminals.

By Taxi: Taxis from the airport cost about £45–70 to west and central London (one hour). For four people traveling together, this can be a deal. Hotels can often line up a cab back to the airport for about £30–40. For the cheapest taxi to the airport, don't order one from your hotel. Simply flag down a few and ask them for their best "off-meter" rate. Locals refer to hired cars that do the trip off-meter as "mini-cabs." These are reliable and generally cost about what you'd pay for a taxi in good traffic, but—with a fixed price—they can save you money when taxis are snarled in congestion with the meter running.

Getting to Bath from Heathrow Airport

By Bus: Direct buses run daily from Heathrow to Bath (£19.10, 10/day direct, 2–3 hours, more frequent but slower with transfer in London, toll tel. 0871-781-8181, www.nationalexpress.com). BritRail passholders may prefer the 2.5-hour Heathrow–Bath bus/train connection via Reading (BritRail passholders just pay £15 for bus; otherwise £46–65 depending on time of day, about £20 cheaper when bought in advance; tel. 0118-957-9425, buy bus ticket from www.railair.com, train ticket from www.firstgreatwestern.co.uk). First catch the RailAir Link shuttle bus (2/hour, 45 minutes) to Reading (RED-ding), then hop on the express train (2/hour, 1 hour) to Bath. Factoring in the connection in Reading—which can add at least an hour to the trip—the train is a less convenient option than the direct bus to Bath.

Gatwick Airport

More and more flights land at Gatwick Airport, halfway between London and the South Coast (toll tel. 0844-335-1802, www.gatwickairport.com). Gatwick has two terminals, North and South, which are easily connected by a free monorail (2-minute trip, runs 24 hours daily). Note that boarding passes say "Gatwick N" or "Gatwick S" to indicate your terminal. British Airways flights generally use Gatwick North. The Gatwick Express trains (described next) stop only at Gatwick South. Schedules in each terminal show only arrivals and departures from that terminal.

Getting to London: Gatwick Express trains are clearly the best way into London from this airport. They shuttle conveniently between Gatwick South and London's Victoria Station, with many of my recommended hotels (£17, £29 round-trip, 4/hour, 30 minutes, runs 5:00–24:00 daily, purchase tickets on train at no extra charge, toll tel. 0845-850-1530, www.gatwickexpress.com). If you buy your tickets at the station before boarding, ask about their deal where three adults travel for the price of two, or four for the price of three. (If you see others in the ticket line, suggest buying your tickets together—you'll save more than £5 each.)

You can save a few pounds by taking Southern Railway's slower and less frequent **shuttle train** between Gatwick South and Victoria Station (£10.90, up to 4/hour, 45 minutes, toll tel. 0845-127-2920, www.southernrailway.com).

A train also runs from Gatwick South to **St. Pancras International Station** (£8.90, 8/hour, 1 hour, www.firstcapital connect.co.uk)—useful for travelers taking the Eurostar train (to Paris or Brussels) or staying in the St. Pancras/King's Cross neighborhood.

Even slower, but cheap and handy to the Victoria Station neighborhood, you can take the **bus** from Gatwick to Victoria (£7.50, hourly, 1.5 hours, toll tel. 0871-781-8181, www.national express.com).

Getting to Bath: To get to Bath from Gatwick, you can catch a bus to Heathrow and take the bus to Bath from there (10/day, 4–5 hours total, £25 one-way, transfer at Heathrow Airport, www.nationalexpress.com—see "Getting to Bath from Heathrow Airport," earlier). By train, the best Gatwick–Bath connection involves a transfer in Reading (£45–54 one-way depending on time of day, £12 in advance, hourly, 2.5 hours, www.firstgreatwestern .co.uk; avoid transfer in London, where you'll have to change stations).

London's Other Airports

Stansted Airport: If you're using Stansted (toll tel. 0870-0000-303, www.stanstedairport.com), you have several options for getting into or out of London. Two different **buses** connect the airport and downtown London's Victoria Station neighborhood: National Express (£10, £17 round-trip, every 20 minutes, 1.75 hours, runs 24 hours a day, picks up and stops throughout London, ends at Victoria Coach Station, toll tel. 0871-781-8181, www.national express.com) and Terravision (£9, 2–3/hour, 1.25 hours, ends at Green Line Coach Station just south of Victoria Station). Or you can take the faster, pricier Stansted Express **train** (£18–20 one-way, £25–27 round-trip, connects to London's Tube system at Tottenham Hale and Liverpool Street, 4/hour, 45 minutes, 5:00–23:00, toll tel. 0845-850-0150, www.stanstedexpress.com). Stansted is expensive by **cab**; figure £120 one-way from central London.

Luton Airport: For Luton (airport tel. 01582/405-100, www .london-luton.co.uk), there are two choices into or out of London.

The fastest way to go is by **rail** to London's St. Pancras International Station (£12 one-way, 1–5/hour, 25–45 minutes—check schedule to avoid the slower trains, toll tel. 0845-712-5678, www.east midlandstrains.co.uk); catch the 10-minute shuttle bus (£1) from outside the terminal to the Luton Airport Parkway Station. The Green Line express **bus #757** runs to Buckingham Palace Road, just south of London's Victoria Station (£13 one-way, £16 round-trip, small discount for easyJet passengers who buy online, 2–4/hour, 1.25–1.5 hours, 24 hours a day, toll tel. 0844-801-7261, www.greenline.co.uk). If you're sleeping at Luton, consider easyHotel (see listing on page 162).

London City Airport: There's a slim chance you might use London City Airport (tel. 020/7646-0088, www.londoncity airport.com). To get into London, take the Docklands Light Railway (DLR) to the Bank Tube station, which is one stop east of St. Paul's on the Central Line (£4 one-way, covered by Travelcard, £2.20–2.70 on Oyster card, 22 minutes, tel. 020/7222-1234, www.tfl.gov.uk/dlr).

Connecting London's Airports by Bus

More and more travelers are taking advantage of cheap flights out of London's smaller airports. A handy **National Express bus** runs between Heathrow, Gatwick, Stansted, and Luton airports—easier than having to cut through the center of London—although traffic can be bad and increase travel times (toll tel. 0871-781-8181, www.nationalexpress.com).

From Heathrow Airport to: Gatwick Airport (1–4/hour, 1.25–1.5 hours, £19.50 one-way, £36.50 round-trip, allow at least three hours between flights), **Stansted Airport** (1–2/hour, 1.5–1.75 hours, £22.50 one-way, £29.30 round-trip), **Luton Airport** (hourly, 1–1.5 hours, £20.30 one-way, £25.60 round-trip).

Discounted Flights from London

London is one of Europe's cheapest places to fly into and out of. For information, see "Cheap Flights" on page 710.

Trains and Buses

Britain is covered by a myriad of rail systems (owned by different companies), which together are called National Rail. London, the country's major transportation hub, has a different train station for each region. There are nine main stations (see the route map on next page):

Euston—Serves northwest England, North Wales, and Scotland.

King's Cross—Serves northeast England and Scotland, including York and Edinburgh.

London's Train Stations

TO NORTH WALES & GLASGOW

TO CANTERBURY, DOVER, PARIS & BRUSSELS VIA CHUNNEL

TO STRATFORD-UPON-AVON

TO CAMBRIDGE, YORK & EDINBURGH

TO HARWICH

RAF MUSEUM LONDON

EUSTON

2012 OLYMPIC PARK

MARYLE-BONE

ST. PANCRAS INT'L.

KING'S CROSS

DOCKLANDS

LONDON CITY AIRPORT

TO HEATHROW AIRPORT, WINDSOR, BATH, S. WALES & COTSWOLDS

PADDINGTON

TRAF. SQ.

LIVERPOOL STREET

L O N D O N

VICTORIA

LONDON BRIDGE

O2 ARENA

WATER-LOO

CANARY WHARF ON ISLE OF DOGS

GREENWICH

WEST-MINSTER PIER

THAMES

KEW GARDENS

WIMBLEDON

TO BRIGHTON

TO SALISBURY

TO GATWICK AIRPORT, CANTERBURY, DOVER & BRIGHTON

HAMPTON COURT PALACE

DCH

□ = CENTRAL LONDON

5 MILES

5 KM

LONDON

Liverpool Street—Serves east England, including Essex and Harwich.

London Bridge—Serves south England, including Brighton.

Marylebone—Serves southwest and central England, including Stratford-upon-Avon.

Paddington—Serves south and southwest England, including Heathrow Airport, Windsor, Bath, South Wales, and the Cotswolds.

St. Pancras International—Serves north and south England, plus the Eurostar to Paris or Brussels (see "Crossing the Channel," later).

Victoria—Serves Gatwick Airport, Canterbury, Dover, and Brighton.

Waterloo—Serves southeast England, including Salisbury.

In addition, there are other, smaller train stations in London that you are not likely to use, such as **Charing Cross** or **Blackfriars.**

Any train station has schedule information, can make reservations, and can sell tickets for any destination. Most stations offer a baggage-storage service (£8/bag for 24 hours, look for *left luggage* signs); because of long security lines, it can take a while to check or pick up your bag (www.excess-baggage.com). For more details on the services available at each station, see www.nationalrail.co.uk /stations.

Buying Tickets: For general information, call 0845-748-4950 (or visit www.nationalrail.co.uk or www.eurostar.com; £5 booking fee for telephone reservations). If you book far enough ahead, you might find discounted train tickets on certain routes at www .megatrain.com (toll tel. 0871-266-3333; as they also sell bus tickets, be careful to specify that you want to take the train).

Railpasses: For train travel outside London, consider getting a BritRail pass. Options include passes that cover England as well as Scotland and Wales, England-only passes, England/Ireland passes, "London Plus" passes (good for travel in most of southeast England but not in London itself), and BritRail & Drive passes (which offer you some rail days and some car-rental days). For specifics, contact your travel agent, or see www.ricksteves.com/rail.

By Train
To Points West
From Paddington Station to: Bath (2/hour, 1.5 hours; also consider a guided Evan Evans tour by bus—see page 190), **Oxford** (2/hour direct, 1 hour, more possible with transfer in Reading, 1 hour), **Penzance** (every 1–2 hours, 5–5.5 hours, possible change in Plymouth), and **Cardiff** (2/hour, 2 hours).

To Points North
From King's Cross Station: Trains run at least hourly, stopping in **York** (2 hours), **Durham** (3 hours), and **Edinburgh** (4.5 hours). Trains to **Cambridge** also leave from here (3/hour, 45–60 minutes).

From Euston Station to: Conwy (nearly hourly, 3.25 hours, transfer in Chester), **Liverpool** (hourly, 2 hours, more with transfer), **Blackpool** (hourly, 3 hours, transfer at Preston), **Keswick** (hourly, 4.5 hours, transfer to bus at Penrith), and **Glasgow** (1–2/ hour, 4.5–5 hours).

From London's Other Stations
Trains run between London and **Canterbury,** leaving from St. Pancras International Station and arriving in Canterbury West (1–2/hour, 1 hour), as well as from London's Victoria Station and arriving in Canterbury East (2/hour, 1.5 hours).

Direct trains leave for **Stratford-upon-Avon** from Marylebone Station, located near the southwest corner of Regents Park (5/day direct, more with transfers, 2.25 hours).

To Other Destinations: Dover (hourly, 1 hour, direct from

Public Transportation near London

St. Pancras International Station; also hourly, 2 hours, direct from Victoria Station or Charing Cross Station), **Brighton** (4–5/hour, 1 hour, from Victoria Station and London Bridge Station), **Portsmouth** (3/hour, 1.5–2 hours, most from Waterloo Station, a few from Victoria Station), and **Salisbury** (1–2/hour, 1.5 hours, from Waterloo Station). For trains to **Windsor, Cambridge, Greenwich,** or **Bath,** see those chapters.

By Bus

Buses are slower but considerably cheaper than trains for reaching destinations around Britain, and beyond. Most depart from **Victoria Coach Station,** which is one long block south of Victoria Station (near many recommended accommodations and Tube: Victoria). Inside the station, you'll find basic eateries, kiosks, and a helpful information desk stocked with schedules and ready to point you to your bus or answer any questions.

Most domestic buses are operated by **National Express** (toll tel. 0871-781-8181, www.nationalexpress.com); their international departures are called **Eurolines** (toll tel. 0871-781-8177, www.eurolines.co.uk). A newer, smaller company called **Megabus** undersells National Express with deeply discounted promotional fares—the further ahead you buy, the less you pay (trips tend to take longer than those on National Express, toll tel. 0900-160-0900, www.megabus.com). They also sell discounted train tickets on selected routes.

Try to avoid bus travel on Friday and Sunday evenings, when weekend travelers are more likely to make buses sell out.

To ensure getting a ticket—and to save money with special promotions—you can book your ticket in advance online (see websites above). The cheapest pre-purchased tickets can be changed (for a £5 fee), but they're nonrefundable. If you have a British mobile phone, you can buy an "M-Ticket," which sends your paperless confirmation number right to your phone.

If you're planning to buy your ticket at the station, try to arrive an hour before the bus departs—or drop by the day before. (For buses to Stansted Airport and Oxford, you can buy the ticket on board; otherwise you'll buy it at a ticket window.) Watch your bags carefully—luggage thieves thrive at the station.

To Bath: The National Express bus leaves from Victoria Coach Station (9/day, 2.75–3.75 hours, avoid those with layover in Bristol, sample fares: one-way-£22, round-trip-£29).

To get to Bath via Stonehenge, consider taking a guided bus tour from London to Stonehenge, Salisbury, and Bath, and abandoning the tour in Bath (be sure to confirm that Bath is the last stop on that particular tour). **Evan Evans'** tour is £69 and includes admissions. The tour leaves from Victoria Coach Station every morning at 8:45 (you can stow your bag under the bus), stops in Salisbury (for a look at its magnificent cathedral) and Stonehenge, and then stops in Bath for a city tour before returning to London (offered year-round; they also offer another tour to Stonehenge and Bath via Windsor Castle). You can book the tour at the Victoria Coach Station or the Evan Evans office (258 Vauxhall Bridge Road, near Victoria Coach Station, tel. 020/7950-1777, US tel. 866-382-6868, www.evanevans.co.uk). **Golden Tours** also runs a Stonehenge–Bath tour (£59, check website for seasonal tour days; departs from Fountain Square, located across from Victoria Coach Station, US tel. 800-548-7083, toll tel. 0844-880-6981, www.goldentours.co.uk).

To Other Destinations: Oxford (2–4/hour, about 1.5 hours), **Cambridge** (hourly, 2–2.5 hours), **Canterbury** (about hourly, 2–2.5 hours), **Dover** (about hourly, 2.5–3.25 hours), **Penzance** (5/day, 8.5-10 hours, overnight available), **Cardiff** (hourly, 3.25 hours), **Liverpool** (8/day direct, 5.25–6 hours, overnight available), **Blackpool** (4/day direct, 6.25–7 hours, overnight available), **York** (4/day direct, 5.25 hours), **Durham** (4/day direct, 6.5–7.5 hours), **Glasgow** (3/day direct, 8–9 hours, train is a much better option), **Edinburgh** (2/day direct, 8.75–9.75 hours, go by train instead).

To Dublin, Ireland: This bus/boat journey, operated by

National Express, takes 10–12 hours (£35–45, 1/da⟩
Victoria Coach Station at 18:00, check in with passport o.
before). Consider a cheap 1.25-hour Ryanair flight instead (.
.ryanair.com).

To the Continent: Especially in summer, buses run to destinations all over Europe, including Paris, Amsterdam, Brussels, and Germany (sometimes crossing the Channel by ferry, other times through the Chunnel). For any international connection, you need to check in with your passport one hour before departure. For details, call toll tel. 0871-781-8177 or visit www.eurolines.co.uk. For information on crossing the Channel by bus, see the end of this chapter.

Crossing the Channel
By Eurostar Train

The fastest and most convenient way to get from Big Ben to the Eiffel Tower is by rail. Eurostar, a joint service of the Belgian,

British, and French railways, is the speedy passenger train that zips you (and up to 800 others in 18 sleek cars) from downtown London to downtown Paris or Brussels (15+/day, 2.25–2.5 hours) faster and more easily than flying. The actual tunnel crossing is a 20–minute, silent, 100-mile-per-hour non-event. Your ears won't even pop. Eurostar's monopoly expired at the beginning of 2010, and Air France has already announced plans to start a competing high-speed rail service between London and Paris (possibly in 2011). Press reports say Germany's national railroad wants to run its high-speed trains to London by the 2012 Olympics.

Eurostar Fares

Channel fares are reasonable but complicated. Prices vary depending on how far ahead you reserve, whether you can live with restrictions, and whether you're eligible for any discounts (children, youths, seniors, round-trip travelers, and railpass holders all qualify).

Fares can change without notice, but typically a **one-way, full-fare ticket** (with no restrictions on refundability) runs about $425 first-class and $300 second-class. **Cheaper seats** come with more restrictions and can sell out quickly (figure $100–160 for second-class, one-way). Those traveling with a railpass that covers France or Britain should look first at the **passholder** fare ($85–130 for second-class, one-way Eurostar trips). For more details, visit my *Guide to Eurail Passes* (www.ricksteves.com/eurostar), Rail

.com), or go directly to Eurostar (www

d **BritainShrinkers** sells one- or two-
o Paris, Brussels, or Bruges, enabling
ties from London for less than most
alone. For example, you'll pay £109 for a one-day
Paris "tour" (unescorted Mon–Sat day trip with Métro pass; tel.
207-713-1311 or www.britainshrinkers.com). This can be a particularly good option if you need to get to Paris from London on short
notice, when only the costliest fares are available.

Buying Eurostar Tickets

Because only the most expensive (full-fare) ticket is fully refundable, don't reserve until you're sure of your plans. But if you wait
too long, the cheapest tickets will get bought up.

Once you're confident about the time and date of your crossing,
you can check and book fares by phone or online. Ordering online
through Eurostar or major agents
offers a print-at-home e-ticket
option. You can also order by
phone through Rail Europe at
US tel. 800-EUROSTAR for
home delivery before you go,
or through Eurostar (French
toll tel. 08 92 35 35 39, priced in
euros) and pick up your ticket at
the train station. In continental Europe, you can buy your
Eurostar ticket at any major
train station in any country or
at any travel agency that handles
train tickets (expect a booking
fee). In Britain, tickets can be
issued only at the Eurostar office

in St. Pancras International Station. You can purchase passholder
discount tickets at Eurostar departure stations, through US agents,
or by phone with Eurostar, but they may be harder to get at other
train stations and travel agencies, and are a discount category that
can sell out.

Remember that Britain's time zone is one hour earlier than
France or Belgium. Times listed on tickets are local times (departure from London is British time, arrival in Paris in French time).

Taking the Eurostar

Eurostar trains depart from and arrive at London's St. Pancras

International Station. Check in at least 30 minutes in advance for your Eurostar trip. It's very similar to an airport check-in: You pass through airport-like security, show your passport to customs officials, and find a TV monitor to locate your departure gate. There are a few airport-like shops, newsstands, horrible snack bars, and cafés (bring food for the trip from elsewhere), pay-Internet terminals, and a currency-exchange booth with rates about the same as you'll find on the other end.

Crossing the Channel Without Eurostar

The old-fashioned ways of crossing the Channel are cheaper than Eurostar (taking the bus is cheapest). They're also twice as romantic, complicated, and time-consuming.

By Train and Boat

To Paris: You'll take a train from London to the port of Dover, then catch a ferry to Calais, France, before boarding another train for Paris. Trains go from London's St. Pancras International to **Dover's** Priory Station (hourly, 1.25 hours; bus or taxi from train station to ferry dock). P&O Ferries sail from Dover to Calais; TGV trains run from Calais to Paris. You'll need to book your own train tickets to Dover and from Calais to Paris. The prices listed here are for the ferry only (from £30 one-way or £60 round-trip online, more at dock or by phone, book early for best fares; 22/day, 1.5 hours, toll tel. 08716-645-645, www.poferries.com).

To Amsterdam: Stena Line's Dutchflyer service combines train and ferry tickets between London and Amsterdam via the ports of **Harwich** and Hoek van Holland. Trains go from London's Liverpool Street Station to Harwich (hourly, 1.75 hours). Stena Line ferries sail from Harwich to Hoek van Holland (7.5 hours), where you can transfer to a train to Amsterdam or other Dutch cities (ferry—from £35, from £57 with cabin, book at least 2 weeks in advance for best price, 13 hours total travel time, Dutchflyer toll tel. 0844-576-2762, www.stenaline.co.uk, Dutch train info at www.ns.nl).

For additional European ferry info, visit www.aferry.to. For UK train and bus info, go to www.traveline.org.uk.

By Bus

You can take the bus from London direct to **Paris** (4/day, 8.25–9.75 hours), **Brussels** (3–4/day, 12 hours), or **Amsterdam** (4/day, 12 hours) from Victoria Coach Station (via ferry or Chunnel, day or overnight). You'll pay the same to Paris, Brussels, or Amsterdam. The price depends on when you book (for example: £28 one-way, £38 round-trip if purchased at least a week ahead; £40 one-way,

£55 round-trip if purchased the day before; £44 one-way, £61 round-trip if purchased same day; no discounts and £5 more for any ticket during peak times such as holiday weekends; toll tel. 0871-781-8177; visit www.eurolines.co.uk and look for "funfares").

By Plane

Check with budget airlines for inexpensive round-trip fares to Paris or Brussels (see "Cheap Flights" on page 710).

GREENWICH, WINDSOR, AND CAMBRIDGE

Three of the best day-trip possibilities near London are Greenwich, Windsor, and Cambridge (listed from nearest to farthest). Greenwich is England's maritime capital; Windsor has a very famous castle; and Cambridge is England's best university town.

Getting Around

By Train: The British rail system uses London as a hub and normally offers same-day round-trip fares that cost virtually the same as one-way fares. For day trips, these "off-peak day return" tickets, available if you depart London outside rush hour (usually after 9:30 on weekdays and anytime Sat–Sun), are best. You can also save a little money if you purchase tickets before 18:00 the day before your trip.

By Train Tour: London Walks offers a variety of "Explorer Days" tours year-round by train, including a Cambridge itinerary (£14 plus transportation and admissions costs, pick up their brochure at the TI or hotels, tel. 020/7624-3978, www.walks.com, see listing on page 67).

Greenwich

Tudor kings favored the palace at Greenwich (GREN-ich). Henry VIII was born here. Later kings commissioned Inigo Jones and Christopher Wren to beautify the town and palace, and built a grand hospital to care for retired seamen (which later became a college for training naval officers). Visitors also come here for all things salty. Greenwich is England's maritime capital, and though its main attraction—the *Cutty Sark* clipper—is closed for restoration until at least late 2011, the town is still worth a visit.

Greenwich is synonymous with timekeeping and astronomy, and at the Royal Observatory Greenwich, you can learn how those pursuits tie into its seafaring status. The town also has stunning Baroque architecture, appealing markets, a fleet of nautical shops, plenty of parks, kid-friendly museums, and hordes of tourists. Since all the major sights here are free to enter, and you can travel between central London and Greenwich on a cheap Tube ticket, it's a wonderfully inexpensive day out. And where else can you set your watch with such accuracy?

Planning Your Time

Upon arrival, stroll past the *Cutty Sark* dry dock to the Discover Greenwich exhibit and TI, then drop into the grand buildings of the Old Royal Naval College and walk the shoreline promenade. Enjoy a lunch or drink in the venerable Trafalgar Tavern, before heading to the National Maritime Museum and then through the park up to the Royal Observatory Greenwich. The town's sights are open daily, but its popular market is closed Monday and Tuesday.

If you like to mix and match public transit, I'd suggest taking the boat to Greenwich for the scenery and commentary, and the DLR (Docklands Light Railway) back, especially if you want to stop at the Docklands on the way home. To visit the Docklands— the glittering forest of skyscrapers rising from a once-derelict port—hop out of the train at the Canary Wharf stop for a quick stroll (see page 127). From there, you can tack on a small detour to check out the Olympics 2012 site (see page 128).

Getting to Greenwich

It's a joy by boat, or a snap by DLR (Docklands Light Railway).

By Boat: From central London, you can cruise scenically

London Day Trips

✈ AIRPORTS

50 MILES

50 KM

CAMBRIDGE

LUTON ✈

+ ✈ STANSTED

NORTH SEA

LONDON

✈ LONDON CITY

BATH

GREENWICH

WINDSOR

HEATHROW

STONE-HENGE

BUS SALISBURY

✈ GATWICK

CHANNEL TUNNEL

DCH

TO PARIS & BRUSSELS

ENGLISH CHANNEL

down the Thames to Greenwich. Various tour boats—with commentary and open-deck seating up top—leave from the piers at Westminster, Waterloo, and the Tower of London (2/hour, about 1 hour); note that most boats have commentary only on the way to Greenwich, not on the way back.

Thames Clippers offer faster trips, with no commentary and only a small deck at the stern (departs every 20 minutes from several piers in central London, 45 minutes). Thames Clippers also connect Greenwich to the Docklands' Canary Wharf Pier (3/hour, 10 minutes).

For cruising details, see page 72.

By DLR (Docklands Light Railway): From Bank station (also accessible from the Monument Tube station) in central London, take the DLR to Cutty Sark station in central Greenwich; it's one stop before the main—but less central—Greenwich station (departs at least every 10 minutes, 20 minutes, all in Zone 2, covered by any Tube pass). Some DLR trains terminate at Island Gardens (from which you can generally catch another train to Greenwich's Cutty Sark station within a few minutes, though it may be more memorable to walk under the river through the long Thames pedestrian tunnel). Many DLR trains terminate at Canary Wharf, so make sure you get on one that continues to Lewisham or Greenwich.

By Train: Mainline trains also go from London (Cannon Street and London Bridge stations) several times an hour to Greenwich station (10-minute walk from the sights). Although the train is fast and cheap, the DLR is preferable because it drops you right in the heart of town.

By Bus: Catch bus #188 from Russell Square near the British Museum (about 45 minutes to Greenwich).

Orientation to Greenwich

(area code: 020)

Still well within the city limits of London, Greenwich feels like a small town all its own. Covered markets and outdoor stalls make

for lively weekends. Save time to browse the town. Wander beyond the touristy Church Street and Greenwich High Road to where flower stands spill onto the side streets, and antique shops sell brass nautical knickknacks. King William Walk, College Approach, Nelson Road, and Turnpin Lane are all worth a look. If you need pub grub, Greenwich has almost 100 pubs, with some boasting that they're mere milliseconds from the prime meridian.

Markets: Thanks to its markets, Greenwich throbs with daytrippers on weekends. The **Greenwich Market** is an entertaining mini-Covent Garden, located in the middle of the block between the Cutty Sark DLR station and the Old Royal Naval College—right on your way to the sights (Wed 11:00–18:00, Thu–Sun 10:00–17:30, closed Mon–Tue; farmers' market on Wed, food court on Thu–Sun, antiques on Thu–Fri, arts and crafts on Fri–Sun; tel. 020/7515-7153, www.greenwichmarket.net). The **Clocktower Market** sells old odds and ends at high prices on Greenwich High Road, near the post office (Sat–Sun only 10:00–16:00, www.clock towermarket.co.uk).

Tourist Information

The TI is inside the Discover Greenwich information center (described later, under "Sights in Greenwich"). From the DLR station, exit straight ahead to the monumental gateway for the Old Royal Naval College complex; Discover Greenwich is just inside the gate on the left (daily 10:00–17:00, Pepys House, 2 Cutty Sark Gardens, toll tel. 0870-608-2000, www.visitgreenwich.org.uk).

Guided walks, which depart from the TI, offer an overview of the town and go past most of the big sights (£6, daily at 12:15 and 14:15, 1.5 hours; the only sights entered are the Painted Hall and Chapel, and only on the 14:15 tour).

Greenwich

TO CANARY WHARF & THE DOCKLANDS

N

TO O₂ ARENA

ISLE OF DOGS

Island Gardens

WEST FERRY ROAD

ISLAND GARDENS

THAMES RIVER

TO LONDON

←PEDESTRIAN TUNNEL

GREENWICH PIER

TUNNEL ENTRANCE

FIVE FOOT WALK

CRANE ST.

TRINITY HOSPITAL

PARK ROW

❸

CHAPEL

OLD ROYAL NAVAL COLLEGE

CUTTY SARK (CLOSED)

❹

Cutty Sark

CHURCH ST.

KING WILLIAM WALK

❺

GREENWICH UNIV.

PAINTED HALL

ROMNEY ROAD

QUEEN'S HOUSE

COLONNADES

ST. ALFEGE'S CHURCH

NELSON ST.

ROAN ST.

❶

GREENWICH STATION

GREENWICH HIGH ROAD

STOCKWELL ST.

NEV.

THE AVE.

NAT'L. MARITIME MUSEUM

PRIME MERIDIAN

❷

GREENWICH PARK

TO LONDON

DCH

ROYAL OBSERVATORY GREENWICH

PETER HARRISON PLANETARIUM

WELLER ASTRONOMY GALLERIES

⊕ DLR Station

View

← Bldg. Entrances

200 YARDS

200 METERS

❶ Greenwich Market
❷ Clocktower Market
❸ Trafalgar Tavern

❹ Marks & Spencer Simply Food
❺ The Old Brewery

GREENWICH

Sights in Greenwich

I've organized these listings as a handy sightseeing walk through town, starting right next to the Cutty Sark DLR station.

▲▲**Cutty Sark**—The Scottish-built *Cutty Sark* was the last of the great China tea clippers, and was the queen of the seas when first launched in 1869. With 32,000 square feet of sail, she could blow with the wind 300 miles in a day. The ship is closed for renovation until at least late 2011—check www.cuttysark.org.uk for updates.

Discover Greenwich—This new visitors center (which also houses the TI) is located at the corner of the Old Royal Naval College closest to the *Cutty Sark*. While it's hardly a museum, it offers a decent introduction to Greenwich. In the center, a model of the town lights up to tell its history. Surrounding the model are displays and artifacts from various people who have left their mark on the town, and exhibits about the architecture and construction of Greenwich's fine buildings (free, daily 10:00–17:00).

Adjoining Discover Greenwich are the TI and a recommended pub, The Old Brewery.

▲**Old Royal Naval College**—The college was originally a hospital founded by Queen Mary II and King William III in 1692 as a charity to care for retired or injured naval officers (called pensioners). William and Mary spared no expense, hiring the great Christopher Wren to design the complex (though other architects completed it). Its days as a hospital ended in 1869, and it served as a college for training naval officers from 1873 to 1998. Now that the Royal Navy has moved out, the public is invited to view the college's elaborate Painted Hall and Chapel, which are in symmetrical buildings that face each other overlooking a broad riverfront park.

Cost and Hours: Free, daily 10:00–17:00, sometimes closed for private events, choral service Sun at 11:00 in chapel—all are welcome. Guides give 1.5-hour tours covering the hall and chapel, along with other areas not open to the general public (£5, daily at 11:30 and 14:00, call ahead to check availability). Tel. 020/8269-4799, www.oldroyalnavalcollege.org.

❍ **Self-Guided Tour:** Good descriptions are free to borrow in each building, or you can buy the fun *Nasty Naval College* brochure, with offbeat facts about the place (50p). Guides called Yeoman Warders are often standing by to answer questions.

Here's an overview of what you'll see:

Painted Hall: Originally intended as a dining hall for pensioners, this sumptuously painted room was deemed too glorious (and, in the winter, too cold) for that purpose. So almost as soon as it was completed, it became simply a place to impress visitors.

Enter the hall, climb the stairs, and gape up at one of the largest painted ceilings in Europe—112 feet long. It's a big propaganda scene, glorifying the building's founders, Queen Mary II and King William III (who, as a Protestant monarch, had recently trounced the Catholic French King Louis XIV in a pivotal battle). Crane your neck—or use the clever wheeled mirrors—to examine the scene. In the center are William and Mary. Under his foot, William is crushing a dark figure with a broken sword...Louis XIV. He is handing a red cap (representing liberty) to the woman on the right, who holds the reins of a white horse

(symbolizing Europe). On the left, a white-robed woman hands him an olive branch, a sign of peace. The message: William has granted Europe liberty by saving it from the tyranny of Louis XIV. Below the royal couple, the Spirit of Architecture shows them the plans for this very building (commemorating the sad fact that Mary died before she saw it completed). Ringing the central image are the four seasons (represented by Zodiac signs), the four virtues, and—at the top and bottom—a captured Spanish galleon and a British man-of-war battleship.

Up the steps at the end of the room, along the wall of the **upper hall,** is a portrait of the family of King George I. On the right is the artist who spent 19 years of his life painting this hall, James Thornhill. He's holding out his hand—reportedly, he didn't feel he was paid enough for this Sistine-sized undertaking.

• *Exit the hall, and cross the field to enter the building with the...*

Chapel: Not surprisingly, you'll sense a nautical air in this fine chapel. Notice the rope motif in the floor tiles down the aisle.

The painting above the altar, by American Benjamin West, depicts the shipwreck of St. Paul on the island of Malta. According to the Bible, Paul came across a poisonous viper and threw it in the fire, miraculously without being injured. Soon after the chapel was completed, it was gutted by a fire, and had to be redecorated all over again. The plans were too ambitious, so they cut corners. Some of the columns and capitals are fake, and the "sculptures" lining the nave high above are actually *trompe l'oeil*—3-D paintings meant to look real. But some items, such as the marble frame around the main door, are finely crafted.

• *Leave the chapel, and walk straight down to the water—enjoying the sweeping views across to the Docklands. When you hit the river, turn right for the...*

Thames to Trafalgar Tavern Stroll—Wander east along the Thames on Five Foot Walk (named for the width of the path). Notice that the Old Royal Naval College is split into two parts; reportedly, Queen Mary didn't want the view from the Queen's House blocked. Looking up from the river, you'll see the college's twin-domed towers (one giving the time, the other the direction of the wind) framing the Queen's House, and the Royal Observatory Greenwich crowning the hill beyond.

Continuing downstream, just past the college, you'll find the **Trafalgar Tavern.** Dickens knew the pub well, and he used

it as the setting for the wedding breakfast in *Our Mutual Friend.* Built in 1837 in the Regency style to attract Londoners downriver, the tavern is popular with locals (and tourists) for its fine lunches. The upstairs Nelson Room is still used for weddings. Its formal moldings and elegant windows with balconies over the Thames are a step back in time. In addition to the casual pub, they also have an elegant ground-floor dining room (£6–11 pub grub; £6–8 starters and £11–17 entrées in restaurant; food served Mon–Sat 12:00–22:00, Sun 12:00–17:00, Park Row, tel. 020/8858-2909).

A mile downstream from the pub, the **O$_2$ Arena** (formerly the "Millennium Dome") languished for nearly a decade after its con-

troversial construction and brief life as a millennial "world's fair" site. Plans for a casino and hotel project fell through, although it has come in handy as an emergency homeless shelter. It was finally bought by a developer a few years ago and rechristened "The O$_2$" in honor of the telecommunications company that paid for the naming rights. Currently, it hosts concerts and sporting events, and will see action during the 2012 Summer Olympics. Whatever it's called, locals will no doubt continue to grumble about its original cost.

• *From the Trafalgar Tavern, walk two long blocks up Park Row, and turn right (through the gate near the corner) into the park. The palatial buildings in the middle of the park are the Queen's House and the Maritime Museum; the Royal Observatory Greenwich is on the hilltop beyond.*

Queen's House—This building, the first Palladian-style villa in Britain, was designed in 1616 by Inigo Jones for James I's wife, Anne of Denmark. All traces of the queen are long gone, and the Great Hall and Royal Apartments now serve as an art gallery for the National Maritime Museum. Predictably, most of the art is nautical-themed, with plenty of paintings of ships and sea battles, and portraits of admirals and captains. The Orangery is home to various Christ-like paintings depicting the death of Admiral Nelson—the naval hero who is so adored here in England's naval capital. Among these is the great J. M. W. Turner painting *Battle of Trafalgar,* his largest and only royal commission. The painting is often out on loan, so ask at the entry before you look for it (free, daily 10:00–17:00, last entry 30 minutes before closing, tel. 020/8858-4422, www.nmm.ac.uk).

▲**National Maritime Museum**—Great for anyone interested in the sea, this museum holds everything from a *Titanic* passenger's

pocket watch to the uniform Admiral Nelson wore when he was killed at Trafalgar (look for the bullet hole, in the left shoulder). A big glass roof tops three levels of slick, modern, kid-friendly exhibits about all things seafaring.

The Explorers exhibit covers early expeditions and an ill-fated Arctic trip, complete with a soundtrack of creaking wooden ships and crashing waves. One room displays stained-glass windows honoring members of London's Baltic Exchange (an important shipping consortium) killed in World War I. Kids like the All Hands and Bridge galleries, where they can send secret messages by Morse code and operate a miniature dockside crane. Along with displays of lighthouse technology, a whaling cannon, and a Greenpeace "survival pod," you'll see model ships, nautical paintings, and various salty odds and ends. Note that some parts of the museum are closed for renovation until 2012, though there's still plenty to see.

Cost and Hours: Free, daily 10:00–17:00, last entry 30 minutes before closing; look for family-oriented events posted at entrance—singing, treasure hunts, storytelling—particularly on weekends; tel. 020/8312-6608, www.nmm.ac.uk.

• *The final sight in town—the Royal Observatory—is at the top of the hill just behind the National Maritime Museum. To reach it, you'll cross through the colonnade connecting the museum and the Queen's House, then follow the crowds as they huff up the steep hill (allow 10-15 minutes).*

▲▲Royal Observatory Greenwich—Located on the prime meridian (0° longitude), the observatory is famous as the point from which all time is measured. However, the observatory's early work had nothing to do with coordinating the world's clocks to Greenwich Mean Time (GMT). The observatory was founded in 1675 by Charles II for the purpose of improving navigation by more accurately charting the night sky. Today, the Greenwich time signal is linked with the BBC (which broadcasts the famous "pips" worldwide at the top of the hour). A visit here gives you a taste of the science of astronomy, timekeeping, and seafaring—and how they all meld together—along with great views over Greenwich and the distant London skyline.

Cost and Hours: Free entry to observatory, daily 10:00–17:00, later in summer—can be as late as 20:00, courtyard sometimes open later than buildings, last entry 30 minutes before closing. Tel. 020/8858-4422, www.nmm.ac.uk.

Planetarium: Shows cost £6.50, last 30 minutes, and generally run every hour (usually Mon–Fri 13:00–16:00, Sat–Sun 11:00–16:00, fewer shows in winter, schedule can change from day to day). Confirm times by calling ahead, checking online, or picking up a flier (which you'll see around the observatory). As these shows can sell out, consider calling ahead to order tickets (see phone number above).

◑ Self-Guided Tour: As you hike up the hill to the observatory, look along the roof to see the orange **Time Ball**—also visible from the Thames—which drops daily at 13:00. Nearby, under the analog clock just outside the courtyard, see how your foot measures up to the foot where the public standards of length are cast in bronze.

Entering the observatory, you're directed to choose between two routes: The meridian route, to the right; and the astronomy route, to the left. Since the meridian route is more interesting, do that first.

Meridian Route: Following signs, you'll have the chance to rent an audioguide (£3.50, 1 hour), then enter the courtyard.

Running through the middle of this space is The Line—the **prime meridian.** Visitors wait patiently in line to have their photographs taken as they straddle the line in front of the monument, with one foot in each hemisphere. While watching all this fuss over a little line, consider that—unlike the equator—the placement of the prime meridian is totally arbitrary. It could well have been at my house, in Timbuktu, or

The Longitude Problem

Around 1700, as England's ships began to venture farther from their home island, the alarming increase in the number of shipwrecks made it clear that navigational tools had to be improved. Determining latitude—the relative position between the equator and the North or South Pole—was straightforward; sailors needed only to measure the angle of the sun at noon. But figuring out longitude, or their east-west position, was not as easy without a fixed point (such as the equator) from which to measure.

In 1714, the British government offered the £20,000 Longitude Prize. Two successful solutions emerged, and both are tied to Greenwich.

The first approach was to map the stars in the night sky over Greenwich. Then, sailors at sea could compare the stars overhead to the Greenwich map and calculate their east-west position. Visitors to the Royal Observatory can still see the giant telescopes—under retractable roofs—that were used to carefully chart the movement of the stars night after night.

The second approach was to create a clock that would remain completely accurate on voyages—no easy feat back then, when turbulence and changes in weather and humidity made timepieces notoriously unreliable at sea. John Harrison spent 45 years working on this problem, finally succeeding in 1760 with his fourth effort, the H4 (which won him the Longitude Prize). You can see all four of his attempts at the Royal Observatory.

So, how can a clock determine longitude? Every 15° of longitude equals an hour when comparing the difference in sunrise or sunset times between two places. For example, the time gap between Greenwich and New York City is five hours, which translates into a longitudinal difference of 75°. Equipped with an accurate timepiece set to Greenwich Mean Time, sailors could figure out their longitude by comparing sunset time at their current position with sunset time back in Greenwich.

Notice that both approaches use Greenwich as a baseline—either on an astral map or on a clock. That's why, to this day, the prime meridian and official world time are both centered in this unassuming London suburb.

just a few feet over—as, for a time, it was (the trough along the building's roofline shows where one astronomer had placed it). While waiting for your turn, set your wristwatch to the digital clock showing GMT to a tenth of a second.

Three different attractions are scattered around this courtyard. First, hiding in a corner is the **camera obscura.** This thrillingly low-tech device projects a live image from Greenwich onto a flat disc in a darkened room, simply by manipulating light, without electricity or machinery. Bizarre as this seems today, imagine how astonishing it was in the days before television.

The smaller building is the **Flamsteed House,** named for the first king-appointed Astronomer Royal (in 1675). It contains the apartments that he lived in, and the Wren-designed Octagon Room, where Flamsteed carried out some of his work. Downstairs is a fascinating exhibit on the "Longitude Problem" and how it was solved (see sidebar on previous page). Also on display are all four of John Harrison's sea clocks. Compared to his other contraptions, the fourth and final attempt looks like an oversized pocket watch. But, in terms of its impact, this little timepiece is right up there with the printing press, the cotton gin, the telegraph, and the money belt on the scale of human achievement.

Finally, the **Telescopes Exhibition,** in the larger house, has a wide assortment of historical telescopes, including a couple of room-sized ones.

• *Now head out back for the...*

Astronomy Route: Walk past the giant rusted-copper cone top of the planetarium. The building beyond houses the **Weller Astronomy Galleries,** where interactive, kid-pleasing displays allow you to guide a space mission and touch a 4.5-billion-year-old meteorite. You can also buy tickets for and enter the state-of-the-art, 120-seat **Peter Harrison Planetarium** from here (for details, see "Planetarium," earlier).

Before you leave the observatory grounds, enjoy the **view** from the overlook—the symmetrical royal buildings, the Thames, the Docklands and its busy cranes (including the tallest building in Britain, Canary Wharf Tower, a.k.a. One Canada Square), the huge O_2 Arena, and the square-mile City of London, with its skyscrapers and the dome of St.

Paul's Cathedral. At night (17:00–24:00), look for the green laser beam the observatory projects into the sky (best viewed in winter), extending along the prime meridian for 15 miles.

Eating in Greenwich

If you're in town on a weekend, be sure to drop by the **Greenwich Market,** which hosts a sprawling food court (Thu–Sun 10:00–17:30, directly in front of Cutty Sark DLR station). Another handy place to pick up ready-made food is **M&S Simply Food,** between the DLR station and the *Cutty Sark* dry dock (Mon–Sat 8:30–

21:00, Sun 10:00–21:00, 55 Greenwich Church Street, tel. 020/ 7228-2545).

The Trafalgar Tavern, described under "Sights in Greenwich" on page 202, is good (Mon–Sat 12:00–22:00, Sun 12:00–17:00, Park Row, tel. 020/8858-2909).

The Old Brewery, in the Discover Greenwich center on the Old Royal Naval College grounds, is an upscale gastropub decorated with all things beer. A brewery formerly on this site used to provide the daily ration of four pints of beer for pensioners at the hospital. Today it's a microbrewery offering 50 different beers, while a beer sommelier suggests the right pairings with food on the menu (£6–12 pub grub; part of the pub becomes a fancier restaurant in the evenings with £5–6 starters and £11–17 entrées; daily 10:00–23:00, lunch 12:00–17:00, dinner from 18:00, tel. 020/3327-1280).

Windsor

Windsor, a compact and easy walking town of about 30,000 people, originally grew up around the royal residence. In 1070, William the Conqueror continued his habit of kicking Saxons out of their various settlements, taking over what the locals called "Windlesora" (meaning "riverbank with a hoisting crane")—which later became "Windsor." William built the first fortified castle on a chalk hill above the Thames; later, kings added on to his early designs, rebuilding and expanding the castle and surrounding gardens.

By setting up primary residence here, modern monarchs increased Windsor's popularity and prosperity—most notably, Queen Victoria, whose stern statue glares at you as you approach the castle. After her death, Victoria rejoined her beloved husband Albert in the Royal Mausoleum at Frogmore House, a mile south of the castle in a private section of the Home Park (house and mausoleum rarely open). The current Queen considers Windsor her primary residence, and the one where she feels most at home. You can tell if Her Majesty is in residence by checking to see which flag is flying above the round tower: If it's the royal standard (a red, yellow, and blue flag) instead of the Union Jack, the Queen is at home.

While 99 percent of visitors just come to the castle and go, some enjoy spending the night. Windsor's charm is most evident when the tourists are gone. Consider overnighting here—parking and access to Heathrow Airport are easy, day-tripping into London is feasible, and an evening at the horse races (on Mondays) is hoof-pounding, heart-thumping fun.

Getting to Windsor

By Train: Windsor has two train stations—Windsor & Eton Central (5-minute walk to palace, TI inside) and Windsor & Eton Riverside (5-minute walk to palace and TI). First Great Western trains run between London's Paddington Station and Windsor & Eton Central (3/hour, 35 minutes, change at Slough; £8 one-way standard class, £8.50–11 same-day return, www.firstgreatwestern .co.uk). South West Trains run between London's Waterloo Station and Windsor & Eton Riverside (2/hour, 1 hour; £8.20 one-way standard class, £9–15 same-day return, info toll tel. 0845-748-4950, www.nationalrail.co.uk).

If you're day-tripping into London from Windsor, ask at the train station about combining a same-day return train ticket with a One-Day Travelcard as one ticket (£12–21, lower price for travel after 9:30, covers rail transportation to and from London and doubles as an all-day Tube and bus pass in town, rail ticket may also qualify you for half-price London sightseeing discounts—ask or look for brochure at station, or go to www.daysoutguide.co.uk).

By Bus: Green Line buses #701 and #702 run from London's Victoria Colonnades (between the Victoria train and coach stations) to the Parish Church stop on Windsor's High Street, before continuing on to Legoland (£1–9 one-way, £9.50–13.50 round-trip, prices vary depending on time of day, 1–2/hour, 1.25 hours to Windsor, tel. 01344/782-222, www.rainbowfares.com).

By Car: Windsor is about 20 miles from London, and just off Heathrow Airport's landing path. The town (and then the castle and Legoland) is well-signposted from the M4 motorway. It's a convenient first stop if you're arriving at and renting a car from Heathrow, and saving London until the end of your trip.

From Heathrow Airport: Buses #71 and #77 run between Terminal 5 and Windsor, dropping you in the center of town on Peascod Street (about £7, 1–2/hour, 45 minutes, toll tel. 0871-200-2233, www.firstgroup.com). London black cabs can charge whatever they like from Heathrow to Windsor (and do); avoid them by calling a local cab company, such as Windsor Radio Cars (£20, tel. 01753/677-677, www.windsorcars.com).

Orientation to Windsor

(area code: 01753)

Windsor's pleasant pedestrian shopping zone litters the approach to its famous palace with fun temptations. You'll find most shops and restaurants around the castle on High and Thames Streets, and down the pedestrian Peascod Street (PESS-cot), which runs perpendicular to High Street.

Tourist Information

The TI is adjacent to Windsor & Eton Central Station, in the Windsor Royal Shopping Centre's Old Booking Hall (May–Sept Mon–Fri 9:30–17:30, Sat 9:30–17:00, Sun 10:00–16:00; Oct–April Mon–Sat 10:00–17:00, Sun 11:00–16:00; tel. 01753/743-900, www.windsor.gov.uk). The TI sells discount tickets to Legoland (adults-£33, children-£23).

Arrival in Windsor

By Train: The train to Windsor & Eton Central Station from Paddington (via Slough) will spit you out in a shady shopping pavilion (which houses the TI), only a few minutes' walk from the castle. If you arrive instead at Windsor & Eton Riverside Station (from Waterloo Station), you'll see the castle as you exit—just follow the wall to the castle entrance.

By Car: Follow signs from the M4 motorway for pay-and-display parking in the center. River Street Car Park is closest to the castle, but pricey and often full. The cheaper, bigger Alexandra Car Park (near the riverside Alexandra Gardens) is farther west. To walk to the town center from the Alexandra Car Park, head east through the tour-bus parking lot toward the castle. At the souvenir shop, walk up the stairs (or take the elevator) and cross the overpass to the Windsor & Eton Central Station. Just beyond the station, you'll find the TI in the Windsor Royal Shopping Centre.

Helpful Hints

Internet Access: Get online for free at the **library,** located on Bachelors' Acre, between Peascod and Victoria Streets (Mon and Thu 9:30–17:00, Tue 9:30–20:00, Wed 14:00–17:00, Fri 9:30–19:00, Sat 9:30–15:00, closed Sun, tel. 01753/743-940, www.rbwm.gov.uk).

Supermarkets: Pick up picnic supplies at **Marks & Spencer** (Mon–Sat 9:00–18:00, Sun 11:00–17:00, 130 Peascod Street, tel. 01753/852-266) or at **Waitrose** (Mon–Tue and Sat 8:30–19:00, Wed–Fri 8:30–20:00, Sun 11:00–17:00, King Edward Court Shopping Centre, just south of the Windsor & Eton Central Station, tel. 01753/860-565). Just outside the castle, you'll find long benches near the statue of Queen Victoria—great for people-watching while you munch.

Bike Rental: Extreme Motion, near the river in Alexandra Gardens, rents 21-speed mountain bikes as well as helmets (£12/4 hours, £17/day, helmets-£1–1.50, £100 credit-card deposit required, bring passport as ID, summer daily 10:00–22:00, tel. 01753/830-220, www.extrememotion.com).

Windsor

TO HEATHROW AIRPORT & LONDON VIA M-4

ETONWICK RD.

ETON COLLEGE

HOME PARK (PUBLIC)

POST

ETON HIGH STREET

SOUTH MEADOW LANE

MEADOW LANE

ROMNEY LOCK ROAD

KING EDWARD VII AVE

THAMES R.

STOVELL

BARRY AVE.

ALEX. GDNS.

CENTRAL STN.

RIVERSIDE STATION

WINDSOR BRIDGE

THAMES

WINDSOR CASTLE

ST. JOHN PARISH CHURCH

ARTHUR ROAD

BEXLEY ROAD

CLARENCE ROAD

CHARLES

PEASCOD ST.

CASTLE HILL

ST. ALBANS ST.

POST

VICTORIA ST.

ST. MARK'S

ST. LEONARDS ROAD

ALEX-ANDRA ROAD

GROVE RD.

SHEET ST.

HOME PARK

KING'S ROAD

FRANCES ROAD

GOSLAR

ALMA ROAD

OSBORNE

ALMA ROAD

DCH

ROAD

LONG WALK

200 YARDS
200 METERS

N

Pedestrian Zone

P Parking

TO ROYAL WINDSOR RACECOURSE

TO PARK FARM B&B & LEGOLAND

TO ASCOT VIA A-332

1 Castle Tickets & Entry
2 Legoland Bus Stops (2)
3 Boat Trips
4 To Royal Windsor Racecourse
5 Mercure Castle Hotel
6 Langton House B&B
7 To Park Farm B&B & Legoland
8 Cornucopia Bistro
9 The Crooked House Teahouse
10 Wagamama
11 Saffron Restaurant
12 Grocery Stores (2)
13 Library (Internet Access)
14 Bike Rental

WINDSOR

Sights in Windsor

▲▲Windsor Castle

Windsor Castle, the official home of England's royal family for 900 years, claims to be the largest and oldest occupied castle in the world. Thankfully, touring it is simple. You'll see immense grounds, lavish staterooms, a crowd-pleasing dollhouse, an art gallery, and the chapel.

Cost and Hours: £16, family pass-£42, daily March–Oct 9:45–17:15, Nov–Feb 9:45–16:15, last entry 1.25 hours before closing, tel. 020/7766-7304, www.royalcollection.org.uk.

Tours: As you enter, ask about the warden's free 30-minute guided walks around the grounds (2/hour). They cover the grounds but not the castle, which is well-described by the included audioguide (skip the official guidebook).

Other Activities: The **Changing of the Guard** takes place Monday through Saturday at 11:00 (April–July) and on alternating days the rest of the year (check website to confirm schedule; ceremonies begin a little earlier—get there by 10:45). There is no Changing of the Guard on Sundays or in very wet weather. There's an **evensong** in the chapel nightly at 17:15—free for worshippers.

➲ Self-Guided Tour: Immediately upon entering, you pass through a simple modern building housing a **historical overview**

of the castle. This excellent intro is worth a close look—you're basically on your own after this. Inside, you'll find the motte (artificial mound) and bailey (fortified stockade around it) of William the Conqueror's castle. Dating from 1080, this was his first castle in England.

Follow the signs to the staterooms/gallery/dollhouse. **Queen Mary's Dollhouse**—a palace in miniature (1:12 scale, from 1924) and "the most famous dollhouse in the world"—often has the longest wait. If dollhouses aren't your cup of tea, you can skip that line and go immediately into the lavish **staterooms.** Strewn with history and the art of a long line of kings and queens, they're the best I've seen in Britain—and well-restored after the devastating 1992 fire. Take advantage of the talkative docents in each room, who are happy to answer your questions.

The adjacent gallery is a changing exhibit featuring the **royal art collection** (and some big names, such as Michelangelo and Leonardo). Signs direct you (downhill) to **St. George's Chapel.** Housing numerous royal tombs, it's a fine example of Perpendicular

Gothic, with classic fan vaulting spreading out from each pillar (dating from about 1500). The simple chapel containing the tombs of the current Queen's parents, King George VI and "Queen Mother" Elizabeth, and younger sister, Princess Margaret, is along the church's north aisle. Next door is the sumptuous 13th-century **Albert Memorial Chapel,** redecorated after the death of Prince Albert in 1861 and dedicated to his memory.

More Sights in Windsor

Legoland Windsor—Paradise for Legomaniacs under 12, this huge kid-pleasing park has dozens of tame but fun rides (often

with very long lines) scattered throughout its 150 acres. The impressive Miniland has 40 million Lego pieces glued together to create 800 tiny buildings and a mini-tour of Europe; the Creation Centre boasts an 80 percent-scale Boeing 747 cockpit, made of two million bricks. Several of the more exciting rides involve getting wet, so dress accordingly or buy a cheap disposable poncho in the gift shop. While you may be tempted to hop on the Hill Train at the entrance, it's faster and more convenient to walk down into the park. Food is available in the park, but you can save money by bringing a picnic.

Cost: Adults-£38, £34.20 in advance online, £33 from Windsor TI; children-£28, £25.20 online, £23 from TI; free for ages 3 and under; optional Q-Bot or Q-Bot Express ride-reservation gadget allows you to bypass lines (£10–40 depending on when you go and how much time you want to save); coin lockers-£1.

Hours: Convoluted schedule, but generally mid-March–July Mon–Fri 10:00–17:00, Sat–Sun 10:00–18:00, sometimes closed Tue–Wed in spring; Aug daily 9:30–20:00; Sept–Oct Thu–Mon 10:00–17:00, until 18:00 Sat–Sun, closed Tue–Wed; closed Nov–mid-March. Call or check website for exact schedule. Toll tel. 0871-222-2001, www.legoland.co.uk.

Getting There: A £4.50 round-trip shuttle bus runs from opposite Windsor's Theatre Royal on Thames Street, and from the Parish Church stop on High Street (2/hour). If day-tripping from London, ask about rail/shuttle/park admission deals from Paddington or Waterloo train stations. For drivers, the park is on B3022 Windsor/Ascot road, two miles southwest of Windsor and 25 miles west of London. Legoland is clearly signposted from the M3, M4, and M25 motorways. Parking is easy and free.

Eton College—Across the bridge from Windsor Castle you'll find many post-castle tourists filing toward the most famous "public" (the equivalent of our "private") high school in Britain. Eton was founded in 1440 by King Henry VI; today it educates about 1,300 boys (ages 13–18), who live on campus. Eton has molded the characters of 19 prime ministers, as well as members of the royal family, most recently princes William and Harry. The college is sparse on sights, but the public is allowed into the schoolyard, chapel, cloisters, and the Museum of Eton Life (£6.20, access only by one-hour guided tour at 14:00 and 15:15; tours available late March–Sept, usually Wed and Fri–Sun but daily during spring and summer holiday; closed Oct–late March and about once a month for special events, so call ahead; no photos in chapel, no food or drink allowed; tel. 01753/671-177, www.etoncollege.com).

Boat Trips—Cruise up and down the Thames River for relaxing views of the castle, the village of Eton, Eton College, and the Royal Windsor Racecourse. Relax onboard and nibble a picnic (£5.20, family pass-from £13, 40 minutes; mid-Feb–Oct 1–2/hour daily 10:00–17:00; Nov Sat–Sun hourly 10:00–16:00, closed Mon–Fri; closed Dec–mid-Feb; tel. 01753/851-900, www.frenchbrothers.co.uk). The same company also offers a longer two-hour circular trip (£8.40, 1–2/day).

Horse Racing—The horses race near Windsor every Monday evening at the Royal Windsor Racecourse (£9–23 entry, off A308 between Windsor and Maidenhead, tel. 01753/498-400, www.windsor-racecourse.co.uk). The romantic way to get there is by a 10-minute shuttle boat (£6 round-trip, www.frenchbrothers.co.uk). The famous Ascot Racecourse (described below) is also nearby.

Near Windsor

Ascot Racecourse—Located seven miles southwest of Windsor and just north of the town of Ascot, this royally owned racecourse is one of the most famous horse-racing venues in the world. Originally opened in 1711, it is best known for June's five-day Royal Ascot race meeting, attended by the Queen and 299,999 of her loyal subjects. For many, the outlandish hats worn on Ladies Day (Thursday) are more interesting than the horses. Royal Ascot is usually the third week in June (June 14–18 in 2011), and the pricey tickets go on sale the preceding November (see website for details). In addition to Royal Ascot, the racecourse runs the ponies year-round—funny hats strictly optional (regular tickets generally £10–20, online discounts, children 17 and under free; parking-£5–7, more for special races; dress code enforced in some areas and on certain days, toll tel. 0870-727-1234, www.ascot.co.uk).

Sleeping in Windsor

(area code: 01753)

Most visitors stay in London and do Windsor as a day trip. But here are a few suggestions for those staying the night.

$$$ Mercure Castle Hotel, with 108 business-class rooms, is as central as can be, just down the street from Her Majesty's weekend retreat (Db-£120–165, nonrefundable online deals, breakfast-£16, air-con, free Wi-Fi, 18 High Street, tel. 01753/851-577, www.mercure.com, h6618@accor.com).

$$ Langton House B&B is a stately Victorian home with three well-appointed rooms lovingly maintained by Paul and Sonja Fogg (Sb-£60, Db-£95, Tb-£115, Qb-£135, 5 percent extra if paying by credit card, lower prices during slow times, family-friendly, guest kitchen, free Internet access and Wi-Fi, 46 Alma Road, tel. 01753/858-299, www.langtonhouse.co.uk, paul@langtonhouse.co.uk).

$$ Park Farm B&B, bright and cheery, is convenient for drivers visiting Legoland (Sb-£65, Db-£85, Tb-£95, Qb-£105, ask about family room with bunk beds, cash only—credit card solely for reservations, free Wi-Fi, access to shared fridge and microwave, free off-street parking, 1 mile from Legoland on St. Leonards Road near Imperial Road, 5-minute bus ride or 1-mile walk to castle, £4 taxi ride from station, tel. 01753/866-823, www.parkfarm.com, stay@parkfarm.com, Caroline and Drew Youds).

Sleep Code

(£1 = about $1.60, country code: 44)

S = Single, **D** = Double/Twin, **T** = Triple, **Q** = Quad, **b** = bathroom, **s** = shower only. Unless otherwise noted, credit cards are accepted.

To help you sort through these listings easily, I've divided the rooms into three categories based on the price for a standard double room with bath:

$$$ **Higher Priced**—Most rooms £100 or more.
 $$ **Moderately Priced**—Most rooms between £60–100.
  $ **Lower Priced**—Most rooms £60 or less.

Prices can change without notice; verify the hotel's current rates online or by email. For other updates, see www.ricksteves.com/update.

Eating in Windsor

Elegant Spots with River Views: Several places flank Windsor Bridge, offering romantic dining after dark. The riverside promenade, with cheap take-away stands scattered about, is a delightful place for a picnic lunch or dinner with the swans.

Touristy Places around the Palace: Strolling the streets and lanes around the palace entrance, you'll find countless trendy and inviting eateries. **Cornucopia Bistro** serves tasty international dishes (£11 two-course lunches, £10–14 dinner entrées, closed Mon, 6 High Street). **The Crooked House** is a touristy 17th-century timber-framed teahouse, serving fresh, hearty £8–10 lunches and cream teas in a tipsy interior or outdoors on its cobbled lane (daily 10:30–18:00, 51 High Street). **Wagamama** offers modern Asian food, mostly in the form of noodle soups, in an informal and communal setting (£7–10 dishes, daily 12:00–23:00, on the left as you face the Windsor Royal Shopping Centre).

Ethnic Food along St. Leonards Road: Locals enjoy the vast selection of unpretentious little eateries (including a fire-station-turned-pub) just past the end of pedestrian Peascod Street. You'll also find a handful of ethnic eateries. **Saffron Restaurant** is the local choice for South Indian cuisine, with a modern interior and attentive waiters who struggle with English but are fluent at bringing out tasty dishes. Their vegetarian *thali* is a treat (open daily for lunch from noon, dinner 17:30–23:00, 99 St. Leonards Road, tel. 01753/855-467).

Cambridge

Cambridge, 60 miles north of London, is world-famous for its prestigious university. Wordsworth, Isaac Newton, Tennyson, Darwin, and Prince Charles are a few of its illustrious alumni. The university dominates—and owns—most of Cambridge, a historic town of 100,000 people. Cambridge is the epitome of a university town, with busy bikers, stately residence halls, plenty of bookshops, and proud locals who can point out where DNA was originally modeled, the atom was first split, and electrons were initially discovered.

In medieval Europe, higher education was the domain of the Church, and was limited to ecclesiastical schools. Scholars lived in "halls" on campus. This academic community of residential halls, chapels, and lecture halls connected by peaceful garden courtyards survives today in the colleges that make up the universities of Cambridge and Oxford. By 1350 (Oxford is roughly 100 years older), Cambridge had eight colleges, each with a monastic-type courtyard, chapel, library, and lodgings. Today, Cambridge has 31 colleges, each with its own facilities. In the town center, these grand old halls date back centuries, with ornately decorated facades that try to one-up each other. While students' lives revolve around their independent college, the university organizes lectures, presents degrees, and promotes research.

The university schedule has three terms: the Lent term from mid-January to mid-March, the Easter term from mid-April to mid-June, and the Michaelmas term from early October to early December. During exam time (roughly the month of May), the colleges are closed to visitors, which can impede access to all the picturesque little corners of the town. But the main sights—King's College Chapel and Trinity Library—stay open, and Cambridge is never sleepy.

If you're choosing between England's two university towns—Cambridge and Oxford—it's hard to go wrong. I prefer Cambridge as a town—it's cozier, more appealing, and very handy from London. However, Cambridge is not really on the way to anything, making it better as a side-trip than as a stopover. For convenience, you can't beat Oxford, which sits near the Cotswolds, Stratford-upon-Avon, and other major sights.

Planning Your Time

Cambridge is worth most of a day but not an overnight. Start by taking the TI's walking tour, which includes a visit to the town's only must-see sight, the King's College Chapel (first tour at 11:00, later on Sun, call ahead to confirm and reserve—see "Tours in Cambridge," later). Spend the afternoon touring the Fitzwilliam Museum (closed Mon), or simply enjoying the ambience of this stately old college town.

Getting to Cambridge

By Train: It's an easy trip from London and less than an hour away. Catch the train from London's King's Cross Station (3/hour, fast trains leave at :15 and :45 past the hour and run in each direction, 45 minutes, £20 one-way standard class, £21 same-day return after 9:30, operated by First Capital Connect, toll tel. 0845-748-4950, www.firstcapitalconnect.co.uk or www.nationalrail.co.uk). Trains also run from London's Liverpool Street Station—though more frequent, they take longer (4/hour, 1.25 hours).

By Bus: National Express coaches run from London's Victoria Coach Station to the Parkside stop in Cambridge (hourly, 2–2.5 hours, £11.50, toll tel. 08717-818-181).

Orientation to Cambridge

(area code: 01223)
Cambridge is congested but small. Everything is within a pleasant walk. There are two main streets, separated from the Cam River by the most interesting colleges. The town center, brimming with tearooms, has a TI and a colorful open-air market square. The train station is about a mile to the southeast.

Tourist Information
Cambridge's TI is well-run and well-signposted, just off Market Square in the town center. They book rooms for £5, and sell bus tickets, a £0.50 town map, and a bigger £1 map/guide (Mon–Sat 10:00–17:00, Easter–Sept also Sun 11:00–15:00—otherwise closed Sun, phones answered from 9:00, Peas Hill, toll tel. 0871-226-8006, room-booking tel. 01223/457-581, www.visitcambridge.org).

Arrival in Cambridge
By Train: Cambridge's train station doesn't have baggage storage, but you can pay to leave your bags at the nearby bike-rental shop (see "Helpful Hints," below). The station also lacks a TI, but it does have automated machines that dispense city maps for a £1 coin.

To get from the station to downtown Cambridge, you have several options. You can **walk** for about 25 minutes (exit straight ahead on Station Road, bear right at the war memorial onto Hills Road, and follow it into town); take a public **bus** marked *Citi1*, *Citi3*, or *Citi7* (£1.30, pay driver, runs every 5–10 minutes, get off at Emmanuel Street stop—look for Grand Arcade shopping mall on the left); pay about £5 for a **taxi;** or book a City Sightseeing **bus tour** (described later).

By Car: Drivers can follow signs from the M11 motorway to any of the handy and central short-stay parking lots. Or you can leave the car at one of five park-and-ride lots outside the city, then take the shuttle into town (free parking, shuttle costs £2.30 round-trip if you buy ticket from machine, or £2.60 from driver).

Helpful Hints
Festival: The **Cambridge Folk Festival** gets things humming and strumming (July 28–31 in 2011, www.cambridgefolkfestival .co.uk).

Bike Rental: Station Cycles, located about a block to your right as you exit the station, rents bikes (£8/4 hours, £10/day, helmets-50p, £75 deposit, cash or credit card) and stores luggage (£3–4/bag depending on size; Mon–Fri 8:00–18:00, Wed until 19:00, Sat 9:00–17:00, Sun 10:00–17:00, tel. 01223/307-125, www.stationcycles.co.uk). They have a second location near the center of town (inside the Grand Arcade shopping mall, Mon–Fri 8:00–19:00, Wed until 20:00, Sat 9:00–18:00, Sun 10:00–18:00, tel. 01223/307-655).

Tours in Cambridge

▲▲Walking Tour of the Colleges—A walking tour is the best way to understand Cambridge's mix of "town and gown." The walks can be more educational (read: dry) than entertaining. But they do provide a good rundown of the historic and scenic highlights of the university, some fun local gossip, and plenty of university trivia. For example, why are entering students called "undergraduates"? Because long ago, new students at Cambridge were assigned a B.A. to mentor them...so they were "under" the supervision of a "graduate."

The TI offers **daily walking tours** that include the King's College Chapel, as well as another college—usually Queen's College (£12.50, 2 hours, includes admission fees; July–Aug daily at 11:00, 12:00, 13:00, and 14:00, no 11:00 tour on Sun; Sept–June Mon–Sat at 11:00, 13:00, and another time—likely at 12:00, Sun only at 13:00 and possibly at 12:00; tel. 01223/457-574, www.visitcambridge.org). It's smart to call ahead to reserve a spot (they'll take your credit-card number), or you can drop by in person (if doing this, try to arrive 30 minutes before the tour). Notice that the 12:00 tour overlaps with the limited opening times of the Wren Library—so you'll miss out on the library if you take the noon tour.

Private guides are also available through the TI (basic 1-hour tour-£3.75/person, £55 minimum; 1.5-hour tour-£4.25/person, £62 minimum; 2-hour tour-£4.75/person, £70 minimum; does not include individual college entrance fees, tel. 01223/457-574, tours @cambridge.gov.uk).

Walking and Punting Ghost Tour—If you're in Cambridge on the weekend, consider a £5 ghost walk Friday evenings at 18:00, or a spooky £17.50 trip on the River Cam followed by a walk most Saturdays at dusk (20:00 in summer; book ahead for either tour, organized by the TI, tel. 01223/457-574).

Bus Tours—City Sightseeing hop-on, hop-off bus tours are informative and cover the outskirts, including the American WWII Cemetery. But keep in mind that walking tours go where buses can't—right into the center (£13, 80 minutes for full 21-stop circuit, cash only, departs every 20 minutes in summer, every 40 minutes

Cambridge

JESUS GREEN

MAGDALENE COLLEGE

200 YARDS
200 METERS

THE

NORTHAMPTON

BRIDGE OF SIGHS

ST. JOHN'S COLLEGE

WESLEY HOUSE

JESUS LANE

SIDNEY SUSSEX COLLEGE

WREN LIBRARY

TRINITY COLLEGE

HOSTEL

GARRET

SENATE HOUSE

CLARE COLLEGE

CHRIST'S COLLEGE

BUS STN.

DRUMMER

GREAT ST. MARY'S

MKT.

MARKET SQUARE

PETTY CURRY

POST

CHAPEL

KING'S COLLEGE

ST. EDWARD'S

GRAND ARCADE

EMMANUEL

To NATIONAL EXPRESS COACH STOP

BENET

WHEELER

CORN EXCH.

ST. TIBBS

QUEEN'S COLLEGE

CLOCK PARADE

ST. BENET'S

ANDREW'S

REGENT ST.

DOWNING COLLEGE

"MATH. BRIDGE"

SILVER ST.

MILL LANE

PEMBROKE

PEMBROKE COLLEGE

DOWNING

To TRAIN STATION (½ MILE)

SIDGWICK

PETER-HOUSE

LAUNDRESS GREEN

TRUMPINGTON ST.

To MUSEUM OF CLASSICAL ARCHAEOLOGY

RIVER CAM

FITZWILLIAM MUSEUM

To

DCH

NOTE: MANY ROADS ARE PEDESTRIAN OR RESTRICTED

CAMBRIDGE

- ☐ OTHER COLLEGES (NOT ALL SHOWN)
- P PARKING
- --- PATHS
- Ⓑ BUS STOPS
- VIEW
- BLDG. ENTRANCES

1. Hotel du Vin
2. To Lensfield Hotel
3. To Beckett B&B
4. The Eagle Pub
5. Michaelhouse Café
6. Café Carringtons
7. Marks & Spencer
8. Sainsbury's
9. Trinity Punt
10. Scudamore's Punts (2)
11. Bus From Train Station
12. Bus To Train Station

in winter, first bus leaves train station at 10:06, last bus at 17:46, recorded commentary, tel. 01223/423-578, www.city-sightseeing .com). If arriving by train, you can buy your ticket from their kiosk directly in front of the station, then ride the bus into town.

Sights in Cambridge

Cambridge has many impressive old college buildings to explore, with fancy facades and tranquil grassy courtyards. I've featured the two most interesting (King's and Trinity), but feel free to wander beyond these. You might notice several bricked-up windows on the old buildings around town. This dates from a time when taxes were calculated per window...so filling them in saved money.

▲**King's Parade and Nearby**—The lively street in front of King's College, called King's Parade, seems to be where everyone in Cambridge gathers. Looming across the street from the college is **Great St. Mary's Church,** with a climbable bell tower (£3, Mon–Sat 9:30–16:30, Sun 12:30–16:00, 123 stairs). The street out front is where students hawk punting tours on the Cam River (gener-

ally £12–15 for 45 minutes; described later, under "Punting on the Cam").

Behind the church is the thriving **Market Square**. The big market is on Sunday (9:30–16:30) and features produce, arts, and crafts. On other days, you'll find mostly clothes and food (Mon–Sat 9:30–16:00).

The imposing Neoclassical building at the top (north) end of the street is the **Senate House,** the meeting place of the university's governing body. In June, you might see green boxes lining the front of this house. Traditionally at the end of the term, students would come to these boxes to see whether or not they'd earned their degree; if their name was not on the list, they had flunked. Amazingly, until 2010 this was the only notification students received about their status. (Now they also get an email.)

In the opposite direction (south), at Benet Street, look for the strikingly modern **Corpus Clock.** Designed and commissioned by alum John Taylor, the clock was ceremonially unveiled by Stephen Hawking in 2008. It uses concentric golden dials with blue LED lights to tell the time, but it's precise only every five minutes; its otherwise-irregular timekeeping mimics the unpredictability of life. Perched on top is Chronophage, the "eater of time"—a grotesque giant grasshopper that keeps the clock moving and periodically winks at passersby. Creepy and disturbing? Exactly, says Taylor...so is the passage of time.

Just down Benet Street on the left is the **Eagle Pub**—Cambridge's oldest pub, and a sight in itself; it's worth poking into the courtyard to learn about its dynamic history, even if you don't eat or drink here (see page 227). Across the street from the pub stands the oldest surviving building in Cambridgeshire, **St. Benet's Church.** The Saxons who built the church included circular holes in its bell tower, to encourage owls to roost there and keep the mouse population under control.

▲▲**King's College Chapel**—Built from 1446 to 1515 by Henrys VI through VIII, England's best example of Perpendicular Gothic is the single most impressive building in town.

Cost and Hours: £5, erratic hours depending on school schedule and events; during academic term usually Mon–Fri 9:30–15:30, Sat 9:30–15:15, Sun 13:15–14:15; during breaks (see page 216) usually Mon–Sat 9:30–16:30, Sun 10:00–17:00. Tel. 01223/331-212, recorded info tel. 01223/331-155, www.kings.cam.ac.uk/chapel.

Evensong: When school's in session, you're welcome to enjoy an evensong service in this glorious space, with a famous choir made up of men and boys (free, Mon–Sat at 17:30, Sun at 15:30).

Getting There: You'll see the regal front facade of King's College along King's Parade. To enter the chapel, curl around the back: Facing the college on King's Parade, head right and take the first left possible (just after the Senate House, on Senate House passage); at the dead-end, bear left on Trinity Lane to reach the gate where you can pay to enter the chapel.

➋ **Self-Guided Tour:** Stand inside, look up, and marvel, as Christopher Wren did, at what was the largest single span of

vaulted roof anywhere—2,000 tons of incredible fan vaulting, held in place by the forces of gravity (a careful balancing act resting delicately on the buttresses visible outside the building).

While Henry VI—who began work on the chapel—wanted it to be austere, his descendants decided instead to use it to glorify the House of Tudor (of which his son, Henry VII, was the first king). Lining the walls are giant **Tudor coats-of-arms.** The shield includes a fleur-de-lis because an earlier ancestor, Edward III, woke up one day and—citing his convoluted lineage—somewhat arbitrarily declared himself king of France. The symbols on the left (a rose and the red dragon of Wales, holding the shield) represent the family of Henry VII's father, the Tudors. On the right, the greyhound holding the shield and the portcullis symbol-ize the family of Henry VII's mother, Lady Margaret Beaufort, who prodded her son for years to complete this chapel.

The 26 **stained-glass windows** date from the 16th century. It's the most Renaissance stained glass anywhere in one spot. (Most of the stained glass in English churches dates from Victorian times, but this glass is much older.) The lower panes show scenes from the New Testament, while the upper panes feature corresponding stories from the Old Testament. Considering their turbulent his-tory, it's miraculous that these windows have survived for nearly half a millennium in such a pris-tine state. After Henry VIII separated from the Catholic Church in 1534, many such windows and other Catholic features around England were destroyed. (Think of all those ruined abbeys dot-ting the English countryside.) However, since Henry had just paid for these windows, he couldn't bear to get rid of them. A century later, in the days of Oliver Cromwell, another wave of iconoclasm destroyed more windows around England. Though these windows were slated for removal, they stayed put. (Historians speculate that Cromwell's troops, who were garrisoned in this building, didn't want the windows removed in the chilly wintertime.) Finally, dur-ing World War II, the windows were taken out and hidden away to keep them safe and then painstakingly replaced.

The **choir screen** that bisects the church was commissioned by King Henry VIII to commemorate his marriage to Ann Boleyn. By the time it was finished, so was she (beheaded). But it was too late to remove her initials, which were carved into the screen (look for *R.A.*, for *Regina Anna*—"Queen Ann").

Behind the screen is the **choir** area, where the King's College Choir performs a daily evensong (see details earlier). On Christmas Eve, a special service is held here and broadcast around the world on the BBC—a tradition near and dear to the hearts of Brits.

Finally, walk to the altar and admire Rubens' masterful *Adoration of the Magi.* It's actually a family portrait: The admirer in the front (wearing red) is a self-portrait of Rubens, Mary looks an awful lot like his much-younger wife, and the Baby Jesus resembles their own newborn at the time.

▲▲**Trinity College and Wren Library**—More than a third of Cambridge's 83 Nobel Prize winners have come from this richest and biggest of the town's colleges, founded in 1546 by Henry VIII. There are three sights to see at the college: the entrance gate, the grounds, and the magnificent Wren Library.

Trinity Gate: You'll notice gates like these adorning facades of colleges around town. Above the door is a statue of **King Henry VIII,** who founded Trinity because he

feared that Cambridge's existing colleges were too cozy with the Church. Notice Henry's right hand holding a chair leg instead of the traditional crown jewels scepter. This is courtesy of Cambridge's Night Climbers, who first replaced the scepter a century ago, and continue to periodically switch it out for other items. According to campus legend, decades ago some of the world's most talented mountaineers enrolled at Cambridge... in one of the flattest parts of England. (Cambridge was actually a seaport until Dutch engineers drained the surrounding swamps.) Lacking opportunities to practice their skill, they began scaling the frilly facades of Cambridge's college buildings under cover of darkness (if caught, they'd be expelled). In the 1960s, climbers actually managed to haul an entire automobile onto the roof of the Senate House. The university had to bring in the army to cut it into pieces and remove it. Only 50 years later, at a class reunion, did the guilty parties finally 'fess up.

In the little park to the right, notice the lone **apple tree.** Supposedly, this tree is a descendant of the very one that once stood in the garden of Sir Isaac Newton (who spent 30 years at Trinity). According to legend, Newton was inspired to investigate gravity when an apple fell from the tree onto his head. This tree stopped bearing fruit long ago; if you do see apples, they've been tied on by mischievous students.

If you like, head through the gate into the...

Trinity Grounds: The grounds are enjoyable to explore, if not quite worth the cost of admission (£3, daily 9:30–17:00, last entry 45 minutes before closing, tel. 01223/338-400, www.trin.cam.ac.uk).

Inside the **Great Court,** the clock (on the tower on the right) double-rings at the top of each hour. It's a college tradition to take

off running from the clock when the high noon bells begin (it takes 43 seconds to clang 24 times), race around the courtyard, touching each of the four corners without setting foot on the cobbles, and return to the same spot by the time the ringing ends. Supposedly only one student (a young lord) ever managed the feat—a scene featured in *Chariots of Fire* (but filmed elsewhere).

The **chapel** (entrance under clock)—which pales in comparison to the stunning King's College Chapel—feels like a shrine to thinking, with statues honoring great Trinity minds both familiar (Isaac Newton, Alfred Lord Tennyson, Francis Bacon) and unfamiliar. Who's missing? The poet Lord Byron, who was such a hellraiser during his time at Trinity that a statue of him was deemed unfit for Church property; his statue stands in the library instead.

Wren Library: Don't miss the 1695 Christopher Wren-designed library, with its wonderful carving and fascinating original manuscripts (free, Mon–Fri 12:00–14:00, Nov–mid-June also Sat 10:30–12:30, always closed Sun; only 19 people allowed in at a time). Just outside the library entrance, Sir Isaac Newton clapped his hands and timed the echo to measure the speed of sound as it raced down the side of the cloister and back. In the library's 12 display cases (covered with cloth that you flip back), you'll see handwritten works by Sir Isaac Newton and John Milton, alongside A. A. Milne's original *Winnie the Pooh* (the real Christopher Robin attended Trinity College). If you just want to see Wren Library (without paying for the grounds), enter from the riverside entrance, located by the Garret Hostel Bridge.

▲▲Fitzwilliam Museum—Britain's best museum of antiquities and art outside of London is the Fitzwilliam, housed in a grand Neoclassical building a 10-minute walk south of Market Square. The Fitzwilliam's broad collection is like a mini-British Museum/ National Gallery rolled into one. The ground floor features an extensive range of antiquities and applied arts—everything from Greek vases, Mesopotamian artifacts, and Egyptian sarcophagi to Roman statues, fine porcelain, and suits of armor. Upstairs is the painting gallery, with works that span art history: Old Masters (such as Titian and Canaletto), a fine English section (featuring Gainsborough, Reynolds, Hogarth, and others), and a nice array of modern and contemporary art (including Picasso, Manet, and Renoir). Rounding out the collection are old manuscripts, including some musical compositions from Handel. Watch your step—in 2006, a visitor tripped and accidentally smashed three 17th-century Chinese vases. Amazingly, the vases were restored and are now on display in Gallery 17...in a protective case (free, suggested £3 donation, audio/videoguide-£3, Tue–Sat 10:00–17:00, Sun 12:00–17:00, closed Mon except Bank Holidays, no photos, Trumpington Street, tel. 01223/332-900, www.fitzmuseum.cam.ac.uk).

Museum of Classical Archaeology—Although this museum contains no originals, it offers a unique chance to see accurate copies (19th-century casts) of virtually every famous ancient Greek and Roman statue. More than 450 statues are on display. If you've seen the real things in Greece, Istanbul, Rome, and elsewhere, touring this collection is like a high school reunion..."Hey, I know you!" But since it takes some time to get here, this museum is best left to devotees of classical sculpture (free, Mon–Fri 10:00–17:00, Sat 10:00–13:00 during term, closed Sun, Sidgwick Avenue, tel. 01223/335-153, www.classics.cam.ac.uk/museum).

Getting There: The museum is a five-minute walk west of Silver Street Bridge; after crossing the bridge, continue straight until you reach a sign reading *Sidgwick Site*. The museum is in the long building on the corner to your right; the entrance is on the opposite side, and the museum is upstairs.

▲**Punting on the Cam**—For a little levity and probably more exercise than you really want, try hiring one of the traditional flat-

bottom punts at the river and pole yourself up and down (or around and around, more likely) the lazy Cam. Once you get the hang of it, it's a fine way to enjoy the scenic side of Cambridge. It's less crowded in late afternoon (and less embarrassing).

Several companies rent punts and offer tours. Hawkers try to snare passengers in the thriving people zone in front of King's College. Prices are soft in slow times—try talking them down a bit before committing.

Trinity Punt, just north of Garret Hostel Bridge, is run by Trinity College students (£12/hour, £40 deposit, 45-minute tours-£30/boat, can share ride and cost with up to 2 others, cash only, ask for quick and free lesson, Easter–mid-Oct Mon–Fri 11:00–17:30, Sat–Sun 10:00–17:30, return punts by 18:30, no rentals mid-Oct–Easter, tel. 01223/338-483). **Scudamore's** has two locations: Mill Lane, just south of the central Silver Street Bridge, and the less convenient Quayside at Magdalene Bridge, at the north end of town (rentals-£16–18/hour, £80 deposit required—can use credit card; 45-minute tours-£15/person; open daily June–Aug 9:00–22:00 or later, Sept–May at least 10:00–16:00, weather permitting, tel. 01223/359-750, www.scudamores.com).

Near Cambridge

Imperial War Museum Duxford—This former airfield, nine miles south of Cambridge, is nirvana for aviation fans and WWII buffs. Wander through seven exhibition halls housing 200 vintage aircraft (including Spitfires, B-17 Flying Fortresses, a Concorde, and a Blackbird), as well as military land vehicles and special displays on Normandy and the Battle of Britain. On many weekends, the museum holds special events, such as air shows (extra fee)—check the website for details (£16.50, show local bus ticket for discount, daily mid-March–late Oct 10:00–18:00, late Oct–mid-March 10:00–16:00, last entry one hour before closing; Concorde interior open Mon-Fri until 15:00, Sat-Sun until 16:00; tel. 01223/835-000, http://duxford.iwm.org.uk).

Getting There: The museum is located off A505 in Duxford. From Cambridge, you can take the bus marked *Citi7* from the train station (45 minutes) or from Emmanuel Street's Stop A (55 minutes, bus runs 2/hour Mon–Sat, www.stagecoachbus.com /cambridge). On Sundays and Bank Holidays, catch the #132 bus, run by private bus operator Myalls, from the train station or the Drummer Street bus station (40 minutes, first bus around 10:00, then every 2 hours until 18:00, tel. 01763/243-225).

Sleeping in Cambridge

(£1 = about $1.60, country code: 44)

While Cambridge is an easy side-trip from London, its subtle charms might convince you to spend the night. Cambridge has very few accommodations in the city center, and none in the tight maze of colleges and shops where you'll spend most of your time. These recommendations are about a 10- to 15-minute walk south of the town center, toward the train station.

$$$ Hotel du Vin blends France, England, and wine. This worthwhile splurge has 41 comfortable, spacious rooms above a characteristic bistro that offers good deals for guests and non-guests. This mod place manages to be classy yet unpretentious (Db-£120–150, fancier suites available, check online for special offers, optional £11 continental or £14 full English breakfast, air-con, elevator, pay Wi-Fi, just down the street from the Fitzwilliam Museum at Trumpington Street 15–17, tel. 01223/227-330, fax 01223/227-331, www.hotelduvin.com).

$$ Lensfield Hotel is a traditional, crank-'em-out hotel with 30 nicely appointed rooms (Sb-£65, Db-£99, pricier rooms also available, pay Wi-Fi, 53 Lensfield Road, tel. 01223/355-017, fax 01223/312-022, www.lensfieldhotel.co.uk, enquiries@lensfield hotel.co.uk).

$ Debbie and Michael Beckett rent one room in their modern home, next door to a big church halfway between downtown and the train station. The room, with a private bathroom on the hall, makes you feel like a houseguest (S-£45, D-£55, includes breakfast, 15 St. Paul's Road, tel. 01223/315-832, debbie.beckett2 @googlemail.com).

Eating in Cambridge

While picnicking is scenic and saves money, the weather may not always cooperate. Here are a few ideas for fortifying yourself with a lunch in central Cambridge.

The Eagle Pub, near the TI, is the oldest pub in town, and a Cambridge institution with a history so rich that a visit here

practically qualifies as sightseeing. Find your way into the delightful courtyard, with outdoor seating and a good look at the place's past. The second-floor windows were once guest rooms, back when this was a coachmen's inn as well as a pub. Notice that the window on the right end is open; any local will love to tell you why. Follow the signs into the misnamed "RAF Bar," where US Air Force pilots signed the ceiling while stationed here during World War II. Science fans can celebrate the discovery of DNA—Francis Crick and James Watson first announced their findings here in 1953 (£6–8 lunches, £6–11 dinners, food served daily 10:00-22:00, drinks until 23:00, 8 Benet Street, tel. 01223/505-020).

The **Michaelhouse Café** is a heavenly respite from the crowds, tucked into the repurposed St. Michael's Church, just north of Great St. Mary's Church. At lunch, choose from salads, soups, and sandwiches, as well as a few hot dishes and a variety of tasty baked goods (£5–10 light meals, Mon–Sat 8:00–17:00, breakfast served 8:00–11:00, lunch served 11:30–15:30, hot drinks and baked goods always available, closed Sun, Trinity Street, tel. 01223/309-147). Near the end of the day—after 14:30—you can pay £4 to fill your plate with whatever they have left.

Café Carringtons is a cozy cafeteria that serves traditional British food at reasonable prices, including a Sunday roast lunch (£6–8 meals, £5 sandwiches, Mon–Sat 8:00–17:00, Sun 10:00–16:00, down the stairs at 23 Market Street, tel. 01223/361-792).

Supermarkets: There's an **M&S Simply Food** at the train station and a larger Marks & Spencer department store on Market Square (Mon–Thu 9:00–18:00, Wed until 20:00, Fri 9:00–19:00, Sat 9:00–18:30, Sun 11:00–17:00, tel. 01223/355-219). **Sainsbury's** supermarket has longer hours (Mon–Sat 8:00–23:30, Sun 11:00–17:00, 44 Sidney Street, at the corner of Green Street).

A good picnic spot is Laundress Green, a grassy park on the river, at the end of Mill Lane near the Silver Street Bridge punts. There are no benches, so bring something to sit on. Remember, the college lawns are private property, so walking or picnicking on the grass is generally not allowed. When in doubt, ask at the college's entrance.

Cambridge Connections

From Cambridge by Train to: York (1–2/hour, 2.5 hours, transfer in Peterborough), **Oxford** (2/hour, 2.5 hours, change in London involves Tube transfer between train stations), **London** (King's Cross Station: 3/hour, 45–60 minutes; Liverpool Street Station: 4/hour, 1.25 hours). Train info: Toll tel. 0845-748-4950, www.nationalrail.co.uk.

By Bus to: London (hourly, 2–2.5 hours), **Heathrow Airport** (1–2/hour, 2–3 hours). Bus info: Toll tel. 08717-818-181, www.nationalexpress.com.

CANTERBURY

Canterbury is one of England's most important religious destinations. For centuries, it has welcomed hordes of pilgrims to its grand cathedral. While these days you'll probably see more iPods than Bibles in this college town, Canterbury's cathedral and medieval core still beckon with rich history and architectural splendor.

Pleasant, walkable Canterbury, like many cities in southern England, was originally founded by the pagan Romans. Then along came St. Augustine, sent by the pope to convert England's King Ethelbert of Kent to Christianity. Ethelbert (who had a Christian wife) joined the Church and allowed St. Augustine to set up a monastery on the edge of town. As Christianity became more established in England, Canterbury became its center, and the Archbishop of Canterbury emerged as one of the country's most powerful men.

The famous pilgrimages to Canterbury began in the 12th century, after the assassination of Archbishop Thomas Becket by followers of King Henry II (with whom Becket had been in a long fight). Becket was canonized as a martyr, rumors of miracles at the cathedral spread, and flocks of pilgrims showed up at its doorstep. Along the way, they'd stop off at inns and entertain each other with tales—sometimes bawdy and just for fun, sometimes devout and meaningful.

Today, much of the medieval city—heavily bombed during World War II—exists only in fragments. Miraculously, the cathedral and surrounding streets are fairly well-preserved. Thanks to its huge student population and thriving pedestrian-and-shopper-friendly zone in the center, Canterbury is an exceptionally livable and fun-to-visit town.

Planning Your Time

Because of its impressive cathedral, compact tourist zone, and relaxing break-from-a-big-city ambience, Canterbury is an ideal day trip from London. With more time, it merits an overnight. (You could even come straight from the airport to Canterbury and sleep here for two nights, with a day of sightseeing.) If visiting for a few hours, head straight for the cathedral, then spend the rest of your time strolling the town's pleasant pedestrian core, and maybe drop into some of Canterbury's other sights. Consider sticking around for an evensong in the cathedral (Mon–Fri at 17:30, Sat–Sun generally at 15:15).

Ambitious sightseers can fit both Canterbury and Dover (see next chapter) into a hectic one-day trip from London: Take an early train to Dover, taxi to Dover Castle, munch a picnic lunch on the train to Canterbury, tour Canterbury Cathedral, then enjoy the evensong and dinner in Canterbury before returning by train to London.

Orientation to Canterbury

(area code: 01227)

With about 45,000 people, Canterbury is big enough to be lively

but small enough to be manageable. The center of town is enclosed by the old city walls, a ring road, and the Stour River to the west. High Street (also known as St. Peter's Street at one end and St. George's Street at the other) bisects the town center. During the day, the action is on High Street and in the knot of medieval lanes surrounding the cathedral. (At night, the city is quiet all around.) The center is walkable—it's only about 20 minutes on foot from one end to the other.

Tourist Information

The TI, in front of Christ Church Gate, assists modern-day pilgrims. Pick up the free Visitors Guide with a map (Mon–Sat 9:00–17:30, Sun 10:00–16:00; 12–13 Sun Street, tel. 01227/378-100, www.canterbury.co.uk).

Combo-Ticket: The TI sells a "Canterbury Attractions Passport" that covers the cathedral, St. Augustine's Abbey, the

Canterbury

1. The White House
2. The Miller's Arms
3. Castle House
4. The Tudor House B&B
5. To Harriet House & Bike Rental
6. St. John's Court Guest House
7. Old Weavers House Rest.
8. Ask Restaurant
9. Wagamama & Morelli's Restaurants
10. The Canterbury Tales Pub
11. Marks & Spencer (Supermarket)
12. Farmers Market
13. Pure Magick Shop (Internet Access)

Canterbury Tales audio-visual show, and either the Roman Museum or another lesser sight. It's a good deal only if you plan to see everything (£20, saves about £3.25, sold only at TI).

Arrival in Canterbury

Canterbury's two train stations (East and West) flank the town center. Trains from London's Victoria Station arrive at Canterbury's East Station; trains from London's St. Pancras and Charing Cross stations arrive at Canterbury's West Station. Each train station is about a 10-minute walk from downtown. The bus station is at the end of the High Street pedestrian area, inside the city walls just past the big Whitefriars shopping center.

Helpful Hints

Guided Walk: Canterbury Tourist Guides offer a 1.5-hour walk departing from the TI (£6, July–Sept daily at 11:00 and 14:00, April–June and Oct daily at 11:00, walks also possible Nov–March—call or check website, www.canterbury-walks.co.uk, tel. 01227/459-779).

Internet Access: For patchouli-scented surfing, drop by the New Agey **Pure Magick** shop, which has three resident ghosts and two Internet terminals upstairs (£3/hour, Mon–Sat 10:00–17:30, Sun 11:00–16:00, on the main shopping drag at 43A St. Peter's Street, tel. 01227/780-000).

Shopping: A **Marks & Spencer** department store, with a supermarket at the back on the ground floor, is located near the east end of High Street (Mon–Sat 9:00–19:00, Sun 11:00–17:00, tel. 01227/462-281). Sprawling behind it is a vast shopping complex called **Whitefriars Centre** (most shops open Mon–Sat 9:00–18:00, Sun 10:00–16:00). A modest **farmers' market** is held every day except Monday at The Goods Shed (Tue–Sat 9:00–19:00, Sun 10:00–16:00), just to the north of the West Station, adjacent to the parking lot.

Bike Rental: Downland Cycles rents and repairs bikes (£15/day, helmets-£3, Mon–Sat 9:00–17:30, closed Sun; up the street from the West Station on Malthouse Road, just off St. Stephen's Road; tel. 01227/479-643, www.downlandcycles .co.uk). For a pleasant daylong ride in the countryside, ask for a map of the Crab and Winkle Way, a popular biking trail from Canterbury to the charming fishing village of Whitstable.

Sights in Canterbury

▲▲▲Canterbury Cathedral

This grand landmark of piety, one of the most important churches in England, is the headquarters of the Anglican Church—in terms of church administration, it's something like the English Vatican. It's been a Christian site ever since St. Augustine, the cathedral's first archbishop, broke ground in 597. In the 12th century, the cathedral became world-famous because of an infamous act: the murder of its then-archbishop, Thomas Becket. Canterbury became a prime destination for religious pilgrims, trumped in importance only by Rome and Santiago de Compostela, Spain. The dramatic real-life history

of Canterbury Cathedral is the tale of two King Henrys (Henry II and Henry VIII), and of the martyred Becket.

Cost and Hours: £8, Easter–Oct Mon–Sat 9:00–17:30, Sun 12:30–14:00, slightly shorter hours Nov–Easter, last entry 30 minutes before closing, tel. 01227/762-862, www.canterbury-cathedral.org.

Tours: Guides wearing golden sashes are posted throughout the cathedral to answer your questions. Guided £5 tours are offered Mon–Fri at 10:30, 12:00, and 14:30 (14:00 in winter); and Sat at 10:30, 12:00, and 13:30 (no tours Sun). At the shop inside the cathedral, you can rent a dry but informative £3.50 audioguide.

Evensong: The choral evensong is easy even for atheists. As you enter, they'll hand you a laminated placard telling you what to say for group responses, when to sit and stand, and when the music begins (free, Mon–Fri at 17:30, Sat–Sun generally at 15:15). Weekend schedules are subject to change, so it's smart to stop by or call to confirm (tel. 01227/762-862).

❍ Self-Guided Tour: Although guided tours and audioguides are available, it's simple just to wander through on your own.

• *Begin your tour in the pedestrian shopping zone just outside the cathedral grounds, by the TI. Before going through the passageway, take a moment to appreciate the...*

Christ Church Gate: This highly decorated gate is the cathedral yard's main entrance. Find the royal seals and symbols on the gate, including the Tudor rose. This rose was the symbol of Henry VIII, who—shortly after the Christ Church Gate was built—divorced both his wife and the Vatican, establishing the Anglican Church.

• *Go through the gate (where you'll buy your ticket) and walk into the courtyard that surrounds this massive, impressive church. Examine the...*

Cathedral Exterior: Notice the cathedral's length, and how each section is distinctive. The church was already considered

Thomas Becket and Canterbury Cathedral

In the 12th century, Canterbury Cathedral had already been a Christian church for more than 500 years. The king at the time was Henry II (who rebuilt and expanded nearby Dover Castle, described in the next chapter). Henry was looking for a new archbishop, someone who would act as a yes-man and allow him to gain control of the Church (and its followers). He found a candidate in his drinking buddy and royal chancellor: Thomas Becket (also called Thomas à Becket). In 1162, the king's friend was consecrated as archbishop.

But Becket surprised the king, and maybe even himself. Inspired by his new position—and wanting to be a true religious leader to his mighty flock—he cleaned up his act, became dedicated to the religious tenets of the Church (dressing as a monk), and refused to bow to the king's wishes. As tensions grew, Henry wondered aloud, "Will no one rid me of this turbulent priest?" Four knights took his words seriously, and assassinated Becket during vespers in the cathedral. The act shocked the medieval world. King Henry later submitted to walking barefoot through town while being flogged by priests as an act of pious penitence.

Not long after Becket's death in 1170, word spread that miracles were occurring in the cathedral, prompting the pope to canonize Becket. Soon the pilgrims came, hoping some of Becket's steadfast goodness would rub off (and perhaps wanting, too, to see the world—just like travelers today).

large in pre-pilgrim days, but in the 15th century, builders began another 100 years of construction (resulting in a patchwork effect that you'll notice in the interior).

• *Enter the church through the side door—the front doors of English cathedrals tend to be used only for special occasions—and pick up a map at the desk before you take a seat in the...*

Nave: The interior of the nave shows the inner workings of this sprawling, eclectic structure. Look around, and you'll see a church that's had many incarnations. Archaeological excavations in the early 1990s showed that the building's core is Roman. Through the ages, new sections were added on, with the biggest growth during the 1400s, when the cathedral had to be expanded to hold all of its pilgrims.

While tourists still flock here, this is also a working church, the headquarters of the Anglican Church, and the seat of the Archbishop of Canterbury. The current archbishop, Rowan Williams, has made headlines with his liberal and accepting views on homosexuality and the ordination of women, as well as his concern about Britain's involvement in the Iraq War. He's been quoted as saying that creationism should not be taught in schools.

• From here, we'll follow the route laid out by the map you picked up when you entered. Head up the left aisle. When you get to the quire (marked by a beautifully carved stone portal in the center of the nave), go down the stairs to the left. On the landing is the...

Thomas Becket Memorial: This is where Thomas Becket was martyred. You'll see a humble plaque and a wall sculpture of lightning-rod arrows pointing to the place where he died.

• Continue down the stairs next to the memorial and enter the...

Crypt: Notice the heavy stone arches. This lower section was started by the Normans, who probably built on top of St. Augustine's original church. Cross over to the other (right) side of the crypt. The small chapel marked *Église Protestante Française* celebrates a Mass in French every Sunday at 15:00. This chapel has been used for hundreds of years by French (Huguenot) and Belgian (Walloon) Protestant communities, who fled persecution in their home countries for the more welcoming atmosphere in Protestant England.

• Facing this chapel, turn right, walk to the end of the crypt, and climb up the stairs. At the landing, turn left to find...

St. Michael's Chapel: Also known as the Warrior's Chapel, this was built by Lady Margaret Holland (d. 1439) to house family tombs. The chapel is also associated with the Royal East Kent Regiment ("The Buffs"). Notice the bell on the wall to the left, which once rang from the HMS *Canterbury*, a ship that waged war against those disobedient colonists during the American Revolution. Each day at 11:00, the bell is rung and a prayer is said here to honor those who have lost their lives in battle.

*• Head up the stairs across from the tomb, and go through the ornate stone portal we passed earlier. This will bring you into the **quire**, where the choir sings evensong. Walk toward the high altar, then turn left through the gate and walk with the quire on your right to the far end of the church (the apse). Behind the quire, you'll see a candle in the center of the floor. This was the site of the...*

Original Becket Shrine: Beginning in the 12th century, hundreds of thousands of pilgrims came to this site to leave offerings. Imagine this site in the Dark Ages. You're surrounded by humble, devout pilgrims who've trudged miles upon miles to reach this spot. (Try to ignore the B.O.) Now that they've finally arrived, they're hoping to soak up just a bit of the miraculous power that's supposed to reside here.

Then came King Henry VIII, who broke away from the pope so he could marry on his own terms. In 1538, he destroyed the original altar (and lots more, including the original abbey on the edge of town). Dictatorial Henry VIII—no fan of a priest who would stand up to a king—had Thomas Becket's body removed from the cathedral. Legend says that Henry had Becket's body burned and the ashes scattered as part of his plan to drive religious pilgrims away from the site.

• *Adjacent to the shrine, in the apse, is the...*

Tomb of the Black Prince: This is the final resting place of the Black Prince, Edward of Woodstock (d. 1376). The Prince of Wales and the eldest son of Edward III, the Black Prince was famous for his cunning in battle and his chivalry—the original "knight in shining armor."

Our tour is finished. As you leave the cathedral, consider this: Even with all their power, wealth, and influence, two English kings were unable to successfully eradicate Thomas Becket's influence (if they had, the line to get into the cathedral would be shorter). A man of conscience—who once stood up to the most powerful ruler in England—continues to inspire visitors, nearly a thousand years after his death.

More Sights in the Old Town

▲**The Canterbury Tales**—If your visit to Canterbury gives you English Lit flashbacks, this corny audio-visual show offers a good review—or, if you're unfamiliar with Chaucer, it provides a decent introduction. Making use of creepy mannequins, primitive lighting effects, and medieval smells, it dramatizes five of the tales. More hokey than literary, the exhibit is useful as a CliffsNotes to Chaucer's masterpiece (£7.75, includes audioguide, daily 10:00–17:00, July–Aug from 9:30, Nov–Feb until 16:30, St. Margaret's Street, tel. 01227/454-888, recorded info tel. 01227/479-227, www.canterburytales.org.uk).

Roman Museum—The colorful displays in this slight museum illustrate Canterbury's Roman origins and end with a view of sections of still-intact foundations and mosaics. Included are several shamelessly self-congratulatory exhibits celebrating the museum archaeologist...nice touch (£3, Mon–Sat 10:00–17:00, in summer also open Sun 13:30–17:00, last entry one hour before closing,

The Canterbury Tales

*"Whan that Aprill, with his shoures soote
The droghte of March hath perced to the roote..."*

So begins *The Canterbury Tales,* one of the earliest and most influential works of English literature. In the late 14th century, author and diplomat Geoffrey Chaucer (c. 1343–1400) was so inspired by the cross-section of humanity undertaking the pilgrimage to Canterbury that he penned a collection of 24 tales told by fictional travelers. *The Canterbury Tales* is arguably the oldest surviving travelogue, and the greatest work written in the Middle English vernacular—a bold move at a time when Latin and French were the literary languages of choice. (Because Middle English is essentially a different language—see the first two lines, above—the work is most often read today in present-day English translation.)

Chaucer demonstrates an impressive range of themes and genres within these tales, ranging from tragedy to romance to humor. *The Canterbury Tales* is a microcosm of human experience, featuring yarns spun by people from diverse walks of life: knight, miller, cook, lawyer, wife, merchant, squire, physician, monk, nun. Despite their obvious differences, all of these travelers were drawn together by a shared faith and the desire to experience the power of the shrine of Thomas Becket...and by a mutual appreciation for a good story.

CANTERBURY

Butchery Lane, across from City Arms Inn, tel. 01227/785-575, www.canterbury-museums.co.uk).

East of the Old Town

While historically significant, these two sights—about a 10-minute walk east of the Old Town walls—aren't worth the trek for most visitors.

St. Augustine's Abbey—These ruins of the original abbey—founded by the man himself, St. Augustine—sit right on the edge of town. At its height, the abbey was a hive of activity, with a large church, cloister, and a cluster of service buildings for the monks. In the 16th century, King Henry VIII grew jealous of the wealth and influence held by England's monks, so he closed down the monasteries, retired the monks, and sold off the land and buildings. The abbey's buildings were converted to houses, while the large church was slowly dismantled and used as a building-material quarry for projects in the area.

Today, the site is dull even compared to other ruined abbeys. A modest museum sets up your visit. Outside, the foundations and some fragments of the original structures are still visible in a grassy field, and the uninspired audioguide struggles to bring the site to life. Pace the square of the cloister and imagine yourself as a monk in the early days of Christianity in England (£4.50, includes audioguide; April–June Wed–Sun 10:00–17:00, closed Mon–Tue; July–Aug daily 10:00–18:00; Sept–March Sat–Sun 10:00–16:00, closed Mon–Fri; sometimes closes at 15:00 for concerts, last entry 30 minutes before closing, tel. 01227/767-345, www.english-heritage.org.uk).

St. Martin's Church—Set in the center of an old, slanted grave-yard, humble little St. Martin's has the honor of being the oldest parish church in England. In continual use since 650, it sits on the foundations of a Roman temple, and features an elegant Norman-era baptismal font to the right of the entrance (free, generally open Tue, Thu, and Sat 11:00–15:00; tel. 01227/768-072). Because the church is run by volunteers, it has very sporadic hours, so call to confirm. To find the church, continue on the busy road 100 yards past the abbey, and turn down the first real road to the left (North Holmes Road); you'll see the churchyard's wooden entry gate from the main road.

Sleeping in Canterbury

Canterbury is a pleasant college town with lots of shops, restaurants, and pubs, making it a fine home base. There are relatively few options within the old walls, but I've listed my favorites. The roads heading out of town, particularly New Dover Road, have clusters of B&Bs that are slim on charm but suitable for tired drivers.

$$$ The White House is a classy and elegant B&B. Its seven recently renovated rooms, on a quiet residential lane just two blocks from the bustle of High Street, offer more modern flair than other Canterbury options in this price range (Sb-£60, Db-£80–105 depending on size, 6 St. Peter's Lane, tel. 01227/761-836, www.whitehousecanterbury.co.uk, info@whitehousecanterbury.co.uk, Adrian and Sharon).

$$$ Castle House, a 10-minute walk from the cathedral, has 13 spacious, inn-like rooms. It overlooks a major roundabout, but the double-glazed windows keep noise to a minimum (Sb-£75, Db-£80–95, family apartment-£97–140, free Wi-Fi, restaurant, free parking, 28 Castle Street, tel. 01227/761-897, www.castlehousehotel.co.uk, enquiries@castlehousehotel.co.uk).

$$$ The Miller's Arms offers 11 comfy rooms adjacent to a cozy pub and restaurant, on a quiet street across from the Stour River (Sb-£60, Db-£75–95, Wi-Fi, parking-£5/day, 1 Mill Lane, tel. 01227/456-057, www.millerscanterbury.co.uk, millersarms@shepherdneame.co.uk).

Sleep Code

(£1 = about $1.60, country code: 44, area code: 01227)
S = Single, **D** = Double/Twin, **T** = Triple, **Q** = Quad, **b** = bathroom,
s = shower only. You can assume credit cards are accepted
and breakfast is included unless otherwise noted.

To help you sort easily through these listings, I've divided
the rooms into three categories based on the price for a
standard double room with bath:

$$$ Higher Priced—Most rooms £80 or more.
  $$ Moderately Priced—Most rooms between £45-80.
   $ Lower Priced—Most rooms £45 or less.

Prices can change without notice; verify the hotel's
current rates online or by email. For other updates, see www
.ricksteves.com/update.

$$ The Tudor House B&B has seven slanted-floor, older-feeling, Victorian-wallpaper rooms in a 1600s home. Located in Canterbury's center, just two blocks from the cathedral, it has a garden with a river view (S-£35, Sb-£50, D-£59, Db-£69, T-£73-75, 6 Best Lane, tel. 01227/765-650, www.tudorhousecanterbury.co.uk, info@tudorhousecanterbury.co.uk, Mazi Gerogan and Mamad Arabnia).

$$ Harriet House, a 15-minute walk from the town center, offers seven tidy, small rooms with sophisticated decor (Sb-£45-50, Db-£65-70, family rooms available, pay Wi-Fi, some road noise, parking, 3 Broad Oak Road, tel. 01227/457-363, fax 01227/470-507, www.harriethouse.co.uk, enquiries@harriethouse.co.uk, Terry and Chris).

$ St. John's Court Guest House has an ideal location on a quiet street in the center of town. No-nonsense Liz Rowe rents eight basic but bright rooms (all with shared bathrooms down the hall) in a quaint brick building (S-£25-30, D-£45, T-£65, cash only, no young children, parking, St. John's Lane, tel. 01227/456-425, www.stjohnscourtguesthouse.co.uk, nigelnrw@aol.com).

Eating in Canterbury

As a student town, Canterbury is packed with eateries—especially along the pedestrianized shopping zone. However, many places serve only lunch, leaving options pretty thin for dinner. Of these listings, only Morelli's is closed for dinner.

Old Weavers House serves solid English food in a pleasant, historic building along the river. Sit inside beneath sunny walls and creaky beams, or outside on their riverside garden patio. This is the most atmospheric of my listings (£6–7 lunch specials, £10–18 dinner plates, daily 11:00–23:00, 1 St. Peter's Street, tel. 01227/464-660).

Ask, over a small bridge from Old Weavers House, is in a renovated home. This chain restaurant offers decent Italian food at moderate prices. The garden in back, while pleasant, lacks the Old Weavers House's river view (£8–12 meals, daily 12:00–23:00, big and splittable salads and pasta bowls, 24 High Street, tel. 01227/767-617).

Wagamama, part of the wildly popular British chain known for slinging delicious pan-Asian fare, has a convenient location just off the main shopping street (£7–13 entrées, daily 12:00–22:00, 7–11 Longmarket Street, tel. 01227/454-307).

Morelli's Restaurant serves typical soups, sandwiches, and "jacket potatoes" with take-away options. You'll find it above the recommended Wagamama on Longmarket Street, with glassy indoor seating or fine outdoor tables (£4–7 light lunches, daily 8:00–17:00, tel. 01227/784-700).

Pubs: **The Canterbury Tales,** across from the Marlowe Theater, has a relaxed living-room atmosphere, but serves no food (Mon–Fri 17:00–24:00, Sat 13:00–24:00, closed Sun, 12 The Friars, tel. 01227/768-594).

Canterbury Connections

Remember that Canterbury has two train stations, East and West.

From Canterbury by Train to: London (2–4/hour, 1–2 hours, some with transfers, trains run from Canterbury West Station to London's St. Pancras or Charing Cross stations, also from Canterbury East Station to London's Victoria Station), **Dover** (2/hour, 20–30 minutes, from Canterbury East to Dover Priory), **Rye** (hourly, 1 hour, from Canterbury West, transfer at Ashford International), **Hastings** (hourly, 1.25 hours, from Canterbury West, transfer at Ashford International), **Brighton** (1–2/hour, 2.25–2.5 hours, 1–3 transfers, can be complicated—best connections through London's St. Pancras or Ashford International, from Canterbury West). Train info: toll tel. 0845-748-4950, www.nationalrail.co.uk.

By Bus to: London's Victoria Coach Station (hourly, 2–2.5 hours), **Dover** (2/hour, 45 minutes). Bus info: toll tel. 0870-781-8181, www.nationalexpress.com.

DOVER AND SOUTHEAST ENGLAND

Dover—like much of southern England—sits on a foundation of chalk. Miles of cliffs stand at attention above the beaches; the most famous are the White Cliffs of Dover. Sitting above those cliffs is the impressive Dover Castle, England's primary defensive stronghold from Roman through modern times. From the nearby port, ferries, hydrofoils, and hovercrafts shuttle people and goods back and forth across the English Channel. France is only 23 miles away—on a sunny day, you can see it off in the distance.

Because of its easy access from the Continent, many travelers have a sentimental attachment to Dover as the first place they saw in England. But in recent years—especially since the opening of the English Channel Tunnel in 1994—this workaday town has lost whatever luster it once had. The run-down town center isn't worth a second look. Focus instead on a fun in-and-out visit to Dover's looming castle, standing guard as it has for almost a thousand years. Geologists and romantics may want to take a cruise to get the best view of the famous White Cliffs. (Or, for a more rural and idyllic white cliff experience, visit Beachy Head near Brighton—described on page 269.)

In the southeast English countryside near Dover, you can explore a castle and charming cottage garden at Sissinghurst; stroll the cobbles of the huggable hill town of Rye; and visit the Battle of Hastings site—in the appropriately named town of Battle—where England's future course was charted in 1066.

Planning Your Time

Dover works best as a day trip from Canterbury or London, and is worth a quick visit if you're passing through anyway. Ambitious sightseers can tackle both Dover and Canterbury as a one-day side-trip from London (see page 230).

Orientation to Dover

(area code: 01304)

Gritty, urban-feeling Dover seems bigger than its population of 30,000. The town lies between two cliffs, with Dover Castle on one side and the Western Heights on the other. While the streets stretch longingly toward the water, the core of the town is cut off from the harbor by the rumbling A20 highway (connecting Dover with cities to the west) and a long, eyesore apartment building. Unless you're taking a boat somewhere, or are interested in the goings-on of a busy industrial harbor, there's not much reason to visit the waterfront. Biggin Street is the town's nondescript, mostly pedestrianized shopping area, running between Market Square and Town Hall.

Tourist Information

You'll find the TI in the center of town, attached to the old jail. The TI sells ferry and bus tickets, and books rooms for a £4 fee (June–Aug daily 9:00–17:30; April–May and Sept Mon–Fri 9:00–17:30, Sat–Sun 10:00–16:00; Oct–March Mon–Fri 9:00–17:30, Sat 10:00–16:00, closed Sun; Old Town Gaol, Biggin Street, tel. 01304/205-108, www.whitecliffscountry.org.uk).

Arrival in Dover

Trains arrive on the west side of town, a five-minute walk from the main pedestrian area and the TI. **Drivers** find that parking is plentiful close to the water—just follow *P* signs. If you arrive by **boat** at the Eastern Docks, walk about 15 minutes along the cliff into town (with the sea on your left), or catch a shuttle bus to the train station (3/hour, daily 7:00–21:00).

Sights in Dover

▲▲Dover Castle

A powerful castle perches grandly atop the White Cliffs of Dover. English troops were garrisoned within the castle's medieval walls for almost 900 years, protecting the coast from European invaders (a record of military service rivaled only by Windsor Castle and the Tower of London). With a medieval Great Keep as its centerpiece and battlements that survey 360 degrees of windswept

Dover

400 YARDS
400 METERS

TO CANTERBURY
+ LONDON

TO WHITE CLIFFS VISITOR CENTRE BY CAR

A-2   A-258

LONDON ROAD

FRITH

CONNAUGHT   ROAD

CASTLE AVE.

MAISON

GOLDWYNE

RIVER   DOUR

HIGH ST.

LADYWELL

BIGGIN

UPPER   ROAD

CASTLE HILL ROAD

TASWELL

PIEU

PENCESTER

CANNON

ST.

CASTLE ST.

DOVER PRIORY TRAIN STN.

🛈 **9**

OLD TOWN GAOL

ROAD

FOLKSTONE B-2011

N. MILITARY RD.

YORK ST.

KING ST.

TOWNWALL

ST.

DOVER CASTLE
4
3
2
1
5

TO WHITE CLIFFS VISITOR CENTRE ON FOOT

EAST CLIFF

MARINE   PARADE

BUS STN. EUROLINES ONLY

7

6

BUS STN.

10

11

8

DOVER MUSEUM Ⓟ

EASTERN DOCKS

DROP REDOUBT

WESTERN HEIGHTS

GRAND SHAFT→ Ⓟ

AYCLIFFE   ROAD

DCH

WATERLOO CRES.

ESPLANADE

HARBOR

WHITE CLIFFS Boat Tours

HOVERPORT

WESTERN DOCKS

A-20 TO SAMPHIRE HOE PARK + FOLKSTONE

TO FRANCE (23 MILES)

⌃ CLIFFS
Ⓟ PARKING
⟳ ROUNDABOUT
- - - FOOTPATH
╱ STAIRS
↗ VIEW

Dover Castle
1 Visitors Centre, Parking & Admiralty Lookout
2 Roman Lighthouse
3 Henry II's Great Tower
4 Medieval Tunnels
5 Secret War Tunnels

Hotels & Restaurants
6 Churchill House
7 Amanda Guest House
8 Premier Inn Dover Central
9 La Scala Restaurant
10 The Eight Bells Pub
11 Market Square: The Ellie Pub & Dickens Corner

coast, Dover Castle has undeniable majesty. Today, the biggest invading menaces are the throngs of school kids on field trips, so it's best to arrive early. While the historic parts of the castle are unexceptional, the tour of the WWII-era Secret War Tunnels is unique and engaging. Until early June of 2011, some of the tunnels' lower levels will be closed for renovation. As a consolation prize for war buffs, other areas normally off-limits to visitors will be open during this period.

Cost and Hours: £14, £35 family ticket; April–Sept daily 10:00–18:00; Oct daily 10:00–17:00; Nov–Jan Thu–Mon 10:00–16:00, closed Tue–Wed; Feb–March daily 10:00–16:00; tel. 01304/211-067, www.english-heritage.org.uk/dovercastle. Arrive early for the fewest crowds (busiest on summer bank holidays and weekends). When you buy your ticket, ask for an assigned entry time for the included Secret War Tunnels tour—they fill up quickly in high season (generally 45–60 minutes, may be as short as 30 minutes during tunnel renovation, runs every 10–20 minutes but can be booked up for hours in advance—or sold out entirely by midday on very busy summer days, 20 people max, last tour departs one hour before closing). Your assigned time will be written on your entry ticket.

Getting There: Drivers follow signs from A20 or the town center. For those without a car, getting up to the castle is tricky. Bus #15 departs hourly from the bus station (on Pencester Road) and heads up to the castle. Otherwise, you can take a taxi from downtown (about £5 one-way) or hoof it up the steep hill (30–45 minutes straight up). By the time you get to the top, you'll know why no invading army ever successfully took the castle. The hike back down is easier, of course—ask for walking directions (using shortcut staircases) at the castle's Visitors Centre before you leave.

Getting Around the Castle: The sporadic and free "land train" does a constant loop around the castle's grounds, shuttling visitors between the Secret War Tunnels, the entrance to the Great Tower, and the Medieval Tunnels (at the lower end of the castle). Though handy for avoiding the ups and downs, the train doesn't run every day. Nothing at the castle is more than a 10-minute walk from anything else—so you'll likely spend more time waiting for the train than you would walking.

Background: A linchpin for English defense starting in the Middle Ages, Dover Castle was heavily used in the time of Henry VIII and Elizabeth I. After a period of decline, the castle was reinvigorated during the Napoleonic Wars, and became a central command in World War II (when naval headquarters were buried deep in the cliffside). Dover Castle was retired from active duty in 1984.

⊘ Self-Guided Tour: Start your tour of strategically located Dover Castle—considered "the key to England" by potential invaders—at the Visitors Centre. Here you can pick up a free map describing the sights, including the Battlements Walk—a great addition if time allows. Adjust the order of this tour based on your assigned time for the Secret War Tunnels.

• *Leave the Visitors Centre to the right, and walk around the officers' barracks to find a grassy slope overlooking...*

Admiralty Lookout: The White Cliffs of Dover are directly beneath you. Take in the superb view across the Channel. Can you see France from here? The statue is of British Admiral Sir Bertram Ramsay, who heroically orchestrated the "Miracle of Dunkirk" by rescuing hundreds of thousands of surrounded Allied troops from the French coast during World War II. You'll learn more about him in the Secret War Tunnels.

• *Backtrack past the Visitors Centre, and hike up the path through the guard tower. Emerging on the other side of the guard tower, look up the hill to your right. The round tower behind the flagpole is the oldest structure at the castle, the...*

Roman Lighthouse: The lighthouse *(pharos)* was built during the first century A.D., when Julius Caesar's Roman fleet for the colony of Britannia was based in the harbor below. To guide the boats, they burned wet wood by day (for maximum smoke), and dry wood by night (for maximum light). When the Romans finally left England 400 years later, the *pharos* is said to have burst into flames as the last ship departed. Adjacent to the lighthouse is the unimpressive St. Mary-in-the-Castle Church, built to guard against invading Saxons in the sixth century.

• *Pass through the archway and into the courtyard of...*

Henry II's Great Tower: The heart of this frontier fortress first beat in 1066, when a castle was built here after the Battle of Hastings (see page 254). In the 12th century, King Henry II (the bad guy in the Thomas Becket story—see page 234 in the Canterbury chapter) added heavy castle fortifications. For centuries, Dover Castle was the most secure fortress in all of England, and an important symbol of royal might on the coast.

Examine the central building, which was the original tower ("keep"). The walls are up to 20 feet thick. King Henry II slept on the top floor, surrounded by his best protection against an invading army. Imagine the attempt: As the thundering enemy cavalry

makes its advance, the king's defenders throw caltrops (four-starred metal spikes meant to cut through the horses' hooves). His knights unsheathe their swords, and trained crossbow archers ring the keep, sending arrows into foreign armor. Later kings added buildings near the keep (along the inner bailey, which lines the keep yard) to garrison troops during war and provide extra rooms for royal courtiers during peacetime.

Inside the keep, on the second floor, you'll find a sparse, kid-oriented exhibit (with sound effects) that gives a sense of what the castle was like in King Henry VIII's time. Find the well, which helped make the keep even more siege-resistant. Fans of Thomas Becket can look for his chapel, a tiny sacristy called the "upper chapel." If you're feeling energetic, climb all the way to the top of the keep's spiral staircase for a sweeping view of the city and sea beyond. Outside, back at ground level, you'll find the entrance to a somewhat silly 12-minute multimedia show that re-creates a 1216 siege on the castle.

• *After leaving the keep, walk a few paces across the courtyard to the...*

Garrison: This structure surrounding the keep once housed knights and men-at-arms. It's now home to the vaguely interesting Princess of Wales's Royal Regiment and Queen's Regiment Museum, a collection of military memorabilia (sorry, no Princess Diana items).

• *Exit the keep yard at the far end through the King's Gate. You'll cross a stone bridge and then descend a wooden staircase. Under these stairs is the entrance to the...*

Medieval Tunnels: This system of tunnels was originally built in case of a siege. While enjoyable for a kid-in-a-castle experience, there's actually little to see in these tunnels. From here, you can catch the tourist train (if it's running) or do the battlements walk. Much of Dover's success as a defendable castle came from these unique concentric walls—the battlements—which protected the inner keep.

• *There's one more thing to see, and it's the castle's undisputed highlight: the Secret War Tunnels. If the "land train" is running today, you can wait for it; otherwise walk (about 10 minutes total) along the inside of the castle's outer wall (with the wall on your right) and through the gate. Continue along the wall until you reach the entrance to the...*

Secret War Tunnels: In the 1790s, with the threat of Napoleon looming, the castle's fortifications were beefed up again. So many troops were stationed here that they needed to tunnel

into the chalk to provide sleeping areas for up to 2,000 men. These tunnels were vastly expanded during World War II, when operations for the war effort moved into a bomb-proofed, underground air-raid shelter safe from Hitler's feared Luftwaffe planes. Winston

Churchill watched air battles from here, while Allied commanders looked out over a battle zone nicknamed "Hellfire Corner."

To tour the tunnels, show your ticket with the entry time. The guided tour—which varies in length depending on crowds and which tunnels are open—usually takes you through the elaborate communications center, an underground hospital, and a command center, while re-creating the wartime atmosphere through sounds and even scents. The original furnishings and equipment have been restored. A 10-minute film at the beginning of the tour gives historical background, and a short film near the end tells you how the evacuation of the battlefield of Dunkirk was coordinated from the tunnels by Admiral Ramsay. Code-named "Operation Dynamo," the mission rescued some 338,000 Allied soldiers from Nazi-occupied France in nine days.

Other Sights in Dover

Dover Museum—This newly refurbished museum, right off the tiny main square, houses a large, impressive, and well-preserved Bronze Age boat unearthed near Dover's shoreline. The boat is displayed on the top floor along with other finds from the site and an exhibit on boat construction techniques (£3; April–Sept

Mon–Sat 10:00–17:30, Sun 12:00–17:00; Oct–March Mon–Sat 10:00–17:30, closed Sun; tel. 01304/201-066, www.dovermuseum .co.uk).

The Cliffs of Dover—The cliff called **Western Heights**—opposite Dover Castle, just outside of town—provides a sweeping view of Dover (and occasionally of France). The trail along the cliff weaves around former gun posts originally installed during Napoleonic times, but used most extensively during World War II. It was here that the British military amassed huge decoy forces in an effort to fool the Germans into thinking that a Dover-based attack was imminent. This fake-out maneuver was meant to disguise the plan for the Normandy D-Day invasion. Today, the bunkers are abandoned, but in decent condition. This is the place where you always wished you could play war as a kid...and with a little imagination, you still can. Peaceniks find it an excellent picnic spot. To drive to Western Heights, take A20 west past the harbor and turn right at the Aycliffe road.

For a different (and many say better) view from the cliffs, as well as a fascinating look at one of the world's busiest ports, head east of town to the **White Cliffs of Dover Visitor Centre**

(free, parking-£3, daily March–Oct 10:00–17:00, Nov–Feb 11:00–16:00, Upper Road, Langdon Cliffs, tel. 01304/202-756, www.nationaltrust .org.uk). You'll find exhibits about the cliffs and local flora and fauna, plus a handy café and ample space for picnicking. You can walk to the Visitor Centre from Dover (about
2.5 miles from the train station—just walk under the cliffs with the sea on your right, following footpath signs from the town center), or you can drive: Head up the Castle Hill Road, pass the castle entrance, then take a sharp right turn onto Upper Road. After crossing over the A2 highway, look for the Visitor Centre entrance at the next hairpin turn. If the first parking area is full, keep going—there are several.

If you have the energy, you can walk two miles along the cliff top from the Visitor Centre to the **South Foreland Lighthouse,** built in 1843, and enjoy the glorious view (£4, admission only with 30-minute guided tour, Fri–Mon 11:00–17:30, closed Tue–Thu except Aug and school holidays, last tour 30 minutes before closing, tel. 01304/852-463, www.nationaltrust.org.uk).

Samphire Hoe—This man-made park, less than two miles south of Dover, makes a good stop for those who wish to see more of the

white cliffs—without the industrial crush of the busy Dover docks. Samphire Hoe, a chalk meadowland beneath the cliffs, was created using more than six million cubic yards of chalk left over from the construction of the Channel Tunnel in the early 1990s. What could have been a dumping ground is now a grassy expanse hosting a rich variety of plants and wildlife. The park has walking paths and a tea kiosk, as well as a mile-long seawall that attracts anglers, wave watchers, and swimmers aiming for France (free, park open daily 7:00–dusk; tea kiosk daily Easter-Sept, weekends only in winter; tel. 01304/225-688, www.samphirehoe.co.uk).

Getting There: From Dover, drivers take A20 heading to Folkestone and watch for the Samphire Hoe exit. After waiting for the green light at the 007-style tunnel, you'll emerge at a pay-and-display parking lot. Walkers can follow the North Downs Way footpath, while cyclists can use the National Cycle Network Route 2; both are signposted from Dover—ask the TI for specifics.

Boat Tours—The famous White Cliffs of Dover are almost impossible to appreciate from town. A 50-minute Dover White Cliffs Boat Tour around the harbor will give you all the photo ops you need (£8, £20 family ticket, more expensive bus-and-boat combos available, July–Aug daily at 12:00, 14:00, and 16:00; Easter–June Sat–Sun only, Sept–Oct by appointment only, mobile 07971/301-379, www.doverwhiteclifftours.com).

Ferries to France—In the mood for a glass of wine and some escargot? A day trip to Calais, France, is only a short boat ride away (walk-on passengers generally £6–8 round-trip, about £30–75 with car, prices double on Sat, 1.25–1.75 hours). Several companies make the journey: P&O Ferries (toll tel. 0871-664-2121, www.poferries.com), SeaFrance (cars only—toll tel. 0871-423-7119, www.seafrance.com), and DFDS Seaways, which was formerly Norfolkline (cars only—to Dunkirk, 2 hours, toll tel. 0871-230-0440, www.norfolkline.com).

Sleeping in Dover

I'd rather sleep in Canterbury, but in a pinch, Dover has a variety of B&Bs spread throughout town (if arriving late at night, take a cab). The guest houses below can recommend another B&B if they're booked up.

$$ Churchill House, neatly run by Alastair and Betty Dimech, is comfortable and perfectly located, just at the base of the castle hill. With eight rooms, one with a four-poster bed, it's a traditional type of place (Sb-£35–45, Db-£50–80, 5-person basement apartment-£80–125, cash only, 6 Castle Hill Road, tel.

Sleep Code

(£1 = about $1.60, country code: 44, area code: 01304)
S = Single, **D** = Double/Twin, **T** = Triple, **Q** = Quad, **b** = bathroom, **s** = shower only. You can assume credit cards are accepted and breakfast is included unless otherwise noted.

To help you sort easily through these listings, I've divided the rooms into three categories based on the price for a standard double room with bath:

  $$$ Higher Priced—Most rooms £80 or more.
    $$ Moderately Priced—Most rooms between £65–80.
      $ Lower Priced—Most rooms £65 or less.

Prices can change without notice; verify the hotel's current rates online or by email. For other updates, see www.ricksteves.com/update.

01304/204-622, www.toastofdover.co.uk, toastofdover@gmail .com).

The homier **$ Amanda Guest House,** on one of the quietest streets in town, works best for drivers (Db-£60–66, cash only but reserve with credit card, easy parking, 20-minute walk from train station to 4 Harold Street, tel. 01304/201-711, www.amandaguest house.com, amandaguesthouse@hotmail.com, Mike and Anne).

Sleeping near the Waterfront: **$$ Premier Inn Dover Central** is handy to the ferry and cruise terminal, with dozens of identical, prefab rooms (Db-£51–71, sleeps up to 2 adults and 2 kids, check website for specials, breakfast-£5–8, restaurant, pay Wi-Fi, free parking, Marine Court, Marine Parade, toll tel. 0871-527-8306, toll fax 0871-527-8307, www.premierinn.com).

Eating in Dover

Your dining options in downtown Dover are few, and not worth writing home about. Consider having lunch at one of the castle's cafés or cafeterias.

La Scala is tiny, but in a romantic way, and serves a good variety of Italian dishes (£8–16 meals, Mon–Sat 12:00–14:00 & 18:00–22:00, Sun 18:00–21:00 except closed Sun Oct–May, 19 High Street, tel. 01304/208-044).

The Eight Bells, smoky and wood-paneled, is a huge pub that feels like a Vegas lounge. It has good beer and an excellent local reputation. Along with La Scala, it's one of two dinner options downtown (£6–9 meals, daily 7:00–23:00, kids OK before 19:00, 19 Cannon Street, tel. 01304/205-030).

Lunch Eateries on Market Square: Dover's main shopping square is surrounded by places for a quick lunch. **The Ellie,** a generic, modern pub at a convenient location (right next door to the Dover Museum), spills out onto Market Square (£4 sandwiches, £6 main dishes, open daily 10:00–24:00, food served 11:00–15:00 only, inviting outdoor seating on the square, tel. 01304/215-685). Across the square is the more genteel **Dickens Corner,** a comfy diner with a tearoom upstairs (£3–5 "jacket potatoes" and soups, Mon–Sat 8:30–17:00, closed Sun, 7 Market Square, tel. 01304/206-692).

Dover Connections

While the train will get you to most big destinations on the South Coast, the bus has better connections to smaller towns. Stagecoach offers good one-day (£5.50) or one-week (£19) tickets covering anywhere they go in south England (toll tel. 0871-200-2233, www .stagecoachbus.com).

The Dover train station is called Dover Priory. Most buses stop at the "bus station" (it's more of a lot) on Pencester Road in the town center. Eurolines buses stop at the Eastern Docks, near the ferries to and from France.

From Dover by Train to: London (hourly, 1 hour, direct to St. Pancras; also hourly, 2 hours, direct to Victoria Station or Charing Cross Station), **Canterbury** (2/hour, 20–30 minutes, arrives at Canterbury East Station), **Rye** (hourly, 1.25 hours, transfer at Ashford International), **Hastings** (hourly, 1.5 hours, transfer at Ashford International), **Brighton** (2/hour, 2.75–3 hours, transfer at Ashford International or London Bridge Station). Train info: toll tel. 0845-748-4950, www.nationalrail.co.uk.

By Bus: National Express (toll tel. 0871-781-8181, www.nationalexpress.com) goes to **London** (roughly hourly, about 3 hours) and **Canterbury** (2/hour, 45 minutes). Stagecoach (toll tel. 0871-200-2233, www.stagecoachbus.com) goes to **Rye** (hourly, 2 hours) and **Hastings** (hourly, 3 hours).

Near Dover

Sissinghurst Castle Garden

For a taste of traditional English gardening, this elegant home and well-maintained garden is worth seeking out. Vita Sackville-West,

socialite and lover of Virginia Woolf, purchased this castle and land in the early 20th century with her husband, diplomat-author Harold Nicolson. The two of them transformed the grounds into a beautiful English cottage garden. The gardens are laid out in sections, each with a theme, such as the Herb Garden and the Lime Walk. Every section feels like a small outdoor room. There is always something blooming here, but the best show is in June, when the famous White Garden bursts with fragrant roses. The castle, formerly a vast and grand affair, has disappeared for the most part, but a tower still stands. Inside are a few small exhibits, and—on the second floor—a series of illustrations that show the development, disintegration, and rebirth of the estate. At the top of the tower, you can survey the garden and orchard from up high. Inside the library wing, a portrait of Vita Sackville-West hangs over the fireplace, along with paintings of other family members, some of whom still live on the property.

Southeast England

Cost and Hours: £9.80, gardens open mid-March–Oct Fri–Tue 11:00–18:00 or until dusk, closed Wed–Thu, shorter hours for castle and library, café, tel. 01580/710-701, www.nationaltrust.org.uk/sissinghurst.

Getting There: Sissinghurst is about 55 miles west of Dover, off A262, near Cranbrook.

Rye

If you dream of half-timbered pubs and wisteria-covered stone churches, Rye is the photo op you've been looking for. A busy seaport village for hundreds of years, Rye was frozen in time as silt built up and the sea retreated in the 16th and 17th centuries, leaving only a skinny waterway to remind it of better days. While shipbuilding and smuggling were the mainstays of the economy back then, antique shops and expensive B&Bs drive business these days.

Rye is England's version of a hill town, packed with tourists trying to soak up some charm.

Arrival in Rye: As you approach town, notice the canal filled with boats. Follow it along to the old quays. The water line used to come up to this area, and the parking lot on Strand Quay would have been the wharf. Drivers should ignore the confusing *P* signs, which direct you to parking lots away from the town center—instead, try to squeeze into the small lot next to the Rye Heritage Centre (by the antique shops) or the larger one across the street.

Tourist Information: The TI is located at the top of the hill, just below the Church of St. Mary the Virgin (daily April–Sept 10:00–17:00, Oct–March 10:00–16:00, 4–5 Lion Street, tel. 01797/229-049, www.visitrye.co.uk).

Sights: Rye's sights try to make too much of this little town, but a stroll along the cobbles is enjoyable. Start at the **Rye Heritage Centre,** which has an impressive scale model of the town, presented in a 17-minute sound-and-light show (£3.50, every 30 minutes, if it's not running you can peek in at the model for free, daily April–Sept 10:00–17:00, Oct–March 10:00–16:00, town audioguide–£4, tel. 01797/226-696, www.ryeheritage.co.uk).

From near the Heritage Centre, Mermaid Street leads up into the medieval heart of Rye. Along this street (on the left), look for the **Mermaid Inn,** rebuilt in 1420 after the original burned down. Step inside and have a peek into Rye's heyday, or splurge for an expensive lunch (£20–24 fixed-price lunches, daily 12:00–14:30 & 19:00–21:30, tel. 01797/223-065). Today, it's a pricey upscale hotel—look for photos of recent celebrity customers just inside the door.

Continuing up Mermaid Street, jog right up West Street to Church Square. The old **Church of St. Mary the Virgin** has a pleasant interior and an 84-step tower you can climb for a country-side view (church—free, daily 9:15–17:15, shorter hours in winter; tower—£2.50, same hours as church but may close in bad weather; tel. 01797/224-935).

Beyond the square, you'll find a miniature castle called the Ypres Tower, housing the **Rye Castle Museum,** with a lookout tower and a modest collection of items from the town's past. Striking up a conversation with the museum's custodian, a lifelong resident, may be the museum's most interesting attraction (£3; April–Oct daily 10:30–17:00; Nov–March Sat–Sun 10:30–16:00, closed Mon–Fri; last entry 30 minutes before closing, tel. 01797/226-728, www.ryemuseum.co.uk).

Getting There: Rye is about 35 miles southwest of Dover

DOVER AND SE ENGLAND

on A259 (the route to Brighton). **Trains** connect to Rye from London (1–2/hour, 1.5 hours from St. Pancras Station, 2 hours from Charing Cross Station, transfer at Ashford International) and Dover (hourly, 1.25 hours, transfer at Ashford International). Stagecoach **bus** #100 provides a direct connection to Dover (hourly, 2 hours, toll tel. 0871-200-2233, www.stagecoachbus.com).

Near Rye: Compared to sugary-sweet Rye, modest **Winchelsea** feels like an antacid. Small, inviting, and just far enough away from the maddening crowd, the town makes a good stop for a picnic lunch. The grocery shop on the square sells all you need for a quiet meal on the little village green. Winchelsea is about three miles southwest of Rye on A259, toward Hastings.

▲Battle of Hastings Abbey and Battlefield

Located about an hour southwest of Dover by car, the town of Battle commemorates a fight no Brit can forget—the Battle of Hastings. In 1066, a Norman (French) king seized control of England, leading to a string of Norman kings and forever changing the course of English history and the English language. The battlefield and adjoining ruined abbey (built soon after the battle to atone for all the spilled blood) are worth ▲▲▲ to British-history buffs, but anyone can appreciate the dramatic story behind the grassy field. Ignore the tourists and take a journey back in time... these fields would have looked almost the same 1,000 years ago. Gaze across the unassuming little valley and imagine thousands of invading troops. Your visit can last from three minutes to three hours, depending on your imagination.

Cost and Hours: £7, includes audioguide, £17.50 family ticket, daily April–Sept 10:00–18:00, Oct–March 10:00–16:00, last entry 30 minutes before closing, children's play area, tel. 01424/775-705, www.english-heritage.org.uk/battleabbey.

Getting There: The town of Battle isn't on a major road, but **drivers** find that it's well-signposted from busy A259, whether you're coming from the east (Dover) or from the west (Brighton). There's a pricey £3 coin-op parking lot next to the abbey. Battle can be reached by **train** from London's Charing Cross or Cannon Street stations (2/hour, 1.5 hours), Hastings (2/hour, 15 minutes), or Dover (2–3/hour, 2–2.5 hours, 1–2 transfers). The entrance to Battle Abbey is at the south end of High Street; follow signs from the train station.

Background: The most epic of all of Europe's medieval *Lord of the Rings*–style battles took place on the most memorable date of the Middle Ages: October 14, 1066. The pivotal Battle of Hastings came about because the celibate King Edward the Confessor of England had died without an heir, and two nobles claimed the throne.

An Anglo-Saxon noble named Harold, Earl of Wessex, claimed that Edward gave him the throne on his deathbed. He was also chosen king by the traditional council, but support for Harold was weak. Meanwhile, across the English Channel, French-born William, Duke of Normandy, claimed that Edward had personally selected *him* as his successor. As the descendant of Vikings who'd once settled England, William claimed he had royal blood. His enemies called him William the Bastard because his mother was the former Duke of Normandy's mistress.

With the pope's blessing, William patiently gathered and trained a large army and sailed across the Channel. Harold raced south to meet him, his own army exhausted from battling enemies in the north. Near the town of Hastings in southern England, Harold assembled his troops into a wall atop the highest hill and waited for William.

Early in the morning on October 14th, the Norman soldiers trudged up the hill, and the battle was on. First, Norman archers rained arrows on the English. Next, foot soldiers on both sides

fought hand-to-hand. William's army began to retreat (a tactical maneuver, say the French). Seeing them flee, the English charged ahead, pursuing them down the hill. Suddenly, the Normans turned and attacked. Riding on horseback, the Norman soldiers were armed with a secret weapon: stirrups, which gave them a foothold to put force behind their lances.

The two sides fought a fierce 14-hour battle, with heavy casualties. Ultimately the Normans decimated the English force. In the battle's climactic finale, Harold was killed (supposedly by an arrow through the eye). William—now "the Conqueror"—marched on to London, where he was crowned King of England in Westminster Abbey on Christmas Day, 1066. William commemorated the dead by building an abbey on the spot of the decisive battle.

The Norman Conquest of England propelled the isolated isle of Britain into the European mainstream. William centralized the government and imported the Romanesque style of architecture—seen at places such as the White Tower at the Tower of London, and Durham Cathedral. The English call this style "Norman." Historians speculate that, were it not for the stirrup, England would have remained on the fringe of Europe (like Scandinavia), French culture and language would have prevailed in the New World...and you'd be reading this book today in French. *Sacré bleu!*

William's conquest also muddied the political waters, setting in motion 400 years of conflict between England and France that would not be resolved until the end of the Hundred Years' War, in 1453.

Visiting the Abbey and Battlefield: A small museum, battle-ground overlook, and remaining Battle Abbey buildings illuminate the historical significance of the Battle of Hastings. After buying your ticket and picking up the essential, included audioguide, head to the nearby Visitors Centre to watch an excellent 15-minute film that recounts the story of the battle, with animated scenes from the famous Bayeux Tapestry (pic-tured on previous page) and impressive live-action reenactments. Also in the center are replicas of weapons used by the fighters—lift them to appreciate how the Brits invented heavy metal long before Led Zeppelin.

Then head outside, where you have two choices with your audioguide: Follow the short tour along a terrace overlooking the battlefield (about 15 minutes), or take the longer version out through the woods and actually across the fateful field (about 40 minutes). With sound effects and a witty but not corny commentary, the audioguide really injects some life into the site. Finally, you'll wind up at the remains of the abbey, where the audioguide relates details of monastic lifestyles. It's interesting and a bit more intact than many other ruined abbeys, but it pales in comparison to the drama of the battle. Walking back to the entrance, you'll notice that the abbey's former Great Hall now houses another famous English institution—a private school.

Eating in Battle: The **Pilgrims Restaurant,** across the street from the abbey, is an atmospherically crooked half-timbered house serving decent but pricey food with outdoor terrace seating (£7-10 soups, sandwiches, and salads, open daily 9:15–17:30, 1 High Street, tel. 01424/772-314).

BRIGHTON

Brighton—brash and flamboyant, with a carnival flair—is refreshing if you're suffering from an excess of doilies and museums. The city boasts a garish 19th-century Royal Pavilion, a loud and flashy carnival pier, England's most thriving gay community, and a long stretch of cobbled beach. It's no wonder that youthful bohemians and blue-collar Londoners alike make this town their holiday destination of choice.

In the 1790s, with Napoleon's armies running rampant on the Continent, aristocrats could no longer travel abroad on a traditional "Grand Tour" of Europe. King George IV chose the village of Brighthelmstone to build a vacation palace for himself, and royal followers began a frenzy of construction on the seashore. Soon this once-sleepy seaside village was transformed into an elegant resort town. With the rise of train travel, connections to London became quick and cheap, making Brighton an inviting getaway for working-class Londoners.

The countryside near Brighton is packed with tempting sights and worthwhile stopovers for drivers. Go for a walk on the South Downs Way, lick an ice-cream cone in the postcard-pretty village of Alfriston, visit the best white cliffs in England at Beachy Head, and explore the evocative ruins of a Roman fort at Pevensey.

Planning Your Time

Brighton's sights—its Royal Pavilion, Museum and Art Gallery, and pleasure pier—can be seen in just a few hours, making this a doable day trip from London. If you've got a full day and a car, spend the rest of your day heading for Alfriston and Beachy Head.

Debating between Brighton and Portsmouth? Younger, hipper travelers are more likely to be turned on by lively Brighton, while older, more conservative visitors might prefer traditional Portsmouth (see next chapter). Either destination works as an easy day trip from London, but with more time, visiting both is a great plan.

Orientation to Brighton

(area code: 01273)

Brighton is big, with 160,000 people. It feels surprisingly urban for a seaside resort—like the Nice of England. Most tourists focus on the area near the waterfront. The heart of Brighton is the Brighton Pier and, several blocks inland, the Royal Pavilion. Between these two landmarks is the twisty old center of town called The Lanes, with good restaurants and lots of shopping. North of The Lanes and past the Royal Pavilion is the popular, recently revived neighborhood of North Laine, with more shopping and eateries, plus occasional street-music performances. The best accommodations cluster to the east of The Lanes, within a block of the seafront, in the colorful neighborhood called Kemptown.

Tourist Information

The TI is in the Royal Pavilion's gift shop. Pick up the free, good color map of Brighton. They also book rooms (£1.50/person) and sell tickets to various sights and theater productions (Mon–Sat 10:00–17:00, Sun 10:00–16:00, maybe slightly shorter hours off-season, you'll pay a greedy 50p/minute to climb through their phone tree at tel. 0300-300-0088, www.visitbrighton.com).

A walking-tour audioguide of Brighton is available for download to your iPod or other MP3 player (£6, www.coolcitywalks.com).

Arrival in Brighton

Trains arrive at Brighton Station, a 15-minute walk from the center. Drivers on A23 enter town on the tree-lined Grand Parade, which goes straight to the water (ending near Brighton Pier). Parking is tricky: Signs will lead you to parking garages near the center, but if you're staying the night, ask your hotelier for the best place to leave your car.

Helpful Hints

Crowd Control: Brighton can overflow with visitors in summer and on weekends. The Brighton Festival (May) and the Summer LGBT Pride Festival (first week of Aug) are the busiest times. Off-season (roughly Oct–March), visitors may

BRIGHTON

Brighton

P PARKING
PEDESTRIAN ZONE

100 YARDS
100 METERS

N

TERMINUS ROAD
TRAIN STATION
TO A-23, GATWICK AIRPORT & LONDON
TO A-27, LEWES & EASTBOURNE

CHEAPSIDE
TRAFALGAR STREET
SURREY
GLOUCESTER ROAD
YORK PLACE
GLOUCESTER PL.
RICHMOND PL.
ALBION HILL

NORTH LAINE
QUEEN'S ROAD
NORTH ROAD
GRAND PARADE
ASHTON RISE
MORLEY
LULL STREET

DYKE ROAD
WINDSOR
PORTLAND
CHURCH STREET
MARLBOROUGH PL.
KINGSWOOD
JOHN
SUSSEX ST.
CARLTON

NORTH ST.
BOND ST.
NEW RD.
BRIGHTON MUSEUM & ART GALLERY
BLAKER

TO WEST PIER RUINS
WEST STREET
DUKE ST.
SHIP ST.
DUKE
MIDDLE ST.
SOUTH ST.
HOUSE LN.
ALBERT ST.
ST. BART.
MARKET
CASTLE SQ.
POST
ROYAL PAVILION
EDWARD STREET
HIGH ST.
KEMPTOWN

THE LANES
KING'S ROAD
GRAND JUNCTION ROAD
EAST ST.
POOL VALLEY
OLD STEINE
BROAD ST.
MADEIRA PL.
JAMES'S ST.
MANCHESTER
NEW
ROCK
TO

BEACH
MARINE PARADE
MADEIRA DR.
VOLK'S ELECTRIC RAILWAY
BEACH
DCH

BRIGHTON PIER

ENGLISH   CHANNEL

1 New Steine Street B&Bs
2 Kempfield House
3 St. Christopher's Inn
4 English's of Brighton
5 Terre à Terre Veggie Rest.
6 Market Street Eateries
7 Bill's Produce Store
8 Cornish Pasties
9 Our Cornish Pasty Shop
10 Wagamama
11 Yo! Sushi
12 La Capannina
13 Launderette
14 To Bike Rental

BRIGHTON

find the city quiet, prices slashed, and attractions shuttered.

Laundry: St. James's Laundry is in Kemptown, near my recommended accommodations (self-service open daily 7:30–21:00, last wash 19:30, or drop-off Mon–Fri 8:30–14:00 for same-day full-service, 53 St. James's Street, tel. 01273/672-395).

Bike Rental: The TI hands out a good, free cycle map listing several rental places. The largest is **Go Cycle Bike Hire,** located 1.5 miles east of my recommended B&Bs at the Brighton Marina (£12/4 hours, £17.50/8 hours, £50 deposit, picture ID required, Mon–Fri 10:30–17:00, Sat–Sun 9:30–17:00, call first in bad weather, catch bus #7 eastbound on St. James's Street to Unit 22, Brighton Marina, tel. 01273/697-104, mobile 01273/697-104, www.gocyclebikehire.com).

Getting Around Brighton

Brighton's well-run bus system is handy, especially if you're staying in one of my recommended guest houses on Kemptown's New Steine Street (£1.50/ride, £3.60 CitySaver day pass; buy from driver, at TI, or online for slight discount; tel. 01273/886-200, www.buses.co.uk).

Sights in Brighton

▲▲**Brighton Royal Pavilion**—Famous for his scandalous secret marriage to Catholic widow Mrs. Fitzherbert, King George IV was lively, decadent, and trendsetting. He loved to vacation by the sea and host glamorous dinner parties. George was enamored with Asian cultures, styling his vacation home with exotic decorations from the East. The result is colorful and exuberant...some would say gaudy. Like Brighton itself, the place smacks of faded elegance— but it's fun to tour. It's free to enter the restored Regency gardens surrounding the Pavilion, and the nearby Brighton Museum and Art Gallery (described later).

Cost and Hours: £9.50, includes audioguide, daily April–Sept 9:30–17:45, Oct–March 10:00–17:15, last entry 45 minutes before closing; head up East Street from The Lanes, bus stop on Old Steine Road; toll tel. 0300-029-0900, www.royalpavilion.org.uk. If there's a line to buy tickets, dip into the TI (at the gift shop next door) and purchase them for the same price.

❍ **Self-Guided Tour:** Pick up the free and informative audioguide as you enter. It'll tell you more about these highlights (and other points of interest) along the one-way route.

While George planned the palace as a royal holiday residence, it was used mainly as a party pad to entertain guests. They'd be suitably impressed by the grand **Long Gallery.** Here and throughout the Pavilion, examine the fine detail work—such as the "bamboo" stairway decoration that's actually carved from wood.

If guests were impressed by the Long Gallery, they were blown away by the **Banqueting Room.** Imagine England's elite nibbling crumpets under the one-ton chandelier...with its dragons exhaling light through lotus-shaped shades. Notice that the ornate table is permanently set for the dessert course.

The elaborate **Kitchen** was one of the most innovative of its time. Smoke from the fireplace rotated a huge rotisserie that could cook enough meat to feed a hundred hungry diners. The king was so particular about his food that he insisted his kitchen be attached to the dining room (unheard-of at the time). He also had a warming table built to keep food at the optimum temperature.

Head through the gallery and salon into a room dedicated to George's true passion: music. In the massive **Music Room,** the royal band serenaded guests. Take a moment to appreciate the Chinese-inspired decor here and throughout the palace. Known as *chinoiserie,* it was the height of fashion in those days.

The **Private Apartments** were on the ground floor, to more easily accommodate the ailing king (who spent less and less time here near the end of his life). Note that this space is more intimate and cozy than the showpiece halls we've seen elsewhere. (If you're intrigued by all this, dip into the dry but informative 18-minute film about the Pavilion's history.)

Continuing upstairs, you'll stroll through the restored **Yellow Bow Rooms,** then **Queen Victoria's Apartments,** where you'll learn the epilogue to the story of George's party palace. George was a big spender, piling up huge debts. No expense was spared. Prudish Queen Victoria, who took the throne seven years after George's death, wanted more privacy than the Pavilion provided and scorned the excesses in George's court—so she quickly offloaded the decadent Pavilion to the local town council (which still owns it today). Only recently did Queen Elizabeth II bring the original furniture out of storage and loan it to the Pavilion.

Brighton Museum and Art Gallery—This gallery, similar to the Victoria and Albert Museum in London, displays decorative arts with a heavy focus on 20th-century art and design. The modern pseudo-kitsch includes the Dalí-inspired *Mae West Lips Sofa* and Frank Gehry's *Wiggle Chair.* The café above the gallery has a pleasant view of the action (free, Tue–Sun 10:00–17:00, closed Mon except holidays, just north of the Royal Pavilion, tel. 03000-290-900, www.virtualmuseum.info).

Brighton Pier—Glittering and shiny with amusement rides and carnival games, Brighton Pier is *the* place to go for a fix of "candy floss" (cotton candy), fortune-tell-

ers, and tacky souvenirs. The pier, opened in 1899 and long known as Palace Pier, has gone in and out of fashion; in recent years, it's come back to life, thanks to a restoration. The main pavilion is a 19th-century gem. If you ignore the fancy video games, you might be able to imagine yourself as a Victorian Londoner out on holiday, seeing brilliant electric lights for the first time (free entry to pier, rides run Mon–Fri 12:00–19:00, Sat–Sun 11:00–22:00, arcade open until 22:00, closing time depends on crowds, tel. 01273/609-361, www.brightonpier.co.uk).

Check out the ruins of the pier to the west. Due to disrepair, the shorter but once equally festive West Pier disintegrated into the water in the 1970s. Watch for construction of a new observation tower here. Designed by the architects of the London Eye, the i360 tower's doughnut-like elevator will lift tourists to a bird's-eye view over the town (may be finished sometime in 2012—get details at TI).

Beach—OK, so it isn't Hawaii, but you can walk along the large, flattened cobbles, called "shingles," and get your feet wet.

Sleeping in Brighton

Brighton's bohemian character is fun during the day, but the town can be a little shady at night. The recommended accommodations are in the gay-friendly Kemptown neighborhood, about a block from the beach and within a 10-minute walk of the Brighton Pier and Royal Pavilion.

The best Brighton accommodations are variations on the same theme: a guest house with about a dozen rooms. A guest house offers more professionalism and anonymity than a B&B, and more character(s) than a hotel. As rooms vary in size, one hotel can have four or five different prices for their doubles. ("Sea views" here are unimpressive, and not worth paying extra for.) To complicate matters, in summer, prices skyrocket by £15–30 on weekends, making otherwise good-value places suddenly way overpriced. Summer weekends are also plagued with noisy partygoers roaming the streets until dawn. Avoid sleeping in Brighton on a summer weekend if you can help it—but if you must sleep here, ask for a quieter room away from the road. I've listed the summer ranges; you can assume the lower rates are for weeknights and smaller rooms, while

Sleep Code

(£1 = about $1.60, country code: 44, area code: 01273)
S = Single, **D** = Double/Twin, **T** = Triple, **Q** = Quad, **b** = bathroom,
s = shower only. You can assume credit cards are accepted
and breakfast is included unless otherwise noted.

To help you sort easily through these listings, I've divided
the rooms into three categories based on the price for a
standard double room with bath:

$$$ Higher Priced—Most rooms £100 or more.
$$ Moderately Priced—Most rooms between £60–100.
$ Lower Priced—Most rooms £60 or less.

Prices can change without notice; verify the hotel's
current rates online or by email. For other updates, see www
.ricksteves.com/update.

the higher rates are for weekends and fancier and/or view rooms.
You'll often get a better deal off-season (especially on weeknights).

On New Steine Street

Kemptown's New Steine Street (pronounced "steen")—essentially
a long square with a park in the middle—is lined with about a

dozen different guest houses.
After visiting all of them, these
are my favorites. Marine View
is more traditional; Sea Spray,
New Steine (and its sister hotel,
Gulliver's), and Hamptons are
mod, stylish, and gay-friendly;
and Strawberry Fields is somewhere in between.

Handy bus #7 runs every
10 minutes from just outside the train station to the top of New
Steine Street (5-minute ride). To return to the center, walk to the
bottom of the road and cross the oceanfront street to the bus stand
(you'll find schedules there).

$$$ Sea Spray is an innovative concept hotel: Each of the 15
rooms has a different theme, from the Renaissance to New York
to Elvis. It's a memorable place to spend the night, with art-filled
public spaces (Db-£60–145, sea views, some with balconies, pricier
suites, free Wi-Fi, sauna and massage, at #26, tel. 01273/680-332,
www.seaspraybrighton.co.uk, seaspray@brighton.co.uk, Neil).

$$$ New Steine B&B, with 22 coffee-and-cream-colored
rooms, combines Old World charm with contemporary chic

(S-£49–55, Db-£85–135, Tb-£132–159, Qb-£181–186, check website for discounts, dinner option, free Wi-Fi, bistro, at #10–11, tel. 01273/695-415, www.newsteinehotel.com, reservation@newsteine hotel.com). **$$$ Gulliver's,** their sister hotel two doors down, has similar decor and slightly cheaper prices (Sb-£44–50, Db-£80–130, Tb-£127–154, at #12a, tel. 01273/681-546, www.gullivershotel .com, reservation@gullivershotel.com).

$$$ Hamptons Brighton has crisp and stylish nautical decor right out of New England—but with Union Jack accents (S-£38–48, Sb-£45–55, D-£70–85, Db-£85–130 depending on size, at #3, tel. 01273/675-436, www.hamptonsbrighton.com, hamptons brighton@hotmail.co.uk).

$$ Strawberry Fields Hotel has 27 rooms with a fun strawberry theme. Sharon and her friendly and competent assistant, Anna, look after you (Ss-£29–45, D-£60–70, Db-£70–98, T-£90–105, free Wi-Fi on lower floors, at #6–7, tel. 01273/681-576, www.strawberry -fields-hotel.com, strawberryfields.brighton@gmail.com).

$$ Marine View has 11 comfortable rooms (S-£35–50, Db-£65–85, family room-£85–150, some with sea and pier view, free Wi-Fi, at #24, tel. 01273/603-870, www.mvbrighton.co.uk, info@mvbrighton.co.uk).

Elsewhere in Brighton

Madeira Place, a few blocks closer to the town center than New Steine Street, has its own stretch of guest houses. The best of these is **$$ Kempfield House,** tastefully run in a Georgian townhouse. The 13 rooms are elegantly simple and nicely appointed (Sb-£50–75, Db-£70–110, huge Db-£85–125, check website for discounts, 2-night minimum on weekends, free Wi-Fi, 18 Madeira Place, tel. 01273/777-740, www.kempfieldhouse.co.uk, info@fieldhouse hotels.co.uk).

$ St. Christopher's Inn is your budget hostel option. Smack-dab in the middle of the action, on the main seafront road across from the Brighton Pier, this self-described "party hostel" offers cheap doubles and dorm beds for young people wanting to live it up in Brighton. The ground-floor bar and basement disco can be noisy—light sleepers can try requesting a higher floor (£19–28 for a bunk in 4- to 8-bed dorms, Db-£45–80, prices change dramatically by season—check online for best deals, elevator, 10–12 Grand Junction Road, booking tel. 020/7407-1856, reception tel. 01273/202-035, www.st-christophers.co.uk).

Eating in Brighton

If you haven't filled yourself up with greasy boardwalk fare, you'll find plenty of good, affordable restaurants around town.

In The Lanes

The area known as The Lanes has the best concentration of both trendy and traditional restaurants. My first two listings are pricey, while the Market Street eateries are easier on a tight budget.

English's of Brighton, hiding on the side of the little square on East Street, is a venerable local institution that's been serving seafood specialties for more than 150 years to luminaries such as Charlie Chaplin and Laurence Olivier. The white-tablecloth-classy interior sprawls through several rooms on two floors, and there's seating out on the square (£13–15 fixed-price lunches, £15–20 fixed-price dinners, £17–25 entrées, Mon–Sat 12:00–22:00, Sun 12:00–21:30, reservations smart, 29–31 East Street, tel. 01273/327-980).

Terre à Terre keeps vegetarians and healthy eaters happy with imaginative dishes and friendly service (£13–15 entrées, Mon–Fri 12:00–22:30, Sat 12:00–23:00, Sun 12:00–22:00, 71 East Street, tel. 01273/729-051).

On Market Street: This bustling area—more a long, wide square than a "street"—is packed with affordable eateries. Take a spin around to choose your favorite, but check out the following: **Fat Leo** gets high marks from locals for big portions of pasta and the best bang-for-your-pound in a bright, modern interior with seating on two levels. It's not haute cuisine, but it's cheap (£3–10 entrées, daily 12:00–22:00, at #16–17, tel. 01273/325-135). For a seafront picnic, pick up some pastries and pasties at **Forfars Fresh**, baking in Brighton since 1818 (eat at their upstairs café for a few pence more, Mon–Fri 8:00–16:30, Sat 8:00–16:00, closed Sun, at #44, tel. 01273/327-458). **Giggling Squid** serves up tasty Thai dishes in a simple, two-story interior (£4–8 light "Thai tapas" lunch dishes, bigger £6–8 dinners, Mon–Sat 11:30–23:00, Sun 11:30–22:00, at #11, tel. 01273/737-373). **The Burger Bar** is a cute little quasi-diner slinging burgers and all-day breakfast fare. As there's no interior seating, you'll have to grab a table on the square (£3–5, cash only, open daily 9:00–18:00, at #11a, tel. 01273/205-979).

In North Laine

Just north of The Lanes and the Royal Pavilion, this former warehouse district is now the cool place to explore, with new restaurants and fun quirky shops popping up all the time.

Bill's Produce Store is a unique café (and yes, produce store) that's immensely popular with locals for its fresh, inventive dishes and smoothies. Get here before the lunch rush to nab a seat and ogle the surroundings—and the fresh-flower-bedecked cakes behind the counter (£3.50–12 lunches, £9–15 dinners, take-away sandwiches, large breakfast menu, Mon–Sat 8:00–22:00, Sun 9:30–16:00, 100 North Road, tel. 01273/692-894).

Cornish Pasties offers excellent versions of its namesake, including vegetarian varieties, and delicious homemade desserts (Mon–Sat 9:00–19:00, Sun 12:00–18:00, 24 Gardner Street, tel. 01273/688-063). It's lovingly run by Ian and Nese Baldry, who also own **Our Cornish Pasty Shop,** just a block down from the train station (also serves salads, Mon–Fri 6:30–18:00, Sat–Sun 9:00–16:00, 55 Queen's Road, tel. 01273/777-363). Arrive an hour before either store closes to get two pasties for the price of one.

Two reliable Asian chains have branches here (a block apart from each other, off North Road). At **Wagamama,** diners slurp pan-fried, pan-Asian noodles at long, shared tables in a single hall as the harried wait staff scurries around (£6–10 entrées, Mon–Sat 12:00–23:00, Sun 12:00–22:00, 30 Kensington Street, tel. 01273/688-892). **Yo! Sushi** features a conveyor belt of tasty and creative raw fish (£2–5/plate, Mon–Sat 12:00–23:00, Sun 12:00–22:30, last orders 30 minutes before closing, 6–7 Jubilee Street, tel. 01273/258-711).

Near the Recommended Accommodations in Kemptown

To dine closer to home, simply wander the lively streets of Kemptown. St. James's Street, running parallel to the seafront a block inland, is lined with all types of cuisine: cheap burgers and fish-and-chips, Thai, Mediterranean, pub grub, and more. For Italian, try **La Capannina,** a cozy one-room restaurant with a run-by-an-Italian-family feel (£6–10 pizzas and pastas, Tue–Fri 12:00–14:30 & 18:00–23:00, Sun 12:00–15:00, Mon 18:00–23:00, just off St. James's Street at 15 Madeira Place, tel. 01273/680-839).

Brighton Connections

Brighton is well-connected to London and most coastal towns.

From Brighton by Train to: London's **Gatwick Airport** (at least hourly, 25–40 minutes), **London's** Victoria Station (1–2/hour direct, 1 hour; also from London Bridge Station, 1–2/hour direct, 1 hour), **Portsmouth** (hourly direct, 1.25 hours, more with transfer), **Hastings** (2/hour direct, 1–1.25 hours), **Dover** (2/hour, 2.75–3 hours, 1–3 transfers), **Canterbury** (1–2/hour, 2.25–2.5 hours, 1–3 transfers). Train info: toll tel. 0845-748-4950, www.nationalrail.co.uk.

By Bus: National Express (toll tel. 0871-781-8181, www.nationalexpress.com) runs buses to London's **Gatwick Airport** (at least hourly, 45 minutes), **Heathrow Airport** (at least hourly, 2.5–3 hours, transfer possible), **London's** Victoria Coach Station (hourly, 2.5 hours), and **Portsmouth** (1/day direct, 1.75 hours). Stagecoach buses (toll tel. 0845-121-0170, www.stagecoachbus.com) go to

Portsmouth (3–4/hour, 4 hours) and **Arundel** (2/hour, fewer on Sun, 1–2.25 hours, some require transfer).

Near Brighton

Stretching east of Brighton is a coastline fringed with broad, rolling green downs, or hills—an area known as the South Downs Way. These hills are an excellent place to practice a favorite sport of the English: walking. Paths, well-tended by local walking clubs, weave through much of the English countryside, attracting weekend and holiday strollers, and anyone looking for fresh air and exercise. On a quick visit, the highlights here are the adorable hamlet of Alfriston and the dramatic chalk cliff of Beachy Head. Just beyond is the ruined Roman fort at Pevensey. I've listed these attractions as you'll reach them traveling eastward from Brighton.

Planning Your Time

These sights can be combined to make a good half-day side trip from Brighton (better in the afternoon; allow more time if you want to squeeze in a South Downs Way walk en route). Drive east on A27, dip down through Alfriston to stroll the cute village center and poke into the clergy house, then continue on to Beachy Head—arriving when the cliffs are gorgeously lit by the late-afternoon sun. Pevensey is skippable but makes for an easy quick visit, as it's just off the main A27/A259 road connecting Brighton to points eastward (Dover or Canterbury).

▲Alfriston

The South Downs Way winds itself inland at Alfriston, set in a peaceful green valley. This tidy, picturesque little one-street village—half redbrick, half half-timbered, all quaint—is packed with tourists and walkers.

Arrival in Alfriston: Drivers follow *Alfriston* signs south from A27. Park in the giant lot at the north end of town, then

stroll up the main drag. Alfriston, while cute, isn't worth the trouble if you don't have a car, but you could take bus #12 or #12A from Brighton south to Seaford, then catch bus #126 to Alfriston (toll tel. 0871-200-2233, www.traveline.org.uk).

Sights: A block behind the main street is the landmark **St. Andrew's Church,** overlooking an

BRIGHTON

Near Brighton

TO LONDON

M-25

TONBRIDGE

TO ASHFORD

GATWICK AIRPORT

M-23

CRAWLEY

KENT

SUSSEX

A-23

M-275

BATTLE (HASTINGS BATTLEFIELD)

TO RYE, DOVER + CANTERBURY

TO PORTSMOUTH A-27

LEWES

A-259

A-27

HASTINGS

PEVENSEY

NEW HAVEN

Seaford

BIRLING GAP

SEVEN SISTERS (CLIFFS)

EASTBOURNE

BEACHY HEAD

BRIGHTON

ALFRISTON

ENGLISH

CHANNEL

---- SOUTH DOWNS WAY FOOTPATH

🏰 CASTLE

10 MILES

20 KM

LONDON

DCH

inviting green (the church sometimes hosts concerts—look for the schedule in the entryway). Tucked behind the church (on the right side) is the humble, thatched **Alfriston Clergy House.** This 14th-century house was the first property ever acquired by the National Trust—for just £10—in 1896. Its small garden is filled with delphiniums and roses, and the interior of the building is well-preserved. This place gives you a look at the lifestyles of the medieval and pious. Docents are sometimes waiting inside to tell you more (£4, skimpy £2.50 guidebook; Sat–Mon and Wed–Thu March–Oct 10:30–17:00, shorter hours off-season; closed Tue and Fri year-round except open Fri in Aug; closed mid-Dec–Feb; last entry 30 minutes before closing, tel. 01323/870-001, www.national trust.org.uk/alfriston).

Sleeping near Alfriston: The **$$ Riverdale House B&B,** perched on a ridge with beautiful views over the South Downs, has three recently renovated rooms that tastefully meld traditional character and modern hues. This family-friendly place also features a shared living room and conservatory with views of the garden and beyond (Db-£80–105 depending on size, family suite-£130–140, just south of Alfriston on Seaford Road—look for sign on right, tel. 01323/871-038, www.riverdalehouse.co.uk, info @riverdalehouse.co.uk).

Eating in Alfriston: The pubs lining the town's main street— such as Ye Olde Smugglers Inn, The George Inn, and The Star Inn—offer typical pub grub in beautiful half-timbered buildings.

▲▲Beachy Head

The highest chalk sea cliff in England is less well-known but more dramatic and scenic than the White Cliffs of Dover. If you see one white cliff in England (and one is enough), make it Beachy Head.

The easiest way to appreciate Beachy Head is to drive to the settlement of **Birling Gap,** with easy access to the coastline below the cliff. From Brighton, make your way to the A259 coastal road. (The most scenic approach is to head east on speedy A27, then turn off and head south when you see signs for *Alfriston;* you can visit this picturesque town—described above—on the way to A259, which you'll follow east.)

Once on A259, you can turn off in Friston directly to Birling Gap or—for a slightly longer and more scenic route—continue east on A259 to make a loop of it, passing through the charming village of East Dean (with a good pub, the Tiger Inn, on the village green). Take a spin around the dial of your car's radio—you'll start to hear more French stations than English ones. Shortly after leaving East Dean, you'll see a turnoff on the right for Beachy Head. Follow this road as it rises over the hills, with views over grassy fields on one side and the English Channel on the other. Soon you'll spot the Countryside Centre, with information for walkers and other visitors (May–Oct daily 10:00–16:00, off-season Sat–Sun

South Downs Way

The South Downs Way (often abbreviated SDW) runs for 100 miles along the chalk hills of England's south coast, from Winchester (25 miles inland in Hampshire) to Eastbourne (on the coast of East Sussex). This long, scenic ridge has attracted walkers for thousands of years, and in April of 2010, the area surrounding the trail became England's 10th national park. Locals consider these trails a birthright.

The SDW is a bridleway, which means you can walk, bike, or ride a horse. To keep on course, look for the blue arrow signs with a white acorn in the middle or dots of blue paint on posts or trees. It's always a good idea to have a map; the UK Ordnance Survey Explorer maps are excellent and widely available (#125 covers the area around Beachy Head).

Walkers have priority over horses and bicycles, but it's polite to step aside and let them pass. While motorized vehicles are not allowed on the SDW itself, much of the path runs along farm tracks, so you may encounter tractors. Keep a safe distance or you may be plowed under.

It's best to walk east, toward Eastbourne. This will keep the wind behind you and the scenery ahead. While you can walk along almost the entire southern coast, the best part for a day hike is the three-mile stretch out to Beachy Head from Eastbourne (find the path at the west end of King Edward's Parade, also called B2103; the small car park is often full, so you may need to park on a nearby street).

Many people walk the entire 100 miles, staying in B&Bs or hostels in towns along the way, or camping in designated areas. The SDW winds its way through or near many towns and villages, including Exton, Buriton, Arundel, Lewes, and Alfriston. Three good websites are www.southdowns.gov.uk, www.southdownsonline.org, and www.nationaltrail.co.uk. You can buy a guidebook at most UK bookshops or online through www.amazon.co.uk. Titles include *South Downs Way* by Jim Manthorpe, *South Downs Way National Trail Guide* by Paul Millmore, and *Walks in the South Downs National Park* by Kev Reynolds.

only 10:00–15:30, tel. 01323/737-273). Then continue on the road, which eventually drops you down into Birling Gap.

Once you arrive in Birling Gap, park at the big, free gravel lot next to the Birling Gap Hotel, and use the staircase to reach the beach. As you stroll under the grand chalky monster, marvel at the otherworldly whiteness of the cliff and the stones underfoot. Pick up a chunk of chalk to feel how soft and crumbly it is—the constant sloughing off is why these cliffs are so steep, dramatic, and pearly-white (signs warn you to stay away from the immediate base of the cliffs). Stretching to your right (as you face the sea) are the Seven Sisters cliffs, also offering chalky splendor as far as the eye can see.

If you have time for a **walk,** there are two good routes to consider. For a clifftop walk with great sea views, but not the best vistas of the cliff face itself, hike from the lighthouse called Belletout (you'll see it as you approach the cliffs from the west) to the Countryside Centre. Or, for head-on views of the cliff as you walk, start out in Seaford and hike up the ridge to Hope Gap. Both of these trails are fairly steep, and it's important to watch your step: Long windblown grass fields come to an abrupt end at the cliff edge, with no barrier between you and the sea crashing hundreds of feet below.

If you don't have a car, take buses #12A or #13X, which offer good daily service between Brighton and Birling Gap, Seaford, and Beachy Head (2/hour, 1–1.75 hours, tel. 01273/886-200, toll tel. 0871-200-2233, www.traveline.org.uk).

Pevensey

This nondescript village, 25 miles east of Brighton (where the A259 coastal route and faster A27 inland route intersect), is a one-street town leading up to a large, brooding Roman fortress. Originally built as a coastal fortification in the fourth century, **Pevensey Castle** was also used by the Normans, who landed in 1066 with William the Conqueror at Norman's Bay, just within sight. The

moat around the inner castle was probably flushed by the incoming tidewater, although the present coastline has moved farther to the south. The ruins of the castle were also put into action during World War II. While you can pay to go into the castle itself, the best activity—wandering the scenic and grassy field around it—is free (castle entry-£4.50, includes audioguide; April–Sept daily 10:00–18:00; Oct daily 10:00–16:00; Nov–March Sat–Sun only 10:00–16:00, closed Mon–Fri; tel. 01323/762-604, www.english-heritage.org.uk/pevensey).

You can also take the train from Brighton to Pevensey (2/hour, 1 hour, possible change in Lewes, toll tel. 0845-748-4950, www.nationalrail.co.uk).

PORTSMOUTH

Portsmouth, the age-old home of the Royal Navy and Britain's second-busiest ferry port after Dover, is best known for its Historic Dockyard and many nautical sights. For centuries, Britain, a maritime superpower, relied on the fleets in Portsmouth to expand and maintain its vast empire and guard against invaders. When sea power was needed, British leaders—from Henry VIII to Winston Churchill to Tony Blair—called upon Portsmouth to ready the ships.

As a major military target, the city of Portsmouth was flattened by WWII bombs (though ironically, the Historic Dockyard was relatively unscathed). Postwar reconstruction was hasty and poorly planned, and the city became infamous for its bad architecture. But an impressive gentrification is underway here. Efforts to rejuvenate tourism have included refurbishing Old Portsmouth, building a sprawling new waterfront shopping complex, and adding an odd, pointy monolith to the skyline. While Brighton rests on its holiday-making laurels—and revels in its shabby-chic—

Portsmouth feels increasingly gentrified.

The old nautical sights are as impressive as ever. Visiting landlubbers can tour the HMS *Victory,* which played a key role in Britain's battles with Napoleon's navy, and see artifacts from the *Mary Rose,* a 16th-century warship. But the new spirit of Portsmouth is equally enticing.

Portsmouth

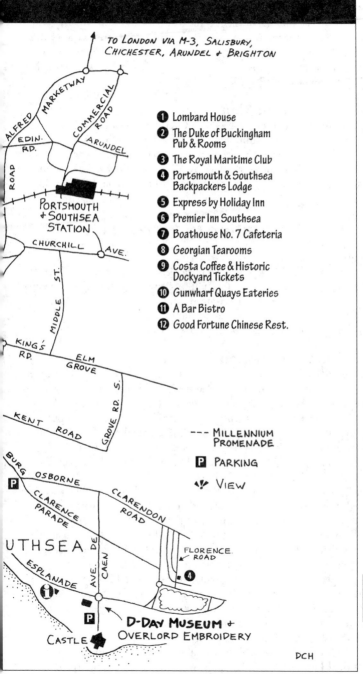

TO LONDON VIA M-3, SALISBURY, CHICHESTER, ARUNDEL & BRIGHTON

1. Lombard House
2. The Duke of Buckingham Pub & Rooms
3. The Royal Maritime Club
4. Portsmouth & Southsea Backpackers Lodge
5. Express by Holiday Inn
6. Premier Inn Southsea
7. Boathouse No. 7 Cafeteria
8. Georgian Tearooms
9. Costa Coffee & Historic Dockyard Tickets
10. Gunwharf Quays Eateries
11. A Bar Bistro
12. Good Fortune Chinese Rest.

--- MILLENNIUM PROMENADE

P PARKING

View

PORTSMOUTH & SOUTHSEA STATION

ALFRED
MARKETWAY
COMMERCIAL ROAD
EDIN. RD.
ARUNDEL
ROAD
CHURCHILL AVE.
MIDDLE ST.
KING'S RD.
ELM GROVE
GROVE RD. S.
KENT ROAD
BURG
OSBORNE
CLARENCE PARADE
CLARENDON ROAD
AVE. DE CAEN
FLORENCE ROAD
UTHSEA
ESPLANADE
CASTLE
D-DAY MUSEUM & OVERLORD EMBROIDERY

DCH

Portsmouth seems to expertly balance its dual status as both a city of the past, and one of the future.

Near Portsmouth, on the road to Brighton, are two very different palaces: the ancient remains of Fishbourne Roman Palace, with its striking mosaics; and thriving Arundel Castle, still the proud home of England's top duke.

Planning Your Time

Portsmouth works well as a day trip from London, Bath, or Salisbury. The city's top sights—at the Historic Dockyard—can be seen in a few hours. But thanks to the bustling Gunwharf Quays and Spinnaker Tower, the D-Day Museum, and a seaside-holiday atmosphere, you'll have no trouble filling a whole day. Consider spending the night.

Orientation to Portsmouth

(area code: 023)

Portsmouth, situated on a large peninsula, feels smaller than its population of 200,000. Almost all of its visit-worthy sights line up along a two-mile stretch of waterfront, from the Historic Dockyard in the north to the Southsea neighborhood in the south—with its D-Day Museum, beaches, and hovercraft to the Isle of Wight.

Tourist Information

The main TI is located on The Hard, just left of the **Historic Dockyard** gate. On most Sundays, the TI offers guided walks, usually at 14:30 for £3—ask for details (open daily 9:30–17:15, tel. 023/9282-6722, www.visitportsmouth.co.uk, vis@portsmouthcc .gov.uk). A second TI is two miles away, near the D-Day Museum in **Southsea**, although its future is uncertain—call first (March–Oct daily 9:30–17:15; Nov–Feb Mon–Fri 9:30–16:30, closed Sat–Sun; Clarence Esplanade, tel. 023/9282-6722).

At either TI, pick up the free, virtually useless black-and-white map, or shell out £1.50 for a good color one. To tempt you to cross the town and see more of Portsmouth, the main TI sells 10-percent-off tickets for the D-Day Museum (located near the Southsea TI), and the Southsea TI gives out 10 percent discount vouchers for the Historic Dockyard (located near the main TI). If you plan to see both sights—and the Southsea TI is open—you'll save about £2 per person if you go to the main TI upon arrival, buy a discounted D-Day Museum ticket, visit that museum, pick up a Historic Dockyard voucher at the Southsea TI, and then head back to the center to visit the Historic Dockyard.

Bus Tours: With vintage double-decker buses and live guides, **Local Haunts** does a 1.5-hour tour through Portsmouth (£8.50, buy tickets from guide or at TI, April–Sept Wed–Thu and Sun at 14:00, leaves from Stand A at The Hard Interchange Bus Station near Historic Dockyard, toll-free tel. 0800-389-6897, www.local haunts.com, info@localhaunts.com).

Arrival in Portsmouth

Portsmouth has two **train** stations. Stay on the train until the final stop at the Portsmouth Harbour Station, conveniently located one long block from the TI and the entrance to the Historic Dockyard. The Hard Interchange Bus Station is just across from the train station (bus #700 runs from here to Southsea). High-speed, passenger-only catamarans to Ryde on the Isle of Wight depart from the waterfront in front of the train station (explained later, under "Portsmouth Connections").

Drivers approach Portsmouth on the M27 motorway. First take the *Portsmouth (W)* exit, then follow signs for *Historic Waterfront*. As you get closer, individual parking lots are well-signposted (the one called "Historic Dockyard" is a garage just two blocks from the TI).

Getting Around Portsmouth

The walkable core contains the main sights: the Historic Dockyard, Spinnaker Tower (views), Gunwharf Quays (shopping complex), Millennium Promenade Walk, and Old Portsmouth. To get to the D-Day Museum two miles away in Southsea, catch bus #700 from the Hard Interchange Bus Station, between the main TI and the train station (90p/ride, £3.50 day pass, 2/hour Mon–Sat, hourly Sun, 10 minutes).

Sights in Portsmouth

I've listed Portsmouth's sights by neighborhood, from north to south.

▲▲Historic Dockyard

When Britannia ruled the waves, it did so from Portsmouth's Historic Dockyard. Britain's great warships, known as the "Wooden Walls of England," were all that lay between the island nation and invaders from the Continent. Today, this harbor is still the base of the Royal Navy. (If you sneak a peek beyond the guard stations, you can see the British military at work.) The shipyard offers visitors a glimpse of maritime attractions new and old. Marvel at the modern-day warships anchored on the docks, then explore the fantastic collection of historic memorabilia and preserved ships.

The museum complex has several parts: HMS *Victory*,

Nelson's Victory over Napoleon

Admiral Lord Horatio Nelson (1758–1805), a small man who suffered seasickness throughout his career, was a brilliant military strategist. He developed a new plan for taking on Napoleon's fleet: Instead of pulling parallel to the ships and firing broadside, he would drive a line of ships head-on, perpendicular to his opponent's fleet. When the English attacked, they decimated the French, who were unable to return adequate fire. Victory was won, but Nelson, who courageously wore his bright uniform to inspire his men, was lost to a sniper's bullet. While sailors are usually buried at sea, Nelson's body was returned to London, where he was given a grand funeral and then buried in St. Paul's Cathedral. The victory at Trafalgar solidified British dominance of the seas. Although Napoleon would menace Europe for another 10 years, he would never again challenge the British Royal Navy.

National Museum of the Royal Naval, *Mary Rose* and *Mary Rose* Museum, HMS *Warrior*, Action Stations, and a harbor cruise. The highlight is the HMS *Victory,* arguably the most important ship in British history. From its deck, Admiral Nelson defeated Napoleon's French fleet at Trafalgar, saving Britain from invasion and escargot. It'll put you in a *Master and Commander* mood—and, in fact, Russell Crowe spent several days here preparing for his role as Captain Jack Aubrey in that 2003 film.

Cost: You can stroll around the shipyard on your own to see the exteriors of the HMS *Victory* and HMS *Warrior* for free (except during special events), but going inside the attractions requires a £19.50 ticket that covers everything (good for one year). The Southsea TI hands out 10 percent discount vouchers for this sight (explained on page 276, under "Tourist Information").

Hours: The Dockyard is open daily April–Oct 10:00–18:00, Nov–March 10:00–17:30 (last tickets sold 1.5 hours before closing, most boats close 30 minutes before the Dockyard closes, tel. 023/9283-9766, recorded info tel. 023/9286-1512, www.historicdockyard.co.uk). Friendly and knowledgeable docents throughout the complex will happily answer your questions and capably tell tales of the sea.

Day-Trip Deal: If visiting the Historic Dockyard as a day trip via train from London, you'll save £3.50 off the admission price by buying a combined rail-and-Dockyard ticket (must depart from London's Waterloo Station, smart to buy at least one day ahead, toll tel. 0845-600-0650, www.southwesttrains.co.uk).

Crowd-Beating Tips: You might have to wait up to 45 minutes to buy tickets in July and August, when school is out—lines are worst at midday, so try to arrive after lunchtime. In summer, there's usually a second, cash-only ticket desk near the HMS *Victory* (ask the greeter as you enter the Dockyard). You can tour the *Victory* on your own in summer, but in winter (Oct–March), you can enter the ship only with a 50-minute tour (you'll get an appointment time for the tour, but as they can fill up by early afternoon, it's best to arrive early in winter).

Because most visitors slowly plod their way back to the *Victory*, the best plan is to do the reverse: Head there first, then work your way back through the other exhibits. This also gets you to the best sights before you get "shipped out." I've listed the attractions in that order.

▲▲▲**HMS *Victory***—This grand historic warship changed the course of world history. At the turn of the 19th century, Napoleon's forces were terrorizing the Continent. In 1805, Napoleon amassed a fleet of French and Spanish ships for the purpose of invading England. The Royal Navy managed to blockade the fleets, but some French ships broke through. Admiral Nelson, commander of the British fleet, pursued the ships aboard the HMS *Victory*, cornering them at Cape Trafalgar, off the coast of Spain (see sidebar). Today, the dry-docked HMS *Victory* is so well-preserved that it feels ready to haul anchor and pull out of the harbor at any moment. In fact, it's still a commissioned warship, the world's oldest. For the British, this ship is more a cathedral than a museum.

◐ Self-Guided Tour: Visitors follow a one-way route that spirals up and down through the ship's six decks. Here are the highlights.

In the **great cabin,** you'll see Admiral Nelson's quarters. Imagine Nelson and his officers dining at the elegant table—or hunched over maps here to plan an attack. While it looks like an officer's stately quarters, this space is also designed for action: All of the wood furniture was foldable and could be stored away during battle. The black-and-white checkerboard "tile" flooring—inspired by Nelson's love of southern Italy (and its women)—is actually painted canvas, which could, like the carpets, be rolled up at a moment's notice. It took the crew less than 10 minutes to clear away all the upper-class trappings and turn this space into a fully functional cannon deck. Leaving the Great Cabin, you'll pass Nelson's hanging bunk—even the master of this ship slept on a glorified hammock rather than a bed. (We'll see humbler hammocks soon.)

The **upper gun deck** is filled with original cannons. To prevent the ship from tipping, the lightest were placed higher on the ship, with the heavy ones below. It took a well-trained British sailor two minutes to ready a cannon for firing, compared to the eight minutes French gunners needed to fire their cannons.

Heading up to the **upper deck,** you'll see Captain Hardy's cabin—not quite as posh as his boss Nelson's, but still not bad. Before descending the stairs, notice the small golden plaque on the deck marking the spot where "Nelson fell" during that fateful Battle of Trafalgar—shot by a sniper. From here, the crew rushed him below deck to care for him during his dying hours.

Down in the **middle gundeck,** you can see how the sailors on the ship lived where they worked. When not in battle, they strung hammocks between the guns and ate at tables wedged under their strung-up beds. Sailors ate from square plates to save space. When a man died, his hammock was his burial cloth—his body was sewn up in the hammock, with a last stitch through the nose to ensure the man was really dead. (Since military service was obligatory, faking death was common.)

As you progress deeper into the bowels of the ship, the space becomes smaller and darker (watch your head). It's down here, in the **orlop deck,** that Nelson died, gasping his final words: "Thank God, I have done my duty." The painting next to the spot of his death shows the admiral glowing like a saint as sailors look on in grief. (Whether or not this is an eyewitness account is suspect, however; check the size of the ship—either people were much smaller back then or the painter had never been onboard the *Victory.*) After his death, Nelson was put in a cask filled with brandy to preserve his body. Legend has it that the cask was not quite as full by the time the sailors arrived in London.

National Museum of the Royal Navy—This museum, situated in three buildings, is packed with model ships, paintings, uniforms, and lots more Nelson hero-worship. While interesting, it gets old quickly for all but serious naval history fans. If you dip into only one part, choose the one nearest the *Victory,* called the Victory Gallery. The corny but informative 15-minute "Trafalgar Experience" multimedia show—with movies, mannequins, sound effects, and smoke—offers a blow-by-blow account of the Battle of Trafalgar. It culminates with a viewing of a panoramic painting of the battle.

▲**Mary Rose**—The eerie, melancholy carcass of the *Mary Rose* is closed to the public while it gets a new, £35 million home. This 16th-century warship was Henry VIII's favorite, named after his sister (Mary) and his family emblem (the rose). In July 1545, when a French fleet approached the English coastline, the *Mary Rose* was sent out to engage the enemy. Suddenly, just two miles offshore, a stiff breeze caught the ship and it tipped over. Since all of the gun bays were open, ready for battle, the water overwhelmed the ship and it began to sink. Netting over the hold was intended to keep boarding parties at bay, but instead it trapped 400 sailors as they frantically scrambled to escape. Eventually, the ship and its doomed crew settled, stuck in the mud, in relatively shallow water.

In 1982, about 15 years after the wreck was located, the half of the ship that was encased in mud—and thus preserved—was raised. Today, the *Mary Rose* is still undergoing restoration. Since allowing the ship to dry out too quickly would cause the structure to disintegrate, its remains are being constantly sprayed with a sealing wax solution. Starting this year, officials will finally start to let the hull dry out—a process that will take five years.

Inside the wreck were found all sorts of Tudor-era items, such as clothes, dishes, weapons, and even a backgammon board and an oboe-like instrument. These items are shown off in the **Mary Rose Museum,** back near the entrance of the Dockyard. A 15-minute film runs every half-hour, telling the story of how they raised the *Rose*. While the museum is a little too kid-oriented and lacks the decorum a shipwreck site deserves, it's still a fascinating look at everyday shipboard life from almost 500 years ago. This museum remains open while the new complex—which will house both the preserved ship and the artifacts—is under construction. Officials hope to finish the new museum in time for the 2012 Summer Olympics.

HMS *Warrior*—This ship, while impressive, never saw a day of battle...which explains why it's in such good condition. The

Warrior was the first ironclad warship, a huge technological advance. Compare this ship, built in 1860, with the *Victory*, which was similar to the common warships at the time. The *Warrior* was unbeatable, and the enemy knew it. Its very existence was sufficient to keep the peace. The late 19th century didn't see many sea battles, however, and by the time warships were needed again, the *Warrior* was obsolete.

Action Stations—Thinly veiled propaganda for the military, this collection of interactive, high-tech exhibits and simulators is aimed mostly at the young and/or prospective Royal Navy recruits. It's like an Army commercial combined with a noisy video arcade—persuasively fun for kids but irritating to weary adults.

Harbor Cruise—You can scoot around the harbor and back to the Historic Dockyard in about 45 minutes by boat (£5, included in £19.50 Historic Dockyard ticket, departs about hourly during the summer starting at 11:00, last cruise usually leaves at 16:00 from just inside Dockyard entrance, weather-dependent, tel. 01983/564-602). As it also stops at Gunwharf Quays, taking this cruise at the very end of your Dockyard visit can be a smart way to eliminate the 10–15-minute walk to the Spinnaker Tower and surrounding mall.

Gunwharf Quays and the Spinnaker Tower

Part of the major (and successful) makeover of Portsmouth, the bustling **Gunwharf Quays** (pronounced "keys") is an American-style outdoor shopping-center-on-steroids, with restaurants, shops, and entertainment. You'll find all the top shops here, as well as a casino, a bowling alley, a 14-screen cinema, trendy eateries with good views of the water, and an Express by Holiday Inn (mall open Mon–Fri 10:00–19:00, Sat 9:00–19:00, Sun 10:00–17:00, tel. 023/9283-6700, www.gunwharf-quays.com).

Out at the far end of the shopping zone is the can't-miss-it **Spinnaker Tower.** Like Seattle's vaguely futuristic Space Needle, the Spinnaker Tower has quickly come to define its city. The 557-foot-tall, £35 million tower is evocative of the billowing ships' sails that have played such a key role in the history of this city and country. Despite massive construction setbacks and cost overruns, the tower finally opened in October 2005. It was not an auspicious beginning: On opening day, the tower's manager became stranded when an elevator broke down. Barring any malfunctions, you can ride to the 330-foot-high view deck for a panorama of the port and sea beyond, or court acrophobia with a stroll across "Europe's biggest glass floor" (£7.25, £6.50 if bought at TI; daily 10:00–18:00, until 19:00 in Aug; since it can be crowded at midday July–Aug, it's smart to book ahead—and doing so online gets you a 10 percent discount; info tel. 023/9285-7520, booking tel. 023/9285-7521, www.spinnakertower.co.uk).

Getting There: If walking to the mall or Spinnaker Tower from the Historic Dockyard, stay on the mainland past the train station, then go through the modern archway marked *Gunwharf Quays* at the old brick rail bridge.

Old Portsmouth

Portsmouth's historic district—once known as "Spice Island" after the ships' precious cargo—is surprisingly quiet. For a long time, the old sea village was dilapidated and virtually empty. Recently, there's been an effort to revitalize the area, which now has a few inviting pubs and B&Bs. It's a pleasant place to stroll around and imagine how different this district was in the old days, when it was filled with salty fishermen and sailors who told tall tales and sang sea shanties in rough-and-tumble pubs.

Getting There: To get to Old Portsmouth from the Historic Dockyard, walk past the train station, and go through the archway on the right marked *Gunwharf Quays* to cut through the giant shopping complex. Follow signs (or ask anyone to point the way) to exit through the gate on the far end of the complex. Turn right and follow the chain links in the sidewalk to skirt the ferry port and reach the old town (the sidewalk markers may be partially obscured by construction).

Old Portsmouth Millennium Promenade Walk—Chain links in the sidewalk mark the Millennium Promenade (also called the Renaissance Trail on some historical markers). The chain symbol recalls the great steel chain that once spanned the mouth of the harbor and was raised to block invading warships. For a pleasant hour-long after-dinner stroll, walk the portion of the trail south of Old Portsmouth along the oceanfront. Interpretive panels along the way give you insights into Portsmouth's fascinating history.

• *From the tip of Old Portsmouth, follow the trail around on the ocean side to small* **Capstan Square,** *where the harbor-spanning chain was raised to keep out enemy ships. Pass through a narrow gate and climb up the stairs to the top of the 15th-century* **Round Tower.** *A plaque shows where the wreck of the* Mary Rose *was found. After taking in the view, follow the top of the old stone fortifications down to the Square Tower.*

The 15th-century **Square Tower,** originally the residence of the governor of Portsmouth, was later used to store gunpowder. South of the Square Tower on the left is the small, roofless Royal Garrison Church. Founded in 1212 as a hospice, it was used as a shelter for overseas pilgrims traveling to Canterbury, Chichester, and Winchester. The church was later used by garrisoned troops before the nave lost its roof in a WWII bombing raid.

• *After walking south about a quarter-mile, you'll see a small moat on the left.*

You've reached the **Spur Redoubt,** part of the outer fortifications (see interpretive sign down by moat)—and the end of our walk. To avoid the huge crowds that had gathered in town to see him, Admiral Nelson supposedly passed through this area on September 14, 1805, on his way to the Battle of Trafalgar. From the beach, he was rowed out to the *Victory*, waiting off the Isle of Wight. He didn't return to England alive.

• *Cross the metal bridge over the moat, pass through a tunnel under the earthen fortifications, and immediately turn right and climb up the short path to the top. Walk back along the top of the grassy fortifications. Benches invite you to stop and watch the many passing ferries and other ships or to simply enjoy the sunset. If the weather's clear, you can see the Isle of Wight from here.*

Southsea

On a sunny day, this appealing seafront neighborhood—with its long, broad, grassy park stretching for miles in front of fine old townhouses—bustles with locals enjoying their city. While it's studded with some humdrum sights, the main reason to venture to Southsea is for its interesting D-Day Museum.

▲D-Day Museum and Overlord Embroidery—This small museum, worth ▲▲ to history buffs, was built to commemorate

the 40th anniversary of the D-Day invasions. Though it feels a bit dated and faded, it still does an excellent job of re-creating both the atmosphere of WWII England and the planning and execution of the Normandy landing.

The centerpiece of the exhibit is the 272-foot long **Overlord Embroidery** (named for the invasion's code name). The 34 appliquéd panels—stitched together over five years by a team of seamstresses, and originally displayed in a brewery's boardroom—were inspired by the Bayeux Tapestry that recorded William the Conqueror's battles during the Norman invasion of England a thousand years earlier. The panels chronologically trace the years from 1940 to 1944, from the first British men receiving their call-up papers in the mail to the successful implementation of D-Day. It celebrates everyone from famous WWII figures to unsung heroes of the home front. A worthwhile 50p audioguide narrates the whole thing, panel by panel (rent when you buy your ticket).

In the center of the embroidery hall, a movie theater shows a good 15-minute film—a montage of archival wartime footage set to period music (included in entry ticket). Then you'll wander through an exhibit that thoughtfully explains the Battle of Britain and D-Day, including some vehicles that were actually used for the landing. Allow at least 1.5 hours for your visit.

Cost and Hours: £6, discounted 10 percent-off tickets sold at main TI—see page 276, daily April–Sept 10:00–17:30, Oct–March 10:00–17:00, last entry 30 minutes before closing. A café is on-site. The museum is on the waterfront about two miles south of the Spinnaker Tower (Clarence Esplanade, Southsea, tel. 023/9282-7261, www.ddaymuseum.co.uk).

Getting There: To get from Portsmouth's Hard Interchange Bus Station to the museum, take bus #700 (2/hour Mon–Sat, hourly on Sun, 10 minutes; ask at info booth about last return-bus times).

Sleeping in Portsmouth

If you just can't get enough of ships and sea air, Old Portsmouth, just a 15-minute walk from the Historic Dockyard (cutting through the outdoor Gunwharf Quays mall), is charming, fairly quiet, and has several accommodation options.

In Old Portsmouth

$$$ Fortitude Cottage, quaint and cozy, rents six modern-feeling rooms and one apartment in two adjoining row houses just a block from the water. Everything is done with care, making these some of the best rooms in Portsmouth. The main building has views, and the top-floor room has its own roof terrace. The new annex rooms are more spacious, with large modern bathrooms (Db-£90–120, Sb pays the Db rate except during slow times, free Wi-Fi, 51 Broad Street, tel. 023/9282-3748, www.fortitudecottage.co.uk, info @fortitudecottage.co.uk, Maggie and Mike).

$$$ Oyster Cottage is for those who want their B&B to themselves. Witty Carol, who might remind you of Carol Channing, has just one large, light-filled, updated room with a bay-window sitting area, ideal for watching passing boats right up close (Db-£70–90, free parking, 9 Bath Square, tel. 023/9282-3683, www.theoystercottage.co.uk, info@theoystercottage.co.uk).

$$ Sailmaker's Loft B&B, next door, is a straightforward, unpretentious B&B. Originally built as a warehouse, it has one en-suite room and two others that share a bathroom. The two rooms on the ocean side offer front-row seats of the bustling harbor.

Sleep Code

(£1 = about $1.60, country code: 44, area code: 023)
S = Single, **D** = Double/Twin, **T** = Triple, **Q** = Quad, **b** = bathroom, **s** = shower only. You can assume credit cards are accepted and breakfast is included unless otherwise noted.

To help you sort easily through these listings, I've divided the rooms into three categories based on the price for a standard double room with bath:

$$$ Higher Priced—Most rooms £75 or more.
$$ Moderately Priced—Most rooms between £40-75.
$ Lower Priced—Most rooms £40 or less.

Prices can change without notice; verify the hotel's current rates online or by email. For other updates, see www .ricksteves.com/update.

Old Portsmouth
Accommodations & Eateries

TO ISLE OF WIGHT

To SPINNAKER TOWER

1 Fortitude Cottage
2 Oyster Cottage
3 Sailmaker's Loft B&B
4 The Spice Island Inn
5 The Still & West Country House Pub
6 Sallyport Tea Rooms

BATH SQ.
EAST ST.
SEAGER'S CT.
WEST TOWER ST.
CAPSTAN SQUARE
ROUND TOWER
FORTIFICATIONS
BROAD ST. (A-3)
WHITE HART ROAD
HIGH ST.
SQUARE TOWER
To SPUR REDOUBT

P PARKING

100 YARDS
100 METERS

OLD PORTSMOUTH MILLENNIUM PROMENADE WALK
P PARKING
VIEW

DCH

Owner Bob is an ex-seaman who loves his home port (S-£35, twin D-£65, Db-£75, free parking, 5 Bath Square, tel. 023/9282-3045, mobile 0796-619-4030, www.sailmakersloft.org.uk, sailmakers loft@aol.com).

Between Old Portsmouth and Gunwharf Quays

$$ **Lombard House** rents two rooms on a quiet residential street next to the cathedral, a five-minute walk from Old Portsmouth. The public areas are tastefully decorated in red and feature original artwork. In 2005, as part of the bicentennial of the Battle of Trafalgar, actor-owners Alex and Finni traveled around Great Britain as Admiral Nelson and his mistress, Lady Emma Hamilton. Alex's museum-quality admiral's costume is on display in their atmospheric breakfast cellar, which also boasts old oak ship beams (Sb-£40–45, Db-£65–68, cash only, free Wi-Fi, 9 Lombard Street, tel. 023/9286-2294, mobile 0776-200-1528, finni@victoryfilms.co.uk).

$$ **The Duke of Buckingham Pub,** a few blocks inland from Old Portsmouth, is likely to have rooms when others are full. While the accommodations take a backseat to the popular pub, the 18 basic rooms—above the bar—are clean and cozy (D-£50, Db-£65, fam-

ily room-£75–80, free Wi-Fi, 119 High Street, tel. 023/9282-7067, www.dukeofbuckingham.com, buckingham119@aol.com). It's also an excellent place to have dinner (£7.50–10 entrées).

Elsewhere in Portsmouth

$$$ The Royal Maritime Club offers a home away from home to sailors in town who don't want to bunk on the boat. Just two blocks up the road from the Historic Dockyard entrance, it also welcomes tourists, who share its grand public spaces, generous facilities (including a swimming pool, fitness center, game room, self-service laundry, even barbershop) and 120 comfortable, surprisingly newish rooms. The catch: They rent out their ballroom for parties, which can sometimes be noisy into the wee hours—if you're a light sleeper, try requesting a quieter room. It's located two blocks from the Historic Dockyard and four blocks from the train station, opposite the oval-shaped Admiralty Tower (Sb-£45, Db-£90, family suites, elevator, free Wi-Fi, Queen Street, tel. 023/9282-4231 or 023/9283-7681, fax 023/9229-3496, www.royal maritimeclub.co.uk, info@royalmaritimeclub.co.uk).

$ Portsmouth & Southsea Backpackers Lodge is your budget option, with dorm beds and some cheap doubles in a faded old house. This strictly-run place is in Southsea, a five-minute walk from the D-Day Museum and about two miles from the central sights (£15 bunks in 4- to 8-bed dorms, D-£34, Db-£38, reception open 7:30–23:00, free Wi-Fi, laundry, 4 Florence Road, tel. 023/9283-2495, www.portsmouthbackpackers.co.uk, info@ports mouthbackpackers.co.uk).

Big Chain Hotels

The following hotels (with elevators and 24-hour reception) may have rooms when the other accommodations are full.

$$$ Express by Holiday Inn, located in the shadow of the Spinnaker Tower and within the Gunwharf Quays shopping complex, rents 130 cookie-cutter rooms not far from the Portsmouth Harbour Train Station and Historic Dockyard (£110–145 per room, check website for specials, includes continental breakfast and discounts at some Gunwharf Quays restaurants; free parking for first 24 hours, then £2/day; US reservations tel. 888-465-4329, British reservations toll-free tel. 0800-405-060, reception tel. 023/9289-4240, fax 023/9289-4241, www.hiexpress.co.uk, portsmouth@kewgreen.co.uk).

$$ Premier Inn Southsea, a half-mile south of Old Portsmouth along the waterfront, offers 48 modern rooms next to the kitschy, cotton-candy-carnival ambience of Clarence Pier (the noisy pier attractions close down at about 22:30). It's popular with business travelers on weeknights and families on weekends—as the hordes of screaming kids in the family restaurant downstairs can attest (Db for up to two adults and two kids-£65, may be up to £110 during special events, check website for specials, continental breakfast-£5.25, full English breakfast-£7.75, pay Wi-Fi, limited free parking, Long Curtain Road, just off Pier Road, Southsea, tel. 023/9273-4622 or toll tel. 0871-527-9015, fax 023/9273-3048, www.premierinn.com).

Eating in Portsmouth

At the Historic Dockyard

The Historic Dockyard has an acceptable **cafeteria** (called Boathouse No. 7) with a play area that kids enjoy (£4–8 meals, daily 10:00–15:00). The **Georgian Tearooms** are across the pedestrian street in Storehouse #9, with good sandwich and cake offerings (daily 10:00–17:00). The **Costa Coffee** inside the entrance building offers surprisingly good grilled sandwiches, and coffee drinks to go (daily 10:00–17:00).

At Gunwharf Quays

Eating options abound at this bustling mega-mall. Most restaurants line up along the waterfront by the Spinnaker Tower. You'll pay too much in this high-rent district—and many of the places are chains selling mall food—but it's the most convenient one-stop neighborhood for dining. Familiar restaurant names include Wagamama, Yo! Sushi, Loch Fyne, and Pizza Express (see descriptions on page 33).

In and near Old Portsmouth

Dinnertime is the best time to head over to Old Portsmouth, eat at a pub, and then stroll along the Millennium Promenade (described earlier, under "Sights in Portsmouth"). The first two pubs listed here sling overpriced pub grub with gorgeous views, within a French fry's toss of the water—the busy maritime traffic makes for a fascinating backdrop. The next two listings are clustered between Old Portsmouth and Gunwharf Quays, along quiet, mostly residential streets. The last listing is a charming tearoom that closes before dinnertime. Also consider **The Duke of Buckingham Pub,** listed earlier under "Sleeping in Portsmouth."

The Spice Island Inn, at the tip of the Old Portsmouth peninsula, has terrific outdoor seating, a family-friendly dining room upstairs, and many vegetarian offerings (£5–9 lunches, £7–12 dinners, food served daily 12:00–21:00, bar open longer, 1 Bath Square, tel. 023/9287-0543).

The Still & West Country House Pub underwent an extensive and expensive renovation a few years ago, and has dining in two appealing zones. Eat from the simpler and cheaper menu on the main floor, or outside on the picnic benches with fantastic views of the harbor (£7 baguette sandwiches and £10 fish-and-chips). Or head upstairs to the dining room, with higher prices (£9–17 entrées) but a gorgeous glassed-in conservatory that offers sea views—especially enticing in cold weather (dining room open Mon–Sat 12:00–15:00 & 18:00–21:00, Sun 12:00–18:00, longer hours in the bar, 2 Bath Square, tel. 023/9282-1567).

The **A Bar Bistro** is a relaxed, seafood-and-wine kind of place, and is handy for those staying near the cathedral or Old Portsmouth (£9–18 entrées, Mon–Sat 11:00–24:00, Sun 12:00–22:30, 58 White Hart Road, tel. 023/9281-1585).

The **Good Fortune**, across the street from the recommended Duke of Buckingham Pub, is a Chinese restaurant favored by locals (£5–9 entrées, £13–20 multi-course meals, Wed–Mon 18:00–23:00, closed Tue, 21 High Street, tel. 023/9286-3293).

Tearoom: If you're in Old Portsmouth before dinner and could do with a proper afternoon tea, visit the **Sallyport Tea Rooms,** named for a gateway in a fortification—specifically the one in Portsmouth's ramparts that Nelson passed through on his final departure (£4–5 sandwiches, £7 afternoon tea—order in advance, daily 10:00–17:00, 35 Broad Street, tel. 023/9281-6265).

Portsmouth Connections

From Portsmouth by Train to: London (3/hour, 1.5–2 hours, most to Waterloo Station, a few to Victoria Station), **Gatwick Airport** (2/hour, 1.5–1.75 hours, some require transfer), **Bath** (hourly, 2.25 hours), **Salisbury** (hourly, 1.25 hours), **Brighton** (direct trains hourly, 1.25 hours, more with transfer), **Exeter** (hourly, 3–3.5 hours, change in Salisbury). Train info: toll tel. 0845-748-4950, www.nationalrail.co.uk.

By Bus: For most connections, the train is faster—take the bus only if you're on a tight budget. Stagecoach runs the #700 Coastliner bus to **Brighton** (3–4/hour, 4 hours; toll tel. 0845-121-0170 or 0871-200-2233, www.stagecoachbus.com). National Express buses also go to **Brighton** (1 direct bus/day, 1.75 hours), **Salisbury** (1 direct bus/day, 1.5 hours), and **Bath** (1 direct bus/day, 3 hours; toll tel. 0871-781-8181, www.nationalexpress.com).

By Ferry to the Isle of Wight: Wightlink Ferries has service to **Fishbourne** (40 minutes, cars and passengers) and a catamaran to **Ryde** (18 minutes, passengers only, toll tel. 0871-376-1000, www.wightlink.co.uk). Hovertravel operates a passenger-only hovercraft from Southsea (2 miles south of Portsmouth) to **Ryde** (£13.50 same-day round-trip, 2/hour, 10 minutes, tel. 023/9281-1000, www.hovertravel.co.uk).

PORTSMOUTH

If you're interested in visiting Queen Victoria's palatial island retreat, **Osborne House,** ask about a combo-ticket that combines the round-trip boat ride, bus #4 to and from the estate, and admission (£26, buy at Hovertravel's Southsea terminal on the day of travel, call Hovertravel—tel. 023/9281-1000—for departure times; Osborne House open April–Sept daily 10:00–17:00; Oct daily 10:00–16:00; Nov–March Wed–Sun 10:00–16:00, closed Mon–Tue; house tel. 01983/200-022, www.english-heritage.org.uk).

By International Ferry: Brittany Ferries (toll tel. 0871-244-1400, www.brittanyferries.com) sails to France: **Caen** (2–4/day, 3.75 hours on high-speed boat, 6–7 hours on slower boat), **Cherbourg** (2–3/day, 3–5 hours), **St. Malo** (night crossing, 1/day, 11 hours); and northern Spain: **Santander** (3/week, 24 hours). LD Lines (toll tel. 0844-576-8836, www.ldlines.co.uk) sails to **Le Havre,** France (1–2/day, 3.25–5.5 hours).

Near Portsmouth

These sights are very near the main A27 road that connects Portsmouth with Brighton. They're worth considering for a stopover if you have time as you pass through.

Fishbourne Roman Palace

In the 1930s, a farmer just outside of Chichester found the remains of a Roman palace on his land. Wary of archaeologists, he didn't disclose his find until 1960. The ensuing dig revealed a huge Roman-era villa, probably owned by a local tribal chief who was loyal to the Roman Empire. In the main museum building, you'll find the collection's impressive centerpiece: well-preserved floor mosaics, which

are on display in their original locations (visitors walk above them on an elevated walkway). Also in the main building is a museum telling the story of the palace and Fishbourne's Roman era. The garden outside was reconstructed to resemble the original Roman plan. Across the parking lot, the Discovery Centre lets you peek into the offices and warehouses of the archaeologists at work— like a zoo for people in lab coats. You'll learn how the artifacts are handled on their long journey from the ground to the display case. The palace is fairly interesting to most, but likely to fascinate true fans of Roman history.

Near Portsmouth

Cost and Hours: £7.60, £2 guidebook outlines a very detailed tour, £2.50 illustrated book is good for kids; March–Oct daily 10:00–17:00, until 18:00 in Aug; Nov–mid-Dec and Feb daily 10:00–16:00; mid-Dec–Jan Sat–Sun 10:00–16:00, closed Mon–Fri; café, tel. 01243/785-859, www.sussexpast.co.uk/fishbourne.

Getting There: It's on the southwestern outskirts of the large town of Chichester, well-signed from the main A27 motorway connecting Brighton and Portsmouth. First head for the town of Fishbourne, then follow *Roman Palace* signs through a very residential-feeling neighborhood to the museum. From the Fishbourne train station, the palace is a five-minute walk.

▲Arundel Castle

This impressive castle of Arundel (AIR-uhn-dull) graces the valley below with straight-out-of-a-storybook appeal. The Duke of Norfolk—the top dog among all the English dukes—still lives here, in what amounts to a museum of his own family (the Fitzalan-Howards). Pompous even for a castle, the self-aggrandizing exhibits, docents who speak in hushed awe of their employers, and opulent interiors offer a somehow off-putting taste of England's affection for its outmoded nobility. Still, castle buffs will find the gorgeous interior worth visiting, and the themed gardens are a delight—check out the Earl's Garden, which is based on 17th-century designs.

Cost and Hours: Castle interior, chapel, and grounds-£14, private bedrooms-£2 more; grounds and chapel only-£7.50. The complex is open April–Oct Tue–Sun, closed Mon (except in Aug) and closed Nov–March. Various parts of the castle are open at different times: grounds and Fitzalan Chapel—10:00–17:00; castle keep—11:00–16:30; main castle rooms—12:00–17:00; last entry at 16:00. Parts of the castle can be unexpectedly closed for private events. Tel. 01903/882-173, www.arundelcastle.org.

Getting There: Arundel Castle is right on A27 between Brighton and Portsmouth—**drivers** just follow signs to the castle, and park at the pay lot across from the castle gate. The town of Arundel is connected by **train** from Portsmouth (2/hour, 1 hour, 1–2 transfers) and Brighton (1–2/hour, 1–1.25 hours, 1 transfer); Stagecoach **buses** also run from Brighton to Arundel (2/hour, 2.25 hours, some require transfer).

Background: The castle seems like the perfect medieval fortress. Well, almost...while the castle dates back to the 11th century, most of what you see today is actually a Victorian restoration. The owners of the castle, the Catholic Dukes of Norfolk, weren't very popular in this Protestant country, and neither was their castle, which endured multiple sieges. The dukes persevered, however, rebuilding their castle in the 18th and 19th centuries along with a large Catholic church. As you explore the castle, posted explanations fill in the story (such as an English Civil War exhibit with a Catholic spin). For a primer before you begin, consider stopping by the little information room in the gate as you enter the castle grounds (across from the ticket booth).

❍ Self-Guided Tour: The castle is all about its intimidating bulk and opulent interior—so little explanation is necessary. But here are a few tidbits to bring meaning to your visit. Notice that various parts of the castle have different opening times (listed earlier); if you're here in the morning, visit them according to when they open.

Castle Keep: This ancient centerpiece of the castle is a classic motte-and-bailey design, with a stout windowless fortress atop a man-made hill—double defense against attackers. Later, as the castle grew around it, the keep became the last resort in case of an attack. Walking across the bridge to the keep, ponder how easy it would be to keep the keep—it's connected to the outside only by one bridge, and is well defended by strategically placed arrow slits. Inside the keep yard, stairs lead down to a cellar used as both a dungeon and a storehouse for resources in case the keep had to be used for a final stand. If the flag is flying up top, it means the Duke of Norfolk or his heir (the Earl of Arundel) is around.

Main Castle Rooms: This was—and remains—the gorgeously appointed residence of the Duke of Norfolk. As you ogle the decor, docents explain what you're looking at, and they are always eager to tell you about the lineage, heraldry, and personalities of their beloved dukes. You'll pass through a spectacular private **chapel** (19th-century "Catholic Revival") before entering the **Baron's Hall,** with a pair of giant fireplaces and some fine furniture (including a gorgeous inlaid-wood chest). This room is still used for functions...and, occasionally, for filming the British version of *Antiques Roadshow.* Then you'll pass through a **picture gallery** displaying a *Who's Who* of the Dukes of Norfolk (no, really... who *are* these people?) and enjoy strolling through the formal state dining room, bedrooms, and drawing rooms. Finally, you'll reach the highlight: a wonderful old **library** with rich mahogany woodwork and 10,000 leather-bound books on two levels.

Fitzalan Chapel: This family church—across a tree-filled garden from the main castle—is the final resting place of many of the Dukes of Norfolk. In the nave of the church, notice the grisly double-decker tomb of a 15th-century earl. Called a *memento mori,* or "reminder of death," this was carved during the earl's lifetime—with his virile, healthy self on the top level, and a rotting corpse on the bottom level—to remind him of his own mortality. Flanking the aisle, find the plaques dedicated to the most recent D.'s of N.: Bernard (who died in 1975) and his cousin Miles Francis (died in 2002). Today's Duke—Edward Fitzalan-Howard—is the 18th to hold the title...and you just walked through his house.

Arundel Town: If you have time to kill, check out the adjacent village of Arundel, where you'll find many fine pubs and shops. The **TI** is also happy to suggest nearby boat trips and activities in town (daily summer 10:00–17:00, Sun until 16:00; winter 10:00–15:00; 1–3 Crown Yard Mews, River Road, tel. 01903/882-268, www.sussexbythesea.com).

DARTMOOR

Windswept and desolate, Dartmoor—one of England's best national parks—is one of the few truly wild places you'll find in this densely populated country. Dartmoor's vast medieval commons are still places where all can pass, anyone can graze their sheep, and ponies run wild. Old stone-slab clapper bridges remind hikers that for thousands of years, humans have trod these same paths. In other parts of England, stone circles, stone rows, and standing stones are cause for a tourist frenzy. In Dartmoor, where the terrain is littered with the highest concentration of prehistoric monuments in the UK, they're barely worth a detour.

Locals brag that Dartmoor is England as it was 50 years ago. Maybe that's why it's increasingly a retreat of the rich and famous. You'll find yourself sharing the narrow roads with luxury SUVs, as many retired CEOs and washed-up celebrities have resettled here, in an idyllic and remote countryside far from prying eyes. The area around Chagford has become known as the "Golden Triangle."

All that wealth aside, Dartmoor remains first and foremost the terrain of hikers. Dartmoor gives you a chance to be alone with England's history, jittery sheep, stately wild ponies, and seemingly endless moors. It's also a moody place: At sunset on a clear evening, the gold-tinged heather and rolling hills can be romantic; but on a gray and misty day, it's foreboding—and if you listen hard enough, you might just hear the howl of the hound of the Baskervilles.

Planning Your Time

Dartmoor works well as a stopover between Cornwall (see next chapter) and the rest of England. While you could get a taste of

Dartmoor with one overnight (after breakfast, do my self-guided driving tour and/or Scorhill Stone Circle before moving on in the afternoon), it really deserves at least one full day and two overnights to fully appreciate its majesty and mystery. This is one of those places where time slows down...and puts a crimp in an ambitious itinerary.

Getting Around Dartmoor

By Car: Drivers have Dartmoor by the tail—but a good map is essential...as is a fair amount of courage. Dartmoor's narrow lanes are the most challenging in England: barely as wide as a single car, and often flanked by tall stone hedges covered in greenery (with an occasional jutting rock near the base that's made to order for slashing tires). As most roads are too narrow for two cars to easily pass, you'll often have to pull up or reverse to the nearest wide spot in the road when encountering another car. Just follow the other driver's lead, pull in your mirrors as needed, and don't be shy to wave a thank you. For driving in Dartmoor, rent the smallest car you can tolerate, and you'll breathe easier.

By Bus: Dartmoor is tricky for visitors without a car, but there are some bus connections. Okehampton and Ivybridge are both on minor rail lines, but the closest major city is Exeter.

From the Exeter bus station, the **Transmoor Link #82** bus departs five times a day Sundays only June through mid-September, and stops in Moretonhampstead, Postbridge, and Princetown (£2, toll tel. 0871-200-2233, www.traveline.org.uk or www.dartmoor -npa.gov.uk/vi-transmoor). On Thursdays and Saturdays in summer, a shorter version of the #82 runs within Dartmoor, between Moretonhampstead and Yelverton, with onward connections to Exeter and Plymouth (June–mid-Sept Thu 3/day and Sat 5/day; April–May and mid-Sept–Oct Sat only 5/day).

Two other bus routes from Exeter also connect to Dartmoor towns (Mon–Fri year-round, no buses Sat–Sun): **Bus #173** to Chagford and Moretonhampstead (4/day), and **bus #359** to Moretonhampstead (7/day).

During high season, the **Haytor Hoppa/#271** bus runs on Thursdays (late May–mid-Sept 3/day) and Saturdays (April–Oct 4/day), looping from Bovey Tracey up to Haytor and on to Widecombe, before returning to Bovey Tracey (£2, www.dartmoor -npa.gov.uk).

The **Sunday Rover** day pass lets you travel on summer Sundays and Bank Holidays on most buses and trains in Dartmoor (£6.50, buy ticket on bus or train, late May–mid-Sept, toll tel. 0871-200-2233, www.carfreedaysout.com/dartrover.html).

Orientation to Dartmoor

Dartmoor National Park is vast (368 square miles), but I've focused on the most accessible chunk at the northeastern end of the park, between the A30 and A38 highways.

Throughout Dartmoor, there are more than 10,000 ancient monuments, all accessible to walkers. Princetown, in the center of the moors, has the park's primary information office, with other branches at Postbridge and Haytor (all described later, under "Tourist Information"). The small villages that encroach on the park are charming, and a few (such as Chagford, Moretonhampstead, and Bovey Tracey) are good as home bases for exploring the moors.

Two pieces of gear are essential: good shoes (resistant to mud and "Dartmoor landmines"—wild-horse patties) and an Ordnance Survey map (essential for drivers). You'll need this highly detailed map, not just because the land can be boggy, but also because roads and walking paths are twisty and confusing. (Only two major roads cross the moor, but there are dozens of lesser roads twisting through the countryside—it seems there are five different ways to get between any two points.) The Ordnance Survey produces two good maps of the region. The 1:25,000 Dartmoor map (Explorer #OL28) is ideal for serious hikers, since it shows every ridge, feature, and landmark, but its detail can be overwhelming for drivers. The 1:50,000 map (called "Okehampton & North Dartmoor," Landranger Map #191) is more useful for drivers, and still includes enough detail to use for basic hikes.

Dangers: Parts of the moors are used by the military for target practice. These areas are clearly shown on maps, and marked by red flags when in use—but before going for a hike, always check with a park information office to ensure your route is OK. Other dangers include ticks and adders (a poisonous snake with a black-and-white zigzag stripe). Weather can change quickly here, so wear layers and be prepared for "four seasons in one day" (as locals say). Because Dartmoor is so vast and empty, getting lost is a real threat—a good map and a compass are essential if you're going more than a short distance from your car.

Tourist Information

Most of the bigger villages surrounding Dartmoor have TIs, but the main information center for the park is the **High Moorland Visitor Centre** in Princetown. In addition to hiking info, this office has an interactive exhibit on the history, wildlife, and "countryside code" for walking the moors (daily Easter–Sept 10:00–17:00, Oct 10:00–16:00, Nov–Easter 10:00–15:30, Tavistock Road, tel. 01822/890-414, www.dartmoor-npa.gov.uk). There are also good

Dartmoor National Park

--- PATHS (NOT ALL SHOWN)

① Sandy Park Inn
② Easton Court
③ The Globe Inn & 22 Mill Street Rest.
④ Eastwrey Barton Country House
⑤ Cookshayes Country Guest House, Sparrowhawk Backpackers & The White Horse Inn

⑥ Brookfield House, The Cromwell Arms, De-Tracey's Bar & Spice Bazaar Rest.
⑦ Bellever Youth Hostel
⑧ Higher Venton Farm & Rugglestone Inn
⑨ Warren House Inn
⑩ Fingle Bridge Inn

branches in **Postbridge** (at the big parking lot near the Clapper Bridge, relaxing video upstairs about Dartmoor ponies, daily Easter–Sept 10:00–17:00, Oct 10:00–16:00, closed Nov–Easter, tel. 01822/880-272) and by **Haytor** (Easter–Sept daily 10:00–17:00; Oct daily 10:00–16:00; Nov–Easter Thu–Sun 10:00–15:30, closed Mon–Wed; tel. 01364/661-520).

At any of these offices, you can buy your Ordnance Survey map and pick up their free information-packed *Dartmoor Guide,* with an insert listing guided walks and events. These offices are the best source of advice on hikes or driving routes, and each one sells an illustrated £1.50 booklet with suggestions for self-guided walks. If you have an iPod or other MP3 player, you can download free, six-mile audio walks starting at the three park information centers (www.dartmoor-npa.gov.uk; click on "Visiting").

Consider taking a **guided walk** offered by the national park (£3–8/person, depends on length; get schedule at www.dartmoor-npa.gov.uk or in *Dartmoor Guide*). You can go with your own guide for a hike of your choosing at a similar price—try Tom Soby, who offers a range of walks, including a popular one exploring the places outlined in *The Hound of the Baskervilles* (£7–10/person to join a scheduled walk, private tours-£36/3 hours, mobile 07516-042-316, tomstors@hotmail.com).

Phil Page, a former Dartmoor park manager, offers walks all year on topics from butterflies to literary novels set in Dartmoor (£10/hour for up to 6 people, under 16 free, book in advance, will pick up within a 10-mile limit, tel. 07858/421-148, mobile 07849-840-126, www.dartmoornaturetours.co.uk, enquiries@dartmoor naturetours.co.uk). His wife, Hanneke, rents two rooms at **$$ Yarrow Lodge**, their home in the midst of Yarner Wood, a nature reserve within the national park between Bovey Tracey and Haytor (D-£55, March–Oct only, tel. 01626/836-589, mobile 07849-840-126, www.yarrowlodge.co.uk).

Self-Guided Driving Tour

▲▲▲Pony, Lamb, and Moor Joyride

This all-day driving route is a convenient framework for your Dartmoor exploration. Linger at the desolate viewpoints you find most appealing, and don't be afraid to venture off this plan for a walk to a secluded stone row or circle. If you have enough time, chase down leads suggested by locals—there are many hidden gems embedded in Dartmoor.

This circular route begins and ends in Chagford, but you can join or leave it wherever you like.

• *Begin in the village of...*

Chagford

Perched on the edge of the moor, this tiny town is not only charming but actually feels like a real, normal slice of English life (www.chagford-parish.co.uk). The small-town ambience here may make you feel like you've stepped into a time warp (or maybe a quaint BBC sitcom). Villages like this one, which was probably established in Saxon times, were built around Dartmoor as tin-mining bases. In 1305, Chagford became one of four Dartmoor stannary towns, a main center for "weighing and paying" the miners. The eight-sided Market House in the village square (known as the "pepper pot") is located on the site of the old stannary court/assayer's office.

St. Michael's Parish Church, at the upper end of town, mostly dates from the 15th century and is built out of the typical stone of the area, gray granite. The hard rock is tough to work, so most buildings here are fairly simple. An incident occurred here that is said to have inspired R. D. Blackmore's *Lorna Doone:* A bride named Mary Whiddon was shot dead by a former suitor as she left the church during her wedding in 1641 (pamphlet available inside). Look among the pews at the needlepoint cushions, a few of which bear a tinner's symbol: three rabbits in a circle that each have two ears, but appear to share only three ears among them. (This motif also shows up in the stained-glass window over the door of the wine store on the town square.)

The little **village square** has all the essentials: bank, post office, small grocery store, pharmacy, butcher, delicatessen, and

a few hardware shops that sell any hiking gear that you might have forgotten (including Ordnance Survey maps). Moorland Dairy, next to the Three Crowns Hotel, sells ice-cream cones, interesting cheeses from the area, and clotted cream by the pound (tel. 01647/432-479). Go gawk inside Bowden's hardware store to see how everything you could possibly ever need can be neatly crammed into one place—don't miss the glassed-in antique-hardware room and the loft full of dozens of Wellington boots (tel. 01647/433-271).

• *Follow* Postbridge *signs directing you to the road south of Chagford, which will take you to busy B3212. Soon after you turn right onto B3212, you'll cross some...*

Cattle Grates

Welcome to wild-pony country. The rumble of your tires over cattle grates—which you'll cross several times on our drive— tells you that you've entered an area without fences, where live- stock of all kinds can roam freely. It's also a reminder to slow down and watch the road closely, espe- cially around blind corners—the animals find cars more interesting than scary, and they are often seen sunning themselves in the middle of the road. I've had to lay on my

horn several times to convince a dozing sheep to let me pass. As throughout England, you'll see sheep grazing and fluffy little lambs bounding through the heather. But Dartmoor adds its own unique touch: famously "wild," but remarkably tame, horses. (Actually, the horses are all owned by local farmers, who keep an eye on them as they graze the moors—notice that some horses are branded.) The horses have free rein of Dartmoor, so you may not see them immediately, but eventually you may find a few (or possibly an entire herd). Horses have wandered here for centu- ries, and the brown ones are probably the most closely related to the ancestral Dartmoor breed. The park discourages people from feeding or even approaching the horses—they get used to mooching, so they often readily come up to people, but may bite or kick without warning.

• *After crossing the cattle grates, you're really into the heart of...*

The Moors

England's green, bucolic landscape is occasionally interrupted by brown, scrubby moorlands like these. It's tricky to define a "moor"—but once you've spent time on one, you'll know them when you see them. A moor is characterized by its relative lack of vegetation, save for high grasses and heather—a dull-brown shrub that thrives here (and briefly turns a brilliant purple when it flow- ers in late summer). The long, undulating expanses of open land, almost unbroken by trees but scattered with long-forgotten prehis- toric stone monuments, makes Dartmoor feel even more evocative and mysterious than other English moors.

• *On the left, you may notice the remains of a hilltop settlement. If you're up for a hike to get a closer look, consider this optional detour: Turn left at the sign to* Widecombe, *and follow the road for a few minutes— keeping an eye on those hilltop ruins above you on the left. Just before the big curve to the right, look for a pullout on the right, and four stone steps on the left. You can park and use these steps to climb up to...*

Grimspound

Dating from 2000 B.C., this Bronze Age fortress was a settlement for 800 years. The outer stone wall was a defense wall, and the inner circles would have been stone huts. Well-populated in ancient times, the moors are thought to have become unlivable in about 1200 B.C. due to climate change, and settlements like these were abandoned.

• *Backtrack to the main road you were on, and continue south. Very soon on the left, just before the little parking lot, look for the worn and weathered stub of a...*

Celtic Cross

All along the road, look for tall stone crosses like this one. These marked the way for villagers to cross the moor, often for funeral processions.

• *Soon after the cross, on the right, you'll see the...*

Warren House Inn

Named for a warrener (rabbit-raiser) who fed bunnies to hungry miners, this pub comes with a fun history. This site has reputedly been occupied by a travelers' rest stop for more than 900 years. In 1845, a pub across the road was falling down from disrepair, so this "new" structure was built. Supposedly embers from the old fire were used to light the fire in the new building—which has burned ever since. While the story is questionable, the food here is good—specializing in (of course) rabbit pie, as well as steak and ale pie. The glorious moorside seating, at picnic benches out front and across the road, make it an enticing stop for a meal or drink (£6–12 entrées, open Easter–mid-Nov daily for lunch and dinner, mid-Nov–Easter closed Mon–Tue evenings, tel. 01822/880-208, www.warrenhouseinn.co.uk).

• *There's a lot "moor" to see, so let's keep moving. Carry on along the same road into the town of...*

Postbridge

This functional village comes with one of Dartmoor's classic views.

As you cross the bridge in the heart of town, on the left you'll see an ancient bridge parallel to the road. This type of stone bridge, essentially a post and a wide flat stone lintel, is called a clapper bridge. These bridges, which dot the moor, date from the Middle Ages, if not earlier. For a closer look, pull over at the big parking lot on the right soon after the bridge, near the handy and very helpful national park office. If you have time, consider a hike—Postbridge is a good base for moor walks (pick up their £1.50 booklet for walks from here).

• *Continue down to the village of Two Bridges, where you hit B3357. Our route turns left (east) on this road, but consider detouring to the right (west) to the town of* **Princetown** *(pronounced "Princeton"), with its High Moorland Visitor Centre (see page 296). Princetown is also home to a high-security prison that held French prisoners during the Napoleonic Wars, and American POWs during the War of 1812. (But if you've already gotten your fill of park info from the Postbridge office, Princetown is skippable.)*

Heading east on B3357, you'll soon have to use some narrower back roads to reach our next stop. You'll feel lost, but use your map and track signs closely: First follow signs down into Dartmeet, then uphill toward Ashburton. After coming back down from the moor, watch for the turn-off on the left to Ponsworthy, then our next stop...

Widecombe-in-the-Moor

Set in the center of the rolling hills, this adorable but shopper-choked village is a scenic stop—and feels crowded after a drive on the empty moor. There's a farm-

ers' market the fourth Saturday of every month (9:30–15:00) and a Thursday craft market during the summer at the 1537 Church House (late May–early Oct 10:00–16:00, www.widecombe -in-the-moor.com). If you're ready for a meal, carry on (turning right at the sign by the Church House) down the country road to the **Rugglestone Inn**—which is more likely to have local farmers drinking a pint than tourists. The prices are surprisingly low, and the quality is good...but watch out for the high-powered local cider (£8–10 entrées, food served daily 12:00–14:00 & 18:30–21:00, tel. 01364/621-327, www.ruggle stoneinn.co.uk).

• *Leave Widecombe, following signs for* Bovey Tracey *and enjoying the sky-high views. (On a clear day, you can see all the way to the ocean.) Now we'll take a look at two of the better-known "tors" of Dartmoor. If you're tight on time, choose one: Haytor is famous and offers better views, but is more difficult to hike to, while Hound Tor is the more impressive formation.*

On the Bovey Tracey road, you'll spot a turnoff on the left toward Moretonhampstead, *which we'll take later (or now, if you want to skip Haytor). To see Haytor, continue 1.5 miles farther on—you'll spot it on the hilltop above you on the left. Use the giant parking lot on the right (after a smaller one on the left) and hike up to the grand...*

Haytor

Dartmoor sits up on a granite plateau, and occasionally bare granite "peaks" poke up through the heather. Like lonesome watchtowers looming above the barren landscape, these "tors" are Dartmoor's most distinctive landmarks— and Haytor is the most famous and popular, thanks to its excellent vantage point for pan-

oramic views. Tors basically look like piles of boulders that you can imagine might have been dragged and dropped on hilltops by prehistoric developers, but they're all natural, caused by weathering. This area is divided into two parts: Haytor itself, and the adjacent Haytor Rocks.

• *If you'd like to detour into the town of **Bovey Tracey** (described on page 306), now's the time—it's 10 minutes away on B3387, in the valley beyond the Haytor park information center.*

Or, to continue our loop, backtrack to the Moretonhampstead turn-off (M'hampstead for short), which you'll now follow north through the moors. Soon you'll see another tor ahead and on the right. When you get to the little fork, follow the P signs to the right and park to walk up to...

Hound Tor

Perhaps the most striking tor in Dartmoor, and the inspiration for the Sherlock Holmes story *The Hound of the Baskervilles,* this

mighty clump of rocks impresses. According to legend, this stand of stones was once a pack of hunting dogs that had disrupted a witches' coven. As a punishment, the pooches were petrified. (The hunter that owned the dogs was turned into the nearby tor called Bowerman's Nose, about a mile north of here.) Hike up and scramble over the many levels. In the valley beyond this ridge are faint remains of old Devon longhouses. These were situated at a gentle angle, with animals in the lower part and people in the upper part—liquids and other waste would run downhill, while the heat generated by the livestock would warm its owners above.

DARTMOOR

Letterboxing

The local pastime of letterboxing began as a way to collect tourist postcards. What has evolved is a secret system of log-books hidden all over Dartmoor—inside metal boxes, squirreled away under rocks, or stuffed in the brush. Your goal: Find the logbook and stamp, and add your name and stamp to as many books as possible (bring your own inkpad just in case). Since this practice is a bit of a secret, you'll need to enlist a local to help you get started. Ask at a local TI or at Bellever Hostel (near Postbridge), or check out www.dartmoorletterboxing.org and www.letterboxingondartmoor.co.uk.

• *Our tour is nearly finished. From the Hound Tor parking lot, backtrack a few yards to the little fork and turn right, following signs to M'hampstead. You'll drive through the countryside before reaching the larger but still charming town of* **Moretonhampstead**—*a nice place for a stroll, dining at the recommended White Horse Inn (see "Eating in Dartmoor," later), or to browse the selection of local guidebooks at the TI (daily 9:30–17:00, off-season Fri–Sun only 10:00–16:30; Internet access—first 10 minutes free, then 50p/30 minutes; New Street, tel. 01647/440-043, www.moretonhampstead.com).*

If you still have daylight left, consider heading north out of Moretonhampstead on A382 until the turnoff (to the right) for Drewsteignton and the **Fingle Bridge;** *or head back through Chagford and venture to the* **Scorhill Stone Circle** *(both described under "Sights in Dartmoor," next).*

Sights in Dartmoor

▲**Walks on the Moors**—Pick up your Ordnance Survey map at any local shop or TI and start walking. The Princetown TI also has a map with suggestions for routes through the moors. Postbridge, in the heart of the moorlands, is a fine launch pad for good walks, and has a park information center that can suggest well-outlined routes. Other good walking bases include Belstone in the north (for rugged scenery) and Ivybridge in the south (more forested). You can go almost anywhere—except the firing ranges. These are technically open for walking when not in use (you'll see red flags if they're closed), but it's probably best to avoid them entirely. For more pointers, read "Orientation to Dartmoor," earlier.

▲▲**Scorhill Stone Circle**—Thousands of Neolithic ruins dot the landscape of Dartmoor, but the Scorhill (SCO-rill) Stone Circle near Gidleigh may be the best. Stonehenge, *the* iconic stone circle, is much bigger—but it's also packed with crowds and right off a busy road (described in the Near Bath chapter). Tranquil, forgotten Scorhill is yours alone—the way a stone circle should be. As it comes with a scenic stroll across a moor, it's a great sampling of what Dartmoor is all about—as much about the journey as about the destination.

Getting There: The trailhead is about a 15-minute drive west of Chagford. The trailhead is tricky to find—be patient, use your Ordnance Survey map, and solicit help from a local. (I wouldn't attempt it in a heavy fog—but if you do, take along a compass.) From Chagford, follow signs to *Gidleigh*—you'll drive west out of town, bear right (uphill) at the fork, then turn right at the next intersection; from there, cross over the very narrow bridge and go through Murchington, then stay straight, going up and down the hills through Gidleigh. Keep following the same off-the-beaten-path road through the hamlet of Berrydown, until you dead-end at a little parking lot (if in doubt, follow signs for *Scorhill*). Park, then walk through the gate and hike about 15 minutes straight ahead up and over the moor (with a long stone fence on either side of you). After cresting the hill, head down into the gentle valley and look for the circle below (slightly to the left—assuming you've walked straight from the gate). Once there, you'll be alone with the heather, broom, ancient history...and, often, sheep and wild ponies.

▲**Teign Gorge and Fingle Bridge**—Near the town of Drew-steignton, a narrow road leads down into the Teign River Valley.

At the end of the road is the **Fingle Bridge Inn,** a pub set along a river and a picturesque old bridge. The food is good and reasonably priced, with daily specials and a hearty ploughman's lunch of open-face sand-wiches (£4–8 lunches served from 12:00–15:00, £7–10

dinners; open June–Sept Mon–Sat 11:00–22:00, Sun 11:00–18:00; Oct–May daily 11:00–16:00, sometimes also open for dinner; tel. 01647/281-287). A popular spot for weddings and fly-fishing, the trail across the road makes for an excellent post-meal amble along the river (from B3219, head to Drewsteignton, then look for signs to *Fingle Bridge*).

Up the road, you'll come across **Castle Drogo,** an elaborate country house—complete with a circular croquet lawn and formal gardens—that has the honor of being the last castle built in England, finished in 1930 (£7.80, grounds only-£5; mid-March-Oct daily 11:00–17:00 except closed Tue mid-March–April and early-Sept–Oct, grounds and visitor

center open at 9:30, sight generally open weekends only off-season, closed Jan–mid-Feb; last entry 30 minutes before closing, on-site café, tel. 01647/433-306, www.nationaltrust.org.uk/castledrogo). Some trails on the estate lead down to Fingle Bridge.

Bovey Tracey—This town on the southeastern side of Dartmoor National Park is a good base and offers a few indoor options to explore when the rains chase you off the moors (just 10 minutes' drive west of Haytor on B3387). With about 7,000 people, it's a metropolis by Dartmoor standards. The **TI** is located at the main pay-and-display lot on the right as you drive into town (March–Oct daily 10:00–16:00, Nov–Feb sporadic hours—usually Sat 10:00–14:00, tel. 01626/832-047, www.boveytracey.gov.uk). You can get online at the library (up to 30 minutes free, Mon–Tue and Thu–Fri 10:00–12:30 & 14:00–17:30, Sat 10:00–12:30 only, closed Wed and Sun, Abbey Road, tel. 01626/832-026, www.devon.gov.uk/library). Accommodations and eateries in Bovey Tracey are suggested later in this chapter.

Bovey Tracey, a pottery town until the 1950s, is becoming known as a center for fine crafts. Clay was quarried nearby, and Josiah Wedgwood even nosed around here when deciding where to locate his china factory (he later chose Staffordshire). The **Devon Guild of Craftsmen** has a gallery/museum and shop in a restored riverside mill downtown (daily 10:00–17:30, Riverside Mill, tel. 01626/832-223, www.crafts.org.uk), and hosts a contemporary arts fair the second weekend in June (www.craftsatboveytracey.co.uk).

The **House of Marbles** sounds goofy enough that you want to visit. It's basically a giant gift shop with some interesting glass-making displays inside. Check out the marble museum displaying antique marbles, ones made of odd materials, and fun, kinetic wire marble mazes in action that always draw a crowd. The place is now the home of Teign Valley Glass Studios, and you can watch artisans at work creating contemporary glassware using traditional skills (in action Tue–Sat 9:00–16:30, Sun 10:00–15:00, lunch and tea breaks posted). Outside in the courtyard are old, circa-1900 "muffle" kilns (signs describe their history). In the gift shop, kids of all ages will love digging through the giant bins of multicolored marbles—they're actually made in Mexico, but big piles of them look really cool (free, Mon–Sat 9:00–17:00, Sun 11:00–17:00, café, about 1.5 miles south of town toward Newton Abbot just off A382, at The Old Pottery on Pottery Road, tel. 01626/835-285, www .houseofmarbles.com).

Sleeping in Dartmoor

Befitting such a mysterious destination, accommodations in Dartmoor tend to be quirkier than the English norm, with more character(s) than the staid, hotelesque accommodations in more mainline destinations. Sleeping here really feels like "going local."

Near Chagford

For a description of the handy home-base town of Chagford, see page 299. Most of these accommodations aren't in Chagford itself, but in other villages (or the countryside) nearby. I've provided general directions, but given the confusing spaghetti of back roads here, it's always smart to call ahead for precise arrival instructions.

$$$ Sandy Park Inn, owned by a local bigwig, rents five well-appointed but overpriced rooms above a busy upmarket pub. Although it's in a creaky old 16th-century shell, it comes with modern touches (Sb-£45, Db-£85, cheaper for longer stays, Wi-Fi, tel. 01647/433-267, www.sandyparkinn.co.uk, sandypark inn@btconnect.com, Matt). It's on A382 east of Chagford, at the turnoff for the Teign Gorge. For more on the pub, see "Eating in Dartmoor," later.

$$$ Along Chagford's main street, several pubs rent rooms upstairs. The best bet is **The Globe Inn,** with seven decent rooms (Sb-£55, Db-£90, 9 High Street, pay parking lot nearby, tel. 01647/433-485, www.globeinnchagford.co.uk, graham@globe innchagford.co.uk, Graham and Mary). They're also open for meals (£7–16, daily 12:00–14:30 & 18:00–21:00).

$$ Easton Court offers five bright, flowery rooms that overlook the gardens where *Brideshead Revisited* was written (decorated with a faux stone circle to ponder). A bit less "colorful" than the other accommodations here (in a good way), it feels like the ideal thatched-roof English guest house (classic Db-£70–75, superior Db-£80–85, Sb-£15 less, free Internet access and Wi-Fi, parking, tel. 01647/433-469, www.easton.co.uk, stay@easton.co.uk, Debra and Paul). It's at the crossroads called Easton, just east of Chagford, right on A382.

In or near Moretonhampstead

Moretonhampstead—larger and less quaint than Chagford or Widecombe-in-the-Moor—is a handy home base with its own share of half-timbered appeal.

DARTMOOR

Sleep Code

(£1 = about $1.60, country code: 44, area code: 01364)
S = Single, **D** = Double/Twin, **T** = Triple, **Q** = Quad, **b** = bathroom, **s** = shower only. You can assume credit cards are accepted and breakfast is included unless otherwise noted.

To help you sort easily through these listings, I've divided the rooms into three categories based on the price for a standard double room with bath:

$$$ Higher Priced—Most rooms £80 or more.
$$ Moderately Priced—Most rooms between £50–80.
$ Lower Priced—Most rooms £50 or less.

Prices can change without notice; verify the hotel's current rates online or by email. For other updates, see www.ricksteves.com/update.

$$$ Eastwrey Barton Country House is set on a terraced lawn halfway up the side of the Wray Valley between Moretonhampstead and Bovey Tracey. It has five warm and spacious rooms in a restored Georgian country house (Sb-£70–80, Db-£100–120, £30 three-course dinners for guests, free Wi-Fi, several nice lounges, on A382 near Lustleigh, tel. 01647/277-338, www.eastwreybarton.co.uk, info@eastwreybarton.co.uk, friendly Sharon and Patrick).

$$ Cookshayes Country Guest House, on the main B3212 road in the heart of Moretonhampstead, has seven traditional, homey rooms in a big house. They also serve good dinners for guests on request (Sb-£40–45, Db-£50–55, 33 Court Street, tel. 01647/440-374, fax 0167/440-453, www.cookshayes.co.uk, cookshayes@aol.com, gregarious Tracy and chef Barry).

$ Sparrowhawk Backpackers rents cheap beds in the Moretonhampstead town center, in the light-filled loft of a restored stone stable (£16 bunks in coed dorm with curtains, D-£36, £45 family room, bedding provided, kitchen, 45 Ford Street, tel. 01647/440-318, mobile 07870-513-570, www.sparrowhawkbackpackers.co.uk, ali@sparrowhawkbackpackers.co.uk).

In or near Bovey Tracey

Sleep here if you want to be close to a real town on the edge of the national park, rather than the rustic villages inside Dartmoor. For more on Bovey Tracey, see page 306.

$$ Brookfield House offers three bedrooms in a spacious 1906 Edwardian house set on two acres of lawns and gardens (Sb-£51–55, D-£72, Db-£72–80, no children under 12, closed Dec–Jan,

Challabrook Lane, tel. 01626/836-181, www.brookfield-house
.com, enquiries@brookfield-house.com, Frances and Laurence).

$$ The Cromwell Arms is a 16th-century coaching inn right
in the middle of the action with 12 simple, comfortable rooms
(Sb-£55–60, Db-£70–75, family Qb-£100–110, Fore Street, tel.
01626/833-473, www.thecromwellarms.co.uk, info@thecromwell
arms.co.uk, Gary and Julie). For more on the downstairs pub, see
"Eating in Bovey Tracey," later.

Near Postbridge
$ Bellever Youth Hostel offers 38 beds in seven rooms on the
moors. It's simple and institutional, but it comes with an impres-
sive wildlife area out front to learn about the local terrain (£16/
bunk in 4- to 8-bed rooms, £1/night discount if arriving by bus,
bicycle, or on foot; £3 more for non-members, £6–7 dinners, £1
self-service laundry, members' kitchen, open all year, reception
open 7:30–10:00 & 17:00–22:30, 10:00–17:00 lockout, toll tel.
0845-371-9622, www.yha.org.uk, bellever@yha.org.uk). It's down
a long road in Bellever just south of Postbridge, well-signed from
the main road.

Near Widecombe-in-the-Moor
$$ Higher Venton Farm is a simple, middle-of-nowhere 1560
farmhouse renting three basic rooms with eclectic, outmoded
decor (S-£32, twin D-£60, Db-£70, tel. 01364/621-235, www
.ventonfarm.com, helenhicks@ventonfarm.fsnet.co.uk). It's about
a half-mile outside the village of Widecombe-in-the-Moor (follow
signs from main intersection to *Rugglestone Inn*, then continue on
the same road beyond the inn to the farm).

Eating in Dartmoor

In or near Chagford
Several pubs in Chagford serve microwaved pub grub, but locals
recommend venturing into the countryside for a better meal. Also
note that many accommodations serve affordable meals to their
guests—but always ask in advance so they have time to shop and
prepare.

22 Mill Street, pricey but well-regarded, is a cut above the
other eateries lining Chagford's main street, both in terms of
class and quality (£23–28 fixed-price lunches, £36–59 fixed-price
dinners, open Tue–Sat, closed Sun-Mon, reservations smart, tel.
01647/432-244). They also rent three good rooms upstairs with
a breakfast and three-course dinner package (Db-£189–219,
www.22millst.com).

Sandy Park Inn, which also rents rooms, has a characteristic

16th-century pub and a cozy dining room that serves pricey but good food with great Old World atmosphere (£5–6 sandwiches at lunch, £5–14 entrées, tel. 01647/433-267). It's a few minutes from Chagford—for location details, see "Sleeping in Dartmoor," earlier.

In Moretonhampstead

The White Horse Inn has tasty Mediterranean-inspired dishes, as well as more traditional pub fare and pizzas. You can sit in the pub or a few steps down in the quieter, more modern dining room (£7.50–11 pizzas, £10–17 main dishes, Tue–Sun 12:00–21:00, Mon 18:00–21:00, 7 George Street, tel. 01647/440-242).

In Bovey Tracey

De-Tracey's Bar offers traditional pub fare in the upper part of the town (£6–10 meals, food served Tue–Sat 12:00–14:00 & 18:30–21:30, Sun–Mon 12:00–14:00, 56 Fore Street, tel. 01626/833-465).

Spice Bazaar offers good Indian food (£7–15 entrées, daily 12:00–14:00 & 18:00–23:30, 38 Fore Street, tel. 01626/833-111).

The Cromwell Arms serves good meals in a traditional atmosphere (food served Mon–Sat 12:00–14:00 & 18:00–21:00, Sun 12:00–14:30 & 18:30–20:30, Fore Street, tel. 01626/833-473).

Elsewhere in Dartmoor

Earlier in this chapter, I've described three restaurants that make for good lunch or dinner stops as you explore the moors: **Warren House Inn,** perched atop a moor south of Chagford (see page 301); **Rugglestone Inn,** just outside the village of Widecombe-on-the-Moor (see page 302); and the **Fingle Bridge Inn,** in the Teign Gorge (see page 305).

CORNWALL

Penzance • St. Ives • The Penwith Peninsula • East Cornwall

Set on a rocky peninsula in the southwest of England, Cornwall has a Celtic vibe. Its rugged scenery and wild, uncultivated appeal make you feel as if you're approaching the end of the world (and many natives would say it's exactly that). Harboring the remnants of an endangered Celtic culture (Cornish), an extinct tin-mining industry, and a gaggle of visit-worthy sights, this is one of England's most popular holiday regions—especially among the English.

Cornwall—part of the "Celtic fringe" of Britain—grew up as a very different place from England, with its own language, called Cornish, which thrived for centuries. Fishing, shipping, and smuggling were the main businesses here for hundreds of years, but in the 18th century, tin-mining became the major industry. The 20th century dealt a double blow to Cornwall: The local pilchard fish became depleted, and cheap Asian and South American tin put an end to mining. Today's predominant trade is tourism, as evidenced by the many tacky tourist traps littering the landscape.

But visitors flock here for good reason. Not only is the area packed with ancient sites, precious villages, and historic monuments, but the climate is also unusually mild. The Gulf Stream often brings warm, almost tropical weather to Cornwall—making it perfect for gardening, walking, basking on the beach, and generally enjoying life.

To see Cornwall, set yourself up in a home base (Penzance or St. Ives) and spend most of your time venturing out on day trips. Romantic St. Ives has an artsy beach-bum ambience and is crowded with holiday-makers in summer. Penzance, on the other hand, is all business—a working-class shipping port with plenty of high-quality accommodations and welcoming eateries. Since Cornwall is best suited for day-tripping, Penzance's relative lack of tourist charm is actually an asset—it's much easier to drive in and out of, and has better public-transportation connections, making it my preferred home base. Sleep in St. Ives only if you're serious about gallery-hopping.

Venture to quaint seaside villages, a dramatic theater, a telegraph museum, a dead tin mine, and a thought-provoking stone circle. Cry "Land Ho!" at Land's End, and consider a chopper or ferry ride to the castaway Isles of Scilly. Farther northeast, the castle of a king named Arthur tickles travelers' imaginations, while unusual gardens thrill green thumbs.

Planning Your Time

Brits spend weeks here on holiday. But for a speedy traveler, two nights based in Penzance or St. Ives, with one solid day rambling around the peninsula, offer a suitable first taste.

Given that it takes so long to get to this edge of the world from the heart of England (figure about a day each way by car or train), it makes sense not to rush your visit. Spending three nights and two days here allows you to slow down, see all the sights, and get a better feel for Cornish culture. Most of the noteworthy sights and villages wrap around the Penwith Peninsula, so you can line them up and see them on a handy circular drive.

The attractions farther east—Tintagel Castle and the gardens—are ideal for breaking up the long journey to or from Cornwall (en route to Bath or Dartmoor).

Getting to Cornwall

By Train: Train travelers arrive in Cornwall at Penzance, the most central and largest city on the coast (see "Penzance Connections" on page 323).

By Plane: Cornwall's main airport is Newquay–Cornwall International (www.newquay-airport.co.uk), 5 miles from Newquay and 35 miles northeast of Penzance. Airlines that serve Newquay include Air Southwest (from London–Gatwick, Bath/Bristol, and more; www.airsouthwest.com) and Flybe (from Edinburgh or London–Gatwick, www.flybe.com). Europcar (www.europcar.co.uk) and Hertz (www.hertz.co.uk) rent cars at the airport. Public-transportation connections into Penzance can be tricky—contact the Newquay TI for suggestions (tel. 01637/854-020,

Cornwall

ATLANTIC OCEAN

AIRPORT

DEVON

TO BARNSTAPLE & BATH

A-39

OKEHAMPTON

LONDON

TINTAGEL

CAMELFORD

A-39

A-375

A-30

BODMIN MOOR

BODMIN

DARTMOOR NAT'L. PARK

A-386

WADE-BRIDGE

SEE PENWITH PENINSULA DETAIL MAP

NEWQUAY

A-30

A-38

TO EXETER + LONDON

ST. IVES

TRURO

EDEN PROJECT

PLYMOUTH

PENZANCE

A-394

LAND'S END

FALMOUTH

ISLES OF SCILLY

ST. MICHAEL'S MOUNT

TREBAH + GLENDURGAN GARDENS

LIZARD PENINSULA

20 MILES

30 KM

ENGLISH CHANNEL

DCH

www.visitnewquay.org), or try BioTravel's airport transfer service (tel. 01637/880-006, www.biotravel.co.uk).

Getting Around Cornwall

This region is most satisfying by car, which allows you to pack a lot into each day. It's challenging but doable by public transportation, in which case you'll have to be more selective. Note that all public-transit routes run less frequently off-season (Oct–April). A tour with Western Discoveries (see page 318) is a handy way to get into the countryside.

By Car: The coastal road—which passes through Penzance and above St. Ives—links together almost all of the best sights. Driving in Cornwall is generally easy, but parking is not, especially in summer—small villages often have tiny parking lots near the water and larger ones outside of town, so it's a good idea to arrive early in the day. Roads can get very congested on Bank Holiday weekends and in August, so allow extra time, especially on main routes such as A30 and A38. Narrow, twisty Cornish lanes criss-cross the spine of the peninsula, and can save time if the main routes are crowded—but you'll need a good map (try the 1:100,000 Ordnance Survey) and, even more importantly, a good navigator. For current traffic conditions, listen to the radio—many rental-car stereos have a setting for automatic traffic updates (often marked by the letters TA or TP, see page 710).

By Bus: It's slow but possible to reach most Cornwall sights

Cornish History

Cornwall's history is almost as old as the history of humanity. Prehistoric huts, stone circles, and other mysterious structures stand witness to the timeless appeal of Cornwall. While a few of these are easy to reach (such as the Merry Maidens), most are hidden away and best uncovered with a local guide (try Western Discoveries tours—described on page 318).

When the Romans arrived in Britain in the first century B.C., the native Celtic inhabitants were forced to the farthest, most inhospitable corners of the island. To this day, a "Celtic fringe" still rings England. This includes several groups struggling to keep alive their fading languages, such as Welsh, Scottish Gaelic, Irish Gaelic, Manx (on the Isle of Man)...and Cornish.

This part of Britain—specifically Penzance—was ideally located for shipping, since boats could launch straight into the Atlantic, rather than having to tack from farther east all the way along the English Channel. It's no wonder that Penzance is best known as the namesake for a Gilbert and Sullivan musical about the high seas. In addition to sailors and pirates, artists love this scenic corner of Britain, which can change from sun-drenched to rainy and windblown in a matter of minutes. Dramatic clouds hit Cornwall like a hammer, and the sea here changes color with the sky.

Rich deposits of metals—especially tin—have linked this rugged spit of land to the rest of the world, making Cornwall unexpectedly cosmopolitan. Cornish tin has been found in ancient plumbing as far away as Turkey and Pompeii (Italy). Cornwall wasn't conquered by the Romans—partly because of its remoteness—but also because the Cornish were already Roman trading partners. (You'll find no Roman forts in Cornwall, but you will find Roman goods.) Cornish trading came with an influx of exotic products—Cornish cooking is unique in England for its use of saffron, likely bartered with the Near East for metals.

In the 18th century, Cornwall's tin-mining industry enjoyed a boom (see sidebar on page 334). But when the industry went bust in the late 19th century, many miners had to find work elsewhere. Though tin-mining was a back-breaking, menial job, it

by bus, some of which go topless May through September. Most buses are run by First (toll tel. 0845-600-1420 or Traveline toll tel. 0871-200-2233, www.firstgroup.com), though Western Greyhound handles the #504 route (tel. 01637/871-871, www.westerngreyhound.com). First has a useful one-day pass called "FirstDay Cornwall" for the region that includes Penzance, St. Ives, Land's End, and the surrounding area (£6.80, buy directly from driver). You'll find the following bus routes useful:

Buses **#1** and **#1A** connect Penzance with Newlyn and Land's End (Mon–Sat every 1–3 hours, Sun 3/day, 10 minutes to Newlyn, also required highly skilled miners. Mine owners from around the world began to recruit and relocate unemployed Cornish miners. Throughout the 1860s, 20 percent of Cornish people emigrated, and this "Cornish diaspora" spread the culture from this corner of England across the face of the earth. For example, hundreds of Cornish miners went to California to get in on the Gold Rush. Locals brag, "Anywhere you find a hole in the ground, you'll find a Cornishman at the bottom of it." Similarly, Cornish graveyards read like a geography textbook, as headstones often list the places where the person lived.

The great migration of the late 19th century also left behind many ghost towns, which still dot the Cornish countryside. Today, many of these long-abandoned homes are being bought up by Londoners and converted into holiday villas—driving up prices and forcing out the few remaining locals.

The Cornish language—related to Welsh, and more distantly related to Scottish Gaelic and Irish Gaelic—was widely spoken here through the late 18th century. As the Industrial Revolution shrunk England and church leaders refused to offer services in Cornish, the language became obsolete. Cornish survived only among a handful of speakers through the 19th and early 20th centuries. But, remarkably, Cornish held on, and—after a recent EU designation as an official minority language—it's now allowed to be taught in schools again. More people speak Cornish today than two centuries ago, and raising kids to be bilingual is in vogue.

Today, feisty Cornwall, with a half-million residents, is officially and for all practical purposes part of England (unlike Wales or Scotland). But native-born Cornishmen and Cornishwomen still cling to what makes them unique—they're Cornish first, British second. The fledgling Cornish independence movement has never really gotten anywhere, but that doesn't stop locals from displaying the flag of Cornwall: a black field (representing the earth) with a white cross (the tin flowing through the earth). Also look for bumper stickers boasting the Cornish word for "Cornwall": *Kernow*.

50 minutes to Land's End); #1A also stops at Porthcurno, near the Telegraph Museum and a steep uphill climb to the Minack Theatre (Mon–Sat 4/day, Sun 2/day, 40 minutes).

Buses **#2** and **#2A** run between Penzance and Falmouth, stopping at Marazion near St. Michael's Mount (Mon–Sat 2/hour, Sun every 2 hours, 10 minutes to Marazion, 1.75 hours to Falmouth).

Buses **#6** and **#6A** connect Penzance with Newlyn and Mousehole (1–2/hour, 10 minutes to Newlyn, 20 minutes to Mousehole). Buses **#5** and **#5A** also go to Newlyn, and sometimes continue to Mousehole (hourly).

Buses **#14**, **#17**, **#17A**, and **#17B** connect Penzance and St. Ives (roughly 2/hour, or 1/hour on Sun, 35–50 minutes). Bus **#17B** also stops at Marazion (St. Michael's Mount).

Bus **#300** does a big, made-for-tourists 3.5-hour loop around the Penwith Peninsula (daily, every 2 hours), connecting Penzance, St. Ives (40 minutes), and Land's End (2.5 hours). Along the way, it stops at Marazion (St. Michael's Mount), the Geevor Tin Mine, Sennen Cove, Porthcurno, and Newlyn.

Bus **#504** connects Penzance to some otherwise difficult-to-reach destinations along the southern edge of Penwith (Mon–Sat 2–4/day, none on Sun): Newlyn (10 minutes), Mousehole (15 minutes), Merry Maidens (35 minutes), Porthcurno (50 minutes), Minack Theatre (55 minutes), Land's End (1.25 hours), and Sennen Cove.

By Train: A scenic (read: slow) rail line connects Penzance and St. Ives, mostly running along the coast (2/day direct, 20 minutes; at least hourly with transfer in St. Erth, 25–60 minutes; toll tel. 0845-748-4950, www.nationalrail.co.uk).

Penzance

Sure enough, Penzance had its share of pirates. Strategically situated near the very tip of Britain, the town was an ideal spot for pirates to hijack and plunder ships returning from the New World with untold treasures. But today's Penzance is less of a rough-and-tumble pirate smuggler's cove and more of a blue-collar transportation hub. Penzance can't compete with the artsy vibe of St. Ives or the precious jewel-box quality of nearby Mousehole, but it's cornered the market on functionality: Well-located B&Bs, good restaurants, train and bus stations, and easy parking make Penzance the most practical home base for exploring the Cornish coast.

Orientation to Penzance

(area code: 01736)

Penzance, with about 20,000 people, is situated on a small peninsula. The eastern part of the peninsula has the TI, harbor, and train and bus stations. The southern part has a broad and inviting promenade, with most of the town's B&Bs nearby. Climbing uphill from the water are various streets, including the bustling Market Jew Street (derived from the Cornish *Marghas Yow*, meaning "Thursday Market") and the more atmospheric, restaurant-

Penzance

P PARKING

— MAIN ROAD (A-30) THROUGH TOWN

TO ST. MICHAEL'S MOUNT, ST. IVES & DARTMOOR

TRAIN STATION (MAY CLOSE IN 2011)

ROCKS

BUS STN.

TO LAND'S END

A-30 ALVERTON ROAD

HARBOR

ALBERT PIER

PENLEE HOUSE MUSEUM

ST. MARY

SOUTH PIER

REGENT TERR.

PROMENADE

CASINO

ROCKS

JUBILEE BATHING POOL

TO ISLES OF SCILLY

MOUNT'S BAY

200 YARDS

200 METERS

TO NEWLYN, MOUSEHOLE & ❽

❶ Regent Terrace Guest Houses

❷ Glencree House & Chiverton House

❸ Penzance Backpackers

❹ The Turks Head Pub & Admiral Benbow

❺ Chapel Street Brasserie

❻ The Navy Inn

❼ The Boatshed

❽ To The Smugglers Restaurant

❾ Launderette

❿ Library (Internet Access)

CORNWALL

lined Chapel Street. The hill is capped by the spire of the Church of St. Mary, and the grandly domed Market House, now a bank.

Tourist Information

Due to uncertainty about funding, the Penzance TI's future is in question. If it's still open for your visit, you'll find it between the train and bus stations (likely hours if open: early July–Aug Mon–Fri 9:00–17:00, Sat 10:00–16:00, Sun 10:00–14:00; Easter–early July and Sept Mon–Sat 9:00–17:00, may close earlier on Sat, closed Sun; Oct–Easter Mon–Fri 9:00–17:00, closed Sat–Sun; tel. 01736/362-207, www.visit-westcornwall.com). The TI offers tips on the many nearby day-trip options, sells helicopter tickets for the Isles of Scilly, and books rooms for a £3 fee.

Helpful Hints

Festival: The annual **Golowan (Midsummer) Festival** engulfs Penzance for nine days in mid- to late-June. Things get especially rowdy on Mazey Day, the last Saturday of the festival, with colorful parades and well-lubricated crowds (tel. 01736/369-686, www.golowan.org).

Art Pass: Art buffs can consider the £12 Art Pass, which provides unlimited access for seven days to the Penlee House Gallery and Museum in Penzance; the Tate Gallery, Barbara Hepworth Museum, and Leach Pottery in St. Ives; and a discount at the shops in the Newlyn Art Gallery and the Exchange in Newlyn (www.tate.org.uk/stives/information).

Internet Access: You can get online at **Steamers Café,** inside the train station (£0.50/10 minutes, Mon–Sat 7:30–17:30, closed Sun, tel. 01736/360-369) or at the **library,** just up from the Penlee House Gallery and Museum on Morrab Road (£0.90/15 minutes, Mon–Fri 9:30–18:00, Sat 9:30–16:00, closed Sun, tel. 0300-1234-111).

Baggage Storage: You can stow your luggage at **Longboat Hotel,** across the street from the train station (£2/bag, daily 7:30–24:00, Market Jew Street, tel. 01736/364-137).

Laundry: Penzance's big waterfront **casino,** along the promenade past the Regent Terrace B&Bs, is attached to a handy little launderette (around the right side of the casino; about £3–5.50/load for self-service, £2.50–5 more for full service, same-day full service possible if you bring it soon after the attendant arrives at 9:00, open daily 7:30–20:00, start last load by 18:30, tel. 01736/333-978).

Taxis: Cabs line up at the train station taxi stand. Or you can call the reliable **Stones Taxi** (tel. 01736/363-400) for the £3–4 fare to my recommended Regent Terrace accommodations.

Swimming Pool: Take a dip next to the sea in the outdoor, Art Deco **Jubilee Pool,** or just watch the action from the promenade (£4, cheaper after 15:30, June–Sept daily 10.30–18:00, tel. 01736/369-224, www.jubileepool.co.uk).

Tours in Penzance

▲**Western Discoveries Tours**—If you want to explore Cornwall's hidden nooks and crannies with a local, a minivan tour is a must. Russ Peake is an enthusiastic, energetic young guide with a broad knowledge of Cornwall's history, geology, and culture. He packs up to eight people into his van and takes them on Cornwall's twistiest back lanes to track down forgotten Neolithic monuments and Iron Age settlements. You won't see any of the big attractions listed in this book—Russ takes you way off the beaten path. The route and specific sights covered change based on the weather and the interests of the group. This is a great way to experience the real Cornwall...away from the tourist congestion on the coast (£25/person for 4 hours, departs Penzance train station at 9:30; can also pick up near St. Ives train station at 9:10 for £5 extra; 5 or more go cheaper with £120 private tour, may also be able to pick up at your Penzance hotel, essential to book ahead by phone or email, tel. 01736/362-763, www.westerndiscoveries .co.uk, info@westcornwallwalks.co.uk).

Boat Tours—The beautiful Cornish coast is best seen from the water, and the catamaran trips run by **Marine Discovery** are a fun way to sample it with an ecological emphasis. A variety of tours are offered, with a chance to see seals, dolphins, porpoises, seabirds, and even basking sharks (£18–32 depending on length of tour, less for kids—though some tours have age restrictions, cash only, April–Oct, may be cancelled in bad weather, depart from either Albert Pier or South Pier depending on tides, best to reserve at least 2 days ahead, tel. 01736/874-907, mobile 07749-277-110, www.marinediscovery.co.uk, info@marinediscovery.co.uk).

Sights in Penzance

Penlee House Gallery and Museum—Filling a Victorian house in Penlee Park, the gallery hosts a fine collection from painters of the local Newlyn School. These Post-Impressionists, attracted to Cornwall in the late 1800s by the quality of light and the low cost of living, painted seascapes, portraits, and scenes of daily life. The ground floor shows off rotating exhibits from the museum's permanent collection. The upstairs has more paintings and a modest museum about Penzance's prehistoric and more recent history (learn how Penzance, Newlyn, and Mousehole were burned by Spanish raiders in 1595). It's smart to call ahead, as several times a year the museum closes some galleries for a week to rearrange its collection (£3, free on Sat and when rearranging galleries, covered by Art Pass, Easter–Sept Mon–Sat 10:00–17:00, Oct–Easter Mon–Sat 10:30–16:30, closed Sun year-round, last entry 30 minutes before closing, café, Morrab Road, tel. 01736/363-625, www.penleehouse.org.uk).

Waterfront Stroll to Newlyn and Mousehole—A broad pedestrian promenade follows the coast around Mount's Bay, from Penzance to Newlyn—perfect for an early-morning or after-dinner stroll (about 30 minutes one-way). From Newlyn, a coastal footpath extends farther to Mousehole (another 30-minute walk; for more on Mousehole, see page 330). Locals say that any fishing that happens these days goes out of Newlyn.

Sleeping in Penzance

Guest Houses on Regent Terrace

Set just a block off the seashore, the upmarket guest houses on this street are central and convenient. Rooms in front usually have views of the sea, while those in back overlook a churchyard. Most breakfast rooms are downstairs on the garden level. Though they're all run by friendly proprietors, these places feel more like small hotels than B&Bs. All offer free parking, along with free Wi-Fi and Internet access to guests. Drivers should get precise directions from their hotelier in order to find the narrow and easy-to-miss Regent Terrace.

$$$ Camilla House is relaxed and modern, with contemporary class, neutral colors, a sophisticated black-and-white lounge, and lots of luxurious touches throughout. Friendly, helpful Simon and Susan rent eight comfy, sunny rooms, and are a great source for travel tips (Sb-£37.50, Db-£75–90 depending on size and view, 3-night minimum April–Oct if booking in advance, at #12, tel. & fax 01736/363-771, www.camillahouse.co.uk, enquiries@camilla house.co.uk).

$$$ Lombard House Hotel offers a chandeliered Georgian townhouse atmosphere. The nine rooms come with slightly older furniture and fixtures than my other listings, but the two top-floor attic rooms are cozy and have fine views (Sb-£40–45, Db-£80–90, Tb-£120–135, large family Qb-£135, at #16, tel. & fax 01736/364-897, www.lombardhousehotel.com, lombardhouse@btconnect .com, Rita and Tom).

$$$ Warwick House has seven fine rooms with a casually posh feel (Sb-£40–44, Db-£80–88, at #17, tel. & fax 01736/363-881, www.warwickhousepenzance.co.uk, enquiry@warwickhouse penzance.co.uk, Chris and Julie). They also rent a two-bedroom cottage in the off-season on the nearby promenade (www.tremor vahcottage.co.uk).

$$$ Chy-an-Mor Guest House has nine rooms, some decorated in a vintage, French-traditional style. Tea and cakes are ready for you upon arrival (Sb-£37–42, Db-£70–90, no children under

---

Sleep Code

(£1 = about $1.60, country code: 44, area code: 01736)
S = Single, **D** = Double/Twin, **T** = Triple, **Q** = Quad, **b** = bathroom,
s = shower only. You can assume credit cards are accepted
and breakfast is included unless otherwise noted.

To help you sort easily through these listings, I've divided
the rooms into three categories based on the price for a
standard double room with bath:

$$$ Higher Priced—Most rooms £75 or more.
$$ Moderately Priced—Most rooms between £50-75.
$ Lower Priced—Most rooms less than £50.

Prices can change without notice; verify the hotel's
current rates online or by email. For other updates, see www
.ricksteves.com/update.

14, closed Dec–mid-March, at #15, tel. 01736/363-441, www.chyan
mor.co.uk, reception@chyanmor.co.uk, Louise and Richard).

$$$ Blue Seas Hotel has eight sleek, modern rooms (Sb-
£40–45, Db-£80–90, check website for special discounts, closed
mid-Dec–Jan, at #13, tel. 01736/364-744, www.blueseashotel
-penzance.co.uk, info@blueseashotel-penzance.co.uk, Arnaud and
Fiona).

Cheaper Options on or near Alexandra Road

Alexandra Road, about a five-minute walk down the promenade
from Regent Terrace (and therefore a bit farther from the town
center and restaurants), is lined with midrange accommodations
and a hostel. All of the below offer free Wi-Fi; additional Internet
access is available nearby at the library for a small fee.

$$ Glencree House, with eight rooms in a beautiful granite
Victorian townhouse, offers charming antique furniture, thought-
ful little touches, and comparable quality to the Regent Terrace
guest houses at a slightly lower price (S-£24–35, Sb-£28–38,
Db-£57–82, Tb-£68–108, Qb-£89–130, price depends on length of
stay and season, just off Alexandra Road on quiet Mennaye Road
at #2, tel. 01736/362-026, www.glencreehouse.co.uk, stay@glen
creehouse.co.uk, Andrew and Lynsey).

$$ Chiverton House is a stone Victorian home with six
smallish rooms packed with wood furnishings (Sb-£30–40,
Db-£50–70, cash only, just off Alexandra Road at 9 Mennaye
Road, tel. 01736/332-733, www.chivertonhousebedandbreakfast
.co.uk, alanwaller@sky.com, Alan and Sally).

$ **Penzance Backpackers,** with 30 beds in seven rooms, is situated in a townhouse on a B&B-studded stretch of Alexandra Road. This is your best bet for budget dorm beds (£16 beds in 6-person dorms, D-£35, reception open 9:00–12:00 & 17:00–23:00, no lockout, tel. 01736/363-836, www.pzbackpack.com, info @pzbackpack.com).

Eating in Penzance

Wherever you eat, check the daily specials lists—most pubs serve fresh local fish and crab, along with the usual options.

On Chapel Street

This historic street, running up into town from the waterfront near Regent Terrace, has several tempting options. Eat before 19:00 to take advantage of early-bird dinner specials.

The Turks Head Pub, the oldest pub in Penzance, is a dark, low-beamed gem. It's an all-around pub, serving tasty food and local ales. This is a popular spot—so be sure to arrive early. There are dining rooms in the back and downstairs, but the pub in front is ideal for rubbing elbows with locals (£6–8 lunches, £9–18 dinners, food served Mon–Sat 11:00–22:00, Sun 12:00–21:00, on Chapel Street near intersection with Abbey Street, no street number, tel. 01736/363-093).

Chapel Street Brasserie offers a bright, mod interior and food with a French flair—a nice change of pace in stodgy, salty Penzance (£5 brunch, £7.50–12.50 fixed-price lunches, £15–25 fixed-price dinners, daily 9:30–21:00, 12 Chapel Street, tel. 01736/350-222).

Admiral Benbow is a memorable tourist trap overloaded with over-the-top nautical decor—it's worth poking inside for a lesson on how a theme can be taken to the extreme (£5–8 lunches, £10–13 dinners, food served daily 12:00–14:30 & 17:30–21:30, 46 Chapel Street, tel. 01736/363-448).

Along the Promenade

The Navy Inn is a friendly, low-key pub that's equal parts traditional/nautical and modern (£5–9 sandwiches, £10–18 entrées, daily 10:00–22:00, just up Queen Street from The Promenade, tel. 01736/333-232).

The Boatshed is a modern wine bar and restaurant tucked across the road from the South Pier and just around the corner from recommended Regent Terrace accommodations (£5–7 sandwiches, £8 pizzas, £8–15 dinners, food served daily 11:00–15:00 & 18:30–21:30, The Quay, tel. 01736/368-845).

Out of Town, in Newlyn

The **Smugglers Restaurant** is the best option for white-tablecloth dining (dinners only). This is where locals go to celebrate special occasions. Located 1.5 miles southwest of my recommended B&Bs, it faces the harbor along the main road in Newlyn (£12–20 entrées; summer daily 19:00–21:30; winter Wed–Sat 19:00–21:30, closed Sun–Tue; 12 Fore Street, tel. 01736/331-501). They also rent out three rooms (Db-£70–82, www.smugglersnewlyn.co.uk, smugglers newlyn@btconnect.com, Stephen).

Penzance Connections

For connections within Cornwall, see page 313.

From Penzance by Train to: London's Paddington Station (about hourly, 5–6 hours, possible transfer in Plymouth or Newton Abbot), **Salisbury** (about hourly, 5–6 hours, 1–2 transfers), **Edinburgh** (every 1–2 hours, 10–17 hours, 1 direct, most transfer in London), **York** (every 1–2 hours, 8–11 hours, 1 direct, most transfer in London), **Exeter** (roughly hourly, 3 hours). Train info: toll tel. 0845-748-4950, www.nationalrail.co.uk.

By Bus to: Exeter (3/day, 5.5-6 hours, transfer in Plymouth), **Brighton** (3/day, 11.5–12.5 hours, transfers in Plymouth and Heathrow), **Portsmouth** (2–3/day, 10.5–13 hours, transfer in Plymouth), **London** (5/day direct, 8.5–10 hours, overnight available). Bus info: toll tel. 0871-781-8181, www.national express.com.

St. Ives

Picturesque St. Ives enjoys three claims to fame: It's a major artists' colony, a top fun-in-the-Cornish-sun holiday destina-

tion, and England's surfing mecca. Tourists hit the town like a tidal wave in summer (July–Sept)—when, as a local told me, "You can smell the sweat and suntan oil for miles around." An annual music and arts festival keeps things humming in September (www.stivesseptemberfestival.co.uk).

But even in the feeding frenzy of peak season, St. Ives remains mellow. British bohemians and British surfers—two kinds of people you probably didn't expect to meet in England—both abound in St. Ives.

The town's artsy aura is nothing new. With golden light reflecting off the aquamarine waves and twisty lanes, St. Ives began to attract artists in the early 20th century. The potter Bernard Leach practiced his craft here, as did sculptor Barbara Hepworth, and both have galleries in town—along with dozens of other, lesser-known artists. (The TI assured me there are an "untold number" of galleries—and handed me two different brochures suggesting gallery-hopping routes through town.) Museum junkies will seek out St. Ives' branch of the Tate Gallery.

Orientation to St. Ives

(area code: 01736)

About half the size of Penzance, with 11,000 people, St. Ives occupies a few steep bits of land between sandy beaches. The town clusters around its sandy harbor, with a bulbous spit of land just beyond called The Island. From the quaint, waterfront old town, newer development sprawls uphill toward the main road. Thanks to its warren of convoluted lanes, small St. Ives can be difficult to navigate.

Tourist Information

The TI, tucked inside the Guildhall, offers a free walking-tour brochure and a current listing of arts events. They also book rooms for a fee (June–Sept Mon–Fri 9:00–17:00, Sat 10:00–16:00, Sun 10:00–14:00; Oct–May Mon–Fri 9:00–17:00, Sat 10:00–13:00, closed Sun; Street an Pol, tel. 01736/796-297, www.visit-westcornwall.com).

Arrival in St. Ives

By Car: St. Ives is a nightmare for drivers—parking is scarce, and the streets are congested with slow-moving pedestrians. If you dare—and if it's not too crowded—you can drive right through the heart of St. Ives. Dip down into town, pass along the harbor, then head back up the hill at the far end to reach a pay lot by The Island (near my recommended accommodations).

However, most drivers avoid the tight, pedestrian-clogged lanes by parking at the huge Trenwith parking lot above town, near the Leisure Centre (£5.50 all day until 20:00; £6.50/24 hours), and take the handy £1 shuttle into town. (To find the parking lot, just before you descend into town, follow the signs to the right with the blue *P* icon.) The shuttle lets you off in town near the movie theater (take note: this is also where you'll catch the bus for the return trip).

By Train or Bus: The train and bus stations are near the waterfront; just exit and walk with the sea on your right into the heart of town. To get here, you can take the cute, historic St. Ives Bay Line that runs above the coast from St. Erth to St. Ives. Catch the train in Penzance, in St. Erth, or at the park-and-ride lot at Lelant Saltings on the way to St. Ives (toll tel. 0871-200-2233 or toll tel. 0845-748-4950, www.nationalrail.co.uk). If you use the train park-and-ride, you get £1 off your Tate Gallery entry fee.

Helpful Hints

Internet Access: You can get online at the **library,** which is just up the street from the TI (£3.60/hour, Tue 9:30–21:30, Wed–Fri 9:30–18:00, Sat 9:30–12:30, closed Sun–Mon, Gabriel Street, tel. 0300-1234-111).

Surf's Up: Find your inner dude by taking surfing lessons from **St. Ives Surf School** on Porthmeor Beach (£25/person, tel. 0966-498-021, www.thesurfschooluk.com).

Sights in St. Ives

Art lovers can save money by buying the Art Pass, which includes the first three sights mentioned here, plus others in Cornwall (see page 318).

Tate Gallery—St. Ives very proudly hosts a branch of the prestigious London art museum. The modern building impresses, but the collection—focusing mostly on modern works by relatively obscure local artists—can be a letdown to non-art-lovers (£5.75, £8.75 combo-ticket includes Barbara Hepworth Museum and Sculpture Garden; March–Oct daily 10:00–17:20; Nov–Feb Tue–Sun 10:00–16:20, closed Mon; last entry 20 minutes before closing, closes periodically to change exhibits, tel. 01736/796-226, www.tate.org.uk/stives).

▲Barbara Hepworth Museum and Sculpture Garden—Many visitors find this collection more accessible than the Tate's. Barbara Hepworth was one of the first sculptors to create non-representational art (that is, totally abstract works that didn't attempt to imitate the real world), and she lived most of her life in St. Ives. This modest museum, with a sculpture garden and replica of her studio, shows off Hepworth's curvaceous, undulating forms—inspired by, if not quite resembling, the sea, wind, sand, and light of St. Ives (£4.75, £8.75 combo-ticket includes the Tate, same hours and tel. as the Tate, at the corner of Ayr Lane and Barnoon Hill, www.tate.org.uk/stives/hepworth).

Leach Pottery Studio and Museum—This studio celebrates Bernard Leach, considered one of the founders of the mid-20th-century British studio-pottery movement. New pieces are produced on-site, and a gallery showcases work by leading contemporary potters (£4.50; March–Sept Mon–Sat 10:00–17:00, Sun 11:00–16:00; Oct–Feb Tue–Sat 10:00–16:00, closed Sun–Mon; last entry 30 minutes before closing, Higher Stennack, tel. 01736/799-703, www.leachpottery.com).

Getting There: The studio is well-marked from the upper outskirts of St. Ives, on the road into town. Park at the Trenwith car park (described earlier under "Arrival in St. Ives"); the studio is a six-minute walk from there (disabled parking only at the studio). During the summer, a frequent shuttle (£1) runs between the studio and the town center.

Stroll the Town—Besides gallery-hopping, the best way to enjoy St. Ives is by taking an ice-cream cone on a waterfront stroll. The slate-tile–clad High Street and pleasant waterfront have plenty of shops and ice-cream stands to entertain even the pickiest kids. Boats departing from the harbor can take you on trips around the cliffs and to the coves, a good way to appreciate why the Cornish coast was so popular with bootleggers and pirates.

Hit the Beach—St. Ives is popular with Brits on a "bucket-and-spade" holiday because it's surrounded by sandy beaches. In addition to the sandy, central harbor—home to boats as well as swimmers—you'll find family-friendly Porthminster Beach (west) and surfer-friendly Porthmeor Beach (east). Tiny, secluded Porthgwidden Beach—hiding between the rocks under the high peninsula called The Island—is worth the hike.

Sleeping in St. Ives

(£1 = about $1.60, country code: 44, area code: 01736)

The town's charm wears thin with the hordes of tourists in high season, but the evenings are quiet enough to consider staying over. Both of these options are in tight, twisty old buildings—climbing to your room can feel like spiraling up through a ship's hull.

$$$ Cornerways rents six rooms with lots of grays, blacks, and exposed beams. It's got a smooth nautical-meets-contemporary vibe, with easygoing Tim at the helm (Sb-£40–60, Db-£70–90, cheaper off-season, free Wi-Fi, 1 Bethesda Place, tel. 01736/796-706, www.cornerwaysstives.com, cornerwaysstives@aol.com).

$$$ The Anchorage has four cozy rooms and claustrophobic ceilings (S-£35–80, Db-£70–90, 5 Bunkers Hill, tel. 01736/797-135, www.anchoragestives.co.uk, info@anchoragestives.co.uk, Christopher).

Eating in St. Ives

The opening times for most St. Ives eateries can change from one day to the next, depending on weather and crowds.

Cornish Pasties

After working all morning underground, Cornish tin miners looked forward to their traditional lunch of a pasty (PASS-tee). Basically a beef stew wrapped in a pastry crust, pasties have a thick, crimped edge that miners could grab with dirty hands without contaminating their food. Because real flour was expensive, early miners skimped by using barley wheat—making for a very tough package. Leftover chunks of dough were often dropped into the mineshaft to appease the Tommyknockers (mischievous Cornish pixies).

Originally a pasty would be filled half with stew, and the rest with dessert, such as jam or apples. Nowadays there's a nice variety of flavors, like lamb and mint, but the full meal deal is rare. The British government is currently seeking trademark protection from the European Union for the Cornish pasty. That means the name could only be applied to those pasties made in Cornwall using traditional techniques and recipes (www.cornishpastyassociation.co.uk).

Look for pasties all over Cornwall, even in posh St. Ives. One of the best places is McFadden and Sons Butchers in St. Just, near Geevor Tin Mine (see page 335).

CORNWALL

Along the Harborfront: The main drag along the harbor has plenty of dining options. Peruse the menus and views, and choose your favorite. I ate well at **Café Coast,** with tasty and well-priced fusion cuisine (English, Thai, and Italian) and a nicely sleek, contemporary, sea-view ambience (£8–12 pizzas, pastas, and entrées; daily 9:00–16:00 & 17:30–22:00, right on the harborfront Wharf Street, tel. 01736/794-925).

Above Porthmeor Beach: Across the street from the Tate Gallery, the **Porthmeor Beach Café** is suspended above this popular surfing beach (£6–9 sandwiches, tapas, salads, and pizzas, £9–13 dinners, daily 9:00–21:30, tel. 01736/793-366).

On Fore Street: Running parallel to the harbor one block inland, Fore Street is lined with tourist shops and some good budget eateries. Near the corner of Salubrious Place, follow the heavenly scent to the **Cornish Bakehouse** for traditional Cornish pasties (tel. 01736/793-632). Just around the corner, **The Dolphin** has good fish-and-chips take-away. Or, for about £1 more, you can eat upstairs, with a sea view—the server will hoist your food up the dumbwaiter for you (tel. 01736/795-701).

On Fish Street: Just up the hill from the harbor and the landmark Sloop Inn, **Saltwater** is a small but upscale place, serving Mediterranean-inspired seafood dishes (£13–16 entrées, Tue–Sat 18:30–21:30, closed Sun–Mon, 14 Fish Street, tel. 01736/794-928).

And for Dessert: You'll see places hawking "Cornish Ice

Cream"—the frozen version of clotted cream, which means it's much creamier than the norm. For something deliciously different, try the lavender-and-honey flavor.

St. Ives Connections

The **bus** is more practical than the train for most connections. The most useful lines are #14, #17, and #17A to Penzance; #17B to Penzance via Marazion (St. Michael's Mount); and #300 to Land's End and Penzance (via Geevor Tin Mine, Sennen Cove, Porthcurno, and Marazion). For details, see page 313.

All **train** connections from St. Ives to points eastward go through St. Erth, where you'll switch from the cute little St. Ives Bay Line to the main line to Penzance (see "Penzance Connections" on page 323).

The Penwith Peninsula

The western tip of Cornwall, called the Penwith Peninsula, is a virtual pincushion of worthwhile stops. Literally meaning "Headland," Penwith features rugged, rocky, windblown scenery and the best-preserved bits of traditional Cornish culture. With Penzance or St. Ives as a home base, all of the following destinations are within easy striking distance for a day trip. I've listed them roughly clockwise from Penzance (the first sight, St. Michael's Mount, is east of—and visible from—Penzance). Drivers: Note that B3315 travels west from Penzance, passing the Merry Maidens stone circle and Porthcurno en route to Land's End.

St. Michael's Mount

Similar to France's Mont St. Michel, but on a smaller scale, this dramatic rock island has been inhabited for 1,500 years. Originally a Benedictine monastery, the castle was built up by the St. Aubyn family, who still own it today in partnership with the National Trust. If the tide is out, a pedestrian causeway connects the island to the town of Marazion. Otherwise, a short ride in a motorboat (£1.50 each way) will bring you up to the lower gates. A steep and rocky path curves its way up to the castle entrance.

Once inside, the castle is surprisingly petite. The most inter-

The Penwith Peninsula

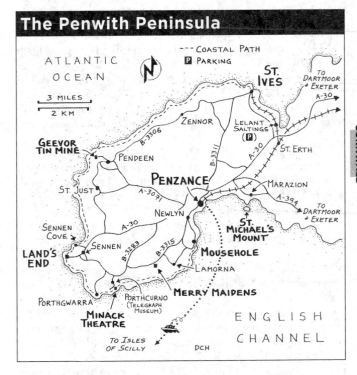

esting rooms are the chapel (probably part of the original monastery) and the Chevy Chase room (which will disappoint *Saturday Night Live* fans). Family portraits, some as recent as 1993, adorn the walls. Contrary to popular belief, most of England's castles are now owned by the state or charities. The Great Depression bankrupted many noble English families, who were forced to sell off family estates and heirlooms. This is one of the few open to the public that has remained associated with the same family since the Middle Ages.

Out on the terrace, views of the Penwith Peninsula are grand, and they get even better when you climb the tower. The windswept gardens below the castle are worth a look for die-hard gardeners.

Locals claim that Jesus Christ visited Cornwall during his teen years. Supposedly he landed here at St. Michael's Mount, then traveled up to Glastonbury (near Bath). While this might seem patently bogus, natives persuasively insist that it could have happened: Joseph of Arimathea, who was a wealthy disciple of Jesus, was also a metal trader. He might have brought Jesus to this metal-rich peninsula on a business trip. All that we know of Jesus' life between his adolescence and age 30 is that he traveled in the "wilderness"... which Britain (and most of Europe) certainly was at that time.

Cost and Hours: Castle and garden-£8.75, castle only-£7, garden only-£3.50; castle open late March–Oct Sun–Fri 10:30–17:00, closed Sat, last entry 45 minutes before closing; Nov–late March castle tours run from the mount's café "when tides and weather are favourable," usually Tue and Fri at 11:00 and 14:00—call to confirm; garden open May–June Mon–Fri 10:30–17:00, July–Oct Thu–Fri only 10:30–17:00, closed off-season; tel. 01736/710-507, ferry and tide info tel. 01736/710-265, www.stmichaelsmount .co.uk.

Getting There: Buses #2, #2A, #17B, and #300 run from Penzance to Marazion, from which you can walk or catch the boat to St. Michael's Mount (Mon–Sat 2/hour, Sun every 1–2 hours, 10 minutes). Drivers can park in either of two waterfront parking lots (£3, fee charged 9:00–20:00).

Eating at St. Michael's Mount: For a convenient and good lunch option, try the mount's café or restaurant.

Mousehole

Tiny and salty as a barnacle on a sloop, Mousehole (MOW-zle) is adorable. Mousehole is typical of the many charming and now touristy fishing villages that sugar this coastline. It's famous for smuggling, for fishing, and for being the last place where the pre-Roman language of Cornish was spoken. Today, Mousehole harvests more tourists than fish. The little harbor maintains a small fleet, but was busier in the past. The tiny passage out of the harbor is said to be what gave the town its curious name. The best time to enjoy the simple charm of Mousehole is early in the day, when it's enhanced by fresh sea air and noisy seagulls. The beachside path from Newlyn makes an excellent 30-minute stroll (described on page 320). Drivers might want to skip Mousehole's maddeningly narrow and twisty lanes.

Getting There: Buses #6 and #6A go from Penzance to Newlyn, then on to Mousehole (1–2/hour, 10 minutes to Newlyn, 20 minutes to Mousehole). Buses #5 and #5A from Penzance also serve Newlyn, and occasionally continue to Mousehole (hourly). Bus #504 provides similar but less frequent service to Newlyn (Mon–Sat 4/day, none on Sun, 10 minutes) and Mousehole (3–4/ day, none on Sun, 15 minutes).

Merry Maidens Stone Circle

In ancient times, stone circles had some sort of significant purpose—probably as a site for religious ceremonies, as a community meeting place, or, most famously, as a calendar. This particular stone circle, far simpler than the famous ones at Stonehenge and Avebury, is a reminder that the Penwith Peninsula was inhabited in the Neolithic Age (roughly 2000 B.C. or earlier). The story behind

CORNWALL

the name, most likely concocted in the Middle Ages, goes like this: A group of village women decided to go into the fields on the Sabbath for some merriment and dancing. This displeased God, who turned the women to stone to serve as a warning to others.

CORNWALL

Getting There: The Merry Maidens are in a grassy field just off B3315 (on the way from Penzance to Land's End). They're easy to miss if you're driving. Coming from Penzance, after passing through Boleigh, look for a pullout on the left near three gates; you'll also see a bus stop and a low-profile stone marker, and, on the right, a green arrow pointing across the road with a faded *Merry Maidens* sign. If you don't have a car, bus #504 takes you from Penzance to the Merry Maidens (2/day Mon–Sat only, none on Sun, 35 minutes).

Porthcurno

This humdrum hamlet, just off B3315 between Penzance and Land's End, has two worthwhile sights.

▲**Minack Theatre**—For good Cornish theater, try the Minack. This local open-air theater has just about the most spectacular set-

ting of any place—theater or otherwise—in England. This gorgeously landscaped facility can seat up to 750 theatergoers. With seats actually carved into a rocky cliff and a terrace stage perched hundreds of feet over the sea, the Minack is quite a sight. Imagine watching *The Tempest* with only the sunset and crashing waves for scenery. If you aren't a theater buff or don't happen to be here during the theater season, the site is still worth a visit for unbeatable views of the rocky cliffs. The small exhibit on the history of the Minack includes a short video on Rowena Cade, the visionary theater-lover who persevered to build it. There's also a cliff-hanging coffee house.

Cost and Hours: You can visit the theater just to see it (£3.50; April–mid-Sept daily 9:30–17:30—except Wed and Fri mid-May–mid-Sept, when it closes at 11:30 for a matinee; call ahead or check website for other sporadic closures; mid-Sept–Oct daily 9:30–17:00; Nov–March 10:00–16:00; last entry 30 minutes before closing), or you can attend a **performance** during peak season (£8–9.50, £1 booking fee if you use a credit/debit card, performances generally mid-May–mid-Sept, usually Mon–Fri at 20:00, also Wed and Fri at 14:00, rarely cancelled but dress for the weather, tel. 01736/810-181, www.minack.com).

Getting There: The theater is up an extremely narrow and twisty road above Porthcurno, well-signed from town, with free parking. From Penzance, bus #504 goes to the theater (2/day Mon–Sat only, none on Sun, 55 minutes). If you're willing to hike, you can also take buses #1A or #300 from Penzance to the stop in Porthcurno, with a steep, quarter-mile uphill climb to the theater (buses run Mon–Sat 5–6/day, Sun 2/day, 40 minutes). During the summer, the last bus #1A leaves Porthcurno for Penzance after the show, at 23:00 (Mon–Sat only).

Telegraph Museum—In 1870, a telegraph cable was laid from Porthcurno to India. By the time World War II broke out, 14 cables tethered this village to the rest of the world. In 1940, defensive tunnels were built to protect the telegraph station and cables from the Nazis—who were now just 80 miles away in France.

Today, those tunnels house a surprisingly interesting museum, tracing the history of the "Victorian Internet." You'll learn how underwater cables were made possible thanks to a new insulating material (a resin from a Malaysian tree called gutta-percha), how the cables were even more heavily armored in shallower water (where they could be damaged by anchors of passing ships), and how they repaired ruptured cables in the briny deep. About once an hour, a docent gives a history lesson on underwater telegraphy... which, like the museum, is better than it sounds.

Cost and Hours: £5.50; April–Oct daily 10:00–17:00, Wed until 19:30 in summer; Nov–March Sun–Mon only 10:00–17:00, closed Tue–Sat; last entry one hour before closing, next to main parking lot in Porthcurno on the road up to Minack Theater—look for big white building marked *Museum,* tel. 01736/810-966, www.porthcurno.org.uk.

Getting There: Buses #1A, #300, and #504 from Penzance stop in Porthcurno near the museum (Mon–Sat 4–6/day, Sun 2/day, 40 minutes).

Land's End

The westernmost point in all of England should seem like a desolate, rugged place. In reality, it's a tacky tourist trap where greedy businesses have chewed up whatever small bit of charm or authenticity this place might once have had. As you approach, you'll see endless signs bragging "the last" (or, in a too-cute spin, "the first and last")...everything: inn, hotel, refreshment stand, postal box, and so on. Come here only if you want to be able to say you've been to Land's End. (Consider lying.)

If you do visit, pay the £4 parking fee (enforced 24 hours/day; coins required 17:00-9:00) and walk straight from the parking lot through the low-budget theme park (stop at your own risk) out to the viewpoint. This once was considered the end of the civilized world, the last (or first) thing to be seen by departing (or arriving) ships. After gazing at the sea and guessing how far away from home you are, find out how close you were by checking your hometown at the picture stand on the right. For £11–14, they'll take your photo with a personalized signpost and mail it to you (theme park toll tel. 0871-720-0044, www.landsend-landmark.co.uk).

"Back Door" Approach to Land's End: To appreciate the majesty of this location while avoiding the tourist logjam, consider hiking in from nearby **Sennen Cove.** From the road just north of Land's End, turn off to drive down the steep and narrow road into the village of Sennen, then park at the harbor (where the road dead-ends at the end of town). It's a steep, uphill, but rewarding one-mile hike over the windswept headlands to Land's End, following the South West Coast Path, Britain's longest national trail (for a description, see www.southwestcoastpath.com).

Getting There: Buses #1, #1A, #300, and #504 connect Penzance with Land's End (Mon–Sat every 1–2 hours, Sun every 2 hours, 40 minutes–2.5 hours depending on bus), while #300 and #504 also stop at Sennen Cove (daily every 2 hours).

▲Geevor Tin Mine

Once 2,100 feet deep and extending almost a mile under the ocean, the Geevor Mine closed in 1990. Today, it's been con-verted into a museum, but it retains most of its original buildings and machinery. Exploring the remnants of this recently defunct industry—which for centuries was an integral part of Cornish life—you'll gain an appreciation for the simple, noble life of miners. Even if you're not into heavy metal, this unique look at tin mining is fascinating—and worth ▲▲▲ to those interested in engineering.

Cornish Tin Mining

Cornwall's history is tied to its tin-mining industry. While Cornwall has always been known for its metal deposits, a major tin boom began here in the mid-1700s, as new steam-engine-powered pumps allowed tin to be mined below the water table. The industry peaked 200 years ago, when tin was the cutting edge of technology, and Cornwall was the Silicon Valley of Britain.

Mines employed the notorious "company store" system, where workers were paid in tokens that could only be redeemed at the store run by the mine (an obvious conflict of interest—which always worked to the company's advantage). To save money, miners made their own "hardhats." They'd take a felt hat and harden it by dipping it alternately in hot tree resin and soil. Then they'd stick a candle on the brim for light while they worked. Since miners had to buy their own candles (from the company store, of course), they'd extinguish them during their lunch break to make them last longer. Imagine miners huddled underground, munching Cornish pasties in the pitch-blackness.

Miners would climb down into the narrow shafts, and use a hammer and a long bit to slowly drive deep, skinny holes into a vein of tin. Then they'd insert sticks of dynamite. Before safety fuses were invented, quills from bird feathers were used as fuses, so miners setting off gunpowder never knew how much time they had to reach safety before the explosion.

Deadly cave-ins were frequent. These were supposedly caused by mischievous Tommyknockers, Cornish pixies similar to leprechauns. But these mysterious creatures might simply have been a creation of the oxygen-starved imaginations of exhausted miners.

The crumbling smokestacks that dot the Cornish landscape today are the last remnants of this now-dead industry, which couldn't compete with cheap tin from Asia and South America. The ground underfoot is still honeycombed with forgotten tin mines. Older Cornish natives can still remember being in their houses and hearing the miners working underground.

Cost and Hours: £9.50, Easter–Oct Sun–Fri 9:00–17:00, Nov–Easter Sun–Fri 9:00–16:00, last entry one hour before closing, closed Sat year-round; self-guided "free flow" visits in summer, but guided tours at 11:00, 13:00, and 15:00 in winter; wear good shoes, pick up the free map at entry to follow the route, café, resident cat available for petting, tel. 01736/788-662, www.geevor .com.

Getting There: It's just off the B3306 road along the north coast of Penwith. Or, if you're driving in from the A30 Penzance bypass, take A3071 to St. Just and follow the brown *Historic Mining Area* signs. Take the right fork on B3318 to Pendeen, turn left at the crossroads to drive through Pendeen, and turn right at the Geevor entrance. You can also get here on buses #10A and #300 from Penzance, or #300 from St. Ives and Land's End (buy combo-ticket for bus plus mine entry from driver).

◑ Self-Guided Tour: Put on your hard hat and wander through the museum. A short film explains the tin-mining process, and a giant model, once used to help engineers keep track of the network of shafts, makes it clear how extensive the mining industry was here.

Then head outside, where you'll walk from shed to shed to see the various parts of the day-to-day workings of the mine. The two-story Hard Rock museum features exhibits for all ages about mining and the rocks that harbor valuable ores. The most interesting area is "The Dry," where the miners showered, changed, and dried their uniforms between shifts. Though it closed almost two decades ago, it feels as though the miners could show up at any time to clock in. Enjoy the old time-punch clock, the fun stickers on the miners' lockers, and graffiti showing their sense of humor (such as the *Ear Protection Must Be Worn* sign posted next to the toilets). In "The Mill," you'll see how a vast warehouse of "shaking tables"—like giant machines panning for gold—separated the miners' haul into its useable parts.

The finale is a half-hour underground tour of an 18th-century mine (which predates the more recent mine that the current buildings supported, and was discovered by modern miners). A docent (often a former mine employee) gives you a coverall and leads you in. The mines—narrow and low (you'll be hunched for most of the tour, and claustrophobes will be miserable)—give you a sense of the difficult life of miners and the perilous conditions under which they worked.

Eating near the Mine: You can get hot, authentic, delicious Cornish pasties on the main square of the humble town of St. Just, at McFadden and Sons Butchers (Mon–Fri 8:00–17:00, Sat 7:30–17:00—or until 16:00 in winter, closed Sun, 11 Market Square, tel. 01736/788-136). For more on pasties, see page 327.

Isles of Scilly

Just off the coast of Cornwall, this group of islands (pronounced "silly") sits right in the path of the Gulf Stream. The warm (or at least warmer) climate is perfect for growing a wide variety of exotic plants, so the islands boast plenty of gardens to visit. But half the fun is getting there: A fleet of old, creaky, Penzance-based **helicopters** is ready to whisk you to precarious heights (£50–176 round-trip depending on time, season, and ticket type, 20-minute flight, Mon–Sat year-round, no flights Sun or winter holidays, £2 shuttle from Penzance train station to heliport 45 minutes before each flight, tel. 01736/363-871, www.islesofscillyhelicopter.com). Alternatively, you can take a very slow **boat** called the *Scillonian III* from Penzance (£35 same-day return, £47.50 one-way, £95 round-trip, 2.75 hours each way, sporadic schedule but generally departs Mon–Sat at 9:15 in summer from the Penzance Quay/Lighthouse Pier, no boats Nov–mid-March, toll tel. 0845-710-5555, www.ios-travel.co.uk). The boat company also runs **planes** out to the islands from the Land's End airport (£86 same-day return, £70 one-way, £125–140 round-trip, 15-minute flight).

East Cornwall

These destinations are a bit farther from Penzance, and closer to Dartmoor National Park (see previous chapter). I've listed them from farthest to nearest to Penzance. Consider visiting them in this order as you approach the tip of Cornwall.

▲▲Tintagel Castle

Wild, rocky, remote, and romantic, Tintagel (tin-TAD-jell) is as dramatic as a castle can be. The real King Arthur—if he actually existed—was supposedly born here and ruled his lands from this rocky point. While the popular tales of Camelot are flights of fantasy, they may be based on a real person. Even though there's no physical record of King Arthur (other than a pottery shard discovered in the 1990s), the verbal tradition is strong enough that experts think a fifth- or sixth-century ruler by that name probably lived in this area, possibly basing himself in modern Camelford (which might be where "Camelot" comes from). Regardless of whether Arthur is fact or fiction, windblown Tintagel Castle is striking. If you can handle lots of steep hiking up and down, this is one of England's most rewarding ruined-castle experiences. And as a bonus, you get to enjoy a spectacularly scenic stretch of Cornish coastline. Bring a picnic to have lunch with a view.

Cost and Hours: £5.20, daily April–Sept 10:00–18:00, Oct 10:00–17:00, Nov–March 10:00–16:00, tel. 01840/770-328, www.english-heritage.org.uk.

Getting There: The castle clings to the coast below the tacky town of Tintagel. If you're arriving by car, look for *Tintagel* signs from A39 as it passes through Camelford. Once you enter town, take your pick of parking lots, then hike down the steep road to the main entrance at the rocky bay. Or, if you prefer, take the Land Rover shuttle (£1.50 each way, runs continuously April–Oct). By public transportation from Penzance, it's a three-hour journey, involving a train and two buses: Take a train from Penzance to Bodmin Parkway, then bus #555 to Wadebridge, where you catch bus #594 to Tintagel (for specifics, call toll tel. 0871-200-2233, or use the journey planner at www.travelinesw.com). For bus info, contact Western Greyhound (tel. 01637/871-871, www.western greyhound.com).

❍ Self-Guided Tour: The main part of the castle is on what's called The Island (actually a rocky peninsula attached by a narrow spit); nearby, on the mainland, is a separate section called the Mainland Courtyard. For the full story, invest in the TI's £4 illustrated guidebook. It's keyed to numbered plaques around the site (which I've also made use of below). Here are the highlights:

After buying your ticket at the main entrance, watch the good seven-minute **film** called *Searching for King Arthur*, which considers the historical and legendary underpinnings of this evocative site.

Head up to the viewpoint overlooking the cove. As you approach the bridge, look for the hole in the cliff below the ruins—supposedly **Merlin's cave.** (If the tide is out, you can climb down to explore the famous wizard's former home...and ponder how he managed to keep the carpet dry and prevent seals from climbing on the furniture.)

Now look up to the top of the giant chunk of rock above Merlin's cave. Appreciate the naturally fortified, easily defendable position of this rock-top castle. Note the narrow and difficult approach to this hunk of land, and you can understand why Tintagel—meaning "fortress with narrow entrance"—is aptly named.

Head up the steps and cross the footbridge, then tackle the very steep climb up to the top of the cliffs, or **The Island.** We'll do a roughly counterclockwise spin around these grounds.

As you enter through the back door, you reach the **Island Courtyard**—castle remnants dating from the Middle Ages (with a *3* plaque). Rather than belonging to Arthur (who would have lived centuries earlier), these structures were built for the brother of a 13th-century king. Notice that the walls are made of stacked sheets of slate, which was mined on this site for many years.

Continue through the ruins and up to the viewpoint platform (marked with a *4* plaque). All around you—including directly below—you'll see the foundations of ruined **Dark Age houses,** which actually date from the time when Arthur most likely lived (the fifth century A.D.). Here archaeologists have found remains of items from as far away as North Africa and the Eastern Mediterranean—evidence of the wealth and status of this castle's owner.

Climb on up to the top of The Island. As you explore, you'll come across several interesting sites. In the walled area called the **garden** (marked *5*), medieval residents could relax and entertain visitors in the summer. The **well** (marked *8*) was the source of water in the Middle Ages, and remains today's last resort in case of fire. The 11th-century **chapel** (marked *10*) is recognizable for the altar at its far end. If you have time, linger up here. The craggy peaks across the tops of the cliffs make a perfect, windblown picnic spot.

After the chapel, you'll head back down the steep steps to the footbridge. From here, for extra credit, consider hiking up the steps across the bridge to the **Mainland Courtyard,** with more medieval remains. If you decide to climb up, you can take a much less steep path behind this courtyard back down to rejoin the main path up the valley.

▲The Eden Project

Set in an abandoned china-clay mine, the Eden Project is an ambitious and futuristic work-in-progress—a theme park of global gardening with an environmental conscience. Exotic plants from all over the world are showcased in two giant biomes, reputedly the largest greenhouses in the world. The displays focus on sustainable farming and ecoconscious planting, but the most interesting thing here is the sheer audacity of the idea. If you're looking for a quaint

English cottage garden, this isn't it. Rather than a flowery look at England's past, this "global garden" gives you a sense of how the shrinking of the world will affect us in the future.

After buying your ticket, zigzag down into the pit and work your way through the various exhibits, including the enormous, hot, and hazy Rainforest Biome (where my camera completely fogged up; you can seek relief in an air-conditioned hut about half-way through); the smaller and more arid Mediterranean Biome; an eatery-filled walkway connecting them called The Link; The Core, with educational exhibits; and lots of gardens. A land train and an elevator from The Core make it easier to get back up to the visitors center when you're done. Kid-oriented programs, rock and pop concerts, and other special events run throughout the year.

It's an impressive concept, and the biomes are striking. But the educational exhibits are a bit too conceptual to be effective—leaving the whole, expensive experience feeling somehow unmoored.

Cost and Hours: £16; mid-March–Oct daily 9:00–18:00; Nov–mid-March daily 10:00–16:30; last entry 1.5 hours before closing, cafés, tel. 01726/811-911, www.edenproject.com.

Crowd Alert: The Eden Project is popular and can be crowded, especially on rainy days and weekdays June–Aug (they told me "wet Wednesdays" are the worst). During peak-of-peak times, you may have to wait up to an hour to get in. Avoid this by arriving after 13:00.

Getting There: Drivers will find the Eden Project well-signposted from both A30 and A39—you'll be directed to A391, and follow signs from there. Park at one of the many outlying lots, note your parking lot's fruity symbol, then walk down into the Project (or take the free park-and-ride shuttle bus). By public transit, first take the train to St. Austell, where you'll meet bus #101 (daily hourly, toll tel. 0871-200-2233 or 0845-600-1420, www.firstgroup.com) or #527 (Mon–Sat hourly, Sun 5/day, tel. 01637/871-871, www.westerngreyhound.com). Buses meet most arriving trains for the 20-minute run to the complex (buy combo-ticket for bus and entry fee from driver).

Gardens near Falmouth

Cornwall has many wonderful gardens, some with subtropical varieties of plants that thrive in this mild climate (www.greatgardensofcornwall.co.uk). These two gardens are a few miles apart on the same backcountry road, just south of Falmouth.

Getting There: If you're driving, take A39 or A394 into Falmouth until you see brown-and-white *Garden* signs—track these closely for four miles through the countryside to the gardens (Glendurgan is the better-signed of the two). If you're without a car, take bus #500 (tel. 01637/871-871, www.westerngreyhound.com) or bus #35 (toll tel. 0845-600-1420, www.firstgroup.com) from Falmouth toward Helston (20-35 minutes, Traveline toll tel. 0871-200-2233, www.travelinesw.com).

Sleeping near the Gardens: If you want to maximize your time exploring the gardens, consider spending the night in salty Falmouth, a tidy harbor town nestled near the Tudor fortress of Pendennis Castle. **$$$ Greenbank Hotel** is right on the water with a seagull-eye's view of the many boats moored in the Fal

Estuary. Look near the hotel lobby for displays about Kenneth Grahame, who wrote parts of *The Wind in the Willows* while staying here (Db-£109–185, check for online deals, Internet access, free Wi-Fi, Harbourside, tel. 01326/312-440, fax 01326/211-362, www.greenbank-hotel.co.uk, reception@greenbank-hotel.co.uk).

▲**Trebah Garden**—The "Garden of Dreams" at Trebah (TREE-bah) is a lush and tropical spectacle. Set on 26 acres that bunny-hop down a ravine to the beach below, this tropical garden is an unexpected treat. While most of England suffers from chilly arctic air, the Cornish peninsula is bathed in warmer air from the Gulf Stream—making average temperatures here much milder (the sea here never drops below 50 degrees Fahrenheit).

Palms, succulents, bamboo, large azaleas, giant rhubarbs, and the prehistoric-looking gunnera might make you think (or wish) that you're in the tropics rather than Cornwall. The garden's exoticism impresses even non-gardeners. While garden-lovers wander in ecstasy, history buffs can ponder the fact that the beach below was used by some US troops in World War II to launch the D-Day attack on Omaha Beach.

Cost and Hours: £7.50 March–Oct, £3 Nov–Feb, show bus ticket for discount, open daily 10:00–18:30, until dusk in winter, last entry 1.5 hours before closing, colorful year-round but flowers are best late March and April, café, tel. 01326/252-200, www.trebahgarden.co.uk.

Glendurgan Garden—Just up the road from Trebah, Glendurgan has a smaller collection of tropical plants mingled with more traditional English garden fare. Similarly set in a broad basin angled to the sea, Glendurgan is bigger but less striking than its neighbor. However, it does come with an extensive, kid-friendly hedge maze (about waist-high—but still entertaining—for an adult), built by the former owner to entertain his 12 children. Gardeners may appreciate its good orchids and its small "Holy Bank" of biblical-themed plants. And down at the seashore, the fishing hamlet of Durgan makes it feel less like just an overblown backyard for aristocrats.

Cost and Hours: £6, worthwhile £3 map/guide, mid-Feb–Oct Tue–Sat 10:30–17:30, closed Sun–Mon except Aug when it's open Mon, last entry 30 minutes before closing, closed Nov–mid-Feb, best in spring, café, tel. 01326/250-906 or 01326/252-020, www.nationaltrust.org.uk.

BATH

The best city to visit within easy striking distance of London is Bath—just a 1.5-hour train ride away. Two hundred years ago, this city of 85,000 was the trendsetting Hollywood of Britain. If ever a city enjoyed looking in the mirror, Bath's the one. It has more "government-listed" or protected historic buildings per capita than any other town in England. The entire city, built of the creamy warm-tone limestone called "Bath stone," beams in its cover-girl complexion. An architectural chorus line, it's a triumph of the Georgian style. Proud locals remind visitors that the town is routinely banned from the "Britain in Bloom" contest to give other towns a chance to win. Bath's narcissism is justified. Even with its mobs of tourists (2 million per year) and greedy prices, Bath is a joy to visit.

Bath's fame began with the allure of its (supposedly) healing hot springs. Long before the Romans arrived in the first century, Bath was known for its warm waters. Romans named the popular spa town Aquae Sulis, after a local Celtic goddess. The town's importance carried through Saxon times, when it had a huge church on the site of the present-day abbey and was considered the religious capital of Britain. Its influence peaked in 973 with King Edgar's sumptuous coronation in the abbey. Later, Bath prospered as a wool town.

Bath then declined until the mid-1600s, wasting away to just a huddle of huts around the abbey, with hot, smelly mud and 3,000 residents, oblivious to the Roman ruins 18 feet below their dirt floors. In fact, with its own walls built upon ancient ones, Bath was no bigger than that Roman town. Then, in 1687, Queen Mary, fighting infertility, bathed here. Within 10 months she gave birth to a son...and a new age of popularity for Bath.

The revitalized town boomed as a spa resort. Ninety percent of the buildings you'll see today are from the 18th century. A father-and-son team of local architects—both named John Wood (the Elder and the Younger)—were inspired by the Italian architect Andrea Palladio to build a "new Rome." The town bloomed in the Neoclassical style, and streets were lined not with scrawny sidewalks but with wide "parades," upon which the women in their stylishly wide dresses could spread their fashionable tails.

Beau Nash (1673–1762) was Bath's "master of ceremonies." He organized both the daily regimen of aristocratic visitors and the city, lighting the streets, improving security, banning swords, and opening the Pump Room. Under his fashionable baton, Bath became a city of balls, gaming, and concerts—the place to see and be seen in England. This most civilized place became even more so with the great Neoclassical building spree that followed.

These days, modern tourism has stoked the local economy, as has the fast morning train to London. (A growing number of Bath professionals catch the 7:13 train to Paddington Station every morning.) With renewed access to Bath's soothing hot springs at the Thermae Bath Spa, the venerable waters are in the spotlight again, attracting a new generation of visitors in need of a cure or a soak.

Planning Your Time

Bath deserves two nights even on a quick trip. On a three-week England getaway, spend three nights in Bath, with one day for the city and one day for side-trips (see next chapter). Ideally, use Bath as your jet-lag recovery pillow, and do London at the end of your trip.

Consider starting a three-week English vacation this way:

Day 1: Land at Heathrow. Connect to Bath by National Express bus—the better option—or the less convenient bus/train combination (for details, see page 184). While you don't need or want a car in Bath, and some rental companies have an office there, those who land early and pick up their cars at the airport can visit Windsor Castle (near Heathrow) and/or Stonehenge on their way to Bath. (You can also consider flying into Bristol.) If you have the evening free in Bath, take a walking tour.

Day 2: 9:00–Tour the Roman Baths; 10:30–Catch the free city walking tour; 12:30–Picnic on the open deck of a Bath tour bus; 14:00–Free time in the shopping center of old Bath; 15:30–Tour the Fashion Museum or Museum of Bath at Work. Take the evening walking tour (unless you did last night), enjoy the Bizarre Bath comedy walk, consider seeing a play, or go for a nighttime soak in the Thermae Bath Spa.

Day 3 (and possibly 4): By car, explore nearby sights. Without a car, consider a one-day Avebury/Stonehenge/cute towns mini-bus tour from Bath (Mad Max tours are best; see "Tours in Bath," later).

Orientation to Bath

(area code: 01225)
Bath's town square, three blocks in front of the bus and train station, is a cluster of tourist landmarks, including the abbey, Roman and Medieval Baths, and the Pump Room. Bath is hilly. In general, you'll gain elevation as you head north from the town center.

BATH

Tourist Information

The TI is in the abbey churchyard (Mon–Sat 9:30–18:00, Sun 10:00–16:00, closes one hour earlier Mon–Sat Oct–May, pricey toll tel. 0906-711-2000—50p/minute, www.visitbath.co.uk). The TI sells various visitor guides and maps—survey your options before buying one (£1–1.50). Only the most basic visitor guide—with a very rudimentary map—is free. The TI books rooms and theater tickets for no extra fee (booking tel. 0844-847-5256). If you're a Jane Austen fan, ask about the walking tours that leave from the TI on weekends. Entertainment listings from the local paper are posted on their bulletin board. You can also buy the Great British Heritage Pass here (see page 20).

Arrival in Bath

The Bath Spa **train station** has a national and international tickets desk and a privately run travel agency masquerading as a TI. Directly in front of the train station is Bath's brand-new SouthGate Bath shopping center. To get from the train station to the TI, exit straight ahead, walk two blocks up Manvers Street, and turn left at the triangular "square" overlooking the riverfront park, following the small TI arrow on a signpost.

The **bus station** is west of the train station, along Dorchester Street.

My recommended B&Bs are all within a 10- to 15-minute walk or a £4–5 taxi ride from the train and bus stations.

Helpful Hints

Festivals: The **Bath Literature Festival** is an open book February 26–March 6 in 2011 (www.bathlitfest.org.uk). The **Bath International Music Festival** bursts into song every spring

Bath

N

200 YARDS
200 METERS

ROYAL CRESCENT

FASHION MUSEUM & ASSEMBLY ROOMS

MARLBOROUGH LANE MARL. GDNS.

R.C. HOTEL

GEORGIAN HOUSE MUSEUM

BROCK ST.

ROYAL AVE.

THE CIRCUS

ROYAL VICTORIA PARK

JANE AUSTEN CENTRE

Charlotte street P

(A-4) UPPER BRISTOL ROAD

CHARLOTTE

TO BRISTOL

MONMOUTH

TINY ARROWS (→) INDICATE ONE WAY STREETS.

CHARLES ST.

FARMERS' MARKET

JAMES

SEE BATH CENTER DETAIL MAP

RIVER AVON

P PARKING
View
Bldg. Entrances

LOWER

WELLS

TO WELLS VIA A-367

DCH

(classical, folk, jazz, contemporary; May 25–June 5 in 2011, www.bathmusicfest.org.uk), overlapped by the eclectic **Bath Fringe Festival** (theater, walks, talks, bus trips; generally similar dates to the Music Festival, www.bathfringe.co.uk). The **Jane Austen Festival** unfolds genteelly in late September (www.janeausten.co.uk/festival). And for three weeks in December, the squares around the abbey are filled with a **Christmas market.**

Bath's festival **box office** sells tickets for most events and can tell you exactly what's on tonight (a block down from the TI at 2 Church Street, tel. 01225/463-362, www.bathfestivals .org.uk). The city's weekly local paper, the *Bath Chronicle,* publishes a "What's On" event listing (www.thisisbath.com).

Internet Access: Ask your hotel or the TI for the closest Internet café. You can also get online at the Bath **library** (£1.20/20 minutes, slightly cheaper with free library membership, Mon 9:30–18:00, Tue–Thu 9:30–19:00, Fri–Sat 9:30–17:00, Sun 13:00–16:00, in the Podium Shopping Centre on Northgate Street near Pulteney Bridge, tel. 01225/394-041, www.bath nes.gov.uk).

Bookstore: Topping & Company, an inviting bookshop, has posters in the windows advertising frequent author readings, free coffee and tea for browsers, and tables filled with tidy stacks of carefully selected volumes (daily 9:00–20:00, near the bottom of the street called "The Paragon"—where it meets George Street, tel. 01225/428-111, www.toppingbooks.co.uk).

Laundry: The **Spruce Goose Launderette** is between the Circus and the Royal Crescent, on the pedestrian lane called Margaret's Buildings. Bring lots of £1 coins for washing and £0.20 coins for drying, as there are no change machines (self-service: about £4–5/load, daily 8:00–20:00, last load at 19:00; full-service: £12/load, Mon–Fri 8:00–12:00; tel. 01225/483-309). **Speedy Wash** can pick up your laundry anywhere in town on weekdays before 11:00 for same-day service (£12/ small bag, Mon–Fri 7:30–17:30, Sat 8:30–13:00 but no pickup, closed Sun, no self-service, most hotels work with them, 4 Mile End, London Road, tel. 01225/427-616).

Car Rental: Enterprise provides a pickup service for customers to and from their hotels (extra fee for one-way rentals, at Lower Bristol Road outside Bath, tel. 01225/443-311, www .enterprise.com). Others include **Thrifty** (pickup service and one-way rentals available, in the Burnett Business Park in Keynsham—between Bath and Bristol, tel. 01179/867-997, www.thrifty.co.uk), **Hertz** (one-way rentals possible, at Windsor Bridge, tel. 0870-850-2691, www.hertz.co.uk), and **National/Europcar** (one-way rentals available, £7 by taxi from the train station, at Brassmill Lane—go west on Upper Bristol Road, tel. 01225/481-982 or 01761/479-205). Skip **Avis**—it's a mile from the Bristol train station; you'd need to rent a car to get there. Most offices close Saturday afternoon and all day Sunday, which complicates weekend pickups. Ideally, take the train or bus from downtown London to Bath, and rent a car as you leave Bath.

Parking: Parking in the city center is difficult. Short-term street parking is available but pricey (about £2.50/hour, 2-hour maximum, buy pay-and-display tickets from machine). You'll pay less per hour in long-stay lots (figure £9/24 hours; the Charlotte Street car park is handy). For more info on parking, visit www.bathnes.gov.uk/bathnes.

Tours in Bath

▲▲▲**Walking Tours**—Free two-hour tours are offered by **The Mayor's Corps of Honorary Guides,** led by volunteers who want to share their love of Bath with its many visitors (as the city's mayor first did when he took a group on a guided walk back in the 1930s). Their chatty, historical, and gossip-filled walks are essential for your understanding of this town's amazing Georgian social scene. How else would you learn that the old "chair ho" call for your sedan chair evolved into today's "cheerio" farewell? Tours leave from outside the Pump Room in the abbey churchyard (free, no tips, year-round Sun–Fri at 10:30 and 14:00, Sat at 10:30 only; additional evening walks May–Sept Tue and Fri at 19:00; tel. 01225/477-411, www.bathguides.co.uk). Tip for theatergoers: When your guide stops to talk outside the Theatre Royal, skip out for a moment, pop into the box office, and see about snaring a great deal on a play for tonight.

For a **private tour,** call the local guides' bureau, Bath Parade Guides (£60/2 hours, tel. 01225/337-111, www.bathparadeguides .co.uk, bathparadeguides@yahoo.com). For **Ghost Walks** and **Bizarre Bath** tours, see "Nightlife in Bath," later.

▲▲**City Bus Tours**—City Sightseeing's hop-on, hop-off bus tours zip through Bath. Jump on a bus anytime at one of 17 sign-posted pickup points, pay the driver, climb upstairs, and hear recorded commentary about Bath. City Sightseeing has two 45-minute routes: a city tour (unintelligible audio recording on half the buses, live guides on the other half—choose the latter), and a "Skyline" route outside town (all live guides, stops near the American Museum—15-minute walk). On a sunny day, this is a multitasking tourist's dream come true: You can munch a sandwich, work on a tan, snap great photos, and learn a lot, all at the same time. Save money by doing the bus tour first—ticket stubs

Bath at a Glance

▲▲▲**Walking Tours** Free top-notch tours, helping you make the most of your visit, led by The Mayor's Corps of Honorary Guides. **Hours:** Sun–Fri at 10:30 and 14:00, Sat at 10:30 only; additional evening walks offered May–Sept Tue and Fri at 19:00. See page 347.

▲▲▲**Roman and Medieval Baths** Ancient baths that gave the city its name, tourable with good audioguide. **Hours:** Daily July–Aug 9:00–22:00, March–June and Sept–Oct 9:00–18:00, Nov–Feb 9:30–17:30. See page 350.

▲▲**The Circus and the Royal Crescent** Stately Georgian (Neoclassical) buildings from Bath's late-18th-century glory days. **Hours:** Always viewable. See page 357.

▲▲**Fashion Museum** 400 years of clothing under one roof, plus opulent Assembly Rooms. **Hours:** Daily March–Oct 10:30–18:00, Nov–Feb 10:30–17:00. See page 359.

▲▲**Museum of Bath at Work** Gadget-ridden circa-1900 engineer's shop, foundry, factory, and office, best enjoyed with a live tour. **Hours:** April–Oct daily 10:30–17:00, Nov and Jan–March weekends only, closed in Dec. See page 360.

▲**Pump Room** Swanky Georgian hall, ideal for a spot of tea or a taste of unforgettably "healthy" spa water. **Hours:** Daily 9:30–12:00 for coffee and breakfast, 12:00–14:30 for lunch, 14:30–16:30 for afternoon tea (open for dinner during Bath International Music Festival, July–Aug, and Christmas holidays only). See page 354.

get you minor discounts at many sights (£11.50, ticket valid for 2 days and both tour routes, generally 4/hour daily in summer 9:30–18:30, in winter 10:00–15:00, tel. 01225/330-444, www.city-sightseeing.com).

Taxi Tours—Local taxis, driven by good talkers, go where big buses can't. A group of up to four can rent a cab for an hour (about £20) and enjoy a fine, informative, and—with the right cabbie—entertaining private joyride. It's probably cheaper to let the meter run than to pay for an hourly rate, but ask the cabbie for advice.

To Stonehenge, Avebury, and the Cotswolds

Bath is a good launch pad for visiting Wells, Avebury, Stonehenge, and more.

Mad Max Minibus Tours—Operating daily from Bath, Maddy and Paul offer thoughtfully organized, informative tours that run

▲**Thermae Bath Spa** Relaxation center that put the bath back in Bath. **Hours:** Daily 9:00–22:00. See page 355.

▲**Abbey** 500-year-old Perpendicular Gothic church, graced with beautiful fan vaulting and stained glass. **Hours:** April–Oct Mon-Sat 9:00–18:00, Sun 13:00–14:30 & 16:30–17:30; Nov–March Mon-Sat 9:00–16:30, Sun 13:00–14:30 & 16:30–17:30. See page 356.

▲**Pulteney Bridge and Parade Gardens** Shop-strewn bridge and relaxing riverside gardens. **Hours:** Bridge—always open; gardens—Easter–Sept daily 11:00–17:00, shorter hours off-season. See page 357.

▲**Georgian House at No. 1 Royal Crescent** Best opportunity to explore the interior of one of Bath's high-rent Georgian beauties. **Hours:** Mid-Feb–Oct Tue–Sun 10:30–17:00, Nov Tue–Sun 10:30–16:00, closed Mon and Dec–mid-Feb. See page 358.

▲**American Museum** An insightful look primarily at colonial/early-American lifestyles, with 18 furnished rooms and eager-to-talk guides. **Hours:** Mid-March–Oct Tue–Sun 12:00–17:00, closed Mon and Nov–mid-March. See page 361.

Jane Austen Centre Exhibit on 19th-century Bath-based novelist, best for her fans. **Hours:** Mid-March–mid-Nov daily 9:45–17:30, July-Aug Thu–Sat until 19:00; mid-Nov–mid-March Sun–Fri 11:00–16:30, Sat 9:45–17:30. See page 361.

with entertaining guides. Book ahead—as far ahead as possible in summer—for these popular tours. Their **Stone Circles** full-day tour covers 110 miles and visits Stonehenge, the Avebury Stone Circles, and two cute villages: Lacock and Castle Combe. Photogenic Lacock (LAY-cock) is featured in parts of the BBC's *Pride and Prejudice* and the Harry Potter movies, and Castle Combe, the southernmost Cotswold village, is as sweet as they come (£32.50 plus £6.90 Stonehenge entry, tours run daily 8:45–16:30, arrive 15 minutes early, leaves early to beat the Stonehenge hordes). Their shorter tour of **Stonehenge and Lacock** leaves daily at 13:15 and returns at 17:15; occasionally, it also leaves at 8:45 and returns at 12:45 (£17.50 plus £6.90 Stonehenge entry). Most of their tours are limited to 16 people, though on busy days, the half-day tour might have up to 24.

Mad Max also offers a **Cotswold Discovery** full-day tour,

a picturesque romp through the countryside with stops and a cream-tea opportunity in the Cotswolds' quainter villages, including Stow-on-the-Wold, Bibury, Tetbury, the Coln Valley, The Slaughters (optional walk between the two villages), and others (£35; runs Sun, Tue, and Thu 8:45–17:15; arrive 15 minutes early). If you request it in advance, you can bring your luggage along and use the tour as transportation to Stow or, for £5 extra, Moreton-in-Marsh, with easy train connections to Oxford.

All tours depart from Bath at the Glass House shop on the corner of Orange Grove, a one-minute walk from the abbey. Arrive 15 minutes before your departure time and bring cash (it's possible to pay with credit card only if you book online at least 48 hours in advance—£1 discount). Online or email reservations are preferable to calling (phone answered daily 8:00–18:00, tel. 07990/505-970, www.madmax.abel.co.uk, maddy@madmax.abel.co.uk). Please honor or cancel your seat reservation.

More Bus Tours—If Mad Max is booked up, don't fret. Plenty of companies in Bath offer tours of varying lengths, prices, and destinations. Note that the cost of admission to sights is usually not included with any tour.

Scarper Tours runs a minibus tour to Stonehenge (£14, 10 percent Rick Steves discount if you book direct, doesn't include £6.90 Stonehenge entry fee, departs from behind the abbey; daily mid-June–Aug at 9:30, 13:00, and 16:30; mid-March–mid-June and Sept–mid-Oct at 10:00 and 14:00; mid-Oct–mid-March at 13:00; tel. 07739/644-155, www.scarpertours.com). The three-hour tour (two hours there and back, an hour at the site) includes driver narration en route.

Celtic Horizons, run by retired teacher Alan Price, offers tours from Bath to a variety of destinations, such as Stonehenge, Avebury, and Wells. He can provide a convenient transfer service (to or from London, Heathrow, Bristol Airport, the Cotswolds, and so on), with or without a tour itinerary en route. Allow about £25/hour for a group (his comfortable minivan seats up to 8 people) and £125 for Heathrow–Bath transfers. It's best to make arrangements and get pricing information by email at alan@celtichorizons .com (cash only, tel. 01373/461-784, http://celtichorizons.com).

Sights in Bath

In the Town Center

▲▲▲**Roman and Medieval Baths**—In ancient Roman times, high society enjoyed the mineral springs at Bath. From Londinium—and throughout the empire—Romans traveled so often to Aquae Sulis, as the city was called, to "take a bath" that finally it became known simply as Bath. Today, a fine museum

Bath Town Center

To THE CIRCUS & ROYAL CRESCENT

← ONE-WAY STREETS
☐ PEDESTRIAN-FRIENDLY AREAS

200 YARDS
200 METERS

JANE AUSTEN CENTRE

GAY ST.
JOHN ST.
MILSOM ST.
BROAD ST.
WALCOT ST.
GROVE ST.
LAURA PLACE
PULTENEY BRIDGE

QUEEN
WOOD
QUIET
GREEN ST.
VICTORIA ART GALLERY
AVON
ARGYLE ST.
BOATS

CHARLES SQUARE
PRINCES ST.
BEAUFORT
BARTON
QUEEN
TRIM
NEW BOND
CLOSED TO CARS 8:30-18:30
BRIDGE
GT. PARADE
HIGH ST.
RIVER

UPPER BOROUGH WALLS
N. HUMB
RUGBY GROUND

MONMOUTH ST.
THEATRE ROYALE
SAW CLOSE
WESTGATE
PARSON
UNION
CORRIDOR
GUILDHALL MARKET

KINGSMEAD SQUARE
BRIDE
ABBEY
CHEAP
PIERREPONT ST.
WC
PARADE GARDENS

JAMES ST. WEST
ST. JOHN BLDGS
ROMAN BATHS & PUMP ROOM
NORTH PARADE

AVON ST.
WEST GATE
CROSS BATH
HETLING
BATH ST.
BEAU ST.
YORK ST.
STALL ST.
DUKE ST.
S. PARADE

SPA MUSEUM
THERMAE BATH SPA
LOWER BOROUGH WALLS
ABBEY GATE
ABBEY GREEN
FESTIVAL BOX OFFICE
OLD ORCH.
MANVERS ST.

WILM
GREEN PARK ROAD
ST. JAMES'S PARADE
SOUTHGATE
NEW ORCHARD
HENRY

CORN ST.
AMERY
THE MALL
NEWARK ST.
TO TRAIN & BUS STATIONS

RAILWAY

DCH

surrounds the ancient bath. With the help of a great audioguide, you'll wander past well-documented displays, Roman artifacts, a

temple pediment with an evocative bearded face, a bronze head of the goddess Sulis Minerva, excavated ancient foundations, and the actual mouth of the spring. At the end you'll have a chance to walk around the big pool itself, where Romans once lounged, splished, splashed, and thanked the gods for the gift of naturally hot water.

Cost and Hours: £11.50, £0.75 more in July–Aug, includes audioguide, £15 combo-ticket includes Fashion Museum—a £3.50 savings, family ticket available, daily July–Aug 9:00–22:00, March–June and Sept–Oct 9:00–18:00, Nov–Feb 9:30–17:30, last entry one hour before closing, tel. 01225/477-785, www.roman baths.co.uk.

Crowd-Beating Tips: As this is the top sight in this touristy town, it can be very busy on Saturdays and any day in the summer (though you'll never wait longer than about 30 minutes to get in). On any day, the least crowded time to visit is before 11:00. If you're here in the summer (July–Aug), the best time is after 19:00, when the baths are romantic, gas-lit, and all yours.

Tours: Take advantage of the included, essential **audioguide,** which will make your visit easy and informative. In addition to the basic commentary, look for posted numbers to key into your audioguide for specialty topics—including a kid-friendly tour and insightful musings from American expat writer Bill Bryson. For those with a big appetite for Roman history, in-depth **guided tours** leave from the end of the museum at the edge of the actual bath (included with ticket, on the hour, a poolside clock is set for the next departure time, 20–40 minutes depending on the guide). You can revisit the museum after the tour.

❍ Self-Guided Tour: Follow the one-way route through the bath and museum complex. This self-guided tour offers a basic overview; for more in-depth commentary, make ample use of the included audioguide.

You'll begin by walking around the upper **terrace,** overlooking the Great Bath. This terrace—lined with sculptures of VIRs (Very Important Romans)—evokes ancient times, but was built in the 1890s. The ruins of the bath complex sat undisturbed for centuries before finally being excavated and turned into a museum in the late 19th century.

Head inside to the museum, where exhibits explain the **dual purpose** of the buildings that stood here in Roman times: a bath complex, for relaxation and for healing; and a temple dedicated to the goddess Sulis Minerva, who was believed to be responsible for the mysterious and much-appreciated thermal springs. Cut-away diagrams and models help resurrect both parts of this complex and give you your bearings for the actual fragments and foundations you'll see.

Peer down into the **spring,** where little air bubbles remind you that 240,000 gallons of water a day emerge from the earth—mag-

ically, it must have seemed to Romans—at a constant 115°F.

Go downstairs to get to know the Romans who built and enjoyed these baths. The fragments of the **temple pediment**—carved by indigenous Celtic craftsmen, but employing Roman themes—represent a remarkable cultural synthesis. Sit and watch for a while, as a slide projection fills in historians' best guess as to what once occupied the missing bits. The identity of the circular face in the middle puzzles researchers. (God? Santa Claus?) It could be the head of the Gorgon monster after it was slain by Perseus—are those snakes peeking through its hair and beard? And yet, the Gorgon was traditionally depicted as female. Perhaps instead it's Neptune, the god of water—appropriate for this aquatic site.

The next exhibits examine the **importance** of Aquae Sulis (the settlement here) in antiquity. Much like the pilgrimage sites of the Middle Ages, this spot exerted a powerful pull on people from all over the realm, who were eager to partake in its healing waters and to worship at the religious site. You'll see some of the small but extremely heavy carved-stone tables that pilgrims hauled here as an offering to the gods.

Walking through the temple's original foundations, keep an eye out for the sacrificial altar. The gilded-bronze head of the goddess **Sulis Minerva** (in the display case) once overlooked a flaming cauldron inside the temple, where only priests were allowed to enter. Similar to the Greek goddess Athena, Sulis Minerva was considered to be a life-giving mother goddess. The next room displays some of the requests (inscribed on sheets of pewter or iron) that visitors made of the goddess. Take time to read some of these—many are comically spiteful and petty, offering a warts-and-all glimpse into day-to-day Roman culture.

Engineers enjoy a close-up look at the **spring overflow** and the original drain system—built two millennia ago—that still carries excess water to the River Avon. Marvel at the cleverness and durability of Roman engineering, created in (what we usually imagine to be) a "primitive" time.

Then you'll head outside to the **Great Bath** itself (where you can join one of the included guided tours—look for the clock with the next start time). Take a slow lap (by foot) around the perimeter, imagining the frolicking Romans who once immersed themselves up to the neck in this five-foot-deep pool. (On busy days, when costumed characters hang out by the bath, you may not have to imagine.) The water is greenish because of algae—don't drink it. The best views are from the west end, looking back toward the abbey. Nearby is a giant chunk of roof span, from a time when this was a cavernous covered swimming hall. At the corner, you'll step over a small canal where hot water still trickles into the main pool. Nearby, find a length of original lead pipe, remarkably well-preserved since antiquity.

Symmetrical bath complexes branch off at opposite ends of the Great Bath (perhaps dating from a conservative period when the Romans maintained separate facilities for men and women). The **East Baths** show off changing rooms and various bathing rooms, each one designed for a special therapy or recreational purpose (immersion therapy tub, sauna-like heated floor, and so on), as described in detail by the audioguide.

When you're ready to leave, head for the **West Baths,** with more facilities (including a sweat bath and a *frigidarium*, or "cold plunge" pool), another look at the spring, and more foundations. After returning your audioguide, you'll exit through the gift shop and have the opportunity to dip into the attached **Pump Room** to drink a spot of tea or to gag on the spa water (described next; for your free sample, head to the little alcove on the right and show them your bath ticket).

▲**Pump Room**—For centuries, Bath was forgotten as a spa. Then, in 1687, the previously barren Queen Mary bathed here, became

pregnant, and bore a male heir to the throne. A few years later, Queen Anne found the water eased her painful gout. Word of its wonder waters spread, and Bath earned its way back on the aristocratic map. High society soon turned the place into one big pleasure palace. The Pump Room,

an elegant Georgian hall just above the Roman Baths, offers visitors their best chance to raise a pinky in this Chippendale grandeur. Above the newspaper table and sedan chairs, a statue of Beau Nash himself sniffles down at you. Drop by to sip coffee or tea or to enjoy a light meal (daily 9:30–12:00 for coffee and £6–9 breakfast, 12:00–14:30 for £6–16 lunches, 14:30–16:30 for £17.50 traditional afternoon tea, tea/coffee and pastries also available in the afternoons; open for dinner July–Aug, during Bath International Music Festival, and Christmas holidays only; live music daily—string trio or piano, times vary; tel. 01225/444-477). For just the price of a coffee (£3), you're welcome to drop in anytime—except during lunch—to enjoy the music and atmosphere.

The Spa Water: This is your chance to eat a famous (but forgettable) "Bath bun" and split a drink of the awful curative water (£0.50 or free with your Roman and Medieval Baths ticket). The water comes from the King's Spring and is brought to you by an appropriately attired server, who explains that the water is 10,000 years old, pumped up from nearly 100 yards deep, and marinated in 43 wonderful minerals. Convenient public WCs (which use plain old tap water) are in the entry hallway that connects the Pump Room with the baths.

▲**Thermae Bath Spa**—After simmering unused for a quarter-century, Bath's natural thermal springs once again offer R&R for the masses. The state-of-the-art

spa is housed in a complex of three buildings that combine historic structures with controversial (and expensive) new glass-and-steel architecture.

Is the Thermae Bath Spa worth the time and money? The experience is pretty pricey and humble compared to similar German and Hungarian spas. Because you're in a tall, modern building in the city center, it lacks a certain old-time elegance. Jets are very limited, and the only water toys you'll see are big foam noodles. There's no cold plunge—the only way to cool off between steam rooms is to step onto a small, unglamorous balcony. The Royal Bath's two pools are essentially the same, and the water isn't particularly hot in either—in fact, the main attraction is the rooftop view from the top one (best with a partner or as a social experience).

That said, this is the only natural thermal spa in the UK, and a chance to bathe in Bath. If you visit, bring your own swimsuit and come for a couple of hours (Fri night and all day Sat-Sun are most crowded). Or consider an evening visit, when—on a chilly day—Bath's twilight glows through the steam from the rooftop pool.

Cost: The cheapest spa pass is £24 for two hours, which gains you access to the Royal Bath's large, ground-floor "Minerva Bath"; the four steam rooms and the waterfall shower; and the view-filled, open-air, rooftop thermal pool. If you want to stay longer, it's £34/4 hours and £54/day (towel, robe, and slippers-£9). The much-hyped £39 Twilight Package includes three hours and a meal (one plate, drink, robe, towel, and slippers). The appeal of this package is not the mediocre meal, but being on top of the building at a magical hour (which you can do for less money at the regular rate).

Thermae also has all the "pamper thyself" extras: massages, mud wraps, and various healing-type treatments, including "watsu"—water shiatsu (£40–70 extra). Book treatments at www .thermaebathspa.com.

Hours: Daily 9:00–22:00, last entry at 19:30. No kids under 16 are allowed. It's 100 yards from the Roman and Medieval Baths, on Beau Street. Tel. 01225/331-234. There's a salad-and-smoothies café for guests.

The Cross Bath: This renovated, circular Georgian structure across the street from the main spa provides a simpler and less-expensive bathing option. It has a hot-water fountain that taps directly into the spring, making its water temperature higher than the spa's (£14/1.5 hours, daily 10:00–20:00, last entry at 18:30, check in at the bath's main office across the street and you'll be escorted to the Cross Bath, changing rooms, no access to Royal Bath, no kids under 12).

Spa Visitor Centre: Also across the street, in the Hetling Pump Room, this free, one-room exhibit explains the story of the spa (Mon–Sat 10:00–17:00, Sun 10:00–16:00, £2 audioguide).

▲**Abbey**—The town of Bath wasn't much in the Middle Ages, but an important church has stood on this spot since Anglo-Saxon times. King Edgar I was crowned here in 973, when the church was much bigger (before the bishop packed up and moved to Wells). Dominating the town center, today's abbey—the last great medieval church of England—is 500 years old and a fine example of Late Perpendicular Gothic, with breezy fan vaulting and enough stained glass to earn it the nickname "Lantern of the West."

The **facade** (c. 1500, but mostly restored) is interesting for some of its carvings. Look for the angels going down the ladder. The statue of Peter (to the left of the door) lost his head to mean iconoclasts; it was re-carved out of his once supersized beard. Take a moment to appreciate the abbey's architecture from the Abbey Green square.

Going **inside** is worth the £2.50 suggested donation (April–Oct Mon–Sat 9:00–18:00, Sun 13:00–14:30 & 16:30–17:30; Nov–March Mon–Sat 9:00–16:30, Sun 13:00–14:30 & 16:30–17:30; handy flier narrates a self-guided 19-stop tour, tel. 0122/422-462, www.bathabbey.org). The glass, red-iron gas-powered lamps, and heating grates on the floor are all remnants of the 19th century. The window behind the altar shows 52 scenes from the life of Christ. A window to the left of the altar shows Edgar's coronation.

Posted on the door (and on the abbey website) is the schedule for **events**, including concerts, services, and evensong.

Climbing to the top of the **tower** is only possible with an official 50-minute guided tour. You'll climb 212 steps for views across the rooftops of Bath and down into the Roman and Medieval Baths complex (£5, sporadic schedule but generally at the top of each hour Mon–Sat April–Oct 10:00–16:00, Nov–March 11:00–

14:00, more often during busy times, no tours Sun, buy tickets in abbey gift shop).

A small but worthwhile exhibit, the abbey's **Heritage Vaults** tell the story of Christianity in Bath since Roman times (free, Mon–Sat 10:00–17:30, until 16:30 Nov–March, closed Sun, entrance just outside church, south side).

▲**Pulteney Bridge, Parade Gardens, and Cruises**—Bath is inclined to compare its shop-lined Pulteney Bridge to Florence's

Ponte Vecchio. That's pushing it. But to best enjoy a sunny day, pay £1 to enter the Parade Gardens below the bridge (Easter–Sept daily 11:00–17:00, shorter hours off-season, includes deck chairs, ask about concerts held some Sun at 15:00 in summer, entrance a block south of bridge, www.bathnes.gov .uk). Taking a siesta to relax peace-fully at the riverside provides a wonderful break (and memory).

Across the bridge at Pulteney Weir, tour boat companies run **cruises** (£8 round-trip, £4 one-way, up to 7/day if the weather's good, one hour to Bathampton and back, WCs on board, tel. 01225/312-900). Just take whatever boat is running—all stop in Bathampton (allowing you to hop off and walk back—about 45–60 minutes). Boats come with picnic-friendly sundecks.

Guildhall Market—The little, old-school shopping mall located across from Pulteney Bridge is a frumpy time warp in this affluent town. It's fun for browsing and picnic-shopping. Its cheap Market Café is recommended in "Eating in Bath," later.

Victoria Art Gallery—This gallery, next to Pulteney Bridge, has two parts: the ground floor houses temporary exhibits, while the upstairs is filled with paintings from the late 17th century to the present, along with a small collection of decorative arts (free, Tue–Sat 10:00–17:00, Sun 13:30–17:00, closed Mon, WC, tel. 01225/477-233, www.victoriagal.org.uk).

Northwest of the Town Center

Several worthwhile public spaces and museums can be found a slightly-uphill 10-minute walk away.

▲▲**The Circus and the Royal Crescent**—If Bath is an archi-tectural cancan, these are its knickers. These first Georgian "condos"—built by the John Woods (the Circus by the Elder, the Royal Crescent by the Younger)—are well-explained by the city walking tours. "Georgian" is British for "Neoclassical," or dat-ing from the 1770s. These two building complexes, conveniently located a block apart from each other, are quintessential Bath.

Circus: True to its name, this is a circular housing complex. Picture it as a coliseum turned inside out. Its Doric, Ionic, and Corinthian capital decorations pay homage to its Greco-Roman origin, and are a reminder that Bath (with its seven hills) aspired to be "the Rome of England." The frieze above the first row of columns has hundreds of different panels, each representing the arts, sciences, and crafts. The first floor was high off the ground, to accommodate aristocrats on sedan chairs and women with sky-high hairdos. The tiny round windows on the top floors were the servants' quarters. While the building fronts are uniform, the backs are higgledy-piggledy, infamous for their "hanging loos." Stand in the middle of the Circus among the grand plane trees, on the capped old well. Imagine the days when there was no indoor plumbing, and the servant girls gathered here to fetch water—this was gossip central. If you stand on the well, your clap echoes three times around the circle (try it).

Royal Crescent: A long, graceful arc of buildings—impossible to see in one glance unless you step way back to the edge of the big park in front—evokes

the wealth and gentility of Bath's glory days. As you cruise the Crescent, pretend you're rich. Then pretend you're poor. Notice the "ha ha fence," a drop-off in the front yard that acted as a barrier, invisible from the windows, for keeping out sheep and peasants. The refined and stylish **Royal Crescent Hotel** sits unmarked in the center of the Crescent (with the giant rhododendron growing over the door). You're welcome to (politely) drop in to explore its fine ground-floor public spaces and back garden. A gracious and traditional tea is served in the garden out back (£12.50 cream tea, £22.50 afternoon tea, daily 15:00–17:00, sharing is OK, reserve a day in advance in summer, tel. 01225/823-333).

▲**Georgian House at No. 1 Royal Crescent**—This museum (corner of Brock Street and Royal Crescent) offers your best look into a period house. Your visit is limited to four roped-off rooms, but if you take your time and talk to the docents stationed in each room, it's worth the £6 admission to get behind one of those classy Georgian facades. The docents are determined to fill you in on all the fascinating details of Georgian life...like how high-class women shaved their eyebrows and pasted on carefully trimmed strips of furry mouse skin in their place. On the bedroom dresser sits a bowl of black beauty marks and a head-scratcher from those pre-shampoo days. Fido spent his days in the kitchen treadmill powering the rotisserie (mid-Feb–Oct Tue–Sun 10:30–17:00, Nov

Tue–Sun 10:30–16:00, last entry 30 minutes before closing, closed Mon and Dec–mid-Feb, £2 guidebook available, no photos, "no stiletto heels, please," tel. 01225/428-126, www.bath-preservation -trust.org.uk). Its WC is accessible from the street (under the entry steps, across from the exit and shop).

▲▲**Fashion Museum**—Housed underneath Bath's Assembly Rooms, this museum displays four centuries of fashion on one

floor. It's small, but the fact-filled, included audioguide can stretch a visit to an informative and enjoyable hour. Like fashion itself, the collection changes all the time. A major feature is usually the museum's choices for "Dress of the Year" dating back to 1963—a fascinating opportunity to see nearly a half-century's fashion trends in one sweep of the head. (The menswear version—awarded sporadically—shows a bit less variation, but has flashes of creativity.) Many of the exhibits are organized by theme (bags, shoes, underwear, wedding dresses, and so on). You'll see how fashion evolved—just like architecture and other arts—from one historical period to the next: Georgian, Regency, Victorian, the Swinging '60s, and so on. If you're intrigued by all those historic garments, take a chance to lace up your own trainer corset (which looks more like a lifejacket) and try on a hoop underdress (£7, £15 combo-ticket covers Roman Baths—saving you £3.50, family ticket available, daily March–Oct 10:30–18:00, Nov–Feb 10:30–17:00, last entry one hour before closing, on-site self-service café, tel. 01225/477-789, www.fashionmuseum.co.uk).

Assembly Rooms: Whether or not you're touring the Fashion Museum, poke into the building that houses it, where you can wander the big, grand, empty Assembly Rooms. Card games, concerts, tea, and dances were held here in the 18th century, before the advent of fancy hotels with grand public spaces made them obsolete. Note the extreme symmetry (pleasing to the aristocratic eye) and the high windows (assuring privacy). After the Allies bombed the historic and well-preserved German city of Lübeck, the Germans picked up a Baedeker guide and chose a similarly lovely city to bomb: Bath. The Assembly Rooms—gutted in this wartime tit-for-tat by WWII bombs—have since been restored to their original splendor. (Only the chandeliers are original.)

Nearby: Below the Fashion Museum (to the left as you leave, 20 yards away, at the door marked *14* and *Alfred House*) is one of the few surviving sets of **iron house hardware.** "Link boys" carried torches through the dark streets, lighting the way for big shots in their sedan chairs as they traveled from one affair to the next. The link boys extinguished their torches in the black conical "snuffers." The lamp above was once gas-lit. The crank on the left was used to hoist bulky things to various windows (see the hooks). Few of these sets survived the dark days of the WWII Blitz, when most were collected and melted down, purportedly to make weapons to feed the British war machine. (Not long ago, these well-meaning Brits finally found out that all of their patriotic extra commitment to the national struggle had been for naught, since the metal ended up in junk heaps.)

Shoppers head down **Bartlett Street,** just below the Fashion Museum, to browse the antique shops.

▲▲Museum of Bath at Work—This modest but lovable place explains the industrial history of Bath. The museum is more interesting than it sounds, serving as a vivid reminder that there's always been a grimy, workaday side to this spa town. The core of the museum is the well-preserved, circa-1900 fizzy-drink business of Mr. Bowler, which includes a Dickensian office, engineer's shop, brass foundry, and factory floor. It's just a pile of meaningless old gadgets—until the included audioguide resurrects Mr. Bowler's creative genius. You'll find that each item has its own story. Upstairs are display cases fea-turing other Bath creations through the years, including a 1914 Horstmann car, wheeled

sedan chairs (this *is* Bath, after all), and the versatile plasti-cine (colorful proto-Play-Doh—still the preferred medium of Aardman Studios, creators of the stop-motion animated *Wallace and Gromit* movies). At the snack bar, you can buy your own his-toric fizzy drink (a descendant of the ones once made here). On your way out, don't miss the small collection of exhibits on the ground floor, featuring cabinetmaking, the traditional methods for cutting the local "Bath Stone," a locally produced six-stroke engine, and more (£5, people over 60 pay £3.50, April–Oct daily 10:30–17:00, Nov–March weekends only except closed in Dec, last entry at 16:00, Julian Road, 2 steep blocks up Russell Street from Assembly Rooms, tel. 01225/318-348, www.bath-at-work .org.uk).

Sightseeing Tip: Notice the proximity of this museum to the very different Fashion Museum (described earlier). Museum atten-dants told me that—while open-minded spouses appreciate both places—it's standard for husbands to visit the Museum of Bath at Work while their wives are touring the Fashion Museum. Maybe it's time to divide and conquer?

Jane Austen Centre—This exhibition focuses on Jane Austen's tumultuous, sometimes-troubled five years in Bath (circa 1800, during which time her father died), and the influence the city had on her writing. There's little of historic substance here; you'll walk through a Georgian townhouse that she didn't live in (one of her real addresses in Bath was a few houses up the road, at 25 Gay Street), and you'll see mostly enlarged reproductions of things associated with her writing. The museum describes various places from two novels set in Bath (*Persuasion* and *Northanger Abbey*). After a live intro (15 minutes, 2/hour, starts at :15 and :45 past the hour) explaining how this romantic but down-to-earth woman dealt with the silly, shallow, and arrogant aristocrats' world, where "the doing of nothings all day prevents one from doing anything," you'll see a 15-minute video and wander through the rest of the exhibit. The well-stocked gift shop—with "I love Mr. Darcy" tote bags and Colin Firth's visage emblazoned on teacups, postcards, and more—is worthy of a shopping spree for Jane Austen fans (£7; mid-March–mid-Nov daily 9:45–17:30, July–Aug Thu–Sat until 19:00; mid-Nov–mid-March Sun–Fri 11:00–16:30, Sat 9:45–17:30; between Queen's Square and the Circus at 40 Gay Street, tel. 01225/443-000, www.janeausten.co.uk).

Upstairs, the award-winning **Regency Tea Rooms** hits the spot for Austenites, with costumed waitstaff and themed teas (£6-10), including the all-out "Tea with Mr. Darcy" for £11.50 (also £6 sandwiches, open same hours as the Centre, last orders 45 minutes before closing).

Jane Austen–themed **walking tours** of the city begin at the TI and end at the Centre (£5, 1.5 hours, Sat–Sun at 11:00, July–Aug also Fri–Sat at 16:00, no reservation necessary).

Building of Bath Collection—This offers an intriguing behind-the-scenes look at how the Georgian city was actually built (£4, mid-Feb–Nov Sat–Mon 10:30–17:00, last entry 30 minutes before closing, closed Tue–Fri and Dec–mid-Feb, a short walk north of the city center on a street called "The Paragon," tel. 01225/333-895, www.bath-preservation-trust.org.uk).

Outer Bath

▲**American Museum**—I know, you need this in Bath like you need a Big Mac. The UK's only museum dedicated to American history, this may be the only place that combines Geronimo and Groucho Marx. It has thoughtful exhibits on the history of Native Americans and the Civil War, but the museum's heart is with the decorative arts and cultural artifacts that reveal how Americans lived from colonial times to the mid-19th century. Each of the 18 completely furnished rooms (from a plain 1600s Massachusetts dining/living room to a Rococo Revival explosion in a New

Orleans bedroom) is hosted by eager guides, waiting to fill you in on the everyday items that make domestic Yankee history surprisingly interesting. (In the Lee Room, look for the original mouse holes, lovingly backlit, in the floor boards.) One room is a quilter's nirvana. You could easily spend an afternoon here, enjoying the surrounding gardens, arboretum, and trails (£8, mid-March–Oct Tue–Sun 12:00–17:00, closed Mon and Nov–mid-March, last entry one hour before closing, at Claverton Manor, tel. 01225/460-503, www.americanmuseum.org). The museum is outside of town and a headache to reach if you don't have a car (10–15-minute walk from bus #18 or the hop-on, hop-off bus stop).

Activities in Bath

Walking—The Bath Skyline Walk is a six-mile wander around the hills surrounding Bath (leaflet at TI). Plenty of other scenic paths are described in the TI's literature. For additional options, get *Country Walks around Bath*, by Tim Mowl (£4.50 at TI or bookstores).

Hiking the Canal to Bathampton—An idyllic towpath leads two miles from the Bath Spa train station, along the Kennet and Avon Canal, to the sleepy village of Bathampton. Immediately behind the station in Bath, cross the footbridge, turn left, and find where the canal hits the River Avon. Head northeast along the small canal, noticing the series of Industrial Age locks and giving thanks that you're not a horse pulling a barge. After the path crisscrosses the canal a few times, you'll mostly walk with the water on your right. You'll be in Bathampton in less than an hour, where The George, a classic pub, awaits with a nice meal and cellar-temp beer (reservations smart, tel. 01225/425-079).

Boating—The Bath Boating Station, in an old Victorian boathouse, rents rowboats, canoes, and punts (£7 per person/first hour, then £3/additional hour, Easter–Sept daily 10:00–18:00, closed off-season, Forester Road, one mile northeast of center, tel. 01225/312-900, www.bathboating.co.uk).

Swimming and Kids' Activities—The Bath Sports and Leisure Centre has a fine pool for laps as well as lots of waterslides. Kids have entertaining options in the mini-gym "Active Club" area, which includes a rock wall and a "Zany Zone" indoor playground (swimming: £3.70 for adults, £2.30 for kids; kids and their parents pay £4 each to use "Active Club" plus pool; Mon–Fri 6:30–22:00, Sat 6:30–19:00, Sun 8:00–20:00, kids' hours limited, call for open-swim times, just across North Parade Bridge, tel. 01225/486-905, www.aquaterra.org).

Shopping—There's great browsing between the abbey and the Assembly Rooms (Fashion Museum). Shops close at about 17:30, and many are open on Sunday (11:00–16:00). Explore the antique shops lining Bartlett Street, below the Fashion Museum.

Nightlife in Bath

For an up-to-date list of events, pick up the local weekly newspaper, the *Bath Chronicle*, which includes a "What's On" schedule (www .thisisbath.com). Younger travelers may enjoy the party-ready bar, club, and nightlife recommendations at www.itchybath.co.uk.

▲▲**Bizarre Bath Street Theater**—For an entertaining walking-tour comedy act "with absolutely no history or culture," follow Dom, J. J., or Noel Britten on their creative and lively Bizarre Bath walk. This 1.5-hour "tour," which combines stand-up comedy with cleverly executed magic tricks, plays off unsuspecting passersby as well as tour members. It's a belly laugh a minute (£8, or £7 if you show your Rick Steves book, April–Oct nightly at 20:00, smaller groups Mon–Thu, promises to insult all nationalities and sensitivities, just racy enough but still good family fun, leaves from The Huntsman pub near the abbey, confirm at TI or call 01225/335-124, www.bizarrebath.co.uk).

▲**Theatre Royal Performance**—The 18th-century, 800-seat Theatre Royal, newly restored and one of England's loveliest, offers a busy schedule of London West End–type plays, including many "pre-London" dress-rehearsal runs (£15–39, shows generally start at 19:30 or 20:00, matinees at 14:30, box office open Mon–Sat 10:00–20:00, Sun 12:00–20:00, £3 extra to book online or by phone with a credit card, tel. 01225/448-844, www.theatreroyal.org.uk).

Forty nosebleed spots on a bench (misnamed "standbys") go on sale at noon Monday through Saturday for that day's evening performance (£5, 2 tickets maximum). If the show is sold out, same-day "standing places" go on sale at 18:00 (12:00 for matinees) for £3 (2 tickets maximum). For either of these cheap options, it's better to pay cash at the box office (£3 fee for online or phone purchases). Also at the box office, you can snatch up any "last minute" seats for £10–15 a half-hour before "curtain up."

A handy, cheap sightseers' tip: During the free Bath walking tour, your guide stops here. Pop into the box office, ask what's playing tonight, and see if there are many seats left. If the play sounds good and plenty of seats remain unsold, you're fairly safe to come back 30 minutes before curtain time to buy a ticket at that cheaper price. Oh...and if you smell jasmine, it's the ghost of Lady Grey, a mistress of Beau Nash.

Evening Walks—Take your choice: comedy (Bizarre Bath, described earlier), history, or ghost tour. The free **city history walks** (a daily standard described on page 347) are offered on some summer evenings (2 hours, May–Sept Tue and Fri at 19:00, leave from Pump Room). **Ghost Walks** are a popular way to pass the after-dark hours (£7, cash only, 1.5 hours, year-round Thu–Sat at 20:00, leave from The Garrick's Head pub to the left and behind Theatre Royal as you face it, tel. 01225/350-512, www.ghostwalks ofbath.co.uk). The cities of York and Edinburgh—which have houses thought to be actually haunted—are better for these walks.

Pubs—Most pubs in the center are very noisy, catering to a rowdy twentysomething crowd. But on the top end of town, you can still find some classic old places with inviting ambience and live music. These are listed in order from closest to farthest away:

The Old Green Tree, the most convenient of all these pubs, is a rare traditional pub right in the town center (locally brewed real ales, no children, 12 Green Street; also recommended for lunch—see "Eating in Bath," later).

The Star Inn is much appreciated by local beer-lovers for its fine ale and "no machines or music to distract from the chat." It's a "spit 'n' sawdust" place, and its long bench, nicknamed "death row," still comes with a complimentary pinch of snuff from tins on the ledge. Try the Bellringer Ale, made just up the road (Mon–Fri 12:00–14:30 & 17:30–24:00, Sat–Sun 12:00–24:00, no food served, 23 The Vineyards, top of The Paragon/A4 Roman Road, tel. 01225/425-072, generous and friendly welcome from Paul, who runs the place).

The Bell has a jazzy, pierced-and-tattooed, bohemian feel, but with a mellow older crowd. There's some kind of activity nearly every night, usually involving live music (the only food served is £2.50 sandwiches, Mon–Sat 11:30–23:00, Sun 12:00–22:30, 103 Walcot Street, tel. 01225/460-426, www.walcotstreet.com).

Summer Nights at the Baths—In July and August, you can stretch your sightseeing day at the Roman Baths, open nightly until 22:00 (last entry 21:00), when the gas lamps flame and the baths are far less crowded and more atmospheric. To take a dip yourself, consider popping in to the Thermae Bath Spa (last entry at 19:30).

Sleeping in Bath

Bath is a busy tourist town. Accommodations are expensive, and low-cost alternatives are rare. By far the best budget option is the YMCA—it's central, safe, simple, very well-run, and has plenty of twin rooms available. To get a good B&B, make a telephone reservation in advance. Competition is stiff, and it's worth asking any of these places for a weekday, three-nights-in-a-row, or off-season deal. Friday and Saturday nights are tightest (with many rates going up by about 25 percent)—especially if you're staying only one night, since B&Bs favor those lingering lon-

Sleep Code

(£1 = about $1.60, country code: 44, area code: 01225)
S = Single, **D** = Double/Twin, **T** = Triple, **Q** = Quad, **b** = bathroom,
s = shower only. Unless otherwise noted, credit cards are accepted.

To help you sort easily through these listings, I've divided the rooms into three categories based on the price for a standard double room with bath:

$$$ **Higher Priced**—Most rooms £100 or more.
  $$ **Moderately Priced**—Most rooms between £60–100.
    $ **Lower Priced**—Most rooms £60 or less.

Prices can change without notice; verify the hotel's current rates online or by email. For other updates, see www.ricksteves.com/update.

ger. If staying only Saturday night, you're very bad news to a B&B hostess. If you're driving to Bath, stowing your car near the center will cost you (though some less-central B&Bs have parking)—see "Parking" on page 347, or ask your hotelier. Almost every place provides Wi-Fi at no charge to its guests.

B&Bs near the Royal Crescent

These listings are all a 15-minute uphill walk or an easy £4–5 taxi ride from the train station. Or take any hop-on, hop-off bus tour from the station, get off at the stop nearest your B&B (likely Royal Avenue—confirm with driver), check in, then finish the tour later in the day. The Marlborough Lane places have easier parking, but are less centrally located.

$$$ The Town House, overlooking the Assembly Rooms, is genteel and deluxe, yet homey, with three fresh, mod rooms that have a hardwood stylishness. In true B&B style, you'll enjoy a gourmet breakfast, likely at a big family table with the other guests. This is a great value for the quality and location (Db-£95–100 or £120–130 Fri–Sat, 2-night minimum, free Wi-Fi, 7 Bennett Street, tel. & fax 01225/422-505, www.thetownhousebath.co.uk, stay@thetownhousebath.co.uk, Alan and Brenda Willey).

$$$ Marlborough House, exuberantly run by Peter, is the most mod-and-trendy B&B I've seen in Bath. Each of the six

Bath Accommodations

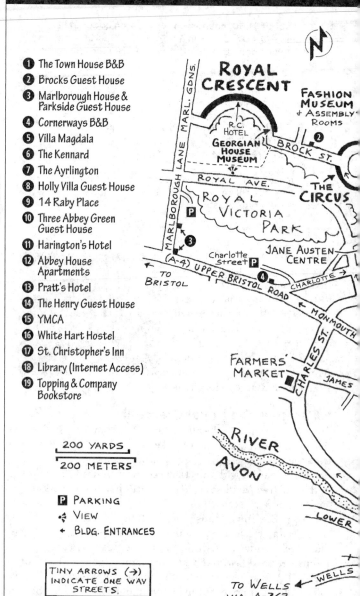

1. The Town House B&B
2. Brocks Guest House
3. Marlborough House & Parkside Guest House
4. Cornerways B&B
5. Villa Magdala
6. The Kennard
7. The Ayrlington
8. Holly Villa Guest House
9. 14 Raby Place
10. Three Abbey Green Guest House
11. Harington's Hotel
12. Abbey House Apartments
13. Pratt's Hotel
14. The Henry Guest House
15. YMCA
16. White Hart Hostel
17. St. Christopher's Inn
18. Library (Internet Access)
19. Topping & Company Bookstore

200 YARDS

200 METERS

P PARKING
VIEW
BLDG. ENTRANCES

TINY ARROWS (→) INDICATE ONE WAY STREETS.

BATH

rooms comes with a sip of brandy (Sb-£70–95, standard Db-£70–110, superior Db-£85–125, Tb-£95–135, organic breakfasts and toiletries, free Wi-Fi, free parking, some street noise, 1 Marlborough Lane, tel. 01225/318-175, fax 01225/466-127, www.marlborough-house.net, mars@manque.dircon.co.uk).

$$ Brocks Guest House has six rooms in a Georgian townhouse built by John Wood in 1765. Located between the prestigious Royal Crescent and the courtly Circus, it was redone in a way that would make the great architect proud (standard Db-£79–85, superior Db-£87–95, Tb-£99–125, Qb-£115–125, higher rates are for Fri–Sat, free Wi-Fi, little top-floor library, 32 Brock Street, tel. 01225/338-374, fax 01225/334-245, www.brocksguesthouse.co.uk, brocks@brocksguesthouse.co.uk, Richard).

$$ Parkside Guest House has five thoughtfully appointed Edwardian rooms. It's a bit older, but it's tidy, clean, homey, and well-priced—and has a spacious back garden (Sb-£60, Db-£80, these prices are for Rick Steves readers, free Wi-Fi, limited free parking, 11 Marlborough Lane, tel. & fax 01225/429-444, www.parksidebandb.co.uk, post@parksidebandb.co.uk, kind Inge Lynall).

$$ Cornerways B&B, located on a noisy street, is simple and well-worn, with three rooms and old-fashioned homey touches (Sb-£45–55, Db-£65–75, 15 percent discount with this book and 3-night stay in 2011, free Wi-Fi, DVD library, free parking, 47 Crescent Gardens, tel. 01225/422-382, www.cornerwaysbath.co.uk, info@cornerwaysbath.co.uk, Sue Black).

B&Bs East of the River

These listings are a 10-minute walk from the city center. While generally a better value, they are not quite as conveniently located.

$$$ Villa Magdala rents 18 stately, hotelesque rooms in a freestanding Victorian townhouse opposite a park. In a city that's so insistently Georgian, it's fun to stay in a mansion that's decorated so enthusiastically Victorian (Db-£95–130 depending on size and demand, family rooms, inviting lounge, free Wi-Fi, free parking, in quiet residential area on Henrietta Street, tel. 01225/466-329, fax 01225/483-207, www.villamagdala.co.uk, enquiries@villamagdala.co.uk, Roy and Lois).

$$$ The Kennard, immaculately maintained by proud owners Giovanni and Mary Baiano, rents 12 rooms a short walk through a genteel neighborhood from the Pulteney Bridge. Each of the rooms is different, but all are colorfully and elaborately decorated (prices are for Sun-Thu/Fri-Sat: S-£58/£65, Sb-£79/£120, Db-£98/£120, Tb-£138/£160, free Wi-Fi, free street parking permits, thoughtfully planned Georgian garden out back, 11 Henrietta Street, tel. 01225/310-472, fax 01225/460-054, www.kennard.co.uk, reception@kennard.co.uk).

$$$ The Ayrlington, next door to a lawn-bowling green, has 16 attractive rooms with Asian decor and hints of a more genteel time. Though this well-maintained hotel fronts a busy street, it's quiet and tranquil. Rooms in the back have pleasant views of sports greens and Bath beyond. For the best value, request a standard top-floor double with a view of Bath (twin Db-£80–100, standard Db-£100–125, superior Db-£120–150, big deluxe Db-£130–170, higher price is for Fri–Sun, free Wi-Fi, fine garden, free and easy parking, 24–25 Pulteney Road, tel. 01225/425-495, fax 01225/469-029, www.ayrlington.com, mail@ayrlington.com, Ling Roper).

$$ Holly Villa Guest House, with a cheery garden, six bright rooms, and a cozy TV lounge, is enthusiastically and thoughtfully run by chatty, friendly Jill and Keith McGarrigle (Db-£70–80, Tb-£90–100, cash only, free Wi-Fi in some areas, free parking; 8-minute walk from station and city center—walk over North Parade Bridge, take the first right, and then take the second left to 14 Pulteney Gardens; tel. 01225/310-331, www.hollyvilla.com, jill@hollyvilla.com).

$$ 14 Raby Place is another good value, mixing Georgian glamour with homey warmth and modern, artistic taste within its five rooms. Muriel Guy—a no-high-tech Luddite—keeps things simple and endearingly friendly. She's a fun-loving live wire who serves organic food for breakfast (S with private bathroom on the hall-£35, Db-£70–75, Tb-£80, cash only; 14 Raby Place—go over bridge on North Parade Road, left on Pulteney Road, cross to church, Raby Place is first row of houses on hill; tel. 01225/465-120).

In the Town Center

You'll pay a premium to sleep right in the center. And, since Bath is so pleasant and manageable by foot, a downtown location isn't essential. Still, these are particularly well-located.

$$$ Three Abbey Green Guest House, with seven rooms, is bright, cheery, and located in a quiet, traffic-free courtyard only 50 yards from the abbey and the Roman Baths. Its spacious rooms are a fine value (Db-£95–145, four-poster Db-£145–175, family rooms-£135–195, price depends on season and size of room, 2-night minimum on weekends, free Internet access and Wi-Fi, tel. 01225/428-558, www.threeabbeygreen.com, stay@three abbeygreen.com, Sue and Derek). They also rent self-catering apartments (Db-£135–165, Qb-£160–195, 2-night minimum).

$$$ Harington's Hotel rents 13 fresh, modern rooms on a quiet street in the town center. This stylish place feels like a boutique hotel, but with a friendlier, laid-back vibe (Sb-£79–155, standard Db-£88–135, superior Db-£98–145, large superior Db-£108–155, Tb-£138–185, prices vary substantially depending on demand, free Wi-Fi, attached bistro for guests only, 10 Queen

Street, tel. 01225/461-728, fax 01225/444-804, www.haringtons hotel.co.uk, post@haringtonshotel.co.uk). Melissa and Peter offer a 5 percent discount with this book for two-night stays except on Fridays, Saturdays, and holidays. They also rent two self-catering apartments down the street—one can sleep up to three (Db-£130, Tb-£145), and the other can sleep up to nine (prices on request; for apartments: 2-night minimum on weekdays, 3-night minimum on weekends).

$$$ Abbey House Apartments consist of three flats on Abbey Green and several others scattered around town—all tastefully restored by Laura (who, once upon a time, was a San Francisco rock musician). The apartments called Abbey View and Abbey Green (which comes with a washer and dryer) both have views of the abbey from their nicely equipped kitchens. These are especially practical and economical if you plan on cooking. Laura provides everything you need for simple breakfasts, and it's fun and cheap to stock the fridge or get take-away for a meal in your flat. When Laura meets you to give you the keys, you become a local (Sb-£90, Db-£100–175, price depends on size, 2-night minimum, rooms can sleep four with Murphy and sofa beds, apartments clearly described on website, free Wi-Fi, Abbey Green, tel. 01225/464-238, www.laurastownhouseapartments.co.uk, laura @laurastownhouseapartments.co.uk).

$$$ Pratt's Hotel is as proper and olde English as you'll find in Bath. Its creaks and frays are aristocratic, and even its public places make you want to sip a brandy. The 46 rooms show their age a bit, but are comfy and spacious. Since it's near a busy street, occasionally it can get noisy—request a quiet room, away from the street (Sb-£60–100, Db-£90–140, price depends on demand, check website for current rates and specials, dogs-£7.50 but children under 15 free with 2 adults, elevator, pay Wi-Fi, attached restaurant-bar, 4–6 South Parade, tel. 01225/460-441, fax 01225/448-807, www .forestdale.com, pratts@forestdale.com).

$$ The Henry Guest House is a simple, vertical place, renting eight clean rooms. It's friendly, well-run, and just two blocks in front of the train station (Sb-£55–65, Db-£85–105, higher prices are for bigger "premier" rooms, extra bed-£15, family room-£135, 2-night minimum on weekends, free Wi-Fi, 6 Henry Street, tel. 01225/424-052, www.thehenry.com, stay@thehenry.com). Steve and Liz also rent two self-catering apartments nearby that sleep up to eight with cots and a sleeper couch (email them for rates).

Bargain Accommodations

Bath's Best Budget Beds: **$** The **YMCA,** centrally located on a leafy square, has 210 beds in industrial-strength rooms—all with sinks and prison-style furnishings. The place is a godsend for budget travelers—safe, secure, quiet, and efficiently run. With lots of twin rooms and no double beds, this is the only easily accessible budget option in downtown Bath (rates for Sun–Thu/Fri–Sat: S-£28/£32, twin D-£44/£52, T-£60/£69, Q-£72/£84, dorm beds-£16/£19, WCs and showers down the hall, includes continental breakfast, cooked breakfast-£2.30, cheap lunches, free linens, rental towels, lockers, pay Internet access, free Wi-Fi, laundry facilities, down a tiny alley off Broad Street on Broad Street Place, tel. 01225/325-900, fax 01225/462-065, www.bathymca.co.uk, stay@bathymca .co.uk).

Sloppy Backpacker Dorms: **$ White Hart Hostel** is a simple nine-room place offering adults and families good, cheap beds in two- to six-bed dorms (£15/bed, S-£25, D-£40, Db-£50–70, kitchen, fine garden out back, 5-minute walk behind train station at Widcombe—where Widcombe Hill hits Claverton Street, tel. 01225/313-985, www.whitehartbath.co.uk). The White Hart also has a pub with a reputation for decent food. **$ St. Christopher's Inn,** in a prime, central location, is part of a chain of low-priced, high-energy hubs for backpackers looking for beds and brews. Their beds are so cheap because they know you'll spend money on their beer. It sits above the lively, youthful Belushi's pub, which is also where you'll find the reception (54 beds in 6- to 12-bed rooms-£15–21, D-£52–58, higher prices are for weekends and walk-ins—it's always cheaper to book online, check website for specials, pay Internet access, free Wi-Fi, laundry facilities, lounge, 9 Green Street, tel. 01225/481-444, www.st-christophers.co.uk).

Eating in Bath

Bath is bursting with eateries. There's something for every appetite and budget—just stroll around the center of town. A picnic dinner of deli food or take-out fish-and-chips in the Royal Crescent Park or down by the river is ideal for aristocratic hoboes. The restaurants I recommend are small and popular—reserve a table on Friday and Saturday evenings. Most pricey little bistros offer big savings with their two- and three-course lunches and "pre-theatre" specials. In general, you can get two courses for £10 at lunch or £12 in the early evening (compared to £15 for a main course after 18:30 or 19:00). Restaurants advertise their early-bird specials, and as long as you order within the time window, you're in for a cheap meal.

Romantic, Upscale French and English

Tilleys Bistro serves healthy French, English, and vegetarian meals with candlelit ambience. Owners Dawn and Dave make you feel as if you are guests at a dinner party in their elegant living

Bath Restaurants

1. Tilleys Bistro & Demuths Vegetarian Rest.
2. The Garrick's Head
3. The Circus Café & Rest.
4. Casanis French Bistro-Rest.
5. Yen Sushi
6. Martini Restaurant
7. Rajpoot Tandoori
8. Thai Balcony, Boston Tea Party & Seafoods Fish & Chips
9. Yak Yeti Yak
10. Ocean Pearl Oriental Buffet & Waitrose Supermarket
11. Wagamama
12. Ask Restaurant
13. Loch Fyne
14. Crystal Palace Pub
15. The Old Green Tree
16. Chandos Deli
17. The Cornish Bakehouse
18. Guildhall Market
19. M&S Kitchen & Café Revive
20. Royal Crescent Hotel (Afternoon Tea)
21. The Star Inn
22. The Bell

BATH

200 YARDS

200 METERS

P PARKING

View

Bldg. Entrances

TINY ARROWS (→) INDICATE ONE WAY STREETS.

TO WELLS ← WELLS VIA A-367

MUSEUM OF BATH AT WORK

To M-4 & LONDON

RIVER AVON

BOATS

LONDON ROAD

LANSDOWN ROAD

JULIAN

GUINEA

BATHWICK

21

22

Building of Bath Museum

BENNETT

4

ALFRED

ST. AND.

GAY

GEORGE

5

11

PARAGON

WALCOT

HENRIETTA ST.

HEN. GDNS.

GREAT PULTENEY ST.

16

6

MILSOM

13

12

BROAD

Victoria Art Gallery & Guildhall Market

ARGYLE

LAURA PLACE

To AMERICAN MUSEUM

QUEEN SQ.

WOOD

JOHN

QUEEN

GREEN

15

10

7

BRIDGE

PULTENEY BRIDGE

BOATS

ABBEY

THEATRE ROYAL

2

WALLS

UPPER

BART. SAW

17

HIGH

18

Rugby Ground

ROAD (A-36)

8

ROMAN BATHS + Pump Room

CHEAP

Parade Gardens

WESTGATE

CHAN.

HET.

BATH ST.

YORK ST.

N. PARADE ROAD

ST. W.

ST.

BEAU

STALL

14

Abbey Green

1

9

S. PARADE

THERMAE BATH SPA

LWR. BOR.

ABBEYGATE

19

ORCH. HENRY

PULT. GDNS.

AVON

2 CORN

ST. JAMES PARADE

SOUTHGATE

SOUTH-GATE MALL

MANVERS ST.

PULTENEY

GREEN PARK RD.

NEWARK

BRISTOL RD.

DORCHESTER

BUS STN.

RAIL STATION

To BATHAMPTON

ROAD

CLAVERTON ST.

ROSSITER RD.

DCH

KENNET & AVON CANAL

BATH

room. Their fun menu lets you build your own meal, and there's an interesting array of £6–9 starters. If you cap things off with the cheese plate and a glass of the house port, you'll realize that's a passion of Dave's. While it's pricey and the portions are modest, this is a memorable splurge (£10–19 entrées; lunch specials: £12.50/2 courses, £15/3 courses; Mon–Sat 12:00–14:30 & 18:00–22:30, Sun 18:00–21:00 only, reservations smart, 3 North Parade Passage, tel. 01225/484-200).

The Garrick's Head is an elegantly simple gastropub right around the corner from the Theatre Royal, with a pricey restaurant on one side and a bar serving affordable snacks on the other. You're welcome to eat from the bar menu, even if you're in the fancy dining room or outside enjoying some great people-watching (£6–10 pub grub, £11–16 entrées on the fancier menu, Mon–Sat 11:00–22:00, Sun 12:00–22:00, drinks until later, 8 St. John's Place, tel. 01225/318-368).

The Circus Café and Restaurant is a relaxing little eatery serving well-executed English cuisine with European flair. Choose between the interior—with a clean, minimalist modern atmosphere either on the main floor or in the cellar—and the four tables on the peaceful street connecting the Circus and the Royal Crescent (£8 lunches, £7 starters and £13 entrées at dinner, open Mon–Sat 12:00–15:00 & 18:00–20:00, closed Sun, reservations smart, 34 Brock Street, tel. 01225/466-020).

Casanis French Bistro-Restaurant is a local hit. Chef Laurent, who hails from Nice, cooks "authentic Provençal cuisine" from the south of France, while his wife Jill serves. The decor matches the cuisine—informal, relaxed, simple, and top-quality. The intimate Georgian dining room upstairs is a bit nicer and more spacious than the ground floor (lunch specials: £13.50/2 courses, £17/3 courses; dinner special available 18:00–19:00: £17/2 courses, £21/3 courses; open Tue–Sat 12:00–14:00 & 18:00–22:00, closed Sun–Mon, immediately behind the Assembly Rooms at 4 Saville Row, tel. 01225/780-055).

Casual, Non-Traditional Alternatives

Whether ethnic food or vegetarian, there are plenty of ways to get some fun culinary variation in this town.

Demuths Vegetarian Restaurant is highly rated and ideal for the well-heeled vegetarian. Its tight, stark, understated interior comes with a vegan vibe (£6–11 lunches, £7 starters and £13–15 entrées at dinner, daily 10:00–16:00 & 17:30–21:00, later on weekends, 2 North Parade Passage, tel. 01225/446-059).

Yen Sushi is your basic little sushi bar—plain and sterile, with stools facing a conveyor belt that constantly tempts you with a variety of freshly made delights on color-coded plates. When you're done, they tally your plates and give you the bill (£1.50–4 plates, you can fill up for £12 or so, daily 12:00–15:00 & 17:30–22:30, 11 Bartlett Street, tel. 01225/333-313).

Martini Restaurant, a hopping, purely Italian place, has class and jovial waiters (£9–12 pastas and pizzas, £14–19 meat and fish dishes, daily 12:00–14:30 & 18:00–22:30—except open all day long on Sat, plenty of veggie options, daily fish specials, extensive wine list, reservations smart on weekends, 9 George Street, tel. 01225/460-818; Nunzio, Franco, and chef Luigi).

Rajpoot Tandoori serves—by all assessments—the best Indian food in Bath. You'll hike down deep into a sprawling cellar, where the plush Indian atmosphere and award-winning cooking make paying the extra pounds palatable. The seating is tight and the ceilings low, but it's air-conditioned (£8.25 three-course lunch special, £9–11 entrées; figure £20 per person with rice, naan, and drink; daily 12:00–14:30 & 18:00–23:00, 4 Argyle Street, tel. 01225/466-833, Ali).

Thai Balcony Restaurant's open, spacious interior is so plush, it'll have you wondering, "Where's the Thai wedding?" While locals debate which of Bath's handful of Thai restaurants serves the best food or offers the lowest prices, there's no doubt that Thai Balcony's fun and elegant atmosphere makes for a memorable and enjoyable dinner (£9 two-course lunch special, £8–9 plates, daily 12:00–14:00 & 18:00–22:00, reservations smart on weekends, Saw Close, tel. 01225/444-450).

Yak Yeti Yak is a fun Nepalese restaurant, with both Western and sit-on-the-floor seating. Sera and his wife Sarah, along with their cheerful, hardworking Nepali team, cook up great traditional food (and plenty of vegetarian plates) at prices that would delight a sherpa (£7–9 lunches, £5 veggie plates, £8–9 meat plates, daily 12:00–14:30 & 17:00–22:30, downstairs at 5 Pierrepont Street, tel. 01225/442-299).

Ocean Pearl Oriental Buffet is famous for being the restaurant Asian tourists eat at repeatedly. It offers a practical, 40-dish, all-you-can-eat buffet in the modern Podium Shopping Centre and spacious seating in a high, bright dining hall overlooking the river. You'll pay £6.50 for lunch, £11.50 for dinner, or you can fill up a take-away box for just £3.50 at lunch or £4.50 at dinner (daily 12:00–15:00 & 18:00–22:30, in the Podium Shopping Centre on Northgate Street, tel. 01225/331-238).

Chain Restaurants

With so many homegrown favorites, I see little reason to frequent a chain restaurant in Bath. But if you're a fan, you'll find these three places: **Wagamama Noodle Bar** specializes in pan-Asian cuisine (£7–9 meals, Mon–Sat 12:00–23:00, Sun 12:00–22:00, 1 York

Buildings, George Street, tel. 01225/337-314, www.wagamama
.com); **Ask** dishes up Italian comfort food (£8-10 pizzas and pastas, good salads, daily 12:00–23:00, George Street but entrance on
Broad Street, tel. 01225/789-997); and **Loch Fyne,** which serves
fresh fish at reasonable prices, fills what was once a lavish bank
building with a bright, airy, youthful, high-energy atmosphere
(£10–18 meals, £10 two-course special from lunch until 19:00 on
weekdays, daily 12:00–22:30, 24 Milsom Street, tel. 01225/750-
120). All of these chains are found all over Britain (see descriptions
on page 33).

Pubs

With so many other tempting options (and since this is not a good
pub-grub town), eating at a pub in Bath isn't as appealing as elsewhere. For the best pub grub, head for **The Garrick's Head** gastropub (described earlier). But if you're looking for a more traditional,
lowbrow place, consider these options.

Crystal Palace Pub is an inviting place just a block away from
the abbey, facing the delightful little Abbey Green. With a focus
on food rather than drink, they serve "pub grub with a Continental
flair" in three different spaces, including a picnic-table back patio
(£9–12 meals, food served Mon–Fri 11:00–21:00, Sat 11:00–20:00,
Sun 12:00–20:00, last orders for drinks at 23:00, no kids after
16:30, Abbey Green, tel. 01225/482-666).

The Old Green Tree, in the old town center, serves satisfying
lunches to locals in a characteristic pub setting (real ales on tap,
£6–7 sandwiches, £9 meals, food served for lunch Mon–Sat 12:00–
15:00 only, open daily for drinks, no children, can be crowded on
weekend nights, 12 Green Street, tel. 01225/448-259).

If you're looking for a pub to drink and hang out in, rather
than eat at, check out **The Star Inn** and **The Bell** (described on
page 364).

Simple Options

These are excellent options for a fast, handy, and tasty meal on the
go. If you get take-away (possible at most of these), you can munch
your picnic while watching street musicians from a bench on the
Abbey Square.

Boston Tea Party feels like a Starbucks—if there were only
one. It's fresh and healthy, serving extensive breakfasts, light
lunches, and salads. The outdoor seating overlooks a busy square.
They also host musical events, and their walls are decorated with
works by local artists (£3–7 breakfasts, £5–7 lunches, Mon–Sat
7:30–19:00, Sun 9:00–19:00, free Wi-Fi, 19 Kingsmead Square,
tel. 01225/313-901).

Chandos Deli has good coffee and tasty £3–5 sandwiches made on artisan breads. This upscale but casual five-table place serves breakfast pastries and lunch to dedicated foodies who don't want to pay too much (Mon–Sat 9:00–17:00, Sun 11:00–17:00, 12 George Street, tel. 01225/314-418).

Seafoods Fish & Chips is respected by lovers of greasy fried fish in Bath. There's diner-style and outdoor seating, or you can get your food to go for a bit cheaper (£4–5 meals, Mon–Sat 11:30–22:00, closed Sun, 38 Kingsmead Square, tel. 01225/465-190).

The Cornish Bakehouse, tucked down a shopping gallery across from the Guildhall Market, has freshly baked £3 take-away pasties (Mon–Sat 8:30–17:30, Sun 10:00–17:00, off High Street at 11A The Corridor, tel. 01225/426-635).

Produce Market and Café: **Guildhall Market,** across from Pulteney Bridge, has produce stalls with food for picnickers. At its inexpensive **Market Café,** you can slurp a curry or sip a tea while surrounded by stacks of used books, bananas on the push list, and honest-to-goodness old-time locals (£3–5 traditional English meals including fried breakfasts all day, Mon–Sat 8:00–17:00, closed Sun, tel. 01225/461-593 a block north of the abbey, on High Street).

Supermarkets: **Waitrose,** at the Podium Shopping Centre, is great for picnics, with a good salad bar (Mon–Fri 8:30–20:00, Sat 8:30–19:00, Sun 11:00–17:00, just west of Pulteney Bridge and across from post office on High Street). **Marks & Spencer,** near the train station, has a grocery at the back of its department store and two eateries: **M&S Kitchen** on the ground floor and the pleasant, inexpensive **Café Revive** on the top floor (Mon–Fri 8:30–19:00, Sat 8:30-18:00, Sun 11:00–17:00, 16–18 Stall Street).

Bath Connections

Bath's train station is called Bath Spa (toll tel. 0845-748-4950). The National Express bus station is just west of the train station (bus info toll tel. 0871-781-8181, www.nationalexpress.com). For all public bus services in southwestern England, see www .travelinesw.com.

From London to Bath: To get from London to Bath and see Stonehenge to boot, consider an all-day organized **bus tour** from London (and skip out of the return trip; see page 190).

From Bath to London: You can catch a **train** to London's Paddington Station (2/hour, 1.5 hours, best deals for travel after 9:30 and when purchased in advance, www.firstgreatwestern .co.uk), or save money—but not time—by taking the National Express **bus** to Victoria Coach Station (direct buses nearly hourly,

3–3.75 hours, one-way-£19.10, round-trip-£27.80).

From Heathrow to Bath: See page 184. Also consider taking a minibus with Alan Price (see "Celtic Horizons" on page 350).

From Bath to London's Airports: You can reach **Heathrow** directly and easily by National Express bus (10/day, 2–3 hours, £19.10 one-way, toll tel. 0871-781-8181, www.nationalexpress .com) or by a train-and-bus combination (take twice-hourly train to Reading, catch twice-hourly airport shuttle bus from there, allow 2.5 hours total, £46–65 depending on time of day, about £10 cheaper when bought in advance, BritRail passholders just pay £15 for bus). Or take the Celtic Horizons minibus to Heathrow.

You can get to **Gatwick** by train (about hourly, 2.5 hours, £45–54 one-way depending on time of day, cheaper in advance, transfer in Reading) or by bus (10/day, 4–5 hours, £25 one-way, transfer at Heathrow Airport).

Between Bristol Airport and Bath: Located about 20 miles west of Bath, this airport is closer than Heathrow, but they haven't worked out good connections to Bath yet. From Bristol Airport, your most convenient options are to take a taxi (£35) or call Alan Price (see "Celtic Horizons" on page 350). Otherwise, at the airport you can hop aboard the Bristol Airport Flyer (bus #A1), which takes you to the Temple Meads train station in Bristol (£7, 2–6/ hour, 30 minutes, buy bus ticket at airport info counter or from driver, tell driver you want the Temple Meads train station). At the Temple Meads Station, check the departure boards for trains going to the Bath Spa train station (4/hour, 15 minutes, £6). To get from Bath to Bristol Airport, just reverse these directions: Take the train to Temple Meads, then catch the Bristol Airport Flyer bus.

From Bath by Train to: Salisbury (1–2/hour, 1 hour), **Portsmouth** (hourly, 2.25 hours), **Exeter** (1–2/hour, 1.5–2 hours, transfer in Bristol or Westbury), **Penzance** (1–2/hour, 4.5–5 hours, one direct, most 1–2 transfers), **Moreton-in-Marsh** (hourly, 2.5–3 hours, 2–3 transfers), **York** (2/hour, 4.25–4.5 hours, 1–2 transfers in Birmingham, Bristol, and/or London), **Oxford** (hourly, 1.25 hours, transfer in Didcot), **Cardiff** (hourly, 1–1.5 hours), **Birmingham** (2/hour, 2 hours, transfer in Bristol), and **points north** (from Birmingham, a major transportation hub, trains depart for Blackpool, Scotland, and North Wales; use a train/bus combination to reach Ironbridge Gorge and the Lake District).

From Bath by Bus to: Salisbury (hourly, 2.75 hours, transfer in Warminster; or 1/day direct at 10:35, 1.5 hours on National Express #300), **Portsmouth** (1/day direct, 3 hours), **Exeter** (4/ day, 3.5–4 hours, transfer in Bristol), **Penzance** (2/day, 7–8 hours, transfer in Bristol), **Cheltenham** or **Gloucester** (4/day, 2.5 hours, transfer in Bristol), **Stratford-upon-Avon** (1/day, 4 hours, transfer in Bristol), and **Oxford** (1/day direct, 2 hours, more with transfer). Buses to **Wells** depart nearly hourly, but the last direct bus back leaves before the evensong service is finished (1.25 hours, last return 17:43—except Sun, when there are also buses at 18:46 and 20:16; or take 18:15 bus to Bristol, then train to Bath—see page 399). For bus connections to **Avebury** and **Glastonbury,** see the next chapter.

NEAR BATH

Glastonbury • Wells • Avebury • Stonehenge • Salisbury

Ooooh, mystery, history. Glastonbury is the ancient home of Avalon, King Arthur, and the Holy Grail. Nearby, medieval Wells gathers around its grand cathedral, where you can enjoy an evensong service. Then get Neolithic at every Druid's favorite stone circles, Avebury and Stonehenge. Salisbury is known for its colorful markets and soaring cathedral.

Planning Your Time

Avebury, Glastonbury, and Wells make a wonderful day out from Bath. With a car, you can do all three in a day if you're selective with your sightseeing in each town (no lingering). Splicing in Stonehenge is possible, but really stretching it. If you want to squeeze a little less into each day, choose either the sights to the west (Wells and Glastonbury), or those to the east (Avebury, Stonehenge, and Salisbury). Ideally, try to see Stonehenge on your way from London, saving your Bath side-tripping day for the other sights.

Everybody needs to see Stonehenge, but I'll tell you now, it looks just like it looks. You'll know what I mean when you pay to get in and rub up against the rope fence that keeps tourists at a distance. Avebury is the connoisseur's circle: more subtle and welcoming.

Wells is simply a cute town, much smaller and more medieval than Bath, with a uniquely beautiful cathedral that's best experienced at the 17:15 evensong service (Sun at 15:00). Glastonbury can be covered well in three to four hours: See the abbey, climb the Tor, and ponder your hippie past (and where you are now). Just an hour from Bath, Salisbury makes a pleasant stop, particularly on a

Sights near Bath

market day (Tue, Sat, and every other Wed), though its cathedral looks striking anytime.

Getting Around the Region

By Car: Drivers can do a 133-mile loop, from Bath to Avebury (25 miles) to Stonehenge (30 miles) to Glastonbury (50 miles) to Wells (6 miles) and back to Bath (22 miles).

By Bus and Train: Wells and Glastonbury are both easily accessible by bus from Bath. Bus #173 goes direct from Bath to **Wells** (hourly, less frequent on Sun, 1.25 hours), where you can catch bus #375, #376, or #377 to continue on to **Glastonbury** (4/hour, 20 minutes). Note that there are no direct buses between Bath and Glastonbury. Wells and Glastonbury are also connected to each other by a 9.5-mile foot and bike path (though, alas, neither town has bike rental).

Many different buses run between Bath and **Avebury,** all requiring one or two transfers (hourly, 2 hours). There is no bus between Avebury and Stonehenge.

A one-hour train trip connects Bath to **Salisbury** (1–2/hour). With the best public transportation of all these towns, Salisbury is a good jumping-off point for Stonehenge or Avebury by bus or car. The Stonehenge Tour runs buses between Salisbury, Old Sarum, and Stonehenge (see page 410). Buses also run regularly from Salisbury to Avebury (1–2/hour, 1.5–2.5 hours; Wilts & Dorset bus #2 leaves from bus station on Endless Street and also from St. Paul's Church on Fisherton Street, near the train station; transfer in Devizes to Stagecoach's bus #49 to Avebury; other combinations possible, some with 2 transfers).

Various bus companies run these routes, including Stagecoach, Bodmans Coaches, the First Bus Company, and Wilts & Dorset. To find fare information, check with Traveline South West, which combines all the information from these companies into an easy-to-use website that covers all the southwest routes (www .travelinesw.com, toll tel. 0871-200-2233). Buses run much less frequently on Sundays.

By Tour: From Bath, if you don't have a car, the most convenient and quickest way to see Avebury and Stonehenge is to take an all-day bus tour, or a half-day tour just to Stonehenge. Of those tours leaving from Bath, Mad Max is the liveliest (see "Tours in Bath" on page 347).

Glastonbury

Marked by its hill, or "tor," and located on England's most powerful line of prehistoric sites (called a "ley line"), the town of Glastonbury gurgles with history and mystery.

In A.D. 37, Joseph of Arimathea—Jesus' wealthy uncle—brought vessels containing the blood of Jesus to Glastonbury, and, with them, Christianity came to England. (Joseph's visit is plausible—long before Christ, locals traded lead to merchants from the Levant.) While this story is "proven" by fourth-century writings and accepted by the Church, the King-Arthur-and-the-Holy-Grail legends it inspired are not.

Those medieval tales came when England needed a morale-boosting folk hero for inspiration during a war with France. They pointed to the ancient Celtic sanctuary at Glastonbury as proof enough of the greatness of the fifth-century warlord Arthur. In 1191, his supposed remains (along with those of Queen Guinevere) were dug up from the abbey garden, and Glastonbury became woven into the Arthurian legends. Reburied in the abbey choir, their gravesite is a shrine today. Many think the Grail trail ends at the bottom of the Chalice Well, a natural spring at the base of the Glastonbury Tor.

The Glastonbury Abbey was England's most powerful by the 10th century, and was part of a nationwide network of monasteries that by 1500 owned one-sixth of all English land and had four times the income of the Crown. Then Henry VIII dissolved the abbeys in 1536. He was particularly harsh on Glastonbury—he not only destroyed the abbey but also hung and quartered the abbot, sending the parts of his body on four different national tours...at the same time.

But Glastonbury rebounded. In an 18th-century tourism campaign, thousands signed affidavits stating that they'd been healed

by water from the Chalice Well, and once again Glastonbury was on the tourist map. Today, Glastonbury and its Tor are a center for searchers, too creepy for the mainstream church but just right for those looking for a place to recharge their crystals.

Part of the fun of a visit to Glastonbury is just being in a town where every other shop and eatery is a New Age place. If you need spiritual guidance or just a rune reading, wander through the Glastonbury Experience, a New Age mall at the bottom of High Street. Locals who are not into this complain that on High Street you can buy any kind of magic crystal or incense, but not a roll of TP. But, as this counterculture is their town's bread and butter, they do their best to sit in their pubs and go "Ommmmm."

Orientation to Glastonbury

(area code: 01458)

Tourist Information

The TI is on High Street—as are many of the dreadlocked folks who walk it. It occupies a fine 15th-century townhouse called The Tribunal (Mon–Thu 10:00–16:00, Fri–Sat 10:00–16:30, closed Sun, pay Internet access, 9 High Street, tel. 01458/832-954, www.glastonburytic.co.uk). The TI sells several booklets about cycling and walking in the area, including the *Glastonbury and Street Guide*, with local listings and a map (£1.50); and the *Glastonbury Millennium Trail* pamphlet, which sends visitors on a historical scavenger hunt, following 20 numbered marble plaques embedded in the pavement throughout the town (£0.60).

Above the TI is the marginally interesting **Lake Village**

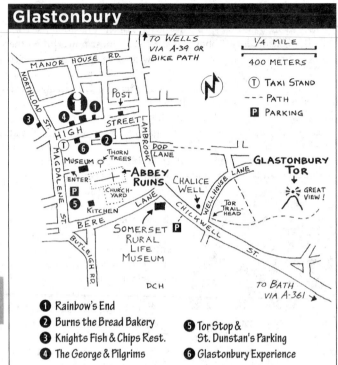

Glastonbury

Museum with two humble rooms featuring tools made of stones, bones, and antlers. Preserved in and excavated from the local peat bogs, these tools offer a look at the lives of marshland people in pre-Roman times (£2.50, extensive descriptions, same hours as TI).

Helpful Hints

Market Day: Tuesday is market day for crafts, knickknacks, and produce on the main street. There's also a country market Tuesday mornings in the Town Hall.

Glastonbury Festival: Every summer (June 22–26 in 2011), the gigantic Glastonbury Festival—billing itself as the "largest music and performing arts festival in the world"—brings all manner of postmodern flower children to its notoriously muddy "Healing Fields." Music fans and London's beautiful people make the trek to see the hottest new English and American bands. If you're near Glastonbury during the festival, anticipate increased traffic and crowds (especially on public transportation; more than 135,000 tickets generally sell out), even though the actual music venue is six miles east of town (www.glastonburyfestivals.co.uk).

NEAR BATH

Sights in Glastonbury

I've listed these sights in the order you'll reach them, moving from the town center to the Tor.

▲▲Glastonbury Abbey

The evocative ruins of the first Christian sanctuary in the British Isles stand mysteriously alive in a lush 36-acre park. Because it

comes with a fine museum, a dramatic history, and enthusiastic guides dressed in period costume, this is one of the most engaging to visit of England's many ruined abbeys.

Cost and Hours: £5.50, daily June–Aug 9:00–18:00, Sept–May 9:30 or 10:00 to dusk, closing times vary in the winter, last entry 30 minutes before closing, nearby pay parking, informative but long-winded 40-minute audioguide-£1, tel. 01458/832-267, www.glastonburyabbey.com. Enter the abbey from Magdalene Street (around the corner from High Street, near the St. Dunstan's parking lot).

Tours and Demonstrations: Costumed guides offer tours and presentations throughout the day (all included with your ticket). These include a fun medieval kitchen demo (described later) and earnest, costumed "Living History" reenactments (generally daily March–Oct at 10:30, 12:00, 14:00, and 16:00). As you enter, confirm these times, and ask about other tour and show times. Or, if you're coming on a slow day (off-season weekdays), call ahead to get the schedule.

Eating: Picnicking is encouraged—bring something from one of the shops in town (see "Eating in Glastonbury," later), or buy food at the small café on site.

Background: The space that these ruins occupy has been sacred ground for centuries. The druids used it as a pagan holy site, and during Joseph of Arimathea's supposed visit here, he built a simple place of worship. In the 12th century—because of that legendary connection with Joseph of Arimathea—Glastonbury was the leading Christian pilgrimage site in all of Britain. The popular abbey grew very wealthy and employed a thousand people to serve the needs of the pilgrims. Then, in 1171, Thomas Becket was martyred at Canterbury, and immediately canonized by the pope (who thanked God for the opportunity to rile up the Christian public in England against King Henry II). This was a classic church-state power struggle. The king was excommunicated, and had to crawl through the streets of London on his knees and submit to a whipping from each bishop in England. Religious pilgrims abandoned Glastonbury for Canterbury, leaving Glastonbury suddenly a backwater.

In 1184, there was a devastating fire in the monastery, and in 1191, the abbot here "discovered"—with the help of a divine dream—the tomb and bodies of King Arthur and Queen Guinevere. Of course, this discovery rekindled the pilgrim trade in Glastonbury.

Then, in 1539, King Henry VIII ordered the abbey's destruction. When Glastonbury Abbot Richard Whiting questioned the king's decision, he was branded a traitor, hung at the top of Glastonbury Tor (after carrying up the plank that would support his noose), and his body cut into four pieces. His head was stuck over the gateway to the former abbey precinct. After this harsh example, the other abbots accepted the king's dissolution of England's abbeys. Many returned to monastic centers in France.

Today, the abbey attracts people who find God within. Tie-dyed, starry-eyed pilgrims seem to float through the grounds, naturally high. Others lie on the grave of King Arthur, whose burial site is marked off in the center of the abbey ruins.

❍ Self-Guided Tour: After buying your ticket, tour the informative **museum** at the entrance building. A model shows the abbey in its pre–Henry VIII splendor, and exhibits tell the story of a place "grandly constructed to entice the dullest minds to prayer." You'll often see costumed guides here who are eager to share the site's story, and might even offer an impromptu tour.

Then head out to explore the green park, dotted with bits of the **ruined abbey.** You come face-to-face with the abbey's west (entrance) end. The abbey was long and skinny, but vast. At 580 feet long, it was the longest in Britain.

Before poking around the ruins, circle to the left behind the entrance building to find the two **thorn trees.** According to legend, when Joseph of Arimathea came here, he climbed nearby Warrell Hill and stuck his staff into the soil. A thorn tree sprouted that still stands there today; these are its offspring. The trees bloom twice a year, at Easter and at Christmas. If the story seems far-fetched to you, don't tell the Queen—a blossom from this tree sits proudly on her breakfast table every Christmas morning.

Now hike along the ruins to the far end of the abbey. You can stand and, from what was the altar, look down at what was the nave. In this area, you'll find the tombstone (formerly in the floor of the church's choir) where the supposed relics of Arthur and Guinevere were interred.

Continue around the far side of the abbey ruins, feeling free to poke around the park. Head back toward the front of the church, noticing all of the foundation rubble in the field adjoining the abbey; among these were the former churchyard, where Arthur and Guinevere's bones were originally found.

Head for the only surviving intact building on the grounds—the abbot's conical **kitchen.** Here, you'll often find Matilda the pilgrim (or another costumed docent) demonstrating life in the abbey kitchen in a kind of medieval cooking show.

Near Glastonbury Tor

These sights are about a 15-minute walk from the town center, toward the Tor (see "Getting There," on page 388).

Somerset Rural Life Museum—Exhibits in this free and extremely kid-friendly museum include peat digging, cidermaking, and cheesemaking. The Abbey Farmhouse is now a collection of domestic and work mementos that illustrate the life of Victorian farm laborer John Hodges "from the cradle to the grave." The fine 14th-century tithe barn (one of 30 such structures that funneled tithes to the local abbey), with its beautifully preserved wooden ceiling, is filled with Victorian farm tools and enthusiastic schoolchildren (free, Tue–Sat 10:00–17:00, closed Sun–Mon, last entry 30 minutes before closing, free parking, at intersection of Bere Lane and Chilkwell Street, tel. 01458/831-197, www.somerset.gov.uk/museums).

Chalice Well—According to tradition, Joseph of Arimathea brought the chalice from the Last Supper to Glastonbury in A.D.

37. Supposedly it ended up in the bottom of a well, which is now the centerpiece of a peaceful and inviting garden. Even if the chalice is not in the bottom of the well and the water is red from iron ore and not Jesus' blood, the tranquil setting is one where nature's harmony is a joy to ponder. To find the well itself, follow the gurgling stream uphill, passing several places to drink from or wade in the healing water, as well as areas designated for silent reflection. The stones of the well shaft date from the 12th century, and are believed to have come from the church in Glastonbury Abbey (which was destroyed by fire). During the 18th century, pilgrims flocked to Glastonbury for the well's healing powers. Have a drink or take some of the precious water home—they sell empty bottles to fill

NEAR BATH

(entry-£3.50, daily April–Oct 10:00–18:00, Nov–March 10:00–16:30, last entry 30 minutes before closing, on Chilkwell Street/A361, drivers park at Rural Life Museum and walk 5 minutes—see instructions below, tel. 01458/831-154, www.chalicewell.org.uk).

▲Glastonbury Tor

Seen by many as a Mother Goddess symbol, the Tor—a natural plug of sandstone on clay—has an undeniable geological charisma.

Climbing the Tor is the essential activity on a visit to Glastonbury. A fine Somerset view rewards those who hike to its 520-foot summit. From its top you can survey a former bogland that is still below sea level at high tide. The ribbon-like man-made drainage canals that glisten as they slice through the farmland are the work of Dutch engineers, imported centuries ago to turn the marshy wasteland into something usable.

Looking out, find Glastonbury (at the base of the hill) and Wells (marked by its cathedral) to the right. Above Wells, a TV tower marks the 996-foot high point of the Mendip Hills. It was lead from these hills that attracted the Romans (and, perhaps, Jesus' uncle Joe) so long ago. Stretching to the left, the hills define what was the coastline before those Dutch engineers arrived.

The Tor-top tower is the remnant of a chapel dedicated to St. Michael. Early Christians often employed St. Michael, the warrior angel, to combat pagan gods. When a church was built upon a pagan holy ground like this, it was frequently dedicated to Michael. But apparently those pagan gods fought back: St. Michael's Church was destroyed by an earthquake in 1275.

Getting There: The Tor is a steep hill at the southeastern edge of the town (it's visible from just about everywhere). The base of the Tor is a 20-minute **walk** from the TI and town center. From the base, a trail leads up to the top (figure another 15–20 uphill minutes, if you keep a brisk pace). While you can hike up the Tor from either end, the less-steep approach (which most people take) starts next to the Chalice Well.

If you have a **car,** drive to the Somerset Rural Life Museum, where you can park for free, then walk five minutes to the trailhead (walk up the lane between the parking lot and the museum, turn right onto Chilkwell Street, and watch on the left for the Chalice Well, then the trailhead).

If you're without a car and don't want to walk to the Tor trailhead, you have two options: The **Tor Bus** shuttles visitors from the town center to the base of the Tor. If you ask, the bus will also stop at the Somerset Rural Life Museum and the Chalice Well (£3 round-trip, 2/hour, on the half-hour, Easter–Sept daily 9:30–13:00 & 14:00–19:30, doesn't run Oct–Easter, catch bus at St. Dunstan's parking lot in the town center—to the right as you face the abbey entrance, pick up schedule at TI). A **taxi** to the Tor trailhead costs about £5 one-way—an easier and more economical choice for couples or groups. Remember, these take you only to the bottom of the Tor; to reach the top, you have to hike.

Eating in Glastonbury

Rainbow's End is one of several fine, healthy, vegetarian lunch cafés for hot meals (different every day), salads, herbal teas, yummy homemade sweets, and New Age people-watching (£7–8 meals, cheaper salads sold by the portion, vegan and gluten-free options, counter service, daily 10:00–16:00, a few doors up from the TI, 17 High Street, tel. 01458/833-896). If you're looking for a midwife or a male-bonding tribal meeting, check their notice board.

Burns the Bread makes hearty pasties (savory meat pies) as well as fresh pies, sandwiches, delicious cookies, and pastries. Ask about the Torsy Moorsy Cake (a type of fruitcake made with cheddar), or try a gingerbread man made with real ginger. Grab a pasty and picnic with the ghosts of Arthur and Guinevere in the abbey ruins (£1.50 pasties and pastries, Mon–Sat 6:00–17:00, Sun 11:00–17:00, 14 High Street, tel. 01458/831-532).

Knights Fish and Chips Restaurant, which has been in the same family since 1909, is the town's top chippy—and another fine option for a picnic at the abbey (£6 to go, about £1 more for table service, Mon 17:00–21:30, Tue–Sat 12:00–14:15 & 17:00–21:30, closed Sun, 5 Northload Street, tel. 01458/831-882).

The George & Pilgrims Hotel's wonderfully Old World pub might be exactly what the doctor ordered for visitors suffering a New Age overdose. The French owners mix a few French dishes into the traditional pub-grub menu (£5 sandwiches, £8–11 meals, Mon–Sat 11:00–23:00, Sun 12:00–22:30, food served 12:00–15:00 & 18:00–21:00, 1 High Street, tel. 01458/831-146). They also rent rooms (Db-£70).

Glastonbury Connections

The nearest train station is in Bath. Local buses are run by First Bus Company (toll tel. 0845-606-4446, www.firstgroup.com).

From Glastonbury by Bus to: Wells (4/hour, 20 minutes, bus #375/#376/#377 runs frequently, bus #29 only 6/day), **Bath** (hourly, allow 2 hours, take bus #375/#376/#377 or #29 to Wells, transfer to bus #173 to Bath, 1.25 hours between Wells and Bath). Buses are sparse on Sundays (generally one bus every other hour). If you're heading to points west, you'll likely connect through **Taunton** (which is a transfer point for westbound buses from Bristol).

Wells

Because this well-preserved little town has a cathedral, it can be

called a city. While it's the biggest town in Somerset, it's England's smallest cathedral city (pop. 9,400), with one of its most interesting cathedrals and a wonderful evensong service. Wells has more medieval buildings still doing what they were originally built to do than any town you'll visit. Market day fills the town square on Wednesday (farmers' market) and Saturday (general goods).

Orientation to Wells

(area code: 01749)

Tourist Information

The TI, on the main square, has information about the town's sights and nearby cheese factories (April–Oct Mon–Sat 10:00–17:00, Sun 10:00–16:00; Nov–March Mon–Sat 11:00–16:00, closed Sun; tel. 01749/672-552, www.wellstourism.com). They have pay Internet access, give out a free schematic map of town, and sell a better one for £0.10. Consider the *Wells City Trail* booklet for £0.60. On Wednesdays and Saturdays at 11:00, they offer a one-hour walking tour of town for £4.

Arrival in Wells

If you're coming by **bus,** you'll arrive at the big, well-organized but unstaffed bus parking lot, about a five-minute walk from the town center. (The big church tower you see is *not* the cathedral.) Find the Wells map at the head of the stalls to get oriented; the signpost at the main exit directs you downtown. **Drivers** will find pay parking right on the main square, but because of confusing one-way streets, it's hard to reach; instead, it's simpler to park at the Princes Road lot near the bus station (enter on Priory Road) and walk five minutes to the cathedral.

Helpful Hints

Local Guide: Edie Westmoreland offers town walks in the summer by appointment (£15/group of 2–5 people, £4/person for 8 or more, 1.5-hour tours usually start at Penniless Porch on town square, book three days in advance, tel. 01934/832-350, mobile 07899-836-706, ebwestmoreland@btinternet.com).

Best Views: It's hard to beat the grand views of the cathedral from the green in front of it...but the reflecting pool tucked inside the Bishop's Palace grounds tries hard. For a fine cathedral-and-town view from your own leafy hilltop bench, hike 10 minutes up Tor Hill.

Sights in Wells

▲▲Wells Cathedral

England's first completely Gothic cathedral (dating from about 1200) is the highlight of the city. Locals claim this church has the largest collection of medieval statuary north of the Alps. It certainly has one of the widest and most elaborate facades I've seen, and unique figure-eight supports in the nave to boot.

Cost and Hours: Requested £5.50 donation—not intended to keep you out, daily Easter–Sept 7:00–19:00, Oct–Easter 7:00–18:00; to take pictures, pay £3 photography fee at info desk or at coin-op machine inside cathedral, no flash in choir; one-hour tours Mon–Sat April–Oct at 10:00, 12:00, 13:00, 14:00, and 15:00—unless other events are going on in the cathedral; good shop, handy Chapter Two restaurant, tel. 01749/674-483, www.wellscathedral.org.uk.

◐ Self-Guided Tour: Begin on the vast, inviting **green** in front of the cathedral. In the Middle Ages, the cathedral was enclosed within the "Liberty," an area free from civil jurisdiction until the 1800s. The Liberty included the green on the west side of the cathedral, which, from the 13th to the 17th centuries, was a burial place for common folk, including 17th-century plague victims. During the Edwardian period, a local character known as Boney Foster used to dig up the human bones and sell them to tourists. The green later became a cricket pitch, then a field for grazing animals. Today, it's the perfect setting for an impressive cathedral.

Peer up at the impressive **facade.** The newly restored west front displays almost 300 original 13th-century carvings of kings and the Last Judgment. The bottom row of niches is empty, too easily reached by Cromwell's men, who were hell-bent on destroying "graven images." Stand back and imagine it as a grand Palm Sunday welcome with a cast of hundreds—all gaily painted back then, choristers singing boldly from holes above the doors and trumpets tooting through the holes up by the 12 apostles.

Now head **inside.** Most of the time, visitors enter by going to the right, through the door under the small spire into the lobby and welcome center. (At certain times—generally 7:00–9:00 and

Wells

A-39 TO BATH ↑

200 YARDS
200 METERS

WOOKEY HOLE ROAD

LOVERS WALK

A-39

WHITING

PORTWAY

CHAMBERLAIN

PRIEST ROW

TUCKER

PRINCES RD.

ST. CUTHBERT

MARKET

WEST ST.

PRIORY RD.

SOUTHOVER

A-39

A-39 TO GLASTONBURY

A-37!

BUS STATION

BROAD ST.

ST. JOHN

HIGH ST.

UNION ST.

NEW ST.

SADLER ST.

THE LIBERTY

VICAR'S CLOSE

MUSEUM

CATHEDRAL GREEN

CATHEDRAL

COLLEGE ROAD

STREET

NORTH RD.

ST. THOMAS PL.

LORLE

TO B-3139 & BATH

BISHOP'S PALACE

TOR FURLONG

TOR ST.

TO TOR HILL

THE PARK

MKT PL.

POST

BIKE PATH TO GLASTONBURY

TO CHEDDAR GORGE, WEDMORE

P PARKING
--- FOOT PATH
--- BIKE PATH
〽 VIEW

DCH

❶ Swan Hotel
❷ The Old Farmhouse
❸ Canon Grange B&B
❹ To Baytree House B&B

❺ Ask Restaurant
❻ West Cornwall Pasty Co.
❼ The Fountain Inn
❽ Chapter Two Restaurant

17:00–19:00—you can enter through the cathedral's main door.)

At the **welcome center,** you'll be warmly greeted and reminded how expensive it is to maintain the cathedral. Pay the donation, buy a £3 photo-permission sticker (if you choose), and pick up a map of the cathedral's highlights. Then head through the cloister and into the cathedral.

At your first glance down the nave, you're immediately struck by the general lightness and the unique "scissors" or hourglass-shaped **double arch** (added in 1338 to transfer weight from the west—where the foundations were sinking under the tower's weight—to the east, where they were firm). The warm tones of the stone interior give the place a modern feel. Until Henry VIII and the Reformation, the interior was painted a gloomy red and green. Later it was whitewashed. Then, in the 1840s, the church experienced the Victorian "great scrape," as locals peeled moldy whitewash off and revealed the bare stone we see today. The floral ceiling painting is based on the original medieval design. A single pattern was discovered under the 17th-century whitewash and repeated throughout.

Small, ornate 15th-century pavilion-like chapels flank the altar, carved in lacy Gothic for wealthy townsmen. The **pulpit** features a post-Reformation, circa-1540 English script—rather than the standard Latin. Since this was not a monastery church, the Reformation didn't destroy it as it did the Glastonbury Abbey church.

We'll do a quick clockwise spin around the cathedral's interior. First walk down the left aisle until you reach the north transept. The medieval **clock** does a silly but much-loved joust on the quarter-hour. If you get to watch the show, notice how—like clockwork—every other rider gets clobbered. The clock's face, which depicts the earth at the center of the universe, dates from 1390. The outer ring shows hours, the second ring shows minutes, and the inner ring shows the dates of the month and phases of the moon. Beneath the clock, the fine **crucifix** was carved out of a yew tree by a German prisoner of war during World War II. After the war ended, many of England's German prisoners figured there was

little in Germany to go home to, so they stayed, assimilating into English culture. Also in the north transept is the door with well-worn steps leading up to the grand fan-vaulted **Chapter House**—an intimate place for the theological equivalent of a huddle among church officials.

Now continue down the left aisle. On the right is the entrance to the **choir** (or "quire," the central zone where the daily services are sung). Go in and take a close look at the embroidery work on the cushions, which celebrate the hometowns of important local church leaders. Up above the east end of the choir is "Jesse's Window," depicting Jesus' family tree. It's also called the "Golden Window," because it's bathed in sunlight each morning.

Head back out to the aisle the way you came in, and continue to the end of the church. In the apse you'll find the **Lady Chapel.** Examine the medieval stained-glass windows. Do they look jumbled? In the 17th century, Puritan troops trashed the precious original glass. Much was repaired, but many of the broken panes were like a puzzle that was never figured out. That's why today many of the windows are simply kaleidoscopes of colored glass.

Now circle around and head up the other aisle. As you walk, notice that many of the black **tombstones** set in the floor have decorative recesses that aren't filled with brass (as they once were).

After the Reformation in the 1530s, the church was short on cash, so they sold the brass to raise money for roof repairs.

Once you reach the south transept, you'll find several items of interest. The **old font** survives from the previous church (A.D. 705) and has been the site of Wells baptisms for almost a thousand years. In the far end of this transept, a little of the muddy green and red that wasn't whitewashed survives.

Nearby, notice the **carvings** at the tops of the pillars, which depict medieval life. On the first pillar, notice the man with a toothache, and another man with a thorn in his foot. The second pillar tells a story of medieval justice: On the left, we see thieves stealing grapes; on the right, the woodcutter (with an axe) is warning the farmer (with the pitchfork) what's happening. Circle around to the back of the pillar for the rest of the story: On the left, the farmer chases one of the thieves, grabbing him by the ear. On the right, he clobbers the thief over the head with his pitchfork—so hard the farmer's hat falls off.

Also in the south transept, you'll find the entrance to the cathedral **Reading Room.** Housing a few old manuscripts, it offers a peek into a real 15th-century library (£1, Fri–Sat 14:30–16:30 only; might also be possible to step in for a quick look on weekday mornings and afternoons).

And finally, the south transept is also where you'll exit the cathedral: Head out into the cloister, then cross the courtyard back to the welcome center, shop, Chapter Two restaurant, and exit. Go in peace.

More Cathedral Sights

▲▲**Cathedral Evensong Service**—The cathedral choir takes full advantage of heavenly acoustics with a nightly 45-minute evensong service. You will sit right in the old "quire" as you listen to a great pipe organ and boys', girls', and men's voices (Mon–Sat at 17:15, Sun at 15:00, generally no service when school is out July–Aug unless a visiting choir performs, to check call 01749/674-483 or visit www.wellscathedral.org.uk). At 17:05 (Sun at 15:05) the verger ushers visitors to their seats. There's usually plenty of room.

On weekdays and Saturdays, if you need to catch the 17:43 bus to Bath, request a seat on the north side of the presbytery, so you can slip out the side door without disturbing the service (10-minute walk to station from cathedral; or go at 18:15 via Bristol—explained under "Wells Connections," later).

The cathedral also hosts several evening **concerts** each month (£10–26, most about £18, generally Thu–Sat at 19:00 or 19:30, box office in cathedral gift shop, open Mon–Sat 14:00–16:30, closed Sun, tel. 01749/832-201). Concert tickets are also available at the TI.

Vicar's Close—Lined with perfectly pickled 14th-century

houses, this is the oldest continuously occupied complete street in Europe (since 1348, just a block north of the cathedral—go under the big arch and look left). It was built to house the vicar's choir, and it still houses church officials (and some of the houses can be rented for a weeklong holiday; contact the cathedral office for details).

▲**Bishop's Palace**—Next to the cathedral stands the moated Bishop's Palace, built in the 13th century and still in use today as the residence of the Bishop of Bath and Wells. While the interior of the palace itself is dull, the grounds and gardens surrounding it are spectacular—the most tranquil and scenic spot in Wells, with wonderful views of the cathedral. It's just the place for a relaxing walk in the park (£5.50, April–Oct daily 10:30–18:00, closed Nov–March, often closed on Sat for special events—call to confirm, last

NEAR BATH

entry one hour before closing, tel. 01749/988-111, www.bishopspalace.org.uk).

The palace's spring-fed moat was built in the 14th century to protect the bishop during squabbles with the borough. Now it serves primarily as a pool for mute swans, who have been trained to ring a bell to ask for food. The bridge was last drawn in 1831. Crossing that bridge, you'll buy your ticket and enter the grounds (past the old-timers playing a proper game of croquet—daily after 13:30). Pass through the evocative ruins of the Great Hall (which was deserted and left to gradually deteriorate), and stroll through the chirpy south lawn. If you're feeling energetic, hike up to the top of the ramparts that encircle the property.

Circling around the far side of the mansion, cross the little bridge and follow the path to the wells (springs) that gave the city its name. Surrounding a reflecting pool with the cathedral towering overhead, these flower-bedecked pathways are idyllic. Nearby are an arboretum, picnic area, and sweet little pea-patch gardens.

After touring the gardens, the mansion's interior is a letdown—despite the borrowable descriptions that struggle to make the dusty old place meaningful. Have a spot of tea in the café (with outdoor garden seating), or climb the creaky wooden staircase to wander long halls lined with portraits of bishops past.

Near Wells

The following stops are best for drivers.

Cheddar Cheese—If you're in the mood for a picnic, drop by any local aromatic cheese shop for a great selection of tasty Somerset cheeses. Real farmhouse cheddar puts American cheddar to Velveeta shame. The **Cheddar Gorge Cheese Company,** eight miles west of Wells, is a dairy farm with a guide and viewing area, giving guests a chance to see the cheesemaking process and enjoy a sample (£2, daily 10:00–16:00; take A39, then A371 to Cheddar Gorge; tel. 01934/742-810, www.cheddargorgecheeseco.co.uk).

Scrumpy Farms—Scrumpy is the wonderfully dangerous hard cider brewed in this part of England. You don't find it served in many pubs because of the unruly crowd it attracts. Scrumpy, at 8 percent alcohol, will rot your socks. "Scrumpy Jack," carbonated mass-produced cider, is not real scrumpy. The real stuff is "rough farmhouse cider." This is potent stuff. It's said some farmers throw a side of beef into the vat, and when fermentation is done only the teeth remain.

TIs list local cider farms open to the public, such as **Mr. Wilkins' Land's End Cider Farm,** a great Back Door travel experience (free, Mon–Sat 10:00–20:00, Sun 10:00–13:00; west of Wells in Mudgley, take B3139 from Wells to Wedmore, then B3151 south for 2 miles, farm is a quarter-mile off B3151—tough to find, get close and ask locals; tel. 01934/712-385).

Apples are pressed from August through December. Hard cider, while not quite scrumpy, is also typical of the West Country, but more fashionable, "decent," and accessible. You can get a pint of hard cider at nearly any pub, drawn straight from the barrel— dry, medium, or sweet.

Castle of Nunney—The centerpiece of the charming village of Nunney (between Bath and Glastonbury, off A361) is a striking 14th-century castle surrounded by a fairy-tale moat. Its rare, French-style design brings to mind the Paris Bastille. The year 1644 was a tumultuous one for Nunney. Its noble family was royalist (and likely closet Catholics). They defied Parliament, so Parliament ordered their castle "slighted" (deliberately destroyed) to ensure that it would threaten the order of the land no more. Looking at this castle, so daunting in the age of bows and arrows, you can see how it was no match for the modern cannon. The pretty Mendip village of Nunney, with its little brook, is also worth a wander.

Sleeping in Wells

Wells is a pleasant overnight stop, with a handful of agreeable B&Bs. The first three places listed below are within a short walk of the cathedral.

$$ Swan Hotel, a Best Western facing the cathedral, is a big, comfortable 50-room hotel. Prices for their Tudor-style rooms vary based on whether you want extras like a four-poster bed or a view of the cathedral (Sb-£104, Db-£136, superior Db-£156, deluxe Db-£176, ask about weekend deals, free Wi-Fi, Sadler Street, tel. 01749/836-300, fax 01749/836-301, www.swanhotelwells.co.uk, info@swanhotelwells.co.uk).

$ The Old Farmhouse, a five-minute walk from the town center, welcomes you with a secluded front garden and two tastefully decorated rooms (Db-£75–80, 2-night minimum, secure parking, next to the gas station at 62 Chamberlain Street, tel.

NEAR BATH

Sleep Code

(£1 = about $1.60, country code: 44, area code: 01749)
S = Single, **D** = Double/Twin, **T** = Triple, **Q** = Quad, **b** = bathroom, **s** = shower only. Unless otherwise indicated, you can assume credit cards are accepted and breakfast is included.

To help you sort easily through these listings, I've divided the rooms into two categories based on the price for a standard double room with bath:

$$ Higher Priced—Most rooms £80 or more.
$ Lower Priced—Most rooms less than £80.

Prices can change without notice; verify the hotel's current rates online or by email. For other updates, see www .ricksteves.com/update.

01749/675-058, www.wellsholiday.com, theoldfarmhousewells@ hotmail.com, charming owners Felicity and Christopher Wilkes).

$ Canon Grange B&B is a 15th-century watch-your-head beamed house directly in front of the cathedral. It has seven homey rooms and a cozy charm (S-£45, Sb-£50, Db-£68, Db with spectacular cathedral view-£74, family room, free Wi-Fi, on the cathedral green, tel. 01749/671-800, www.canongrange.co.uk, canongrange@email.com, Annette and Ken).

$ Baytree House B&B is a modern and practical home at the edge of town (on a big road, a 10-minute walk to the center) renting five fresh, bright, and comfy rooms. Amanda and Paulo Bellini run the place with Italian enthusiasm (Db-£68, Tb-£80, two rooms have private bathrooms on the hall, family rooms, free Wi-Fi, plush lounge, free parking, near where Strawberry Way hits the A39 road to Cheddar at 85 Portway, tel. 01749/677-933, mobile 07745-287-194, www.baytree-house.co.uk, stay@baytree -house.co.uk).

Eating in Wells

Downtown Wells is tiny. A fine variety of eating options is within a block or two of its market square, including classic pubs, **Ask Restaurant** (a popular Italian chain, £8–10 pizza and pastas, £9–12 entrées, open daily, right on the square in the Market Hall, outdoor tables, tel. 01749/677-681); a branch of **West Cornwall Pasty Company,** selling good savory pasties to go (Mon–Sat 8:00–18:00, Sun 10:00–17:00, 1a Sadler Street, tel. 01749/671-616); and little delis and bakeries serving light meals.

The Fountain Inn, on a quiet street 50 yards behind the cathedral, serves good pub grub (£9–10 lunches, £10–13 dinners, open daily, St. Thomas Street, tel. 01749/672-317).

Chapter Two, the modern restaurant in the cathedral welcome center, offers a handy if not heavenly lunch (£6–7 lunches, Mon–Sat 10:00–17:00, Sun 11:00–17:00, may close earlier in winter, tel. 01749/676-543).

Wells Connections

The nearest train station is in Bath. The bus station in Wells is at a well-organized bus parking lot at the intersection of Priory and Princes roads. Local buses are run by First Bus Company (for Wells, toll tel. 0845-606-4446, www.firstgroup.com), while buses to and from London are run by National Express (toll tel. 0871-781-8181, www.nationalexpress.com).

From Wells by Bus to: Bath (hourly, 1.25 hours, last bus #173 leaves at 17:43—except Sun, when there are also buses at 18:46 and 20:16; if you miss the Mon–Sat 17:43 bus to Bath, catch the 18:15 bus to Bristol, then a 15-minute train ride to Bath, arriving 19:35), **Glastonbury** (4/hour, 20 minutes, bus #375/#376/#377 runs frequently, bus #29 only 6/day), **London**'s Victoria Coach Station (£28–30, 1/day direct, departs Wells at 6:55, arrives London at 11:20; otherwise hourly with a change in Bristol, 4 hours).

Avebury

Avebury is a prehistoric open-air museum, with a complex of fascinating Neolithic sites all gathered around the great stone henge (circle). Because the area sports only a thin skin of topsoil over chalk, it is naturally treeless (similar to the area around Stonehenge). Perhaps this unique landscape—where the land connects with the big sky—made it the choice of prehistoric societies for their religious monuments. Whatever

the case, Avebury dates to 2800 B.C.—six centuries older than Stonehenge. This complex, the St. Peter's Basilica of Neolithic civilization, makes for a fascinating visit. Many enjoy it more than Stonehenge.

Arrival in Avebury

(area code: 01672)

Avebury, just a little village with a big stone circle, is easy to reach by car, but may not be worth the hassle by public transportation (see "Getting Around the Region," page 381).

Tourist Information

The TI is located within the town chapel. Notice the stone work: It's a mix of bricks and broken stones from the ancient circle (April–Oct Tue–Sat 9:30–17:00, Sun 9:30–14:30, closed Mon; Nov–March likely open Thu–Sat 9:30–16:00, Sun 9:30–14:30, likely closed Mon–Wed; Green Street, tel. 01672/539-179, www.visitwiltshire.co.uk). For good information on the Avebury sights, see the websites of the English Heritage (www.english-heritage.org.uk) and the National Trust (www.nationaltrust.org.uk).

Arrival by Car in Avebury

If **driving,** you must pay to park in Avebury, and your only real option is the flat-fee National Trust parking lot, which is a three-minute walk from the village (£5, £3 after 15:00, summer 9:00–18:00, off-season 9:00–16:00). No other public parking is available in the village.

Sights in Avebury

▲▲**Avebury Stone Circle**—The stone circle at Avebury is bigger (16 times the size), less touristy, and, for many, more interesting than Stonehenge. You're free to wander among 100 stones, ditches, mounds, and curious patterns from the past, as well as the village of Avebury, which grew up in the middle of this fascinating 1,400-foot-wide Neolithic circle.

In the 14th century, in a kind of frenzy of religious paranoia, Avebury villagers buried many of these mysterious pagan stones. Their 18th-century descendants hosted social events in which they broke up the remaining pagan stones (topple, heat up, douse with cold water, and scavenge broken stones as building blocks). In modern times, the buried stones were dug up and re-erected. Concrete markers show where the missing broken-up stones once stood.

To make the roughly half-mile walk around the circle, you'll hike along an impressive earthwork henge—a 30-foot-high outer bank surrounding a ditch 30 feet deep, making a 60-foot-high rampart. This earthen rampart once had stones standing around the perimeter, placed about every 30 feet, and four grand causeway entries. Originally, two smaller circles made of about 200 stones stood within the henge (free, always open).

Avebury

- —— ROAD
- --- FOOTPATH
- **P** PARKING
- ••• STANDING STONES

TO SWINDON

Direction of Summer Sunrise

ALEXANDER KEILLER MUSEUM

EARTHEN RAMPARTS

GREEN ST.

TO CALNE

HIGH ST.

1 **2**

AVEBURY STONE CIRCLE

P

BECKHAMPTON RD.

B-4003

RITUAL PROCESSION WAY

TO CHERHILL HORSE & BATH

3

A-4 A-4361

SILBURY HILL

A-361

TO DEVIZES

ROMAN ROAD

A-8

½ MILE
800 METERS

B-4003

TO MARL-BOROUGH
A-4

RIVER KENNET

1 Circle Restaurant
2 The Red Lion Pub
3 Mrs. Dixon's B&B

WEST KENNET LONG BARROW

THE SANCTUARY "WOOD HENGE"

Direction of Winter Sunrise

DCH

NEAR BATH

▲**Ritual Procession Way**—Also known as West Kennet Avenue, this double line of stones provided a ritual procession way leading from Avebury to a long-gone wooden circle dubbed "The Sanctuary." This "wood henge," thought to have been 1,000 years older than everything else in the area, is considered the genesis of Avebury and its big stone circle. Most of the stones standing along the procession way today were reconstructed in modern times.

▲**Silbury Hill**—This pyramid-shaped hill is a 130-foot-high, yet-to-be-explained mound of chalk just outside of Avebury.

More than 4,000 years old, this mound is considered the largest man-made object in prehistoric Europe (with the surface area of London's Trafalgar Square and the height of the Nelson Column). It's a reminder that we've only just scratched the surface of England's mysterious and ancient religious landscape.

Inspired by a legend that the hill hid a gold statue in its center, locals tunneled through Silbury Hill in 1830, undermining the structure. Work is currently underway to restore the hill, which remains closed to the public. Archaeologists (who date things like this by carbon-dating snails and other little critters killed in its construction) figure Silbury Hill took only 60 years to build in about 2200 B.C. This makes Silbury Hill the last element built at Avebury and contemporaneous with Stonehenge. Some think it may have been an observation point for all the other bits of the Avebury site. You can still see evidence of a spiral path leading up the hill, and a moat at its base.

The Roman road detoured around Silbury Hill. (Roman engineers often used features of the landscape as visual reference points when building roads. Their roads would commonly kink at the crest of hills or other landmarks, where they realigned with a new visual point.) Later, the hill sported a wooden Saxon fort, which likely acted as a lookout for marauding Vikings. And in World War II, the Royal Observer Corps stationed men up here to count and report Nazi bombers on raids.

West Kennet Long Barrow—A pull-out on the road just past Silbury Hill marks the West Kennet Long Barrow (a 15-minute walk from Silbury Hill). This burial chamber, the best-preserved Stone Age chamber tomb in the UK, stands intact on the ridge. It lines up with the rising sun on the summer solstice. You can walk inside the barrow.

Cherhill Horse—Heading west from Avebury on A4 (toward Bath), you'll see an obelisk (a monument to some important earl) above you on the downs, or chalk hills, near the village of Cherhill. You'll also see a white horse carved into the chalk hillside. Above it are the remains of an Iron Age hill fort known as Oldbury Castle—described on an information board at the roadside pull-out. There is one genuinely prehistoric white horse in England (the Uffington White Horse); the Cherhill Horse, like all the others, is just an 18th-century creation. Prehistoric discoveries were all the rage in the 1700s, and it was a fad to make your own fake ones. Throughout southern England, you can cut into the thin layer of topsoil and find chalk. Now, so they don't have to weed, horses like this are cemented and painted white.

Alexander Keiller Museum—This archaeology museum has an interactive exhibit in a 17th-century barn (£4.50, daily April–Oct 10:00–18:00, Nov–March 10:00–16:30, last entry 30 minutes before closing, tel. 01672/539-250).

Eating and Sleeping in Avebury

The pleasant **Circle Restaurant** serves healthy, hearty à la carte lunches, including vegan and gluten-free dishes, and cream teas on most days (daily April–Oct 10:00–17:30, Nov–March 10:00–15:30, next to National Trust store and the Alexander Keiller museum, tel. 01672/539-514).

The Red Lion has inexpensive, greasy pub grub; a creaky, well-worn, dart-throwing ambience; and a medieval well in its dining room (£6–12 meals, daily 12:00–22:00, tel. 01672/539-266).

Sleeping in Avebury makes lots of sense, since the stones are lonely and wide-open all night. **$ Mrs. Dixon's B&B,** up the road from the public parking lot, rents three cramped and homey rooms. Look for the green-and-white *Bed & Breakfast* sign from the main road (S-£40, D-£60, these prices promised with this book in 2011, cash only, parking available in back, 6 Beckhampton Road, tel. 01672/539-588, run by earthy Mrs. Dixon and crew).

Stonehenge

As old as the pyramids, and older than the Acropolis and the Colosseum, this iconic stone circle amazed medieval Europeans, who figured it was built by a race of giants. And it still impresses visitors today. As one of Europe's most famous sights, Stonehenge does a valiant job of retaining an air of mystery and majesty (partly because cordons, which keep hordes of tourists from trampling all over it, foster the illusion that it stands alone in a field). Although some people are underwhelmed by Stonehenge, most of its almost one million annual visitors find that it's worth the trip. And the ancient site continues to reveal its mysteries: In 2010, within sight of Stonehenge, archaeologists discovered another 5,000-year-old henge, or ditch, which they believe once encircled a wooden "twin" of the famous circle.

Getting to Stonehenge

By Public Transportation: Catch a train to Salisbury, then go by bus or taxi to Stonehenge (for details, see page 410). Note that there is no public transportation between Avebury and Stonehenge.

By Car: Stonehenge is well-signed just off A303. It's about 15 minutes north of Salisbury, an hour east of Glastonbury, and an hour south of Avebury. From Salisbury, head north on A345 (Castle Road) through Amesbury, go west on A303 for 1.5 miles, veer right onto A344, and it's just ahead on the left, with the parking lot on the right.

By Bus Tour: For tours of Stonehenge from Bath, see page 350 (Mad Max is best); for tours from Salisbury, see page 410.

Orientation to Stonehenge

Cost: £6.90, covered by English Heritage Pass and Great British Heritage Pass (see page 20).

Hours: Daily June–Aug 9:00–19:00, mid-March–May and Sept–mid-Oct 9:30–18:00, mid-Oct–mid-March 9:30–16:00, last entry 30 minutes before closing.

When to Go: Shorter hours and possible closures June 20–22 due to huge, raucous solstice crowds; £3 parking fee likely in summer—refundable with paid admission.

Information: Entry includes a worthwhile hour-long audio-guide—though they sometimes run out. Tel. 01980/623-108 or toll tel. 0870-333-1181, www.english-heritage.org.uk/stonehenge.

Reaching the Inner Stones: Special one-hour access to the stones' inner circle—before or after regular visiting hours—costs an extra £14.50 and must be reserved well in advance. Details are on the English Heritage website (go to "Explore Stonehenge," then click on the Stone Circle Access link) or by calling 01722/343-830.

Planned Changes: Future plans for Stonehenge call for the creation of a new visitors center and museum, designed to blend in with the landscape and make the stone circle feel more pristine. Visitors will park farther away and ride a shuttle bus to the site.

Self-Guided Tour

The entrance fee includes a good audioguide, but this commentary will help make your visit even more meaningful.

Walk in from the parking lot, buy your ticket, pick up your included audioguide, and head through the ugly underpass beneath the road. On the way up the

Stonehenge

SEE DETAIL BELOW

INNER STONES

- STANDING STONES
- FALLEN STONES
- MISSING STONES

ramp, notice the artist's rendering of what Stonehenge once looked like. As you approach the massive structure, walk right up to the knee-high cordon and let your fellow 21st-century tourists melt away. It's just you and the druids...

England has hundreds of stone circles, but Stonehenge—which literally means "hanging stones"—is unique. It's the only one that has horizontal cross-pieces (called lintels) spanning the vertical monoliths, and the only one with stones that have been made smooth and uniform. What you see here is a bit more than half the original structure—the rest was quarried centuries ago for other buildings.

Now do a slow counterclockwise spin around the monument, and ponder the following points. As you walk, mentally flesh out the missing pieces and re-erect the rubble. Knowledgeable guides posted around the site are happy to answer your questions.

This was a hugely significant location to prehistoric peoples. There are some 500 burial mounds within a three-mile radius of Stonehenge—most likely belonging to kings and chieftains. Built in phases between 3000 and 1000 B.C., Stonehenge's original function may have been simply as a monumental gravestone for a ritual burial site. (So goes one recently popular theory.) But that's not the end of the story, as the monument was expanded over the millennia.

Stonehenge still functions as a remarkably accurate celestial calendar. As the sun rises on the summer solstice (June 21), the "heel stone"—the one set apart from the rest, near the road—lines up with the sun and the altar at the center of the stone circle. A study of more than 300 similar circles in Britain found that each was designed to calculate the movement of the sun, moon, and stars, and to predict eclipses in order to help early societies know when to plant, harvest, and party. Even in modern times, as the summer solstice sun sets in just the right slot at Stonehenge, pagans boogie.

In addition to being a calendar, Stonehenge is built at the precise point where six ley lines intersect. Ley lines are theoretical lines of magnetic or spiritual power that crisscross the globe. Belief in the power of these lines has gone in and out of fashion over time: They are believed to have been very important to prehistoric peoples, but then were largely ignored until the New Age movement of the 20th century. Without realizing it, you follow these ley lines all the time: Many of England's modern highways are built on top of prehistoric paths, and many churches are built on the site of prehistoric monuments where ley lines intersect. If you're a skeptic, ask one of the guides at Stonehenge to demonstrate the ley lines with a pair of L-shaped divining rods...it's creepy and convincing.

Notice that two of the stones (facing the entry passageway) are blemished. At the base of one monolith, it looks like someone has pulled back the stone to reveal a concrete skeleton. This is a clumsy repair job to fix damage done by souvenir-seekers long ago, who actually rented hammers and chisels to take home a piece of Stonehenge. Look to the right of the repaired stone: The back of another stone is missing the same thin layer of protective lichen that covers the others. The lichen—and some of the stone itself—was sandblasted off to remove graffiti. (No wonder they've got Stonehenge roped off now.)

Stonehenge's builders used two different types of stones. The tall, stout monoliths and lintels are made of sandstone blocks called sarsen stones. Most of the monoliths weigh about 25 tons (the largest is 45 tons), and the lintels are about seven tons apiece. These sarsen stones were brought from "only" 20 miles away. The shorter stones in the middle, called "bluestones," came from the south coast of Wales—240 miles away. (Close if you're taking a train, but far if you're packing a megalith.) Imagine the logistical puzzle of floating six-ton stones up the River Avon, then rolling them on logs about 20 miles to this position...an impressive feat, even in our era of skyscrapers.

Why didn't the builders of Stonehenge use what seem like perfectly adequate stones nearby? This, like many other questions about Stonehenge, remains shrouded in mystery. Think again about the ley lines. Ponder the fact that many experts accept none of the explanations of how these giant stones were transported. Then imagine congregations gathering here 5,000 years ago, raising thought levels, creating a powerful life force transmitted along the ley lines. Maybe a particular kind of stone was essential for maximum energy transmission. Maybe the stones were levitated here. Maybe psychics really do create powerful vibes. Maybe not. It's as unbelievable as electricity used to be.

Salisbury

Salisbury, set in the middle of the expansive Salisbury Plain, is a favorite stop for its striking cathedral and intriguing history.

Salisbury was originally settled during the Bronze Age, possibly as early as 600 B.C., and later became a Roman town called Sarum. The modern city of Salisbury developed when the old settlement outgrew its boundaries, prompting the townspeople to move the city from a hill to the river valley below. Most of today's visitors come to marvel at the famous Salisbury Cathedral, featuring England's tallest spire and largest cathedral green. Collectors, bargain hunters, and foodies will savor Salisbury's colorful market days. And archaeologists will dig the region around Salisbury, with England's highest concentration of ancient sites. The town itself is pleasant and walkable, and is a convenient base camp for visiting the ancient sites of Stonehenge and Avebury, or for exploring the countryside.

Orientation to Salisbury

(area code: 01722)

Salisbury (pop. 45,000) stretches along the River Avon in the shadow of its huge landmark cathedral. The heart of the city clusters around Market Square, which is also a handy parking lot on non-market days. High Street, a block to the west, leads to the medieval North Gate of the Cathedral Close. Shoppers explore the streets south of the square. The area north of Market Square is generally residential, with a few shops and pubs.

Tourist Information

The TI, just off Market Square, hands out free city maps, books rooms for no fee, and sells train tickets with a £1.10 surcharge (May Mon–Sat 9:30–17:00, Sun 10:00–16:00; June–Sept Mon–Sat 9:30–18:00, Sun 10:00–16:00; Oct–April Mon–Sat 9:30–17:00, closed Sun; Fish Row, tel. 01722/334-956, www.visitwiltshire .co.uk).

Ask the TI about 1.5-hour **walking tours** (£4, April–Oct daily at 11:00, Nov–March Sat–Sun only, depart from TI; other itineraries available, including £4 Ghost Walk May–Sept Fri at 20:00; tel. 01722/320-349, www.salisburycityguides.co.uk).

Arrival in Salisbury

By Train: From the train station, it's a 10-minute walk into the town center. Leave the station to the left, walk about 50 yards down South Western Road, and take the first right (at The Railway Tavern) onto Mill Road, following it around the bend and through the traffic roundabouts. Soon you'll see the Queen Elizabeth Gardens and the cathedral spire on your right. The road becomes Crane Bridge Road, then Crane Street, and finally New Street before intersecting with Catherine/St. John Street. Market Square and the TI are one long block north (left) on Catherine Street, and it's another two short blocks beyond that to the bus station. The Salisbury Cathedral and recommended Exeter Street B&Bs are to the south (right), down St. John Street (which becomes Exeter Street).

By Car: Drivers will find several pay parking lots in Salisbury—simply follow the blue *P* signs. The "Central" lot, behind the giant red-brick Sainsbury's store, is within a 10-minute walk of the TI or cathedral and is best for overnight stays (enter from Churchill Way West or Castle Street, lot open 24 hours). The "Old George Mall" parking garage is closer to the cathedral and has comparable daytime rates (£1/hour, 1 block north of cathedral, enter from New Street; garage open Mon–Sat 7:00–20:00, Sun 10:00–17:00).

Salisbury

P PARKING
— WALLS
☐ PEDESTRIAN ZONE

TO OLD SARUM

CHURCHILL WAY NORTH

TO LONDON VIA M-3

CASTLE ROAD

WEST WALK

CHURCHILL WAY

CASTLE ST.

ENDLESS ST.

SCOTS LANE

BEDWIN LANE

GREENCROFT ST.

CHURCHILL WAY EAST

A-36

TO STONEHENGE VIA A-360

DEVIZES ROAD

WILTON RD.

ST. PAUL'S

FISHERTON ST.

CITY HALL

POST

SALT LANE

CHIP

BLUE BOAR

WINCHESTER ST.

MILFORD ST.

BROWN ST.

GIGANT ST.

MILFORD HILL

TRAIN STATION

CHURCHFIELDS

MILL ROAD

WATER STREET

BRIDGE ST.

HIGH ST.

SILVER ST.

BUTCHER ROW

FISH ROW

NEW CANAL

ST. JOHN ST.

CATHERINE ST.

EXETER ST.

IVY ST.

TRINITY ST.

ST. ANN ST.

FRIARY LANE

WATER-MEADOWS

Q.E. II GARDENS

CRANE BR.

MOMPESSON HOUSE

THE WARDROBE

NEW ST.

NORTH GATE

NORTH WALK

ST. ANNE'S GATE

WEST WALK

SALISBURY & SOUTH WILTSHIRE MUSEUM

CATHEDRAL

CATHEDRAL CLOSE

ST. NICHOLAS RD.

NEW ST.

HARNHAM GATE

CHURCHILL WAY SOUTH

TO SOUTHAMPTON & PORTSMOUTH VIA A-36

RIVER AVON

NEW BR. RD.

TO BLANDFORD & "DORSET COUNTRYSIDE JOYRIDE"

200 YARDS
200 METERS

DCH

1 To Cricket Field House, Wilton House & Stourhead

2 Sarum College Rooms

3 Spire House & Cathedral View B&Bs

4 To Premier Inn

5 Charter 1227 Rest. & Market Square

6 The Haunch of Venison Pub

7 Reeve the Baker (2)

8 Anokaa Indian Rest.

9 The King's Head Inn

10 Launderette

11 Library (Internet Access)

12 Bus to Avebury

NEAR BATH

Helpful Hints

Market Days: For centuries, Salisbury has been known for its lively markets. On Tuesdays and Saturdays, Market Square hosts the charter market, with general goods. Every other Wednesday is the farmers' market. There are also special markets, such as one with French products. Ask the TI for a current schedule.

Festivals: The **Salisbury International Arts Festival** runs for just over two weeks at the end of May and beginning of June (likely May 20–June 4 in 2011, www.salisburyfestival.co.uk).

Internet Access: The **library** has 12 terminals for visitors, who can use them free of charge for 30 minutes (Mon–Wed and Fri 9:00–19:00, Thu and Sat 9:00–17:00, closed Sun, computers turned off 10 minutes before closing, Market Place, tel. 01722/324-145).

Laundry: Washing Well has full-service (£7.50–13/load depending on size, 2-hour service, Mon–Sat 8:30–17:30) as well as self-service (Mon–Sat 16:00–20:30, Sun 7:00–20:30, last self-service wash 30 minutes before closing; 28 Chipper Lane, tel. 01722/421-874).

Getting to the Stone Circles: You can get to Stonehenge from Salisbury on **The Stonehenge Tour** bus. Their distinctive red-and-black double-decker buses leave from the Salisbury train station and make a circuit to Stonehenge and Old Sarum (£11, £18 with Stonehenge and Old Sarum admission, tickets good all day, buy ticket from driver, June–Aug daily 9:30–17:00, 1–2/hour, may not run June 21 due to solstice crowds, shorter hours off-season, 30 minutes from station to Stonehenge, tel. 01983/827-005, check www.thestonehengetour.info for timetable).

A **taxi** from Salisbury to Stonehenge can be a good deal for groups (£40–50, call or email for exact price, includes round-trip from Salisbury to Stonehenge plus an hour at the site, entry fee not included, 5–6 people maximum, best to reserve ahead, tel. 01722/339-781 or mobile 07971-255-690, www.salisburytaxis.com, brian@salisburytaxis.co.uk, Brian MacNeillie). Brian also offers a three-hour Stonehenge visit for £80, which includes Old Sarum, Woodhenge, Durrington Walls, and Woodford's thatched cottages.

For buses to Avebury's stone circle, see "Salisbury Connections," later.

Sights in Salisbury

▲▲**Salisbury Cathedral**—This magnificent cathedral, visible for miles around because of its huge spire (the tallest in England at 404 feet), is a wonder to behold. The surrounding enormous grassy field (called a "close") makes the Gothic masterpiece look even larger. What's more impressive is that all this was built in a mere 38 years—astonishingly fast for the Middle Ages. When the old hill town of Sarum was moved down to the valley, its cathedral had to be replaced in a hurry. So, in 1220, the townspeople began building, and in 1258 their sparkling-new cathedral was ready for ribbon-cutting. Since the structure was built in just a few decades, its style is uniform, rather than the patchwork of styles common in cathedrals of the time (which often took centuries to construct).

Cost and Hours: £5.50 suggested donation; mid-June–Aug Mon–Sat 7:15–19:15, Sun 7:15–18:15; Sept–mid-June daily 7:15–18:15; Chapter House usually opens Mon–Sat at 9:30, Sun at 12:45, closes 30–45 minutes before the rest of the cathedral, and closes entirely for special events; choral evensong Mon–Sat at 17:30, Sun at 15:00; excellent cafeteria, tel. 01722/555-120, recorded info tel. 01722/555-113, www.salisburycathedral.org.uk. This working cathedral opens early for services—be respectful if you arrive when one is in session.

Tower Tours: Imagine building a cathedral on this scale before the invention of cranes, bulldozers, or modern scaffolding. An excellent tower tour (1.5–2 hours) helps visitors understand how it was done. You'll climb in between the stone arches and the roof to inspect the vaulting and trussing; see a medieval winch that was used in the construction; and finish with the 330-step climb up the narrow tower for a sweeping view of the Wiltshire countryside (£8.50; early June–Aug Mon–Sat at 11:15, 13:15, 14:15, and 15:15, Sun at 14:00 and 16:00; May–early June and Sept Mon–Sat at 11:15, 14:15, and 15:15, Sun at 14:00 and 16:00; fewer off-season but usually one at 14:15, no tours in Dec except Christmas week; maximum 12 people, can reserve by calling 01722/555-156).

⊙ Self-Guided Tour: Entering the church, you'll instantly feel the architectural harmony. Volunteer guides posted at the entry are ready to answer your questions. (Free guided tours of the cathedral nave are offered—about twice hourly—when enough people assemble.)

As you look down the nave, notice how the stone columns march identically down the aisle, like a thick gray forest of tree trunks. The arches overhead soar to grand heights, helping churchgoers appreciate the vast and amazing heavens.

From the entrance, head to the far wall (the back-left corner). You'll find a model showing how this cathedral was built so quickly in the 13th century. Next to that is the "oldest working clock in existence," dating from the 14th century (the hourly bell has been removed, so as not to interrupt worship services). On the wall by the clock is a bell from the decommissioned ship HMS *Salisbury*. Look closely inside the bell to see the engraved names of crew members' children who were baptized on the ship.

Wander down the aisle past monuments and knights' tombs. When you get to the transept, examine the columns where the arms of the church cross. These posts were supposed to support a more modest bell tower, but when a heavy tower was added 100 years later, the columns bent under the enormous weight, causing the tower to lean sideways. Although the posts were later reinforced, the tower still tilts about two and a half feet.

Continue down the left side of the choir and dip into the Morning Chapel. At the back of this chapel, find the spectacular glass prism engraved with images of Salisbury—donated to the church in memory of a soldier who died at the D-Day landing at Normandy.

The oldest part of the church is at the apse (far end), where construction began in 1220: the Trinity Chapel. The giant, modern stained-glass window ponders the theme "prisoners of conscience."

After you leave the nave, pace the cloister and follow signs to the medieval **Chapter House.** All English cathedrals have a chapter house, so called because it's where the daily Bible verse, or chapter, is read. These spaces often served as gathering places for conducting church or town business. Here you can see a modest display of cathedral items plus one must-see display: one of the four original copies of the Magna Carta, a document as important to the English as the Constitution is to Americans. This "Great Charter," dating from 1215, settled a dispute between the slimy King John and some powerful barons. Revolutionary for limiting the monarch's power, the Magna Carta constitutionally guaranteed that the monarch was not above the law. This was one of the first major victories in the long battle between monarchs and nobles.

▲**Cathedral Close**—The enormous green surrounding the cathedral is the largest in England, and one of the loveliest. It's cradled in the elbow of the River Avon and ringed by row houses, cottages, and grand mansions. The church owns the houses on the green and rents them to lucky people with holy connections. A former prime minister, Edward Heath, lived on the green, not because of his political influence, but because he was once the church organist.

The benches scattered around the green are an excellent place for having a romantic moonlit picnic or for gazing thoughtfully at the leaning spire. Although you may be tempted to linger until it's late, don't—this is still private church property...and the heavy medieval gates of the close shut at about 23:00.

A few houses are open to the public, such as the overpriced Mompesson House and the medieval Wardrobe. The most interesting attraction is the...

▲**Salisbury and South Wiltshire Museum**—Occupying the building just opposite the cathedral entry, this eclectic and sprawling collection was heralded by American expat travel writer Bill Bryson as one of England's best. While that's a stretch, the museum does offer a little something for everyone, including exhibits on local archaeology and history, a costume gallery, the true-to-its-name "Salisbury Giant" puppet once used by the tailors' guilds during parades, some J. M. W. Turner paintings of the cathedral interior, and a collection of exquisite Wedgwood china and other ceramics. The highlight is the "Stonehenge Gallery," with informative and interactive exhibits explaining the ancient structure. Since there's not yet a good visitors center at the site itself, this makes for a good pre- or post-Stonehenge activity (£6, Mon–Sat 10:00–17:00, July–Aug Sun 12:00–17:00, Sept–June closed Sun, 65 The Close, tel. 01722/332-151, www.salisburymuseum.org.uk).

Sleeping in Salisbury

(£1 = about $1.60, country code: 44, area code: 01722)
Salisbury's town center has very few affordable accommodations, and I've listed them below—plus a couple of good choices a little farther out. The town gets particularly crowded during the arts festival (late May through early June).

$$ Cricket Field House, outside of town on A36 toward Wilton, overlooks a cricket pitch and golf course. It has 17 clean, comfortable rooms, a gorgeous garden, and plenty of parking (Sb-£60–68, Db-£85–105, price depends on season, Wilton Road, tel. & fax 01722/322-595, www.cricketfieldhouse.co.uk, cricketfield cottage@btinternet.com, Brian and Margaret James). While this place works best for drivers, it's just a 15-minute walk from the train station or a 5-minute bus ride from the city center.

$$ Sarum College is a theological college that rents 48 rooms in its building right on the peaceful Cathedral Close. Much of the year, it houses visitors to the college, but it usually has rooms for tourists as well—except the week after Christmas, when they close. The slightly institutional but clean rooms share hallways with libraries, bookstores, and offices, and the five attic rooms come with grand cathedral views (S-£45, Sb-£60, D-£70, Db-£95–105 depending on size, meals available at additional cost, elevator, 19 The Close, tel. 01722/424-800, fax 01722/338-508, www.sarum .ac.uk, hospitality@sarum.ac.uk).

$$ Spire House B&B, just off the Cathedral Close, is classy and cozy. The four bright, surprisingly quiet rooms come with busy wallpaper, and two have canopied beds (Db-£80, Tb-£90, cash only, no kids under age 8, free Wi-Fi, 84 Exeter Street, tel. 01722/339-213, www.salisbury-bedandbreakfast.com, spire .enquiries@btinternet.com, friendly Lois).

$ Cathedral View B&B, with four rooms next door at #83, is similar and offers a good value in an outstanding location (Db-£75, Tb-£90, cash only, 2-night minimum on weekends, no kids under age 10, free Wi-Fi, 83 Exeter Street, tel. 01722/502-254, www .cathedral-viewbandb.co.uk, enquiries@cathedral-viewbandb .co.uk, Wenda and Steve).

$ Premier Inn, two miles from the city center, offers dozens of prefab and predictable rooms ideal for drivers and families (Db-£66-87, more during special events, 2 kids ages 15 and under sleep free, breakfast-£5–8, pay Wi-Fi, possible noise from nearby trains, off roundabout at A30 and Pearce Way, toll tel. 0871-527-8956, toll fax 0871-527-8957, www.premierinn.com).

Eating in Salisbury

There are plenty of atmospheric pubs all over town. For the best variety of restaurants, head to the Market Square area. Many places offer great "early bird" specials before 20:00.

Charter 1227, an upstairs eatery overlooking Market Square, is a handy place for a nice meal (£12.50 two-course lunch, open Tue–Sat 12:00–14:30 & 18:00–21:30, closed Sun–Mon, dinner reservations smart, 6 Ox Row, tel. 01722/333-118).

The Haunch of Venison, possibly dating back to 1320, is a Salisbury institution with creaky, crooked floors and the mummified hand of a cheating card player on display (actually a replica; to the left of the fireplace in the House of Lords room). Downstairs, the "occasionally haunted" half-timbered pub serves nouvelle pub grub (£5–8 meals). The restaurant upstairs, while a little pretentious, has a good reputation for its traditional fare (£8–13 entrées; pub open Mon–Sat 11:00–23:00, Sun 12:00–22:00, food served 12:00–14:30 & 18:00–21:00, reservations smart for dinner, 1 Minster Street, tel. 01722/411-313).

Reeve the Baker, with a branch just up the street from the TI, crafts an array of high-calorie delights and handy pick-me-ups for a fast and affordable lunch. The long cases of pastries and savory treats will make you drool (Mon–Fri 8:00–17:30, Sat 8:00–17:00, Sun 10:00–16:00, cash only; one location is next to the TI at 2 Butcher Row, another is at the corner of Market and Bridge streets at 61 Silver Street, tel. 01722/320-367).

Anokaa is a splurge that's highly acclaimed for its updated Indian cuisine. You won't find the same old chicken *tikka* here, but clever newfangled variations on Indian themes, dished up in a dressy contemporary setting (£9–15 entrées, £9 lunch buffet, daily 12:00–14:00 & 17:30–22:30, 60 Fisherton Street, tel. 01722/414-142).

The King's Head Inn is a youthful chain pub with a big, open, modern interior and fine outdoor seating overlooking the pretty little River Avon. Its extensive menu has something for everyone (£3–5 sandwiches, £4–9 entrées, Mon–Fri 7:00–24:00, Sat–Sun 8:00–24:00, food served until 22:00, kids welcome during the day but they must order meals by 20:30, free Wi-Fi, 1 Bridge Street, tel. 01722/342-050).

Salisbury Connections

From Salisbury by Train to: London's Waterloo Station (1–2/hour, 1.5 hours), **Bath** (1–2/hour, 1 hour), **Oxford** (hourly, 2 hours, transfer in Reading and Basingstoke), **Portsmouth** (hourly, 1.25 hours), **Exeter** (1–2/hour, 2 hours, some require transfers), **Penzance** (about hourly, 5.5–6 hours, 1–2 transfers). Train info: toll tel. 0845-748-4950, www.nationalrail.co.uk.

By Bus to: Bath (hourly, 2.75 hours, transfer in Warminster, www.travelinesw.com; or one direct bus/day at 10:35, 1.5 hours on National Express #300, toll tel. 0871-781-8181, www.national express.com), **Avebury** (1–2/hour, 1.5–2.5 hours, transfer in Devizes, Pewsey, or Marlborough, www.travelinesw.com). Many of Salisbury's long-distance buses are run by Wilts & Dorset (tel. 01722/336-855 or 01983/827-005, www.wdbus.co.uk). National Express buses go once a day to **Bath** (morning only at 10:35, 1.5 hours) and **Portsmouth** (evenings only at 18:25, 1.5 hours, toll tel. 0871-781-8181, www.nationalexpress.com).

Near Salisbury

Old Sarum

Right here, on a hill overlooking the plain below, is where the original town of Salisbury was founded many centuries ago. While little remains of the old town, the view of the valley is amazing...and a little imagination can transport you back to *very* olde England.

Near Salisbury

Human settlement in this area stretches back to the Bronze Age, and the Romans, Saxons, and Normans all called this hilltop home. From about 500 B.C. through A.D. 1220, Old Sarum flourished, giving rise to a motte-and-bailey castle, a cathedral, and scores of wooden homes along the town's outer ring. The town grew so quickly that by the Middle Ages, it had outgrown its spot on the hill. In 1220, the local bishop successfully petitioned to move the entire city to the valley below, where space and water was plentiful. So, stone by stone, Old Sarum was packed up and shipped to New Sarum, where builders used nearly all the rubble from the old city to create a brand-new town with a magnificent cathedral.

Old Sarum was eventually abandoned altogether, leaving only a few stone foundations. The grand views of Salisbury from here have "in-spired" painters for ages and provided countless picnickers with a scenic backdrop: Grab a sandwich or snacks from one of the grocery stores in Salisbury or at the excellent Waitrose super-market at the north end of town—just west of where A36 meets A345.

Cost and Hours: £3.50, daily July–Aug 9:00–18:00, April–June and Sept 10:00–17:00, Feb–March and Oct 10:00–16:00, Nov–Jan 11:00–15:00, last entry 30 minutes before closing, tel. 01722/335-398, www.english-heritage.org.uk.

Getting There: It's two miles north of Salisbury off A345, accessible by Wilts & Dorset bus #5 or #6 or via The Stonehenge Tour bus (see page 410).

Wilton House

This sprawling estate, with a grand mansion and lush gardens, has been owned by the Earls of Pembroke since King Henry VIII's time. Inside the mansion, you'll find a collection of paintings by Rubens, Rembrandt, Van Dyck, and Brueghel, along with quirky odds-and-ends, such as a lock of Queen Elizabeth I's hair. The perfectly proportioned Double Cube Room has served as everything from a 17th-century state dining room to a secret D-Day planning room during World War II...if only the portraits could talk. The Old Riding School houses a skippable 20-minute film that dramatizes the history of the family. Outside, classic English gardens feature a river lazily winding its way through grasses and under Greek-inspired temples. Jane Austen fans particularly enjoy this stately home, where parts of 2005's Oscar-nominated *Pride and Prejudice* were filmed. But, alas, Mr. Darcy has checked out.

Cost and Hours: House and gardens-£12, gardens only-£5; house open Easter weekend and May–Aug Sun–Thu 11:30–16:30, last entry 45 minutes before closing, closed Fri–Sat except holiday weekends; gardens open 2 weeks in mid-April and May–Aug daily 11:00–17:00, Sept Sat–Sun 11:00–17:00, last entry 30 minutes before closing; house and gardens closed Oct–April, except house open Easter weekend and gardens open mid-April; recorded info tel. 01722/746-729, tel. 01722/746-714, www.wiltonhouse.com.

Getting There: It's five miles west of Salisbury via A36 to Wilton's Minster Street; or buses #2, #13, #25, #26, #27, or #R3 from Salisbury to Wilton.

Stourhead

For a serious taste of traditional English landscape, don't miss this 2,650-acre delight. Stourhead, designed by owner Henry Hoare II in the mid-18th century, is a wonderland of rolling hills, meandering paths, placid lakes, and colorful trees, punctuated by classically inspired bridges and monuments. It's what every other English estate aspires to be—like nature, but better (house and garden-£11.60, or £7 to see just one; house open mid-March–Oct

Fri–Tue 11:00–17:00, closed Wed–Thu; garden open year-round daily 9:00–18:00, last entry 30 minutes before closing, 28 miles west of Salisbury off B3092 in town of Stourton, 3 miles northwest of Mere, tel. 01747/841-152, www.nationaltrust.org.uk).

Drivers or ambitious walkers can visit nearby **King Alfred's Tower** and climb its 205 steps for glorious views of the estate and surrounding countryside (£2.80 to climb tower, same opening times as house, 2.5 miles northwest of Stourhead, off Tower Road).

Dorset Countryside Joyride

The region of Dorset, just southwest of Salisbury, is full of rolling fields, winding country lanes, quaint cottages, and villages stuffed with tea shops. Anywhere you go in the area will take you someplace charming, so consider this tour only a suggestion and feel free to get pleasantly lost in the English countryside. You'll be taking some less-traveled roads, so bring along a good map.

Starting in Salisbury, take A354 through Blandford Forum to Winterborne Whitechurch. From here, follow signs and small back roads to the village of Bere Regis, where you'll find some lovely 15th-century buildings, including one with angels carved on the roof. Follow A35 and B3075 to Wareham, where T. E. Lawrence (a.k.a. Lawrence of Arabia) lived; he's buried in nearby Moreton. Continue south on A351 to the dramatic and romantic **Corfe Castle.** This was a favorite residence for medieval kings until it was destroyed by a massive gunpowder blast during a 17th-century siege (£6.20, daily April–Sept 10:00–18:00, March and Oct 10:00–17:00, Nov–Feb 10:00–16:00, last entry 30 minutes before closing, tel. 01929/481-294, www.nationaltrust.org.uk). Retrace A351 to Wareham, and then take A352 to Dorchester.

Just northeast of Dorchester on A35, near the village of Stinsford, novelist Thomas Hardy was born in 1840; you'll find **Hardy's family's cottage** nearby in Higher Bockhampton (£4, May–Oct Thu–Mon 11:00–17:00, closed Tue–Wed and Nov–April, last entry 30 minutes before closing, tel. 01305/262-366, www.nationaltrust.org.uk). While Hardy's heart is buried in Stinsford with his first wife, Emma, the rest of him is in Westminster Abbey's Poets' Corner. Take A35 back to Dorchester. Just west of Dorchester, stay on A35 until it connects to A37; then follow A352 north toward Sherborne.

About eight miles north of Dorchester, on the way to Sherborne, you'll find the little town of **Cerne Abbas** (surn AB-iss), named for an abbey in the center of town. There are only two streets to wander down, so take this opportunity to recharge with a cup of tea and a scone. Abbots Tea Room has a nice cream tea (pot of tea, scone, jam, and clotted cream, 7 Long St., tel.

01300/341-349). Up the street, you can visit the abbey and its well, reputed to have healing powers.

Just outside of town, a large chalk figure, the **Cerne Abbas Giant,** is carved into the green hillside. Chalk figures such as this one can be found in many parts of the region. Because the soil is only a few inches deep, the overlying grass and dirt can easily be removed to expose the bright white chalk bedrock beneath, creating the outlines. While nobody is sure exactly how old the figures are, or what their original purpose was, they are faithfully maintained by the locals, who mow and clear the fields at least once a year. This particular figure, possibly a fertility god, looks friendly...maybe a little too friendly. Locals claim that if a woman who's having trouble getting pregnant sleeps on the giant for one night, she will soon be able to conceive a child. (A few years back, controversy surrounded this giant, as a 180-foot-tall, donut-hoisting Homer Simpson was painted onto the adjacent hillside. No kidding.)

Leaving Cerne Abbas on country roads toward Piddletrenthide (on the aptly named River Piddle), continue through Cheselbourne to **Milton Abbas.** (This area, by the way, has some of the best town names in the country, such as Droop, Plush, Pleck, and Folly.) The village of Milton Abbas looks overly perfect. In the 18th century, a wealthy man bought up the town's large abbey and estate. His new place was great...except for the neighbors, a bunch of vulgar villagers with houses that cluttered his view from the garden. So, he had the town demolished and rebuilt a mile away. What you see now is probably the first planned community, with identical houses, a pub, and a church. The estate is now a "public school," which is what the English call an expensive private school. From Milton Abbas, signs lead you back to Winterborne Whitechurch, and A354 to Salisbury.

OXFORD

England is home to two world-renowned universities: Oxford and Cambridge. While I prefer the town of Cambridge for its charm (see page 215), Oxford's historic university makes it a heavyweight sight. While Cambridge feels like a lazy, easygoing small town, Oxford has a slightly more urban vibe, and even more stately buildings than its rival. For centuries, Oxford's stellar graduates have influenced Western civilization—ever since the first homework was assigned here in 1167.

But that doesn't mean that Oxford is stodgy. Although you may see professors in their traditional black robes, this is a fun, young college town, filled with lots of shopping, cheap eats around every corner, and rowdy, rollicking pubs.

While a typical American-style university has one campus, Oxford (like Cambridge) has colleges scattered throughout town. But the sightseers' Oxford is walkable and compact. Many of the streets in the center are pedestrian-only during the day. Stick to the center, and you'll get a feel for workaday Oxford, where knowledge is the town business—and procrastinating over a pint is the students' main hobby. (Local shops sell T-shirts that say, "Don't ask me about my thesis.")

Sample the spirit of Oxford. Step off the busy, urban-feeling High Street into the hushed sanctuary of a grassy college quad. See the dining hall that inspired the one where Harry Potter eats his meals, or the pub where J. R. R. Tolkien first spoke about the Hobbits.

If you haven't yet tried pub grub—or sampled a local British ale—make a point to do so in Oxford, just as its local famous writers did. In Oxford, a town known for traditions, the pubs are where the action is.

Perhaps better than anything in Oxford itself is the excellent Blenheim Palace. It's England's best countryside estate, just outside Oxford and described at the end of this chapter. Don't miss it.

Planning Your Time

Oxford is a convenient stop for people visiting the Cotswolds, Blenheim Palace (a 30-minute drive away), Stratford-upon-Avon, and Bath. Both Oxford and Cambridge are easy day trips from London...and both are miserable from a budget-accommodations standpoint. A stop-off here on the way to somewhere else is ideal.

Oxford's colleges are generally open to visitors, but each has its own visiting hours (which can be unpredictable). There are three terms: Michaelmas (Oct–Dec), Hilary (Jan–March), and Trinity (April–June). Public spaces in the colleges are more likely to be closed during exams in early to mid-June.

Orientation to Oxford

(area code: 01865)

Oxford was first built where oxen crossed, or forded, the Cherwell and Isis rivers. (The Isis is another name for the Thames; back then you could row to London from Oxford...in just five days.) Property in the town center is divided about evenly among three different groups: the university; the colleges (which are independent entities); and private shops and homes.

Despite its relatively compact town center, Oxford can be confusing to navigate. All those colleges start to look alike, and streets tend to change names from block to block. Use the biggest buildings as navigational landmarks, and don't be shy about asking students for directions.

The main arteries are the north-south Cornmarket/St. Aldate's, and the east-west Queen Street/High Street. At the intersection of these streets stands the stubby, 14th-century Carfax Tower (named for the French *carrefour*, or "crossroads"). From here, pedestrianized Cornmarket—essentially an outdoor mall lined with shops and chain restaurants—heads north, where it intersects with another pedestrian zone at George Street/Broad Street.

Tourist Information

The TI offers walking tours (£7), a good town map (£1.50), and the do-it-yourself walking-tour brochure, *Welcome to Oxford* (£1). They also book rooms for a £4 fee, and sell tickets for the City Sightseeing Oxford bus. If you're headed to Blenheim Palace, buy your tickets here for a £2.50 discount (TI open Mon–Sat

9:30–17:00, Sun 10:00–16:00, 15–16 Broad Street, tel. 01865/252-200, www.visitoxford.org, tic@oxford.gov.uk). For more on the tours and the bus, see "Tours in Oxford," later.

Arrival in Oxford

From the **train** station, the city center is a 10-minute walk (exit straight ahead and follow the signs) or a £5 taxi ride. The "city information" desk in the train station is actually just a sales outlet for City Sightseeing's skippable hop-on, hop-off bus tours; the real TI (described above) is in the city center. There are no lockers at the station, but day-trippers can leave their luggage at either of two youth hostels 400 yards in front of the train station toward the town center; confusingly, both are called "Backpackers" (Oxford Backpackers Hostel, 9A Hythe Bridge Street, £3/bag, no lock-out times; and Central Backpackers, 13 Park End Street, £2/bag, 7:00–23:00). Note: The official Oxford YHA youth hostel, which sits behind the station, does not store bags.

The **bus** station, a bit closer to downtown at Gloucester Green, is just a five-minute walk from the heart of Oxford and the TI: Turn left onto George Street and follow it straight into town (no lockers at station—leave your bags at the hostels mentioned above).

Drivers day-tripping into Oxford have several options. The cheapest but least convenient is to use one of the outlying park-and-ride lots, which are about a 10-minute shuttle-bus ride from the town center. There are some pay parking lots closer to the center (including a handy one between the train station and downtown), but they're much more expensive. There's also pay-and-display street parking north of the Ashmolean Museum, on St. Giles Street (carefully monitored, so get back in time or you're likely to get ticketed).

Helpful Hints

Bookstore: One of the world's largest bookstores, **Blackwell's,** boasts miles of shelves in its main location (additional satellite shops around town). The vast Norrington Room in the basement holds stacks of books (Mon–Sat 9:00–18:30, Sun 11:00–17:00, coffee shop upstairs, WC on top floor, 48–51 Broad Street, tel. 01865/792-792, http://bookshop.blackwell .co.uk). Ask here about literary walking tours (see "Tours in Oxford," later).

Best Views: At the University Church of St. Mary the Virgin, climb the 127 narrow, twisting stairs of the 13th-century bell tower for views of Oxford's many spires and colleges (church free, tower-£3, daily 9:00–17:00, July–Aug until 18:00, tower opens Sun at 11:45, last entry to tower 30 minutes before closing, coffee shop in vault, High Street, tel. 01865/279-111, www.university-church.ox.ac.uk). For an easier climb, skip up the 99 steps of Carfax Tower (£2.20, daily April–Oct 10:00–17:30, Nov–March 10:00–15:00).

Harry Potter Sights: In the movies, the look of Hogwarts School was partially based on a few real-life Oxford sights. For details, see page 714, and consider taking a Harry Potter tour (see below).

Tours in Oxford

▲**Walking Tours**—The TI's **"City and University" walking tours,** led by Blue Badge guides, explain the local history and traditions and take you inside one or two of the colleges. More informative than entertaining, these dry talks give you a solid historical background (£7, 2 hours, daily at 10:45 and 14:00, Sat also at 11:00 and 13:00, additional tours on busy days—ask at TI for schedule; 10:45 tours generally include Divinity School and cost £0.50 extra; book any tour inside TI, tours depart from sidewalk out front). They also have a wide variety of themed tours, including **Harry Potter tours** (£11) and **literary tours** about C. S. Lewis, J. R. R. Tolkien, and others (£7.50); pick up the latest schedule at the TI, or check online to see what's offered during your visit (www.visitoxford.org). All of these tours are popular and can sell out (especially on Sat); it's smart to reserve at least an hour ahead (drop by, call, or go online).

Blackwell's Walking Tours, led by proper British gentlemen, focus on literary and historic Oxford. Their Inklings tour visits J. R. R. Tolkien's and C. S. Lewis' former haunts. Check Blackwell's bookstore for current tours and times (£7, mid-April–Oct Tue–Fri, 1.5 hours, 48–51 Broad Street, tour info tel. 01865/333-606).

Bike Cart Tours—Rickshaws called **Oxon Carts** pedal you on a tour around the major sights of central Oxford (one-hour tour-£30, 15-minute spin-£10, cart holds 2 people, weather permitting, reserve in advance, mobile 07747-024-600, www.oxoncarts.com, info@oxoncarts.com).

Hop-on, Hop-off Bus Tours—**City Sightseeing Oxford** runs bright-red double-decker buses around town, shuttling tourists from one sight to the next (20 stops in all). Because Oxford is fairly compact, with colleges that have to be seen on foot, consider this tour only if you've missed a walking tour or have tired feet. If you do go, take a seat up top to see over the college walls (£12.50, pay driver or buy tickets at TI, 4/hour, daily 9:30–18:30, last bus at 18:00; in winter goes 2/hour and stops running earlier; commentary is live on some buses and recorded on others, tel. 01865/790-522, www.citysightseeingoxford.com).

OXFORD

Oxford

TO WOODSTOCK,
BLENHEIM PALACE
& COTSWOLDS
VIA A-4144

THE
ASHMOLEAN
MUSEUM

GLOUCESTER
GREEN +
BUS STN.

BEAUMONT

TRAIN
STATION

ST. GILES MAG.

HYTHE BR. ST.

GEORGE

ST.

NEW INN

SHIP

MIC. CORNMKT.

MKT.

PARK   END   STREET

NEW ROAD

QUEEN

CARFAX
TOWER

A-
420

BECKET

HOLLYBUSH ROW

ST. THOMAS

NORFOLK

CASTLE

ST. EBBE'S

WEST-
GATE
SHOP.
CTR.

POST

PEM.

ST. ALDATES

BL.

TOM
TOWER

BREWER

VISITORS'
ENTRANCE

OXPENS

THAMES

SPEEDWELL

ST. M's.

ISIS
RIVER →
(A.K.A. THAMES)

❶ The Tower House
❷ Bath Place Hotel
❸ The Buttery Hotel
❹ Holywell B&B
❺ Oxford Backpackers Hostel
❻ Central Backpackers Oxford
❼ To The Coach & Horses Inn
❽ The King's Arms
❾ The Bear
❿ The Turf Tavern
⓫ The Eagle & Child
⓬ Taylors Sandwich Shop

OXFORD

13 Covered Market
14 The News Café
15 Jamie's Italian
16 The Randolph Hotel (Afternoon Tea)
17 Blackwell's Bookstore
18 St. Mary the Virgin Church (Viewpoint)
19 Christ Church Picture Gallery
20 Clarendon Building
21 "Bridge of Sighs"
22 Radcliffe Camera
23 Blenheim Palace Bus Stops (2)

Minivan Tours—Run by Philip Baum, **Cotswold Roaming** offers a different minivan tour each day with scenic itineraries that include the Cotswolds, Blenheim Palace, Stratford/Warwick Castle, Bath/Castle Combe, and Salisbury/Stonehenge/Avebury (includes admissions for everywhere but Bath and Shakespeare sights). They can also arrange custom tours for small groups on request (£25 for half-day tours to the Cotswolds, £40–50 for full-day tours, tours may not run if there aren't enough people, tel. 01865/308-300, www.cotswold-roaming.co.uk).

Sights in Oxford

The Colleges

You could spend a lot of time going from college to college here—but since they all have similar features, frankly, if you've seen one, you've seen them all. If you just take the TI's walking tour, you'll get a sufficient taste of one or two—for most visitors, it's overkill to visit more. Save your time for the excellent Ashmolean Museum, Bodleian Library, or punting.

The entrance to each college is easy to spot—just look for a doorway with crests and a flagpole on the top. Each entry has an office with a porter (a live-in caretaker, not a janitor). Inquire there to find out which buildings are open to visitors, and if any plays, music, or lectures are scheduled.

▲**Christ Church College**—This is the alma mater of William Penn (founder of Pennsylvania), John Wesley (influential Methodist leader), Charles Dodgson (a.k.a. Lewis Carroll), and 13 prime ministers. Its grounds include a grand old dining hall, a giant quad, and an impressive chapel that doubles as a cathedral. Of Oxford's colleges, Christ Church is the largest and most prestigious (and, some think, most pretentious). It's also the most popular (and most expensive) for tourists to visit—partly thanks to its historic fame, but mostly because scenes in the Harry Potter movies were filmed here. While Christ Church is fun to see, it's no better or more representative than any other of Oxford's colleges; if your time is short and you can live without seeing the dining hall that inspired Harry's, a visit here isn't obligatory.

Cost and Hours: £6, Mon–Sat 9:00–17:30, Sun 14:00–17:30, church closes at 16:30, dining hall closes at 17:00, tel. 01865/286-573, www.chch.ox.ac.uk.

Dining Hall Closure: Note that the dining hall—the prime attraction for Harry Potter fans—is closed to outsiders when students are actually lunching here (usually Mon–Sat 11:30–14:30 during term). Plan your visit accordingly.

Evensong: Every day in Christ Church Cathedral, an excellent choir of students (and fidgety little boys) sings along to the church's pipe organ. This delightful service is open to anyone; linger after the service ends to hear the organist jam (free, daily at 18:00, enter at Tom Tower).

❷ Self-Guided Tour: The college is located on St. Aldate's; follow *Vistors' Entrance* signs (past the big tower and all the way at the end of the biggest building, toward the river).

As you enter the grounds through the visitors' entrance, you'll pass through a bit of countryside spreading out to the river. This is actually part of the college. Called **Christ Church Meadow,** it was the setting Lewis Carroll used for the croquet scenes in *Alice's Adventures in Wonderland* (free, open in summer 7:00–dusk). Consider taking a stroll here, either now or after your college visit (though you'll exit at the opposite end of the college complex).

Buy your ticket and pick up the essential self-guided tour booklet with map. Follow the one-way route to be sure you don't miss anything. Gentlemen wearing derby hats, called Custodians, are posted around the college to answer questions.

First you'll head into the small **cloister** (where some Harry Potter scenes were filmed), then you'll reach the base of the grand staircase leading up to the **dining hall** (closed Mon–Sat 11:30–14:30 during term). Appreciate its grand scale and the splendid, Gothic, hammer-beam roof. While Harry Potter scenes were filmed along the staircase, they never actually filmed in the dining hall itself; set designers merely based their dining hall on this grand space. (Custodians report that astute kids who visit immediately know it's not the "real" Hogwarts—since there are three long rows of tables, not four.)

You'll then enter the impressive **Tom Quad,** a grassy field surrounded by college buildings. In the middle is a small fish pond with a statue of Mercury. Notice the outlines of archways ringing the quad; the architect wanted to create a giant cloister here, but funding ran out.

The tall tower, designed by Christopher Wren, holds a seven-

ton bell called **Great Tom.** According to tradition, this clangs out 101 times every night at 21:05. Why not on the hour? When the tradition began, time zones had yet to be standardized—and since Oxford was five minutes of longitude west of Greenwich, clocks here were set five minutes earlier. That means 21:05 Greenwich Mean Time was 21:00 on the dot Oxford time.

Continue a few steps along the quad, and enter the 800-year-old **chapel** (on the right). This is the only university chapel in the

The Colleges of Oxford

While we think of it as one big university, Oxford consists of 38 autonomous, self-funded colleges. Students directly apply to—and study at—one of these colleges, rather than the university (though the university does administer exams and award degrees). Rivalry among the colleges is fierce, both academically and in sports (rowing is a favorite). Many of the colleges, dating back hundreds of years, have historic old buildings that are open to the public. While some of these are free to enter, the more famous and interesting ones charge admission. Most are open only in the afternoons, but they can be unexpectedly closed due to exam schedules and special events.

History: The first school is thought to have been founded here in the 11th century, but Oxford really took off in 1167, when, during a period of political tension between England and France, Henry II banned English students from attending the University of Paris. The students—mostly poor peasant kids who'd been fortunate enough to be educated at monastic schools in Latin (the language of higher learning of the day)—gathered in Oxford to pursue their studies. The teachers took students under their wing, rented out boarding houses, and lived with and taught their charges in an almost monastic environment. Students often clashed with residents in this market town, just as university students tussle with "townies" the world over. In Oxford, these "town-and-gown fights" were often violent and claimed many casualties in the Middle Ages.

Anatomy of a College: Gradually, little campuses evolved that consisted of four parts: a library, dormitories, a dining hall, and a chapel. In its purest form, a college would have these four buildings surrounding a central courtyard, where students could exercise and which could be locked at night for security—the origin of today's quadrangle (though planting those spaces with golf course-quality grass was a much later innovation). Today, visitors touring a college will still find these same four components.

Notice that many of the chapels are shaped like a capital "T," rather than like a typical cross-shaped church floor plan. One of the earliest chapels (at New College) planned on a cross shape, but wasn't able to acquire the land they needed. Their modified, truncated plan (missing the top, or apse) caught on with the other colleges. Many chapels host evensong services at 18:00, which are usually open to the public.

In the Harry Potter-esque dining halls, long rows of tables

(for students) lead toward the elevated high table, where the faculty dines. Hanging above the high table is usually a portrait of the college's founder, while portraits of other rectors and important alums also decorate the space. Students actually still eat in these halls at these long tables—which is why during term periods, you can't enter them at lunchtime (generally from about 11:00 to 14:30, depending on the college).

Oxford Today: About a quarter of applicants are accepted, and about a third of the student body hails from other countries—giving the city an international feel. You'll hear more American accents here than just about anywhere in England. Tuition, room, board, and books run about £10,000 a year for UK and EU residents; non-EU students pay double.

Students enter the college in October and spend their first year (through the following June) preparing for preliminary exams, which they must pass to remain enrolled. Once that hurdle is cleared, they study for two more years preparing for their final exams. If you visit in June, you might see students wearing traditional academic robes on their way to their finals. (Well, not entirely traditional—while students can be penalized if they're not properly clad, the faculty years ago refused to legislate the length of female students' skirts. Many of today's young women express their individuality amid all that stuffiness by raising their gowns' hemlines...sometimes dramatically.) Students taking their finals wear carnations on their lapels: white on the first day, pink on the second day, and red on the final day. When students emerge from their final exam wearing a red carnation, they're greeted by friends and family who douse them with flour, glitter, and champagne or beer (a tradition called "trashing"). There's usually a happy ending: Among those who remain at Oxford all three years, the graduation rate is nearly 100 percent.

world that also serves as a cathedral (bishop's seat). The interior feels dark and mysterious. Pick up the free sheet identifying the highlights, including the shrine to the obscure local saint, St. Frideswide, and a 1320 stained-glass window honoring Thomas Becket (whose face was blacked out to help him survive the Reformation). For information on the evensong that takes place here nightly, see earlier.

Exiting the chapel, you'll be steered back around the cloister, where you can view a 15-minute video about Christ Church. Then circle back around past the base of the dining hall stairs, pass through the Tom Quad again, and head straight to exit out the far end.

As you pass by the library, look for the tall **chestnut tree** behind the wall. Lewis Carroll would watch a cat belonging to a little girl named Alice (the dean's daughter) sitting in the tree. When he later wrote his story about Alice's visit to Wonderland, it inspired him to include the Cheshire Cat character.

Continue past more buildings. On the right just before the exit is Christ Church's final sight, the picture gallery described next.

Christ Church Picture Gallery—This sleepy but good collection houses a rotating exhibition of drawings and sketches by Albrecht Dürer, Michelangelo, Leonardo da Vinci, Raphael, and other Old Masters. Because the drawings are fragile, they need to "rest" periodically—so don't be disappointed if your favorite is missing. There's also a permanent collection of oil paintings by the likes of Tintoretto, Veronese, Van Dyck, and Frans Hals.

Cost and Hours: £3, £1.50 if you paid to enter the college; May–Sept Mon–Sat 10:30–17:00, Sun 14:00–17:00; Oct–April Mon–Sat 10:30–13:00 & 14:00–16:30, Sun 14:00–16:30; tel. 01865/276-172.

Getting There: If you're visiting Christ Church College, the one-way tour route will eventually lead you here—look for signs to the *Picture Gallery*. To visit only the gallery—or if the main campus is closed to visitors—you can enter the gallery directly from the street (at Canterbury Gate, off Oriel Square).

Magdalen College—Sitting on the upper edge of town, this college (pronounced "maudlin") has the largest grounds (big enough to include its own deer park). The best-known path through the college, Addison's Walk across the river, was frequented by C. S. Lewis. Visitors can see the chapel, the dining hall, and the expansive grounds (£4.50, daily mid-June–Sept 12:00–18:00, Oct–mid-June 13:00–18:00 or dusk, last entry 30 minutes before closing;

evensong with the renowned boys' choir Oct–June Mon and Wed–Sat at 18:00, none July–Sept; High Street next to Magdalen Bridge, tel. 01865/276-000, www.magd.ox.ac.uk).

Merton College—The third-oldest college (at not quite 750 years old), Merton boasts the oldest quad (Mob Quad, from the 14th century). *The Lord of the Rings* author J. R. R. Tolkien taught here. Visitors have access to the quad and the chapel, but to get inside the superb medieval "chained" library—the oldest in Oxford—you'll have to take a tour (college entry without tour-£2, Mon–Fri 14:00–17:00, Sat–Sun 10:00–17:00, last entry at 16:30, Merton Street, tel. 01865/276-310, www.merton.ox.ac.uk). Tours, which are available in the summer for £3, include the college, chapel, and library (usually July–Sept at 14:00, 15:00, and 16:00; confirm times at the Porters' Lodge, 45 minutes).

Exeter College—A smaller college, Exeter is worth a peek. The

highlight is Sir George Gilbert Scott's jewel-like Neo-Gothic chapel. This replica of Paris' Sainte-Chapelle was recently cleaned, so the stone is gleaming. It features William Morris' *The Adoration of the Magi* tapestry (free, usually open daily 14:00–17:00, Turl Street, tel. 01865/279-600).

University Buildings

While each individual college has its own admirable complex of historic buildings, Oxford University's facilities aren't too shabby, either. As if trying to one-up all the colleges, the biggest and best university buildings cluster near the intersection of Broad Street/Holywell Street and Parks Road/Catte Street. These are the classic, iconic Oxford buildings you often see in movies.

Landmark University Buildings—Across the little square from the Sheldonian Theatre, the big Neoclassical building with the columns out front is the **Clarendon Building,** originally built to house the Oxford University Press. Among the books printed here was the Lincoln Bible—used to inaugurate Presidents Lincoln and Obama.

Across the street, you'll see the **"Bridge of Sighs,"** modeled after the one in Venice. It was built to connect the two parts of Hetford College.

The next two buildings sit in a quaint cobblestoned square, just down Catte Street from the others.

The most distinctive university building of all is the round, columned **Radcliffe Camera.** Built as a medical library, today it's used as a reading room for a gigantic library complex that runs through tunnels underneath the square. (It's named for the alum who funded it, not for the Harry Potter film star.)

The tall steeple belongs to the **Church of St. Mary the Virgin,** which is the university church and has a climbable tower (see page 422) and a café in the crypt.

The following two are the only university facilities that welcome visitors: Bodleian Library and Sheldonian Theatre.

▲**Bodleian Library**—With some 11 million books and more than 100 miles of shelving in its underground stacks, "the Bod" is one of the world's largest and most famous libraries. Founded by Thomas Bodley in 1602, this is one of six "legal deposit" libraries in the UK—so it must receive a copy of every book printed in the nation. The palatial building—with a big courtyard and frilly spires along the roofline—has two areas that are open to the public: the Divinity School on the ground floor (which you can visit with a £1 ticket, or on a tour), and the medieval Duke Humfrey's Library (only with a tour).

The **Divinity School,** an impressive fan-vaulted hall, has a ceiling carved with intricately detailed religious symbolism. Above the entry, notice that the crucifix (directly over the door) and St. Peter were defaced by Reformation forces. The colorful stained-glass windows that once lined the hall were another casualty. Above the door at the far end of the hall is a statue of Mary...holding a book. Students gather here to put on their gowns before walking to their graduation ceremony at the theater next door. Before leaving, imagine hospital beds lining this hall...yes, it's the infirmary from the Harry Potter films.

Upstairs in **Duke Humfrey's Library** are the musty, creaky old shelves of ancient-looking books, stacked neatly under a beautifully painted wooden ceiling. The required tour shows you only a small section of the library—basically one hall, and a view down another—but even at that, it gives you a good feel for the place. You'll learn about the library's history, and about the huge stockpile of books that sits beneath this part of Oxford. Because this is purely a reference library—none of the books can be taken out—they need plenty of space. They have a rare-books collection—with everything from a Shakespearean First Folio to a couple of Magna Cartas—that they're hoping to eventually display to the public after a planned renovation (in 2015 at the soonest).

Cost and Hours: You'll pay £1 to enter the Divinity School on your own (Mon–Fri 9:00–17:00, Sat 9:00–16:30, closed Sun), but to see the library you must take a dry but informative **tour** (£4.50/30-minute tour of Divinity School and library, £6.50/one-hour version). Tours run several times daily—check the schedule and buy your ticket at the kiosk in the passage across the courtyard from the library entrance (or call 01865/277-178).

Sheldonian Theatre—Graduations, matriculations, and other important campus events take place in this grand theater.

Before it was built, these ceremonies took place in churches—but the music and celebratory tone were deemed inappropriate for a sacred space, so this theater was purpose-built. (Despite its misleading name, no theatrical presentations take place here...though music concerts sometimes do.) This was the first major building project designed by Sir Christopher Wren, then a physics professor and budding architect who went on to rebuild much of London after the great fire (including the landmark St. Paul's Cathedral). While the interior isn't too exciting, you'll see the round main hall, with its painted ceiling, gold trim, stone columns, pipe organ, and chandeliers. Your ticket also includes admission to the building's cupola, with 360-degree views over the many spires of Oxford (£2.50, Mon–Sat 10:00–12:30 & 14:00–16:30, until 15:30 in winter, sometimes closed for special events, closed Sun, Broad Street, tel. 01865/277-299).

Literary Oxford

Oxford's list of alums is almost laughably impressive. A virtual factory for famous politicians—among them a couple dozen prime ministers (including current PM David Cameron), Indira Gandhi, and Bill Clinton (who took classes here as a Rhodes scholar)—it's also the home of some of the most important scientists of the 20th century. Stephen Hawking (*A Brief History of Time*) went to Oxford, Richard Dawkins (*The Selfish Gene*) teaches at Oxford, and Tim Berners-Lee—inventor of the World Wide Web—got in trouble for hacking into Oxford's computers. But Oxford may be most famous for its literary past.

J. R. R. Tolkien (1892–1973) graduated from the university and was a professor at Oxford, teaching the glories of Anglo-Saxon language and English literature through one of his favorite works, the epic poem *Beowulf*. He spent years in Oxford writing the books he's most famous for: *The Hobbit* and the three volumes of *The Lord of the Rings,* beloved by millions of readers.

C. S. Lewis (1898–1963), Tolkien's good friend, was a fellow at Oxford for almost 30 years. Lewis sent generations of children through the back of a wardrobe in his series *The Chronicles of Narnia*. During his time in Oxford, Lewis was also the ringleader of a famous writing society called the Inklings, who met regularly at The Eagle and Child pub (which they called the "Bird and Baby"—see page 439). Picture these literary geniuses sitting in the pub's familiar confines. Lewis orders another round, while Tolkien tells Frodo's tale—with a pipe in hand—for the first time.

The Oxford-educated poet **W. H. Auden** (1907–1973) was a lifelong friend and correspondent of Tolkien's. (He was one of the first critics to publicly praise *The Lord of the Rings*.) Auden may be most familiar to Americans for the line of his poem "Funeral Blues" that was quoted in the film *Four Weddings and a Funeral*: "He was my North, my South, my East and West, / My working week and my Sunday rest, / My noon, my midnight, my talk, my song; / I thought that love would last for ever: I was wrong."

Lewis Carroll (1832–1898), the pen name of Charles Lutwidge Dodgson, was a mathematician who taught at Oxford, where he met young Alice Liddell, the dean's daughter and the real-life inspiration for his most famous book, *Alice's Adventures in Wonderland*. The author lived at Christ Church College, and

OXFORD

Other Sights

▲▲The Ashmolean Museum of Art and Archaeology—This eclectic museum was founded in 1683 by a royal gardener, John Tradescant, who loved to collect interesting items while traveling in search of plants. All these years later, the collection is huge, and the building recently underwent a thorough £63 million renovation.

While the collection doesn't rank with the big-league muse-

Carroll and Liddell would regularly play croquet—without the Queen of Hearts—in The Meadow.

Aldous Huxley (1894–1963), a prolific novelist and Oxford student, wrote the early science-fiction classic *Brave New World*, about a disturbing, mindless future. His later book, *The Doors of Perception,* was written under the influence of mescaline. (Jim Morrison, another fan of mind-altering experiences, named his band The Doors after the book.)

Literary great **Virginia Woolf** (1882–1941) was banned from using Oxford's library because she was a woman (Oxford didn't begin admitting women until 1920 though they could attend some classes before that). She later wrote her most important essay, "A Room of One's Own," where she parodied the university she nicknamed "Oxbridge," a combination of Oxford and Cambridge.

Oscar Wilde (1854–1900) did well at Oxford (graduating with the highest grade possible) and went on to become famous for his novels *(The Picture of Dorian Gray)*, plays *(The Importance of Being Earnest),* homosexuality (his famous trial sent him to jail), and memorably witty quotes, such as "Men marry because they are tired; women, because they are curious: both are disappointed." Another of his quotes: "I can resist everything except temptation." And another: "We are all in the gutter, but some of us are looking at the stars."

Oxford's other notable literary stars include the poet **Percy Bysshe Shelley, Jonathan Swift** (*Gulliver's Travels*), **T. S. Eliot** (*The Waste Land*), **John le Carré** (*The Spy Who Came in from the Cold*), **Philip Pullman** (*The Golden Compass,* part of his children's book series *His Dark Materials*), **Martin Amis** (*Time's Arrow*), **Helen Fielding** (*Bridget Jones's Diary*), and—maybe most important of all to generations of children's book readers—Theodor Seuss Geisel (a.k.a. **Dr. Seuss**).

In addition to the **Harry Potter** connection, visiting Brits are enthralled by locations relating to the Oxford-set **Inspector Morse** television series, which was an enormous hit in the UK from 1987 to 2000 (the sequel, **Inspector Lewis,** is now being filmed here). Sort of the British Columbo or a modern-day Sherlock Holmes, this fictional police detective was quirky, cultured, and extremely effective.

ums of London, it's very impressive for a small city. The vast collection features everything from antiquities to fine porcelain to Old Masters paintings. Rather than featuring any particularly famous items, it has a broad range of offbeat bits and pieces (such as Lawrence of Arabia's ceremonial dress, prehistoric Cycladic figurines from Greece, gorgeous Turkish and Middle Eastern tiles, a Stradivarius violin, and so on). What distinguishes this place is that it's all exceptionally well-presented, with engaging descriptions that pull you in to topics you didn't realize were interesting.

The museum is loosely organized chronologically, starting in the basement and working up through five floors of history; it's also arranged geographically, with excellent collections of Chinese, Middle Eastern, Indian, Mediterranean, and other regional art and artifacts. As you move up the building, the exhibit shows how these very different civilizations came together as the world shrunk. For an engaging introduction, head for the basement and peruse the "Exploring the Past" themed exhibits, which bring together various eras of history and corners of the globe while examining a particular topic (such as money, the human image, and reading and writing). Then browse the collection to your heart's content, and find your own favorites (I enjoyed the paintings of royal elephants from India).

There's also a fine painting gallery, showcasing lesser-known pieces by Degas, Pissarro, Van Gogh, and others. It's fun to see artist J. W. M. Turner's view down High Street in Oxford...then walk a block to see today's version. If nothing else, the Ashmolean provides visitors to this university town a way to see a respectable range of English glass, Chinese porcelain, ancient sculpture, and tapestries without having to ride the train.

Cost and Hours: Free, £3 audioguide, Tue–Sun 10:00–18:00, closed Mon, rooftop café, Beaumont Street, tel. 01865/278-000, www.ashmolean.org.

Punting—Long, flat boats can be rented for punting (pushing with a long pole) along the River Cherwell. Chauffeurs are available, but the do-it-yourself crowd is having more fun, even if they are a little wet (£14/hour—or £16–20/hour on busy weekends, £30 deposit, chauffeured punts-£23/30 minutes, rowboats and paddle boats available for the less adventurous, cash only, daily March–Nov 9:30–dusk, closed off-season and in bad weather, Magdalen Bridge Boathouse, tel. 01865/202-643, www.oxford punting.co.uk).

Sleeping in Oxford

Sleeping cheaply in Oxford is not easy. The colleges and university own much of the town, so boarding space is at a premium. There are a few high-end hotels in the center, and B&Bs crowd the main roads out of town. Noise is an issue in this college town—mostly students conversing or singing loudly in the streets on the way home from the pub. Try requesting a quiet room, but expect

Sleep Code

(£1 = about $1.60, country code: 44, area code: 01865)
S = Single, **D** = Double/Twin, **T** = Triple, **Q** = Quad, **b** = bathroom,
s = shower only. Unless otherwise noted, breakfast is included
and credit cards are accepted.

To help you sort easily through these listings, I've divided
the rooms into three categories based on the price for a
double room with bath:

$$$ **Higher Priced**—Most rooms £100 or more.
$$ **Moderately Priced**—Most rooms between £50-100.
$ **Lower Priced**—Most rooms £50 or less.

Prices can change without notice; verify the hotel's
current rates online or by email. For other updates, see www
.ricksteves.com/update.

some noise regardless. Given the easy connections by train to the
Cotswolds (Moreton-in-Marsh) and London, I'd make Oxford a
day trip, and sleep elsewhere. But if you're spending the night, here
are some centrally located, reasonable options.

$$$ **The Tower House,** with tight spaces and low ceilings,
has small but sweet rooms, and couldn't be more central. Three of
the seven rooms share a bathroom with a spacious shower (S-£70,
Sb-£90, D-£80, Db-£110, includes continental breakfast, free
Wi-Fi, no parking, request a quieter back room, 15 Ship Street,
tel. 01865/246-828, fax 01865/247-508, www.oxfordhotelsandinns
.com, thetowerhouse@btconnect.com).

$$$ **Bath Place Hotel** is a creaky place with 16 cute, flow-
ery, slightly worn rooms connected by a maze of impossibly steep
and narrow stairways. It's tucked down a tiny lane—just follow
the trail of students going to the very popular pub below. The pub
closes and things calm down after 23:30 on weeknights, or 24:00
on weekends—if you're a light sleeper and want to turn in early,
request a quieter room (Sb-£85–95—or £110 on Fri-Sat, Db-£110–
140, Tb-£160, Qb-£180–195, price depends on room size, includes
buffet breakfast, free Wi-Fi, limited parking-£10/day, free parking
farther away, 4 Bath Place, tel. 01865/791-812, fax 01865/791-834,
www.bathplace.co.uk, info@bathplace.co.uk, Yolanda).

$$ **The Buttery Hotel,** up steep steps above a café/bakery
(hence the name) and two doors down from the TI, rents 16
comfortable, good-value rooms. The "deluxe" rooms are larger
and have big windows overlooking bustling Broad Street—nice
for views but not for noise; the cheaper "standard" rooms are
quieter (tiny Sb-£55, bigger Sb-£80–85, standard Db-£95–100,

OXFORD

deluxe Db-£120–130, Tb-£120–160, higher rates are for Fri–Sat, free Wi-Fi, no parking, 11–12 Broad Street, tel. 01865/811-950, fax 01865/811-951, www.thebutteryhotel.co.uk, enquiries@the butteryhotel.co.uk, Felicity).

$$ Holywell Bed & Breakfast is hidden away in an ancient row house on quiet Holywell Street, across from New College. Its four twin rooms share two bathrooms (S-£60–80, D-£70–90, higher prices are for Fri–Sat, book well in advance, no children under age 12, steep stairs, free Wi-Fi, free parking in adjacent lot, 14 Holywell Street, tel. 01865/721-880, www.holywellbed andbreakfast.com, info@holywellbedandbreakfast.com, Stuart and Carrie).

Hostels

This youthful town has two different hostels that are called "Backpackers," at opposite sides of the same block (a 3-minute walk from the train station on the way to the town center). Both of them are willing to store non-guests' bags for a fee (£3/bag at Oxford Backpackers, £2/bag at Central Backpackers).

$ Oxford Backpackers Hostel rents 92 beds in single-sex and mixed dorms. While the ambience is somewhere between grotty and funky, hard-core hostelers appreciate the cheap beds (£15–17/ bed in large dorm, £19/bed in 4-person dorm, includes continental breakfast, reception open 8:00–10:00 & 17:00–19:00, free Wi-Fi, laundry service, 9A Hythe Bridge Street, tel. 01865/721-761, fax 01865/203-293, www.hostels.co.uk, oxford@hostels.co.uk).

$ Central Backpackers Oxford, loosely run by gregarious Aussie Mick, rents 50 beds in 4- to 12-bed dorms around an invit- ing covered patio. It feels a bit more tame than Oxford Backpackers (£18–21/bed depending on room size, includes basic continental breakfast, free Internet access and Wi-Fi, laundry service, 13 Park End Street, tel. 01865/242-288, www.centralbackpackers.co.uk).

Near Oxford

$$ The Coach & Horses Inn, a charming 16th-century inn and pub, is located seven miles southeast of Oxford in Chislehampton, across the street from a bus stop that connects the two towns (Sb- £62, Db-£75, free Wi-Fi, tel. 01865/890-255, fax 01865/891-995, www.coachhorsesinn.co.uk, enquiries@coachhorsesinn.co.uk).

Eating in Oxford

Pubs

These pubs perfectly conform to what Americans imagine a British pub to be: a rambling series of cozy, well-worn rooms on sloping wooden floors filled with tight clusters of friends enjoying food and ale around ancient-feeling tables. The hours listed below are for when food is served—most stay open later to serve drinks.

The King's Arms, across from Blackwell's Bookstore and the Sheldonian Theatre, has an approachable, open, convivial atmosphere. They offer good traditional English fare (£5 sandwiches, £8–10 pub grub, daily 10:30–24:00, 40 Holywell Street at corner of Parks Road, across from the Sheldonian, tel. 01865/242-369).

The Bear, hidden down a side street and close to the Christ Church Picture Gallery, is one of Oxford's oldest and most

charming pubs. This teensy place proudly sports no right angles (go ahead—check) since 1242. Peruse the framed collections of amputated clothing on the walls and hold on to your tie if you're wearing one. If you're coming for lunch, arrive before 13:00, when they're typically swamped and tables are in short supply (£7–10 meals, food served daily 12:00–21:00, 6 Alfred Street at corner of Blue Boar Street, tel. 01865/728-164). There are a few picnic tables out back—leave through the pub's side door to find them, or walk to the left as you're facing the front.

The Turf Tavern—big, boisterous, and tucked into a short alley—is popular for its good food, outdoor beer garden, and warren of claustrophobic rooms nestled against the old city wall (£6–9 pub grub, Mon–Sat 11:00–23:00, Sun 12:00–22:30, 4 Bath Place, tel. 01865/243-235). To find it from Holywell Street, listen for the chatter of students enjoying a beer (down Bath Lane); otherwise, head for the gap marked *St. Helen's Passage* under the Bridge of Sighs on New College/Queen's Lane.

OXFORD

The Eagle and Child, a long and thin series of rooms, is subdued, smaller, and more intimate than the other pubs listed. A five-minute walk from the city center, it's more famous for its history and ambience than its very traditional food. This was the gathering place of the writers known as the Inklings (see sidebar on page 434), and a literary vibe still haunts the place. If you're a fan of Middle-earth and Narnia, stop in for a drink under photos of J. R. R. Tolkien and C. S. Lewis (£6–10 pub grub, read the history on the menu, Mon–Sat 10:00–23:00, Fri–Sat until 24:00, Sun 10:00–22:30, 49 St. Giles Street, tel. 01865/302-925).

Eating Cheaply

Taylors is a student favorite for affordable £3–5 hot or cold sandwiches with a wide range of fillings. There are a few tables, but most people get food to go and find a scenic spot for a picnic (daily 8:00–20:00, closes at 17:00 July–Aug and other times students are away, 58 High Street, tel. 01865/723-152). You'll see several Taylors locations around Oxford.

The **Covered Market**—a farmers'-market maze of shops, fruit stands, deli counters, and cafés—has a fine selection for breakfast, lunch, or a picnic (Mon–Sat 9:00–17:30, closed Sun, between Market Street and High Street, near Carfax Tower).

Other Eateries

The News Café, with a cheerful and bright interior, buzzes with locals. They serve light food for lunch and early dinner, and hearty entrées, big salads, and cheaper cream teas than at the large hotels. It's a nice break from the chain eateries on nearby Cornmarket (£7–10 meals, Sun–Thu 9:00–19:00, Fri–Sat 9:00–22:00, 1 Ship Street, tel. 01865/242-317).

Chain Restaurants on Cornmarket and Nearby: On Cornmarket, you'll find a slew of chain eateries, including **Pret à Manger** and **West Cornwall Pasty Company.** Nearby is **Jamie's Italian,** part of a chain owned by British TV's celebrity chef Jamie Oliver and serving up classic Italian cuisine in a sprawling, industrial-mod interior (£6–8 pastas, £11–16 entrées, Mon–Sat 12:00–23:00, Sun 12:00–22:30, 24–26 George Street, tel. 01865/838-383). There's a **Marks & Spencer** on Queen Street, across from Carfax Tower.

Afternoon Tea: The **Randolph Hotel** is a swanky place where proud parents take their graduating students for a fancy afternoon tea (reserve ahead, especially near the end of the term). You'll enjoy impeccable service and classic English afternoon tea under high ceilings and chandeliers (afternoon tea-£19, traditional cream tea-£12.25, daily 12:00–22:00, tea served until 18:00, Beaumont Street, directly opposite Ashmolean Museum, tel. 01865/256-400).

Oxford Connections

From Oxford by Train to: London's Paddington Station (2/hour direct, 1 hour, more possible with transfer in Reading; cheap £20 "day return" ticket good Mon–Fri after 9:01 from Oxford or 9:21 from London, or all day Sat–Sun), **Bath** (hourly, 1.25 hours, transfer in Didcot), **Moreton-in-Marsh** (about hourly, 40 minutes), **Stratford-upon-Avon** (every 2 hours, 1.5 hours, transfer in Leamington Spa or Banbury), **Salisbury** (hourly, 2 hours, transfer in Reading and Basingstoke), **Portsmouth** (2–4/hour, 2.5–2.75

hours, 1–2 transfers), **York** (hourly, 4 hours). Train info: tel. 0845-748-4950, www.nationalrail.co.uk.

By Bus: The Oxford Tube bus runs every 12–20 minutes to **London**'s Marble Arch and Victoria Coach Station (£14 one-way, £20 round-trip, tel. 01865/772-250, www.oxfordtube.com). The competing Oxford Espress runs every 15 minutes during peak times to the same London stops (otherwise about 2–3/hour; £13 one-way, £20 round-trip, tel. 01865/785-400, www.oxfordbus .co.uk) Both companies take about 1.75 hours to make the trip, and all buses depart from the Gloucester Green bus station—just show up and ask which leaves first.

An independent bus service called The Airline shuttles students and visitors directly between Oxford and **Heathrow Airport** 24 hours a day (2/hour, 1.5 hours, £20 one-way, £25 round-trip) and to **Gatwick Airport** (hourly, 2–2.5 hours, £25 one-way, £35 round-trip, tel. 01865/785-400, www.oxfordbus.co.uk).

National Express (toll tel. 0871-781-8181, www.national express.com) runs buses to **Stratford-upon-Avon** (2 direct buses/ day, 1 hour). For details on taking a public bus to **Blenheim Palace,** see the next section.

Near Oxford: Blenheim Palace

Just 30 minutes' drive from Oxford (and convenient to combine with a drive through the Cotswolds), Blenheim Palace is one of England's best—worth ▲▲▲. Too many palaces can send you into

a furniture-wax coma, but everyone should see Blenheim. The Duke of Marlborough's home—the largest in England—is still lived in, which is wonderfully obvious as you prowl through it. The 2,000-acre yard, well-designed by Lancelot "Capability" Brown, is as majestic to some as the palace itself.

The view just past the outer gate as you enter is a classic. Note: Americans who pronounce the place "blen-HEIM" are the butt of jokes. It's "BLEN-em."

Cost and Hours: £18, discount tickets that save £2.50 are available at TIs in surrounding towns—including Oxford and Moreton-in-Marsh; family ticket for two adults and two kids-£48, £5 guidebook; open mid-Feb–Oct daily 10:30–17:30, last tour departs at 16:45; Nov–mid-Dec Wed–Sun 10:30–17:30; park open but palace closed Nov–mid-Dec Mon–Tue and mid-Dec–mid-Feb; tel. 01993/810-530, recorded info tel. 0800-849-6506, www .blenheimpalace.com.

Getting There: Blenheim Palace sits at the edge of the cute cobbled town of Woodstock. The train station nearest the palace (Hanborough, 1.5 miles away) has no taxi or bus service.

From **Oxford,** take bus #S3 (Mon-Sat 2/hour, less frequent on Sun, 30 minutes; bus tel. 01865/772-250, www.stagecoachbus .com). It departs from downtown Oxford at George Street (near the corner with Magdalen Street), then stops at Oxford's bus station at Gloucester Green and sometimes also at Oxford's train station (check the schedule). It stops twice near Blenheim Palace: the "Blenheim Palace Gates" stop is along the main road about a half-mile walk to the palace itself; the "Woodstock/Marlborough Arms" stop puts you right in the heart of the village of Woodstock (handy if you want to poke around town before heading to the palace; this adds just a few more minutes' walking than the other bus stop). The Woodstock gate also offers the most spectacular view of the palace and lake.

If you're coming from the **Cotswolds,** your easiest train connection is from Moreton-in-Marsh to Oxford, where you can catch the bus to Blenheim (note that bus #S3 doesn't always stop at the Oxford train station—you may have to walk five minutes to the bus station).

Drivers head for Woodstock (from the Cotswolds, follow signs for *Oxford* on A-44); the palace is well-signposted once in town, just off the main road. Buy your ticket at the gate, then drive up the long driveway to park near the palace.

Background: John Churchill, first duke of Marlborough, defeated Louis XIV's French forces at the Battle of Blenheim in 1704. This pivotal event marked a turning point in the centuries-long struggle between the English and the French, and some historians claim that if not for his victory, we'd all be speaking French today. (They're probably exaggerating, but *qui sait?*) A thankful Queen Anne rewarded Churchill by building him this nice home, perhaps the finest Baroque building in England (designed by playwright-turned-architect John Vanbrugh). Ten dukes of Marlborough later, it's as impressive as ever. (The current, 11th duke considers the would-be 12th more of an error than an heir, and what to do about him is quite an issue.) In 1874, a later John Churchill's daughter-in-law, Jennie Jerome gave birth at Blenheim to another historic baby in that line...and named him Winston. The history continues.

❍ Self-Guided Tour: From the parking lot, stop off at the "Falstaff" info booth to pick up a free map and head through the small courtyard. You'll emerge into a grand courtyard in front of the palace's columned yellow facade. Most of the attractions are reached by going through the palace's main entry.

You'll enter into the truly great **Great Hall.** Before taking the well-organized tour, spend some time on your own in the fine **Winston Churchill Exhibition,** displaying letters, paintings, and other artifacts of the great statesman who was born here. The highlight is the bed in which Sir Winston was born in 1874 (prematurely...his mother went into labor suddenly while attending a party here).

When you've had your fill of Churchill, catch the 45-minute guided tour of the **state rooms**—the fancy halls the dukes use to impress visiting dignitaries (tours leave every 10 minutes, included with ticket, last one at 16:45). This fascinating tour lets visitors ogle some of the most sumptuous rooms in the palace, ornamented with fine porcelain, gilded ceilings, portraits of past dukes (and photos of the present duke's family), and "chaperone" sofas designed to give courting couples just enough privacy...but not too much. When the palace is really busy (most likely on Sun), they dispense with guided tours and go "free flow," allowing those with an appetite for learning to strike up conversations with docents in each room.

Enjoy the series of 10 Brussels tapestries that commemorate military victories of the First Duke of Marlborough, including the Battle of Blenheim. After winning that pivotal conflict, he scrawled a quick note on the back of a hotel bill notifying the Queen of his victory (you'll see a replica). The tour offers insights into the quirky ways of England's fading nobility—for example, in exchange for this fine palace, the duke still pays "rent" to the Queen in the form of one ornamental flag per year (called "quit-rent standard").

The palace items come with tales of past dukes of Marlborough and their families. You'll learn about Consuelo Vanderbilt—of the New York Vanderbilts—who was forced against her will to marry into this aristocratic family. She was miserable, but dutifully produced two sons (whom she dubbed "the heir and the spare") before the marriage fell apart after 10 years.

Finish with the remarkable "long library"—with its tiers of books and stuccoed ceilings—before exiting through the chapel, near the entrance to the gardens (described later). But before taking off to explore the gardens, consider two more attractions inside the main palace.

Blenheim Palace: The Untold Story (to the left as you enter the Great Hall) is a modern, 45-minute, multimedia "visitors' experience" (runs every 10 minutes, included in your ticket). You'll travel from room to room—as doors open and close behind you—guided through 300 years of history by a maid named Grace Ridley. (If you have limited time to spend at the palace, this is skippable.)

For a more extensive visit, follow up the general tour with a 30-minute guided walk through the **private apartments** of the duke. Tours leave at the top and bottom of each hour; however, since you'll see where the duke's family actually resides today, tours are cancelled if His Grace is in his jammies (£4.50, irregular schedule but generally May–Sept daily 12:00–16:30, tickets are limited, buy from table in library or at Flagstaff info booth outside main gates, enter in corner of courtyard to left of grand palace entry).

The palace's expansive **gardens** stretch nearly as far as the eye can see in every direction. Access them from the courtyard, by

going through the little door near the "Churchill Shop" (as you face the main palace entrance, it's to the right). You'll emerge into the Water Terraces; from there, you can loop around to the left, behind the palace, to see (but not enter) the Italian Garden. Or, head down to the lake to walk along the waterfront trail; going left takes you to the rose gardens and arboretum, while turning right brings you to the Grand Bridge. You can explore on your own (using the map and good signposting), or rent a £3 audioguide that outlines three different walks around the property (40–90 minutes depending on tour; rent it in the "Churchill Shop" next to the door to the gardens).

Finally, in the "stables block" (under the gateway to the right, as you face the main palace entrance) is the **"Churchill's Destiny" exhibit,** which traces the military leadership of two great men who shared that name: John, who defeated Louis XIV at the Battle of Blenheim in the 18th century, and in whose honor this palace was built; and Winston, who was born in this palace, and who won the Battle of Britain and helped defeat Hitler in the 20th century. The exhibit offers a painstaking, blow-by-blow account of each of the battles. It's remarkable that arguably two of the most important military victories in the nation's history were overseen by distant cousins—England is a small island indeed. (Winston Churchill fans can visit his tomb, just over a mile away in the Bladon town churchyard—the church is faintly visible from inside the palace.)

The final attraction is actually on the way out of the palace complex: the kid-friendly **pleasure garden,** where a lush and humid greenhouse flutters with butterflies. A kid zone includes a few second-rate games and the "world's largest symbolic hedge maze." The maze is worth a look if you haven't seen one and could use some exercise. If you have a car, you'll pass these gardens as you drive down the road toward the exit; otherwise, you can take the tiny train from the palace parking lot to the garden (2/hour).

Sleeping near Blenheim Palace, in Woodstock

(£1 = about $1.60, country code: 44, area code: 01993)

$$ Blenheim Guest House, charming and 200 years old, has six rooms in the town center. A bit musty, it's located above a tea-room literally next door to the gateway into the palace grounds (Sb-£55, Db-£65–75 depending on size, free Wi-Fi, 17 Park Street, tel. 01993/813-814, fax 01993/813-810, www.theblenheim.com, theblenheim@aol.com).

$$ The Townhouse is a refurbished 18th-century stone house where Eddie rents five plush rooms (Sb-£55, Db-£75–90 depending on size, includes breakfast, free Wi-Fi in garden, in town center at 15 High Street, tel. & fax 01993/810-843, www.woodstock-townhouse.com, info@woodstock-townhouse.com).

THE COTSWOLDS

Chipping Campden • Stow-on-the-Wold •
Moreton-in-Marsh

The Cotswold Hills, a 25-by-90-mile chunk of Gloucestershire, are dotted with enchanting villages. As with many fairy-tale regions of Europe, the present-day beauty of the Cotswolds was the result of an economic disaster. Wool was a huge industry in medieval England, and Cotswold sheep grew the best wool. A 12th-century saying bragged, "In Europe the best wool is English. In England the best wool is Cotswold." The region prospered. Wool money built fine towns and houses. Local "wool" churches are called "cathedrals" for their scale and wealth. Stained-glass slogans say things like "I thank my God and ever shall, it is the sheep hath paid for all."

With the rise of cotton and the Industrial Revolution, the woolen industry collapsed. Ba-a-a-ad news. The wealthy Cotswold towns fell into a depressed time warp; the homes of impoverished nobility became gracefully dilapidated. Today, visitors enjoy a harmonious blend of man and nature—the most pristine of English countrysides decorated with time-passed villages, rich wool churches, tell-me-a-story stone fences, and "kissing gates" you

wouldn't want to experience alone. Appreciated by throngs of 21st-century Romantics, the Cotswolds are enjoying new prosperity.

The north Cotswolds are best. Two of the region's coziest towns, Chipping Campden and Stow-on-the-Wold, are eight and four miles, respectively, from Moreton-in-Marsh, which has the best public transportation connections. Any of these three towns makes a fine home base for your exploration of the thatch-happiest of Cotswold villages and walks.

Planning Your Time

The Cotswolds are an absolute delight by car and, with patience, enjoyable even without a car. On a three-week British trip, I'd spend at least two nights and a day in the Cotswolds. The Cotswolds' charm has a softening effect on many uptight itineraries. You could enjoy days of walking from a home base here.

Home Bases: Chipping Campden and Stow-on-the-Wold are quaint without being overrun, and both have good accommodations. Stow has a bit more character for an overnight stay, and offers the widest range of choices. The plain town of Moreton-in-Marsh is the only one of the three with a train station, and only worth visiting as a transit hub. While Moreton has the most convenient connections, non-drivers can also make it work to home-base in Chipping Campden or Stow—especially if you don't mind sorting through bus schedules or springing for the occasional taxi to connect towns. (But note that this becomes even more challenging on Sundays, when bus schedules are dramatically reduced.) With a car, consider really getting away from it all by staying in one of the smaller villages.

Nearby Sights: If you want to take in some Shakespeare, note that Stow, Chipping Campden, and Moreton are only a 30-minute drive from Stratford, which offers a great evening of world-class entertainment (see next chapter). And England's greatest countryside palace, Blenheim, is located at the eastern edge of the Cotswolds, between Moreton and Oxford (see previous chapter).

One-Day Driver's 100-Mile Cotswold Blitz: Use a good map and reshuffle this plan to fit your home base:

9:00	Browse through Chipping Campden, following my self-guided walk.
10:30	Joyride through Snowshill, Stanway, and Stanton.
12:30	Have lunch in Stow-on-the-Wold, then follow my self-guided walk there.
15:00	Drive to the Slaughters, Bourton-on-the-Water, and Bibury; or, if you're up for a hike instead of a drive, walk from Stow to the Slaughters to Bourton, then catch the bus back to Stow.
18:00	Have dinner at a countryside gastropub (reserve in advance by phone), then head home; or drive 30 minutes to Stratford-upon-Avon for a Shakespeare play.

Cotswold Appreciation 101

Much history can be read into the names of the area. *Cotswold* could come from the Saxon phrase meaning "hills of sheep's cotes" (shelters for sheep). Or it could mean shelter ("cot" like cottage) on the open upland ("wold").

In the Cotswolds, a town's main street (called High Street) needed to be wide to accommodate the sheep and cattle being marched to market (and today, to park tour buses). Some of the most picturesque cottages were once humble row houses of weavers' cottages, usually located along a stream for their waterwheels (good examples in Bibury and Lower Slaughter). The towns run on slow clocks and yellowed calendars. An entire village might not have a phone booth.

Fields of yellow (rapeseed) and pale blue (linseed) separate pastures dotted with black and white sheep. In just about any B&B, when you open your window in the morning you'll hear sheep baa-ing. The decorative "toadstool" stones dotting front yards throughout the region are medieval staddle stones, which buildings were set upon to keep the rodents out.

Cotswold walls and roofs are made of the local limestone. The limestone roof tiles hang by pegs. To make the weight more bearable, smaller and lighter tiles are higher up. An extremely strict building code keeps towns looking what many locals call "overly quaint."

Don't miss Blenheim Palace, which deserves a half-day. Thanks to its location at the Cotswolds' eastern edge, Blenheim fits well on the way into or out of the region.

Two-Day Plan by Public Transportation: This plan is best for any day except Sunday—when virtually no buses run—and assumes you're home-basing in Moreton-in-Marsh.

Day 1: Take the morning bus (likely around 9:30) to Chipping Campden to explore that town. If you want to stretch your legs, hike 30 minutes (each way) into Broad Campden. Then take the bus from Chipping Campden to Moreton and transfer to a Stow-bound bus. After poking around Stow, hike from Stow through the Slaughters to Bourton-on-the-Water (about 3 hours at a relaxed pace), then return by bus to Moreton for dinner. (For less walking and more time for an early dinner in Stow, do just part of the hike, or take the bus from Stow to Bourton and back.) Note that the last bus back to Moreton departs Stow at about 19:20 (departs Bourton at 19:10, this bus runs Mon-Sat only—sparse connections on Sun,

While you'll still see lots of sheep, the commercial wool industry is essentially dead. It costs more to shear a sheep than the 50 pence the wool will fetch. In the old days, sheep lived long lives, producing lots of wool. When they were finally slaughtered, the meat was tough and eaten as "mutton." Today, you don't find mutton much because the sheep are raised primarily for their meat, and slaughtered younger. When it comes to Cotswold sheep these days, it's lamb (not mutton) and dinner (not sweaters).

Towns are small, and everyone seems to know everyone. The area is provincial yet ever-so-polite, and people commonly rescue themselves from a gossipy tangent by saying, "It's all very...mmm...yaaa."

In contrast to the village ambience are the giant manors and mansions whose private, gated driveways you'll drive past. Many of these now belong to A-list celebrities, who have country homes here. If you live in the Cotswolds, you can call Madonna, Elizabeth Hurley, Kate Moss, and Kate Winslet your neighbors.

This is walking country. The English love their walks and vigorously defend their age-old right to free passage. Once a year the Rambling Society organizes a "Mass Trespass," when each of the country's 50,000 miles of public footpaths is walked. By assuring that each path is used at least once a year, they stop landlords from putting up fences. Any paths found blocked are unceremoniously unblocked.

Questions to ask locals: Do you think foxhunting should have been banned? Who are the Morris men? What's a kissing gate?

THE COTSWOLDS

confirm times locally).

Day 2: Take a day trip to Blenheim Palace via Oxford (train to Oxford, bus to palace—explained on page 442); or rent a bike and ride to Chastleton House; or take a daylong countryside walk (best to bus to Stow or Chipping Campden and walk from there).

Tourist Information

Local TIs stock a wide array of helpful resources. Ask for the *Cotswold Lion* weekly newspaper, which includes suggestions for walks and hikes (summers only); the monthly *Cotswold Events* guide; the *Explore the Cotswolds by Public Transport* bus timetable brochure, as well as individual bus schedules for the routes you'll be using; and the *Attractions and Events Guide 2011* (with updated prices and hours for Cotswolds sights). Each village also has its own assortment of brochures about the place itself, and the surrounding countryside, often for a small fee (£0.50–1). While paying for these items seems chintzy, realize that Cotswolds TIs

The Cotswolds

TO WORCESTER

A-44

A-46

TO M-5

B-4084

EVESHAM

HIDCOTE MANOR GARDEN

B-4632

MICKLETON

CHIPPING CAMPDEN

A-44

A-44

B-

B-4081

BROAD CAMPDEN

BROADWAY

A-44

STANTON

11

SNOWS-HILL

12

BLOCKLEY

7

A-44

TO TEWKES-BURY

1

2

A-424

STANWAY

STANWAY HOUSE

WINCHE-COMBE

FORD

6

B-4077

COTSWOLD FARM PARK

UPPER SWELL

LOWER SWELL

B-4632

COTSWOLD WAY FOOTPATH

B-4068

TO CHELTENHAM

A-436

UPPER & LOWER SLAUGHTER

9

A-429

— MAJOR ROAD
— MINOR ROAD
--- FOOTPATH

NOTE: NOT ALL ROADS OR SHEEP ARE SHOWN

TO 3, BIBURY, NORTHLEACH & CIRENCESTER

THE COTSWOLDS

1. The Vine B&B
2. Sheepscombe House B&B
3. To The William Morris B&B
4. The Horse and Groom Village Inn (Upper Oddington)
5. The Fox Inn (Lower Oddington)
6. The Plough Inn
7. Horse and Groom (Bourton-on-the-Hill)
8. The Fox Inn (Broadwell)
9. "Slaughter Pike" Bus Stop
10. Broadway Tower
11. Cotswolds Riding Centre
12. Snowshill Lavender
13. Batsford Falconry Centre & Arboretum

TO STRATFORD-UPON-AVON

A.34

ILMINGTON

A035

B.4479

A.429

SHIPSTON-ON-STOUR

5 MILES

5 KM

MORETON-IN-MARSH

CHASTLETON HOUSE

A-44

A.34

CHIPPING NORTON

TO OXFORD & BLENHEIM PALACE

A-436

STOW-ON-THE-WOLD

B-4450

BOURTON-ON-THE-WATER

TO OXFORD

A-424

TO BURFORD & OXFORD

DCH

LONDON

N

have lost much of their funding and are struggling to make ends meet (some even have volunteer staff).

Getting Around the Cotswolds

By Bus

The Cotswolds are so well-preserved, in part, because public transportation to and within this area has long been miserable.

Fortunately, a train line and a few key buses connect the more interesting villages. Centrally located Moreton-in-the-Marsh is the region's transit hub—with the only train station and several bus lines.

To explore the towns, use the bus routes that hop through the Cotswolds about every 1.5 hours, lacing together main stops and ending at rail stations. In each case, the entire trip takes about an hour. Individual fares are around £2. (There is an all-day, unlimited Cotswold Rover Ticket for £6, but of the handy buses described below, it covers only #855. You can buy it from the driver on participating routes.)

The TI hands out easy-to-read bus schedules for the key lines described below (or check www.traveline.org.uk, or call the Traveline info line, toll tel. 0871-200-2233). Put together a one-way or return trip by public transportation, making for a fine Cotswolds day. Ask the TI for the *Explore the Cotswolds by Public Transport* timetables, which summarize all of the bus routes in the area in separate central, north, and south sections (or download them at www.cotswoldsaonb.org.uk). If you're traveling one-way between two train stations, remember that the Cotswold villages—generally pretty clueless when it comes to the needs of travelers without a car—have no official baggage-check services. You'll need to improvise; ask sweetly at the nearest TI or business. Note that bus service is essentially nonexistent on Sundays.

Here are the most helpful bus lines:

Buses **#21** and **#22** run from Moreton-in-Marsh to Batsford to Bourton-on-the-Hill to Blockley, then either to Broadway (#21) or Broad Campden (#22) on their way to Chipping Campden, before ending at Stratford-upon-Avon (operated by Johnsons Coaches, tel. 01564/797-000, www.johnsonscoaches.co.uk). Note that this route is the only one that goes all the way through to Chipping Campden.

Bus **#801** goes from Moreton-in-Marsh to Stow-on-the-Wold to "Slaughter Pike" (on the main road just south of the two Slaughters) to Bourton-on-the-Water, and then usually continues on to Cheltenham (operated by Pulham & Sons Coaches, tel.

01451/820-369, www.pulhamscoaches.com).

Bus **#855** (called the Fosse Link) goes from Moreton-in-Marsh to Stow-on-the-Wold to Bourton-on-the-Water to Northleach to Cirencester, and then (in the morning and evening) on to the Kemble train station (operated by Pulham & Sons Coaches, tel. 01451/820-369, www.pulhamscoaches.com).

Note that no single bus connects the three major towns described in this chapter (Chipping Campden, Stow, and Moreton); to get between Chipping Campden and Stow, you'll have to change buses in Moreton.

By Bike

Despite narrow roads, high hedgerows (blocking some views), and even higher hills, bikers enjoy the Cotswolds free from the constraints of bus schedules. For each area, TIs have fine route planners that indicate which peaceful, paved lanes are particularly scenic for biking. In summer, it's smart to book your rental bike a couple of days ahead.

In **Moreton-in-Marsh,** the nice folks at the **Toy Shop** rent mountain bikes. You can stop in the shop to rent a bike, or call ahead to pick up or drop off at other times—they're flexible (£15/day with route maps, bike locks, and helmets; shop open Mon and Wed–Fri 9:00–13:00 & 14:00–17:00, Sat 9:00–17:00, closed Sun and Tue, High Street, tel. 01608/650-756).

In **Chipping Campden,** you have two options: **Cycle Cotswolds,** right in town at the Volunteer Inn pub, is the most convenient (£10/day, £15/24 hours, daily 7:00-21:00, Lower High Street, tel. 01789-720-193, www.cyclecotswolds.co.uk). Otherwise, try **Cotswold Country Cycles** (£15/day, tandem-£30/day, includes helmets and route maps, delivery for a fee, daily 9:30–dusk, 2 miles north of town at Longlands Farm Cottage, tel. 01386/438-706, mobile 07746-107-728, www.cotswoldcountrycycles.com); they also offer self-led bike tours of the Cotswolds and surrounding areas (2–7 days, see website for details).

Stow-on-the-Wold does not have any bike rental shops.

By Foot

Walking guidebooks and leaflets abound, giving you a world of choices for each of my recommended stops (choose a book with clear maps). If you're doing any hiking whatsoever, get the excellent Ordnance Survey Explorer OL #45 map, which shows every road, trail, and ridgeline (£8 at local TIs). Nearly every hotel and B&B has a box or shelf of local walking guides and maps, including Ordnance Survey #45. Don't hesitate to ask for a loaner. For a quick circular hike from a particular village, peruse the books and brochures offered by that village's TI. Villages are generally no more than three miles apart, and most have pubs that would love to feed and water you. For a list of guided walks, ask at any TI for the free *Cotswold Lion* newspaper. The walks range from 2 to 12 miles, and often involve a stop at a pub or tearoom (April–Sept; *Lion* newspaper also online at www.cotswoldsaonb.org.uk—click on "Publications").

There are many options for hikers, ranging from the "Cotswold Way" path that leads 100 miles from Chipping Campden all the way to Bath, to easy loop trips to the next village. Serious hikers enjoy doing a several-day loop, walking for several hours each day and sleeping in a different village each night. One popular route is the **"Cotswold Ring"**: Day 1—Moreton-in-Marsh to Stow-on-the-Wold to the Slaughters to Bourton-on-the-Water (12 miles); Day 2—Bourton-on-the-Water to Winchcombe (13 miles); Day 3—Winchcombe to Stanway to Stanton (7 miles), or all the way to Broadway (10.5 miles total); Day 4—On to Chipping Campden (just 5.5 miles, but steeply uphill); Day 5—Chipping Campden to Broad Campden, Blockley, Bourton-on-the-Hill or Batsford, and back to Moreton (7 miles).

Realistically, on a short visit, you won't have time for that much hiking. But if you have a few hours to spare, consider venturing across the pretty hills and meadows of the Cotswolds. Each of the home-base villages I recommend has several options. Stow-on-the-Wold, immersed in pretty but not-too-hilly terrain, is within easy walking distance of several interesting spots, and is probably the best starting point. Chipping Campden sits along a ridge, which means that hikes from there are extremely scenic, but also more strenuous. Moreton—true to its name—sits on a marsh, offering flatter and less picturesque hikes.

Here are a few hikes to consider, in order of difficulty (easiest first). I've selected these for their convenience to the home-base towns, and because the start and/or end points are on bus lines, allowing you to hitch a ride back to where you started (or on to the next town) rather than backtracking by foot.

Stow, the Slaughters, and Bourton-on-the-Water: Walk from Stow to Upper and Lower Slaughter, then on to Bourton-on-the-Water (which has bus service back to Stow on #801 or #855). One big advantage of this walk is that it's mostly downhill (4 miles, about 2–3 hours one-way). For details, see page 478.

Chipping Campden, Broad Campden, Blockley, and Bourton-on-the-Hill: From Chipping Campden, it's an easy mile walk into charming Broad Campden, and from there, a more strenuous hike to Blockley and Bourton-on-the-Hill (which are both connected by bus #21/#22 to Chipping Campden and Moreton). For more details, see page 458.

Winchcombe, Stanway, Stanton, and Broadway: You can

reach the charming villages of Stanway and Stanton by foot, but it's tough going—lots of up and down. The start and end points (Winchcombe and Broadway) have decent bus connections, and in a pinch some buses do serve Stanton (but carefully check schedules before you set out).

Broadway to Chipping Campden: The hardiest hike of those I list here, this takes you along the Cotswold Ridge. Attempt it only if you're a serious hiker (5.5 miles).

Bibury and the Coln Valley are pretty, but lack of bus access makes hiking there less appealing.

By Car

Joyriding here truly is a joy. Winding country roads seem designed to spring bucolic village-and-countryside scenes on the driver at every turn. Distances here are wonderfully short—but only if you invest in the Ordnance Survey map of the Cotswolds, sold locally at TIs and newsstands (the £8 Explorer OL #45 map is excellent but almost too detailed for drivers; the £5 Tour Map #8 covers a wider area in less detail). Here are driving distances from Moreton: **Stow-on-the-Wold** (4 miles), **Chipping Campden** (8 miles), **Broadway** (10 miles), **Stratford-upon-Avon** (17 miles), **Warwick** (23 miles), **Blenheim Palace** (20 miles).

Car hiking is great. In this chapter, I cover the postcard-perfect (but discovered) villages. With a car and the local Ordnance Survey map, you can easily ramble about and find your own gems. The problem with having a car is that you are less likely to walk. Consider taking a taxi or bus somewhere, so that you can walk back to your car and enjoy the scenery (see suggestions earlier).

Car Rental: Two places near Moreton-in-Marsh rent cars by the day. **Value Self Drive,** based in Shipston-on-Stour (about six miles north of Moreton) and run by accommodating Julian, has affordable rates (£23–33/day including insurance and taxes, automatic for no extra charge, Mon–Sat 8:30–19:00, might also be open Sun, call ahead to arrange, mobile 07974-805-485, valueselfdrive @btinternet.com). Conveniently, Julian will deliver a car to you in Moreton for £5 extra, provided you drive him back to Shipston (or a taxi from Moreton to Shipston costs £20). **Robinson Goss Self Drive,** also six miles north of Moreton-in-Marsh, is a bit more expensive, and won't bring the car to you in Moreton (£29–58/day including everything but gas, Mon–Fri 8:30–17:00, Sat 8:30–12:00, closed Sun, tel. 01608/663-322, www.robgos.co.uk).

By Taxi

Two or three town-to-town taxi trips can make more sense than renting a car. While taking a cab cross-country seems extravagant

THE COTSWOLDS

(about £2.50/mile), the distances are short (Stow to Moreton is 4 miles, Stow to Chipping Campden is 10), and one-way walks are lovely. If you call a cab, confirm that the meter will start only when you are actually picked up. Consider hiring a cab at the hourly "touring rate" (generally around £30), rather than the meter rate (e.g., £20–25 Stow to Chipping Campden). For a few more bucks, you can have a joyride peppered with commentary.

Note that the drivers listed are not typical city taxi services (with many drivers on call), but are mostly individuals—it's smart to book ahead if you're arriving in high season, since they can book up in advance on weekends.

To scare up a driver in Moreton, call **Moreton Taxis** (toll-free tel. 0800-955-8584), Richard at **Four Shires** (mobile 07747-802-555), or **Iain's Taxis** (mobile 07789-897-966); in Stow, call Iain (above) or **Tony Knight** (mobile 07887-714-047); and in Chipping Campden, call Iain (above) or Paul at **Cotswold Private Hire** (mobile 07980-857-833). Tim Harrison at **Tour the Cotswolds** specializes in tours of the Cotswolds and its gardens (mobile 07779-030-820, www.tourthecotswolds.co.uk; Tim co-runs a recommended B&B in Snowshill—see page 471).

By Tour

Departing from Bath, **Mad Max Minibus Tours** offers a "Cotswold Discovery" full-day tour, and can drop you off in Stow with your luggage if you arrange it in advance (see page 348 of the Bath chapter).

While none of the Cotswold towns offers regularly scheduled walks, many have voluntary warden groups who love to meet visitors and give walks for just a small donation (about £3/person; specific contact information appears below for Chipping Campden).

Chipping Campden

Just touristy enough to be convenient, the north Cotswolds town of Chipping Campden (CAM-den) is a ▲▲ sight. This market town, once the home of the richest Cotswold wool merchants, has some incredibly beautiful thatched roofs. Both the great British historian G. M. Trevelyan and I call Chipping Campden's High Street the finest in England.

Orientation to Chipping Campden

(area code: 01386)

Walk the full length of High Street; its width is characteristic of market towns. Go around the block on both ends. On one end, you'll find impressively thatched homes (out Sheep Street, past the public WC, and right on Westington Street). Walking north on High Street, you'll pass the Market Hall, the wavy roof of the first great wool mansion, a fine and free memorial garden, and, finally, the town's famous 15th-century Perpendicular Gothic "wool" church. (This route is the same as my self-guided town walk.)

Tourist Information

Chipping Campden's TI is tucked away in the old police station on High Street. Get the £1 town guide, which includes a map (April–Oct daily 9:30–17:00; Nov–March Mon–Thu 10:00–13:00, Fri–Sun 10:00–16:00; tel. 01386/841-206, www.chippingcampden online.org).

Helpful Hints

Festivals: Chipping Campden's biggest festival is the **Cotswold Olimpicks,** a series of tongue-in-cheek countryside games (such as competitive shin-kicking) atop Dover's Hill, just above town (first Fri–Sat after Late May Bank Holiday, www .olimpickgames.co.uk). They also have an **open gardens festival** the third weekend in June and a **music festival** in mid-May.

Internet Access: Try the occasionally open **library** (closed Tue, Thu, and Sun; High Street, tel. 01386/840-692) or **Butty's at the Old Bakehouse**, a casual eatery and Internet café (£1.50/15 minutes, £2.50/30 minutes, £4/hour, free Wi-Fi, Mon–Sat 7:30–14:30, closed Sun, Lower High Street, tel. 01386/840-401).

Bike Rental: Call **Cycle Cotswolds** or **Cotswold Country Cycles** (see page 453).

Taxi: Try **Cotswold Private Hire** or **Tour the Cotswolds** (see page 456).

Parking: Find a spot anywhere along High Street and park for free with no time limit. There's also a pay-and-display lot (1.5-hour maximum) on High Street (across from TI).

Tours: The local members of the **Cotswold Voluntary Wardens** would be happy to show you around town for a small donation to their conservation society (£3/person, 1-hour walk, walks July–Sept Tue at 14:30, meet at Market Hall). Tour guide and coordinator Ann Colcomb can help arrange for a walk on other days as well (tel. 01386/832-131, www.cotswoldsaonb.com).

Walks and Hikes from Chipping Campden: Since this is a particularly hilly area, long-distance hikes are challenging. The easiest and most rewarding stroll is to the thatch-happy Hobbit village of **Broad Campden** (about a mile, mostly level). From there, you can walk or take the bus (#22) back to Chipping Campden.

Or, if you have more energy, continue from Broad Campden up over the ridge and into picturesque **Blockley**—and, if your stamina holds out, all the way to **Bourton-on-the-Hill** (Blockley and Bourton-on-the-Hill are also connected by bus #21/#22 to Chipping Campden and Moreton).

Alternatively, you can hike up to **Dover's Hill,** just north of the village. Ask locally about this easy circular one-hour walk that takes you on the first mile of the 100-mile-long Cotswold Way (which goes from here to Bath).

For more about hiking, see "Getting Around the Cotswolds—By Foot" on page 453.

Self-Guided Walk

Welcome to Chipping Campden

This stroll through "Campden" (as locals call their town) takes you from the Market Hall west to the old silk mill, and then back east the length of High Street to the church. It takes about an hour.

Market Hall: Begin at Campden's most famous monument—the Market Hall. It stands in front of the TI, marking the town center. The Market Hall was built in 1627 by the 17th-century Lord of the Manor, Sir Baptist Hicks. (Look for the Hicks family coat of arms in the building's facade.) Back then, it was an elegant—even over-the-top—shopping hall for the townsfolk who'd come here to buy their produce. In the 1940s, it was almost sold to an American, but the townspeople heroically raised money to buy it first, then gave it to the National Trust for its preservation.

The timbers inside are true to the original. Study the classic Cotswold stone roof, still held together with wooden pegs nailed in from underneath. (Tiles were cut and sold with peg holes, and stacked like waterproof scales.) Buildings all over the region still use these stone shingles. Today, the hall, which is rarely used, stands as a testimony to the importance of trade to medieval Campden.

Chipping Campden

TO BROADWAY

TO HIDCOTE MANOR GARDEN

TO STRATFORD-UPON-AVON

KINGCOMBE LANE

B-4035

B-4081

ASTON RD

P PARKING

NOT TO SCALE

COTSWOLD WAY FOOTPATH

BACK ENDS

CIDERMILL

PARK ROAD

HIGH STREET

STATION ROAD

ALMS-HOUSES

CHURCH

CALF LANE

COURT BARN MUSEUM

TO SNOWSHILL VIA B-4081

THATCHED HOUSES

WESTINGTON

SHEEP ST.

WC

CATBROOK

GEORGE LANE

COTSWOLD WAY FOOTPATH

TO MORETON & STOW VIA A-44

Self-Guided Walk

❶ Market Hall
❷ Magistrate's Court (above TI)
❸ "Green Dragons" House
❹ Silk Mill & Silversmith Workshop
❺ High Street
❻ Grevel House
❼ Ernest Wilson Memorial Garden
❽ Baptist Hicks Land & Ruined Mansion
❾ St. James Church

Hotels and Restaurants

❿ Noel Arms Hotel
⓫ The Lygon Arms Hotel & Pub
⓬ Badgers Hall Tea Room/ B&B; Bantam Tea Rooms
⓭ Cornerways B&B
⓮ Dragon House B&B
⓯ Sandalwood House B&B
⓰ The Old Bakehouse & Butty's (Internet Café)
⓱ The Chance B&B
⓲ Eight Bells Pub
⓳ Michael's Restaurant
⓴ Maharaja Indian Rest. & Cycle Cotswolds
㉑ Le Petit Croissant
㉒ Co-op Grocery

THE COTSWOLDS

   Adjacent to the Market Hall is the sober WWI monument—a reminder of the huge price paid by every little town. Walk around it, noticing how 1918 brought the greatest losses.

   The TI is just across the street, in the old police courthouse. If it's open, you're welcome to climb the stairs and peek into the **Magistrate's Court** (free, same hours as TI, ask at TI to go up). Under the open-beamed courtroom, you'll find a humble little exhibit on the town's history.

• *Walk west a few steps, to the Red Lion Pub. Across High Street (and a bit to the right) from the pub, look for the house with a sundial, called...*

"Green Dragons": The house's decorative black cast-iron fixtures once held hay and functioned much like salad bowls for horses. Fine-cut stones define the door, but "rubble stones" make up the rest of the wall. The pink stones are the same limestone but have been heated, and likely were scavenged from a house that burned down.

• *At the Red Lion Pub, leave High Street and walk a block down Sheep Street. Just past the public loo, on the right-hand side, is the old...*

Silk Mill: The tiny Cam River powered a mill here since about 1790. Today it houses the handicraft workers guild and some interesting history. In 1902, Charles Robert Ashbee (1863–1942) revitalized this sleepy hamlet of 2,500 by bringing a troupe of London artisans and their families (160 people in all) to town. Ashbee was a leader in the romantic Arts and Crafts movement—craftspeople repulsed by the Industrial Revolution who idealized the handmade crafts and preindustrial ways. Ashbee's idealistic craftsmen's guild lasted only until 1908, when most of his men grew bored with their small-town, back-to-nature ideals. Today, the only shop surviving from the originals is that of **silversmith David Hart.** His grandfather came to town with Ashbee, and the workshop (upstairs in the mill building) is an amazing time warp—little changed since 1902. Mr. Hart is a gracious man as well as a fine silversmith, and he welcomes browsers six days a week. (While you could continue 200 yards farther to see some fine thatched houses, this walk doesn't.)

• *Return to High Street, turn right, and walk through town.*

High Street: Chipping Campden's High Street has changed little architecturally since 1840. (The town's street plan and property lines survive from the 12th century.) Notice the harmony of the long rows of buildings. While the street comprises different styles through the centuries, everything you see was made of the same Cotswold stone—the only stone allowed today.

To remain level, High Street arcs with the contour of the hillside. Because it's so wide, you know this was a market town. In past centuries, livestock and packhorses laden with piles of freshly shorn fleece would fill the streets. Campden was a sales and distribution center for the wool industry, and merchants from as far away as Italy would come here for the prized raw wool.

High Street has no house numbers: Locals know the houses by their names. In the distance, you'll see the town church (where this walk ends). Notice that the power lines are buried underground, making the scene delightfully uncluttered.

As you stroll High Street, you'll find the finest houses on the uphill side—which gets more sun. You'll pass several old sundials as you wander. Decorative features (like the Ionic capitals near the TI) are added for non-structural touches of class. Most High Street buildings are half-timbered, but with cosmetic stone facades. You may see some exposed half-timbered walls. Study the crudely beautiful framing, made of hand-hewn oak (you can see the adze marks) and held together by wooden pegs.

Peeking down alleys, you'll notice how the lots are narrow but very deep. Called "burgage plots," this platting goes back to 1170. In medieval times, rooms were lined up long and skinny like train cars: Each building had a small storefront, followed by a workshop, living quarters, staff quarters, stables, and a pea patch-type garden at the very back. Now the private alleys that still define many of these old lots lead to comfy gardens. While some of today's buildings are wider, virtually all the widths are exact multiples of that basic first unit (for example, a modern building may be three times wider than its medieval counterpart).

• *Hike up High Street toward the church, to just before the first intersection, to find the….*

Grevel House: In 1367, William Grevel built what's considered Campden's first stone house (on the left). Sheep tycoons had big homes. Imagine back then, when this fine building was surrounded by humble wattle-and-daub huts. It had newfangled chimneys, rather than a crude hole in the roof. (No more rain inside!) Originally a "hall house" with just one big, tall room, it got its upper floor in the 16th century. The finely carved central bay window is a good early example of the Perpendicular Gothic style. The gargoyles scared away bad spirits—and served as rain spouts. The boot scrapers outside each door were fixtures in that muddy age—especially in market towns, where the streets were filled with animal dung.

• *Continue up High Street for about 100 yards. Go past Church Street (which we'll walk up later). On the right, you'll find a small Gothic arch leading into a garden.*

Ernest Wilson Memorial Garden: Once the church's vegetable patch, this small and secluded garden is a botanist's delight today. It's filled with well-labeled plants that the Victorian botanist Ernest Wilson brought back to England from his extensive travels in Asia. There's a complete history of the garden on the board to the left of the entry (free, open daily until dusk).

• *Backtrack to Church Street. Turn left, walk past the recommended Eight Bells Inn, and hook left with the street. Along your right-hand side stretches…*

Baptist Hicks Land: Sprawling adjacent to the town church, the area known as Baptist Hicks Land held Hicks' huge estate and manor house. This influential Lord of the Manor was from "a family of substance," who were merchants of silk and fine clothing as well as moneylenders. Beyond the ornate gate (which you'll see ahead, near the church), only a few outbuildings and the charred corner of his **mansion** survive.

The mansion was burned by Royalists in 1645 during the Civil War—notice how Cotswold stone turns red when burned. Hicks housed the poor, making a show of his generosity, adding a long row of almshouses (with his family coat of arms) for neighbors to see as they walked to church. These almshouses (lining Church Street on the left) house pensioners today, as they have since the 17th century.

On the right, filling the old **Court Barn,** is a museum about crafts and designs from the Arts and Crafts movement, with works by Ashbee and his craftsmen (£3.50, Tue–Sun 10:30–17:30, closed Mon, tel. 01386/841-951, www.courtbarn.org.uk).

• *Next to the Court Barn, a scenic, tree-lined lane leads to the front door of the church. On the way, notice the 12 lime trees, one for each of the apostles, that were planted in about 1760 (sorry, no limes).*

St. James Church: One of the finest churches in the Cotswolds, St. James Church graces one of its leading towns. Both the town and the church were built by wool wealth. Go inside. The church is Perpendicular Gothic, with lots of light and strong verticality. Notice the fine vestments and altar hangings (intricate c. 1460 embroidery) behind protective blue curtains (near the back of the church). Tombstones pave the floor in the chancel (often under protective red carpeting)—memorializing great wool merchants through the ages.

At the altar is a brass relief of William Grevel, the first owner

of the Grevel House (described earlier), and his wife. But it is Sir Baptist Hicks who dominates the church. His huge, canopied tomb is the ornate final resting place for Hicks and his wife, Elizabeth. Study their faces, framed by fancy lace ruffs (trendy in the 1620s). Adjacent—as if in a closet—is a statue of their daughter, Lady

THE COTSWOLDS

Juliana, and her husband, Lutheran Yokels. Juliana commissioned the statue in 1642, when her husband died, but had it closed until *she* died in 1680. Then, the doors were opened, revealing these two people holding hands and living happily ever after—at least in marble. The hinges were likely used only once.

As you leave the church, look immediately around the corner to the left of the door. A small tombstone reads "Thank you Lord for Simon, a dearly loved cat who greeted everyone who entered this church. RIP 1980."

Sleeping in Chipping Campden

In Chipping Campden—as in any town in the Cotswolds—B&Bs offer a better value than hotels. Rooms are generally tight on Saturdays (when many charge a bit more and are reluctant to rent to one-nighters) and in September, which is considered a peak month. Parking is never a problem. Always ask for a discount if staying longer than one or two nights.

$$$ **Noel Arms Hotel,** the characteristic old hotel on the main square, has welcomed guests for 600 years. Its lobby was recently remodeled in a medieval-meets-modern style, and its 27 rooms are well-furnished with antiques (Sb-£110, standard Db-£130, bigger Db-£160, fancier four-poster Db-£180–200, midweek deals, some ground-floor doubles, free Wi-Fi in lobby, attached restaurant/bar and café, free parking, High Street, tel. 01386/840-317, fax 01386/841-136, www.noelarmshotel.com, reception@noelarmshotel.com).

$$$ **The Lygon Arms Hotel** (pronounced "lig-un"), attached to the popular pub of the same name, has small public areas and 10 cheery, open-beamed rooms (one small older Db-£75–80, huge "superior" Db-£100–120, lovely courtyard Db-£130–160, lower prices are for midweek or multi-night stays, family deals, free Wi-Fi, free parking, High Street, go through archway and look for hotel reception on the left, tel. 01386/840-318, www.lygonarms .co.uk, sandra@lygonarms.co.uk, Sandra Davenport).

$$$ **Badgers Hall Tea Room,** also listed later under "Eating in Chipping Campden," rents three pricey rooms (Db-£98, or £110 on weekends, 2-night minimum, includes breakfast and tea, no kids under age 10, free Wi-Fi, High Street, tel. 01386/840-839, www.badgershall.com, Karen).

$$ **Cornerways B&B** is a fresh, bright, and comfy modern home (not "oldie worldie") a block off High Street. It's run by the delightful Carole Proctor, who can "look out the window and see the church where we were married." The two huge, light, airy loft rooms are great for families (Db-£70, Tb-£90, Qb-£110, 2-night minimum, £5 off for 3 or more nights, children's discount,

---

Sleep Code

(£1 = about $1.60, country code: 44, area code: 01386)
S = Single, **D** = Double/Twin, **T** = Triple, **Q** = Quad, **b** = bathroom,
s = shower only. Unless noted otherwise, you can assume credit cards are accepted and breakfast is included.

    To help you sort easily through these listings, I've divided the rooms into three categories based on the price for a standard double room with bath:

$$$ Higher Priced—Most rooms £90 or more.
  $$ Moderately Priced—Most rooms between £65-90.
    $ Lower Priced—Most rooms £65 or less.

    Prices can change without notice; verify the hotel's current rates online or by email. For other updates, see www .ricksteves.com/update.

---

cash only, free Wi-Fi, off-street parking, George Lane, just walk through the arch beside Noel Arms Hotel, tel. 01386/841-307, www.cornerways.info, carole@cornerways.info).

$$ Dragon House B&B rents two tidy rooms—with medieval beams and a shared lounge—right on the center of High Street. They have laundry machines and a sumptuous, stay-awhile garden (Db-£68, £5 off for 3 or more nights, cash only, free Wi-Fi, free off-street parking available, near Market Hall, tel. & fax 01386/840-734, www.dragonhouse-chipping-campden.com, info@dragonhouse-chipping-campden.co.uk, Valerie and Graeme the retired potter). They also have a cottage that sleeps up to six (Sat–Sat only, £250–750/week depending on month).

$$ Sandalwood House B&B is a big, comfy, heavily potpourri-scented home with a pink flowery lounge and a sprawling back garden. Just a five-minute walk from the center of town, it's in a quiet, woodsy setting. Its two cheery, pastel rooms are bright and spacious (D/Db-£73, T-£90, 2-night minimum, cheaper if you order a light breakfast instead of full, self-catering apartment sleeps four-£450/week, cash only, no kids under age 10, free Wi-Fi, free off-street parking, tel. & fax 01386/840-091, sandalwoodhouse @hotmail.com, Diana Bendall). To get to Sandalwood House, go west on High Street, and at the church and the Volunteer Inn, turn right and then right again; look for a sign in the hedge on the left, and head up the long driveway.

$$ The Old Bakehouse rents two small but pleasant twin-bedded rooms in a 600-year-old home with a plush fireplace lounge. As this place is under new management in 2011, some of these details might change (Sb-£45, Db-£70, family deals, £5 off for 2 or more nights, cash only, free Wi-Fi, Lower High Street, tel. & fax 01386/840-979, www.chippingcampden-cotswolds.co.uk, oldbakehouse@chippingcampden-cotswolds.co.uk).

$ The Chance B&B rents two rooms in a modern home with Cotswolds charm about a 10-minute walk from the town center (Db-£65, cash only, free Wi-Fi, free parking, 1 Aston Road, tel. 01386/849-079, www.the-chance.co.uk, enquiries@the-chance .co.uk, Sally and Paul).

Eating in Chipping Campden

This town—so filled with wealthy residents and tourists—comes with many choices. I've listed some local favorites below. If you have a car, consider driving to one of the excellent countryside pubs mentioned in the sidebar on page 482.

Eight Bells Pub is a charming 14th-century inn on Leysbourne with a classy and woody restaurant and a more colorful pub. For over a decade now, Neil and Julie have enjoyed keeping their seasonal menu as locally sourced as possible. They serve a daily special, are proud of their fish dishes, and always have a good vegetarian dish. As this is rightly considered the best deal going in town for top-end pub dining, reservations are smart (£13-16 dinners, daily 12:00–14:00 & 18:30–21:00, later Fri-Sat, tel. 01386/840-371).

The Lygon Arms Pub is cozy and inviting, with a good, basic bar menu. You can order from the same menu in the colorful pub or the more elegant dining room across the passage (£7 sandwiches, £8–15 meals, daily 11:30–14:30 & 18:00–22:00).

Michael's, a fun Mediterranean restaurant on High Street, serves hearty portions and breaks plates at closing every Saturday night. Michael, who runs his place with a contagious passion and love of life, is from Cyprus: The forte here is Greek, with plenty of *mezes*—small dishes for £5–10 (also £14–17 entrées, Tue–Sun 11:00–14:30 & 19:00–22:00, closed Sun nights and Mon, tel. 01386/ 840-826).

Maharaja Indian Restaurant in the Volunteer Inn, while forgettable, is the only Indian place in town (£8–12 meals, daily 17:00–22:30, grassy courtyard out back, Lower High Street, tel. 01386/849-281).

Light Meals
If you want a quick, take-away sandwich, consider these options. Munch your lunch on the benches on the little green near the Market Hall.

Le Petit Croissant, a cheery little French deli with a tearoom in the back, serves pastries, quiche, cheese, and wine (£4 sandwiches, more to eat in, Mon–Fri 9:00–17:00, Sat 8:30–17:00, closed Sun, Lower High Street, tel. 01386/841-861).

Butty's at the Old Bakehouse offers tasty £2-4 sandwiches and wraps made to order (Mon–Sat 7:30–14:30, closed Sun, Lower High Street, tel. 01386/840-401). They also have Internet access (see "Helpful Hints," earlier).

Picnic: The **Co-op** grocery store is the town's small "supermarket" (Mon–Sat 7:00–22:00, Sun 8:00–22:00, next to TI on High Street).

Tearooms

To visit a cute tearoom, try one of these places, located in the town center.

Badgers Hall Tea Room is great for a wide selection of savory dishes and desserts. A tempting table of homemade cakes, crumbles, and scones just inside the door lures passersby into its delightful half-timbered dining room. Along with light lunches, they serve a generous afternoon tea—a tall and ritualistic tray of dainty sandwiches, pastries, and scones with tea—for half the London price (£25 for 2 people, daily 10:00–17:00, High Street).

Bantam Tea Rooms, near the Market Hall, is also a good value (£7 teas, £6 sandwiches, Mon–Sat 10:00–17:00, Sun 10:30–17:00, High Street, tel. 01386/840-386).

Near Chipping Campden

Because the countryside around Chipping Campden is particularly hilly, it's also especially scenic. This is a very rewarding area to poke around and discover little thatched villages.

West of Chipping Campden

Due west of Chipping Campden lies the famous and touristy town of Broadway. Just south of that, you'll find my nominations for the cutest Cotswold villages. Like marshmallows in hot chocolate, Stanway, Stanton, and Snowshill nestle side by side, awaiting your arrival. (Note the Stanway House's limited hours when planning your visit.)

Broadway

This postcard-pretty town, a couple of miles west of Chipping Campden, is filled with inviting shops and fancy teahouses. With a "broad way" indeed running through its middle, it's one of the bigger towns in the area. This means you'll likely pass through at some point if you're driving—but, since all the big bus tours seem to stop here, I usually give Broadway a miss. However, with a new road that allows traffic to skirt the town, Broadway has gotten cuter than ever. Broadway has good bus connections with Chipping Campden (on bus #21).

Just outside Broadway, on the road to Chipping Campden, you might spot signs for the **Broadway Tower,** which looks like a turreted castle fortification stranded in the countryside without a castle in sight. This 55-foot-tall observation tower is a "folly"—a uniquely English term for a quirky, outlandish novelty erected as a giant lawn ornament by some aristocrat with more money than taste. If you're also weighted down with too many pounds, you can relieve yourself of £4 to climb to its top for a view over the pastures.

Stanway

More of a humble crossroads community than a true village, sleepy Stanway is worth a visit mostly for its manor house, which offers an intriguing insight into the English aristocracy today. If you're in the area when it's open, it's well worth visiting.

▲▲**Stanway House**—The Earl of Wemyss (pronounced "Weemz"), whose family tree charts relatives back to 1202, opens

his melancholy home and grounds to visitors just two days a week in the summer. Walking through his house offers a unique glimpse into the lifestyles of England's eccentric and fading nobility.

Cost and Hours: £7, June–Aug Tue and Thu only 14:00–17:00, tel. 01386/584-469, www.stanwayfountain.co.uk. His lordship himself narrated the audioguide to his home (£2).

Getting There: By car, leave B4077 at a statue of (the Christian) George slaying the dragon (of pagan superstition); you'll round the corner and see the manor's fine 17th-century Jacobean gatehouse. There's no public transportation to Stanway.

➲ **Self-Guided Tour:** Start with the grounds, then head into the house itself.

The Earl recently restored "the tallest **fountain** in Britain" on the grounds—300 feet tall, gravity-powered, and quite impressive (fountain spurts for 30 minutes at 14:45 and 16:00 on opening days).

The bitchin' **Tithe Barn** (near where you enter the grounds) dates to the 14th century, and predates the manor. It was originally where monks—in the days before money—would accept one-tenth of whatever the peasants produced. Peek inside: This is a great hall for village hoedowns. While the Tithe Barn is no longer used to greet motley peasants and collect their feudal "rents," the lord still gets rent from his vast landholdings, and hosts community fêtes in his barn.

Stepping into the obviously very lived-in **manor,** you're free to wander around pretty much as you like, but keep in mind that a family does live here. His lordship is often roaming about as well. The place feels like a time warp. Ask a staff member to demonstrate the spinning rent-collection table. In the great hall, marvel at the one-piece oak shuffleboard table and the 1780 Chippendale exercise chair (half an hour of bouncing on this was considered good for the liver).

The manor dogs have their own cutely painted "family tree," but the Earl admits that his last dog, C. J., was "all character and no breeding." Poke into the office. You can psychoanalyze the lord by the books that fill his library, the videos stacked in front of his bed (with the mink bedspread), and whatever's next to his toilet.

The place has a story to tell. And so do the docents stationed in each room—modern-day peasants who, even without family trees, probably have relatives going back just as far in this village. Really. Talk to these people. Probe. Learn what you can about this side of England.

From Stanway to Stanton: These towns are separated by a row of oak trees and grazing land, with parallel waves echoing the furrows plowed by medieval farmers. Centuries ago, farmers were allotted long strips of land called "furlongs." The idea was to dole out good and bad land equitably. (One square furlong equals an acre.) Over centuries of plowing these, furrows were formed. Let someone else drive, so you can hang out the window under a canopy of oaks, passing stone walls and sheep.

Leaving Stanway on the road to Stanton, the first building you'll see (on the left, just outside Stanway) is a thatched cricket pavilion overlooking the village cricket green. Dating only from 1930, it's raised up (as medieval buildings were) on rodent-resistant staddle stones. Stanton is just ahead; follow the signs.

▲Stanton

Pristine Cotswold charm cheers you as you head up the main street of the village of Stanton. Go on a photo safari for flower-bedecked doorways and windows. (A scant few buses serve Stanton, but they're unpredictable—inquire locally.)

Stanton's **Church of St. Michael** (with the pointy spire) betrays a pagan past. It's safe to assume any church dedicated to St. Michael (the archangel who fought the devil) sits upon a sacred pagan site. Stanton is actually at the intersection of two ley lines (geographic lines along which many prehistoric sights are found). You'll see St. Michael's well-worn figure (and, above that, a sundial) over the door as you enter. Inside, above the capitals in the nave, find the pagan symbols for the sun and the moon. While the church probably dates back to the ninth century, today's building is mostly from the 15th century, with 13th-century transepts. On the north transept (far side from

entry), medieval frescoes show faintly through the 17th-century whitewash. (Once upon a time, these frescoes were considered too "papist.") Imagine the church interior colorfully decorated throughout. Original medieval glass is behind the altar. The list of rectors (at the very back of the church, under the organ loft) goes back to 1269. Finger the grooves in the back pews, worn away by sheepdog leashes. (A man's sheepdog accompanied him everywhere.)

Horse Riding—Anyone can enjoy the Cotswolds from the saddle. Jill Carenza's **Cotswolds Riding Centre,** set just outside

Stanton village, is in the most scenic corner of the region. The facility has 50 horses, and takes rank beginners on a scenic "hack" through the village and into the high country (per-hour prices: £29/person for a group hack, £39/person for a semi-private hack, £49 for a private one-person hack; lessons, longer rides, rides for experts, and pub tours available; tel. 01386/584-250, www.cotswoldsriding.co.uk). From Stanton, head toward Broadway and watch for the riding center on your right after about a third of a mile.

Sleeping in Stanton: **$$ The Vine B&B** has five rooms in a characteristic old Cotswolds house near the center of town. Owned by Jill from the riding center (described earlier), it takes a backseat to the horses: It's basically self-service, so there's no greeting or check-in, and guests wander around wondering which room is theirs. Still, it's the best option in Stanton, and convenient if you want to ride all day (Ds-£69, Db-£95, cottage with kitchen and 2 bedrooms-£150, most rooms with 4-poster beds, some stairs, tel. 01386/584-250, info@cotswoldsriding.co.uk).

Snowshill

Another nearly edible little bundle of cuteness, the village of Snowshill (SNOWS-hill) has a photogenic triangular square with a characteristic pub at its base.

▲**Snowshill Manor**—Dark and mysterious, this old palace is filled with the lifetime collection of Charles Paget Wade. It's one big,

musty celebration of craftsmanship, from finely carved spinning wheels to frightening samurai armor to tiny elaborate figurines carved by prisoners from the bones of meat served at dinner. Taking seriously his family motto, "Let Nothing Perish," Wade dedicated his life and fortune to preserving things finely crafted. The house (whose management made me promise not to promote it as an eccentric collector's pile of curiosities) really shows off Mr. Wade's ability to recognize and acquire fine examples of craftsmanship. It's all very...mmm... yaaa.

Cost and Hours: £9, manor house open mid-March–Oct Wed–Sun 12:00–17:30, gardens and ticket window open at 11:00, last entry 50 minutes before closing, closed Mon–Tue and Nov–March, restaurant, tel. 01386/852-410, www.nationaltrust.org.uk /snowshillmanor.

Getting There: The manor overlooks the town square, but there's no direct access from the square; instead, the entrance and parking lot are about a half-mile up the road toward Broadway. Park there and follow the long walkway through the garden to get to the house. A golf-cart–type shuttle to the house is available for those who need assistance.

Getting In: This popular sight strictly limits the number of entering visitors by doling out entry times. No reservations are possible; to get a slot, you must report to the ticket desk. It can be up to an hour's wait—even more on busy days, especially weekends (when they can sell out for the day as early as 14:00). Tickets go on sale and the gardens open at 11:00; the manor house opens at 12:00. Therefore, a good strategy is to arrive close to the opening time, and if there's a wait, enjoy the gardens (it's a 10-minute walk to the manor). If you have more time to kill, head into the village of Snowshill itself (a half-mile away) to wander and explore—or get a time slot for later in the day, and return in the afternoon.

Snowshill Lavender—In 2000, farmer Charlie Byrd realized that tourists love lavender. He planted his farm with 250,000

plants, and now visitors come to wander among his 53 acres, which burst with gorgeous lavender blossoms from mid-June through late August. His fragrant fantasy peaks late each July. Lavender—so famous in France's Provence—is not indigenous to this region, but it fits the climate and soil just fine. A free flier in the shop explains the variations of flowers blooming. Farmer Byrd produces lavender oil (an herbal product valued since ancient times for its healing, calming, and fragrant qualities) and sells it in a delightful shop, along with many other lavender-themed items. In the café, enjoy a pot of lavender-flavored tea with a lavender scone.

Cost and Hours: £2.50 to walk through the fields and the distillery, free to enter shop and café; late May–late Aug daily 10:00–17:00; Easter–late May and late Aug–Christmas Wed–Sun 10:00–17:00, closed Mon–Tue; closed Jan–Easter; tel. 01386/854-821, www.snowshill-lavender.co.uk, info@snowshill-lavender .co.uk.

Getting There: It's a half-mile out of Snowshill on the road toward Chipping Campden (easy parking). Entering Snowshill from the road to the manor (described above), take the left fork, then turn left again at the end of the village.

Sleeping near Snowshill: The pretty, one-pub village of Snowshill holds a gem of a B&B. **$$$ Sheepscombe House B&B** is a clean and pristine home on a working sheep farm. It's immersed in the best of Cotswold scenery, with plenty of sheep in the nearby fields. Jacki and Tim Harrison rent three modern, spacious, and thoughtfully appointed rooms (Db-£90–100, Tb-£130–150, folding cots available, free Wi-Fi, just a third of a mile south of Snowshill—look for signs, tel. 01386/853-769, www.broadway-cotswolds.co.uk/sheepscombe.html, reservations @snowshill-broadway.co.uk). Tim, who's happy to give you a local's perspective on this area, also runs Tour the Cotswolds car service (see page 456).

East of Chipping Campden

These lie roughly between Chipping Campden and Stow (or Moreton)—handy if you're connecting those towns.

▲Hidcote Manor Garden

Located northeast of Chipping Campden, this is less "on the way" to other towns than the other sights in this section—but the grounds around this manor house are still worth a look if you like gardens. Hidcote is where garden designers pioneered the notion of creating a series of outdoor "rooms," each with a unique theme (e.g., maple room, red room, and so on) and separated by a yew-tree hedge. The manor

house itself is closed to the public, but you're invited to follow your nose through a clever series of small gardens that lead delightfully from one to the next. Among the best in England, Hidcote Gardens are at their fragrant peak from May through August.

Cost and Hours: £9.50; July–Aug daily 10:00–18:00; mid-March–June and Sept Sat–Wed 10:00–18:00, closed Thu–Fri; Oct Sat–Wed 10:00–17:00, closed Thu–Fri; last entry one hour before closing; closed Nov–mid-March except Nov–Christmas Sat–Sun 12:00–15:00; tearoom, restaurant, 4 miles northeast of Chipping Campden—roughly toward Ilmington, tel. 01386/438-333, www .nationaltrust.org.uk/hidcote.

▲Broad Campden, Blockley, and Bourton-on-the-Hill

This trio of pleasant villages lines up along an off-the-beaten-path

road between Chipping Campden and Moreton or Stow. **Broad Campden,** just on the outskirts of Chipping Campden, has some of the cutest thatched-roof houses I've seen. **Blockley,** nestled higher in the picturesque hills, is a popular setting for films. The same road continues on to **Bourton-on-the-Hill** (pictured), with fine views looking down into a valley and an excellent gastropub (Horse and Groom, described on page 482). All three of these towns are connected to Chipping Campden by bus #22 (#21 goes only to Bourton and Blockley), or you can walk (easy to Broad Campden, more challenging to the other two—see page 454).

Stow-on-the-Wold

Located 10 miles south of Chipping Campden, Stow-on-the-Wold—with a name that means "meeting place on the uplands"—is the highest point of the Cotswolds. Despite its crowds, it retains its charm, and it merits ▲▲. Most of the tourists are day-trippers, so nights—even in the peak of summer—are peaceful. Stow has no real sights other than the town itself, some good pubs, antiques stores, and cute shops draped seductively around a big town square. Visit the church, with its evocative old door guarded by ancient yew trees and the tombs of wool tycoons. A visit to Stow is not complete until you've locked your partner in the stocks on the village green.

Orientation to Stow-on-the-Wold

(area code: 01451)

Tourist Information

Stow's TI, an independent business called Go Stow, is on a little alley right between the main street and Market Square. Get the handy little £0.50 walking-tour brochure called *Town Trail* and the free monthly *Cotswold Events* guide (Mon–Sat 10:00–17:00, Sun 11:00–16:00—except Oct–April until 16:30, 12 Talbot Court, tel. 01451/870-150, www.go-stow.co.uk).

At the TI, you can rent an **audioguide** town tour (£8, £12/2 people). You'll borrow an iPod Shuffle with the tour, and follow it to a dozen or so points around town for 80 minutes. While well-produced and easy to follow, there's not a lot of substance beyond my self-guided walk.

Helpful Hints

Internet Access: Try the erratically open **library** in St. Edwards Hall on the main square (closed Sun–Mon and Thu, tel. 01451/830-352), or the **youth hostel** (open long hours daily).

Taxi: See "Getting Around the Cotswolds—By Taxi" (page 455).

Parking: Park anywhere on Market Square free for two hours, or overnight between 16:00 and 11:00 (free 18:00–9:00 plus any 2 hours—they note your license, so you can't just move to another spot; £50 tickets for offenders). There's a pay-and-display lot for longer stays at the bottom of town (toward the Oddingtons), and a free long-stay lot 400 yards north of the town square at the Tesco supermarket (follow the signs).

Self-Guided Walk

Welcome to Stow-on-the-Wold

This little four-stop walk covers about 500 yards and takes about 45 minutes.

Start at the **Stocks on the Market Square.** Imagine this village during the time when people were publicly ridiculed here as

a punishment. Stow was born in pre-Roman times; it's where three trade routes crossed at a high point in the region (altitude: 800 feet). This square was the site of an Iron Age fort, and then a Roman garrison town. This main square hosted an international fair starting in 1107, and people came from as far away as Italy for the wool fleeces. This grand square was a vast, grassy expanse. Picture it in the Middle Ages (before the buildings in the center were added): a public commons and grazing ground, paths worn through the grass, and no well. Until the late 1800s, Stow had no running water; women fetched water from the "Roman Well" a quarter-mile away.

With as many as 20,000 sheep sold in a single day, this square was a thriving scene. And Stow was filled with inns and pubs to keep everyone housed, fed, and watered. A thin skin of topsoil covers the Cotswold limestone, from which these buildings were made. The **Stow Lodge** (next to the church) lies a little lower than the church; the lodge sits on the spot where locals quarried stones for the church. That building, originally the rectory, is now a hotel. The church (where we'll end this little walk) is made of Cotswold stone, and marks the summit of the hill upon which the town was built. The stocks are a great photo op (lock dad up for a great family Christmas card).

• *Walk past the youth hostel and White Hart inn to the market, and cross to the other part of the square. Notice how locals seem to be a part of a tight-knit little community.*

For 500 years, the **Market Cross** stood

Stow-on-the-Wold

TO BROADWAY & CHIPPING CAMPDEN

TO MORETON-IN-MARSH, STRATFORD-UPON-AVON, WARWICK

NOT TO SCALE

TESCO SUPERMKT

P Free

PATH TO BROADWELL

TO UPPER SWELL, FORD & STANWAY

BUS STOP

PARSON'S CORNER

START

P PARKING
SELF-GUIDED WALK

WC

STOCKS

THE SQUARE

CHURCH

TO LOWER SWELL

POST

SHEEP

CHURCH ST.

DIGBETH

TO UPPER & LOWER ODDINGTON

PARK ST.

WC

"GO STOW"

FLEECE ALLEY

BACK WALLS

DCH

Pay & Display

TO

TO BOURTON-ON-THE-WATER & THE SLAUGHTERS

1 The Stow Lodge Hotel & Rest.
2 The Kings Arms Hotel & Pub; Co-op Grocery
3 The Old Stocks Hotel & Rest.
4 Number Nine B&B; Park Street Eateries
5 Cross Keys Cottage; Chipping House B&B
6 The Pound B&B
7 West Deyne B&B
8 Tall Trees B&B
9 Youth Hostel & Café
10 To Little Broom B&B
11 The Queen's Head Pub
12 The Talbot Restaurant
13 The Coffee House
14 Market Cross
15 St. Edwards Hall & Library (Internet)

THE COTSWOLDS

in the market reminding all Christian merchants to "trade fairly under the sight of God." Notice the stubs of the iron fence in the concrete base—a reminder of how countless wrought-iron fences were cut down and given to the government to be melted down during World War II. (Recently, it's been disclosed that all that iron ended up in junk heaps—frantic patriotism just wasted.) The plaque on the cross honors the Lord of the Manor, who donated money back to his tenants, allowing the town to finally finance running water in 1878.

Scan the square for a tipsy shop that locals call the "wonky house" (next to The Kings Arms). Because it lists (tilts) so severely, it's a listed building—the facade is protected (but the interior is modern and level). The Kings Arms, with its great gables and scary chimney, was once where travelers parked their horses before spending the night. In the 1600s, this was considered the premium "posting house" between London and Birmingham. Today, the Kings Arms cooks up pub grub and rents rooms upstairs.

During the English Civil War, which pitted Parliamentarians against Royalists, Stow-on-the-Wold remained staunchly loyal to the king. (Charles I is said to have eaten at the Kings Arms before a great battle.) Because of its allegiance, the town has an abundance of pubs with royal names (King's This and Queen's That).

The stately building in the center of the square with the wooden steeple is **St. Edwards Hall.** Back in the 1870s, a bank couldn't locate the owner of an account containing a small fortune, so it donated the funds to the town to build this civic center. It serves as a city hall, library, and meeting place. When it's open for some local event, you can wander around upstairs to see the largest collection of Civil War portrait paintings in England.

• *Walk past The Kings Arms down Digbeth Street to the little triangular park located in front of the Methodist Church and across from the Royalist Hotel. This hotel—along with about 20 others—claims to be the oldest in England, dating from 947.*

Just beyond the small grassy triangle with benches was the place where locals gathered for bloody cockfights and bearbaiting (watching packs of hungry dogs tear at bears). Today this is where—twice a year, in May and October—the Stow Horse Fair attracts nomadic Roma (Gypsies) and Irish Travellers from far and wide. They congregate down the street on the Maugersbury Road. Locals paint a colorful picture of the Roma, Travellers, and horses inundating the town. The young women dress up because the fair also functions as a marriage market.

• *Hook right and hike up the wide street.*

As you head up **Sheep Street,** you'll pass a boutique-filled former brewery yard (on the left). Notice its fancy street-front office, with a striking flint facade. Sheep Street was originally not a street, but a staging place for medieval sheep markets. The sheep would be gathered here, then paraded into the Market Square down narrow alleys—just wide enough for a single file of sheep to walk down, making it easier to count them. You'll see several of these so-called "fleece alleys" as you walk up the street.

• *Just past a fine antique bookstore (Wychwood Books), turn right onto*

Church Street, which leads past the best coffee shop in town (The Coffee House), and find the church.

Before entering the **church,** circle it. On the back side, a door is flanked by two ancient yew trees. While many view it as the Christian "Behold, I stand at the door and knock" door, J. R. R. Tolkien fans see something quite different. Tolkien hiked the Cotswolds, and had a passion for sketching evocative trees such as this. *Lord of the Rings* enthusiasts are convinced this must be the inspiration for the door into Moria.

While the church (open daily— apart from services—9:00–18:00) dates from Saxon times, today's structure is from the 15th century. Its history is played up in leaflets and plaques just inside the door. The floor is paved with the tombs of big shots who made their money from wool and are still boastful in death. (Find the tombs crowned with the bales of wool.) Most of the windows are Victorian (19th-century), but the two sets high up in the clerestory are from the dreamier Pre-Raphaelite school (c. 1920).

On the right wall as you approach the altar, a monument remembers the many boys from this small town who were lost in World War I (50 out of a population of 2,000). There were far fewer in World War II. The biscuit-shaped plaque (to the left) remembers an admiral from Stow who lost four sons defending the realm. It's sliced from an ancient fluted column (which locals believe is from Ephesus, Turkey).

During the English Civil War (1615), the church was ransacked, and more than 1,000 soldiers were imprisoned here. The tombstone in front of the altar remembers the Royalist Captain Keyt. His long hair, lace, and sash indicate he was a "cavalier," and true-blue to the king (Cromwellians were called "round heads"— named for their short hair). Study the crude provincial art—child-like skulls and (in the upper corners) symbols of his service to the king (armor, weapons).

Finally, don't miss the kneelers tucked in the pews. These are made by a committed band of women known as "the Kneeler Group." They meet most Tuesday mornings (except sometimes in summer) at 10:30 in the Church Room to needlepoint, sip coffee, and enjoy a good chat. (The vicar assured me that any tourist wanting to join them would be more than welcome. The help would be appreciated and the company would be excellent.)

Hiking from Stow

Stow/Lower Slaughter/Bourton Day Hike

Stow is made-to-order for day hikes. The most popular is the downhill, four-mile stroll to Lower Slaughter, then on to Bourton-on-the-Water. It's a two-hour walk if you don't stop. Allow about three hours if you dawdle. From Bourton-on-the-Water, a bus can bring you back to Stow. Any B&B or hotel can loan you a map for this hike. Note that these three towns are described in more detail starting on page 484.

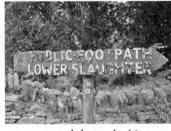

Leaving Stow, walk through the cemetery and down the big A429 road for about 200 yards, then cross the road and catch the well-marked trail. Follow it for a delightful hour across farms, over romantic gates, and past Gainsborough-painting vistas. You'll enjoy an intimate backyard look at local farm life. Although it seems like you might lose the trail, tiny signs keep you on target. Finally, passing a cricket pitch, you reach **Lower Slaughter,** with its fine church and a mill creek leading up to its mill.

Hiking from Lower Slaughter up to **Upper Slaughter** is a worthwhile one-mile, 15-minute detour each way, if you have the time and energy.

From Lower Slaughter, it's a less-scenic 15-minute walk to the bigger town of **Bourton-on-the Water.** Leave Lower Slaughter along its mill creek, then follow a bridle path back to A429 and into Bourton. Walking into Bourton, you'll pass the bus stop for the ride back to Stow (buses #801 or #855 depart roughly hourly Mon–Sat, only 3/day Sun, 10-minute ride, £1.30).

Sleeping in Stow

(£1 = about $1.60, country code: 44, area code: 01451)
$$$ The Stow Lodge Hotel fills the historic church rectory with lots of old English charm. Facing the town square, with its own sprawling and peaceful garden, this lavish old place offers 21 large, thoughtfully appointed rooms with soft beds, stately public spaces, and a cushy-chair lounge (slippery rates but generally Db-£120, £10 extra on Sat, cheaper Oct–April, closed Jan, pay Internet access and free Wi-Fi, free off-street parking, The Square, tel. 01451/830-485, fax 01451/831-671, www.stowlodge .com, enquiries@stowlodge.com, helpful Hartley family).

$$$ The Kings Arms, with nine rooms above a pub, manages to keep its historic Cotswolds character while still feeling fresh and modern in all the right ways (Sb-£60, Db-£100, steep stairs, three "cottages" out back, free Wi-Fi, free off-street parking, Market Square, tel. 01451/830-364, www.kingsarmsstow.co.uk, info@kingsarmsstow.co.uk, Lucinda and Richard).

$$$ The Old Stocks Hotel, facing the town square, is a good value, even though the building itself is classier than its 18 big, simply-furnished rooms. It's friendly and family-run, yet professional as can be. With man-killer beams and all beds equipped with footboards, it's a challenge for anyone over six feet tall (Sb-£45, standard Db-£90, refurbished "superior" Db-£110, Tb-£120, each room £10 extra on Sat, family deals, ground-floor room, free Wi-Fi in some rooms, attached bar and restaurant, garden patio, free off-street parking, The Square, tel. 01451/830-666, fax 01451/870-014, www.oldstockshotel.co.uk, info@oldstockshotel .co.uk, Allen family).

$$ Number Nine has three large, bright, recently refurbished, and tastefully decorated rooms. This 200-year-old home comes with watch-your-head beamed ceilings and old wooden doors (Sb-£45-55, Db-£60-75, free Internet access and Wi-Fi, 9 Park Street, tel. 01451/870-333, mobile 07779-006-539, www.number-nine .info, enquiries@number-nine.info, James and Carol Brown).

$$ Cross Keys Cottage offers four smallish but smartly updated rooms with bright floral decor and modern bathrooms. Kindly Margaret and Roger Welton take care of their guests in this 350-year-old beamed cottage (Sb-£55-65, Db-£65-75, cash discount if you book direct, free Wi-Fi, Park Street, tel. & fax 01451/831-128, rogxmag@hotmail.com).

$ Chipping House B&B is a fine, warm, old place with three rooms with modern touches and a welcoming lounge—it feels like a visit to Auntie's house (Db-£65, cash only, free Wi-Fi, Park Street, tel. 01451/831-756, chippinghouse@tesco.net, dog-lovers Merv and Carolyne Oliver).

$ The Pound is the quaint, 500-year-old, slanty, cozy, and low-beamed home of Patricia Whitehead. She offers two bright, inviting, twin-bedded rooms and a classic old fireplace lounge (D-£50-60, T-£85, cash only, downtown on Sheep Street, tel. & fax 01451/830-229, patwhitehead1 @live.co.uk).

$ West Deyne B&B has two grandmotherly rooms, a garden, a fountain, and a small conservatory overlooking the countryside (D-£50-60, T-£85, cash only, a short walk across the busy road from downtown Stow on Lower Swell Road, tel. 01451/831-011, Joan Cave).

$ Tall Trees B&B, on Oddington Road at the bottom end of Stow, comes with horses and chickens on four acres of land. Run by no-nonsense Jennifer, the five contemporary rooms are in an old-style building (Sb-£40–50, Db-£60–70, price depends on size, family room-£100; she also rents out the whole place for up to 8 people—£400/3 days, £800/week; cash only, two ground-floor rooms, free Wi-Fi, free off-street parking, tel. 01451/831-296, fax 01451/870-049, www.self-cateringcotswolds.co.uk, talltreestow @aol.com).

$ *Hostel:* The Stow-on-the-Wold Youth Hostel, on Stow's main square, is the only hostel in the Cotswolds, with 48 beds in nine rooms. It has a friendly atmosphere and a members' kitchen (dorm bed-£18, non-members-£3 extra, includes sheets, some family rooms with private bathrooms, evening meals, pay Internet access and Wi-Fi, lockers, reserve long in advance, tel. 01451/830-497, fax 01451/870-102, www.yha.org.uk, stow@yha .org.uk, manager Rob).

Near Stow

$$ Little Broom B&B hides out in the neighboring hamlet of Maugersbury, which enjoys the peace Stow once had. It rents three cozy rooms that share a fine garden and a pool (S-£30, Sb-£45–65, D-£50, Db-£55–75, apartment Db-£75–85 for two people plus £10–15 for each extra person, cash only, pay Wi-Fi, tel. & fax 01451/830-510, www.cotswolds.info/webpage/little-broom.htm, brendarussell@hotmail.co.uk). Brenda has racehorses, and her greenhouse keeps the pool warm throughout the summer (guests welcome). It's an easy eight-minute walk from Stow: Head east on Park Street until the fork. Take the gravel road (marked *private property/no parking*) to the right of the toilet kiosk, and it'll take you to the B&B.

Eating in and near Stow

While Stow has several good dining options, consider venturing out of town for a meal. You can walk to the pub in nearby Broadwell, or—better yet—drive to one of the many enticing gastropubs in the surrounding villages (see sidebar on page 482).

In Stow

These places are all within a five-minute walk of each other, either on the main square or downhill on Queen and Park streets. For dessert, consider munching a treat or fruit (there's plenty for sale at the late-hours grocery on the square) under the trees on the square's benches and watching the sky darken, the lamps come on, and visitors having their photo fun in the stocks.

THE COTSWOLDS

Restaurants and Pubs

The Stow Lodge is the choice of the town's proper ladies. There are two parts: The formal but friendly bar serves fine pub grub (hearty £8–11 lunches and dinners, daily 12:00–14:00 & 19:00–20:30). The restaurant serves a popular £25 three-course dinner (nightly, veggie options, good wines, just off main square, tel. 01451/830-485, Val). On a sunny day, the pub serves lunch in the well-manicured garden, where you'll feel quite aristocratic.

The Old Stocks Hotel Restaurant, which might at first glance seem like a tired and big hotel dining room, is actually a classy place to dine. With attentive service and an interesting menu, they provide tasty and well-presented food. It's good, basic pub grub at pub prices served in a fancy dining room with views of the square. In good weather, the garden out back is a hit (£8–9 lunches, £10–13 dinners, cheaper "snack" menu before 17:00, dinner served nightly 18:30–20:30, reservations recommended on weekends, tel. 01451/830-666).

The Queen's Head faces the Market Square, next to the Stow Lodge. With a classic pub vibe, it's a great place to bring your dog and watch the eccentrics while you eat pub grub and drink the local Cotswold brew, Donnington Ale (£6–7 sandwiches, £8–10 lunches, £9–13 dinners, beer garden out back, daily 12:00–14:30 & 18:30–21:00, tel. 01451/830-563, John).

The Talbot has a more stylish and contemporary feel, with creative, modern dishes (£6–8 lunches, £10–12 dinners). They serve drinks until midnight or later (meals served 12:00–14:30 & 18:30–21:00). With couches to cuddle up on and free Wi-Fi, it works hard to be a popular hangout. On Friday and Saturday evenings after 22:00, they crank up the music, making it the liveliest place in town (The Square, tel. 01451/870-934).

The Old Butchers feels like a breath of fresh air in staid old Stow. Trendy, with good food and slow, snooty service, it dishes up classic English cuisine with a French foodie flair and a passion for meat (£14–18 entrées, daily 11:00–15:30 & 18:00–21:30, open all day long Sat–Sun, 7 Park Street, reservations likely necessary, tel. 01451/831-700).

Cheaper Options and Ethnic Food

Head to the grassy triangle where Digbeth hits Sheep Street; there you'll find take-out fish-and-chips, Chinese, and Indian food. You can picnic at the triangle, or on the benches by the stocks on Market Street.

Greedy's Fish and Chips, on Park Street, is a favorite with locals for take-out. There's no seating, but they do have benches in front (£4.50 fish-and-chips, Mon–Sat 12:00–14:00 & 16:30–21:00, closed Sun, tel. 01451/870-821).

Great Country Gastropubs

These places—known for their high-quality meals and fine settings—are very popular. Arrive early or phone in a reservation. (If you show up at 20:00, it's unlikely that they'll be able to seat you for dinner if you haven't called first.) These pubs allow "well-behaved children," and are practical only for those with a car. If you have wheels, make a point to dine at one (or more) of these—no matter where you're sleeping.

Near Stow

The first two (in Oddington, about three miles from Stow) are more trendy and fresh, yet still in a traditional pub setting. The Plough (in Ford, a few miles farther away) is your jolly olde dark pub.

The Horse and Groom Village Inn in Upper Oddington is a smart place in a 16th-century inn, serving modern English and

Continental food with a good wine list (32 wines by the glass) and serious beer (lunch: £7–10 sandwiches, £10–15 entrées; dinner: £14–17 entrées; daily 12:00–14:00 & 18:30–21:00, tel. 01451/830-584).

The Fox Inn, a different Fox Inn than the one in Broadwell (see "Pub Dinner Hike from Stow"), is old but fresh and famous among locals for its quality cooking (£12–17 entrées, daily 12:00–14:00 & 18:30–22:00, garden and winter garden, in Lower Oddington, tel. 01451/870-555). They also rent three rooms (Db-£75–95, www.foxinn.net)

Jade Garden Chinese Take-Away is appreciated by locals who don't want to cook (Wed–Sun 17:00–23:00, closed Tue, Park Street, tel. 01451/870-288).

The Prince of India offers good Indian food to take out or eat in (£7–8 entrées, nightly 18:00–23:30, 5 Park Street, tel. 01451/830-099).

The Coffee House provides a nice break from the horses-and-hounds traditional cuisine found elsewhere. You can get your food to go, or eat here—there's pleasant garden seating out back (£9–10 soups, salads, and sandwiches; good coffee, Mon–Sat 9:30–17:00, Sun 10:00–16:00, Church Street, tel. 01451/870-802).

The **Youth Hostel Café** (facing the Market Square) serves drinks and meals all day and is family-friendly, with great prices and tables in the backyard garden (£5 breakfast, £6–7 dinner, tel. 01451/830-497).

Even Cheaper: Small grocery stores face the main square

The Plough Inn, in the hamlet of Ford, fills a fascinating old building, once an old coaching inn and later a courthouse. Ask

the bar staff for some fun history—like what "you're barred" means. Eat from the same traditional English menu in the restaurant, bar, or garden. They are serious about both their beer and—judging by the extensive list of home-made temptations—their desserts (£11–16 meals, food served daily 12:00–14:00 & 18:00–21:00, all day long Fri–Sun and June–Aug, 4

miles from Stow on Tewkesbury Road, reservations smart, tel. 01386/584-215).

Near Moreton-in-Marsh, in Bourton-on-the-Hill

The hill-capping Bourton—about a five-minute drive (or two-mile uphill walk) above Moreton—offers sweeping views over the Cotswold countryside. Perched at the top of this steep, picturesque burg is an enticing destination pub.

Horse and Groom is a new-feeling gastropub serving delicious modern English fare in a light and spacious modern-meets-traditional interior. The service is friendly, and the place is lively (£12–19 meals, food served daily 12:00–14:00 & 19:00–21:00, until 21:30 on Fri–Sat, tel. 01386/700-413). They also rent rooms (Db-£110–160 depending on size, www.horseandgroom.info). Don't confuse this with The Horse and Groom Village Inn in Upper Oddington, near Stow (described earlier).

(**Co-op,** open daily 7:00–22:00, is next to the Kings Arms), and a big **Tesco** supermarket is 400 yards north of town.

Pub Dinner Hike from Stow

From Stow, consider taking a half-hour countryside walk to the village of Broadwell, where you'll find a traditional old pub serving good basic grub in a convivial atmosphere. **The Fox Inn** serves pub dinners and draws traditional ales—including the local Donnington ales (£8–10 meals, food served Mon–Sat 11:30–14:00 & 18:30–21:00, Sun 12:00–14:00 only, outdoor tables in garden out back, on the village green, tel. 01451/870-909, Mike and Carol).

Getting There: If you walk briskly, it's just 20 minutes downhill from Stow. While the walk is not particularly scenic (it's one-third paved lane, and the rest on an arrow-straight bridle path), it is peaceful, and the exercise is a nice way to start and finish your meal. The trail is poorly marked, but it's hard to get lost:

THE COTSWOLDS

Leave Stow at Parson's Corner, continue downhill, pass the town well, follow the bridle path straight until you hit the next road, then turn right at the road and walk downhill into the village of Broadwell. You can often hitch a ride with someone from the pub back to Stow after you eat.

Near Stow-on-the-Wold

These sights are all south of Stow: Some are within walking distance (the Slaughters and Bourton-on-the-Water), and one is 20 miles away (Cirencester). The Slaughters and Bourton are tied together by the countryside walk described on page 478.

▲Lower and Upper Slaughter

"Slaughter" has nothing to do with lamb chops. It comes from the sloe tree (the one used to make sloe gin). You can reach these towns on bus #801 at the "Slaughter Pike" stop (along the main road, near the villages).

Lower Slaughter is a classic village, with ducks, a charming little church, a working water mill, and usually an artist busy at her easel somewhere. The Old Mill Museum is a folksy ensemble with a tiny museum, shop, and tea house complete with a delightful terrace overlooking the mill pond, enthusiastically run by Gerald and his daughter Laura (who just can't resist giving generous tastes of their homemade ice cream). Just behind the Old Mill, two kissing gates lead to the path that goes to nearby Upper Slaughter (a 15-minute walk or 2-minute drive away). And if you follow the mill creek downstream, a bridle path leads to Bourton-on-the-Water (described next).

In **Upper Slaughter,** walk through the yew trees (sacred in pagan days) down a lane through the raised graveyard (a buildup of centuries of graves) to the peaceful church. In the back of the fine graveyard, the statue of a wistful woman looks over the tomb of an 18th-century rector (sculpted by his son).

If driving, the small roads from Upper Slaughter to **Ford** and **Kineton** (and the Cotswold Farm Park, described later) are some of England's most scenic. Roll your window down and joyride slowly.

▲Bourton-on-the-Water

I can't figure out whether they call this "the Venice of the Cotswolds" because of its quaint canals or its miserable crowds. Either way, it's very pretty. This town—four miles south of Stow and a mile from Lower Slaughter—gets overrun by midday and weekend hordes. Surrounding Bourton's green are sidewalks jammed with disoriented tourists wearing nametags. If you can avoid them, it's worth a drive-through and maybe a short stop. While it can be mobbed with tour groups during the day, it's pleasantly empty in the early evening and after dark. It's conveniently connected to Stow and Moreton by buses #801 and #855.

Parking: Finding a spot here is predictably tough. Even during the busy business day, rather than park in the pay-and-display parking lot a five-minute walk from the center, drive right into town and wait for a spot on High Street just past the village green (where the road swings left, turn right to go down High Street; there's a long row of free two-hour spots in front of the Edinburgh Woolen Mills Shop, on the right).

Tourist Information: The TI is tucked across the stream a short block off the main drag, just off Victoria Street (April–Oct Mon–Fri 9:30–17:00, Sat 9:30–17:30, closed Sun, closes one hour earlier Nov–March, tel. 01451/820-211, www.bourtoninfo.com).

Sights: Bourton's attractions are tacky tourist traps, but the three listed below might be worth considering. All are on High Street in the town center. In addition to these, families also enjoy Bourton's kid-perfect **leisure centre** (big pool and sauna, 5-minute walk from town center, open daily, call for public hours, tel. 01451/824-024).

▲**Motor Museum**—Lovingly presented, this good, jumbled museum shows off a lifetime's accumulation of vintage cars, old lacquered signs, threadbare toys, and prewar memorabilia. If you appreciate old cars, this is nirvana. Wander the car-and-driver displays, from the automobile's early days to the stylish James Bond era. Don't miss the back door (marked *village life exhibition*), which leads to old carriage houses filled with even more cars. Talk to an elderly Brit who's touring the place for some personal memories (£4.10, mid-Feb–early Dec daily 10:00–18:00, closed off-season, in the mill facing the town center, tel. 01451/821-255, www.cotswold-motor-museum.com).

THE COTSWOLDS

Model Railway Exhibition—This exhibit of three model railway layouts is impressive only to train buffs (£2.50, June–Aug daily 11:00–17:00, Sept–May Sat–Sun only, limited Jan hours, located in the back of a hobby shop, tel. 01451/820-686, www.bourton modelrailway.co.uk).

Model Village—This light but fun display recreates the town on a 1:9 scale in a tiny outdoor park, and has an attached room full of tiny models showing off various bits of British domestic life (£3.50 for the park, £1 more for the model room, daily 10:00–17:45, until 15:45 in winter, tel. 01451/820-467).

Walk to the Slaughters—From Bourton-on-the-Water, it's about a 30-minute walk (or a two-minute drive) to Upper and Lower Slaughter (described previously); taken together, they make for an easy two-hour round-trip walk from Bourton. (You could also walk from Stow through the Slaughters to Bourton—hike described on page 478.)

▲Cotswold Farm Park

Here's a delight for young and old alike. This park is the private venture of the Henson family, who are passionate about preserving ing rare and endangered breeds of local animals. While it feels like a kids' zone (with all the family-friendly facilities you can imagine), it's actually a fascinating chance for anyone to get up close and (very) personal with piles of mostly cute animals, including the sheep that made this region famous—the big and woolly Cotswold Lion. A

busy schedule of demonstrations gives you a look at local farm life—check the events board as you enter for times for the milking, "farm safari," shearing, and well-done "sheep show." Join the included, 20-minute tractor ride, with recorded narration by the founder's son, Adam Henson, filled with the family passion for the farm's mission. Buy a bag of seed (£0.50) upon arrival, or have your map eaten by munchy goats as I did. Tykes love the little tractor rides, maze, and zip line, but the "touch barn" is where it's at for little kids.

Cost and Hours: £7, kids-£5.65, family ticket for 2 adults and 2 kids-£22.75, daily mid-March–early Sept 10:30–17:00, last entry 30 minutes before closing, closed off-season, good £2 guidebook, decent cafeteria, tel. 01451/850-307, www.cotswoldfarmpark .co.uk.

Getting There: It's well-signposted about halfway between Stow and Stanway (15 minutes from either) just off Tewkesbury

Road (B4077, toward Ford from Stow). A visit here makes sense if you're traveling from Stow to Chipping Campden.

Northleach

One of the "untouched and untouristed" Cotswold villages, Northleach is worth a short stop. The town's impressive main

square and church attest to its position as a major wool center in the Middle Ages. Park in the square called The Green or the adjoining Market Place. The town has no TI, but you can pick up a free town map and visitor guide at Keith Haring's World of Mechanical Music (described next) or at the post office on the Market Place (Mon–Fri 9:00–13:00 & 14:00–17:30, Sat 9:00–12:30, closed Sun) and at other nearby shops. Information: www.northleach.gov.uk.

Getting There: Northleach is nine miles south of Stow, down A429. Bus #855 connects it to Stow and Moreton (toll tel. 0871-200-2233, www.traveline.org.uk).

▲**Keith Harding's World of Mechanical Music**—In 1962, Keith Harding, tired of giving ad-lib "living room tours," opened this delightful little one-room place. It offers a unique opportunity to listen to 300 years of amazing self-playing musical instruments. It's run by people who are passionate about the restoration work they do on these musical marvels. The curators delight in demonstrating about 20 of the museum's machines with each hour-long tour. You'll hear Victorian music boxes and the earliest polyphones (record players) playing cylinders and then discs—all from an age when music was made mechanically, without the help of electricity. The admission fee includes an essential hour-long tour (£8, daily 10:00–17:00, last entry at 16:00, tours go constantly—join one in progress, High Street, Northleach, tel. 01451/860-181, www.mechanicalmusic.co.uk).

Church of Saints Peter and Paul—This fine Perpendicular Gothic church has been called the "cathedral of the Cotswolds." It's one of the Cotswolds' finest two "wool" churches (along with Chipping Campden's), paid for by 15th-century wool tycoons. Find the oldest tombstone. The brass plaques on the floor memorialize big shots, showing sheep and sacks of wool at their long-dead feet, and inscriptions mixing Latin and the old English.

▲Bibury

Six miles northeast of Cirencester, this village is a favorite with British picnickers fond of strolling and fishing. Bibury (BYE-bree)

offers some relaxing sights, including a row of very old weavers' cottages, a trout farm, a stream teeming with fat fish and proud ducks, and a church surrounded by rosebushes, each tended by a volunteer of the parish. A protected wetlands area on

the far side of the stream hosts newts and water voles. Walk up the main street, then turn right along the old weavers' Arlington Row and back on the far side of the marsh, peeking into the rushes for wildlife.

For a closer look at the fish, cross the little bridge to the 15-acre **Trout Farm,** where you can feed them—or catch your own (£3.75 entrance fee to walk the grounds, fish food-£0.50, rod rental-£3.75, daily April–Sept 9:00–18:00, March and Oct 9:00–17:00, Nov–Feb daily 9:00–16:00, catch-your-own only available weekends daily July–Aug and March–June and Sept–Oct, tel. 01285/740-215, www.biburytroutfarm.co.uk).

Don't miss the scenic **Coln Valley drive** from A429 to Bibury through the enigmatic villages of Coln St. Dennis, Coln Rogers, Coln Powell, and Winson. Unfortunately, no buses reach Bibury.

Sleeping in Bibury: If you'd like to spend the night in tiny Bibury, consider **$$ The William Morris B&B,** named for the 19th-century designer and writer (small Db-£75, big Db-£85, £10 more Fri–Sun, cash only, 2 rooms, 200 yards from the bridge toward the church at 11 The Street, tel. 01285/740-555, www.thewilliammorris.com, info@thewilliammorris.com).

▲Cirencester

Almost 2,000 years ago, Cirencester (SIGH-ren-ses-ter) was the ancient Roman city of Corinium. It's 20 miles from Stow down A429, which was called Fosse Way in Roman times. Bus #855 connects Cirencester to Stow and Moreton. Drivers follow *town centre* signs and try to find parking right on the market square; if it's parked up, retreat to the

THE COTSWOLDS

Waterloo pay-and-display lot (a five-minute walk away).

In Cirencester, stop by the impressive **Corinium Museum** to find out why they say, "If you scratch Gloucestershire, you'll find

Rome." The museum chronologically displays well-explained artifacts from the town's rich history, with a focus on Roman times—when Corinium was the second-biggest city in the British Isles (after Londinium). You'll see column capitals and fine mosaics, before moving on to the Anglo-Saxon and Middle Ages exhibits (£4.50; April–Oct Mon–Sat 10:00–17:00, Sun 14:00–17:00; Nov–March Mon–Sat 10:00–16:00, Sun 14:00–16:00; Park Street, tel. 01285/655-611, www.cirencester .co.uk/coriniummuseum).

The **TI,** in the Corinium Museum shop, answers questions and sells a £0.50 town map and a £1 town walking-tour brochure (same hours as museum, tel. 01285/654-180).

Cirencester's church is the largest of the Cotswolds "wool" churches. The cutesy New Brewery Arts crafts center entertains visitors with traditional weaving and potting, workshops, an interesting gallery, and a good coffee shop. Monday and Friday are general-market days, Friday features an antiques market, and a crafts market is held on most Saturdays.

Moreton-in-Marsh

This workaday town—worth ▲—is like Stow or Chipping Campden without the touristy sugar. Rather than gift and

antiques shops, you'll find streets lined with real shops: ironmongers selling cottage nameplates and carpet shops strewn with the remarkable patterns that decorate B&B floors. A shin-kickin' traditional market of 100-plus stalls fills High Street each Tuesday, as it has for the last 400 years (8:00–16:00, handicrafts, farm produce, clothing, great people-watching, best if you go early). The Cotswolds has an economy aside from tourism, and you'll feel it here.

Orientation to Moreton-in-Marsh

(area code: 01608)

Moreton has a tiny, sleepy train station two blocks from High Street, lots of bus connections, and the best **TI** in the region. The TI offers a room-booking service, pay Internet access, and discounted tickets for major sights (such as Blenheim Palace). Peruse the racks of fliers, confirm rail and bus schedules, and consider the £0.50 *Town Trail* self-guided walking tour leaflet (Mon 8:45–16:00, Tue–Thu 8:45–17:15, Fri 8:45–16:45, Sat 10:00–13:00—or until 12:30 in winter, closed Sun, good public WC, tel. 01608/650-881).

Helpful Hints

Internet Access: It's available for a price at the **TI** and free at the erratically open **library** (down High Street where it becomes Stow Road, tel. 01608/650-780).

Baggage Storage: While there is no formal baggage storage in town, the **Black Bear Inn** (next to the TI) might let you leave bags there—especially if you buy a drink. Or you can pay £2 to leave a bag at the **launderette** (see below).

Laundry: The handy launderette is a block in front of the train station on New Road (daily 7:00–19:00, last wash at 18:00, £3.40 self-service wash, £2–3 self-service dry, or drop off Mon–Fri 8:00–11:00 for £2.50 extra and same-day service—pick up by 17:00, tel. 01608/650-888).

Bike Rental, Taxis, and Car Rental: See "Getting Around the Cotswolds" (page 452).

Parking: It's easy—anywhere on High Street is fine any time, as long as you want, for free (though there's a 2-hour limit for parking in the small lot in the middle of the street). On Tuesdays, when the market makes parking tricky, you can park at the Budgens supermarket for £3—refundable if you spend at least £5 in the store.

Hikes and Walks from Moreton-in-Marsh: As its name implies, Moreton-in-Marsh sits on a flat, boggy landscape, making it a bit less appealing for hikes; I'd bus to Chipping Campden or to Stow, both described earlier, for a better hike (this is easy, since Moreton is a transit hub). If you do have just a bit of time to kill in Moreton, consider walking a mile out to the arboretum and falconry center in **Batsford** (described later).

Sleeping in Moreton-in-Marsh

(£1 = about $1.60, country code: 44, area code: 01608)

$$$ Manor House Hotel is Moreton's big old hotel, dating from 1545 but sporting such modern amenities as toilets and

Moreton-in-Marsh

TO WORCESTER

TO STRATFORD-UPON-AVON VIA A-429

TO BATSFORD

BATSFORD

TODENHAM RD.

VICTORIA PARK

HIGH ST.

TRAIN STATION

TO BATSFORD

PATH

NEW

POST

TO CHASTLETON HOUSE & OXFORD VIA A-44

LONDON ROAD

OXFORD ST.

WC

BOURTON ROAD

EAST ST.

TO OXFORD & LONDON

TO BROADWAY VIA A-44

CHURCH ST.

LIBRARY

DCH

P PARKING

NOT TO SCALE

① Manor House Hotel
② Kymalton House
③ Treetops B&B
④ Warwick House
⑤ The Marshmallow Restaurant
⑥ The Black Bear Inn
⑦ Hassan Balti Rest.

⑧ Tilly's Tea House & Mermaid Fish Shop
⑨ Ask Restaurant
⑩ Co-op & Tesco Express
⑪ Budgens Supermarket
⑫ Launderette
⑬ Toy Shop Bike Rental

THE COTSWOLDS

electricity. Its 35 classy-for-the-Cotswolds rooms and its garden invite relaxation (Sb-£115, Db-£145, family suite-£210, £40 more for Sat night, rates are soft—often a bit less, includes breakfast, elevator, pay Wi-Fi, log fire in winter, attached restaurants, free parking, on far end of High Street away from train station, tel. 01608/650-501, fax 01608/651-481, www.cotswold-inns-hotels .co.uk, info@manorhousehotel.info).

$$ Kymalton House (KYE-mal-ton) has two bright, tastefully decorated rooms in a gracious modern house. With a pleasant garden, it's set back off of a busy street just outside the town center

(Db-£70, cheaper for 3 or more nights, double beds only, cash only, closed Dec–Jan, tel. 01608/650-487, kymalton@uwclub.net, Sylvia and Doug Gould). It's a seven-minute walk from town (walk past Budgens supermarket, turn right on Todenham Road, look for house on the right). They'll happily pick up and drop off train travelers at the station.

$ Treetops B&B is plush, with seven spacious, attractive rooms, a sun lounge, and a three-quarter-acre backyard. Liz and Ben (the family dog) will make you feel right at home—if you meet their two-night minimum on weekends (large Db-£65, gigantic Db-£70, two wheelchair-accessible ground-floor rooms have patios, free Wi-Fi, set far back from the busy road, London Road, tel. & fax 01608/651-036, www.treetopscotswolds.co.uk, treetops1@talk21.com, Liz and Brian Dean). It's an eight-minute walk from town and the railway station (exit station, keep left, go left on bridge over train tracks, look for sign, then long driveway).

$ Warwick House, just down the road from Treetops, is where "half-American" Charlie Grant rents three rooms in a contemporary, casual, slightly rough-around-the-edges house. It's on a busy road, but the windows keep out most noise. Charlie will do your laundry if you stay three or more nights (Sb-£38, Db-£62, Tb-£75, 3 percent extra with credit card, no kids under age 12, healthy breakfast option, free Wi-Fi and loaner laptop, free parking, will pick up from train station, London Road, tel. 01608/650-773, www.snoozeandsizzle.com, whbandb@yahoo.com).

Eating in Moreton-in-Marsh

A stroll up and down High Street lets you survey your small-town options.

The Marshmallow is relatively upscale but affordable, with a menu that includes traditional English dishes as well as lasagna and salads (£9–11 entrées, 14 fancy teas, Sun–Mon 10:00–19:00, Tue 10:00–16:00, Wed–Sat 10:00–20:00, reservations smart, shady back garden for summer dining, tel. 01608/651-536).

The Black Bear Inn offers traditional English food. As you enter, choose between the dining room on the left or the pub on the right (£5–10 meals and daily specials, restaurant open daily 12:00–14:00 & 18:30–21:00—except no dinner on Sun, pub open daily 11:00–1:00 in the morning, tel. 01608/652-992).

Hassan Balti, with tasty Bangladeshi food, is a fine value for sit-down or take-out (£7–12 meals, daily 12:00–14:00 & 17:30–23:30, High Street, tel. 01608/650-798).

Tilly's Tea House serves fresh soups, salads, sandwiches, and pastries for lunch in a cheerful spot on High Street across from the TI (£5–7 light meals, good cream tea-£5, Mon–Sat 9:00–16:30,

THE COTSWOLDS

closed Sun, tel. 01608/650-000).

Ask, a chain restaurant across the street, has decent pastas, pizzas, and salads, and a breezy, family-friendly atmosphere (£8–11 pizzas, daily 12:00–23:00, take-out available, tel. 01608/651-119).

Mermaid fish shop is popular for its take-out fish and tasty selection of traditional savory pies (£5 fish-and-chips, £2 pies, Mon–Sat 12:00–14:00 & 17:00–22:30, closed Sun).

Picnic: There's a small **Co-op** grocery on High Street in the town center (Mon–Sat 7:00–20:00, Sun 8:00–20:00), and a **Tesco Express** one door down (Mon–Fri 6:00–23:00, Sat–Sun 7:00–23:00). The big **Budgens** supermarket is indeed super (Mon–Sat 8:00–22:00, Sun 10:00–16:00, far end of High Street). There are picnic tables across the busy street, in pleasant Victoria Park.

Nearby: The excellent **Horse and Groom** gastropub in Bourton-on-the-Hill is a quick drive or uphill two-mile walk away (see page 482).

Moreton-in-Marsh Connections

Moreton, the only Cotswolds town with a train station, is also the best base for exploring the region by bus (see "Getting Around the Cotswolds," page 452).

From Moreton by Train to: London's Paddington Station (one-way-£27–29, round-trip after 8:15-£27, every 1–2 hours, 1.5–1.75 hours), **Bath** (hourly, 2.5–3 hours, 2–3 transfers), **Oxford** (about hourly, 40 minutes), **Ironbridge Gorge** (hourly, 2.75–3.5 hours, 2–3 transfers; arrive Telford, then catch bus or cab 7 miles to Ironbridge Gorge—see page 523). While you can reach **Stratford** by train, it's faster by bus (#21 and #22 end there, Mon–Sat about hourly, none on Sun, 1–1.25 hours). Train info: tel. 0845-748-4950, www.nationalrail.co.uk.

Near Moreton-in-Marsh

▲Chastleton House

This stately home, located about five miles southeast of Moreton-in-Marsh, was actually lived in by the same family from 1607 until 1991. It offers a rare peek into a Jacobean gentry house. (Jacobean, which comes from the Latin for "James," indicates the style from the time of King James I—the early 1600s.) Built, like most Cotswold palaces, with wool money, it gradually declined with the fortunes of its aristocratic family until, according to the last lady of the house, it was "held together by cobwebs." It came to the National Trust on condition that they would maintain its musty Jacobean ambience. Wander on creaky floorboards, many of them original, and chat with volunteer guides stationed in each room. It's an uppity place that doesn't encourage spontaneity. The docents are proud to play on one of the best croquet teams in the region (the rules of croquet were formalized in this house in 1868). Page through the early 20th-century family photo albums in the room just off the entry.

Cost and Hours: £8.65; April–Sept Wed–Sat 13:00–17:00, closed Sun–Tue; Oct Wed–Sat 13:00–16:00, closed Sun–Tue; last entry one hour before closing; closed Nov–March; 10-minute drive southeast of Moreton, well-signposted, 5-minute hike to house from free parking lot, recorded info tel. 01494/755-560, www.nationaltrust.org.uk/chastleton.

Getting In: Only 175 visitors a day are allowed into the home (25 people every 30 minutes), and reservations are not possible—it's first-come, first served. At the busiest times, you might have to wait a bit to enter the house. Wednesday and Thursday are the quietest days, with the shortest wait times.

Batsford

This village, just a mile west of Moreton, has two side-by-side attractions that might appeal if you have a special interest or time to kill. These are also connected to Moreton by buses #21 and #22.

Cotswold Falconry Centre—Along with the Cotswolds' hunting heritage comes falconry—and this place, with dozens of specimens of eagles, falcons, owls, and other birds, gives a sample of what these deadly birds of prey can do. You can peruse the cages to see all the different birds, but there's little point in visiting unless you make it to the hour-long falconry presentation (£6.50, £11 combo-ticket with Arboretum, mid-Feb–mid-Nov daily 10:00–17:30, last entry at 17:00; flying displays at 11:30, 13:30, and 15:00, plus in summer at 16:30; Batsford Park, tel. 01386/701-043, www.cotswold-falconry.co.uk).

Batsford Arboretum—This sleepy grove, with 2,800 trees from around the world, pales in comparison to some of the Cotswolds' genteel manor gardens. But it's next door to the Falconry Centre, and handy to visit if you'd enjoy strolling through a diverse wood (£6.50, £11 combo-ticket with Falconry Centre, daily 9:00–18:00, last entry at 16:45, closed Wed in Dec–Jan, tel. 01386/701-441, www.batsarb.co.uk).

STRATFORD-UPON-AVON

Stratford is Shakespeare's hometown. To see or not to see? Stratford is a must for every big bus tour in England, and one of the most popular side-trips from London. English majors and actors are in seventh heaven here. Sure, it's touristy, and non-literary types might find it's much ado about nothing. But nobody back home would understand if you skipped Shakespeare's house.

Shakespeare connection aside, the town's riverside and half-timbered charm, coupled with its hardworking tourist industry,

makes Stratford a fun stop. But the play's the thing to bring the Bard to life—and with the Royal Shakespeare Company (the world's best Shakespeare ensemble) finally moving back into its newly renovated home in 2011, this is sure to be a banner year for visitors. If you'll ever enjoy a Shakespeare performance, it'll be here...even if you flunked English Lit.

While you're in the area, explore Warwick, England's finest medieval castle, and stop by Coventry, a blue-collar town with a spirit that the Nazis' bombs couldn't destroy.

Planning Your Time

Stratford, Warwick, and Coventry are a made-to-order day for drivers connecting the Cotswolds with points north (such as Ironbridge Gorge or North Wales). While connections from the Cotswolds to Ironbridge Gorge are tough, Stratford, Warwick, and Coventry are well-served by public transportation.

If you're just passing through Stratford, it's worth a half-day, but to see a play, you'll need to spend the night, or drive in from the nearby Cotswolds (doable—just 30 minutes away; see previous chapter).

Warwick is England's single most spectacular castle. It's very touristy, but it's also historic and fun (worth three hours of your time). Have lunch in Warwick town. Coventry, the least important stop on a quick trip, is most interesting as a chance to see a real, struggling, Midlands industrial city (with some decent sightseeing).

If you're very speedy, you can hit all three sights on a one-day drive-through (you'll find driving tips at the end of this chapter). If you're more relaxed, see a play and stay in Stratford, then stop at Warwick and Coventry the following morning en route to your next destination.

Orientation to Stratford

(area code: 01789)

Stratford's old town is compact, with the TI and theater along the riverbank, and Shakespeare's Birthplace a few blocks inland; you can easily walk to everything except Anne Hathaway's and Mary Arden's places. The core of town is lined with half-timbered houses. The river has an idyllic yet playful feel, with a park along both banks, paddleboats, hungry swans, and a fun old crank-powered ferry.

Arrival in Stratford

By Train: It's simple: Exit straight ahead from the train station, bear right up the hill (alongside the parking lot), and you'll follow the main drag straight to the river. (For the Grove Road B&Bs, turn right at the first big intersection.) If you need to buy a picnic for your return train trip, there's a Morrison's grocery store nearby (you can see it across the tracks).

By Car: If you're sleeping in Stratford, ask your B&B for arrival and parking details (many have a few free parking spaces, but it's best to reserve ahead). If you're just here for the day, and coming from the south (i.e., the Cotswolds), cross the big bridge and pass the TI for the best parking. Veer right (following *Through Traffic, P,* and *Wark* signs), go around the block—turning right and right and right—and enter the multistory Bridgefoot garage (first hour free, £6/6 hours, £20/10–24 hours, you'll find no place easier or cheaper). The TI and City Sightseeing bus stop are a block away.

Tourist Information

The TI has moved around in recent years, but in 2011 you'll probably find it where the main street hits the river. Otherwise, ask around, or get information from your B&B (likely open daily 9:00–16:00, on Bridgefoot, tel. 01789/264-293, www.shakespeare -country.co.uk).

Helpful Hints

Name That Stratford: If you're coming by train or bus, be sure to request a ticket for "Stratford-upon-Avon," not just "Stratford." Another Stratford—also known as Stratford Langthorne, just outside London—is the location for several events in the 2012 Olympics, and is nowhere near where you're trying to go.

Festival: Every year on the weekend following Shakespeare's birthday (traditionally considered to be April 23—also the day he died), Stratford celebrates. The town hosts free events, including activities for children. In 2011, expect tours and hotels to be booked up long in advance surrounding the weekend of April 23–24.

Internet Access: Get online at **Cyber Junction** (£3.50/hour, Mon–Thu and Sat 10:30–20:00, Fri 10:30–17:00, closed Sun, 28 Greenhill Street, tel. 01789/263-400, www.thecyber junction.co.uk) or the **library,** on Henley Street just a few doors down from Shakespeare's Birthplace (£5/hour, Mon–Fri 9:00–17:30, Sat 9:30–17:00, Sun 12:00–16:00; if all computers are in use, reserve a time at the desk; tel. 01789/292-209).

Baggage Storage: Located directly behind the TI, **The Old Barn** shop stores bags—but be back to pick them up before the store closes, or you're out of luck for the night (£2/bag, Mon–Sat 10:00–17:00, Sun 10:00–16:00, tel. 01789/269-567).

Laundry: Sparklean is a 10-minute walk from the city center, or about five minutes from the Grove Road B&Bs (self-serve wash-£8.50, daily 8:00–21:00, last wash at 20:00, 74 Bull Street, tel. 01789/269-075). On weekdays, Sparklean's kindly Jane will do the wash for you for £10–12 in a few hours if you drop it off by 12:00 (if you're in a pinch, she may even be able to pick up or drop off at your B&B). **Greenhill Launderette** is more central, but also more expensive and not as friendly (self-service wash and dry-about £10–12, daily 8:00–22:00, last wash at 20:45, Greenhill Street).

Taxis: Try **007 Taxis** (tel. 01789/414-007) or the taxi stand on Woodbridge, near the intersection with High Street. To arrange for a private car and driver, contact **Platinum Cars** (£25/hour, tel. 01789/264-626, www.platinum-cars.co.uk).

Stratford-upon-Avon

TO WORCESTER VIA A-46

ALCESTER RD.

TRAIN STATION

ARDEN ST.

GREENHILL

WINDSOR

PEDESTRIAN ZONE

P PARKING

T TAXI

TO ANNE HATHAWAY'S COTTAGE

MARKET PLACE

GROVE

ROTHER

ELY

SHOTTERY

EVESHAM PL.

BROAD WALK

CHESTNUT

NASH'S HOUSE

CHURCH

HALL'S CROFT

OLD TOWN

COURTYARD THEATRE

SOUTHERN

TO OXFORD VIA A-439

RIVER

HOLY TRINITY CHURCH (SHAKESPEARE'S GRAVE)

❶ Ambleside, Woodstock, Adelphi & Salamander Guest Houses

❷ Mercure Shakespeare Hotel

❸ The Emsley Guest House

❹ To Hemmingford House Hostel

❺ The Windmill Inn

❻ Le Bistro Pierre

❼ Lambs, Oppo, The Coconut Lagoon & Barnaby's Fish & Chips

❽ The Vintner Restaurant

❾ The Garrick Inn

❿ The Old Thatch Tavern

⓫ Henley Street Tea Rooms & Bensons House of Tea

TO MARY ARDEN'S FARM

BIRM. ROAD

200 YARDS
200 METERS

TO WARWICK VIA A-439

SHAKESPEARE'S BIRTHPLACE

SOR.

HENLEY
MEER
WOOD
11
18
GUILD
POST ST.
PAYTON ST.
WARWICK ROAD

BUS STATION

HIGH
9
BRIDGE
14
15
P Bridgefoot

TUDOR WORLD

SHEEP
2
7
WATERSIDE
20
TRAMWAY BRIDGE→
22
BRIDGEFOOT
21
25
BRIDGEWAY

PARK

AVON

CHAPEL LANE
23
SWAN THEATRE

BOAT HOUSE
24
CLOPTON BR.
SWAN'S NEST
6
TIDDINGTON RD.
TO 4

ROYAL SHAKESPEARE THEATRE

SHIPSTON RD.
BANBURY RD.
TO OXFORD VIA A-3400 & THE COTSWOLDS

DCH

12 Avon Spice Restaurant
13 Kingfisher Fish & Chips
14 Marks & Spencer
15 Sainsbury's Local
16 Somerfield Grocery
17 Internet Café & Greenhill Launderette
18 Library (Internet)
19 Sparklean Launderette

20 Swan Fountain (Town Walks)
21 City Bus Tours
22 River Cruises (2)
23 Chain Ferry
24 Cox's Yard
25 The Old Barn Shop (Bag Storage)

Tours in Stratford

Stratford Town Walks—These entertaining, award-winning 1.5-hour walks introduce you to the town and its famous play-wright. Tours run daily year-round, rain or shine. Just show up at the Swan fountain (on the waterfront, opposite Sheep Street) in front of the Royal Shakespeare Theatre and pay the guide (£5, kids-£2, ticket stub offers good discounts to some sights, Mon–Wed at 11:00, Thu–Sun at 14:00, tel. 01789/292-478 or 07855/760-377, www.stratfordtownwalk.co.uk). They also run an evening ghost walk led by a professional magician (£6, kids-£3, Mon, Thu, and Fri–Sat at 19:30, must book in advance).

City Sightseeing Bus Tours—Open-top buses constantly make the rounds, allowing visitors to hop on and hop off at all the Shakespeare sights. Given the far-flung nature of two of the Shakespeare sights, and the value of the fun commentary pro-vided, this tour makes the town more manageable. The full 12-stop circuit takes about an hour, and comes with a steady and informa-tive commentary (£11.50, buy tickets on bus or as you board, ticket good for 24 hours, buses leave from the TI every 20 minutes in high season from 9:30–17:00, every 30 minutes off-season; buses alternate between tape-recorded commentary and live guides—for the best tour, wait for a live guide; tel. 01789/412-680, www.citysightseeing-stratford.com).

Shakespearean Sights

Stratford's five biggest Shakespeare sights are run by the same organization, the Shakespeare Birthplace Trust (www.shakespeare.org.uk). While these sights are promoted as if they were tacky tourist attractions—and are designed to be crowd-pleasers rather than to tickle academics—they're well-run and genuinely interesting. Shakespeare's Birthplace, Nash's House, and Hall's Croft are in town; Mary Arden's Farm and Anne Hathaway's Cottage are just outside Stratford. Each of these sights has a tranquil garden and helpful, eager docents who love to tell a story; and yet, each is quite different, so visiting all five gives you a well-rounded look at the Bard.

If you're here for Shakespeare sightseeing—and have time to venture to the countryside sights—you might as well buy the "Five House" combo-ticket and drop into them all. If your time is more limited, visit only Shakespeare's Birthplace, which is the most convenient to reach (right in the town center) and offers the best historical introduction to the playwright.

Combo-Tickets: Admission to the three Shakespeare Birthplace Trust sights in town requires one of two combo-tickets; no individual tickets are sold. Individual tickets are sold for the out-lying sights, Anne Hathaway's Cottage (£7.50) and Mary Arden's Farm (£8.50), but make sense only if you visit just these two sights. To visit only Shakespeare's Birthplace, Hall's Croft, and Nash's House, get the £12.50 **Shakespeare Birthplace combo-ticket.** To add Anne Hathaway's Cottage and Mary Arden's Farm, get the £19 **Shakespeare Five House combo-ticket.** If you've taken a walking tour with Stratford Town Walks (described under "Tours in Stratford," earlier), show your ticket stub to get the Shakespeare Five House combo-ticket for just £12.50. Tickets are sold at participating sights, and are good for one year. Shakespeare's grave isn't covered by either combo-ticket.

Closing Times: What the Shakespeare sights list as their "closing time" is actually their last-entry time. If you show up at the closing time I've noted below, you'll still be able to get in, but will have limited time to enjoy the sight (since they start closing things down soon after).

In Stratford
▲▲Shakespeare's Birthplace

Touring this sight, you'll experience a modern multimedia exhibit before seeing Shakespeare's actual place of birth. While the birthplace itself is a bit underwhelming, the exhibit, helpful docents, and sense that Shakespeare's ghost still haunts these halls make it good introduction to the Bard.

Cost and Hours: Covered by either combo-ticket, daily April–Oct 9:00–17:00, July–Aug until 18:00, Nov–March 10:00–16:00, in town center on Henley Street, tel. 01789/204-016.

❍ Self-Guided Tour: The "**Shakespeare: Life, Love, and Legacy**" exhibit provides an entertaining and easily digestible introduction (or, for some, review) about what made the Bard so great. You'll walk through a series of four rooms, and in each one you'll watch a four-minute video clip about Shakespeare's life and career: movie clips of his works; his upbringing in Stratford and his family life; his career in London; and the impact he's had on many facets of our culture. You'll also see fancy displays (such as a manne-quin Shakespeare hunched over his desk), as well as actual historic artifacts that are illuminated when they're described in the video presentation, including an original 1623 First Folio of Shakespeare's work. It would be nice to linger over the First Folio, but the presentation hustles you into the next room after just a short glance.

William Shakespeare
(1564–1616)

William Shakespeare is the greatest author in any language, period. He expanded and helped define modern English. In one fell swoop, he made the language of everyday people as important as Latin. In the process, he gave us phrases like "one fell swoop," which we quote without knowing it's Shakespeare.

William Shakespeare was born in Stratford-upon-Avon (at today's Shakespeare's Birthplace attraction, described on page 501), and married local girl Anne Hathaway at the age of 18. A few years later, he moved to London, where he spent most of his career and founded (along with his troupe) the Globe Theatre, a replica of which now sits along the Thames' South Bank (see page 115). It was in London that Shakespeare taught his play-going public about human nature, with plots that entertained both the highest and the lowest minds. His tool was an unrivaled mastery of the English language. He retired—rich and famous—back in Stratford, spending his last five years at a house called New Place (now long gone, but its foundations next to Nash's House are being excavated—see page 504).

Using borrowed plots, outrageous puns, and poetic language, Shakespeare wrote comedies (c. 1590—*Taming of the Shrew, As You Like It*), tragedies (c. 1600—*Hamlet, Othello, Macbeth, King Lear*), and fanciful combinations (c. 1610—*The Tempest*), exploring the full range of human emotions and reinventing the English language.

Perhaps as important was his insight into humanity. Think of his stock of great characters and great lines: Hamlet ("To be or not to be, that is the question"), Othello and his jealousy ("It is the green-eyed monster"), ambitious Mark Antony ("Friends,

Leaving the exhibit, you'll walk through the garden and to the **birthplace,** a half-timbered Elizabethan building where young William grew up. I find the old house a bit disappointing, as if millions of visitors have rubbed it clean of anything authentic. It was restored in the 1800s, and, while the furnishings seem tacky and modern, they're supposed to be true to

Romans, countrymen, lend me your ears"), rowdy Falstaff ("The better part of valor is discretion"), and the star-crossed lovers Romeo and Juliet ("But soft, what light through yonder window breaks"). Shakespeare probed the psychology of human beings 300 years before Freud. Even today, his characters strike a familiar chord.

Shakespeare wrote his plays to be performed, not read. He published a few, but as his reputation grew, unauthorized "bootleg" versions began to circulate. Some of these were written by actors who were trying (with faulty memories) to re-create plays they had appeared in years before. It wasn't until seven years after his death, in 1623, that a complete collection of Shakespeare's plays was published, commonly known as the First Folio. Of the 700 printed, about 150 survive. (Most are in the US, but three are in Stratford.) Western literature owes much to this folio, which collects 36 of the 37 known Shakespeare's plays (*Pericles* missed out). It came with an engraving of the only portrait from living memory of Shakespeare, and likely the most accurate depiction of the great playwright.

Little is known about Shakespeare the man. The scope of his brilliant work, his humble beginnings, and the fact that no original Shakespeare manuscripts survive raise a few scholarly eyebrows. Some scholars have wondered if maybe Shakespeare had help on several of his plays. After all, they reasoned, how could a journeyman actor, with little education, have written so many masterpieces? And he was surrounded by other great writers, such as his friend and fellow poet, Ben Jonson. Most modern scholars, though, agree that Shakespeare did indeed write the plays and sonnets attributed to him.

1575, when William was 11. To liven up the otherwise dead-feeling house, chat up the well-versed attendants posted here and there, eager to answer your questions. You'll be greeted by a costumed guide who offers an introductory talk, then set free to explore on your own. Shakespeare's father, John—who came from humble beginnings, but bettered himself by pursuing a career in glove-making (you'll see the window where he sold them to customers on the street)—provided his family with a comfortable, upper-middle-class existence. The guest bed in the parlor was a major status symbol: They must have been rich to afford such a nice bed that wasn't even used every day. This is also the house where

Shakespeare and his bride, Anne Hathaway, began their married life together. Upstairs you'll see the rooms where young Will, his siblings, and his parents slept. After Shakespeare's father died and William inherited the building, the thrifty playwright converted it into a pub to make a little money.

You'll exit into the fine **garden.** The ugly modern building in the middle of the complex sometimes hosts temporary exhibits.

If you hear a commotion in the garden, it's likely Shakespearean **actors,** who perform brief scenes here. Pull up a bench and listen, imagining the playwright as a young boy stretching his imagination in this very place.

Nash's House—Nash was the first husband of Shakespeare's granddaughter...not exactly a close connection. However, this

house is next to the garden that was once the site of New Place, the house where Shakespeare retired. Archaeologists have recently been excavating the remains of New Place, and an engaging, kid-friendly temporary exhibit (called "Dig for Shakespeare") has filled the otherwise dull parlor of Nash's House. Even better, you might be able to walk around the garden, watch the archaeologists at work, and (sometimes) lend a hand with the excavation and cleaning of the artifacts. Because Shakespeare is, in many ways, still shrouded in mystery, this work is important to learn about his lifestyle. This opportunity will only last as long as the excavation does, so the house might be back to its boring old self for your visit (covered by either combo-ticket, daily April–Oct 10:00–17:00, Nov–March 11:00–16:00, Chapel Street, tel. 01789/292-325).

Hall's Croft—This former home of Shakespeare's daughter, Susanna, is in the Stratford town center. A fine old Jacobean house,

it's the fanciest of the group. Since she married a doctor, the exhibits here are focused on 17th-century medicine. If you have time to spare and one of the combo-tickets, it's worth a quick pop-in. To make the exhibits interesting, ask the docent for the 15- to 20-minute introduction, which helps bring the plague—and some of the bizarre remedies of the time—to life (covered by either combo-ticket, same hours as Nash's House, on-site tearoom, between Church Street and the river

---

Stratford Thanks America

Residents of Stratford are thankful for the many contributions Americans have made to their city and its heritage. Along with pumping up the economy day in and day out with tourist visits, Americans paid for half the rebuilding of the Royal Shakespeare Theatre after it burned down in 1926. The Swan Theatre renovation was funded entirely by American aid. Harvard University inherited—you guessed it—the Harvard House, and it maintains the house today. London's much-loved theater, Shakespeare's Globe, was the dream (and gift) of an American. And there's even an odd but prominent "American Fountain" overlooking Stratford's market square on Rother Street, which was given in 1887 to celebrate the Golden Jubilee of the rule of Queen Victoria.

---

on Old Town Street, tel. 01789/292-107).

Shakespeare's Grave—To see his final resting place, head to the riverside Holy Trinity Church. Shakespeare was a rector for this church when he died. While the church is surrounded by

an evocative graveyard, the Bard is entombed in a place of honor, right in front of the altar inside (£1.50, not covered by either combo-ticket, free to view for churchgoers, April–Sept Mon–Sat 8:30–17:30, Sun 12:30–17:00, Oct–March until 17:00 or 16:00, 10-minute walk past the theater—see its graceful spire as you gaze down the river, tel. 01789/266-316, www.stratford-upon-avon.org). The church marks the ninth-century birthplace of the town, which was once a religious settlement.

Just Outside Stratford

To reach either of these sights, it's best to drive or take the hop-on, hop-off bus tour (see "Tours in Stratford," earlier). Both sights are well-signposted (with brown signs) from the major streets and ring roads around Stratford. If driving between the sights, ask for directions at the sight you're leaving.

▲▲**Mary Arden's Farm**—Along with Shakespeare's Birthplace, this is my favorite of the Shakespearean sights. Famous as the girlhood home of William's mom, this homestead is in Wilmcote (about three miles from Stratford). Built around two historic farmhouses, it's an open-air folk museum depicting 16th-century farm life...which happens to have ties to Shakespeare. The Bard is basically an afterthought here.

The museum hosts many special **events,** including the falconry show described below. The day's events are listed on a chalkboard by the entry, or you can call ahead to find out what's on. There are always plenty of activities to engage kids: It's an active, hands-on place.

Follow the Tudor roses from building to building, through farmhouses with good displays about farm life. Throughout the complex, you'll see period interpreters in Tudor costumes. They'll likely be going through the day's chores as people back then would have done—activities such as milking the sheep and cutting wood to do repairs on the house. They're there to answer questions and provide fun, gossipy insight into what life was like at the time.

The first building, **Palmer's farm** (mistaken for Mary Arden's home for hundreds of years, and correctly identified in 2000), is furnished as it would have been in Shakespeare's day.

Mary Arden actually lived in the neighboring **farmhouse,** seemingly less impressive and covered in brick facade. Dorothy Holmes, who lived here until 1979, left it as a 1920s time warp, and that's just what you'll see today.

Of the many events here, the most enjoyable is the **falconry demonstration** with lots of mean-footed birds (only on weekends and local school holidays—including July–Aug; usu-

ally at 11:00, 13:00, and 15:00). Chat with the falconer about their methods for earning the birds' trust. The birds' hunger sets them to flight (a round-trip earns the bird a bit of food; the birds fly when hungry—but don't have the energy if they're *too* hungry). Like Katherine, the wife described as "my falcon" in *The Taming of the Shrew,* these birds are tamed and trained with food as a reward. If things are slow, ask if you can feed one.

Cost and Hours: £8.50 or covered by £19 combo-ticket, daily April–Oct 10:00–17:00, visitors must leave by 17:30, likely closed Nov–March, tel. 01789/293-455.

Getting There: The most convenient way to get here is by car (free parking) or the hop-on, hop-off bus tour, but it's also possible to reach by train. The Wilmcote train station is directly across the street from Mary Arden's House (£2 round-trip fare, one stop from Stratford-upon-Avon on Birmingham-bound train, 5-minute trip, train runs about every hour, call London Midland to confirm departure time—tel. 0844-811-0133, www.london midland.com).

▲**Anne Hathaway's Cottage**—Located 1.5 miles out of Stratford (in Shottery), this home is a 12-room farmhouse where the Bard's

wife grew up. William courted Anne here—she was 26, he was only 18—and his tactics proved successful. (Maybe a little too much, as she was several months pregnant at their wedding.) They were married for 34 years, until his death in 1616 at age 52. The Hathaway family lived here for 400 years, until 1911, and much of the family's 92-acre farm remains part of the sight.

After buying your ticket, turn left and head down through the garden to the thatch-roofed **cottage,** which looks cute enough to eat. The house offers an intimate peek at life in Shakespeare's day. In some ways, it feels even more authentic than his birthplace, and it's fun to imagine the writer of some of the world's greatest romances wooing his favorite girl right here during his formative years. Docents are posted in the first and last rooms to provide meaning and answer questions; while most tourists just stampede through, you'll have a more informative visit if you pause to listen to their commentary. (If the place shakes, a tourist has thunked his or her head on the low beams.)

Maybe even more interesting than the cottage are the **gardens,** which have several parts (including a prizewinning "traditional cottage garden"). If you head uphill (to the right from the entry), you'll find a "Woodland Walk," along with a fun sculpture garden littered with modern interpretations of Shakespearean characters (such as Falstaff's mead gut, and a great photo-op statue of the British Isles sliced out of steel). In the middle is a yew maze (planted only in 2001, so not yet a challenge). You might also find rotating exhibits, generally on a gardening theme.

Cost and Hours: £7.50 or covered by £19 combo-ticket, daily April–Oct 9:00–17:00, Nov–March 10:00–16:00, tel. 01789/292-100.

Getting There: It's a 30-minute walk, a stop on the hop-on, hop-off tour bus, or a quick taxi ride from Stratford; well-signposted for drivers entering Stratford from any direction, easy £1 parking.

▲▲▲Plays Performed by the Royal Shakespeare Company

The Royal Shakespeare Company (RSC), undoubtedly the best Shakespeare company on earth, performs year-round in Stratford and in London (see page 140). Seeing a play here in the Bard's birthplace is a must for Shakespeare fans, and a memorable experience for anybody. Between its excellent acting and remarkable staging, the RSC makes Shakespeare as accessible and enjoyable as it gets.

The RSC expects to have a banner year in 2011, as their completely refurbished flagship theater is finally re-opening after a three-year renovation. In addition to the main Royal Shakespeare Theatre, the smaller, attached Swan Theatre is also coming out of mothballs. Meanwhile, the Courtyard Theatre—which filled in for the other two theaters while they were out of commission—will continue to operate at some capacity, likely staging mostly non-Shakespearean plays. All told, Stratford now has three great venues.

The Royal Shakespeare Company makes it easy to take in some theater, thanks to their very user-friendly website (www.rsc.org.uk), painless ticket-booking system, and chock-a-block schedule that fills the summer with mostly big-name Shakespeare plays (with a few more obscure titles to please the die-hard aficionados, as well).

Performances: Performances take place most days (Mon–Sat generally around 19:00 or 19:30, matinees around 13:00, sporadic Sun shows). Shows generally last three hours or more, with one intermission; for an evening show, don't count on getting home much before 23:00. There's no strict dress code—and people dress casually (nice jeans and short-sleeve shirts are fine)—but shorts are discouraged. You can buy a program for £3.50. If you're feeling bold, buy a £5 standing ticket and then slip into an open seat as the lights dim—if there's not something available during the play's first half, something might open up after intermission.

Getting Tickets: Tickets range from £5 (standing) to £45, with most around £35. Saturday evening shows—the most popular—are most expensive. You can book tickets as you like it: online (www.rsc.org.uk), by phone (toll tel. 0844-800-1110), or in person at the box office (Mon–Sat 9:30–20:00, closed Sun). You'll pay by credit card, get a confirmation number, then pick up your tickets at the theater 30 minutes before "curtain up." Because it's so easy to get tickets online or by phone, it makes absolutely no sense to pay extra to book tickets through any other source.

Tickets go on sale months in advance. Saturdays and very famous plays (such as *Romeo and Juliet* or *Hamlet*) sell out the fastest; the earlier in the week the performance is, the longer it takes to sell out (e.g., Thursdays sell out faster than Mondays). Before your trip, check the schedule on their website, and consider buying tickets if something strikes your fancy. But demand is difficult to predict, and some tickets do go unsold. On my last visit, on a sunny Friday in June, the riverbank was crawling with tourists. I stepped into the RSC on a lark to see if they had any tickets. An hour later, I was watching King Lear lose his marbles.

Even if there aren't any seats available, you can sometimes buy a returned ticket on the evening of an otherwise sold-out show. Ask for details at the box office.

Theaters

The Royal Shakespeare Theatre—The newly restored flagship theater of the RSC has an interesting past. The original theater

was built in 1879 to honor the Bard, but burned down in 1926. The big replacement building you see today (facing the riverside park) was erected in 1932. During the design phase, no actors were consulted; as a result, they built the stodgy Edwardian "picture frame"–style stage, even though the more dynamic "thrust"-style stage—which makes it easier for the audience to become engaged—is the actors' choice. (It's also closer in design to Shakespeare's Globe stage, which juts into the crowd.) The original, ill-conceived design was the reason for the recent multiyear renovation. Now, post-renovation, the theater has an updated, thrust-style stage. While the new theater is bigger, it still respects its history; for example, floorboards from the 1932 stage have been re-laid in the theater's entry foyer, so as you wait for your play, you're walking on theater history.

The Swan Theatre—Adjacent to the RSC Theatre is the smaller, Elizabethan-style Swan Theatre, a galleried playhouse that opened in 1986. Seating about 450, this venue is a much smaller space.

The Courtyard Theatre—A two-minute walk down Southern Lane from the original Royal Shakespeare Theatre, this 1,000-seat theater was expanded (and the so-called "giant rusty box" attached to its side) as a replacement venue while the Royal Shakespeare Theatre was being renovated. It was actually designed as a prototype for the main theater—a testing ground for the lights, seats, and structure of its big brother. With a dramatic thrust stage and a vertical, wrap-around seating arrangement that makes it unusually intimate for a theater of its size, the Courtyard Theatre puts you right on top of the action—literally, as the cheapest "gallery" seats literally look down onto Othello's bald spot.

Non-Shakespearean Sights

Tudor World at the Falstaff Experience—This attraction is tacky, gimmicky, and more about entertainment than education. (And, while it's named for a Shakespeare character, the exhibit isn't about the Bard.) Filling Shrieve's House Barn with fun exhibits (mannequins and descriptions, but few real artifacts), it sweeps through Tudor history from the plague to Henry VIII's privy chamber to a replica 16th-century tavern. If you're into ghost-spotting, their nightly ghost tours may be your best shot (museum-£5, daily 10:30–17:30, last entry 30 minutes before closing; ghost

tours-£7.50, daily at 18:00; Sheep Street, tel. 01789/298-070, www .falstaffexperience.co.uk).

Avon Riverfront—The River Avon is a playground of swans and canal boats. The swans have been the mascots of Stratford since 1623, when, seven years after the Bard's death, a poem in his First Folio nicknamed him "the sweet swan of Avon." Join in the bird-scene fun and buy **swan food** (£0.50) to feed swans and ducks; ask at the ice-cream stand for details. Don't feed the Canada geese, which locals disdain (they say the geese are vicious and have been messing up the eco-balance since they were imported by a king in 1665).

The **canal boats** saw their workhorse days during the short window of time between the start of the Industrial Revolution

and the establishment of the railways. Today, they're mostly pleasure boats. The boats are long and narrow, so two can pass in the slim canals. There are 2,000 miles of canals in England's Midlands, built to connect centers of industry with seaports and provide vital transportation during the early days of the Industrial Revolution.

Stratford was as far inland as you could sail on natural rivers from Bristol; it was the terminus of the man-made Birmingham Canal, built in 1816. Even today, you can motor your canal boat all the way to London from here.

For a little bit of mellow river action, rent a **rowboat** (£4/hour per person) or, for more of a challenge, pole yourself around on a Cambridge-style **punt** (canal is poleable—only 4 or 5 feet deep;

STRATFORD-UPON-AVON

The Look of Stratford

There's much more to Stratford than Shakespeare sights. Take time to appreciate the look of the town itself. While the main street goes back to Roman times, the key date for the city was 1196, when the king gave the town "market privileges." Stratford was shaped by its marketplace years. The market's many "departments" were located on logically named streets, whose names still remain: Sheep Street, Corn Street, and so on. Today's street plan—and even the 57' 9" width of the lots—survives from the 12th century. (Some of the modern storefronts in the town center are still that exact width.)

Starting about 1600, three great fires gutted the town, leaving very few buildings older than that era. Since those fires, tinderbox thatch roofs were prohibited—the Old Thatch Tavern on Greenhill Street is the only remaining thatch roof in town, predating the law and grandfathered in.

The town's main drag, Bridge Street, is the oldest street in town, but looks the youngest. It was built in the Regency style—a result of a rough little middle row of wattle-and-daub houses being torn down in the 1820s to double the street's width. Today's Bridge Street buildings retain that early 19th-century style: Regency.

Throughout Stratford, you'll see striking black-and-white, half-timbered buildings, as well as half-timbered structures that were partially plastered over and covered up in the 19th century. During Victorian times, the half-timbered style was considered low-class, but in the 20th century—just as tourists came, preferring the ye olde style—timbers came back into vogue, and the plaster was removed on many old buildings. But any black and white you see is likely to be modern paint. The original coloring was "biscuit yellow" and brown.

same price as the rowboat and more memorable/embarrassing if you do the punting—don't pay £8/hour per person for a waterman to do the punting for you).

Take a short stop on your lazy tour of the English countryside, and moor your canal boat at Stratford's Canal Basin. You can try a sleepy half-hour **river cruise** (£4.50, no commentary, Avon Boating, board boat in Bancroft Gardens near the RSC theater or at Swan's Nest Boathouse across the Tramway Footbridge, tel. 01789/267-073, www.avon-boating .co.uk), or jump on the oldest surviving **chain ferry** (c. 1937) in Britain (£0.50), which shuttles people across the river just beyond the theater.

Cox's Yard, a riverside timber yard until the 1990s, is a rare physical remnant of the days when Stratford was an industrial port. Today, Cox's is a touristy entertainment center with pubs that have live music most nights (£5–15, schedule at tel. 01789/404-600 or www.coxsyard.co.uk).

Sleeping in Stratford

If you want to spend the night after you catch a show, options abound. Ye olde timbered hotels are scattered through the city center. Most B&Bs are a short walk away on the fringes of town, right

on the busy ring roads that route traffic away from the center. (The recommended places below generally have double-paned windows for rooms in the front, but still get some traffic noise.)

Local hoteliers expect huge demand in 2011 since the Royal Shakespeare Theatre is finally reopening: Book as far ahead as possible. In general, the weekend after Shakespeare's birthday (April 23–24 in 2011) is particularly tight, but Fridays and Saturdays are busy through the season. This town is so reliant upon the theater for its business that some B&Bs have secondary insurance covering their loss if the Royal Shakespeare Company ever stops performing in Stratford.

On Grove Road

These accommodations are at the edge of town on busy Grove Road, across from a grassy park. From here, it's about a 10-minute walk either to the town center or to the train station (opposite directions).

$$ Ambleside Guest House is run with quiet efficiency and attentiveness by owners Peter and Ruth. Each of the seven rooms has been completely renovated, including the small but tidy bathrooms. The place has a homey, airy feel, with none of the typical B&B clutter (S-£28–38, Db-£60–80, Tb-£85–115, Qb-£100–140, ground-floor rooms, free parking, free Wi-Fi, 41 Grove Road, tel. 01789/297-239, fax 01789/295-670, www.amblesideguesthouse .com, ruth@amblesideguesthouse.com—include your phone num-

Sleep Code

(£1 = about $1.60, country code: 44, area code: 01789)

S = Single, **D** = Double/Twin, **T** = Triple, **Q** = Quad, **b** = bathroom, **s** = shower only. Unless noted otherwise, you can assume credit cards are accepted and breakfast is included.

To help you sort easily through these listings, I've divided the rooms into three categories based on the price for a standard double room with bath:

$$$ Higher Priced—Most rooms £90 or more.
$$ Moderately Priced—Most rooms between £60-90.
$ Lower Priced—Most rooms £60 or less.

Prices can change without notice; verify the hotel's current rates online or by email. For other updates, see www .ricksteves.com/update.

ber in your request, since they like to call you back to confirm with a personal touch).

$$ Woodstock Guest House is a friendly, frilly, family-run, and flowery place with five comfortable rooms (Sb-£35–45, Db-£60–80, family room-£75–120 depending on number of people, cash only, deals for 2 or more nights, ground-floor room, free Wi-Fi, free parking, 30 Grove Road, tel. 01789/299-881, www .woodstock-house.co.uk, jackie@woodstock-house.co.uk, owners Denis and bubbly Jackie).

$$ Adelphi Guest House has six rooms, two with four-poster beds. Martin and Ellen have filled the house with antiques and run the place with Scottish charm. For breakfast, they offer a wide variety beyond the standard "English fry" (S-£40, Db-£75–80, Tb-£120, 5 percent surcharge on credit cards, 10 percent discount if you stay at least 2 nights in 2011—mention this book when you reserve, free Wi-Fi, free parking if booked in advance, 39 Grove Road, tel. 01789/204-469, www.adelphi-guesthouse.com, info @adelphi-guesthouse.com).

$ Salamander Guest House, run by gregarious Frenchman Pascal and his wife, Anna, rents seven well-priced but basic rooms (S-£30–35, Db-£50–60, Tb-£60–75, Qb-£80–90, free Wi-Fi, free on-site parking, 40 Grove Road, tel. & fax 01789/205-728, www .salamanderguesthouse.co.uk, p.delin@btinternet.com).

Elsewhere in Stratford

$$$ Mercure Shakespeare Hotel, centrally located in a black-and-white building just up the street from Nash's House, has 73 spacious and elegant rooms, each one named for a Shakespearean play or character. Some of the rooms are old-style Elizabethan higgledy-piggledy (with modern finishes), while others are contemporary style—note your preference when you reserve (Sb-£80, standard Db-£100, deluxe Db-£130–150, breakfast-£15/person, prices soft depending on demand, parking-£10/day, free Wi-Fi in lobby, pay Wi-Fi in rooms, Chapel Street, tel. 01789/294-997, fax 01789/415-411, www.mercure.com, h6630-re@accor.com).

$$ **The Emsley Guest House** holds five bright, modern rooms named after different counties in England. It's conscientiously run by Melanie and Ray Coulson, who give it a homey and inviting atmosphere (Sb-£45–50, Db-£60–80, Tb-£90–120, Q-£120–160, 5-person family room with extra bathroom-£150–200, families welcome, free Wi-Fi, free off-street parking, 5 minutes from station at 4 Arden Street, tel. 01789/299-557, www.theemsley.co.uk, mel@theemsley.co.uk).

$ *Hostel:* **Hemmingford House,** with 130 beds in 2- to 10-bed rooms, is a 10-minute bus ride from town (from £26 for non-members, includes breakfast; take bus #15, #18, or #18A two miles to Alveston; tel. 01789/297-093 or 0845-371-9661, stratford @yha.org.uk).

Eating in Stratford

Stratford's numerous eateries vie for your pre-theater business, with special hours and meal deals. (Most offer light two- and three-course menus from 17:30–19:00.) You'll find many hardworking places lined up along Sheep Street and Waterside. Unfortunately, post-theater dinners are more challenging, as most eateries close early.

The Windmill Inn serves modestly priced but elegant fare in a 17th-century inn. It combines old and new style, and—since it's a few steps beyond the heart of the tourist zone—actually attracts some locals as well. Order drinks and food at the bar, settle into a comfy chair, and wait for your meal to be served (£7–10 pub grub, daily 12:00–22:00, Church Street, tel. 01789/297-687).

Le Bistro Pierre, across the river near the boating station, is a relatively new French eatery that's been impressing Stratford residents. They have indoor or outdoor seating and slow service (£9.25 two-course lunches; £13.50 two-courses meals before 19:00, otherwise £10–13 entrées; Mon–Fri 12:00–15:00 & 17:00–22:30, Sat 12:00–16:00 & 17:00–23:00, Sun 12:30–16:00 & 18:00–22:00, Swan's Nest, Bridgefoot, tel. 01789/264-804). They also have a pub with a different menu.

The next three places, part of the same chain, line up along Sheep Street, offering trendy ambience and "modern English" cuisine, with relatively high prices and small portions (you'll pay separately for side dishes): **Lambs** is intimate, and serves meat, fish, and veggie dishes with panache. The upstairs feels dressy, under low half-timbered beams (specials before 19:00: £11.50 two-course meals, £15 three-course meals; otherwise £12–16 entrées, Mon 17:00–21:30, Tue–Sat 12:00–14:00 & 17:00–21:30, Sun 12:00–14:00 & 18:00–21:00, 12 Sheep Street, tel. 01789/292-554). **Oppo,** next door, has a less formal "bistro" ambience (£11.50 two-course meals before 19:00; otherwise £8–10 light meals, £13–15 entrées; Mon–Thu 12:00–14:00 & 17:00–21:30, Fri–Sat 12:00–14:00 & 17:00–23:00, Sun 18:00–21:00, tel. 01789/269-980). **The Vintner,** just up the street, feels even trendier than its siblings, but still with old style. They're known for their £10 burger (£7–10 light meals, £11–15 entrées, Mon–Thu 12:00–21:45, Fri–Sat 12:00–22:00, Sun 12:00–21:00, 4–5 Sheep Street, tel. 01789/297-259).

The **Garrick Inn** bills itself as the oldest pub in town, and comes with a cozy, dimly lit restaurant vibe. Choose between the pub or table-service section; either way, you'll dine on pricey pub grub (£8–11 dishes, daily 12:00–23:00, 25 High Street, tel. 01789/292-186).

Drinking: The **Old Thatch Tavern** is, according to natives, the best place in town for beer, including local brews from the Purity Brewery. Since the food is mediocre, come here only to drink—not to eat (daily 11:00–23:00, on Greenhill Street overlooking the market square).

Tea Room: **Henley Street Tea Rooms**, across the street from Shakespeare's Birthplace, has indoor seating plus outdoor tables right on the main pedestrian mall (£4 cream tea, £10 afternoon tea, teas available all day, daily 9:00–17:30, 40 Henley Street, tel. 01789/415-572). The same people run Bensons House of Tea & Gift Shop, just down the street (at #33).

Indian: **The Coconut Lagoon** serves tasty, spicy nouvelle South Indian cuisine and offers pre-theater specials until 19:00: a £10.50 two-course deal or £13.25 for three courses (otherwise £10–13 entrées, daily 12:00–14:30 & 17:00–23:00, 21 Sheep Street, tel. 01789/293-546). Closer to the Grove Road B&Bs, the simpler **Avon Spice** has a good reputation and lower prices (£7–11 entrées, daily 17:00–23:30, 7 Greenhill Street, tel. 01789/267-067).

Fish-and-Chips: **Barnaby's** is a greasy fast-food fish-and-chips joint near the waterfront—but it's convenient if you want to get takeout for the riverside park just across the street (£4–6 fish-and-chips, daily 11:00–20:00, at Sheep Street and Waterside). For better food, queue up with the locals at **Kingfisher** (£6–7 fish-and-chips, Mon–Sat 11:30–13:45 & 17:00–22:00, closed Sun, a long block up at 13 Ely Street, tel. 01789/292-513).

Picnics: For groceries, you'll find **Marks & Spencer** on Bridge

Street (Mon–Sat 9:00–18:00, Sun 10:30–16:30, small coffee-and-sandwiches café upstairs, tel. 01789/292-430). Across the street, the **Sainsbury's Local** stays later than other supermarkets in town (daily 7:00–22:00). Nearby, **Somerfield** is in the Town Centre mall (Mon–Sat 8:00–19:00, Sun 10:00–16:00, tel. 01789/292-604). To picnic, head to the canal and riverfront park between the Royal Shakespeare Theatre and the TI. Choose a bench with views of the river or of vacation houseboats, and munch your fish-and-chips while tossing a few fries into the river to attract swans. It's a fine way to spend a midsummer night's eve.

Stratford Connections

Remember: When buying tickets or checking schedules, ask for "Stratford-upon-Avon," not just "Stratford" (which is a different town). Notice that a single train (running about every 2 hours) connects most of these destinations: Warwick, Leamington Spa (change for Coventry or Oxford), then London.

From Stratford-upon-Avon by Train to: London (every 2 hours, 2.25 hours, direct to Marylebone Station), **Warwick** (10/day, 30 minutes), **Coventry** (at least hourly, 1.75 hours, change in Leamington Spa or Birmingham), **Oxford** (every 2-3 hours, 1.25, change in Leamington Spa or Banbury). Train info: toll tel. 0845-748-4950, www.nationalrail.co.uk.

By Bus to: Cotswolds towns (bus #21 or #22, Mon–Sat about hourly, none on Sun, 35 minutes to **Chipping Campden,** 1–1.25 hours to **Moreton-in-Marsh;** also stops at Broadway, Blockley, and Bourton-on-the-Hill; Johnsons Coaches, tel. 01564/797-000, www.johnsonscoaches.co.uk), **Warwick** (hourly by bus, 20 minutes, tel. 01788/535-555, www.stagecoachbus.com), **Coventry** (hourly, 1.25 hours, tel. 01788/535-555, www.stagecoachbus.com). A direct bus runs to **Oxford** only on Sundays; otherwise, you'll change in Chipping Norton (train is better). Most intercity buses stop on Stratford's Bridge Street (a block up from the TI). For bus info that covers all the region's companies, call Traveline at toll tel. 0871-200-2233 (www.travelinemidlands.co.uk).

By Car: Driving is easy and distances are brief: **Stow-on-the-Wold** (22 miles), **Warwick** (8 miles), **Coventry** (19 miles).

Route Tips for Drivers: Stratford to Points North via Warwick and Coventry

Leaving the Bridgefoot garage in downtown Stratford (see page 496), circle to the right around the same block, but stay on "the Wark" (Warwick Road, A439). Warwick is eight miles away. The castle is just south of town on the right. (For parking advice, see page 521.) When you're trying to decide whether to stop in

Coventry or not, factor in Birmingham's rush hour—try to avoid driving through that city between 14:00–20:00, if you can.

If You're Including Coventry: After touring Warwick Castle, carry on through the center of Warwick town and follow signs to Coventry (still A439, then A46). If you're stopping in Coventry, follow signs painted on the road to the *City Centre*, and then to *Cathedral Parking*. Grab a place in the high-rise parking lot. Leaving Coventry, follow signs to *Nuneaton* and *M6 North* through lots of sprawl, and you're on your way. (See below.)

If You're Skirting Coventry: Take M69 (direction: Leicester) and follow M6 as it threads through giant Birmingham.

Once You're on M6: The highway divides into a free M6 and an "M6 Toll" road (designed to help drivers cut through the Birmingham traffic chaos). Take the toll road—£5 is a small price to pay to avoid all the nasty traffic (www.m6toll.co.uk).

When battling through sprawling Birmingham, keep your sights on M6. If you're heading for any points north—Ironbridge Gorge (Telford), North Wales, Liverpool, Blackpool, or the Lakes (Kendal for the South Lake District, Keswick for the North Lake District)—just stay relentlessly on M6 (direction: North West). Each destination is clearly signed directly from M6. For specifics on getting to Ironbridge Gorge, see page 532.

Near Stratford-upon-Avon

Warwick

The pleasant town of Warwick—home to England's finest medieval castle—goes about its business almost oblivious to the busloads of tourists passing through. From the castle, a lane leads into the old town center a block away, where you'll find the **TI** (Mon–Fri 9:30–17:00, Sat–Sun 10:00–16:30, closes earlier in winter, tel. 01926/492-212, www.warwick-uk.co.uk), plenty of eateries (including the Ask restaurant chain), and several minor attractions. The TI can also sell same-day tickets to Warwick Castle; there's no discount, but it can save you time in line at the castle.

Sights in Warwick

▲▲Warwick Castle

Almost *too* groomed and organized, this theme park of a castle gives its crowds of visitors a decent value for the stiff entry fee. The cash-poor but enterprising lord hired the folks at Madame

Near Stratford

Tussauds (now part of Merlin Entertainments, which also owns the London Eye and Legoland) to wring maximum tourist dollars out of his castle. The greedy feel of the place is a little annoying, considering the already-steep admission. But—especially for kids—there just isn't a better medieval castle experience in England.

With a lush, green, grassy moat and fairy-tale fortifications, Warwick will entertain you from dungeon to lookout. Standing inside the castle gate, you can see the mound where the original Norman castle of 1068 stood. Under this "motte," the wooden stockade (or "bailey") defined the courtyard in the way the castle walls do today. The castle is a 14th- and 15th-century fortified shell, holding an 18th- and 19th-century royal residence, surrounded by another one of dandy "Capability" Brown's landscape jobs (like at Blenheim Palace).

Within the castle's mighty walls, there's something for every taste. The Great Hall and six lavish staterooms are the sumptuous highlights. You'll also find a Madame Tussauds–mastered re-creation of a royal weekend party—an 1898 game of statue-maker (look for a young Winston Churchill). You can ponder the weapons in the fine and educational armory, then see demonstrations outside of a trebuchet (like a catapult) and ballista (a type of giant slingshot). The "King Maker" exhibit (set in 1471, when the townsfolk are getting ready for battle) is highly promoted, but not quite as good as a

Disney ride. From the classic ramparts, the tower is a one-way, no-return, 250-step climb, offering a fun perch from which to fire your imaginary longbow. A recently restored mill and engine house come with an attendant who explains how the castle was electrified in 1894. Surrounding everything is a lush, peacock-patrolled, picnic-perfect park, complete with a Victorian rose garden. The castle grounds are often enlivened by a knight in shining armor on a horse that rotates with a merry band of musical jesters.

Cost and Hours: Steep £20 entry fee (£12 for kids under age 12, £13 for seniors), includes gardens and most castle attractions, add £6 to see the gory dungeon, discounted tickets available in advance on the castle's website and at the TI in Stratford. It's open daily April–Oct 10:00–18:00, Nov–March 10:00–17:00. Driving and parking tips are noted under "Warwick Connections—By Car," later. For train travelers, it's a 15-minute, one-mile walk from the Warwick train station to the castle (recorded info tel. 0871-265-2000, www.warwick-castle.com).

Audioguide: Three audioguides provide descriptions of the State Apartments, the Royal Weekend Party exhibit, and A Knight's Tale (£3 apiece, or all three for £6, can be combined with online ticket purchase or rented upon arrival). The £5 guidebook

gives you nearly the same script in souvenir-booklet form. Either is worthwhile if you want to understand the various rooms. If you tour the castle without help, pick the brains of the earnest and talkative docents.

Events: During summer, special events (great for kids) are scheduled every half-hour throughout the day (jousting, longbow demo, sword fights, jester acts, and so on). Pick up the daily events flier (which also lists kiosks that sell snacks) and plan accordingly.

Eating in Warwick

The castle has three main lunch options. **The Coach House** has cafeteria fare and grungy seating (located just before the turnstiles). **The Undercroft** offers the best on-site cooked food, and has a sandwich buffet line (located inside, in basement of palace); you can sit under medieval vaults or escape with your food and picnic outside. The **riverside pavilion** sells sandwiches and fish-and-chips, and has fine outdoor seating (in park just before the bridge, behind castle).

Literally a hundred yards from the castle turnstiles—through a tiny gate in the wall—is the workaday commercial district of the town of **Warwick,** with several much more elegant and competitive eateries that serve fine lunches at non-Tussauds prices. It's worth the walk.

Warwick Connections

From Warwick by Train to: London (3/hour, 1.75 hours), **Stratford** (10/day, 30 minutes—buses are better, see below). Warwick's little train station is a 15-minute walk (or £3 taxi) from the castle. It has no official baggage check, but you can ask politely. The castle has a baggage-check facility. Train info: toll tel. 0845-748-4950, www.nationalrail.co.uk.

By Bus to: Stratford (hourly, 20 minutes, bus #X17, also slower #15/ #18), **Coventry** (10/day, 1 hour, bus #X17, www.stage coachbus.com).

By Car: The main Stratford–Coventry road cuts right through Warwick. Coming from Stratford (8 miles to the south), you'll hit the castle parking lots first (£4; if these are full, lurk until a few cars leave and they'll let you in). The four castle lots are expensive, and three of them are a 10- to 15-minute walk from the actual castle; "premium" £6 parking lot next to the entrance, off Castle Lane. Consider continuing into the town center (on the main road). At the TI (near the big square church spire), grab any street-side parking (free for 2 hours). The castle is a block behind the TI.

Coventry

Coventry, a ▲ sight, was bombed to smithereens in 1940 by the Nazi Luftwaffe. From that point on, the German phrase for "to really blast the heck out of a place" was "to coventrate" it. But Coventry rose from its ashes, and its message to our world is one of forgiveness, reconciliation, and the importance of peace. Browse through Coventry, the closest thing to normal, everyday, urban England that most tourists will ever see. Get a map at the **TI,** located at the cathedral ruins (Mon–Fri 10:00–17:00, Sat 10:00–16:30, Sun 10:00–12:30 & 13:30–16:30, shorter hours off-season, tel. 02476/227-264, www .visitcoventryandwarwickshire.co.uk, tic@cvone.co.uk).

The symbol of Coventry is the bombed-out hulk of its old **cathedral,** with the huge new one adjoining it. The inspirational complex welcomes visitors. Climb the tower (£2.50, daily 10:30–16:00, 180 steps, tel. 02476/521-257, www.coventrycathedral .org.uk).

According to legend, Coventry's most famous hometown girl, Lady Godiva, rode bareback and bare-naked through the town in the 11th century to help lower taxes. You'll see her bronze statue a block from the cathedral (near Broadgate). Just beyond that is the **Coventry Transport Museum,** which features the first, fastest, and most famous cars and motorcycles that came from this "British Detroit" (free, daily 10:00–17:00, tel. 02476/234-270, www.transport-museum.com).

St. Mary's Guildhall has 14th-century tapestries, stained glass, and an ornate ceiling (free, Easter–Sept Sun–Thu 10:00–16:00, closed Fri–Sat, during events, and off-season, tel. 02476/833-325, www.coventry.gov.uk/stmarys).

Coventry Connections

From Coventry by Train to: Telford Central (near Ironbridge Gorge; 2/hour, 1.5 hours, change in Birmingham or Wolverhampton), **Warwick** (hourly, 30 minutes, change in Leamington Spa), **Stratford-upon-Avon** (at least hourly, 1.75 hrs, change in Leamington Spa or Birmingham). Train info: toll tel. 0845-748-4950, www.nationalrail.co.uk.

IRONBRIDGE GORGE

The Industrial Revolution was born in the Severn River Valley. In its glory days, this valley (blessed with abundant deposits of iron ore and coal, and a river for transport) gave the world its first iron wheels, steam-powered locomotive, and cast-iron bridge (begun in 1779). The museums in Ironbridge Gorge, which capture the flavor of the Victorian Age, take you back into the days when Britain was racing into the modern era, and pulling the rest of the West with her.

Near the end of the 20th century, the valley went through a second transformation: Photos taken just 30 years ago show an industrial wasteland. Today the Severn River Valley is lush and lined with walks and parkland. Even its bricks, while still smoke-stained, seem warmer and more inviting.

Planning Your Time

Without a car, Ironbridge Gorge isn't worth the headache. Drivers can slip it in between the Cotswolds/Stratford/Warwick and points north (such as the Lake District or North Wales). Speed demons zip in for a midday tour of the Blists Hill Victorian Town, look at the famous Iron Bridge and quaint Industrial Age town that sprawls around it, and speed out. For an overnight visit, arrive in the early evening to browse the town, see the bridge, and walk along the river. Spend the morning touring the Blists Hill Victorian Town, have lunch there, and head to your next destination.

With more time—say, a full month in Britain—I'd spend two nights and a leisurely day: 9:30–Iron Bridge and the town; 10:30–Museum of the Gorge; 11:30–Coalbrookdale Museum of

Ironbridge Gorge

1 Library House B&B
2 Tontine Hotel
3 Calcutts House B&B
4 Coalport Youth Hostel
5 To Wilderhope Manor Youth Hostel
6 Restaurant Severn
7 Pondicherry Restaurant
8 Da Vinci's Restaurant
9 Golden Ball Inn
10 The Coalbrookdale Inn
11 The Malt House Bar & Rest.

B   BUS STOP
—   ROAD
⊙   ROUNDABOUTS
P   PARKING
---   PATH

TO A-4169 &
WELLINGTON
JIGGERS BANK
CHERRY HILL
DARBY HOUSES
COALBROOK-DALE
DARBY FURNACE
COALBROOKDALE MUSEUM OF IRON
ENGINUITY
CHURCH
WELL. RD.
TO SHREWSBURY
B-4380
BUILDWAS RD.
DALE RD.
IRON TO
SEVERN
MUSEUM OF THE GORGE
TOLLHOUSE
THE IRON BRIDGE

1 MILE
1 KILOMETER

Iron; 14:30–Blists Hill Victorian Town; then dinner at the recommended Golden Ball Inn.

Orientation to Ironbridge Gorge

(area code: 01952)

The town is just a few blocks gathered around the Iron Bridge, which spans the peaceful, tree-lined Severn River. While the smoke-belching bustle is long gone, knowing that this wooded, sleepy river valley was the "Silicon Valley" of the 19th century makes wandering its brick streets almost a pilgrimage. The actual museum sites are scattered over three miles. The modern cooling towers (for coal, not nuclear energy) that loom ominously over these red-brick remnants seem strangely appropriate.

Tourist Information

The TI is in the Museum of the Gorge, just west of the town center (Mon–Fri 9:00–17:00, Sat–Sun 10:00–17:00, tel. 01952/884-

TO A-4169

TREE

TO IRONBRIDGE OPEN-AIR
MUSEUM OF STEEL SCULPTURE
+ TELFORD VIA B-4373

MADELEY

Telford
Ski Centre

A-4169

TO
TELFORD, M-54,
M-6 TO BIRMINGHAM
+ RAF MUSEUM
COSFORD

A-442

BEECH

BRIDGE
WN

MADELEY ROAD

MUSEUM
ENTRANCE

COALPORT ROAD

TO
BRIDGNORTH +
KIDDERMINSTER

NEW
ROAD

SHROPSHIRE
CANAL

BLISTS HILL
VICTORIAN
TOWN

HIGH ⑦

WATERLOO

⑥ ⑧

B-4373

CALCUTTS RD.

COALPORT

IRONBRIDGE RD.

COALPORT
CHINA MUSEUM

④

③

JACKFIELD
TILE MUSEUM

JACKFIELD

R

I

V

E

R

TO
BROSELEY,
MUCH WENLOCK,
LONG MYND GORGE
+ ⑤

TO BROSELEY

DCH

391, www.ironbridge.org.uk). The TI has lots of booklets for sale, including pamphlets describing nearby walks.

Getting Around Ironbridge Gorge

On weekends from Easter through October, **Gorge Connect** buses link the museum sites (£0.50/ride, £2.50 day ticket, free with Museum Passport—described below, 1–2/hour, 9:00–18:00 only, no buses Mon–Fri, several morning and afternoon runs go to the Telford rail station—schedule at www.visitironbridge.co.uk, tel. 01952/200-005).

Sights in Ironbridge Gorge

▲▲Iron Bridge

While England was at war with her American colonies, this first cast-iron bridge was built in 1779 to show off a wonderful new building material. Lacking experience with cast iron, the builders erred on the side of sturdiness and constructed it as if it were made

out of wood. Notice that the original construction used traditional
timber-jointing techniques rather
than rivets. (Any rivets are from
later repairs.) The valley's centerpiece is free, open all the time,
and thought-provoking. Walk
across the bridge to the tollhouse.
Read the fee schedule and notice

the subtle slam against royalty. (England was not immune to the
revolutionary sentiment brewing in the colonies at this time.)
Pedestrians paid half a penny to cross; poor people crossed cheaper
by coracle—a crude tub-like wood-and-canvas shuttle ferry. Cross
back to the town and enjoy a pleasant walk downstream along the
towpath. Where horses once dragged boats laden with Industrial
Age cargo, locals now walk their dogs.

▲▲Ironbridge Gorge
Industrial Revolution Museums

Ten museums located within a few miles of each other focus on the
Iron Bridge and all that it represents. Not all the sights are worth
your time. The Blists Hill Victorian Town is by far the best. The
Museum of the Gorge attempts to give a historic overview, but the
displays are humble—its most interesting feature is the 12-minute
video. The Coalbrookdale Museum of Iron tells the story of iron—
interesting to metalheads. Enginuity is just for kids. And the
original Abraham Darby Furnace is a free shrine to 18th-century
technology. The sights share the same opening hours and contact
info (daily 10:00–17:00, tel. 01952/884-391, www.ironbridge.org
.uk, tic@ironbridge.org.uk).

Museum Passport: This group of widely scattered sights has
varied admission charges (usually £3–7; Blists Hill is £15). The £22
Museum Passport (families-£60) covers admission to all attrac-
tions. If you're visiting the area's top three sights—Blists Hill
Victorian Town, the Museum of the Gorge, and the Coalbrookdale
Museum of Iron—you'll save about £3 by using the £22 Passport.

Sightseeing Strategies: It helps to see the introductory
movie at the Museum of the Gorge first, to help put everything
else into context. To see the most significant sights by car, you'll
park three times: once in town (either in the pay lot just over
the bridge or in the lot at the Museum of the Gorge—the Iron
Bridge and Gorge Museum are connected by an easy, flat walk);
once at the Blists Hill parking lot; and once outside of the
Coalbrookdale Museum of Iron (Enginuity is across the lot, and
the Darby Houses are a three-minute uphill hike away). While
you'll pay separately to park at the Museum of the Gorge, a single

ticket is good for both "pay and display" lots at the Coalbrookdale Museum and Blists Hill.

If you're visiting on a weekend, you can leave your car in a town lot and take the Gorge Connect bus instead (runs Easter–Oct).

Museum of the Gorge

Orient yourself to the valley here in the Severn Warehouse (£4, daily 10:00–17:00, 500 yards upstream from the bridge, parking-£1.10). The 12-minute introductory movie (on a continuous loop) lays the groundwork for what you'll see in the other museums. Check out the exhibit and the model of the gorge in its heyday. Farther upstream from the museum parking lot is the fine riverside Dale End Park, with picnic areas and a playground.

Blists Hill Victorian Town

Save most of your time and energy for this wonderful town—an immersive, open-air folk museum. You'll wander through 50 acres

of Victorian industry, factories, and a re-created community from the 1890s. Pick up the Blists Hill guidebook for a good step-by-step rundown (£15, daily 10:00–17:00, closes at 16:00 in winter, tel. 01952/601-048).

The map you're given when entering is very important—it shows which stops in the big park are staffed with lively docents in Victorian dress. Pop in to say hello to the banker, the lady in the post office, the blacksmith, and the girl in the candy shop. Maybe the boys are singing in the pub. It's fine to take photos. Asking questions and chatting with the villagers is encouraged. What's a shilling? How was the pay? What about health care in the 1800s?

Stop by the pharmacy and check out the squirm-inducing setup of the dentist's chair—it'll make you appreciate the marvel of modern dental care. Down the street, kids like watching the candlemaker at work. Check the events in the barn across the path, where hands-on candle-making and other activities take place.

Just as it would've had in Victorian days, the village has a working pub, a greengrocer's shop, a fascinating squatter's cottage, and a snorty, slippery pigsty. Don't miss the explanation of the "winding engine" at the Blists Hill Mine (demos throughout the day). Walk along the canal to the "inclined plane."

Eating in Blists Hill: There are three places serving lunches: the New Inn Pub for beer and pub snacks, a traditional fish-and-chips joint, and the cafeteria near the children's old-time rides.

Coalbrookdale Museum of Iron and Abraham Darby's Furnace

The **museum,** while old-school, does a fine job of explaining the original iron-smelting process, and how iron (which makes up 95 percent of all industrial metal) changed our world. Compared to the fun and frolicking Blists Hill village, this museum is sleepy (£8.50, includes entry to the Darby Houses, listed later; £1 less in winter—when Darby Houses are closed for lack of light).

Across from the museum, standing like a shrine to the Industrial Revolution, is the **Abraham Darby Furnace.** The Coalbrookdale neighborhood is the birthplace of modern technology, where locals like to claim that mass production was invented. Darby's blast furnace sits inside a big glass pyramid (free), surrounded by evocative Industrial Age ruins. It was here that, in 1709, Darby first smelted iron, using coke as fuel. To me, "coke" is a drink, and "smelt" is the past tense of smell...but around here, these words recall the event that kicked off the modern Industrial Age.

All the ingredients of the recipe for big industry were here in abundance—iron ore, top-grade coal, and water for power and shipping. Wander around Abraham Darby's furnace. Before this furnace was built, iron ore was laboriously melted by charcoal. With huge waterwheel-powered bellows, Darby burned top-grade coal at super-hot temperatures (burning off the impurities to make "coke"). Local iron ore was dumped into the furnace and melted. Impurities floated to the top, while the pure iron sank to the bottom of a clay tub in the bottom of the furnace. Twice a day, the plugs were knocked off, allowing the "slag" to drain away on the top and the molten iron to drain out on the bottom. The low-grade slag was used locally on walls and paths. The high-grade iron trickled into molds formed in the sand below the furnace. It cooled into pig iron (named because the molds look like piglets suckling their mother). The pig-iron "planks" were broken off by sledgehammers and shipped away. The Severn River became one of Europe's busiest, shipping pig iron to distant foundries, where it was melted again and made into cast iron (for projects such as the Iron Bridge), or to forges, where it was worked like toffee into wrought iron.

Enginuity

Located across the parking lot from the Coalbrookdale Museum of Iron, Enginuity is a hands-on funfest for kids. Riffing on Ironbridge's engineering roots, this converted 1709 foundry is full of entertaining-to-kids water contraptions, pumps, magnets, and laser games. Build a dam, try your hand at earthquake-proof construction, navigate a water maze, operate a remote-controlled robot, or power a turbine with your own steam (£8).

Darby Houses

The Darby family, Quakers who were the area's richest residents by far, lived in these two homes located just above the Coalbrookdale Museum.

The 18th-century Darby mansion, **Rosehill House,** features a collection of fine china, furniture, and trinkets from various fam-

ily members. It's decorated in the way the family home would have been in 1850. If the gilt-framed mirrors and fancy china seem a little ostentatious for the normally wealth-shunning Quakers, keep in mind that these folks were rich beyond reason, and—as docents will assure you—considering their vast wealth, this was relatively modest (included in £8.50 Coalbrookdale Museum of Iron ticket, otherwise £4.60, closed Nov–Easter).

Skip the adjacent **Dale House.** Dating from the 1780s, it's older than Rosehill, but almost completely devoid of interior furniture, and its exhibits are rarely open.

Coalport China Museum, Jackfield Tile Museum, and Broseley Pipeworks

Housed in their original factories, these showcase the region's porcelain, decorated tiles, and clay tobacco pipes. These industries were developed to pick up the slack when the iron industry shifted away from the Severn Valley in the 1850s. Each museum features finely decorated pieces, and the china and tile museums offer low-energy workshops (£5–8).

Ironbridge Open-Air Museum of Steel Sculpture

This park is a striking tribute to the region's industrial heritage. Stroll the 10-acre grounds and spot works by Roy Kitchin and other sculptors stashed in the forest and perched in rolling grasslands (£3, March–Nov Tue–Sun 10:00–17:00, closed Mon except bank holidays, closed Dec–Feb, 2 miles from Iron Bridge, Moss House, Cherry Tree Hill, Coalbrookdale, Telford, tel. 01952/433-152, www.go2.co.uk/steelsculpture).

Near Ironbridge Gorge

Skiing and Swimming—There's a small, brush-covered ski slope with two Poma lifts at Telford Snowboard and Ski Centre in Madeley, two miles from Ironbridge Gorge; you'll see signs for it as you drive into Ironbridge Gorge (£11/hour including gear, less for kids, open practice times Mon and Thu 10:00–20:00, Tue and

Fri 12:00–22:00, Wed 10:00–19:00, Sat 16:00–18:00, Sun 10:00–16:00, tel. 01952/382-688, www.telford.gov.uk/skicentre). A public swimming pool is up the road on Court Street (5-minute drive from town, Madeley Court Sports Centre, tel. 01952/382-770).

Royal Air Force (RAF) Museum Cosford—This Red Baron magnet displays more than 80 aircraft, from warplanes to rockets. Get the background on ejection seats and a primer on the principles of propulsion (free, daily 10:00–18:00, last entry at 17:00, Shifnal, Shropshire, on A41 near junction with M54, tel. 01902/376-200, www.rafmuseum.org.uk).

More Sights—If you're looking for reasons to linger in Ironbridge Gorge, these sights are all within a short drive: the medieval town of Shrewsbury, the abbey village of Much Wenlock, the scenic Long Mynd gorge at Church Stretton, the castle at Ludlow, and the steam railway at the river town of Bridgnorth. Shoppers like Chester (en route to points north).

Sleeping in Ironbridge Gorge

$$$ Library House is *Better Homes and Gardens* elegant. Located in the town center, a half-block downhill from the bridge, it's a classy, friendly gem that actually used to be a library. Each of its three rooms is a delight. The Chaucer Room, which includes a small garden, is the smallest and least expensive. Lizzie Steel offers a complimentary drink upon arrival (small Db-£75, larger Db-£90, £15 less for Sb, DVD library, Wi-Fi, free parking just up the road, 11 Severn Bank, Ironbridge Gorge, tel. 01952/432-299, www.libraryhouse.com, info@libraryhouse.com). Lizzie may be able to pick you up from the Telford train station if you request it in advance.

$$ Tontine Hotel is the town's big, 12-room, musty, Industrial Age hotel. Check out the historic photos in the bar (S-£25, Sb-£40, D-£40, Db-£56, en-suite rooms include breakfast—otherwise it's £5 extra, family rooms, 10 percent discount with this book if you ask while booking in advance, The Square, tel. 01952/432-127, fax 01952/432-094, www.tontine-hotel.com, tontinehotel@tiscali.co.uk).

Outside of Town

$$$ Calcutts House rents seven rooms in their 18th-century ironmaster's home and adjacent coach house. Rooms in the main house are elegant, while the coach-house rooms are bright, modern, and less expensive. Their inviting living room and garden are a plus. Ask the owners, Colin and Sarah Williams, how the rooms were named (Db-£52–85, price depends on room size, Wi-Fi, located on Calcutts Road, tel. 01952/882-631, www.calcuttshouse.co.uk, enquiries@calcuttshouse.co.uk). From Calcutts House, it's

Sleep Code

(£1 = about $1.60, country code: 44, area code: 01952)
S = Single, **D** = Double/Twin, **T** = Triple, **Q** = Quad, **b** = bathroom,
s = shower only. You can assume credit cards are accepted and breakfast is included unless noted otherwise.

To help you sort easily through these listings, I've divided the rooms into three categories based on the price for a standard double room with bath during high season:

$$$ Higher Priced—Most rooms £65 or more.
  $$ Moderately Priced—Most rooms between £45–65.
    $ Lower Priced—Most rooms £45 or less.

Prices can change without notice; verify the hotel's current rates online or by email. For other updates, see www.ricksteves.com/update.

a delightful 15-minute stroll down a former train track into town.

$ Coalport Youth Hostel, plush for a hostel, fills an old factory at the China Museum in Coalport (£15–20 bunks in mostly 4-bed dorms, bunk-bed Db-£32–48, £3 more for non-members, includes sheets, kitchen, self-service laundry, tel. 01952/588-755, ironbridge@yha.org.uk). Don't confuse this hostel with the area's other hostel, Coalbrookdale, which is only available for groups.

$ Wilderhope Manor Youth Hostel, a beautifully remote 425-year-old manor house, is one of Europe's best hostels. On Wednesday and Sunday afternoons, tourists actually pay to see what hostelers get to sleep in (£19–23 bunks, under 18-£13.50, £3 more for non-members, single-sex dorms, family rooms available, reservations recommended, reception closed 10:00–17:00, restaurant open 17:30–20:00, tel. 01694/771-363, wilderhope@yha.org .uk). It's in Longville-in-the-Dale, six miles from Much Wenlock down B4371 toward Church Stretton.

Eating in Ironbridge Gorge

Restaurant Severn is the local favorite for a place with style that serves contemporary dishes. You'll choose from a £25 two-course fixed-price meal or a £28 three-course offering (evenings Wed–Sun, closed Mon–Tue, across from the Iron Bridge in the town center, reservations smart—especially on weekends, 33 High Street, tel. 01952/432-233).

Pondicherry, in a renovated former police station, serves delicious Indian curries and a few British dishes to keep the less adventurous happy. The mixed vegetarian sampler is popular even with meat-eaters. The basement holding cells are now little plush lounges—a great option if you'd like your pre-dinner drink "in prison" (£12–16 plates, Mon–Sat 17:00–23:00, Sun 17:00–21:30—starts to get hopping after 19:00, 57 Waterloo Street, tel. 01952/433-055).

Da Vinci's serves good, though pricey, Italian food and has a dressy ambience (£15–20 main courses, Tue–Sat 19:00–22:00, closed Sun–Mon, 26 High Street, tel. 01952/432-250).

Golden Ball Inn, a brewery back in the 18th century, is a popular pub known for its quality food and great atmosphere. Check out chef/owner Kevin Price's creative dishes listed on the big blackboard. You can dine with the friendly local crowd in the "bar," eat in back with the brewing gear in the more quiet—and formal—dining room, or munch on the lush garden patio. Kevin is serious about his beer, listing featured ales daily (£10–15 meals, daily 11:30–23:00, reservations smart on weekends, 5-minute hike up Madeley Road from the town roundabout, 1 Newbridge Road, tel. 01952/432-179).

The Coalbrookdale Inn is filled with locals enjoying excellent ales and good food. This former "best pub in Britain" has a tradition of offering free samples from a lineup of featured beers. Ask which real ales are available (Mon–Thu 17:00–23:30, Fri–Sun 12:00–23:30, food served 12:00–14:00 & 18:00–21:00, no food Sun evening, reservations unnecessary for the bar but a good idea for the fancier restaurant, lively ladies' loo, across street from Coalbrookdale Museum of Iron, 1 mile from Ironbridge Gorge, 12 Wellington Road, tel. 01952/433-953, www.coalbrookdaleinn .co.uk).

The Malt House, located in an 18th-century beer house, is a very popular scene with the local twentysomething gang (£9–15 main courses, bar menu at their Jazz Bar, daily 12:00–21:30, Sun until 22:00, near Museum of the Gorge, 5-minute walk from center, The Wharfage, tel. 01952/433-712). For nighttime action, The Malt House is *the* vibrant spot in town, with live rock music and a fun crowd (generally Thu–Sat).

Ironbridge Gorge Connections

Ironbridge Gorge is five miles from Telford, which has the nearest train station. To get between Ironbridge Gorge and Telford, take bus #9, #39, #76, #77, or #99 (£5 "Day Saver" fare, 1–2/hour, 20–45 minutes, none on Sun) or a taxi (about £10). Although Telford's train and bus stations are an annoying 15-minute walk apart, you can connect them in five minutes on bus #44 (every 10 minutes, covered by "Day Saver") or #55 (every 15 minutes), or with a £3 cab ride. The Telford bus station is part of a large modern mall, an easy place to wait for the bus to Ironbridge Gorge. Buses are run by Arriva (www.arrivabus.co.uk), but you can also call Traveline for departure times and other information (toll tel. 0871-200-2233, www.traveline.org.uk).

The Gorge Connect bus service, which runs among Ironbridge Gorge sights on weekends, makes several morning and afternoon runs between Ironbridge Gorge and the Telford train station (doesn't run off-season, schedule at www.visitironbridge.co.uk). If you need a **taxi** while in Ironbridge Gorge, call Central Taxis at tel. 01952/501-050.

By Train from Telford to: Birmingham (2/hour, 1.25 hours, change in Wolverhampton), **Conwy** in North Wales (9/day, 2.25 hours, some change in Chester or Shrewsbury), **Blackpool** (hourly, 2.75 hours, 2 changes), **Keswick/Lake District** (every 1–2 hours, 5.5 hours; 3.5–4 hours to Penrith with 1–2 changes, then catch a bus to Keswick, hourly except Sun 6/day, 1.5 hours, www.stage coachbus.com), **Edinburgh** (every 1–2 hours, 4.5–5.5 hours, 1–2 changes). Train info: tel. 0845-748-4950, www.nationalrail.co.uk.

By Car from the South: Driving in from the **Cotswolds** and **Stratford,** take M40 to Birmingham, then M6 (direction northwest) through Birmingham. The traffic northbound through Birmingham is miserable from 14:00 to 20:00, especially on Fridays. Take one of two M6 options: free with traffic through the city center; or M6 Toll, which, for £5, skirts you north of the center with nearly no traffic—a very good bet during rush hour. After Birmingham, follow signs to *Telford* via M54 (if on toll road, it'll be via A5). Leave M54 at the Telford/Ironbridge exit (Junction 4). Follow the brown *Ironbridge* signs through several roundabouts to Ironbridge Gorge. (Note: On maps, Ironbridge Gorge is often referred to as "Iron Bridge" or "Iron-Bridge.")

BLACKPOOL AND LIVERPOOL

These two bustling cities—wedged between serene North Wales and the even-more-serene Lake District—provide an opportunity to sample the "real" England, both at work (Liverpool) and at play (Blackpool). Scream down roller coasters and eat "candy floss" until you're deliriously queasy in fun-loving Blackpool. In Liverpool, experience industrial England and relive the early mop-top days of some famous Liverpudlians...meet the Beatles.

Blackpool

Blackpool is Britain's tacky, laid-back underbelly. It's one of England's most-visited attractions, the private domain of its working class, a faded and sticky mix of Coney Island, Las Vegas, and Denny's. It can be fun or depressing, thought-provoking or mind-numbing. Some people love it...others hate it. But it is, without a doubt, an amazing spectacle.

Blackpool grew up with the Industrial Revolution. In the mid-1800s, entire mill towns would close down and take a two-week break here. They came to drink in the fresh air (much needed after a hard year in the mills) and—literally—the seawater. (Back then they figured it was healthy.) Supposedly, because Blackpool lies in a "rain shadow," it gets fewer rainy days than some other parts of England.

Blackpool's heyday is long past now, as more and more working people can afford the cheap charter flights to sunny Spain.

Blackpool

SEE DETAIL MAP

TO M-55
TO M-55

TALBOT
TOWER
CHURCH ST.
CENTRAL DRIVE
RIGBY RD.
BLOOMFIELD RD.
WATER LOO RD.
SOUTH STATION
WATSON RD.
NORTH STATION
LYTHAM RD.
PLEASURE BEACH RIDES
TO HOTELS
PROMENADE
6 MILES OF TRAMWAY
WALKWAY,
& TACKINESS
NORTH PIER
CENTRAL PIER
SOUTH PIER
SAND-CASTLE WATER PARK
DCH
½ MILE
IRISH
SEA

BLACKPOOL

The resort has become popular for "stag" and "hen" (bachelor and bachelorette) parties—basically a cheap drunk weekend for the twentysomething crowd. Consequently, there are two Blackpools: the daytime Blackpool of kids riding roller coasters and grannies getting early-bird specials; and the drunken, debauched, late-night Blackpool of glass-dance-floor clubs and bars.

Blackpool is working to reinvent itself and draw more visitors. An overhaul of The Promenade has begun, as well as numerous renovations in the city center. No matter what, the town remains an accessible and affordable fun zone for the Flo and Andy Capps of northern England. People come year after year. They stay for a week, and they love it.

Be warned: Some of you will get to Blackpool and wonder, "Why did Rick send me *here*?" Most Americans don't even consider a stop in Blackpool. Many won't like it. It's an ears-pierced-while-you-wait, tipsy-toupee kind of place. Tacky, yes. Lowbrow, OK. More than a little run-down in parts, sure. If you're before or beyond kids, and not into kitsch and greasy spoons, skip it. But if you have kids, they'll enjoy Blackpool (hey, it's cheaper than Disneyland). And for those who are into nightlife, this town delivers. If you believe (as I do) that an itinerary should feature as many different facets of a culture as possible, consider a stop here. Blackpool is as English as the Queen—and considerably more fun.

Spend the day "muckin' about" the beach promenade of fortune-tellers, fish-and-chips joints, amusement piers, warped mirrors, and Englanders wearing hats with built-in ponytails. A million greedy doors try every trick to get you inside. Huge arcade halls advertise free toilets and broadcast bingo numbers into the streets; the wind machine under a wax Marilyn Monroe blows at a steady gale; and the smell of fries, tobacco, and sugar is everywhere. Milk comes in raspberry or banana in this land where people under incredibly bad wigs look normal.

Planning Your Time

Ideally, get to Blackpool around lunchtime for an afternoon and evening of making bubbles in this cultural mud puddle. A good overall plan is to ride the tram down to Pleasure Beach, and then walk back along the waterfront to the North Pier and Blackpool Tower, dipping into whatever fun zones appeal. To see a more pristine beach, just keep walking north.

The evening light here is great, with the sun setting over the sea. Walk out along the peaceful North Pier at twilight. Blackpool's Illuminations, when much of the waterfront is decorated with lights, draws crowds in fall, particularly on weekends (September through early November).

Blackpool is easy by car or train. Speed demons with a car can treat it as a midday break (it's just off M6 on M55) and continue north. If the weather's great and you love nature, the lakes are just a few hours north. A visit to Blackpool sharpens the wonders of Windermere.

Orientation to Blackpool

(area code: 01253)

Everything clusters along The Promenade, a tacky, glittering six-mile-long beachfront good-time strip mall punctuated by three fun-filled piers reaching out into the sea. The Pleasure Beach rides are near the South Pier. Jutting up near the North Pier is Blackpool's stubby Eiffel-type tower. The most interesting shops, eateries, and theaters are inland from the North Pier. For a break from glitz, walk north along The Promenade or sandy beach—a residential neighborhood stretches for miles. When you've had enough, just hop on the tram or a bus for a quick ride back.

Tourist Information

The TI sits about 50 yards inland from the North Pier (Mon–Sat 9:00–17:00, Easter–early Nov Sun 10:00–16:30, closed Sun off-season, 1 Clifton Street; tel. 01253/478-222—answered during the day, gives recorded entertainment info after hours; www.visitblackpool.com). There you'll find a city map, brochures on the amusement centers, and a helpful staff. The free *What's On* booklet lists local events; the TI can book shows for you for a £2 fee. If you're going to Sandcastle Waterpark, buy your tickets here to save a few pounds. The TI books rooms for no fee (but collects a 10 percent deposit, which hotels don't recoup; room-finding service closes at 16:30).

Arrival in Blackpool

The main (north) **train** station is three blocks from the town center (no maps given but one is posted). There's no luggage storage in town.

If arriving by **car,** the motorway funnels you down Yeadon Way into a giant parking zone. If you're just spending the day, head for one of the huge £6/day garages. If you're spending the night, drive to the waterfront and head north. My top accommodations are north on The Promenade (easy parking). Leaving Blackpool to go anywhere, follow signs to *M55,* which starts at Blackpool and zips you to M6 (for points north or south).

Helpful Hints

Markets: At the indoor **Abingdon Street Market,** vendors sell baked goods, fruit, bras, jewelry, eggs, and more (Mon–Sat 9:00–17:00, closed Sun). Eight miles north, the **Fleetwood Market** is huge, with two buildings full of produce, clothes, and crafts spilling out onto the street (May–Oct Mon–Tue and Thu–Sat 8:00–17:00, closed Wed and Sun; Nov–April Tue and Fri–Sat only; catch tram marked *Fleetwood,* 30 minutes, £2.70 one-way, www.fleetwoodmarket.co.uk).

Tipping: The pubs of Blackpool have a unique tradition of "and (name an amount) your own, luv." Say that here, and your barmaid will add that amount to your bill and drop it into her tip jar. (Say it anywhere else...and they won't know what you mean.)

Internet Access: The public library, in the big domed building on Queen Street, lets visitors stand and use its computers for 15 minutes (free, Mon and Fri 9:00–17:00, Tue and Thu 9:00–19:00, Wed and Sat 10:00–17:00, Sun 11:00–14:00, tel. 01253/478-111).

Post Office: The main P.O. is in the basement of the WH Smith store, at 12–16 Bank Hey Street (Mon–Sat 9:00–17:30, closed Sun).

Car Rental: In case you decide to tour the Lake District by car, you'll find plenty of rental agencies in Blackpool (closed Sat afternoon and Sun), including **Avis** (at the airport—just south of the South Pier, tel. 01253/408-003) and **Budget** (434 Waterloo Road—just north of the South Pier, tel. 01253/691-632).

Getting Around Blackpool

Trams trundle 13 miles up and down the waterfront, connecting all the sights. They come in all shapes and colors (some vintage, some modern, some dressed up like boats), but are all on the same system and take the same tickets. This electric tramway—the first in Europe—dates from 1885 (about £2 per ride depending on length of trip, pay conductor, trams come every 10–15 minutes or so year-round 6:00–23:15). Many **buses** also run along The Promenade—make sure you're not standing at a tram stop if you're waiting for a bus (similar prices, pay conductor, tel. 01253/473-001, www.blackpooltransport.com). For £6, you can purchase a day pass that covers both trams and buses; buy it on board, or at their office on Market Street.

City Sightseeing's one-hour, 16-stop **hop-on, hop-off bus** has a recorded commentary and leaves from the Blackpool Tower every 30 minutes (£7.50, June–early Nov daily from 9:00 until last departure at 19:00, mid-April–May Sat–Sun only, none off-season, tel. 01253/473-001, www.city-sightseeing.com).

Taxis are easy to snare in Blackpool, and three to five people travel cheaper by cab than by tram. Hotels can get you a taxi by phone within three minutes (no extra charge).

Sights in Blackpool

▲▲▲**People-Watching**—Blackpool's top sight is its people. You'll see England here as nowhere else. Grab someone's hand and a big baton of "rock" (candy), and stroll. Grown men walk around with huge teddy bears looking for places to play "bowlingo," a short-lane version of bowling. Ponder the thought of actually retiring here and spending your last years, day after day, wearing plaid pants and a bad toupee, surrounded by Blackpool. This place puts people in a talkative mood. Start up conversations. Ask a young couple on the street, "What's there to do here?" Find someone to explain the difference between tea and supper. Back at your hotel, join in the chat sessions in the lounge.

▲▲**The Piers**—Blackpool's famous piers were originally built for Victorian landlubbers who wanted to go to sea but were afraid of getting seasick. Each of the three amusement piers has its own personality and is a joy to wander. The sedate **North Pier** is most traditional and refreshingly uncluttered (open first Sat in March to first weekend in Nov, daily 10:00–23:00, £0.50 admission 10:00–17:30 includes discounts on an ice cream or drink and the carousel ride, free admission after 17:30). Dance down its empty planks at twilight to the early English rock playing on its speakers. Its **Carousel Bar** at the end is great for families—with a free kids' DJ nightly from 19:00 to 23:00 (parents drink good beer while the kids bunny-hop and boogie). The something-for-everyone **Central Pier** is lots of fun. Ride its great Ferris wheel for the best view in Blackpool (rich photography at twilight, get the operator to spin you as you bottom out). The family bar at the end of the pier is a hit with kids. The rollicking **South Pier** is all rides.

From the far end of any pier, look out at the horizon to see the natural-gas drilling platforms in the Irish Sea. In the distance, off the North Shore, a castaway gaggle of wind turbines capture energy.

▲**Blackpool Tower**—This mini–Eiffel Tower is a 100-year-old vertical fun center. You pay £17 to get in (£14 for kids, family tickets available); after that, the fun is free. Work your way up from the bottom through layer after layer of noisy entertainment: a circus (2–3 acts a day, runs Easter–first weekend in Nov), a 3-D cinema, an aquarium, and a wonderful old ballroom with barely live music and golden oldies dancing to golden oldies all day. Enjoy a break at the dance-floor-level pub or on a balcony perch. Kids love this place. With a little marijuana, adults would, too. Ride the elevator to the tip of the 500-foot-tall symbol of Blackpool for a chance to stroll across the "Walk of Fear" glass floor and enjoy a smashing view,

especially at sunset (Easter–June daily 10:00–17:00; July–early Nov daily 10:00–20:00; early Nov–Easter Wed 10:00–17:00, Sat–Sun 10:00–18:00; may be closed for events, top of tower closed when windy, tel. 01253/622-242, www.theblackpooltower.co.uk). If you want to leave and return, request a hand stamp.

▲**Pleasure Beach**—Rated ▲▲▲ for roller-coaster enthusiasts, these 42 acres across The Promenade from the beach attract nearly six million visitors annually, and are littered with rides galore, an

ice show, circus and illusion shows, and varied amusements. Many rides are tame enough for the under-10 set, but the top few offer some of the best thrills in Europe: the Pepsi Max Big One (with a peak of 235 feet and 85 mph, it's one of the world's fastest, highest, and steepest roller coasters), the Infusion (a twisty, loopy speed rush that you ride with feet dangling), and the IceBlast (which rockets you straight up before letting you bungee down). The Bling ride spins gondola riders in three different directions 100 feet above the ground at speeds of more than 60 mph. Also memorable is the Steeplechase—carousel horses stampeding down a roller coaster track (a dream come true for *National Velvet* and *Mary Poppins* fans). The Irn Bru Revolution speeds you over a steep drop and upside-down in a loop, then does it again backwards. The Valhalla ride zips you on a Viking boat in watery darkness past scary Nordic things like lutefisk. With two 80-foot drops and lots of hype, first you're scared, then you're soaked, and—finally—you're just glad you survived. The park also offers several old wooden-framed rides full of historic charm—but brittle travelers will want to consider their necks and backs. The tame-looking Wild Mouse, built in 1958, is the jerkiest, and has no doubt kept generations of Blackpool chiropractors in the money.

Admission to Pleasure Beach is £5, which includes a few attractions, then you can pay individually for rides with your £1 tickets (2–8 tickets per ride), or get unlimited rides with a £25–30 armband (price varies with season and day of week, cheaper if purchased in advance on their website). If you haven't pre-purchased your pass, pay the £5 entry fee and have a look around (check to see how long lines are for the top rides)—once you've paid admission to the park, you can upgrade to the armband by paying the difference (daily Easter–early Nov, also open some weekends in winter, opens at about 10:00 and closes as early as 17:00 or as late as 21:30, depending on season, weather, and demand—check website; toll tel. 0871-222-1234, www.pleasurebeachresort.com). Note: Pleasure Beach is about two miles (a 45-minute walk) south of the North Pier, so consider taking the tram or bus.

Sandcastle Waterpark—This popular indoor attraction, across the street from Pleasure Beach, has a big pool, long slides, a wave machine, and water, water, everywhere, at a constant temperature of 84 degrees. Featuring the longest tube waterslide in the world, this is a place where most kids could easily spend a day (£12 limited entry/£15 full admission, £10/£13 for kids, family passes, discount tickets online and at TI; roughly July–Aug daily 10:00–17:30; April–June and Sept–Oct Sat–Thu 10:00–17:00, Fri 13:30–20:00; Nov–March Sat–Sun only 10:00–16:30—confirm as hours may vary; last admission one hour before closing, tel. 01253/343-602, www.sandcastle-waterpark.co.uk).

▲**Illuminations**—Blackpool was the first town in England to "go electric" in 1879. Now, every fall, from early September through early November, Blackpool stretches its tourist season by illuminating its six miles of waterfront with countless lights, all blinking and twinkling (www.blackpool-illuminations.net). People here speak with wonder about these lights. The American in me kept saying, "I've seen bigger, and I've seen better," but I stuffed his mouth with cotton candy and just had some simple fun like everyone else on my specially decorated tram. Look for the animated tableaux up along the North Shore.

St. Annes-on-Sea—Had enough greasy food and flashing lights? The seaside village of St. Annes is an easy 20-minute bus ride away to the south, and offers a welcome break (buses #7 and #11 run from the Blackpool Tower every 10 minutes, covered by the all-day tram/bus pass). Get off at St. Annes Square, which is the first stop after the bus turns left following the long, dune-side straightaway. The town's promenade and the end of the simple Victorian pier (once you pass the noisy game arcade) feel like a breath of sanity. The broad sand beach is perfect for flying a kite, building a sand-castle, or watching happy dogs play in the surf. Consider strolling the beach northward all the way to the southern edge of The Promenade (about three miles—you can see the Pleasure Beach roller coaster from here); if you max out on sand and sea before that, simply cross the dunes back to the seaside road and find the nearest bus stop.

Nightlife in Blackpool

▲**Showtime**—Blackpool always has a few razzle-dazzle music, dancing-girl, racy-humor, magic, and tumbling shows. Box offices around town can give you a rundown on what's available (£7–30 tickets). Your hotel has the latest. Blackpool is a staging ground for some London West End plays—giving you a chance to enjoy a show for a fraction of the London cost. You might try the Opera House for musicals (booking toll tel. 0844-856-1111, info tel. 01253/625-252) and the Grand Theatre for drama and ballet (£15–25, tel. 01253/290-190, www.blackpoolgrand.co.uk). Both are on Church Street, a couple of blocks behind the tower. For the latest in evening entertainment, see the window displays at the TI on The Promenade (www.blackpoollive.com).

▲▲**Funny Girls**—Blackpool's hot bar is in a dazzling venue a couple of blocks from the tower. Most nights from 20:00 to

23:30, Funny Girls puts on a "glam bam thank you ma'am" burlesque-in-drag show that delights footballers and grannies alike. A troop of a dozen or so gorgeous guys go through an entire wardrobe, putting on skits and dances that range from the Charleston to Beyoncé to a very vampy *Sound of Music*. Between songs, the high-heeled MC entertains.

Get your drinks at the bar...unless the transvestites are dancing on it. The show, while racy, is not raunchy. The music is very loud. The crowd is young, old, straight, gay, very down-to-earth, and fun-loving. A weeknight is both a less-expensive and less-crushed experience, as Fridays and Saturdays are jammed. While the area up front can be a mosh pit, there are more sedate tables in back, where service comes with a vampish smile. If you want to experience the show without being immersed in a bar crowd, pay extra to sit.

There are two admissions: sitting and standing (Sun £4 to stand, £14 to sit; Tue–Thu £3.50 to stand, £11 to sit; Fri £6 to stand, £17.50 to sit; Sat £8 to stand, £19.50 to sit; no shows Mon). Getting dinner here before the show runs about £16 (dinner reservations required, must be 18 to enter, 5 Dickson Road, TI sells tickets; to reserve in advance, call 01253/624-901, or visit box office at 44 Queen Street—open 9:30–17:15, www.funnygirlsshowbar.co.uk).

Other Nightspots—The **Mitre Pub** serves beer in a truly rare, old-time Blackpool ambience. Drop in anytime to survey the fun photos of old Blackpool and for the great people scene (daily 11:00–23:00, 3 West Street, tel. 01253/623-718).

Blackpool's clubs and discos are cheap, with live bands and an interesting crowd (nightly 22:00–2:00 in the morning). With all the stag and hen parties, the late-night streets can be clotted with rude rowdies.

Sleeping in Blackpool

Blackpool's 140,000 people provide 120,000 beds in 3,500 mostly dumpy, cheap, nondescript hotels and B&Bs. Remember, this town's in the business of accommodating the people who can't afford to go to Spain. Most places have the same design—minimal character, maximum number of springy beds—and charge £20-25 per person. Empty beds abound except summer weekends and from September through early November (during Illuminations, when everyone bumps up prices). With the huge number of hotels

---

Sleep Code

(£1 = about $1.60, country code: 44, area code: 01253)

S = Single, **D** = Double/Twin, **T** = Triple, **Q** = Quad, **b** = bathroom, **s** = shower only. You can assume credit cards are accepted unless otherwise noted.

To help you sort easily through these listings, I've divided the rooms into three categories based on the price for a standard double room with bath:

$$$ **Higher Priced**—Most rooms £90 or more.

$$ **Moderately Priced**—Most rooms between £45-90.

$ **Lower Priced**—Most rooms £45 or less.

Prices can change without notice; verify the hotel's current rates online or by email. For other updates, see www.ricksteves.com/update.

Central Blackpool

NOT TO SCALE
NORTH PIER TO CENTRAL PIER
IS ABOUT ½ MILE (800 METERS)

++ TROLLEY LINE
Ⓟ PARKING
▨ PEDESTRIAN ZONE

BLACKPOOL NORTH
TRAIN STN.

BUS STN.

TO M-55

KING

CHURCH STREET

DICKSON RD.

TO ②

⑧

⑦

MARKET

OPERA HOUSE +
WINTER GARDENS

LIBRARY

ABINGDON

SPRINGFIELD ROAD

QUEEN ST.

ROAD

CLIFTON

CHEAPSIDE

STREET

④

①

⑥

CORONATION STREET

VICTORIA ST.

ALBERT RD.

CENTRAL DRIVE

BONNY ST.

CHAPEL

TO M-55

CORPORATION

TALBOT SQ.

WEST ST.

MARKET ST.

Ⓟ

ST. POST

⑤

TOWER

ST. JOHN'S CHURCH

TO SOUTH PIER

P R O M E N A D E

TO ① ③

TRAMWAY

♙ B E A C H

♙ B E A C H

♙

NORTH PIER

CENTRAL PIER

I R I S H ⛵ S E A

DCH

① To Hotels North of the Tower
② To The Lonsdale & Valdene Hotels
③ To Red Bank Road Eateries
④ Clifton Street Eateries

⑤ The Mitre Pub
⑥ Marks & Spencer
⑦ Funny Girls (Bar & Show)
⑧ Funny Girls (Box Office)

BLACKPOOL

in town, prices get really soft off-season. I've listed regular high-season prices. There's likely a launderette within a five-minute walk of your hotel; ask your host.

North of the Tower

These listings are on or near the waterfront in the quiet area they call "the posh end," a mile or two north of Blackpool Tower, with easy parking and easy access to the center by tram or bus. The first two listings have classy extras you wouldn't expect in Blackpool, and aren't far from the North Pier. The last two are B&Bs with welcoming owners and lots of stairs, a short tram ride or approximately 35-minute walk from the North Pier.

$$$ Barceló Imperial Hotel is where the Queen would stay in Blackpool. (They boast that every prime minister since they opened has visited their #10 Bar.) With dark-paneled Old World elegance, this splurge has all the comforts at its posh address (standard Db-£115–168 depending on size of room, season, and day of week—check website for deals but call front desk for best standard room available; children stay free, parking-£2.50/day, tram stop: Imperial Hotel, North Promenade, tel. 01253/623-971, fax 01253/751-784, www.barcelo-hotels.co.uk, imperialblackpool @barcelo-hotels.co.uk).

$$$ The **Hilton Hotel** is good if you need a splurge. Yes, I know, staying at the Hilton in Blackpool is like wearing a tux to eat falafel. But this is a grand 270-room place with lots of views, a pool, sauna, gym, and comfortable rooms (Db-£110–170, "club deal" Db with lots of extras-£25 more, ask if there are any "special rates" being advertised, best deals online, call front desk to request room with view for no extra charge, air-con, tram stop: Warley Road, North Promenade, tel. 01253/623-434, fax 01253/627-864, www.hilton.com).

$$ **Beechcliffe Private Hotel** has seven clean rooms run by a friendly couple, Ken and Carol Selman. The rooms are tight and simple, but this place has a homey touch, and the decor is being nicely updated (Sb-£25, Db-£50, kids half-price, tram stop: Cabin; turn left from tram stop, then right at Shaftesbury Avenue, and walk a block away from beach; 16 Shaftesbury Avenue, North Shore, tel. 01253/353-075, www.beechcliffe.co.uk, info@beech cliffe.co.uk). Ken offers guests rides to or from the train station for no charge.

$$ **Robin Hood Hotel** is a cheery place with a big, welcoming living room and nine spacious rooms with big beds and sea views. If you don't mind the stairs, the top room, #9, is great (Sb-£25, Db-£50, discount for kids, under 6 free, facial and massage treatments available, tram stop: St. Stephen's Avenue and walk a block north, 1.5 miles north of tower across from a peaceful stretch of beach, 100 Queens Promenade, North Shore, tel. 01253/351-599, www.robinhoodhotel.co.uk, info@robinhoodhotel.co.uk, Paul and Kathy).

Near the Train Station

Both of these hotels are located on quiet Cocker Street, which provides an oasis of sanity and affordable comfort in a handy, if rough, neighborhood just a few blocks from the train station and the Blackpool Tower and North Pier. These hotels are family-run, have strict security and noise standards, and cater to couples and families rather than to revelers.

$$ **The Lonsdale Hotel** offers five rooms in an oasis of peace behind a lush front porch garden. The plush lounge, with Edwardian paintings and furnishings, takes you to another era. Steve has managed the place for 25 years (Db-£60, Wi-Fi, free parking, at the corner of Lord Street and Cocker Street at 25 Cocker Street, tel. 01253/621-628, www.blackpoolaccommodation .net, lonsdalehotel@hotmail.co.uk).

$$ The Valdene Hotel, with a small garden facing the street, rents 10 rooms above its generous and inviting lounge. Old-time Blackpool photos on the walls create a peaceful and nostalgic atmosphere (Db-£50, 16 Cocker Street, tel. 01253/291-080, valdenehotel@aol.com, www.valdene-hotel.co.uk, Bob, Linda, and Simon Ablett).

Eating in Blackpool

Considering what's in demand here, I wouldn't hope for great food in Blackpool. Generally, food in the tower and along The Promenade is terrible.

Red Bank Road: Locals recommend riding the tram north to Bishpam, where Red Bank Road has several good eateries including Indian, Italian, and steakhouse choices. Try the Bishpam Kitchen (at #14-16) for good fish-and-chips.

Clifton Street: This street is lined with decent ethnic-food eateries, including Italian, Indian, and Chinese.

Supermarket: **Marks & Spencer** has a big supermarket in its basement (Mon–Wed and Fri 9:00–18:00, Thu 9:00–19:00, Sat 8:30–18:00, Sun 10:30–16:30, near recommended eateries, on Coronation Street and Church Street). Buy some food here and go picnic at the beach.

Blackpool Connections

If you're heading to (or from) Blackpool by train, you'll usually need to transfer at **Preston** (5/hour, 30 minutes). The following trains leave from Blackpool's main (north) station.

From Blackpool to: Liverpool (hourly, 1.5 hours), **Keswick/ Lake District** (roughly hourly, allow at least 3.5 hours total for journey: transfer in Preston—30 minutes away, then 1 hour to Penrith, then catch a bus to Keswick, hourly except Sun 8/day, 40 minutes), **Conwy** in North Wales (roughly hourly, 3 hours, 3 transfers), **Edinburgh** (roughly hourly, 3.5 hours, transfer in Preston), **Glasgow** (1–2/hour, 3.25–3.5 hours, transfer in Preston), **York** (hourly, 3 hours, more with change in Manchester), **Moreton-in-Marsh** in the Cotswolds (hourly, 4.25–5 hours, 3 transfers), **Bath** (hourly, 4.5–4.75 hours, 2–3 transfers), **London**'s Euston Station (1–2/hour, 2.75–3.25 hours, 1–2 transfers), Telford near **Ironbridge Gorge** (hourly, 2.25 hours, 2 transfers), **Oban** (2/day, 7.25–7.75 hours, 3 transfers). Train info: toll tel. 0845-748-4950, www.nationalrail.co.uk.

Liverpool

Liverpool, a large, bustling city with a downtown full of shopping malls, is a fascinating stop for Beatles fans and those who would like to look urban England straight in the eye. The city, while long known as a depressed industrial center, has enjoyed a cultural renaissance. In 2008, Liverpool was one of the European Capitals of Culture; to prepare for the honor, the city rode a building-boom wave of new construction and architectural face-lifts. And today, it welcomes guests with a new confidence and energy.

Planning Your Time

For a quick visit (which basically ignores the core of this workaday city), every major sight is in or near the Albert Dock, and the Beatles bus tours also depart from there.

If you're a casual Beatles fan, make Liverpool an afternoon pit stop: Spend most of your time at the Albert Dock, popping in to see The Beatles Story museum, having lunch at the Tate's lunchtime café (and appreciating the art upstairs), and visiting the Maritime Museum. Consider getting a ticket to ride the ferry across the Mersey, which leaves from the docks north of the Albert Dock.

Serious Beatles fan will need more time. There are three main Beatles-related activities: touring The Beatles Story, taking a Beatles bus tour, and visiting the boyhood homes of John and Paul. The first two are easy (and you'll see the homes from the outside on the tour). To actually visit the home interiors, you'll need to make arrangements in advance.

Orientation to Liverpool

(area code: 0151)

Tourist Information

Liverpool's main TI is on **Whitechapel Street,** a six-minute walk downhill from Lime Street Station. Ignore the pavilion with the information symbol on it—the real TI is a glossy silver storefront on this main shopping street (Mon–Sat 10:00–17:00, Sun 11:00–16:00, tel. 0151/233-2008, www.visitliverpool.com). There's another TI at the **Albert Dock** (daily 10:00–17:30, inland from

The Beatles Story, tel. 0151/707-0729). Get the free, small map at either place.

Arrival in Liverpool

By Train: Most trains use the **Lime Street train station.** Look for baggage-storage services on the station's main concourse (£7/item for 24 hours, open daily 7:00–21:00; most bus tours and private minivan/car tours are able to accommodate people with luggage). From this station to the Albert Dock, it's about a 20-minute walk, a short ride on bus #C4 (£1.60 one-way, £3.30 all-day ticket, 3/hour), or a £4 taxi trip. For public-transportation information, visit the Merseytravel center at the main bus center, between Lime Street Station and the TI (Mon–Sat 9:00–17:30, Sun 10:30–16:30, Queen Square, toll tel. 0871-200-2233, www.merseytravel.gov.uk).

Regional trains also arrive at the much smaller **Central Station,** which is essentially a subway stop, located just a few blocks south.

By Plane: From Liverpool John Lennon Airport, take bus #500 to the city center (£2.60, 2/hour).

By Car: Drivers approaching Liverpool follow signs to *City Center* and *Albert Dock,* where you'll find a huge parking lot at the dock. If coming from Wales, take the toll tunnel under the Mersey River (£1.40) and follow signs for *Albert Dock.*

Tours in Liverpool

Beatles Bus Tours

The "sights" covered by these tours are basically houses where the Fab Four grew up (exteriors only), places they performed, and spots made famous by the lyrics of their hits ("Penny Lane," "Strawberry Fields," the Eleanor Rigby grave-yard, and so on). While boring to anyone not into the Beatles, fans will enjoy the commentary and seeing the shelter on the roundabout, the fire station with the clean machine, and the barber who shaves another customer.

Magical Mystery Big Bus Tour—Beatles fans may want to invest a couple of hours taking this tour, which hits the lads' homes (from the outside), Penny Lane, and so on. With an enthusiastic, live commentary and Beatles tunes cued to famous landmarks, it leaves people happy (£15, 1.75 hours; Easter–Oct tours daily at 12:00, also at 14:30 on weekends and July–Aug; Oct–Easter Sat–Sun only at

LIVERPOOL

Liverpool

1. Sir Thomas Hotel
2. Premier Inns (2)
3. To Cocoon Pod Hotel & International Inn Hostel
4. National Trust Beatles Tour Pick-Up Point (Mornings Only)
5. Magical Mystery Tour Pick-Up Point
6. Yellow Duckmarine Tickets
7. Mathew Street & Site of Original Cavern Club

400 YARDS

400 METERS

TO SOUTHPORT

LEEDS

NEW QUAY

CHAPEL

TITHE

WATER

ROYAL LIVER BLDG.

BRUNS.

James Street

M

STRAND

MERSEY FERRIES DOCK

P

MUSEUM OF LIVERPOOL

MARITIME & SLAVERY MUSEUMS

TATE GALLERY LIVERPOOL

B   QUEEN SQUARE BUS HUB

M   MERSEYRAIL SUBWAY STOP

P   PARKING

THE BEATLES STORY

6

2

P

RIVER

MERSEY

DCH

12:00; buses depart from the Albert Dock near The Beatles Story and TI, tel. 0151/233-2459, www.cavernclub.org). As these tours often fill up, you're wise to book ahead by phone, or in person at any TI.

Phil Hughes Mini-Bus Beatles Tours—For something more extensive, fun, and intimate, consider a four-hour minibus Beatles tour from Phil Hughes. It's longer because it includes information on historic Liverpool, along with the Beatles stuff. Phil organizes his tour to fit your schedule and will do his best to accommodate you (£17/person, £88/private group tour, can coordinate times with National Trust tour of Lennon and McCartney homes, 8-seat minibus, mobile 07961-511-223, tel. 0151/228-4565, www.tour liverpool.co.uk, tourliverpool@hotmail.com).

Jackie Spencer Private Tours—To tailor a visit to your schedule and interests, Jackie Spencer is at your service...just say when and where you want to go (up to 5 people in her minivan-£140, 2.5 hours, longer tours available, will pick you up at hotel or train station, mobile 0799-076-1478, www.beatleguides.com, jackie @beatleguides.com).

Beware of cheaper private-taxi tours promoted by some hotels—kickbacks, not quality, motivate concierges to recommend these tours.

▲Lennon and McCartney Homes

John and Paul's boyhood homes are now owned by the National Trust and have both been restored to how they looked during their 1950s childhoods. This isn't Graceland—you won't find an over-the-top rock-and-roll extravaganza here. And if you don't know the difference between John and Paul, you'll likely be bored. But for die-hard Beatles fans who want to get a glimpse into the time and place that created these musical masterminds, this tour is worth ▲▲▲.

Because the houses are in residential neighborhoods—and still share walls with neighbors—the National Trust runs only four tours per day in summer (Wed–Sun only), limited to 14 Beatlemaniacs each. Just 7,000 people pass through these doors each year. While some Beatles bus tours stop here for photo ops, only the National Trust tour gets you inside the homes.

Tour Options: From mid-March to October, tours run four times per day Wed–Sun (no tours Mon–Tue). Morning tours (at 10:00 and 10:50) follow a more scenic route that includes a quick pass by Penny Lane; these are more convenient, as they depart from the Jurys Inn at the Albert Dock (south of and visible from The Beatles Story). Afternoon tours (at 14:30 and 15:00) leave from Speke Hall, an out-of-the-way National Trust property located eight miles southeast of Liverpool. Allow 30 minutes to drive from the city center to Speke Hall—follow the brown *Speke Hall* signs through dozens of roundabouts, heading in the general direction of the airport. If you don't have a car, you'll need to hop a taxi.

Off-Season: From early to mid-March and in November, tours leave Wed–Sun at 10:00, 12:30, and 15:00, and all depart from the handy Jurys Inn at the Albert Dock. No tours run in winter (Dec–Feb).

Cost and Reservations: £17; because only 14 people are allowed on each tour, it's smart to make a reservation ahead of time, especially for the morning tours. You can reserve online (www.nationaltrust.org.uk/beatles), or by calling 0151/427-7231. If you haven't reserved ahead, you can try to book a same-day tour (for the morning tours, call 0151/707-0729). The afternoon tours generally don't fill up, but remember that it takes 30 minutes (by car or taxi) to reach the tour's starting point from central Liverpool.

Guides: Each home has a live-in caretaker who acts as your guide. These folks give an entertaining, insightful-to-fans 20- to 30-minute talk, and then leave you time (10–15 minutes) to wander through the house on your own. Ask lots of questions if their spiel peters out early—the docents are a wealth of information.

Mendips (John Lennon's Home)—Even though he sang about being a working-class hero, John grew up in the suburbs of

Liverpool, surrounded by doctors, lawyers, and—beyond the back fence—Strawberry Field (he added the "s" for the song).

This was the home of John's Aunt Mimi, who raised him in this house from the time he was five years old and once told him, "A guitar's all right, John, but you'll never earn a living by it." John moved out at age 23, but his first wife, Cynthia, bunked here for a while when John made his famous first trip to America. Yoko Ono bought the house in 2002, and gave it as a gift to the National Trust (generating con-

troversy among the neighbors). The stewards, Colin and Sylvia, make this place come to life.

On the surface, it's just a 1930s house carefully restored to how it would have been in the past. But delve deeper. It's been lovingly cared for—restored to be the tidy, well-kept place Mimi would have recognized (down to her apron hanging in the kitchen). It's a lucky quirk of fate that the house's interior remained mostly unchanged after the Lennons left—the bachelor who owned it for the previous decades didn't upgrade much, so even the light switches are true to the time.

If you're a John Lennon fan, it's fun to picture him as a young boy drawing and imagining at his dining room table. It also makes for an interesting comparison to Paul's humbler home, which is the second part of the tour.

20 Forthlin Road (Paul McCartney's Home)—In comparison to Aunt Mimi's house, the home where Paul grew up is simpler,

 much less "posh," and even a little ratty around the edges. Michael, Paul's brother, wanted it that way—their mother, Mary (famously mentioned in "Let It Be"), died when the boys were young, and it never had the tidiness of a woman's touch. It's been intentionally scuffed up around the edges to preserve the historical accuracy. Notice the differences—Paul has said that John's house was vastly different and more clearly middle class; at Mendips, there were books on the bookshelves.

More than a hundred Beatles songs were written in this house (including "I Saw Her Standing There") during days Paul and John spent skipping school. The photos from Michael, taken in this house, help make the scene of what's mostly a barren interior much more interesting.

Other Tours

City Bus Tour—The City Sightseeing bus is a hop-on, hop-off bus tour with a canned soundtrack, but considering the size of the city center, it's a quick way to get an overview that links all the major sights in 55 breezy minutes (£8, buy ticket from driver, valid for 24 hours, daily March–Oct 10:00–17:00, Jan–Feb 10:00–16:30, runs every 30 minutes, tel. 0151/203-3920, www.city-sightseeing.com).

Ferry Cruise—Mersey Ferries offers narrated cruises that depart from Mersey Dock, an easy five-minute walk from the Albert Dock. The 50-minute cruise makes two brief stops on the other side of the river; you can hop off and catch the next boat back (£6.50, year-round, Mon–Fri 10:00–15:00, Sat–Sun 10:00–18:00, leaves at top of hour, café, WCs onboard, tel. 0151/330-1444, www.merseyferries.co.uk).

Harbor and City Tour—The Yellow Duckmarine runs wacky tours of Liverpool's waterfront, city, and docks by land and by sea in its amphibious WWII-era tourist assault vehicles. Be prepared to quack (£12, or £10 midweek and off-peak, family deals, one hour, buy tickets at office on the Albert Dock near The Beatles Story, departs from the Albert Dock every 30 minutes daily 10:30–

17:00, more frequently with demand, tel. 0151/708-7799, www
.theyellowduckmarine.co.uk).

Sights in Liverpool

At the Albert Dock

All of the following sights are at the Albert Dock. Opened in 1852
by Prince Albert, and enclosing seven acres of water, the Albert
Dock is surrounded by five-story brick
warehouses. In its day, Liverpool was
England's greatest seaport, but at the
end of the 19th century, the port wasn't
deep enough for the big new ships; trade
declined after 1890, and by 1972 it was
closed entirely. Like Liverpool itself,
the docks have enjoyed a renaissance,
and today, they contain the city's main
attractions. A half-dozen trendy eateries are lined up here, out of the rain, and
padded by lots of shopping mall–type
distractions. There's plenty of parking. And just strolling along the
thriving harborside promenade, you'll find plenty of fun people-
watching and local energy.

▲**The Beatles Story**—It's sad to think the Beatles are stuck in
a museum (and their music turned into a Las Vegas show). Still,
this exhibit—while overpriced—is
excellent, the story's a fascinating one,
and even an avid fan will pick up some
new information.

Listen to the included audioguide
as you study the knickknacks. Cynthia
Lennon, John's first wife, still marvels
at the manic power of Beatlemania,
while the narrator reminds listeners
of all that made the group earth-
shattering—and even a little edgy—at
the time. For example, performing
before the Queen Mother, John Lennon famously quips: "Will the
people in the cheaper seats clap your hands? And the rest of you,
if you'll just rattle your jewelry." The great audioguide captures
the Beatles' charm and cheekiness in the way the stuffy wax mannequins can't.

The last few rooms trace the members' solo careers, and the
last few steps are reserved for reverence about John's peace work,
including a re-creation of the white room he used while writing
"Imagine."

Cost and Hours: £13, includes audioguide, daily 9:00–19:00 in summer, 10:00–18:00 in winter, last entry two hours before closing, tel. 0151/709-1963, www.beatlesstory.com. The shop has an impressive pile of Beatles buyables.

▲**Merseyside Maritime Museum and International Slavery Museum**—These museums tell the story of Liverpool, once the second city of the British Empire. The port prospered in the 18th century as one corner of a commerce triangle with Africa and America. The British shippers profited greatly through exploitation: About 1.5 million enslaved African people passed through Liverpool's docks (if you have African ancestors who arrived in America as slaves, chances are high they came through here). From Liverpool, the British exported manufactured goods to Africa in exchange for enslaved Africans; the slaves were then shipped to the Americas, where they were traded for raw material (cotton, sugar, and tobacco); and the goods were then brought back to Britain. While the merchants on all three sides made money, the big profit came home to England. As Britain's economy boomed, so did Liverpool's. Not all the money made was above-board—a gallery in the basement discusses customs, duties, and the profitable business of smuggling.

Three galleries on the third floor make up the International Slavery Museum. They describe life in West Africa, enslavement and the Middle Passage to America, and the legacy of slavery. At the music desk, you can listen to more than 300 songs from many different genres that were influenced by African music.

After participation in the slave trade was outlawed in Britain in the early 1800s, Liverpool kept its port busy as a transfer point for emigrants. If your ancestors came from Scandinavia, Ukraine, or Ireland, they likely left Europe from this port. Between 1830 and 1930, nine million emigrants sailed from Liverpool to find their dreams in the New World. Awe-inspiring steamers such as the *Lusitania* called this port home. One exhibit shows footage and artifacts of three big Liverpool-related shipwrecks: the *Lusitania*, the *Empress of Ireland*, and the *Titanic*.

Cost and Hours: Free, daily 10:00–17:00, café, tel. 0151/478-4499, www.liverpoolmuseums.org.uk.

Tate Gallery Liverpool—This prestigious gallery of modern art is near the Maritime Museum. It won't entertain you as well as its London sister, the Tate Modern, but if you're into modern art, any Tate's great. Its two airy floors, dedicated to the rotating collection of statues and paintings from the 20th century, are free; the third floor is devoted to special exhibits (free but £3 suggested donation, £8 for special exhibits; Tue–Sun 10:00–17:50, closed Mon except in July–Aug; tel. 0151/702-7400, www.tate.org.uk/liverpool). The Tate has a nice, inexpensive café.

Museum of Liverpool—Opening in 2011, this museum promises to "capture Liverpool's vibrant character and demonstrate the city's unique contribution to the world." Displays will fill a big, splashy, white building on the harborfront next to the Albert Dock, and be divided into four main themes: Port City, Global City, People's City, and Creative City. On my last visit, the details of the new museum were uncertain...all anyone could tell me was that they were moving Ringo's house there, brick by brick (www.liverpool museums.org.uk/mol).

Sleeping in Liverpool

(£1 = about $1.60, country code: 44, area code: 0151)
Your best budget options in this thriving city are the boring, predictable, and central chain hotels. Many hotels, including the ones listed below, charge more on weekends, especially when Liverpool's soccer team plays a home game. Rates shoot up even higher two weekends a year: during the Grand National horse race (April 7–9 in 2011) and during Beatles Week at the end of August—avoid these times if you can.

$$ Sir Thomas Hotel is a centrally located hotel that was once a bank, and feels like it. The 39 recently renovated rooms are comfortable, and deluxe rooms are outfitted with stately, heavy decor (Db-£65 midweek, £85–99 on non-event weekends, includes breakfast, free Wi-Fi, 10-minute walk from station, 24 Sir Thomas Street at the corner of Victoria Street, tel. 0151/236-1366, fax 0151/227-1541, www.sirthomashotel.co.uk, reservations@sir thomashotel.co.uk).

$$ Premier Inn, which has pleasant, American-style rooms and a friendly staff, is right on the Albert Dock (Db-£64-108, check website for specific rates, discounted parking in nearby lot-£7.50, next to The Beatles Story, toll tel. 0871-527-8622, www .premierinn.com). There's a second, downtown **$$ Premier Inn** as well. While it's a much less desirable location than the Albert Dock branch, it's just a 10-minute walk from the Lime Street train station (Vernon Street, just off Dale Street, tel. 0151/242-7650). Both locations can fill up quickly on weekends.

$$ Cocoon Pod Hotel, in the basement of the hostel (next listing), offers 32 no-nonsense, modern rooms with your choice of two twins or a king. As all the rooms are underground, there are no windows—but at least it's quiet (Sb or Db-£43 Sun–Thu, £53 Fri–Sat, 1- to 3-bedroom apartments from £65, free Wi-Fi, breakfast not included but café next door—with £1/30 minutes Internet access, laundry, same location and contact info as hostel below, www.cocoonliverpool.co.uk).

$ International Inn Hostel, run by the daughter of the Beatles' first manager, rents 100 budget beds in a former Victorian warehouse. Most nights, the hostel puts on fun, free food-themed events for guests—like a traditional Liverpudlian stew (Db-£36–45, bed in 2- to 10-bed room-£15–20, includes sheets and towels, all rooms have bathrooms, free toast and tea/coffee, free Wi-Fi, laundry room, games in lobby, TV lounge, video library, 24-hour reception, café, 4 South Hunter Street, tel. & fax 0151/709-8135, www.internationalinn.co.uk, info@internationalinn.co.uk). From the Lime Street Station, it's an easy 15-minute walk. Or take bus #80A or #86A (3–6/hour, direction: Liverpool Airport or Garston). If taking a taxi, tell them it's on South Hunter Street near Hardman Street.

Eating in Liverpool

Not much distinguishes restaurants in Liverpool. Your best bet is to survey your options at the **Albert Dock.** Here you'll find a slew of trendy restaurants that come alive with club energy at night, but are sedate and pleasant in the afternoon and early evening. For lunch, consider the café in the Tate Gallery (described earlier).

Liverpool Connections

By Train
From Liverpool by Train to: Blackpool (hourly, 1.5 hours), **Keswick/Lake District** (train to Penrith—roughly hourly with 1–2 changes, 1.75–2.25 hours; then bus to Keswick—hourly except Sun 8/day, 40 minutes), **York** (hourly, 2.25 hours), **Edinburgh** (hourly, 3.5–3.75 hours, 1–2 changes), **Glasgow** (1–2/hour, 3.25–3.75 hours, 1–2 changes), **London**'s Euston Station (1–2/hour, 2.25–2.5 hours, some with change), **Crewe** (2/hour, 45 minutes), **Chester** (2/hour, 45 minutes). Train info: toll tel. 0845-748-4950, www.nationalrail .co.uk.

By Ferry
By Ferry to Dublin, Republic of Ireland: It's a seven- to eight-hour trip between Liverpool and Dublin by boat. Both ferry companies require you to check in 1.25–2 hours before the sailing time—call to confirm the details.

P&O Irish Sea Ferries runs a car ferry only—no foot passengers (prices vary widely, roughly £109–195 for car and 2 passengers, Tue–Sat at 9:30 and daily at 21:30, 8-hour trip, overnight ferry includes berth and meals, 20-minute drive north of the city center at Liverpool Freeport—Gladstone dock, toll tel. 0871-664-4777, www.poirishsea.com).

On foot or by car, you can use DFDS Seaways (formerly Norfolkline) from nearby Birkenhead. Ferries sail at 10:00 (Tue–Sat) and nightly at 22:00 (£25–30 for foot passengers on daytime ferry, £20 more for overnight ferry, sleeper cabins extra; prices vary widely, roughly £125–175 for car and 2 passengers on daytime ferry, £215–275 for overnight ferry includes cabin and meals; book online at least one day ahead to avoid additional £10 phone/in-person/day-of-sailing fee, 7-hour trip, Birkenhead Port, toll tel. 0871-230-0330, from the US dial 011-44-208-127-8303, www.norfolkline.com). Birkenhead's dock is a 15-minute walk from Hamilton Square Station on Merseyrail's Wirral Line. You can also take a ferry to Dublin via the Isle of Man (www.steam-packet.com).

By Ferry to Belfast, Northern Ireland: DFDS Seaways (formerly Norfolkline) sails most mornings (Tue–Sun) at 10:30, and every evening (Mon at 22:00, Tue–Sun at 22:30) year-round (8 hours, toll tel. 0871-230-0330, from the US dial 011-44-208-127-8303, www.norfolkline.com). You can also take a ferry to Belfast via the Isle of Man (www.steam-packet.com).

Route Tips for Drivers

From Liverpool to Blackpool: Leaving Liverpool, drive north along the waterfront, following signs to *M58* (Preston). Once on M58 (and not before), follow signs to *M6*, and then *M55* into Blackpool.

THE LAKE DISTRICT

In the pristine Lake District, William Wordsworth's poems still shiver in trees and ripple on ponds. This is a land where nature rules, and humanity keeps a wide-eyed but low profile. Relax, recharge, take a cruise or a hike, and maybe even write a poem. Renew your poetic license at Wordsworth's famous Dove Cottage.

The Lake District, about 30 miles long and 30 miles wide, is nature's lush, green playground. Explore it by foot, bike, bus, or car. While not impressive in sheer height (Scafell Pike, the tallest peak in England, is only 3,206 feet), there's a walking-stick charm about the way nature and the culture mix here. Locals are fond of declaring that their mountains are older than the Himalayas and were once as tall, but have been worn down by the ages. Walking along a windblown ridge or climbing over a rock fence to look into the eyes of a ragamuffin sheep, even tenderfeet get a chance to feel very outdoorsy. The tradition of staying close to the land remains true—albeit in an updated form—in the 21st century; you'll see restaurants serving organic foods as well as stickers advocating for environmental causes in the windows of homes.

Dress in layers, and expect rain mixed with brilliant "bright spells" (pubs offer atmospheric shelter at every turn). Drizzly days can be followed by delightful evenings.

Plan to spend the majority of your time in the unspoiled North Lake District. In this chapter, I focus on the town of Keswick, the lake called Derwentwater, and the vast, time-passed Newlands Valley. The North Lake District works great by car or by bus (with easy train access via Penrith), delights nature-lovers, and has good accommodations to boot.

The South Lake District—famous primarily for its Wordsworth and Beatrix Potter sights—is slightly closer to London, and gets the promotion, the tour crowds, and the tackiness that comes with them. I strongly recommend that you focus on the north. Ideally, enter the region from the north, via Penrith. Make your home base in or near Keswick, and side-trip from here into the South Lake District only if you're interested in the Wordsworth and Beatrix Potter sights.

Planning Your Time

On a three-week trip to England, I'd spend two days and two nights in this area. Penrith is the nearest train station, just 40 minutes by bus or car from Keswick. Those without a car will use Keswick as a springboard: Cruise the lake and take one of the many hikes in the Catbells area. Non-hikers can hop on a minibus tour. If great scenery is commonplace in your life, the Lake District can be more soothing (and rainy) than exciting. If you're rushed, you could make this area a one-night stand—or even a quick drive-through.

Two-Day Driving Plan: Here's the most exciting way for drivers coming from the south—who'd like to visit South Lake District sights en route to the North Lake District—to max out their time here:

Day 1: Get an early start, aiming to leave the motorway at Kendal by 10:30; drive along Windermere and through Ambleside.

11:30   Tour Dove Cottage and the Wordsworth Museum.

13:00   Backtrack to Ambleside, where a small road leads up and over the dramatic Kirkstone Pass (far more scenic northbound than southbound—get out and bite the wind) and down to Glenridding on Lake Ullswater.

15:00   Catch the Ullswater boat and ride to Howtown. Hike six miles (3–4 hours, roughly 15:30–19:00) from Howtown back to Glenridding.

19:00   Drive to your Keswick hotel or farmhouse B&B near Keswick, with a stop as the sun sets at Castlerigg Stone Circle.

Day 2: Spend the morning (3-4 hours) splicing the Catbells high-ridge hike into a circular boat trip around Derwentwater. In the afternoon, make the circular drive from Keswick through the Newlands Valley, Buttermere, Honister Pass, and Borrowdale. You could pitch-and-putt nine holes in Keswick before a late dinner.

Getting Around the Lake District
With a Car

Nothing is very far from Keswick and Derwentwater. Pick up a good map (any hotel can loan you one), get off the big roads, and

The Lake District

SEE DETAIL MAPS

5 MILES
5 KM

TO GLASGOW & OBAN

COCKER-MOUTH

A-66

B-5292

BASSENTHWAITE LAKE

M-6

PENRITH

B-5289

KESWICK

A-66

CRUMMOCK WATER

NEWLANDS VALLEY

HAWES END

CASTLERIGG STONE CIRCLE

ULLS-WATER

POOLEY BRIDGE

BUTTER-MERE

CATBELLS HIKE

DERWENT-WATER

STRIDING EDGE WALK

HOWTOWN

HIGH BRANDELHOW

LODORE

GLENRIDDING

BUTTER-MERE (LAKE)

HONISTER PASS

BORROW-DALE

SEATOLLER

SEATHWAITE

HELVELLYN

THIRLMERE

PATTERDALE

A-591

A-592

N

DCH

HARD KNOTT PASS

TO RAVENGLASS

GRASMERE

DOVE COTTAGE

RYDAL

KIRKSTONE PASS

AMBLESIDE

BROCKHOLE

CONISTON

TARN HOWS

WINDERMERE

A-591

CONISTON-WATER

HAWKS-HEAD

HILL TOP FARM

BOWNESS

KENDAL

OXENHOLME

WINDERMERE LAKE

AQUARIUM

NEWBY BRIDGE

TO ULVERSTON

A-592

TO LONDON

LONDON

leave the car, at least occasionally, for some walking. In summer, the Keswick–Ambleside–Windermere–Bowness corridor (A591) suffers from congestion.

Keswick Motor Company rents cars in Keswick (from £32/ day with insurance, Mon–Sat 8:30–17:15, closed Sun, ages 25–70 only, must have an International Driving Permit and passport, Lake Road, a block from Moot Hall in town center, tel. 017687/72064).

Parking is tight throughout the region. It's easiest to just park in the pay-and-display lots (gather small coins, as most machines don't make change). If you're parking free on the roadside, don't block the vital turnouts. Never park on double yellow lines.

Without a Car

Those based in Keswick without a car manage fine. Because of the region's efforts to "green up" travel and cut down on car traffic, the bus service is quite efficient for your hiking and sightseeing. (You could even make a case for leaving your car in town and using the bus for many sightseeing and hiking agendas.)

By Bus: Keswick has no real bus station; buses stop at a turnout in front of the Booths Supermarket. Local buses take you quickly and easily (if not always frequently) to all nearby points of interest. Check the schedule carefully to make sure you can catch the last bus home. The exhaustive *Cumbria & Lakes Rider* bus brochure (50 pages, free, at TI or on any bus) explains the schedules. On board, you can purchase one-day Explorer passes (£10), or get one-day passes for certain routes. A four-day pass is available at the Keswick TI/National Park Visitors Centre. For bus and rail info, visit www.traveline.org.uk.

Buses **#X4** and **#X5** connect Penrith train station to Keswick (hourly Mon–Sat, 8/day Sun, 40 minutes, £5.50).

Bus **#77/#77A,** the Honister Rambler, makes the gorgeous circle from Keswick around Derwentwater, over Honister Pass, through Buttermere, and down the Whinlatter Valley (4/day clockwise, 4/day "anticlockwise," daily Easter–Oct, weekends only in Nov, 1.5-hour loop, £6.50 Honister Dayrider all-day pass).

Bus **#78,** the Borrowdale Rambler, goes topless in the summer, affording a wonderful sightseeing experience in and of itself, heading from Keswick to Lodore Hotel, Grange, Rosthwaite, and Seatoller at the base of Honister Pass (hourly, 2/hour mid-July–Aug, 8/day on Sun, 25 minutes each way, £5.75 Borrowdale Dayrider all-day pass).

Bus **#108** runs between Penrith and Glenridding, stopping in Pooley Bridge (daily 4–6/day, no Sun service Sept–Easter, 45 minutes, £14 Ullswater Bus & Boat day pass covers this bus route as well as steamers on Ullswater).

Bus **#208** runs between Keswick and Glenridding (5/day mid-July–Aug, Sat–Sun only late May–mid-July, 45 minutes).

Bus **#505,** the Coniston Rambler, connects Windermere with Hawkshead (daily Easter–Oct, hourly, 35 minutes).

Bus **#517,** the Kirkstone Rambler, runs between Windermere and Glenridding (3/day mid-July–Aug, Sat–Sun only Easter–mid-July, 1 hour).

Buses **#555** and **#556** connect Keswick with the south (hourly,

The Lake District at a Glance

North Lake District

In Keswick

▲▲**Theatre by the Lake** Top-notch theater a pleasant stroll from Keswick's main square. **Hours:** Shows at 20:00 in summer, usually 19:30 in spring and fall, 19:00 in winter; box office open from 9:30 until curtain time. See page 578.

▲**Derwentwater** Lake immediately south of Keswick, with good boat service and trails. See page 572.

▲**Pencil Museum** Peaen to graphite-filled wooden sticks. **Hours:** Daily 9:30–17:00. See page 570.

▲**Pitch-and-Putt Golf** Cheap, easygoing nine-hole course in Keswick's Hope Park. **Hours:** Daily from 9:30, last start at 19:45 or dusk, may close Nov–Easter. See page 571.

Bond Museum Vehicles and more from *007* films. **Hours:** Daily 10:00–17:00, closed roughly Jan–Easter. See page 571.

Near Keswick

▲▲▲ **Scenic Circle Drive South of Keswick** Hour-long drive through the best of the Lake District's scenery, with plenty of fun stops (including the fascinating Honister Slate Mine) and short side-trip options. See page 576.

▲▲**Castlerigg Stone Circle** Evocative and extremely old (even by British standards) ring of Neolithic stones. **Hours:** Always viewable. See page 571.

▲▲**Catbells High Ridge Hike** Two-hour hike along dramatic ridge southwest of Keswick. See page 572.

▲▲**Buttermere Hike** Four-mile, low-impact lakeside loop in a gorgeous setting. See page 574.

▲▲**More Hikes from Keswick** Scenic hikes with varying degrees of difficulty: Latrigg Peak, Latrigg Trail, Walla Crag. See page 575.

▲▲**Ullswater Hike and Boat Ride** Long lake best enjoyed via steamer boat and seven-mile walk. **Hours:** Boats run June–Aug daily 9/day, April–May and Sept 6/day, fewer off-season. See page 587.

South Lake District

William Wordsworth Sights

▲▲**Dove Cottage and Wordsworth Museum** The poet's humble home, with a museum that tells the story of his remarkable life. **Hours:** Feb–Dec daily 9:30–17:30, closed Jan. See page 590.

Rydal Mount Wordsworth's later, more upscale home. **Hours:** March–Oct daily 9:30–17:00; Nov–Dec and Feb Wed–Sun 11:00–16:00, closed Mon–Tue; closed Jan. See page 592.

Beatrix Potter Sights

▲▲**Beatrix Potter Gallery** Collection of artwork by and background on the creator of Peter Rabbit. **Hours:** April–Oct Sat–Thu 10:30–16:30, mid-Feb–March Sat–Thu 11:00–15:30, closed Fri and Nov–mid-Feb. See page 593.

Hill Top Farm Potter's painstakingly preserved cottage. **Hours:** April–Oct Sat–Thu 10:30–16:30, mid-Feb–March Sat–Thu 11:00–15:30, closed Fri and Nov–mid-Feb, often a long wait to visit—call ahead. See page 593.

The World of Beatrix Potter Touristy exhibition about the author. **Hours:** Daily Easter–Sept 10:00–18:00, Oct–Easter 10:00–17:00. See page 594.

Other Sights

▲**Brockhole National Park Visitors Centre** Best place to gather info on Lake Windermere and the surrounding area, grandly situated in a lakeside mansion. **Hours:** Daily April–Oct 10:00–17:00, Nov–March 10:00–16:00. See page 595.

1 hour to Windermere).

Bus #599, the open-top Lakes Rider, runs along the main Windermere corridor, connecting the big tourist attractions in the south (3/hour daily Easter–Aug, 50 minutes each way, £6.50 Central Lakes Dayrider all-day pass, route: Grasmere and Dove Cottage–Rydal Mount–Ambleside–Brockhole–Windermere–Bowness Pier).

By Bike: Several shops in Keswick rent road bikes and mountain bikes. Bikes come with helmets, touring maps, and advice for good trips. Keswick works well as a springboard for several fine days out on a bike; consider a three-hour trip up Newlands Valley and the Latrigg loop up a former train track (now a biking path), and back via Castlerigg Stone Circle.

Good places to rent bikes in Keswick include **Whinlatter Bikes** (£12/half-day, £15/day, daily 10:00–17:00, 82 Main Street, tel. 017687/73940) and **Keswick Mountain Bikes** (£15–20/day depending on model, Mon–Sat 9:00–17:30, Sun 10:00–17:30; right off the town square, at the recommended Lakeland Pedlar Restaurant; tel. 017687/75202, www.keswickbikes.co.uk).

By Boat: A circular boat service glides you around Derwentwater, with several hiker-aiding stops along the way (for a cruise/hike option, see "Derwentwater Lakeside Walk," page 572).

By Foot: Hiking information is available everywhere. Don't hike without a good, detailed map (wide selection at Keswick TI and at the many outdoor gear stores, or borrow one from your B&B). Helpful fliers at TIs and B&Bs describe the most popular routes. For an up-to-date weather report, ask at TI or call 0844-846-2444. Wear suitable clothing and footwear (you can rent boots in town; B&Bs can often loan you a good coat if weather looks threatening). Plan for rain. Watch your footing. Injuries are common. And every year, several people die while hiking in the area (some from overexertion; others are blown off ridges).

By Tour: For organized bus tours that run the roads of the Lake District, see "Tours in Keswick," later.

Keswick and the North Lake District

As far as touristy Lake District towns go, Keswick (KEZ-ick, population 5,000) is far more enjoyable than Windermere, Bowness, or Ambleside.

Many of the place names around Keswick have Norse origins, inherited from the region's 10th-century settlers. An important mining center for slate, copper, and lead through the Middle Ages, Keswick became a resort in the 19th century. Its fine Victorian buildings recall those Romantic days when city slickers first learned about "communing with nature." Today, the compact town is lined with tearooms, pubs, gift shops, and hiking-gear shops. The lake called Derwentwater is a pleasant 10-minute walk from the town center.

Orientation to Keswick

(area code: 017687)

Keswick is an ideal home base, with plenty of good B&Bs, an easy bus connection to the nearest train station at Penrith, and a prime location near the best lake in the area, Derwentwater. In Keswick, everything is within a 10-minute walk of everything else: the pedestrian town square, the TI, recommended B&Bs, grocery stores, the wonderful municipal pitch-and-putt golf course, the main bus stop, a lakeside boat dock, the post office (with Internet access upstairs), and a central parking lot. Thursdays and Saturdays are market days in the town square, but the square is lively every day throughout the summer.

Keswick town is a delight for wandering. Its centerpiece, Moot Hall (meaning "meeting hall"), was a 16th-century copper warehouse upstairs with an arcade below (closed after World War II). "Keswick" means "cheese farm"—a legacy from the time when the town square was the spot to sell cheese. When the town square went pedestrians-only a few years back, locals were all abuzz about people tripping over the curbs. (The English, seemingly thrilled by ever-present danger, are endlessly warning

THE LAKE DISTRICT

Keswick

TO NEWLANDS VALLEY B&B's

1 Stanger Street B&Bs
2 Howe Keld & Parkfield Guest House
3 Hazeldene Hotel
4 Burleigh Mead B&B;
   Brundholme Guest House
5 Keswick Youth Hostel
6 To Derwentwater Hostel
7 The Dog and Gun
8 To The Pheasant
9 Star of Siam
10 Abraham's Tea Room
11 The Lakeland Pedlar &
    Keswick Mountain Bikes
12 Bryson's Bakery & Tea Room
13 Good Taste Café
14 Maysons Restaurant
15 Supermarket
16 The Oddfellows Arms
17 Post Office & Internet Café
18 Launderette, Grocery &
    Whinlatter Bikes
19 Theatre by the Lake
20 Keswick Launch Cruises
21 Keswick Motor Co.
22 Cricket Pitch
23 Lawn Bowling, Tennis,
    Putting Green
24 Photo Fun with Sheep

RIVER GRETA

CAMPING

CROWN HIGH

P PARKING

PEDESTRIAN ZONE

TO NICHOL END PIER

DERWENTWATER

TO ASHNESS GATE PIER

DCH

visitors to "watch your head," "duck or grouse," "watch the step," and "mind the gap.")

Keswick and the Lake District are popular with English holiday-makers who prefer to bring their dogs with them on vacation. The town square in Keswick can look like the Westminster Dog Show, and the recommended Dog and Gun pub, where "well-behaved dogs are welcomed," is always full of patient pups. If you are shy about connecting with people, pal up to an English pooch—you will often find they are happy to introduce you to their owners.

Tourist Information

The National Park Visitors Centre is in Moot Hall, right in the middle of the town square (daily Easter–Oct 9:30–17:30, Nov–Easter 9:30–16:30, tel. 017687/72645, www.lake-district.gov.uk and www.keswick.org). Staffers are pros at advising you about hiking routes. They'll also help you figure out public transportation to outlying sights, and book rooms (you'll pay a £4 booking fee; it's cheaper to call B&Bs direct).

The TI sells theater tickets, Keswick Launch tickets (at a £1 discount), fishing licenses, and brochures and maps that outline nearby hikes (£0.60–1.80, including a very simple and driver-friendly £1.70 *Lap Map* featuring sights, walks, and a mileage chart). The TI also has books and maps for hikers, cyclists, and drivers (more books are sold at shops all over town).

Check the "What's On Locally" boards (inside the TI's foyer) for information about walks, talks, and entertainment. The daily weather forecast is posted just outside the front door (weather tel. 0844-846-2444). For information about the TI's guided walks, see "Tours in Keswick," later.

Helpful Hints

Book in Advance: Keswick hosts a variety of festivals and conventions, especially during the summer, so it's smart to book ahead. Please honor your bookings—the B&B proprietors here lose out on much-needed business if you don't show up.

A sampling of events for 2011: The Keswick Jazz Festival mellows out the town in mid-May, followed immediately by the Mountain Festival, then a beer festival in early June (June 3–4 in 2011). The Keswick Religious Convention packs the town with 4,000 evangelical Christians the last three weeks in July.

Several Bank Holiday Mondays in spring and summer (May 2, May 30, and Aug 29 in 2011) draw vacationers from all over the island for three-day weekends.

If you have trouble finding a room (or a B&B that accepts

small children), try www.keswick.org to search for available rooms.

Internet Access: U-Compute, located above the store that contains the post office, provides Internet access in a pleasant and airy perch (£2/30 minutes, £3/hour, unused time valid for 2 weeks, daily May–mid-Sept 8:30–21:00, mid-Sept–April 9:00–17:30, 16 terminals and Wi-Fi—same price, corner of Main and Bank streets, tel. 017687/75127). The **launderette** listed next also has Wi-Fi (£2/hour).

Laundry: It's around the corner from the bus station on Main Street, next to the Co-op grocery (self-service Mon–Fri 8:00–19:00, Sat–Sun 9:00–18:00, £6/load wash and dry, change machine and coin-op soap dispenser; full-service for a reasonable £1.20 service charge extra; tea and Wi-Fi for £2, tel. 017687/75448).

Midges: Tiny biting insects might bug you from late May through September, particularly at dawn and dusk, but insect repellant fends them off.

Tours in Keswick

Guided Walks—Walks of varying levels of difficulty depart from the TI several times a week at 10:00. They're led by local guides, leave regardless of the weather, and sometimes incorporate a bus ride into the outing (£12, Easter–Oct, no tours during religious convention in July, wear suitable clothing and footwear, bring lunch and water, return by 17:00, tel. 017687/72645, www.keswick rambles.org.uk). TIs throughout the region also offer free walks led by "Voluntary Rangers" (generally from Keswick on Sun and Wed in summer, ask for the *Events Guide*).

Bus Tours—These are great for people with bucks who'd like to wring maximum experience out of their limited time and see the area without lots of hiking or messing with public transport. For a cheaper alternative, take public buses.

Mountain Goat Tours is the region's dominant tour company. Unfortunately, they run their minibus tours out of Windermere, with pick-ups in Ambleside and Grasmere, but not Keswick—adding about an extra hour of driving, round-trip, for those based in Keswick (£25/half-day, £35/day, year-round if there are sufficient sign-ups, minimum 4 to a maximum of 16 per hearty bus, book in advance by calling 015394/45161, www.mountain -goat.com).

Show Me Cumbria Private Tours runs personalized tours all around the area, and can pick you up in Keswick. They charge per tour, not per person (for 1–5 people), so their tours are a fine value for small groups (£35/first hour, £25/hour after that, tel.

01768/866-880, mobile 0780-902-6357, based in Penrith, www
.showmecumbria.co.uk, andy@showmecumbria.co.uk).

Sights in Keswick

▲Derwentwater—One of Cumbria's most photographed and popular lakes, Derwentwater has four islands, good circular boat service, and plenty of trails. The pleas-
ant town of Keswick is a short stroll from the shore, near the lake's north end. The roadside views aren't much, and while you can walk around the lake (fine trail, floods in heavy rains, 9 miles, 4 hours), much of the walk is boring. You're better off mixing a hike and boat ride (see "Hikes and Drives in the North Lake District," later), or

simply enjoy the circular boat tour of the lake (described next).

Boating on Derwentwater: Keswick Launch runs two **cruises** an hour, alternating clockwise and "anticlockwise" (departing on the half-hour, daily 10:00–16:30, July–Aug until 17:30, in winter 5/day weekends only, at end of Lake Road, tel. 017687/72263, www.keswick-launch.co.uk). Boats make seven stops on each one-hour round-trip. The boat trip costs £9 per circle (£1 less if you book through TI) with free stopovers, or about £2 per segment. Stand on the pier Gilligan-style, or the boat may not stop. Keswick Launch also rents **rowboats** for two (£8/30 minutes, £12/hour).

Keswick Launch's **evening cruise** is a delightful little trip that comes with a glass of wine and a mid-lake stop for a short commentary (£9.50, £21 family ticket, 1 hour, mid-July–Aug at 19:30 every evening—weather permitting and if enough people show up; 6 is the minimum). You're welcome to bring a picnic dinner and munch scenically as you cruise.

▲Pencil Museum—Graphite was first discovered centuries ago in Keswick. A hunk of the stuff proved great for marking sheep in the 15th century. In 1832, the first crude Keswick pencil factory opened, and the rest is history (which is what you'll learn about here). While you can't actually tour the 150-year-old factory where the famous Derwent pencils were made, you can enjoy the smell of thousands of pencils getting sharpened for the first time. The adjacent charming and kid-friendly museum is a good way to pass a rainy hour; you may even catch an artist's demonstration. Take a look at the "war pencils" made for WWII bomber crews (filled with tiny maps and compasses) and relax for 10 minutes watching *The Humble Pencil* video in the theater, followed by a sleepy animated-snowman short (£3.50, daily 9:30–17:00, last entry at

16:00, humble café on-site, 3-minute walk from the town center, signposted off Main Street, tel. 017687/73626, www.pencil museum.co.uk).

Bond Museum—Next door to the Pencil Museum, and dedicated to all things Bond...James Bond, this museum features an impressive collection of cars from each movie, from *Dr. No*'s dragon tank to *Quantum of Solace*'s Aston Martin DBS V12. For many, it's more exciting than pencils (£6, open "007 days a week" 10:00–17:00, closed roughly Jan–Easter, tel.—what else?—01768/775-007).

Fitz Park—An inviting, grassy park stretches alongside Keswick's tree-lined, duck-filled River Greta. There's plenty of room for kids to burn off energy. Consider an after-dinner stroll on the footpath. You may catch men in white (or frisky schoolboys in uniform) playing a game of cricket. There's the serious bowling green (where you're welcome to watch the experts play, and enjoy the cheapest cuppa—i.e., tea—in town), and the public one where tourists are welcome to give lawn bowling a go (£3). You can try tennis on a grass court (£7/hour for 2 people, includes rackets) or enjoy the putting green (£2). Find the rental pavilion across the road from the art gallery (open daily 9:30–19:45 or until dusk).

▲**Golf**—A lush nine-hole pitch-and-putt golf course near the gardens in Hope Park separates the town from the lake and offers a classy, cheap, and convenient chance to golf near the birthplace of the sport. This is a great, fun, and inexpensive experience—just right after a day of touring and before dinner (£3.70 for 9 holes, £2.20 for putting, £2.50 for 18 tame holes of "obstacle golf," daily from 9:30, last round starts at 19:45 or dusk, may close Nov–Easter, tel. 017687/73445).

Swimming—While the Leisure Centre doesn't have a serious adult pool, it does have an indoor pool kids love, with a huge waterslide and wave machine (pool-£4.75, kids-£3.75, family-£14, Mon–Tue 11:00–15:00, Wed 11:00–16:00, Thu 11:00–18:00, Fri 11:00–17:00, Sat–Sun 10:00–17:00, shorter hours off-season, longer during school break, no towels or suits for rent, lockers-£1 deposit, 10-minute walk from town center, follow Station Road past Fitz Park and veer left, tel. 017687/72760).

Near Keswick

▲▲**Castlerigg Stone Circle**—For some reason, 70 percent of England's stone circles are here in Cumbria. Castlerigg is one of the best and oldest in Britain, and an easy stop for drivers. The circle—90 feet across and 5,000 years old—has 38 stones mysteriously laid out on a line between the two tallest peaks on the horizon. They served as a celestial calendar for ritual celebrations. Imagine the ambience here, as ancient people filled this clearing in spring to celebrate fertility, in late summer to commemorate the harvest, and in the winter to celebrate the winter solstice and the coming renewal of light. Festival dates were dictated by how the sun rose and set in relation to the stones. The more that modern academics study this circle, the more meaning they find in the placement of the stones. The two front stones face due north, toward a cut in the

mountains. The rare-for-stone-circles "sanctuary" lines up with its center stone to mark where the sun rises on May Day. (Party!) For maximum "goose pimples" (as they say here), show up at sunset (free, open all the time, 3 miles east of Keswick—follow brown signs, 3 minutes off A66, easy parking).

Hikes and Drives in the North Lake District

From Keswick

Derwentwater Lakeside Walk—There's a trail all along Derwentwater, but much of it (especially the Keswick-to-Hawes End stretch) is not that interesting. The best hour-long section is the 1.5-mile path between the docks at High Brandelhow and Hawes End in Keswick, where you'll stroll a level trail through peaceful trees. This walk works best in conjunction with the lake boat (see "Boating on Derwentwater," earlier).

▲▲Catbells High Ridge Hike—For a great "king of the mountain" feeling, 360-degree views, and a close-up look at the weather

blowing over the ridge, hike above Derwentwater about two hours from Hawes End up along the ridge to Catbells (1,480 feet) and down to High Brandelhow. From there, you can catch the boat back to Keswick, or take the easy path along the shore of Derwentwater to your Hawes End starting point. (Extending the hike farther around the lake to Lodore takes you to a waterfall, rock climbers, a fine café, and another boat dock for a convenient return to Keswick—see "Car Hiking: A Scenic Circle Drive South of Keswick," later.)

Catbells is probably the most dramatic family walk in the area (but wear sturdy shoes, bring a raincoat, and watch your footing). From Keswick, the lake, or your farmhouse B&B, you can see

Derwentwater & Newlands Valley

TO COCKERMOUTH

B-5292

B 77

WHIN-LATTER PASS

BRAITHWAITE

KESWICK

TO PENRITH VIA B X-4 & X-5

LATRIGG PEAK

A-66

B 77 & 78

CASTLERIGG STONE CIRCLE

DERWENT-WATER

NEWLANDS VALLEY

STAIR

SKEL-GILL

LITTLE TOWN

NEWLANDS PASS

TO BUTTER-MERE

CATBELLS RIDGE HIKE

CAT GHYL

WALLA CRAG

ASHNESS BRIDGE

SURPRISE VIEW

TO GRASMERE, WINDERMERE & AMBLESIDE VIA B 555, 556 & 599

GRANGE

LODORE FALLS

WATENDLATH

BOWDER-STONE

TO BUTTERMERE & CRUMMOCK-WATER VIA B 77

HONISTER PASS

B-5289

SLATE MINE

SEATHWAITE

ROSTHWAITE

BORROWDALE

STONETHWAITE

SEATOLLER

B 79 (END POINT)

DCH

1 MILE

1 KM

THE LAKE DISTRICT

B 78 BUS ROUTES
— ROAD
═ SCENIC DRIVE
P PARKING

••• BOAT
--- PATH
▲ PEAK
■ POINT OF INTEREST

B&Bs
❶ Uzzicar Farm
❷ Ellas Crag Guest House
❸ Gill Brow Farm B&B
❹ Keskadale Farm B&B
❺ Ashness Farm

Derwentwater Piers
❻ Keswick Launch Pier
❼ Ashness Gate Pier
❽ Lodore Pier
❾ High Brandelhow Pier
❿ Low Brandelhow Pier
⓫ Hawes End Pier
⓬ Nichol End Pier

silhouetted figures hiking along this ridge.

Getting There: To reach the trailhead from Keswick, catch the "anticlockwise" boat (see "Boating on Derwentwater," earlier) and ride for 10 minutes to the second stop, Hawes End. (You can also ride to High Brandelhow and take this walk in the other direction, but I don't recommend it—two rocky scrambles along the way are easier, and safer, to navigate going uphill from Hawes End.) Note the schedule for your return boat ride, as boats generally run only hourly. Drivers can park free at Hawes End. The Keswick TI sells a *Catbells* brochure about the hike (£0.60).

The Route: The path is not signposted, but it's easy to follow, and you'll see plenty of other walkers. From Hawes End, walk away from the lake, through a kissing gate to the turn just before the car park. Then turn left and go up, up, up. After about 20 minutes, you'll hit the first of two short scrambles (where the trail vanishes into a cluster of steep rocks—the far-left route is easiest through this), which leads to a bluff. From the first little summit, and then along the ridge, you'll enjoy sweeping views of the lake on one side, and of Newlands Valley on the other. The bald peak in the distance is Catbells. Broken stones crunch under each step, wind buffets your ears, clouds prowl overhead, and the sheep baa comically. To anyone looking up from the distant farmhouse B&Bs, you are but a stick figure on the ridge. Just below the summit, the trail disintegrates into another short, steep, scramble. Your reward is just beyond: a magnificent hilltop perch. After Catbells summit, descend along the ridge to a saddle ahead. The ridge continues much higher, and while it may look like your only option, at its base a small, unmarked lane with comfortable steps leads left. Unless you're up for extending the hike (see "Longer Catbells Options," next), take this path down to the lake. To get to High Brandelhow Pier, take the first left fork you come across down through a forest to the lake. When you reach Abbot's Bay, go left through a swinging gate, following a lakeside trail around a gravelly bluff, to the idyllic High Brandelhow Pier, a peaceful place to wait for your boat back to Keswick. (You can pay your fare when you board.)

Longer Catbells Options: Catbells is just the first of a series of peaks all connected by a fine ridge trail. Hardier hikers continue up to nine miles along this same ridge, enjoying valley and lake views as they arc around the Newlands Valley toward (and even down to) Buttermere. After High Spy, you can descend an easy path into Newlands Valley. The ultimate, very full day-plan would be to take a bus to Buttermere, climb Robinson, and follow the ridge around to Catbells and back to Keswick.

▲▲**Buttermere Hike**—The ideal little lake with a lovely, circular four-mile stroll offers nonstop, no-sweat Lake District beauty. If you're not a hiker (but kind of wish you were), take this walk. If you're very short on time, at least stop here and get your shoes dirty.

Buttermere is connected with Borrowdale and Derwentwater by a great road that runs over rugged Honister Pass. Buses #77/#77A make a 1.5-hour round-trip loop between Keswick and Buttermere that includes a trip over this pass. The two-pub hamlet of Buttermere has a pay-and-display parking lot, but many drivers park free along the side of the road. You're welcome to leave your car at the Fish Hotel if you eat in their pub. There's also a pay parking lot at the Honister Pass end of the lake (at Gatesgarth Farm, £3). The Syke Farm in Buttermere is popular for its homemade ice cream (tel. 01768/770-277).

▲▲More Hikes from Keswick—The area is riddled with wonderful hikes. B&Bs all have good advice, but consider these as well:

Latrigg Peak: For the easiest mountain-climbing sensation around, take the short drive to the Latrigg Peak parking lot just north of Keswick, and hike 15 minutes to the top of the 1,200-foot-high hill, where you'll be rewarded with a commanding view of the town and lake. At the traffic circle just outside of Keswick, take the A591 Carlisle exit, then an immediate right (direction: Ormathwaite/Underscar). Take the next right, a hard right, at the *Skiddaw* sign, where a long, steep, one-lane road leads to the Latrigg car park at the end of the lane.

Latrigg Trail: Right from downtown Keswick, you can walk the seven-mile Latrigg trail, which includes a stretch along an old train track and the Castlerigg Stone Circle described earlier (pick up £0.60 map/guide from TI).

Walla Crag: From your Keswick B&B, a fine two-hour walk to Walla Crag offers great fell (mountain) walking and a ridge-walk experience without the necessity of a bus or car. Start by strolling along the lake to the Great Wood parking lot (or drive to this lot), and head up Cat Ghyl (where "fell runners"—trail-running enthusiasts—practice) to Walla Crag. You'll be treated to great panoramic views over Derwentwater and surrounding peaks. You can do a shorter version of this walk from the parking lot at Ashness Bridge.

▲▲▲Car Hiking: A Scenic Circle Drive South of Keswick—This hour-long drive, which includes Newlands Valley, Buttermere, Honister Pass, and Borrowdale, gives you the best scenery you'll find in the North Lake District. (To do a similar route without a car from Keswick, take loop bus #77/#77A.) Distances are short, roads are narrow and have turn-outs, and views are rewarding. Get a good map and ask your B&B host for advice.

From Keswick, leave town on Crosthwaite Road, then, at the roundabout, head west on Cockermouth Road (A66). Don't take the first Newlands Valley exit, but do take the second one (through Braithwaite), and follow signs up the majestic **Newlands Valley.** If the place had a lake, it would be packed with tourists. But it doesn't—and it isn't.

The valley is dotted with 500-year-old family-owned farms. Shearing day is reason to rush home from school. Sons get school out of the way ASAP, and follow their dads into the family business. Neighbor girls marry those sons and move in. Grandparents retire to the cottage next door. With the price of wool depressed, most of the wives supplement the family income by running B&Bs (virtually every farm in the valley rents rooms). The road has one lane, with turnouts for passing. From the Newlands Pass summit, notice the glacial-shaped wilds, once forested, now not.

From the parking lot at Newlands Pass, at the top of Newlands Valley, there's an easy hike to a little waterfall. There's also an easy one-mile hike up to **Knottrigg,** which probably offers more TPCB (thrills per calorie burned) than any walk in the region. If you don't have time for even a short hike, at least get out of the car and get a feel for the setting.

After Newlands Pass, descend to **Buttermere** (scenic lake, tiny hamlet with a pub and ice-cream store—see "Buttermere Hike," earlier), turn left, and climb over rugged **Honister Pass**—strewn with glacial debris, remnants from the old slate mines, and curious, shaggy Swaledale sheep (looking more like goats with their curly horns). The valleys you'll see are textbook examples of those carved out by glaciers. Look high on the hillsides for "hanging valleys"—small glacial-shaped scoops cut off by the huge flow of the biggest glacier, which swept down the main valley.

The **Honister Slate Mine,** England's last still-functioning slate mine, stands at the summit of Honister Pass. The youth hos-

tel next to it was originally built to house miners in the 1920s. The mine closed in 1986, but was recently purchased and reopened by flamboyant entrepreneur Mark Weir, who now offers worthwhile tours. (As you await your tour, you'll see a video featuring views from Weir's helicopter ride to

work.) You'll put on a hardhat, load onto a bus for a short climb, then hike into a shaft to learn about the region's slate industry. It's a long, stooped hike into the mountain, made interesting by the guide, and punctuated by the sound of your helmet scraping against low bits of the shaft. Standing deep in the mountain, surrounded by slate scrap and the beams of thirty headlamps fluttering around like fireflies, you'll learn of the hardships of miners' lives and how "green gold" is trendy once again, making the mine viable. Call ahead to confirm tour times and to book a spot (£10, 1.5-hour tour; departs daily at 10:30, 12:30, 14:00, and 15:30; Dec–Jan 12:30 tour only, tel. 017687/77230, www.honister.com). Even if you don't have time to take the tour, stop here for its slate-filled shop (café and nice WCs).

After stark and lonely Honister Pass, drop into sweet and homey **Borrowdale,** with a few lonely hamlets and fine hikes from Seathwaite. Circling back to Keswick past Borrowdale, B5289 takes you past a number of popular attractions: You can climb stairs to the top of the house-size **Bowder Stone** (signposted, a few minutes walk off the main road). Farther along, **Lodore Falls** is a short walk from the road (behind Lodore Hotel). **Shepherds Crag,** a cliff overlooking Lodore, was made famous by pioneer rock climbers. (Their descendants hang from little ridges on its face today.) This is serious climbing, with several fatalities a year.

For a great lunch, or tea and cakes, drop into the much-loved **High Lodore Farm Café,** where sheep farmer Martin is busy feeding hikers and day-trippers (Easter–Oct daily 9:00–17:00, closed Nov–Easter, short drive uphill from the main road and over a tiny bridge, tel. 017687/77221).

A hard right off B5289 (signposted *Ashness Bridge, Watendlath*) and a steep half-mile climb on a narrow lane takes you to the postcard-pretty **Ashness Packhorse Bridge** (a quintessential Lake District scene, parking lot just above on right). A half-mile farther up (parking lot on left, no sign), and you're startled by the "surprise view" of Derwentwater (great for a lakes photo op). Continuing from here, the road gets extremely narrow en route to the hamlet of **Watendlath,** which has a tiny lake and lazy farm animals.

Return to B5289, the Borrowdale Valley Road, and back to Keswick. If you have yet to see it, cap your drive with a short detour from Keswick to the Castlerigg Stone Circle (described earlier).

Nightlife in Keswick

▲▲Theatre by the Lake—Keswickians brag that they enjoy "London theater quality at Keswick prices." Their theater offers events year-round and a wonderful rotation of six plays through the summer (plays vary throughout the week, with music concerts on Sun). There are two stages: The main one seats 400, and the smaller "studio" theater seats 100 (and features edgier plays with rough language and nudity). Attending a play here is a fine opportunity to enjoy a classy night out (£10–23, box office open from 9:30 until curtain time, discounts for old and young, 20:00 shows in summer, usually at 19:30 in spring and fall, at 19:00 in winter, café, smart to book ahead, parking at the adjacent lot is free after 18:30, tel. 017687/74411; book by phone, at TI, or online: www .theatrebythelake.com).

▲▲Evening Activities—For a small and remote town, Keswick has lots going on in the evening. Remember, at this latitude it's light until 22:00 in midsummer. Along with the Theatre by the Lake (described above), you can **golf** (fine course, pitch-and-putt, goofy golf, or just enjoy the putting green, last start at 19:45) or **walk** among the grazing sheep in Hope Park as the sun gets ready to set (between the lake and the golf course, access from just above the beach, great photo ops on balmy evenings).

To socialize with locals, head to a pub for one of their special evenings: There's **quiz night** at The Dog and Gun (21:30 on most Thu; £1, proceeds go to Keswick's Mountain Rescue team, which rescues hikers and the occasional sheep). At a quiz night, tourists are more than welcome. Drop in, say you want to join a team, and you're in. If you like trivia, it's a great way to get to know people here.

Also in the town center, The Oddfellows Arms has free **live music** most nights (usually classic rock, from 21:30).

You can join Bob, the **Town Crier,** when he does his routine many summer Tuesday evenings (£2.50, 1.5 hours, usually starts at 19:30, weekly late May–early July, details at TI). Catch a **movie** at the Alhambra Cinema, a restored old-fashioned movie theater a few minutes' walk from the town center. An **evening lake cruise** is perfect for an extremely scenic and relaxing picnic dinner (£10, with narration, mid-July–Aug at 18:30 and 19:30, 55 minutes).

Sleeping in Keswick

The Lake District abounds with attractive B&Bs, guest houses, and hostels. It needs them all when summer hordes threaten the serenity of this Romantic mecca.

Reserve your room in advance in high season. From October through April, you should have no trouble finding a room. But to get a particular place (especially on Saturdays), call ahead. If you're using public transportation, you should sleep in Keswick. If you're driving, staying outside Keswick is your best chance for a remote farmhouse experience. Lakeland hostels offer £20 beds and come with an interesting crowd of all ages.

For Keswick, I've featured B&Bs and small hotels on two streets, each within three blocks of the bus station and town square. Stanger Street, a bit humbler but quiet and handy, has smaller homes and more moderately priced rooms. "The Heads" is a classier area lined with proud Victorian houses, close to the lake and theater, overlooking a golf course.

Many of my Keswick listings charge extra for a one-night stay. Most won't book one-night stays on weekends (but if you show up and they have a bed free, it's yours) and don't welcome children under 12 (unless extremely well-behaved). Owners are enthusiastic about offering plenty of advice to get you on the right walking trail. Most accommodations have inviting lounges with libraries of books on the region and loaner maps. Take advantage of these

---

Sleep Code

(£1 = about $1.60, country code: 44, area code: 017687)
S = Single, **D** = Double/Twin, **T** = Triple, **Q** = Quad, **b** = bathroom, **s** = shower only. You can assume credit cards are accepted unless otherwise noted, and all B&B stays include breakfast.

To help you sort easily through these listings, I've divided the rooms into three categories based on the price for a double room with bath:

$$$ Higher Priced—Most rooms £75 or more.
$$ Moderately Priced—Most rooms between £30-75.
$ Lower Priced—Most rooms £30 or less.

Prices can change without notice; verify the hotel's current rates online or by email. For other updates, see www.ricksteves.com/update.

lounges to transform your humble B&B room into a suite.

This is still the countryside—expect huge breakfasts (often with a wide selection, including vegetarian options), no phones in the rooms, and shower systems that might need to be switched on to get hot water. Parking is pretty easy (each place has a line on parking).

On Stanger Street

This street, quiet but just a block from Keswick's town center, is lined with B&Bs situated in Victorian slate townhouses. Each of these places is small, family-run, and accepts cash only. They are all good, offering comfortably sized rooms and a friendly welcome.

$$ Dunsford Guest House rents four rooms decorated with a Victorian feel, at a good price. Stained glass and wooden pews give the blue-and-cream breakfast room a country-chapel vibe (Db-£66, this price promised with this book in 2011, no children under age 16, free Wi-Fi, parking, 16 Stanger Street, tel. 017687/75059, www.dunsford.net, enquiries@dunsford.net, accommodating Richard and Linda).

$$ Heckberry House's two light, airy rooms are both on the first floor (Db-£64, 2-night minimum, no children, will pick up from bus station, 12 Stanger Street, tel. 017687/71277, www.heckberry.co.uk, enquiries@heckberry.co.uk, friendly Judith and David).

$$ Badgers Wood B&B, at the top of the street, has six modern, bright, un-frilly view rooms, each named after a different tree (Sb-£38, Db-£70, 2-night minimum, no children under age 12, special diets accommodated, Wi-Fi, 30 Stanger Street, tel. 017687/72621, www.badgers-wood.co.uk, enquiries@badgers-wood.co.uk, Andrew and Anne).

$$ Abacourt House, with a daisy-fresh breakfast room, has five pleasant doubles (Db-£68, no children, Wi-Fi, 26 Stanger Street, tel. 017687/72967, www.abacourt.co.uk, abacourt.keswick@btinternet.com, John and Heather).

On The Heads

These B&Bs are in an area known as The Heads. This area is classier, with bigger and grander Victorian architecture and great views overlooking the pitch-and-putt range and out into the hilly distance. The golf-course side of The Heads has free parking, if you can snare a spot (easy at night).

$$$ Howe Keld has the polished feel of a boutique hotel, but offers all the friendliness of a B&B. Its 14 contemporary-posh rooms are spacious and tastefully decked out in native woods and slate. It's warm, welcoming, and family-run, with one of the best breakfasts I've had anywhere in England (Sb-£45–50, standard Db-£80, superior Db-£95, cash preferred, 2 ground-floor rooms, family deals, free Wi-Fi, 017687/72417, www.howekeld .co.uk, david@howekeld.co.uk, run with care by David and Valerie Fisher).

$$$ Parkfield Guest House, thoughtfully run and decorated by John and Susan Berry, is a big Victorian house. Its seven bright and pastel rooms have fine views (Sb-£55, Db-£78 with this book through 2011, Db suite-£98, 2-night minimum, no children under age 16, Wi-Fi, off-street parking available, tel. 017687/72328, www .parkfield-keswick.co.uk, susanberryparkfield@hotmail.com).

$$$ Burleigh Mead B&B is a slate mansion from 1892 with wild carpeting. Gill (pronounced "Jill," short for Gillian) rents seven lovely rooms for a great value, and offers a friendly welcome, as well as a lounge and peaceful front-yard sitting area that's perfect for enjoying the view (Db-£75, cash only, tel. 017687/75935, www.burleighmead.co.uk, info@burleighmead.co.uk).

$$$ Hazeldene Hotel, on the corner of The Heads, rents 10 spacious rooms, many with commanding views (Db-£70–90, Tb-£105, £5 extra for one-night stay, free Wi-Fi, tel. 017687/72106, www.hazeldene-hotel.co.uk, Helen).

$$ Brundholme Guest House has three bright and comfy rooms, all with grand views—especially from the front side—and a friendly and welcoming atmosphere (Db-£68 in 2011, cash only, tel. 017687/73305, www.brundholme.co.uk, barbara@brundholme .co.uk, the Thompsons).

Hostels in and near Keswick

The Lake District's inexpensive hostels, mostly located in great old buildings, are handy sources of information and social fun. These two hostels—both part of the Youth Hostels Association (www .yha.org.uk)—are former hotels, offering Internet access, laundry machines, and three cheap meals daily; at these, non-members pay about £3 extra a night, or buy a £16 membership.

$ Keswick Youth Hostel, with 85 beds in a converted old mill that overlooks the river, has a great riverside balcony and plenty of handy facilities, including a big lounge and library. Travelers of all ages feel at home here, but book ahead—beds here can be hard to come by from July through September (£22/bed, mostly 3- to 6-bed rooms, includes sheets and breakfast, café, bar, laundry, center of town just off Station Road before river, tel. 017687/72484, keswick@yha.org.uk).

$ Derwentwater Hostel, in a 200-year-old mansion on the shore of Derwentwater, is two miles south of Keswick and has 88 beds (£20 beds in 4- to 22-bed rooms, family rooms, 23:00 curfew, follow B5289 from Keswick, look for sign 100 yards after Ashness exit, tel. 017687/77246, derwentwater@yha.org.uk).

West of Keswick, in the Newlands Valley

If you have a car, drive 10 minutes past Keswick down the majestic Newlands Valley (described earlier, under "Car Hiking: Scenic Circle Drive South of Keswick"). This valley is studded with 500-year-old farms that have been in the same family for centuries, and now rent rooms to supplement the family income. Each place offers easy parking, grand views, and perfect tranquility. The rooms are plainer and generally more dated than the B&Bs in town, and come with steep and gravelly roads, plenty of dogs, and an earthy charm. Traditionally, farmhouses lacked central heating, and while they are now heated, you can still request a hot-water bottle to warm up your bed.

Getting to the Newlands Valley: Leave Keswick via the roundabout at the end of Crosthwaite Road, and then head west on Cockermouth Road (A66). Take the second Newlands Valley exit through Braithwaite, and follow signs through Newlands Valley (drive toward Buttermere). All of my recommended B&Bs are on this road: Uzzicar Farm (under the shale field, which local kids love hiking up to glissade down), Ellas Crag Guest House, then Gill Brow Farm, and finally—the last house before the stark summit—Keskadale Farm (about four miles before Buttermere). The one-lane road has turnouts for passing. These are listed in geographical order, the first being a 10-minute drive from Keswick and the last being at the top of the valley (about a 15-minute drive from Keswick).

$$ Uzzicar Farm is a big, rustic place with a comfy B&B in a low-ceilinged, circa-1650 farmhouse—watch out for ducks. It's a particularly intimate and homey setting, where you'll feel like part of the family (S-£35, D or Db-£65, family deals, cash only, tel. 017687/78026, www.uzzicarfarm.co.uk, uzzicar@googlemail.com, Helen, David, and three daughters).

$$ Ellas Crag Guest House, with three rooms—each with a great view—is more of a comfortable stone house than a farm. This homey B&B offers a good mix of modern and traditional decor, including beautifully tiled bathrooms (Ss-£45, Sb-50, Ds-£60, Db-£64, these prices guaranteed with this book through 2011, cash only, 2-night minimum, local free-range meats and eggs for breakfast, sack lunches available, huge DVD library, laundry-£10, tel. 017687/78217, www.ellascrag.co.uk, info@ellascrag.co.uk, Jane and Ed Ma and their children).

$$ Gill Brow Farm is a rough-hewn, working farmhouse where Anne Wilson rents two simple but fine rooms (D or Db-£58, 10 percent discount with this book and 2-night stay in 2011, tel. 017687/78270, www.gillbrow-keswick.co.uk, wilson_gillbrow @hotmail.com).

$$ Keskadale Farm is another good farmhouse experience, with Ponderosa hospitality. One of the valley's oldest, the house—with two rooms to rent and a cozy lounge—is made from 500-year-old ship beams. This working farm is an authentic slice of Lake District life and is your chance to get to know lots of curly-horned sheep and the dogs who herd them. Now that her boys are old enough to help Dad in the fields, Margaret Harryman runs the B&B (Sb-£40, Db-£60–70, £2 extra for one-night stays, cash only, closed Dec–Feb, tel. 017687/78544, www.keskadalefarm.co.uk, info@keskadalefarm.co.uk). They also rent a two-bedroom apartment (£400/week).

Southwest of Keswick, in Buttermere

$$$ Bridge Hotel, just beyond Newlands Valley at Buttermere, offers 21 beautiful rooms—most of them quite spacious—and a classic Old World countryside-hotel experience. On Fridays and Saturdays, a £31 dinner is required (standard Db-£130, fancier rooms for more, free Wi-Fi in lobby, tel. 017687/70252, fax 017687/70215, www.bridge-hotel.com, enquiries@bridge-hotel .com). There are no shops within 10 miles—only peace and quiet a stone's throw from one of the region's most beautiful lakes. The hotel has a dark-wood pub/restaurant on the ground floor.

$ Buttermere Hostel, a quarter-mile south of Buttermere village on Honister Pass Road, has good food, 70 beds, family rooms, and a peacefully rural setting (£20 beds in 4- to 6-bed rooms, £2 cheaper mid-week, includes breakfast, inexpensive lunches and dinners, laundry, office open 8:30–10:00 & 17:00–22:30, 23:00 curfew, toll tel. 0845-371-9508, buttermere@yha.org.uk).

South of Keswick, near Borrowdale

$$$ Ashness Farm sits alone, ruling its valley high above Derwentwater. If you want to be immersed in farm sounds and lakeland beauty, this is the place. On this 750-acre working farm, now owned by the National Trust, people have raised sheep and cattle for centuries. Today Anne and her son are "tenant farmers" keeping this farm operating, and renting five rooms to boot (Db-£75–86, less for 2 nights, cozy lounge, eggs and sausage literally fresh off the farm for breakfast, just above Ashness Bridge, tel. 017687/77361, www.ashnessfarm.co.uk, inquiries@ashness farm.co.uk).

$$ Seatoller Farm B&B is a rustic 17th-century house in a five-building hamlet where Christine Simpson rents three rooms. The old windows are small, but the abundant flower boxes keep things bright (Db-£70, less for 2 or more nights, tel. 017687/77232, www.seatollerfarm.co.uk, info@seatollerfarm.co.uk).

$ Borrowdale Hostel, in secluded Borrowdale Valley just south of Rosthwaite, is a well-run place surrounded by many ways to immerse yourself in nature. The hostel serves cheap dinners, offers sack lunches, and keeps the pantry well-stocked (86 beds, £18–22 beds in 2- to 8-bed dorms, D-£44, £3 more for non-members, family rooms, pay Internet access and Wi-Fi, laundry machines, 3 cheap meals daily, 23:00 curfew, toll tel. 0845-371-9624, borrowdale@yha.org.uk). To reach this hostel from Keswick by bus, take #78, the "Borrowdale Rambler" (hourly, 2/hour mid-July–Aug, 8/day on Sun; last bus from Keswick at 17:40 most of year, at 18:00 mid-July–Aug).

Eating in Keswick

Keswick has a huge variety of eateries catering to its many visitors, but I've found nothing particularly enticing at the top end; the places listed here are just good, basic values. Most stop serving by 21:00.

The Dog and Gun serves good pub food, but mind your head, and tread carefully: Low ceilings and wooden beams loom overhead, while paws poke out from under tables below, as Keswick's canines wait patiently for their masters to finish their beer (£6–10 meals, daily 12:00–21:00, goulash, no chips and proud of it, 2 Lake Road, tel. 017687/73463).

The Pheasant is a walk outside town, but locals trek here regularly for the food. The menu offers Lake District pub standards (fish pie, Cumbrian sausage, guinea fowl), as well as more inventive choices. Check the walls for caricatures of pub regulars, sketched at these tables by a Keswick artist. While they have a small restaurant section, I much prefer eating in the bar (£9–13 meals, daily 12:00–14:00 & 18:00–21:00, Crosthwaite Road, tel. 017687/72219). From the town square, walk past the Pencil Museum, hang a right onto Crosthwaite Road, and walk 10 minutes. For a more scenic route, cross the river into Fitz Park, go left along the riverside path until it ends at the gate to Crosthwaite Road, turn right, and walk five minutes.

Star of Siam serves wonderful and authentic Thai dishes in a tasteful dining room (£8–10 plates, daily 12:00–14:30 & 17:30–22:30, 89 Main Street, tel. 017687/71444).

Abraham's Tea Room, popular with townspeople, is a fine value for lunch. It's tucked away on the first floor of the giant George Fisher outdoor store (£4–6 soups and sandwiches, Mon–Fri 10:00–17:00, Sat 9:30–17:00, Sun 10:30–16:30, on the corner where Lake Road turns right).

The Lakeland Pedlar, a wholesome, pleasant café (with a bike shop upstairs), serves freshly baked vegan and vegetarian fare, including soups, organic bread, and daily specials. Their interior is cute. Outside tables face a big parking lot (£8 meals, daily 9:00–

17:00, Thu–Sat until 21:00 in summer, Hendersons Yard, find the narrow walkway off Market Street between pink Johnson's sweet shop and The Golden Lion, tel. 017687/74492).

Bryson's Bakery and Tea Room has an enticing ground-floor bakery, with sandwiches and light lunches. The upstairs is a popular tearoom. Order lunch to go from the bakery, or for a few pence more, eat there, either sitting on stools or at a couple of sidewalk tables (£4–8 meals, Mon–Sat 8:30–17:30—tearoom opens at 9:30, Sun 9:30–17:00, 42 Main Street, tel. 017687/72257). Consider their £16 two-person Cumberland Cream Tea, which is like afternoon tea in London, but cheaper, and made with local products. Sandwiches, scones, and little cakes are served on a three-tiered platter with tea.

Good Taste has a small café space but a huge following, and is known for its fresh ingredients and its chef's expertise. Stop by for a light snack of homemade muffins and an espresso, or try a wild-boar burger (Mon–Sat 8:30–16:30, closed Sun, 19 Lake Road, tel. 017687/75973).

Maysons Restaurant, with Californian ambience, is fast and easy, with a buffet line of curry, Cajun, and vegetarian options. The food is cooked fresh on the premises, but it's nothing fancy: You point, and they dish up and microwave (£6–8 plates, cash only; April–Oct daily 11:30–20:45; Nov–March Mon–Thu 11:45–17:00, Fri–Sun 11:45–20:30; family-friendly, also take-out—great for evening cruise picnic, 33 Lake Road, tel. 017687/74104).

Picnic: The fine **Booths supermarket** is right where all the buses arrive (Mon–Sat 8:00–21:00, Sun 10:00–16:00, The Headlands). The recommended **Bryson's Bakery** does good sandwiches to go (described earlier). **The Keswickian,** on the town square, serves up old-fashioned fish-and-chips to go (daily 11:00–23:30, upstairs restaurant closes earlier). Just around the corner, **The Cornish Pasty** offers an enticing variety of fresh meat pies to go (£2–3 pies, daily 9:30–17:30 or until the pasties are all gone, across from The Dog and Gun on Borrowdale Road).

In the Newlands Valley

The farmhouse B&Bs of Newlands Valley don't serve dinner, so their guests have two good options: Go into Keswick, or take the lovely 10-minute drive to Buttermere for your evening meal at the **Fish Hotel Pub,** which has fine indoor and outdoor seating, but takes no reservations (£8–10 meals, daily 12:00–14:00 & 18:00–21:00, family-friendly, good fish and daily specials with fresh vegetables, tel. 017687/70253). The neighboring **Bridge Hotel Pub** is a bit cozier and serves "modern-day nibbles and good classic pub grub" (£10–12 meals, daily 12:00–21:30, tel. 017687/70252).

Keswick Connections

The nearest train station to Keswick is in Penrith (ticket window open Mon–Sat 5:30–21:00, Sun 11:30–21:00, no lockers). For train and bus info, check at a TI, visit www.traveline.org.uk, or call 0845-748-4950 (for train), or 0871-200-2233 (£0.10/minute). Most routes run less frequently on Sundays.

From Keswick by Bus: For connections, see page 561.

From Penrith by Bus to: Keswick (Mon–Sat roughly hourly 7:20–22:45, only 8/day on Sun, 40 minutes, £5.50, pay driver, Stagecoach buses #X4 and #X5), **Ullswater** and **Glenridding** (6/day, 45 minutes, bus #108). The Penrith bus stop is just outside the train station (bus schedules posted inside and outside station).

From Penrith by Train to: Blackpool (12/day, 1.75 hours, change in Preston), **Liverpool** (roughly hourly, 2 hours, change in Wigan or Preston), **Birmingham**'s New Street Station (roughly hourly, 2.5–3 hours, some with change in Preston), **Durham** (hourly, 2.5–3 hours, change in Carlisle and Newcastle), **York** (2/hour, 3.5–4 hours, 1–2 transfers), **London**'s Euston Station (9/day, 3–3.5 hours), **Edinburgh** (nearly hourly, 1.75 hours), **Glasgow** (10/day, 1.5–2 hours), **Oban** (2/day, morning train 5.75 hours, evening train 6.75 hours, both require changing stations in Glasgow, evening train requires additional change in Carlisle).

Route Tips for Drivers

Coming from (or Going to) the West: Only 1,300 feet above sea level, Hard Knott Pass is still a thriller, with a narrow, winding, steeply graded road. Just over the pass are the scant but evocative remains of the Hard Knott Roman fortress. The great views can come with miserable rainstorms, and it can be very slow and frustrating when the one-lane road with turnouts is clogged by traffic. Avoid it on summer weekends.

From Points South (such as Blackpool, Liverpool, or North Wales) to the Lake District: The direct, easy way to Keswick is to leave M6 at Penrith, and take the A66 highway for 16 miles to Keswick. For the scenic sightseeing drive through the south lakes to Keswick, exit M6 on A590/A591 through the towns of Kendal and Windermere to reach Brockhole National Park Visitors Centre. From Brockhole, the A road to Keswick is fastest, but the high road—the tiny road over Kirkstone Pass to Glenridding and lovely Ullswater—is much more dramatic.

Near Keswick: Ullswater

▲▲Ullswater Hike and Boat Ride

Long, narrow Ullswater, which some consider the loveliest lake in the area, offers eight miles of diverse and grand Lake District scenery. While you can drive it or cruise it, I'd ride the boat from the south tip halfway up (to Howtown—which is nothing more than a dock) and hike back. Or walk first, then enjoy an easy ride back. Old-fashioned "steamer" boats (actually diesel-powered) leave **Glenridding** regularly for Howtown (£5.50 one-way, £9 round-trip, covered by £14 Ullswater Bus & Boat day pass, family rates, June–Aug daily 9/day 9:45–16:45, April–May and Sept 6/day 9:45–15:50, fewer off-season, 35 minutes one-way, drivers can use safe pay-and-display parking lot—£2/2 hours, £4/12 hours; take bus #108 from Penrith, bus #208 from Keswick, or bus #517 from Windermere; café at dock, brochure shows walking route, tel. 017684/82229, www.ullswater-steamers.co.uk).

From Howtown, spend three to four hours hiking and dawdling along the well-marked path by the lake south to Patterdale, and then along the road back to Glenridding. This is a serious seven-mile walk with good views, varied terrain, and a few bridges and farms along the way. For a shorter hike from Howtown Pier, consider a three-mile loop around Hallin Fell. A rainy-day plan is to ride the covered boat up and down the lake to Howtown and back, or to Pooley Bridge at the northern tip of the lake (£12 round-trip, 2–5/day, 2 hours). Boats don't run in really bad weather—call ahead if it looks iffy.

Helvellyn

Considered by many the best high-mountain hike in the Lake District, this breathtaking round-trip route from Glenridding includes the spectacular Striding Edge—about a half-mile along the ridge. Be careful; do this six-hour hike only in good weather, since the wind can be fierce. While it's not the shortest route, the Glenridding ascent is best. Get advice from the Keswick TI, which has a helpful *Helvellyn from Glenridding* leaflet on the hike (£0.60).

South Lake District

The South Lake District has a cheesiness similar to other popular English resort destinations. Here, piles of low-end vacationers suffer through terrible traffic, slurp ice cream, and get candy floss caught in their hair. The area around Windermere is worth a drive-through if you're a fan of Wordsworth or Beatrix Potter, but you'll still want to spend the majority of your Lake District time (and book your accommodations) up north.

Getting Around

By Car: Driving is your best option to see the small towns and sights clustered in the South Lake District; consider combining your drive with the bus trip mentioned below. If you're coming to or leaving the South Lake District from the west, you could take the Hard Knott Pass for a scenic introduction to the area.

By Bus: Buses are a fine and stress-less way to lace together this gauntlet of sights in the congested Lake Windermere neighborhood. The open-top Lakes Rider bus #599 stops at Bowness Pier (lake cruises), Windermere (train station), Brockhole (National Park Visitors Centre), Ambleside, Rydal Mount, and Grasmere (Dove Cottage). Consider leaving your car at Grasmere and enjoying the breezy and extremely scenic ride, hopping off and on as you like (3/hour daily Easter–Aug, 50 minutes each way, Central Lakes Dayrider all-day pass–£6.50—buy from driver). Buses #555 and #556 run between Windermere and Keswick.

Sights in the South Lake District

Wordsworth Sights

William Wordsworth was one of the first writers to reject fast-paced city life. During England's Industrial Age, hearts were muzzled and brains ruled. Science was in, machines were taming nature, and factory hours were taming humans. In reaction to these brainy ideals, a rare few—dubbed Romantics—began to embrace untamed nature and undomesticated emotions.

Back then, nobody climbed a mountain just because it was there—but Wordsworth did. He'd "wander lonely as a cloud" through the countryside, finding inspiration in "plain living and high thinking." He soon attracted a circle of like-minded creative friends.

The emotional highs the Romantics felt weren't all natural. Wordsworth and his poet friends Samuel Taylor Coleridge and Thomas de Quincey got stoned on opium and wrote poetry, combining their generation's standard painkiller drug with their

Wordsworth at Dove Cottage

William Wordsworth (1770–1850) was a Lake District home-boy. Born in Cockermouth (in a house now open to the public), he was schooled in Hawkshead. In adulthood, he married a local girl, settled down in Grasmere and Ambleside, and was buried in Grasmere's St. Oswald's churchyard.

But the 30-year-old man who moved into Dove Cottage in 1799 was not the carefree lad who'd roamed the district's lakes and fields. At Cambridge University, he'd been a C student, graduating with no job skills and no interest in a nine-to-five career. Instead, he and a buddy hiked through Europe, where Wordsworth had an epiphany of the "sublime" atop Switzerland's Alps. He lived a year in France, watching the Revolution rage. It stirred his soul. He fell in love with a Frenchwoman who bore his daughter, Caroline. But lack of money forced him to return to England, and the outbreak of war with France kept them apart.

Pining away in London, William hung out in the pubs and coffeehouses with fellow radicals, where he met poet Samuel Taylor Coleridge. They inspired each other to write, edited each other's work, and jointly published a groundbreaking book of poetry.

In 1799, his head buzzing with words and ideas, William and his sister (and soul mate) Dorothy moved into the white-washed, slate-tiled former inn now known as Dove Cottage. He came into a small inheritance, and dedicated himself to poetry full time. In 1802, with the war over, William returned to France to finally meet his daughter. (He wrote of the rich experience: "It is a beauteous evening, calm and free.../Dear child! Dear Girl! that walkest with me here,/If thou appear untouched by solemn thought,/Thy nature is not therefore less divine.")

Having achieved closure, Wordsworth returned home to marry a former kindergarten classmate, Mary. She moved into Dove Cottage, along with an initially jealous Dorothy. Three of their five children were born here, and the cottage was also home to Mary's sister, the family dog Pepper (a gift from Sir Walter Scott; see Pepper's portrait), and frequent houseguests who bedded down in the pantry: Scott, Coleridge, and Thomas de Quincey, the Timothy Leary of opium.

After almost nine years here, Wordsworth's family and social status had outgrown the humble cottage. They moved first to a house in Grasmere before settling down in Rydal Hall. Wordsworth was changing. After the Dove years, he would write less, settle into a regular government job, quarrel with Coleridge, drift to the right politically, and endure criticism from old friends who branded him a sellout. Still, his poetry—most of it written at Dove—became increasingly famous, and he died honored as England's Poet Laureate.

South Lake District

tree-hugging passions. Today, opium is out of vogue, but the Romantic movement thrives as visitors continue to inundate the region.

▲▲Dove Cottage and Wordsworth Museum—For poets, this two-part visit is the top sight of the Lake District. Take a short tour of William Wordsworth's humble cottage and be inspired in its excellent museum, which displays original writings, sketches, personal items, and fine paintings.

The poet whose appreciation of nature and a back-to-basics lifestyle put this area on the map spent his most productive years (1799–1808) in this well-preserved stone cottage on the edge of Grasmere. After functioning as the Dove and Olive Bow pub for almost 200 years, it was bought by

Wordsworth's Poetry at Dove

At Dove Cottage, Wordsworth was immersed in the beauty of nature and the simple joy of his young, growing family. It was here that he reflected on both his idyllic childhood and his troubled twenties. The following are select lines from two well-known poems from this fertile time.

Ode: Intimations of Immortality

There was a time when meadow, grove, and stream,
The earth, and every common sight, to me did seem
Apparelled in celestial light, the glory and the freshness
    of a dream.
It is not now as it hath been of yore; turn wheresoe'er I
    may, by night or day,
The things which I have seen I now can see no more.
Now while the birds thus sing a joyous song...
To me alone there came a thought of grief...
Whither is fled the visionary gleam?
Where is it now, the glory and the dream?
Our birth is but a sleep and a forgetting:
The Soul...cometh from afar...
Trailing clouds of glory do we come
From God, who is our home.

I Wandered Lonely as a Cloud

I wandered lonely as a cloud
That floats on high o'er vales and hills,
When all at once I saw a crowd,
A host, of golden daffodils;
Beside the lake, beneath the trees,
Fluttering and dancing in the breeze...
For oft, when on my couch I lie
In vacant or in pensive mood,
They flash upon that inward eye
Which is the bliss of solitude;
And then my heart with pleasure fills,
And dances with the daffodils.

his family. This is where Wordsworth got married, had kids, and wrote much of his best poetry. Still owned by the Wordsworth family, the furniture was his, and the place comes with some amazing artifacts, including the poet's passport and suitcase (he packed light). Even during his lifetime, Wordsworth was famous, and Dove Cottage was turned into a museum in 1891—predating even the National Trust, which protects the house today.

Even if you're not a fan, Wordsworth's appreciation of nature, his Romanticism, and the ways his friends unleashed their creative talents with such abandon are appealing. The 30-minute cottage **tour** (departures on the hour and half-hour) and adjoining **museum**—with lots of actual manuscripts handwritten by Wordsworth and his illustrious friends—are both excellent. In dry weather, the garden where the poet was much inspired is worth a wander. (Visit this after leaving the cottage tour, and pick up the description at the back door. The garden is closed when wet.) Allow 1.5 hours for this visit.

Cost and Hours: £7.50, daily Feb–Dec 9:30–17:30, last entry at 17:00, last tour at 16:50, closed Jan, bus #555 or #556 from Keswick, tel. 015394/35544, www.wordsworth.org.uk. Parking costs £5 in the Dove Cottage lot facing the main road (A591), 50 yards from the site (coins only; grants you £4 rebate on Dove Cottage ticket).

Poetry Readings: On Tuesday evenings in summer, the Wordsworth Trust puts on poetry readings, where national poets read their own works. They're hoping to continue the poetry tradition of the Lake District. Readings are held at the St. Oswald's Church in Grasmere Village (every other Tue at 18:45, runs May–mid-Oct only, two 45-minute sessions followed by an optional dinner, £7 at the door or £6 pre-booked, £15 pre-booked dinner, tel. 015394/35544).

Rydal Mount—Located just down the road from Dove Cottage, this sight is well worthwhile for Wordsworth fans. The poet's final,

higher-class home, with a lovely garden and view, lacks the humble charm of Dove Cottage, but still evokes the time and creative spirit of the literary giant who lived here for 37 years. His family repurchased it in 1969 (after a 100-year gap), and his great-great-great-granddaughter still calls it home on occasion, as shown by recent family photos sprinkled throughout the house.

After a short intro by the attendant, you'll be given an explanatory flier and are welcome to roam. Wander through the garden William himself designed, which has changed little since then. Surrounded by his nature, you can imagine the poet enjoying them with you. "O happy gardens! Whose seclusion deep, so friendly to industrious hours; and to soft slumbers, that did gently steep our spirits carry with them dreams of flowers, and wild notes warbled among leafy bowers."

Cost and Hours: £6; March–Oct daily 9:30–17:00; Nov–Dec and Feb Wed–Sun 11:00–16:00, closed Mon–Tue; closed Jan, 1.5 miles north of Ambleside, well-signed, free and easy parking, bus #555 or #556 from Keswick, tel. 015394/33002, www.rydalmount .co.uk.

Beatrix Potter Sights

Of the many Beatrix Potter commercial ventures in the Lake District, there are two serious Beatrix Potter sights: her farm (Hill Top Farm); and her husband's former office, which is now the Beatrix Potter Gallery, filled with her sketches and paintings. The sights are two miles apart, in or near Hawkshead, a 20-minute drive south of Ambleside. If you're coming over from Windermere, catch the cute little 15-car ferry (runs constantly except when it's extremely windy, 10-minute trip, £4 car fare includes all passengers). Note that both of the major sights are closed on Friday.

On busy summer days, the wait to get into Hill Top Farm can last several hours (only eight people are allowed in every five minutes, and the timed-entry tickets must be bought in person). If you like cutesy tourist towns (Hawkshead), this can be a blessing. Otherwise, you'll wish you were in the woods somewhere with Wordsworth.

Hill Top Farm—A hit with Beatrix Potter fans (and skippable for others), this dark and intimate cottage, swallowed up in the inspirational and rough nature around it, provides an enjoyable if quick experience. The six-room farm was left just as it was when she died in 1943. At her request, the house is set as if she had just stepped out—flowers on the tables, fire on, low lights. While there's no printed information here, room guides are eager to explain things.

Cost and Hours: £6.50, tickets often sell out by 14:00, April–Oct Sat–Thu 10:30–16:30, mid-Feb–March Sat–Thu 11:00–15:30, closed Fri and Nov–mid-Feb, last entry 30 minutes before closing, in Near Sawrey village, 2 miles south of Hawkshead, bus #505 or #525 from Hawkshead, Mountain Goat Tours' hourly shuttle bus from ferry dock, tel. 015394/36269, www.nationaltrust.org.uk/beatrixpotter. Drivers can park and buy tickets 150 yards down the road, and walk back to tour the place. Call the farm for the current wait times (if no one answers, leave a message for the administrator; someone will call you back).

▲▲**Beatrix Potter Gallery**—Located in the cute but extremely touristy town of Hawkshead, this gallery fills her husband's former law office with the wonderful and intimate drawings and watercolors that Potter did to illustrate her books. The best of the Potter sights, the gallery has plenty of explanation about her life and work. Even non-Potter fans find her art surprisingly interesting. Of about 700 works in the gallery's possession, a rotation of about 50 are shown at any one time. As you enter, pick up a page identifying each work of art—then you'll know (for example) that it's Mrs. Tittle Mouse meeting Bappity Bumble.

Cost and Hours: £4.50, tiny discount with Hill Top Farm, same hours as Hill Top Farm, bus #505 from Windermere, Main Street, drivers use the nearby pay-and-display lot and walk 200

THE LAKE DISTRICT

Beatrix Potter
(1866–1943)

As a girl growing up in London, Beatrix Potter vacationed in the Lake District, where she became inspired to write her popular children's books. Unable to get a publisher, she self-published the first two editions of *The Tale of Peter Rabbit* in 1901 and 1902. When she finally landed a publisher, sales of her books were phenomenal. With the money she made, she bought Hill Top Farm, a 17th-century cottage, and fixed it up, living there from 1905 until she married in 1913. Potter was more than a children's book writer; she was a fine artist, an avid gardener, and a successful farmer. She married a lawyer and put her knack for business to use, amassing a 4,000-acre estate. An early conservationist, she used the garden-cradled cottage as a place to study nature. She willed it—along with the rest of her vast estate—to the National Trust, which she enthusiastically supported. The events of Potter's life were dramatized in the 2007 movie *Miss Potter*, starring Renée Zellweger as Beatrix.

yards to the town center, tel. 015394/36355, www.nationaltrust.org.uk/beatrixpotter.

Hawkshead—The town of Hawkshead is engulfed in Potter tourism, and the extreme quaintness of it all is off-putting. Just across from the pay-and-display parking lot is the interesting Hawkshead Grammar School Museum, founded in 1585, where William Wordsworth studied from 1779 to 1787. It shows off old school benches and desks whittled with penknife graffiti (£2 includes guided tour; April–Sept Mon–Sat 10:00–13:00 & 14:00–17:00, Sun 13:00–17:00; Oct Mon–Sat 10:00–13:00 & 14:00–15:30, Sun 13:00–15:30; closed Nov–March; bus #505 from Windermere, tel. 015394/36735, www.hawksheadgrammar.org.uk).

The World of Beatrix Potter—This tour, a hit with children, is a gimmicky exhibit with all the historical value of a Disney ride. The 45-minute experience features a 5-minute video trip into the world of Mrs. Tiggywinkle and company, a series of Lake District tableaux starring the same imaginary gang, and an all-about-Beatrix section, with an 8-minute video biography (£7, kids-£3.50, daily Easter–Sept 10:00–18:00, Oct–Easter 10:00–17:00, last entry 30 minutes before closing, in Bowness near Windermere town, tel. 015394/88444, www.hop-skip-jump.com).

More Sights at Lake Windermere

▲Brockhole National Park Visitors Centre—Set in a nicely groomed lakeside park, the center offers a free 30-minute video on life in the Lake District (played upon request), an information desk, organized walks (see the park's free *Visitor Guide*), exhibits, a bookshop (excellent selection of maps and guidebooks), a cafeteria, gardens, nature walks, and a large parking lot. Check the events board as you enter (free entry but steep £3 parking fee—coins only, or buy ticket at the Visitors Centre 100 yards away from parking lot; daily April–Oct 10:00–17:00, Nov–March 10:00–16:00, bus #555 from Keswick, buses #505 and #599 from Windermere, tel. 015394/46601, www.lake-district.gov.uk). It's in a stately old lakeside mansion between Ambleside and Windermere on A591. For a joyride around famous Windermere, catch the Brockhole "Green" cruise (£7, hourly April–Oct, more sailings mid-July–Aug, 45-minute circle, scant narration).

Lakes Aquarium—This aquarium gives a glimpse of the natural history of Cumbria. Exhibits describe the local wildlife living in lake and coastal environments, including otters, eels, pike, sharks, and the "much maligned brown rat." Experts give various talks throughout the day (£9, kids under 15-£6, family deals, daily 9:00–18:00, until 17:00 in winter, last entry one hour before closing, in Lakeside, by Newby Bridge, at south end of Lake Windermere, tel. 015395/30153, www.lakesaquarium.co.uk).

Hayes Garden World—This extensive gardening center, a popular weekend excursion for locals, offers garden supplies, a bookstore, a playground, and gorgeous grounds. Gardeners could wander this place all afternoon. Upstairs is a fine cafeteria-style restaurant (Mon–Sat 9:00–18:00, Sun 11:00–17:00, at south end of Ambleside on main drag, see *Garden Centre* signs, located at north end of Lake Windermere, tel. 015394/33434, www.hayesgarden world.co.uk).

YORK

Historic York is loaded with world-class sights. Marvel at the York Minster, England's finest Gothic church. Ramble The Shambles, York's wonderfully preserved medieval quarter. Enjoy a walking tour led by an old Yorker. Hop a train at Europe's greatest railway museum, travel to the 1800s in the York Castle Museum, and head back a thousand years to Viking York at the Jorvik exhibit.

York has a rich history. In A.D. 71, it was Eboracum, a Roman provincial capital—the northernmost city in the empire. Constantine was actually proclaimed emperor here in A.D. 306. In the fifth century, as Rome was toppling, a Roman emperor sent a letter telling England it was on its own, and York became Eoforwic, the capital of the Anglo-Saxon kingdom of Northumbria.

A church was built here in 627, and the town became an early Christian center of learning. The Vikings later took the town, and from the 9th through the 11th centuries, it was a Danish trading center called Jorvik. The invading and conquering Normans destroyed then rebuilt the city, fortifying it with a castle and the walls you see today.

Medieval York, with 9,000 inhabitants, grew rich on the wool trade and became England's second city. Henry VIII used the city's fine Minster as his Anglican Church's northern capital. (In today's Anglican Church, the Archbishop of York is second only to the Archbishop of Canterbury.)

In the Industrial Age, York was the railway hub of northern England. When it was built, York's train station was the world's largest. Today, York's leading industry is tourism.

Planning Your Time

York is the best sightseeing city in England after London. On even a 10-day trip through England, it deserves two nights and a day. For the best 36 hours, follow this plan: Catch the 18:45 free city walking tour on the evening of your arrival (evening tours offered mid-June through Aug). The next morning, be at the Castle Museum when it opens (at 9:30)—it's worth a good two hours. Then browse and sightsee the rest of town. Train buffs love the National Railway Museum, and the Yorkshire Museum displays artifacts from throughout the region's history. Tour the Minster at 16:00 before catching the 17:15 evensong service (16:00 on Sun, usually none on Mon). Finish your day with an early-evening stroll along the wall (wall gates close at 20:00), and perhaps through the abbey gardens. This schedule assumes you're here in the summer (when the evening orientation walk is going) and that there's an evensong on. Confirm your plans with the TI.

Orientation to York

(area code: 01904)

York has about 190,000 people; about one in ten is a student. But despite the city's size, the sightseer's York is small. Virtually everything is within a few minutes' walk: sights, train station, TI, and B&Bs. The longest walk a visitor might take (from a B&B across the old town to the Castle Museum) is 30 minutes.

Bootham Bar, a gate in the medieval town wall, is the hub of your York visit. (In York, a "bar" is a gate and a "gate" is a street. Go ahead—blame the Vikings.) At Bootham Bar and on Exhibition Square, you'll find the starting points for most walking tours and bus tours, handy access to the medieval town wall, a public WC, and Bootham Street—which leads to the recommended B&Bs. To find your way around York, use the Minster's towers as a navigational landmark, or follow the strategically placed green signposts, which point out all places of interest to tourists.

Tourist Information

The **Museum Street** TI sells a £1 *York Map and Guide*. Ask for the free monthly *What's On* guide and the *York MiniGuide*, which includes a map and some discounts (April–Oct Mon–Sat 9:00–18:00, Sun 10:00–17:00; Nov–March Mon–Sat 9:00–17:00, Sun 10:00–16:00; 1 Museum Street, tel. 01904/550-099, www.visityork.org). The TI books rooms for a £4 fee. A screen lists "Today's Events in Town."

York and Yorkshire Pass: The TI sells an expensive pass that covers most York sights and a lot of other major sights in the region, and gives you discounts on the City Sightseeing hop-on, hop-off bus tours. You'd have to be a very busy sightseer to make this pass worth it—most will want to skip it (£28/1 day, £38/2 days, £44/3 days, £68/6 days, www.yorkshirepass.com).

Arrival in York

By Train: The train station is a 10-minute walk from town. Day-trippers can store baggage at the Europcar office on platform 1 (£5/24 hours, Mon–Sat 8:00–20:30, Sun 9:00–20:30). To walk downtown from the station, turn left down Station Road, and follow the crowd toward the Gothic towers of the Minster. After the bridge, a block before the Minster, you'll come upon the TI on your right. Recommended B&Bs are a 10-minute walk or a £5 taxi ride from the station—for specific walking directions to the B&Bs, see page 619.

By Car: As you near York (and your B&B), you'll hit the A1237 ring road. Follow this to the A19/Thirsk roundabout (next to river on northeast side of town). From the roundabout, follow signs for *York City,* traveling through Clifton into Bootham. All recommended B&Bs are four or five blocks before you hit the medieval city gate (see neighborhood map, page 620). If you're approaching York from the south, take M1 until it becomes A1M, exit at junction 45 onto A64, and follow it for 10 miles until you reach York's ring road (A1237), which allows you to avoid driving through the city center. If you have more time, A19 from Selby is a slower and more scenic route into York.

Helpful Hints

Festivals: Book a room well in advance during festival times, and on weekends any time of year. The **Viking Festival** features *lur* horn-blowing, warrior drills, and re-created battles in mid-February (www.jorvik-viking-centre.co.uk). The **Early Music Festival** (medieval minstrels, Renaissance dance, and so on) zings its strings in mid-July (July 8–16 in 2011, www.ncem.co.uk/yemf.shtml). York claims to be the "Ascot of the North," and the town fills up on horse-race weekends, especially during the **Ebor Races** in mid-August (once a month May–Oct, check schedules at www.yorkracecourse.co.uk). And the **York Festival of Food and Drink** takes a bite out of the last two weekends of September (www.yorkfoodfestival.com). For a complete list of festivals, see www.yorkfestivals.com.

Internet Access: Evil Eye Lounge has 10 terminals in a hip bar (Mon–Sat 10:00–23:00, Sun 11:00–23:00, upstairs at 42 Stonegate, tel. 01904/640-002). **The Basement Internet**

Café-Bar overlooks the river (£3/hour, daily 11:00–18:00, 9 terminals, lower level of City Screens Cinema, at 13 Coney Street, tel. 01904/612-940). The **York Public Library**'s reference desk, on the first floor up, provides Internet access to visitors (£1/hour, Mon–Thu 9:00–19:45, Fri 9:00–18:00, Sat 9:00–17:00, Sun 11:00–16:00, Museum Street, tel. 01904/552-828).

Laundry: The nearest place is **Haxby Road Launderette,** a long 15-minute walk north of the town center (about £8/load self-service, about £1.50 more for drop-off service, Mon–Wed and Fri 9:00–17:45, Thu 10:00–18:00, Sat 9:00–17:15, Sun 9:00–16:15, start last loads 1.5 hours before closing, 124 Haxby Road, tel. 01904/623-379). Some B&Bs will do laundry for a small charge.

Bike Rental: With the exception of the pedestrian center, the town's not great for biking. But there are several fine country-side rides from York, and the riverside New Walk bike path is pleasant. **Bob Trotter Cycles,** just outside Monk Bar, rents bikes and has free cycling maps (£15/day, helmet and map free with this book in 2011, Mon–Sat 9:00–17:30, closed Sun, 13–15 Lord Mayor's Walk, tel. 01904/622-868, www.bobtrotter cycles.com). **Europcar,** at platform 1 at the train station, also rents bikes (£10/day, includes helmet and lock, Mon–Sat 8:00–20:30, Sun 9:00–20:30, toll tel. 0844-846-4003, www .autohorn.co.uk).

Taxi: From the train station, taxis zip new arrivals to their B&Bs for £5. Queue up at the taxi stand, or call 01904/638-833; cabbies don't start the meter until you get in.

Car Rental: If you're nearing the end of your trip, consider dropping your car upon arrival in York. The money saved by turning it in early just about pays for the train ticket that whisks you effortlessly to London. In York, you'll find these agencies: **Avis** (Mon–Fri 8:00–18:00, Sat 8:00–13:00, closed Sun, 3 Layerthorpe, toll tel. 0844-544-6117); **Hertz** (Mon–Fri 8:00–17:00, Sat 9:00–13:00, closed Sun, at train station, tel. 01904/612-586); **Budget** (Mon–Fri 8:00–18:00, Sat 8:00–13:00, closed Sun, near the National Railway Museum at 75 Leeman Road, tel. 01904/644-919); and **Europcar** (Mon–Sat 8:00–20:30, Sun 9:00–20:30, train station platform 1, toll tel. 0844-846-4003).

Beware: Except for Europcar, most car-rental agencies close early on Saturday afternoons and all day Sunday—when dropping off is OK, but picking up is only possible by prior arrangement (and for a fee).

YORK

York

TO A-19 & THIRSK

CLIFTON
BOOTH CRES.
GROS. TERR.

QUEEN ANNES
BOOTHAM TERR.
ST. MARYS

SYCAMORE

LONGFIELD
FREDERIC
MARYGATE

N

- 🔲 ACCESS STAIRS TO WALL
- ⬜ PEDESTRIAN ZONE
- 🅿 PARKING
- --- FOOTPATH

EARLS

RIVER

RAILWAY MUSEUM

🅿

LEEMAN

ROAD

STATION RD.

TRAIN STATION

200 YARDS

200 METERS

L. MICKL.

QUEEN

NUNNER.

BLOSSOM

MICKLEGATE BAR

Ⓐ Start of Museum Gardens
& Wall Walk
Ⓑ Start of Riverside Walk
or Bike Ride

TO A-64
& LEEDS

DCH

Tours in York

▲▲▲Walking Tours

Free Walks with Volunteer Guides—Charming locals give energetic, entertaining, and free two-hour walks through York (daily at 10:15 all year, plus 14:15 April–Oct, plus 18:45 June–Aug, depart from Exhibition Square in front of the art gallery). These tours often go long because the guides love to teach and tell stories. You're welcome to cut out early—but say so or they'll worry, thinking they lost you.

Yorkwalk Tours—These are more serious 1.5- to 2-hour walks with a history focus. They do four different walks: Essential York, Roman York, Secret York, and York's Snickelways (£5.50 each, Feb–Nov daily at 10:30 and 14:15, Dec–Jan weekends only, depart from Museum Gardens Gate, just show up, tel. 01904/622-303, www.yorkwalk.co.uk—check website, TI, or call for schedule). Tours go rain or shine, with as few as two participants.

Haunted Walks—Numerous ghost tours, all offered after dusk, are more fun than informative. "Haunted Walk" relies a bit more on storytelling and history than on masks and surprises (£4, Easter–Oct nightly at 20:00, weekends only Nov–Easter, 1.5 hours, just show up, depart from Exhibition Square in front of the art gallery, end in The Shambles, tel. 01904/621-003).

Local Guide—**Julian Cripps** offers good private walking tours (£25/hour, tel. 01904/709-755, mobile 077-6323-4156, travellers intime@googlemail.com), as well as guided day trips to the North York Moors, Whitby, and Goathland.

▲City Bus Tours

Two companies run hop-on, hop-off bus tours circling York. While you can hop on and off all day, these have no real transportation value because York is so compact. If taking a bus tour, I'd catch either one at Exhibition Square (near Bootham Bar) and ride it for an orientation all the way around. Consider getting off at the National Railway Museum, skipping the last five minutes.

City Sightseeing—This outfit's half-enclosed, bright-red, double-decker buses take tourists past secondary York sights that the city walking tours skip—the mundane perimeter of town. Buses that leave Exhibition Square at the top and bottom of each hour usually have live guides in summer—look for a sign in the front window (£9, £13.50 combo-ticket with boat cruise through YorkBoat—described later, pay driver cash, ticket good for 24 hours, can also buy tickets online or from TI with credit card, Easter–Sept buses run 9:15–17:00, every 10 minutes, less frequent off-season, tel. 01904/655-585, www.yorktourbuses.co.uk).

York Pullman Bus Tours—These classic old-time buses are slightly less expensive, with fewer stops, live guides, and two overlapping routes (£7.50, buy ticket from driver, office, or TI; mid-June–Oct departs 6/hour from Exhibition Square daily 9:20–17:15, off-season 2–3/hour until about 16:00, 45 minutes, enclosed bus used when wet, tel. 01904/622-992, www.yorkpullmanbus.co.uk).

Boat Cruise

YorkBoat does a lazy, narrated 45-minute lap along the River Ouse (£7.50, £13.50 combo-ticket with City Sightseeing bus tours—see above, 4/day Feb–Nov 10:30–15:00; runs every 30–45 minutes April–Oct; 1.25-hour evening cruise at 21:15 for £9.50; leaves from Lendal Bridge and King's Staith landings, near Skeldergate Bridge, tel. 01904/628-324, www.yorkboat.co.uk).

Self-Guided Walk

Museum Gardens and Wall

Get a taste of Roman and medieval York on this easy stroll along a segment of York's wall.

• *Start just inside the Museum Gardens Gate (near the river, where Lendal Street hits Museum Street; gate closes at 20:00). About 20 yards to the right of the gate stands...*

Abbey Hospital: The 13th-century facade of the Abbey hospital is interesting mostly because of the ancient Roman tombs stacked just under its vault. These were buried outside the Roman city and discovered in the last century with the building of the train line.

• *Continue into the garden. About 50 yards ahead (on the right) is another remnant of ancient Rome, the...*

Multangular Tower: This 12-sided tower (A.D. 300) was likely a catapult station built to protect the town from enemy river traffic. The red ribbon of bricks was a Roman trademark—both structural and decorative. The lower stones are Roman, while the upper, bigger stones are medieval. After Rome fell, York suffered through two centuries of a dark age. Then the Vikings ruled from 780. They built with wood, so almost nothing from that period remains. The Normans came in 1066 and built in stone, generally atop Roman structures (like this wall). The Roman wall which defined the ancient garrison town worked for the Norman town, too. From the 1600s on, no such fortified walls were needed in England's interior.

• *Continue about 100 yards (past the Neoclassical building holding the fine Yorkshire Museum on the right—worth a visit and described on page 615) to York's ruined...*

York at a Glance

▲▲▲**York Minster** York's pride and joy, and one of England's finest churches, with stunning stained-glass windows, textbook Decorated Gothic design, and glorious evensong services. **Hours:** Open for worship daily from 7:00 and for sightseeing Mon–Sat from 9:00 (9:30 Nov–March), Sun from 12:00; flexible closing time (roughly May–Oct at 18:30, earlier off-season); shorter hours for tower and undercroft; evensong services Tue–Sat 17:15, Sun 16:00, occasionally on Mon, sometimes no services mid-July–Aug. See page 606.

▲▲▲**York Castle Museum** Excellent, far-ranging collection displaying everyday objects from Victorian times to the present. **Hours:** Daily 9:30–17:00. See page 612.

▲▲**National Railway Museum** Train buff's nirvana, tracing the history of all manner of rail-bound transport. **Hours:** Daily 10:00–18:00. See page 614.

▲▲**Yorkshire Museum** Sophisticated archaeology and natural history museum with York's best Viking exhibit, plus Roman, Saxon, Norman, and Gothic artifacts. **Hours:** Daily 10:00–17:00. See page 615.

▲**The Shambles** Atmospheric old butchers' quarter, with colorful, tipsy medieval buildings. **Hours:** Always open. See page 612.

▲**Jorvik** Cheesy, crowded, but not-quite-Disney-quality exhibit/ride exploring Viking lifestyles and artifacts. **Hours:** Daily April–Oct 10:00–17:00, Nov–March 10:00–16:00. See page 613.

▲**Fairfax House** Glimpse into an 18th-century Georgian family house, with enjoyably chatty docents. **Hours:** Mon–Thu and Sat 11:00–16:30, Sun 13:30–16:30, Fri by tour only at 11:00 and 14:00. See page 616.

St. Mary's Abbey: This abbey dates to the age of William the Conqueror—whose harsh policies of massacres and destruction in this region (called the "Harrowing of the North") made him unpopular. His son Rufus, who tried to improve relations in the 12th century, established a great church here. The church became an abbey that thrived from the 13th century until the Dissolution of the Monasteries in the 16th century. The Dissolution, which came with the Protestant Reformation and break with Rome, was a power play by Henry VIII. He took over the land and riches of the monasteries. Upset with the pope, he wanted his subjects to pay him taxes rather than give the Church tithes. (For more information, see the sidebar on page 609.)

As you gaze at this ruin, imagine magnificent abbeys like this scattered throughout the realm. Henry VIII destroyed most of them, taking the lead from their roofs and leaving the stones to scavenging townsfolk. Scant as they are today, these ruins still evoke a time of immense monastic power. The one surviving wall was the west half of a very long, skinny nave. The tall arch marked the start of the transept. Stand on the plaque that reads *Crossing beneath central tower,* and look up at the air that now fills the space where a huge tower once stood.

• *Now, backtrack about 50 yards and turn left, walking between the museum and the Roman tower. Continuing between the abbot's palace and the town wall, you're walking along a "snickelway"—a small, characteristic York lane or footpath. The snickelway pops out on...*

Exhibition Square: With the Dissolution, the Abbot's Palace became the **King's Manor** (from the snickelway, make a U-turn to the left and through the gate). Today, it's part of the University of York. Because the northerners were slow to embrace the king's reforms, Henry VIII came here to enforce the Dissolution. He stayed 17 days in this mansion and brought along a thousand troops to make a statement of his determination. You can wander into the grounds and building. The Refectory Café serves cheap cakes, soup, and sandwiches to students, professors, and visitors like you (Mon–Fri 9:30–15:30, closed Sat–Sun).

Exhibition Square is the departure point for various walking and bus tours. You can see the towers of the **Minster** in the distance. (Travelers in the Middle Ages could see the Minster from miles away as they approached the city.) Across the street is a public WC, and **Bootham Bar**—one of the fourth-century Roman gates in York's wall—with access to the best part of the city walls (free, walls open 8:00–dusk).

• *Climb up and...*

Walk the Wall: Hike along the top of the wall behind the Minster to the first corner. York's 12th-century walls are three miles long. Norman kings built the walls to assert control over northern England. Notice the pivots in the crenellations (square notches at the top of a medieval wall), which once held wooden hatches to provide cover for archers. At the corner with the benches—Robin Hood's Tower—you can lean out and see the moat outside. This was originally the Roman ditch that surrounded the fortified garrison town. Continue walking for a fine view of the Minster (better when the scaffolding comes down in 2014), with its truncated main tower and the pointy rooftop of its chapter house.

• *Continue on to the next gate, **Monk Bar** (skip the tacky museum in the* *tower house). Descend the wall at Monk Bar, and step past the portcullis to emerge outside the city's protective wall. Lean against the last bollard and gaze up at the tower, imagining 10 archers behind the arrow slits. Keep an eye on the 12th-century guards, with their stones raised and primed to protect the town. Return through the city wall and go left at the fork in the road to follow Goodramgate a couple of blocks into the old town center. Hiding off Goodramgate on the right is...*

Holy Trinity Church: This church holds rare box pews atop a floor that is sinking as bodies rot and coffins collapse (open Tue–Sun 10:00–16:00, closed Mon). The church is built in the late Perpendicular Gothic style, with lots of clear and precious stained glass from the 13th to 15th centuries. Enjoy the peaceful picnic-friendly gardens.

• *Goodramgate dead ends at...*

King's Square: This lively people-watching zone, with its inviting benches, is prime real estate for buskers and street performers. Just beyond (crossing the square diagonally) is the most characteristic and touristy street in old York: The Shambles (described on page 612). Our walk ends here, at the midpoint between York's main sights.

Sights in York

▲▲▲York Minster

The pride of York, this largest Gothic church north of the Alps (540 feet long, 200 feet tall) brilliantly shows that the High Middle

Ages were far from dark. The word "minster" comes from the Old English for "monastery," but is now simply used to imply that it's an important church. As it's the seat of a bishop, York Minster is also a cathedral. While Henry VIII destroyed England's great abbeys, this was not part of a monastery and was therefore left standing. It seats 2,000 comfortably; on Christmas and Easter, at least 4,000 worshippers pack the place. Today, more than 250 employees and 500 volunteers work to preserve its heritage and welcome the 1.3 million visitors each year.

Cost and Hours: The cathedral opens for worship daily at 7:00. It's open for sightseeing Mon–Sat from 9:00 (9:30 Nov–March) and Sun from 12:00, when they begin charging £8 admission (includes free guided tour and entry to the undercroft, treasury, and crypt). Closing time flexes with activities (roughly May–Oct at 18:30, earlier off-season—check the day's closing time posted outside the church, or call for details, tel. 01904/557-217,

York Minster

CHAPTER HOUSE

50 YARDS
50 METERS

NAVE

TRANSEPT

CHOIR

SHOP

TOURIST ENTRY

1. West Door & Great West Window
2. Central Tower
3. North Transept
4. South Transept
5. Dragon
6. Choir Screen
7. Choir
8. Chapter House
9. East End
10. Tower & Undercroft

YORK

www.yorkminster.org). The Minster may also close for special events (check calendar on their website). The tower (£5) and undercroft have shorter hours, typically opening a half-hour later and closing at 17:00 (as early as 16:45 for the tower).

Tours: After buying your ticket, go directly to the welcome desk, pick up the worthwhile *Welcome to the York Minster* flier, and ask when the next free guided tour departs (roughly 2/hour, Mon–Sat 10:30–15:00, one hour, they go even with just one or two people; you can join one in progress, or if none is scheduled, request a departure). The helpful Minster guides, some wearing blue badges, are happy to answer your questions. Stained-glass enthusiasts can take a special behind-the-scenes tour to learn about the restoration of the Minster's glass-terpiece, the Great East Window (£5, Wed and Fri at 14:00, one hour, 10-person maximum).

Evensong and Church Bells: To experience the cathedral in musical and spiritual action, attend an evensong (Tue–Sat at 17:15, Sun at 16:00, visiting choirs occasionally perform on Mon, 45 minutes). When the choir is off on school break (mid-July–Aug), visiting choirs usually fill in (confirm at church or TI). Arrive 10 minutes early and wait just outside the choir in the center of the church. You'll be ushered in and can sit in one of the big wooden stalls.

If you're a fan of church bells, you'll experience ding-dong ecstasy daily except Monday (Sun morning about 10:00, Tue practice 19:30–21:30, and Tue–Sat at 16:45 to announce evensong). These performances are especially impressive, as the church now holds a full carillon of 35 bells (it's the only English cathedral to have such a range). Stand in front of the church's west portal and imagine the gang pulling on a dozen ropes (halfway up the right tower—you can actually see the ropes through a little window) while one talented carillonneur plays 22 more bells with a baton-keyboard and foot pedals. On special occasions, you might even catch them playing a Beatles tune.

❍ Self-Guided Tour: Upon entering, head left, to the back (west end) of the church. Stand in front of the grand **west door** (used only on Sundays) on the *Deo Gratias 627–1927* plaque—a place of worship for 1,300 years, thanks to God. Flanking the door, the list of bishops goes unbroken back to the 600s. The statue of Peter with the key and Bible is a reminder that the church is dedicated to St. Peter, and the key to heaven is found through the word of God. While the Minster sits on the remains of a Romanesque church (c. 1100), today's church was begun in 1220 and took 250 years to complete.

Grab a chair and enjoy the nave. Looking down the church, your first impression might be the spaciousness and brightness of the nave (built 1280–1360). The nave—from the middle period of Gothic, called "Decorated Gothic"—is one of the widest Gothic naves in Europe. Rather than risk a stone roof, builders spanned the space with wood. Colorful shields on the arcades are the coats of arms of nobles who helped tall and formidable Edward I, known as "Longshanks," fight the Scots in the 13th century.

The coats of arms in the clerestory (upper-level) glass represent the nobles who helped his son, Edward II, in the same fight. There's more medieval glass in this building than in the rest of England combined. This precious glass survived World War II—hidden in stately homes throughout Yorkshire.

Walk to the very center of the church, under the **central tower.** Look up. Look down. Ask a Minster guide about how gifts and skill saved this tower—which weighs the equivalent of 40 jumbo jets—from collapse. (The first tower collapsed in 1407.) While the tower is 197 feet tall, it was intended to be much taller. Use the neck-saving mirror to marvel at it.

From here, you can survey many impressive features of the church:

In the **north transept,** the grisaille windows—dubbed the "Five Sisters"—are dedicated to British women who died in all wars. Made in 1260 (before colored glass was produced in England), these contain more than 100,000 pieces of glass.

England's Anglican Church

The Anglican Church (a.k.a. the Church of England) came into existence in 1534 when Henry VIII declared that he, and not Pope Clement VII, was the head of England's Catholics. The pope had refused to allow Henry to divorce his wife to marry his mistress Anne Boleyn (which Henry did anyway, resulting in the birth of Elizabeth I). Still, Henry regarded himself as a faithful Catholic—just not a *Roman* Catholic—and made relatively few changes in how and what Anglicans worshiped.

Henry's son, Edward VI, instituted many of the changes that Reformation Protestants were bringing about in continental Europe: an emphasis on preaching, people in the pews actually reading the Bible, clergy being allowed to marry, and a more "Protestant" liturgy in English from the revised Book of Common Prayer (1549). The next monarch, Edward's sister Mary I, returned England to the Roman Catholic Church (1553), earning the nickname of "Bloody Mary" for her brutal suppression of Protestant elements. When Elizabeth I succeeded Mary (1558), she soon broke from Rome again. Today, many regard the Anglican Church as a compromise between the Catholic and Protestant traditions.

Is the York Minster the leading Anglican church in England? Yes and no (but mostly no). After a long feud, the archbishops of Canterbury and York agreed that York's bishop would have the title "Primate of England" and Canterbury's would be the "Primate of All England," directing Anglicans on the national level.

The **south transept** features the tourists' entry, where stairs lead down to the undercroft. The new "bosses" (carved medallions decorating the point where the ribs meet on the ceiling) are a reminder that the roof of this wing of the church was destroyed by fire in 1984. Some believe the fire was God's angry response to a new bishop, David Jenkins, who questioned the literal truth of Jesus' miracles. Others blame an electricity box hit by lightning. Regardless, the entire country came to York's aid. *Blue Peter* (England's top kids' show) conducted a competition among their young viewers to design new bosses. Out of 30,000 entries, there were six winners (the blue ones—e.g., man on the moon, feed the children, save the whales).

Look back at the west end to marvel at the **Great West Window,** especially the stone tracery. While its nickname is the "Heart of Yorkshire," it represents the sacred heart of Christ, meant to remind people of his love for the world.

Find the **dragon** on the right of the nave (two-thirds of the way up). While no one is sure of its purpose, it pivots and has a hole through its neck—so it was likely a mechanism designed to raise a lid on a baptismal font.

The **choir screen** is an ornate wall of carvings separating the nave from the choir. It's lined with all the English kings from William I (the Conqueror) to Henry VI (during whose reign it was carved, 1461). Numbers indicate the years each reigned. To say "it's slathered in gold leaf" sounds impressive, but the gold is very thin...a nugget the size of a sugar cube is pounded into a sheet the size of a driveway.

Step into the **choir** (or "quire"), where a service is held daily. All the carving was redone after an 1829 fire, but its tradition of glorious evensong services (sung by choristers from the Minster School) goes all the way back to the eighth century.

In the **north transept,** the 18th-century astronomical clock is worth a look (a sign to its left helps you make sense of it). It's dedicated to the heroic Allied aircrews from bases here in northern England who died in World War II (as Britain kept the Nazis from invading in its "darkest hour"). The Book of Remembrance below the clock contains 18,000 names.

A corridor that functions as a small church museum leads to the Gothic, octagonal **Chapter House,** the traditional meet-

ing place of the governing body (or chapter) of the Minster. Above the doorway, the Virgin holds Baby Jesus while standing on the devilish serpent. Look for the panel of stained glass that is often on display here (it may also be in the undercroft). The panel is exquisitely detailed—its minute features would be invisible from the floor of the church and therefore would be "for God's eyes only."

The Chapter House, without an interior support, is remarkable (almost frightening) for its breadth. The fanciful carvings decorating the canopies above the stalls date from 1280 (80 percent are originals) and are some of the Minster's finest. Stroll slowly around the entire room and imagine that the tiny sculpted heads are a 14th-century parade—a fun glimpse of medieval society. Grates still send hot air up robes of attendees on cold winter mornings. A model of the wooden construction illustrates the impressive 1285 engineering.

The Chapter House was the site of an important moment in England's parliamentary history. Fighting the Scots in 1295, Edward I (the "Longshanks" we met earlier) convened the "Model Parliament" here, rather than down south, in London. (The Model Parliament is the name for its early version, back before the legislature was split into the Houses of Commons and Lords.) The government met here through the 20-year reign of Edward II, before moving to London during Edward III's rule in the 14th century.

The church's **east end** is square, lacking a semicircular apse, typical of England's Perpendicular Gothic style (15th century). Monuments (almost no graves) were once strewn throughout the church, but in the Victorian Age, they were gathered into the east end, where you see them today.

The **Great East Window,** the size of a tennis court, is currently behind scaffolding. In the meantime, an interesting display explains the ongoing work. Also, a chart (on the right as you face the window) highlights the core Old Testament scenes in this masterpiece (hard to read from below, even when you can actually see the window). Because of the window's immense size, there's an extra layer of supportive stonework, parts of it wide enough to walk along. In fact, for special occasions, the choir sings from the walkway halfway up the window.

The tower and undercroft are two extra sights to consider, both accessed from the south transept. One gets you exercise and a view; the other is a basement full of history. You can scale the 275-step **tower** for the panoramic view (£5, last entry varies—can be as early as 16:45 in summer and 30 minutes before dusk in winter, no children under 8, not good for acrophobes, closes in bad weather). The **undercroft** consists of the crypt, treasury, and foundations (included in church admission, last entry at 17:00, no photos). The crypt is an actual bit of the Romanesque church, featuring 12th-century Romanesque art, excavated in modern times. The foundations give you a chance to climb down—archaeologically and physically—through the centuries to see the roots of the much smaller, but still huge, Norman (Romanesque) church from 1100 that stood on this spot and, below that, the Roman excavations. Today's Minster stands upon the remains of a Roman fort. Peek also at the modern concrete save-the-church foundations.

Outside the Minster entrance, you'll find the **Roman Column.** Erected in 1971, this column commemorates the 1,900th anniversary of the Roman founding of Eboracum (later renamed York). Across the street is a statue of Constantine, who was in York when his father died. The troops declared him the Roman emperor in A.D. 306 at this site, and six years later, he went to Rome to claim his throne. In A.D. 312, Constantine legalized Christianity, and in A.D. 314, York got its first bishop.

More Sights in York

▲**The Shambles**—This is the most colorful old street in the half-timbered, traffic-free core of town. Walk to the midway point,

at the intersection with Little Shambles. This 100-yard-long street, next to the old market, was once the "street of the butchers" (the name is derived from *shammell*—a butcher's cutting block). In the 16th century, it was busy with red meat. On the hooks under the eaves once hung rabbit, pheasant, beef, lamb, and pigs' heads. Fresh slabs were displayed on the fat sills. People lived above—as they did even in Roman times. All the garbage was flushed down the street to a mucky pond at the end—a favorite hangout for the town's cats and dogs. Tourist shops now fill the fine 16th-century, half-timbered Tudor buildings. Look above the modern crowds and storefronts to appreciate the classic old English architecture. The soil here wasn't great for building. Notice how things settled in the absence of a good soil engineer.

Little Shambles leads to the frumpy Newgate Market (popular for cheap produce and clothing), created in the 1960s with the demolition of a bunch of lanes as colorful as The Shambles. Return to The Shambles a little farther along, through a covered lane (one of York's "snickelways"). Study the 16th-century oak carpentry—mortise-and-tenon joints with wooden plugs rather than nails.

For a cheap lunch, consider the cute, tiny **St. Crux Parish Hall**. This medieval church is now used by a medley of charities that sell tea, homemade cakes, and light meals. They each book the church for a day, often a year in advance. Chat with the volunteers (Mon–Sat 10:00–16:00, closed Sun, on the left at bottom end of The Shambles, at intersection with Pavement).

▲▲▲**York Castle Museum**—Truly one of Europe's top museums, this is a Victorian home show, the closest thing to a time-tunnel experience England has to offer. Even a speedy museumgoer will want a couple of hours here.

Stroll down the museum's two re-created streets: Kirkgate, from the Victorian era, with roaming live guides in period dress; and a fun exhibit that depicts the spirit of the swinging 1960s—

"a time when the cultural changes were massive but the cars and skirts were mini." The newest exhibit is the York Castle Prison, which re-creates the experiences of actual people who were thrown into the clink here. Actors are projected onto the walls of individual cells in eerie hologram-style scenes.

The "From Cradle to Grave" clothing exhibit and fine costume collection are also impressive. The one-way plan assures that you'll see everything: remakes of rooms from the 17th to 20th centuries, the domestic side of World War II, a giant dollhouse from 1715, Victorian toys, and a century of swimsuit fashions.

The museum's £4 guidebook isn't necessary, but it makes a fine souvenir. The museum proudly offers no audioguides, as its roaming guides are enthusiastic about talking—engage them.

Cost and Hours: £8, ticket good for one year, £12 combo-ticket with Yorkshire Museum, kids under 16 free with paying adult, daily 9:30–17:00, cafeteria midway through museum, tel. 01904/687-687, www.yorkcastlemuseum.org.uk. It's at the bottom of the hop-on, hop-off bus route. The museum can call you a taxi (worthwhile if you're hurrying to the National Railway Museum).

Clifford's Tower—Perched high on a knoll across from the Castle Museum, this ruin is all that's left of York's 13th-century

castle, the site of an 1190 massacre of local Jews (read about this at base of hill). If you climb inside, you can enjoy fine city views from the top of the ramparts (not worth the £3.50, daily April–Sept 10:00–18:00, Oct 10:00–17:00, Nov–March 10:00–16:00, last entry 15 minutes before closing, tel. 01904/646-940).

▲**Jorvik**—Take the "Pirates of the Caribbean," sail them northeast and back 1,000 years, and you get Jorvik—more a ride than a museum. Innovative 20 years ago, the commercial success of Jorvik (YOR-vik) inspired copycat ride/museums all over England.

Some love this attraction, while others call it a gimmicky rip-off. If you're looking for a grown-up museum, skip Jorvik and head instead to the Viking exhibit at the Yorkshire Museum. If you're thinking Disneyland with a splash of history, Jorvik's fun. To me, Jorvik is a commercial venture designed for kids, with nearly as much square footage devoted to its shop as to the museum. You'll ride a little Disney-type people-mover for 20 minutes through the re-created Viking street of Coppergate. It's the year 975, and you're in the village of Jorvik. Next, your little train takes you through the actual excavation site that inspired the reconstructed village. Everything is true to the dig—even the faces of the models are derived by computer from skulls dug up here. Finally, you'll browse through an impressive gallery of Viking shoes, combs, locks, and other intimate glimpses of that redheaded culture. More than 40,000 artifacts were dug out of the peat bog here in the 1970s. The exhibit on bone archaeology is fascinating.

Cost and Hours: £8.95, £13 combo-ticket with Dig—see below, daily April–Oct 10:00–17:00, Nov–March 10:00–16:00, these are last-entry times, tel. 01904/615-505, www.jorvik-viking -centre.co.uk.

Dig—This kid-oriented archaeological site gives young visitors an idea of what York looked like during Roman, medieval, Viking, and Victorian eras. Sift through "dirt" (actually shredded tires), reconstruct Roman wall plaster, and have a look at what archae- ologists have dug up recently (£5.50, £13 combo-ticket with Jorvik, daily 10:00–17:00, last entry one hour before closing, St. Saviour's Church, Saviourgate, tel. 01904/615-505, www.digyork.com).

▲▲National Railway Museum—If you like model railways, this is train-car heaven. The thunderous museum shows 200 illustri-

ous years of British railroad history. Fanning out from a grand roundhouse is an array of historic cars and engines, including Queen Victoria's lavish royal car and the very first "stagecoaches on rails," with a crude steam engine from 1830. A working steam engine is sliced open, showing cylinders, driving wheels, and smoke box in action. You'll trace the evolution of steam-powered transportation to the era of the aerodynamic Mallard, famous as the first train to travel at a startling two miles per minute (a marvel back in 1938). There's much more, including exhibits on dining cars, post cars, sleeping cars, train posters, and videos. At the Works section, you can see live train switchboards. And don't miss the English Channel Tunnel video (showing the first handshake at the breakthrough). Purple-shirted "explainers" are everywhere, eager to talk trains. This biggest and best railroad museum anywhere is interesting even to people who think "Pullman" means "don't push."

Cost and Hours: Free, £2.50 audioguide with 60 bits of railroad lore is worthwhile for train buffs, daily 10:00–18:00, tel. 08448/153-139, www.nrm.org.uk.

Getting There: It's about a 15-minute walk from the Minster (southwest of town, up the hill behind the train station). A cute little "road train" shuttles you more quickly between the Minster and the Railway Museum (£2 each way, runs daily Easter–Oct, leaves Railway Museum every 30 minutes 11:00–16:00 at the top and bottom of the hour; leaves the town—from Duncombe Place, 100 yards in front of the Minster—at :15 and :45 minutes after the hour).

▲▲**Yorkshire Museum**—Located in a lush, picnic-perfect park next to the stately ruins of St. Mary's Abbey, the Yorkshire Museum is the city's serious "archaeology of York" museum. While the hordes line up at Jorvik, this museum has no crowds and provides a better historical context (and includes a kid-friendly dinosaur exhibit to boot).

You can't dig a hole in York without hitting some remnant of the city's long past, and most of what's found ends up here. The museum has recently had a makeover, with freshly redone exhibits on life in York during prehistoric, Roman, and medieval times.

The Roman collection includes slice-of-life exhibits from Roman baths, a huge floor mosaic, and the skull of a man killed by a sword blow to the head. (The latter makes it graphically clear that the struggle between Romans and barbarians was a violent one.) These artifacts are particularly interesting when you consider that you're standing in one of the farthest reaches of that empire.

An eighth-century Anglo-Saxon helmet shows a bit of barbarian refinement; you'll notice that the Vikings wore some pretty decent shoes and actually combed their hair.

The Middleham Jewel, an exquisitely etched 15th-century pendant, is considered the finest piece of Gothic jewelry in Britain. The noble lady who wore this on a necklace believed that it helped her worship and protected her from illness. The back of the pendant, which rested near her heart, shows the Nativity. The front shows the Holy Trinity crowned by a sapphire (which people believed put their prayers at the top of God's to-do list).

Cost and Hours: £7, kids under 16 free with paying adult, ticket good for one year, £12 combo-ticket with York Castle Museum, daily 10:00–17:00, within Museum Gardens, tel. 01904/687-687, www.yorkshiremuseum.org.uk.

Nearby: Before leaving, enjoy the evocative ruins of St. Mary's Abbey in the park (described on page 604).

▲**Fairfax House**—This well-furnished townhouse is perfectly Georgian inside, with wonderfully pleasant docents in each room eager to talk with you. Built in 1740, the house is compact and bursting with stunning period furniture, all of it giving insights into aristocratic life in 18th-century England (£6, Mon–Thu and Sat 11:00–16:30, Sun 13:30–16:30, Fri by guided tour only at 11:00 and 14:00—the tours are worthwhile, closed Jan–mid-Feb, on Castlegate, near Jorvik, tel. 01904/655-543, www.fairfaxhouse .co.uk).

Traditional Tea—York is famous for its elegant teahouses. Drop into one at 16:00 for tea and cakes. Ladies love **Bettys Café Tea Rooms,** where you pay £8 for a Yorkshire Cream Tea (tea and scones with clotted Yorkshire cream and strawberry jam), or £17 for a full traditional English afternoon tea (tea, delicate sandwiches, scones, and sweets). Your table is so full of doily niceties that the food is served on a little three-tray tower. While you'll pay a little extra here (and the food's nothing special), the ambience and people-watching are hard to beat. If there's a line, it moves quickly (except at dinnertime). Wait for a seat by the windows on the ground level rather than in the much bigger basement (daily 9:00–21:00, "afternoon tea" served all day, piano music nightly 18:00–21:00, tel. 01904/659-142, St. Helen's Square, fine view of street scene from a window seat on the main floor). Near the WC downstairs is a mirror signed by WWII bomber pilots—read the story.

Riverside Walk or Bike Ride—The New Walk is a mile-long, tree-lined riverside lane created in the 1730s as a promenade for York's dandy class to stroll, see, and be seen—and is a fine place for today's visitors to walk or bike. This hour-long walk along a bike path is a great way to enjoy a dose of countryside away from York. It's clearly described in the TI's *New Walk* flier (£0.60). Start from the riverside under Skeldergate Bridge (near the York Castle Museum), and walk away from town for a mile until you hit the modern Millennium Bridge (check out its thin, modern, stainless-steel design). Cross the river and walk back home, passing through Rowntree Park (a great Edwardian park with lawn bowling for the public, plus family fun including a playground and adventure rides for kids). Energetic bikers can continue past the Millennium Bridge 18 miles to the market town of Selby.

Honorable Mentions

York has a number of other sights and activities (described in TI brochures) that, while interesting, pale in comparison to the biggies.

Merchant Adventurers' Hall—Claiming to be the finest surviving medieval guildhall in Britain (from 1357), it's basically a vast half-timbered building with marvelous exposed beams and 15 minutes' worth of interesting displays about life and commerce back in the days when York was England's second city (£5, includes audioguide; Easter–Sept Mon–Thu 9:00–17:00, Fri–Sat 9:00–15:30, Sun 12:00–16:00; Oct–Easter Mon–Sat 9:00–15:30, closed Sun; south of The Shambles off Piccadilly, tel. 01904/654-818, www.theyorkcompany.co.uk).

Barley Hall—Uncovered behind a derelict office block in the 1980s, this medieval house has been restored to replicate a 1483 dwelling (£5, combo-tickets with Jorvik or Dig, daily April–Oct 10:00–17:00, until 16:00 in winter, last entry one hour before closing, 2 Coffee Yard off Stonegate, tel. 01904/615-505, www.barley hall.org.uk).

Micklegate Bar Museum—This new museum, at one of the city's main gateways, gives a feel for how families lived here inside the city wall, and how enemies of the crown were punished in medieval, Tudor, and Stuart times (£3, 2 kids free with paying adult, daily Feb–Oct 10:00–15:00, closed Nov–Jan, tel. 01904/615-505, www.micklegatebar.com).

Richard III Museum—This goofy exhibit is like seeing a high school history project. It's interesting only for Richard III enthusiasts (£2.50, daily March–Oct 9:00–17:00, Nov–Feb 9:30–16:00, longer hours possible in summer, filling the top floors of Monk Bar, tel. 01904/634-191, www.richardiiimuseum.co.uk).

Shopping in York

With its medieval lanes lined with classy as well as tacky little shops, York is a hit with shoppers. I find the **antiques malls** interesting. Three places within a few blocks of each other are filled with stalls and cases owned by antiques dealers from the countryside. The malls sell the dealers' bygones on commission. Serious shoppers do better heading for the country, but York's shops are a fun browse: The **Antiques Centre York** (Mon–Sat 9:00–17:30, Sun 9:00–16:00, 41 Stonegate, tel. 01904/635-888, www.theantiques centreyork.co.uk), the **Red House Antiques Centre** (Mon–Fri 9:30–17:30, Sat 9:30–18:00, Sun 10:30–17:30, a block from Minster at Duncombe Place, tel. 01904/637-000, www.redhouseyork .co.uk), and **Cavendish Antiques and Jewellers** (Mon–Sat 9:30–17:30, Sun 10:00–17:00, 44 Stonegate, tel. 01904/621-666, www .cavendishjewellers.co.uk).

You'll find **thrift shops** run by various charity organizations from the beginning of Goodramgate by the wall to just past Deangate. Good deals abound on clothing, purses, accessories, children's toys, books, CDs, and maybe even a guitar. If you buy something, you're getting a bargain and at the same time helping the poor, elderly, or even a pet in need of a vet (Mon–Sat 9:30–17:00, Sun 11:00–16:00). On Goodramgate alone you'll find shops run by the British Heart Foundation, Save the Children, and Oxfam (selling donated items as well as free-trade products such as coffee, tea, culinary goods, stationery items, and jewelry and purses made in developing countries and purchased directly from the producers and artisans).

Nightlife in York

Theatre Royal—A full variety of dramas, comedies, and works by Shakespeare entertain the locals in either the main theater or the little 100-seat theater-in-the-round (£10–20, usually Tue–Sat at 19:30, tickets easy to get, on St. Leonard's Place near Bootham Bar and a 5- to 10-minute walk from recommended B&Bs, booking tel. 01904/623-568, www.yorktheatreroyal.co.uk). Those under 25 and students of any age get tickets for only £7.

Ghost Tours—You'll see fliers, signs, and promoters hawking a variety of not-so-spooky after-dark tours; of these, I'd go for the "Haunted Walks" (for details, see "Tours in York," earlier).

Pubs—Atmospheric, half-timbered pubs abound. One of my favorites for old-school York ambience is **The Blue Bell,** a tiny, traditional establishment with a time-warp Edwardian interior. This smallest pub in York serves no food. It has two distinct little rooms—each as cozy as can be—and the owners only recently allowed women to enter (near the east end of town at 53 Fossgate).

Movies—The centrally located City Screens Cinema is right on the river, playing both art-house and mainstream flicks (13 Coney Street, toll tel. 0871-704-2054).

Sleeping in York

I've listed peak-season, book-direct prices. Don't use the TI. Outside of July and August, some prices go soft. B&Bs will often charge £10 more for weekends and sometimes turn away one-night bookings, particularly for peak-season Saturdays. (York is worth two nights anyway.) Prices spike up for horse races and Bank Holidays (about 20 nights a season). Remember to book ahead during festival times (mid-Feb, early June, early July, mid-Aug, and late Sept—see "Helpful Hints," page 598) and weekends year-round.

B&Bs and Small Hotels

These B&Bs are all small and family-run. They come with plenty of steep stairs (and no elevators) but no traffic noise. Rooms can be tight; if maneuverability is important to you, say so when

---

Sleep Code

(£1 = about $1.60, country code: 44, area code: 01904)
S = Single, **D** = Double/Twin, **T** = Triple, **Q** = Quad, **b** = bathroom,
s = shower only. You can assume credit cards are accepted
unless otherwise noted.

To help you sort easily through these listings, I've divided
the rooms into three categories based on the price for a
standard double room with bath (during high season):

$$$ Higher Priced—Most rooms £90 or more.
$$ Moderately Priced—Most rooms between £65–90.
$ Lower Priced—Most rooms £65 or less.

Prices can change without notice; verify the hotel's
current rates online or by email. For other updates, see www
.ricksteves.com/update.

---

booking. For a good selection, call well in advance. B&B owners
will generally hold a room with a phone call and work hard to
help their guests sightsee and eat smartly. Most have permits to
lend for street parking.

The handiest B&B neighborhood is the quiet residential area
just outside the old town wall's Bootham gate, along the road called
Bootham. All of these are within a 10-minute walk of the Minster
and TI, and a 10- to 15-minute walk or £5 taxi ride from the station. If driving, head for the cathedral and follow the medieval
wall to the gate called Bootham Bar. The street called Bootham
leads away from Bootham Bar.

Getting There: Here's the most direct way to walk to this
B&B area from the train station: Exit the station to the left on
Station Road. When the road swings right and goes through the
old gate, turn left onto the busy street (Leeman Road). Just before
that street goes under the rail bridge, turn right and follow the
walkway along the tracks, then cross the bridge over the river.
From the far end of the bridge, the Abbey Guest House is a few
yards to your left, facing the river. To reach the B&Bs closer to the
town wall, walk from the bridge along the river until just before
the short ruined tower, then turn inland up onto Marygate. For
other B&Bs, follow the path from the bridge, turning left immediately onto a path that skirts the big parking lot (parallel to the
train tracks). At the end of the parking lot, you'll turn depending
on your B&B: for the places on or near Bootham Terrace, turn left
and go under the tracks; or, for B&Bs on St. Mary's Street, take
the short stairway on your right.

York Accommodations

YORK

TO A-19 & THIRSK

1. Abbeyfields Guest House
2. St. Raphael Guesthouse
3. Arnot House
4. Hedley House Hotel
5. The Sycamore
6. Bootham Guest House
7. Amber House & Number 34
8. Queen Annes Guest House
9. Abbey Guest House
10. Number 23 St. Mary's B&B
11. Crook Lodge B&B
12. Airden House
13. The Hazelwood
14. The Coach House Hotel & Rest.
15. Ardmore Guest House
16. Dean Court Hotel
17. Travelodge York Central
18. Premier Inns (2)
19. Ace Hotel York
20. Internet Cafés (2)
21. To Launderette
22. Library (Internet)
23. Bike Rental

RAILWAY MUSEUM

RIVER

LEEMAN

ROAD

TRAIN STATION

STATION RD.

MICKLE

QUEEN

NUNNERY

BLOSSOM

MICKLEGATE BAR

TO A-64 & LEEDS

200 YARDS
200 METERS

ACCESS STAIRS TO WALL

PEDESTRIAN ZONE

P PARKING

- - - FOOTPATH

CLIFTON

BOOTH CRES.

GROS TERR.

QUEEN ANNES

BOOTHAM TERR.

ST. MARYS

SYCAMORE

LONGFIELD

FREDERIC

MARYGATE

EARLS.

YORK

On or near Bootham Terrace

$$ Abbeyfields Guest House has eight comfortable, bright rooms. This doily-free place, which lacks the usual B&B clutter, has been designed with care (Sun–Thu: Sb-£44, Db-£72; Fri–Sat: Sb-£49, Db-£82; doesn't price-gouge during races, free Wi-Fi, 19 Bootham Terrace, tel. 01904/636-471, www.abbeyfields.co.uk, enquire@abbeyfields.co.uk, charming Al and Les).

$$ At St. Raphael Guesthouse, young, creative, and energetic Dom and Zoe understand a traveler's needs. You'll be instant friends. Dom's graphic design training brings a dash of class to their seven comfy rooms, each themed after a different York street, and each lovingly accented with a fresh rose (Sb-£65; Db-£76 Sun–Thu, £88 Fri–Sat; less off-season, free drinks in their guests' fridge, family rooms, free Internet access and Wi-Fi, 44 Queen Annes Road, tel. 01904/645-028, www.straphaelguesthouse.co.uk, info@straphaelguesthouse.co.uk).

$$ Arnot House, run by a hardworking daughter-and-mother team, is homey and lushly decorated with Victorian memorabilia. The three well-furnished rooms even have little libraries (Db-£70–80 depending on size of room, 2-night minimum stay unless it's last-minute, no children, free Wi-Fi, huge DVD library, 17 Grosvenor Terrace, tel. 01904/641-966, www.arnothouseyork .co.uk, kim.robbins@virgin.net, Kim).

$$ Hedley House Hotel, well-run by a wonderful family, has 30 clean and spacious rooms. The outdoor hot tub is a fine way to end your day (Sb-£55–90, Db-£70–100, ask for a deal with stay of 3 or more nights, family rooms, good 3-course evening meals from £18, free Wi-Fi, free parking, 3 Bootham Terrace, tel. 01904/637-404, www.hedleyhouse.com, greg@hedleyhouse.com, Greg and Louise Harrand). They also have two luxury studio apartments—see their website for details.

$$ The Sycamore is a fine value, with six homey rooms at the end of a quiet street opposite a bowling green. A little cramped, it's friendly and well-run (Db-£60–75, Tb-£90–102, Qb-£110, lower price is for weekdays, these are special prices in 2011 if you mention this book when you reserve and pay cash, may be cheaper off-season, free Wi-Fi, 19 Sycamore Place off Bootham Terrace, tel. 01904/624-712, www.thesycamore.co.uk, mail@thesycamore .co.uk, accommodating Elizabeth and Spiros freely dispense sight-seeing advice).

$ Bootham Guest House features gregarious Emma, who welcomes you to her eight simple but cheery and thoughtfully renovated rooms (S-£35; D-£56, £60 Fri–Sat; Db-£60, £70 Fri–Sat; these prices in 2011 if you mention this book when reserving, free Wi-Fi, 56 Bootham Crescent, tel. 01904/672-123, www .boothamguesthouse.com, boothamguesthouse1@hotmail.com).

$ Amber House is a small place with three breezy and well-tended rooms (Db-£64 Sun–Thu, £72 Fri–Sat; Tb-£90; mention Rick Steves when booking for these prices in 2011, free Wi-Fi, 36 Bootham Crescent, tel. 01904/620-275, www.amberhouse-york .co.uk, amberhouseyork@hotmail.co.uk, John and Linda).

$ Number 34, run by hardworking Amy and Jason, has four simple, light, and airy rooms at fair prices (May–Oct: Sb-£35–45, Db-£60, Tb-£84; Nov–April: Sb-£35, Db-£56, Tb-£75; free Wi-Fi, 34 Bootham Crescent, tel. 01904/645-818, www.number 34york.co.uk, enquiries@number34york.co.uk).

$ Queen Annes Guest House has nine basic rooms in two adjacent houses at the best prices in the neighborhood. If you're looking for plush beds and rich decor, look elsewhere. If you'd simply like an affordable and clean place to sleep, this is it (high season: S-£30, D-£48, Db-£55; off-season: S-£26, D-£44, Db-£48; these prices with this book through 2011, family room, ground-floor room, free Wi-Fi, lounge, 24 Queen Annes Road, tel. 01904/629-389, www.queen-annes-guesthouse.co.uk, info @queen-annes-guesthouse.co.uk, Jason).

YORK

On the River
$$ Abbey Guest House is a peaceful refuge overlooking the River Ouse, with five cheerful, beautifully updated rooms and a cute little garden (Db-£78–86, four-poster Db with river view, less off-season, ask for Rick Steves discount when booking, free Wi-Fi, free parking, £7 laundry service, 13–14 Earlsborough Terrace, tel. 01904/627-782, www.abbeyghyork.co.uk, info@abbeyghyork.co.uk, delightful couple Gill—pronounced "Jill"—and Alec Saville, and a dog aptly named Loofah).

On St. Mary's Street
$$ Number 23 St. Mary's B&B is extravagantly decorated. Chris and Julie Simpson have done everything just right and offer nine spacious and tastefully comfy rooms, a classy lounge, and all the doily touches (Sb-£48–55, Db-£80–95 depending on room size and season, discount for longer stays, family room, DVD library and DVD players, free Wi-Fi, 23 St. Mary's, tel. 01904/622-738, www.23stmarys.co.uk, stmarys23@hotmail.com).

$$ Crook Lodge B&B, with seven tight but elegantly charming rooms, serves breakfast in an old Victorian kitchen (Db-£74–80, cheaper off-season, check for specials online, one ground-floor room, free Internet access and Wi-Fi, parking, quiet, 26 St. Mary's, tel. 01904/655-614, www.crooklodge.co.uk, crooklodge @hotmail.com, Brian and Louise Aiken).

$$ Airden House rents nine nice rooms (Db-£70–78, this price with 2-night minimum if you mention this book when reserving in 2011, cheaper off-season, lounge, free parking, 1 St. Mary's, tel. 01904/638-915, www.airdenhouse.co.uk, info@airden house.co.uk).

Closer to the Town Wall

$$$ The Hazelwood, my most hotelesque listing, is plush and more formal than a B&B. This spacious house has 14 beautifully decorated rooms with modern furnishings and lots of thoughtful touches (Sb-£65, Db-£80–125 depending on room size and day of week, two ground-floor rooms, free Internet access and Wi-Fi, laundry service-£7, free parking, light breakfast option, garden patio; a fridge, ice, and travel library in the pleasant basement lounge; 24 Portland Street, tel. 01904/626-548, www.thehazelwoodyork.com, reservations @thehazelwoodyork.com, Ian and Carolyn). Ask about their bright top-floor two-bedroom apartment, great for families and those with strong legs (continental breakfast only).

$$$ The Coach House Hotel is a labyrinthine, well-located 17th-century coach house. Facing a bowling green and the abbey walls, it offers 14 huge ceiling-beamed rooms, some with views of the Minster (Sb-£55, Db-£85–100, family room for £150 sleeps up to 6, one ground-floor room, free Internet access and Wi-Fi, tea and cake at check-in, laundry service, free parking, 20–22 Marygate, tel. 01904/652-780, www.coachhousehotel-york.com, info@coachhousehotel-york.com, Julie). This is also a good place for a cozy pub dinner, with veggie options and homemade sweets (£9-13 dishes, nightly 17:00–21:00).

$$ Ardmore Guest House is a fine little four-room place enthusiastically run by Irishwoman Vera, who's given it a green theme. It's about 15 minutes' walk from the station, but only five minutes from Bootham Bar (Sb-£40, Db-£60–75, Tb-£75, discount off-season for 3 or more nights, cash only, 31 Claremont Terrace, tel. 01904/622-562, mobile 079-3928-3588, www.ardmore york.co.uk).

Hotels in the Center and Big-Budget Hotel Options

$$$ Dean Court Hotel, a Best Western facing the Minster, is a big, stately hotel with classy lounges and 37 comfortable rooms (Ss/Sb-£105, small Db-£140, standard Db-£170, superior Db-£200, spacious deluxe Db-£220, cheaper midweek and off-season, elevator, free Wi-Fi, bistro, restaurant, Duncombe Place, tel. 01904/625-082, fax 01904/620-305, www.deancourt-york.co.uk).

$$ Travelodge York Central offers 93 identical, affordable, slightly worn rooms near the Castle Museum. If you book long in advance on their website, this can be amazingly cheap. River views make some rooms slightly less boring—after booking online, call the front desk to try to arrange a view (Db and Tb-£70 Sun–Thu, £65 Fri–Sat, often much lower with online deals, kids' bed free, continental breakfast-£4.50, pay Internet access and Wi-Fi, parking-£6.50/day, 90 Piccadilly, central reservations toll tel. 08719-848-484, front desk tel. 01904/651-852, www.travelodge.co.uk).

$$ Premier Inn offers 200 rooms in two side-by-side hotels that I hate to recommend, but York has few budget options. They have little character (at one, you enter through a coffee shop), but they offer industrial-strength efficiency and a decent value (Db-£74 Sun–Thu, £85 Fri–Sat, check for specials online, up to 2 kids stay free, breakfast-£8 extra, pay Internet access and Wi-Fi, free parking, 5-minute walk to train station, 20 and 28–40 Blossom Street, toll tel. 0871-527-9194, www.premierinn.com, yorkcitycentre .pi@premierinn.com).

YORK

Hostel

$ Ace Hotel York is a boutique hostel in a large, classy, nicely renovated Georgian house that provides a much-needed option for backpackers. They rent 129 beds in 2- to 14-bed rooms, most with great views and all with private bathrooms and thoughtful touches such as reading lights for each bed. They also offer fancier, hotel-quality doubles (£20–30/bed depending on size of dorm, Db-£80, family room-£100, includes continental breakfast, air-con, pay Internet access, free Wi-Fi, laundry-£3, TV lounge, bar, lockers, no curfew, 5-minute walk from train station at 88–90 Mickelgate, tel. 01904/627-720, www.acehotelyork.co.uk, reception @ace-hotelyork.co.uk).

Eating in York

York is bursting with inviting eateries. There seems to be a pub serving grub on every corner. And in the last decade or so, the city has become a hot spot for the new British cuisine—every year seems to bring another bistro serving classy dishes made with fresh, local ingredients. I've listed five of my favorites here: Café No. 8, Café Concerto, The Blue Bicycle, J. Baker's, and Melton's Too. These places are each romantic, laid-back, and popular with natives (so reservations are wise for dinner). All have several creative vegetarian options on the menu. Main courses at these places cost about £15–20—not exorbitant by British standards, but not cheap, either.

Fortunately, picnic and light-meals-to-go options abound, and it's easy to find a churchyard, bench, or riverside perch upon which

York Restaurants

YORK

TO A-19 & THIRSK

CLIFTON
BOOTH CRES.
GROS. TERR.
QUEEN ANNE'S
BOOTHAM TERR.
ST. MARY'S
SYCAMORE
LONGFIELD
FREDERIC
MARYGATE
EARLS.

1. St. William's Tea Rooms
2. Grays Court Tea Rooms
3. Bettys Café Tea Rooms
4. York Hogroast (2)
5. Café Concerto
6. El Piano Restaurant
7. Evil Eye Lounge
8. Ask Restaurant
9. Siam House
10. Bengal Brasserie & Caesars
11. The Viceroy of India
12. Little Italy
13. Café No. 8
14. Mamma Mia
15. The Exhibition Hotel Pub & Sainsbury's Grocery
16. The Blue Bicycle
17. J. Baker's
18. Melton's Too
19. The Blue Bell
20. The Coach House

RAILWAY MUSEUM

RIVER

LEEMAN

ROAD

STATION RD.

TRAIN STATION

STATION RD.

MICKLE

QUEEN

NUNNERY

BLOSSOM

TO A-64 & LEEDS

MICKLEGATE BAR

⊿ ACCESS STAIRS TO WALL

▢ PEDESTRIAN ZONE

P PARKING

--- FOOTPATH

200 YARDS

200 METERS

to munch cheaply. On a sunny day, perhaps the best picnic spot in town is under the evocative 12th-century ruins of St. Mary's Abbey in the Museum Gardens (near Bootham Bar).

Just Lunch

St. William's Tea Rooms, signed as the "York Minster Tea Rooms," are nestled just behind the Great East Window of the Minster in a wonderful half-timbered 15th-century building (read the history on the menu). They serve quick and tasty lunches. Eat outside (with a scaffolded Minster view), inside (cafeteria under timbers), or in the peaceful cobbled courtyard (tea and pastries served daily 10:30–16:00, £7–8 lunches served daily 12:00–15:00, College Street, tel. 01904/634-830).

Grays Court is also tucked away behind the Minster, around the corner from St. William's Tea Rooms. For centuries, this was the residence of the Norman Treasurers of York Minster; today it's home to a pleasant tea room. Enjoy lunch or tea in the garden or in the Jacobean gallery—ask to see the medieval wall of the original Treasurer's House behind the oak paneling (daily 10:00–17:00, Chapter House Street, tel. 01904/612-613).

Bettys Café Tea Rooms, a favorite among local ladies, is popular for its traditional English afternoon tea (which works as a meal—£17 for tea, delicate sandwiches, scones, and sweets; for details, see page 616).

York Hogroast is a fixture, serving its delicious £3 hearty pork sandwiches with a choice of traditional fillings—try the apple (take-away only, Mon–Thu 11:00–16:00, Fri 11:00–16:00 & 20:00–24:00, Sat 11:00–24:00, Sun 11:00–17:00, 82–84 Goodramgate; second location with similar hours at 4 Stonegate). Grab a sandwich and munch in the yard at the nearby Holy Trinity Church (to your left as you exit, peaceful) or in King's Square (to your right as you exit, lively with buskers).

Near the Minster

Café Concerto, a casual bistro with a fun menu, wholesome food, and a charming musical theme, has an understandably loyal following (soup, sandwich, and salad meals–£9–10; fancier dinners–£12–17; daily 8:30–22:00, smart to reserve for dinner—try for a window seat, also offers take-away, facing the Minster, 21 High Petergate, tel. 01904/610-478).

El Piano Restaurant, a few blocks from the Minster on charming Grape Lane, is a popular veggie option that serves only vegan, gluten-free, and low-sodium dishes in tapas-style portions. The dishes have Indian/Asian/Middle Eastern flavors, and the inside ambience is bubble gum with blinking lights; they also have a pleasant patio out back. If you're eating family-style, three or four plates serve two. Save money at the take-away window (£3–4 to-go "bamboo boats," Mon–Sat 11:00–23:00, Sun 12:00–17:00, between Low Petergate and Swinegate at 15–17 Grape Lane, tel. 01904/610-676).

Evil Eye Lounge serves large portions of Southeast Asian cuisine to a hip crowd in a creaky, funky space (£7 entrées, food served Mon–Fri 10:00–21:00, Sat 12:00–19:00, 42 Stonegate, tel. 01904/640-002). On Sundays, the Asian cuisine takes a break, and a full multi-course traditional Sunday roast is served instead (good deal at £7 for adults, £9 for "monsters," Sun 12:00–18:00).

Ask Restaurant is a cheap and cheery Italian chain, similar to those found in historic buildings all over England. But York's version lets you dine in the majestic marble-columned yellow hall of its Grand Assembly Rooms. The food may be Italian-chain dull—but the atmosphere is 18th-century deluxe (£8–9 pizza, pastas, and salads; daily, Blake Street, tel. 01904/637-254). Even if you're just walking past, peek inside to gape at the interior.

Along Goodramgate

Goodramgate is lined with a fun variety of competitive eateries dishing up everything from fish-and-chips and pub grub to tastes of Thailand, India, and Italy. Strolling this lane, you'll find plenty of good options. Working roughly from the center to the medieval gate, Monk Bar, my favorites are:

Siam House serves creative Thai food popular with locals (£7 lunches, £11–13 dinners, Sun–Fri 18:00–22:00, Wed–Fri also 12:00–14:00, Sat 12:00–15:00 & 17:00-23:00, 63a Goodramgate, tel. 01904/624-677).

Bengal Brasserie is a town favorite for Indian cuisine (Sun–Fri 18:00–24:00, Sat 12:00–24:00, 21 Goodramgate, tel. 01904/613-131). I also like the **Viceroy of India,** just outside Monk Bar and therefore outside the tourist zone (£6–11 plates, daily 18:00–24:00, out Monk Bar to 26 Monkgate, tel. 01904/622-370).

Two popular Italian places along Goodramgate offer pizzas and pastas for £8: **Little Italy** is a little more intimate and classy (Mon–Tue and Thu–Sat 10:30–22:00, Sun 11:30–21:00, closed Wed, at #12, tel. 01904/623-539), while **Caesars** is bright and boisterous (Mon–Fri 12:00–14:30 & 17:30–23:00, Sat–Sun 12:00–23:00, at #27, tel. 01904/670-914).

Near Bootham Bar and Recommended B&Bs

Café No. 8 is your best bistro choice on Gillygate, serving modern European and veggie options. Grab one of eight tables inside or enjoy a shaded little garden out back if the weather's good. No. 8 feels like Café Concerto (described earlier) but is more romantic, with jazz, modern art, candles, and hardworking Martin bringing it all together. Chef Chris Pragnell uses what's fresh in the market to shape his menu. The food is simple, elegant, and creative—with appetizers such as figs with Yorkshire bleu cheese (£6–10 lunches, £15–17 dinners, Mon–Fri 11:00–22:00, Sat-Sun 10:00–22:00, 8 Gillygate, tel. 01904/653-074).

Mamma Mia is the locals' choice for affordable Italian. The casual eating area features a tempting gelato bar, and in nice weather the back patio is *molto bella* (£8 pizza and pasta, daily 11:30–14:00 & 17:30–23:00, 20 Gillygate, tel. 01904/622-020).

The handsome **Exhibition Hotel pub** has a nice bar area inside, as well as a glassed-in conservatory and patio seating out back that's great for kids (daily 12:00–21:00, just outside Bootham Bar at 19 Bootham Street, tel. 01904/624-248).

Supermarket: **Sainsbury's** grocery store is handy and open late (daily 7:00–23:00, 50 yards outside Bootham Bar, on Bootham).

YORK

At the East End of Town

This neighborhood is across town from my recommended B&Bs, but still central (and a short walk from the Castle Museum). All three of these places are worth the longer after-dinner stroll.

The Blue Bicycle is no longer a brothel (but if you explore downstairs, you can still imagine when the tiny privacy snugs needed their curtains). Today, it is passionate about fish. The energy of its happy eaters, its charming canalside setting, and its location just beyond the tourist zone make it worth the splurge. Of my recommended York restaurants, this wins the best ambience award. It's a velvety, hardwood scene, a little sultry but fresh...like its fish. Reservations are a must (£5–10 starters, £17–24 entrées, vegetarian and meat options, nightly 18:00–21:30, Thu–Sun also 12:00–14:30, 34 Fossgate, tel. 01904/673-990).

J. Baker's is popular for how it turns local produce into high-brow versions of classic dishes. At lunchtime, their "grazing menu" makes it affordable to sample several dishes (available à la carte, or £12 for three courses). At dinnertime, the two earth-tone dining rooms—one downstairs, one upstairs—tend to fill up fast, so reservations are smart (£25 two-course meals, £29 three-course meals, £33 seven-course "grazing" meal, Tue–Sat 12:00–14:30 & 18:00–22:00, closed Sun–Mon, near the end of The Shambles at 7 Fossgate, tel. 01904/622-688). Across the street is the recommended Blue Bell pub (see page 618).

Melton's Too is a fun and casual place to eat. This homey, spacious, youthful restaurant serves up elegantly simple meals and a nice a selection of tapas, all with a focus on local ingredients (£9–11 entrées, Mon–Sat 10:30–22:30, Sun 10:30–21:30, just past Fossgate at 25 Walmgate, tel. 01904/629-222).

York Connections

From York by Train to: Durham (1-3/hour, 45 minutes), **London**'s King's Cross Station (2/hour, 2 hours), **Bath** (2/hour, 4.25–4.5 hours, 1–2 changes), **Cambridge** (roughly hourly, 2.5 hours, change in Peterborough), **Birmingham** (2/hour, 2–2.5 hours), **Keswick/Lake District** (train to Penrith: 1–2/hour, 3.5 hours, 1–2 transfers; then bus, allow about 4.5 hours total), **Manchester Airport** (2/hour, 1.75 hours), **Edinburgh** (1–2/hour, 2.5–2.75 hours). Train info: toll tel. 0845-748-4950, www.nationalrail.co.uk.

Connections with London's Airports: Heathrow (allow 3 hours minimum; from airport take Heathrow Express train to London's Paddington Station, transfer by tube to King's Cross, train to York—2/hour, 2 hours; for details on cheaper but slower Tube or bus option from airport to London see page 182), **Gatwick** (allow 3 hours minimum; from Gatwick South, catch First Capital Connect train to London's St. Pancras Station; from there, walk to neighboring King's Cross Station, and catch train to York—2/hour, 2 hours).

YORK

NORTH YORKSHIRE

Near York • North York Moors •
The North Yorkshire Coast

The countryside to the north of York—dubbed "North Yorkshire"—is speckled with pleasant attractions: the house and office of the "real" rural vet James Herriot, the desolately beautiful North York Moors, an eclectic mansion often used in movies, an engaging folk museum, a quirky World War II museum at a former POW camp, a kitschy scenic steam train, and several looming skeletons of destroyed abbeys. On the Yorkshire coast, you'll find an appealing pair of salty seaside towns—one big and one small. While none of these is a top-tier sight in itself, they complement each other nicely, so a day driving to several is time well spent.

Getting Around North Yorkshire

By Car: Driving is the best option—distances are short, the towns are small and easy to navigate, and there are plenty of tempting stopovers along the way. Get a good map, and use it thoughtfully to craft an efficient itinerary. As you drive, watch out for "wild" pheasants absentmindedly crossing the road. These birds are bred and fed by locals, and left to range freely through the woods...until autumn, when hunting season begins, and the fat, tame, and naive pheasants become easy prey.

By Bus and Train: You can reach most of these destinations by public transportation, but it requires patience (and in some cases—such as Rievaulx Abbey—a long walk from where the bus or train drops you off). York serves as a fine hub (buses leave from in front of the railway station), with bus connections to Thirsk, Castle Howard, Eden Camp, Pickering, and Whitby (most run by Coastliner, tel. 01653/692-556, www.coastliner.co.uk); Hutton-le-

North Yorkshire

TO DURHAM, HOLY ISLAND & EDINBURGH
SALTBURN-BY-THE-SEA
NORTH SEA
MIDDLES-BROUGH
STAITHES
A-66
To A-1
A-174
A-171
A-173
GUIS-BOROUGH
A-174
SANDSEND
WHITBY
A-172
A-19
BATTERSBY
B-1257
DANBY
A-171
GROS-MONT
ROBIN HOOD'S BAY
GOATHLAND
A-171
NORTH YORK MOORS
TO DURHAM & EDINBURGH
RIEVAULX ABBEY
HUTTON-LE-HOLE
A-169
SCARBOROUGH
THIRSK
A-170
HELMSLEY
A-170
PICKERING
A-170
KILBURN
WHITE HORSE
EDEN CAMP
A-64
TO YORKSHIRE DALES
COXWOLD
HOVING-HAM
B-1257
MALTON
TO DURHAM & EDINBURGH
CASTLE HOWARD
NORTON
A-19
WELLBURN
WHITEWELL-ON-THE-HILL
A-59
A-64
A-166
A-1
YORK
A-64
A-1079
TO LONDON
A-64
A-19
TO KINGSTON-UPON-HULL

5 MILES
3 KM

DCH

++ NORTH YORKSHIRE MOORS RAILWAY — ROAD --- PATH
++ OTHER RAIL ❶ MOORS VISITORS CENTRE

Hole and Rievaulx Abbey (via Helmsley) are sparsely connected to York by Moorsbus (www.northyorkmoors.org.uk/moorsbus). A fun old steam train chugs through the middle of the North York Moors, from Pickering to Grosmont, then sometimes on to Whitby. Buses also follow the coastal road north and south of Whitby, including Staithes. I've explained particularly handy connections with each listing below. As specific bus schedules change frequently with the season, always confirm the details at the York TI.

By Tour: Various tour companies offer guided bus excursions from York, focusing on Yorkshire Dales/James Herriot country, the North York Moors, Castle Howard, and more (different tour every day, see website for tours and prices; try Eddie Brown, tel. 01423/321-246, www.eddiebrowntours.com; or York Pullman, tel. 01904/622-992, www.yorkpullmanbus.co.uk).

Near York

The following sights are between York and the North York Moors. I've listed them in order from west to east. If you have a car and are very speedy, you could see all of these in one day—but it makes more sense to pick a few that appeal to you, then link them with lazy countryside drives. Sparse public-transportation connections mean you'll have to choose one or two if you lack a car.

▲World of James Herriot

Devotees of the *All Creatures Great and Small* books and television series can visit the folksy veterinarian's digs in Thirsk, a pleasant market town west of York. James Herriot was an autobiographical character created by Alfred Wight, once the Thirsk town vet. Today Wight's home and office have been converted into a museum that painstakingly re-creates the 1940s Skeldale House featured in the novels, and also explores the development of veterinary science. The worthwhile audioguide, narrated by the vet's son, James Wight, adds even more intimacy to the exhibits. Even non-fans will find the slice-of-1940s-life decor fascinating, and the trivia intriguing. (For example, Alf Wight chose the name James Herriot for his protagonist to avoid violating an anti-advertising law...and named himself for his favorite Scottish soccer goalie.) But fans will be tickled by the museum's reverence for all things Herriot. Even the studio sets from the TV show have been re-created. The interactive children's section is particularly engaging, even for adults: Try your hand at horse dentistry and find out if you're strong enough to calve a cow.

Cost and Hours: £6, recommended £2 audioguide is loud enough to be shared, daily April–Oct 10:00–17:00, Nov–March 11:00–16:00, last entry one hour before closing, 23 Kirkgate, tel. 01845/524-234, www.worldofjamesherriot.org.

Getting There: The museum is just a block up Kirkgate from the main market square in Thirsk. Buses connect York with Thirsk (4/day Mon–Sat, 1/day on Sun, 45 minutes, www.yorkshiretravel.net). There are more connections by train and it takes the same amount of time, but you're left at a station about a mile outside of

Thirsk, while the bus drops you at the main square. Drivers can zip there from York on A19 in about 40 minutes.

Nearby: Die-hard Herriot fans might enjoy exploring the **Yorkshire Dales,** westward from and much tamer than the North York Moors. Get details about the region—and information about guided tours—at the TI in York. Approaching Thirsk, keep an eye out on the right side of the road for the **"White Horse"**—a gigantic image in the hillside that overlooks the town of Kilburn. The figure was created by a schoolmaster and his students in 1857, who removed the soil to expose the light-colored bedrock.

▲Rievaulx Abbey

Rievaulx (ree-VOH) is the sprawling ruins of a 12th-century abbey. Since it's not near any major towns, its pre-cut stones were

less susceptible to plunder—so it's been left a bit more intact than many other ruined abbeys. Its beautiful and secluded setting—tucked away in a gentle, sheep-speckled valley—is appealing, but if you've seen other fine old abbeys, this is a rerun. Start with the little museum, then follow the included audioguide through the ruins. You'll learn how monastic life changed during the four centuries between its founding and its destruction by Henry VIII.

Cost and Hours: £5.30, includes audioguide; generally April–Sept daily 10:00–18:00; Oct Thu–Mon 10:00–17:00, closed Tue–Wed; Nov–March Thu–Mon 10:00–16:00, closed Tue–Wed; café, tel. 01439/798-228, www.english-heritage.org.uk.

Getting There: Drivers get there in a snap (just a short detour from A170). Bus transportation is trickier. From York, first catch a bus to Helmsley (6/day Mon–Sat, 1/day on Sun, 1.25 hours). From Helmsley, you can get to the abbey on foot (2 miles), by taxi (call 01439/770-981), or by infrequent bus (#M9, runs daily mid-July–Aug, but only on Sun mid-March–mid-July and Sept–Oct, bus may not run Nov–mid-March, confirm schedules before you set out, www.yorkshiretravel.net).

▲Hutton-le-Hole

This postcard-pretty town, lining up along a river as if posing for its close-up, is an ideal springboard for a trip into the North York Moors. It has some touristy shops and inviting picnic benches, but Hutton-le-Hole's (pronounced "HOO-ton le hole") biggest attraction is its engaging folk museum. **Ryedale Folk Museum** illustrates farm life in the moors through reconstructed and furnished 18th-century buildings. At this open-air complex, you'll wander along a line of shops, including a village store—one-stop shopping (the original Costco) to save locals the long trek into the closest market town. Then you'll come to a humble cluster of traditional, lived-in-feeling thatch-roof cot-

tages. If the beds are unmade, notice the "mattress" is made of rope stretched across a frame, which could be tightened for a firmer night's sleep (giving us the phrase "sleep tight"). The museum is most worthwhile on summer Thursdays and during frequent special weekends, when lively costumed docents explain what you're seeing along the way (check online schedule or call ahead).

Cost and Hours: £5.50; mid-March–late Oct daily 10:00–17:30, last entry at 16:30; late Oct–mid-March 10:00–dusk, closes early Dec–mid-Jan; tel. 01751/417-367, www.ryedalefolkmuseum .co.uk.

Getting There: Drivers find it just north of A170. From Hutton-le-Hole, you can plunge northward directly into the North York Moors (which begin suddenly as you leave town). Non-drivers will rely on the sporadic Moorsbus (tel. 01845/597-000, www.northyorkmoors.org.uk/moorsbus).

▲Castle Howard

Especially popular since the filming of the *Brideshead Revisited* TV miniseries here in 1981, this fine, palatial, 300-year-old home (more a manor than a "castle") is a bit overrated but still worth considering. It was commissioned on a whim to John Vanbrugh, a playwright who previously had no architectural training whatsoever—which explains some of his unique flourishes (like the grand, domed entryway that would seem more at home in a Baroque church). Vanbrugh went on to build the even grander Blenheim Palace near Oxford (which is at least twice as interesting, if you're choosing between them—see page 441). After being damaged in a 1940 fire, Castle Howard lay in ruins for years before being refurbished in the 1950s and opened to the public. The Howard family, whose precocious daughters are pictured throughout the place, still lives in one wing—and in winter, when the place is closed to the public, they actually use the rooms that are normally on the tour route. The 2008 big-screen version of *Brideshead Revisited*, starring Emma Thompson and Michael Gambon, was also filmed here.

The sprawling grounds include several pools, lakes, and

fountains, a rose garden, and a quiet wood. As you follow the one-way route through the house, chatty docents posted in key rooms explain what you're seeing. Many of the decorations are "souvenirs" from the Howards' travels—such as replicas of Roman busts and Greek statues, or paintings that attempt to jam several of a Grand Tour city's landmarks onto a single canvas like today's collage postcards. (Outside, the mini-pyramid on the horizon—behind the big Atlas Fountain—was inspired by a trip to Egypt.) Also watch for the elaborate, multistory, blue Delft porcelain tulip vase—dating from the "Tulip Fever" era of the late 17th century, when a single flower could cost £1,000. Imagine the extravagance of filling this whole vase.

Cost and Hours: £12.50 for house and grounds, or £8.50 for grounds only in winter, when the house is closed. The gardens are open daily 10:00–18:30, last entry at 17:30, closes at dusk in winter; the house is open daily mid-March–Oct 11:00–16:00, last entry at 16:00; house closed Nov–mid-March except late Nov–mid-Dec, when it's decorated for Christmas. Tel. 01653/648-333, www.castlehoward.co.uk.

Getting There: It's in the countryside between Helmsley and Malton. It's ideal by car, but the bus connection (via Malton) eats up the better part of a day, which the castle isn't worth for most travelers (for public-transit options, see the castle's website or visit www.yorkshiretravel.net).

Eden Camp

Once an internment camp for German and Italian POWs during World War II, this is now a theme museum on Britain's war experience. Sprawling, cluttered, and a bit hokey, the exhibit works best for Brits who want to help their kids (or grandkids) understand the war years. But, even though it's overpromoted, its earnestness will win over WWII buffs, as it energetically tries to convey the spirit of a country Hitler couldn't conquer.

Various barracks detail the rise of Hitler, the fury of the Blitz, and the efforts on the home front—such as rationing and the Local Defense Volunteers, affectionately dubbed "Dads Army." A detailed map and ample posted information are helpful, if a bit overwhelming. Focus your visit on the topics that interest you most. An intense exhibit on the Blitz comes with the sound of bombs, the acrid smell of burning, and quotes such as, "Hitler will send no warning—so always carry your gas mask." Don't miss hut #10, which details the actual purpose of the camp—a prison for captured Nazis and Italians during World War II (think *Hogan's Heroes* in reverse). Enjoy the quirky handmade items—such as a miniature pair of shoes carved out of bread—created by bored POWs who were killing time. Consider the relative delight of

NORTH YORKSHIRE

being in the care of the gentlemanly English rather than in a Nazi camp. It's no wonder the Germans and Italians settled right in.

Cost and Hours: £5.50, daily 10:00–17:00, last entry at 16:00, closed late Dec–mid-Jan, cash only, mess-kitchen cafeteria, tel. 01653/697-777, www.edencamp.co.uk.

Getting There: It's near Malton, 18 miles northeast of York. From York, drivers take A169 toward Scarborough, then follow signs to the camp (notice its proximity to Castle Howard—it's easy to combine these two and more on a day's drive). Or, from York, you can catch Coastliner bus #840 (every 1–2 hours Mon–Sat, fewer on Sun, 50–60 minutes, www.yorkshiretravel.net).

Pickering

This functional town is a major crossroads and a proud hub of sorts for this region's meager public transit (**TI** tel. 01751/473-791). The main reason to visit Pickering is to catch the **North Yorkshire Moors Railway** steam train into the moors (described later). Otherwise, you can browse its Monday market (produce, knick-knacks) and consider its rural-life museum (Hutton-le-Hole's is better)—but don't bother visiting Pickering unless you're passing through anyway.

With more time, consider stopping by Pickering's ruined 13th-century Norman **castle,** built on the site of a wooden castle from William the Conqueror's 11th-century heyday. Appreciate its textbook motte-and-bailey (stone fort on a grassy hilltop) design, and climb to the top to understand its strategic location (£3.70, April–Sept daily 10:00–17:00, closed Oct–March, on the ridge above town, tel. 01751/474-989, www.english-heritage.org.uk).

Getting There: Drivers find Pickering right on A169 north of York (en route to the coast). Or you can catch Coastliner bus #840 from York (every 1–2 hours Mon–Sat, fewer on Sun, 1.25 hours, www.yorkshiretravel.net); you can shave a few minutes off the trip by taking the train to Malton, then catching bus #840 from there.

North York Moors

In the lonesome North York Moors, sheep seem to outnumber people. In this high, desolate-feeling plateau, with a spongy and inhospitable soil, bleating flocks jockey for position against scrubby heather for control of the terrain. You can almost imagine the mysterious Heathcliff (from *Wuthering Heights,* which was set here) plodding across this terrain. As you pass through this haunting landscape, crisscrossed by only a few roads, notice how the gloomy brown heather—which blooms briefly with purple flowers at summer's end—is actually burned back by wardens to clear the way for new growth. The vast, undulating expanses of nothingness are punctuated by greener, sparsely populated valleys called dales. Park your car and take a hike across the moors on any small road. You'll come upon a few tidy villages and maybe even old Roman roads.

Drivers can consider The Moors Centre; non-drivers can take the steam train; and anyone might want to stop in Goathland.

The Moors Centre

This visitor facility near Danby provides the best orientation for exploring North York Moors National Park. (Unfortunately, it's at the northern end of the park—not as convenient if you're coming from York.) This grand old lodge offers exhibits, shows, nature walks, an information desk, plenty of books and maps, brass rubbing, a cheery cafeteria, and brochures on several good walks that start right outside the front door.

Cost and Hours: Free entry but £2.20 parking fee; April–Oct daily 10:00–17:00; March and Nov–Dec daily 11:00–16:00; Jan–Feb Sat–Sun 11:00–16:00, closed Mon–Fri; café, tel. 01439/772-737, www.northyorkmoors.org.uk.

Getting There: The Centre is three-fourths of a mile from Danby in Esk Valley, in the northern part of the park (follow signs from Danby, which is a short drive from A171 running along the northern edge of the park).

▲North Yorkshire Moors Railway

This 18-mile, one-hour steam-engine ride between Pickering and Grosmont (GROW-mont) runs almost hourly through some of the best parts of the moors. Sometimes the train continues from Grosmont on to the seaside town of Whitby; otherwise, you might be able to transfer in Grosmont to another, non-steam train to reach Whitby (check schedules before you plan your trip). Once in Whitby, you can use the bus to connect along the coast (such as to Staithes) or to return to York. (For details on getting to Pickering, see previous page.)

Even with the small and dirty windows (try to wipe off the outside of yours before you roll), and with the track situated mostly in a scenic gully, it's a good ride. You can stop along the way for a walk on the moors (or at the appealing village of Goathland—

described next) and catch the next train (£16 round-trip to Grosmont, or £21 round-trip to Whitby, includes hop-on, hop-off privileges; runs daily late March–Oct, and some Dec weekends, no trains Nov and Jan–late March, schedule flexes with the season but generally the first train departs Pickering at 9:00, last train departs Grosmont about 18:30; trip takes about one hour one-way to Grosmont, allow about 2.75 hours round-trip to come back on the same train; tel. 01751/472-508 or 24-hour timetable info at tel. 01751/472-508, www.nymr.co.uk). There's nowhere to leave luggage at any stop on the steam-train line—pack light if you decide to hike.

Goathland

This tranquil village, huddled along a babbling brook, is worth considering for a sleepy stopover, either on the steam-train trip or for drivers (it's an easy detour from A169, which cuts through the moors). Movie buffs will enjoy Goathland's train station, which was used to film scenes at "Hogsmeade Station" for the early Harry Potter movies (for more on Harry Potter sights, see page 714). But Brits know and love Goathland as the setting for the beloved, long-running TV series *Heartbeat,* about a small Yorkshire town in the 1960s. You'll see TV sets intermingled with real buildings, and some shops are even labeled "Aidensfield," for the TV town's fictional name.

The North Yorkshire Coast

Two salty Yorkshire towns—one big (Whitby) and one small (Staithes)—are seaside escapes worth a stop for the seagulls, surf, and Captain Cook lore. If you're not seeing the English coast anywhere else on your trip, and you have an extra day in York, side-tripping here is worthwhile.

Getting to the North Yorkshire Coast

Various buses connect **York** to Whitby (1–2/hour, 1.75–2.75 hours, www.yorkshiretravel.net).

To connect Whitby to the **North York Moors,** you can take the historic steam train from Pickering to Grosmont, which often continues into Whitby (otherwise you can sometimes transfer in Grosmont to a Whitby-bound train).

From **Durham,** you can get to Whitby by train via Darlington and Middlesbrough (Durham–Middlesbrough: at least hourly, 1 hour with transfer in Darlington; then Middlesbrough–Whitby: 4/day, 1.5 hours). The Durham–Middlesbrough train also stops at two towns on the North York Moors (both described earlier): Grosmont (where you can catch the Moors steam train south to Pickering) and Danby (near The Moors Centre).

Getting Around the North Yorkshire Coast

Once in Whitby, Arriva buses #5 and #5A run at least hourly in each direction up and down the coast, connecting you to Staithes and Sandsend (north); buses #93 and #X93 run at least hourly from Whitby south to Robin Hood's Bay (www.arrivabus.co.uk).

Whitby

An important port since the 12th century, Whitby is today a fun coastal resort town with about 14,000 people and a gaggle of steep

and salty old streets. Its busy harbor is squeezed into a narrow canyon flanked on one side by the stately skeleton of its 11th-century abbey, and on the other by the bluff-topping West Cliff neighborhood. The harborfront zone is a carousel of Coney Island–type amusements and city-dwellers from inland Yorkshire whooping it up. Rounding out Whitby's claim to fame are its connections to Captain Cook and Bram Stoker (whose *Dracula* was partly written here).

Orientation to Whitby

(area code: 01947)

Tourist Information

The TI is on the harbor next to the train and bus stations (daily May–Sept 9:30–17:00, July–Aug until 18:00, Oct–April 10:00–16:30, often closed for lunch in winter, tel. 01723/383-636, www.discoveryorkshirecoast.com).

Arrival in Whitby

If driving, consider first stopping by the hilltop sights (the abbey on one side of town, and West Cliff on the other). Then drive down into the old town center and drop your car across the street from the TI in the pay-and-display parking lot near the train and bus stations. Walk a few steps toward the harbor—and the lone bridge spanning it—to get oriented.

From the bridge, face the sea to consider your options (described in more detail below): On the left is the waterfront promenade called Pier Road/Fish Quay, lined with tacky carnival distractions, as well as the recommended Magpie Café (popular fish-and-chips) and a tacky Dracula exhibit (skip it); above this scene is the West Cliff area, with fine views over town. On the right (across the bridge) is a warren of touristy lanes filled with hard-candy stores, knickknack shops, and the Captain Cook Memorial Museum; overhead is the ruined abbey.

Sights in Whitby

Whitby's main landmark is its ruined **abbey,** set on a bluff overlooking the harbor. Built on the site of a seventh-century monastic settlement, the remains of this 11th-century version echo with the chants of ages past...enough to raise goose bumps even on a vampire (*Dracula* was partly set here). Many of the stones from this formerly grand abbey were used to build houses in the town below (£5.80, includes audio-

guide; April–Sept daily 10:00–18:00; Oct–March Thu–Mon 10:00–16:00, closed Tue–Wed; tel. 01947/603-568, www.english -heritage.org.uk).

The abbey is connected to the streets below by a **staircase** of 199 steps called Caedmon's Trod. In the olden days, poor people would carry the coffins of the departed up these steps, resting occasionally on broader steps called "coffin rests"...which, for practical reasons, are more frequent near the top.

Down below, the small **Captain Cook Memorial Museum,** in an old shipowner's house where Cook lodged for a few years, offers a dull look at the famous hometown sailor and his exotic voyages. The most interesting bit is the Voyages Room, with a cutaway model of one of Cook's ships, and miniature replicas of everything that went on board (£4.50, pick up free pamphlet as you enter, daily March 11:00–15:00, April–Oct 9:45–17:00, last entry 30 minutes before closing, closed Nov–Feb; tucked down little Grape Lane behind the Dolphin Hotel, near the bridge on the abbey side of town; tel. 01947/601-900, www.cookmuseumwhitby.co.uk). Two of Captain Cook's boats (*Resolution* and *Endeavour*) were built in the Whitby shipyards; a full-size replica of the *Endeavour,* which has been used in many swashbuckling films, is often moored in Whitby.

Across the harbor from the abbey is a fun little hilltop park called **West Cliff,** with inviting benches and a lively kids' area. Supposedly it was from this vantage point that Bram Stoker con-

NORTH YORKSHIRE

templated Whitby's abbey...and inspiration bit him in the neck. In *Dracula*, a boat docks at the long pier, and a black dog—the Count in disguise—jumps off the boat and runs up the 199 steps to the abbey...where he hides out for the next three chapters, until he takes to the sea again. Nearby, the whale bones forming an archway over the path recall Whitby's former status as a major whaling city. When whalers returned to port, they'd prop up bones like these on their ships, as a sign to their wives and mothers (who were anxiously waiting ashore) that the trip had gone safely.

To go for a **walk along the beach,** consider strolling to nearby villages, then walking or catching an Arriva bus back: Sandsend to the north (buses #5 and #5A) is closer than Robin Hood's Bay to the south (buses #93 and #X93, www.arrivabus.co.uk).

Sleeping in Whitby

A collection of inviting B&Bs perches atop the plateau behind West Cliff. Among these, **$$ Crescent Lodge B&B** is a good choice (8 rooms, Sb-£35, Db-£60, just off the main drag as you enter the upper part of town at 27 Crescent Avenue, tel. 01947/820-073, http://crescentlodgewhitby.co.uk, carol@carolyates.wanadoo.co.uk, Carol).

$$ The Dolphin Hotel, in the old-town center at the bridge overlooking the harbor, is a colorful old pub with seven renovated rooms upstairs with miniscule yacht-type bathrooms (Db-£60–90, apartment with kitchen-£100, pub closes at 23:00, 3 blocks from train station, Bridge Street, tel. 01947/602-197, www.dolphin whitby.co.uk).

Sleep Code

(£1 = about $1.60, country code: 44, area code: 01947)
S = Single, **D** = Double/Twin, **T** = Triple, **Q** = Quad, **b** = bathroom, **s** = shower only. Unless otherwise noted, you can assume breakfast is included and credit cards are accepted.

To help you sort easily through these listings, I've divided the rooms into three categories based on the price for a standard double room with bath (during high season):

$$$ Higher Priced—Most rooms £80 or more.
$$ Moderately Priced—Most rooms between £50–80.
$ Lower Priced—Most rooms £50 or less.

Prices can change without notice; verify the hotel's current rates online or by email. For other updates, see www.ricksteves.com/update.

$ Whitby's **Abbey House youth hostel** is one of England's most impressive. Right on the abbey grounds above town—and literally built with bits and pieces of that abbey—this 17th-century building has recently undergone an extensive restoration. Now it houses 100 beds in 22 rooms, most of them 4- to 6-bed dormitories with bathrooms. Many rooms have information plaques on the walls explaining the architecture and renovation (£16–22/bed, Db twin-£40–55, price depends on day and season, breakfast-£5, reception open 7:30–10:00 & 13:00–22:30, no curfew, family rooms, fully wheelchair-accessible rooms, pay Internet access and free Wi-Fi, laundry, kitchen, cafeteria-style restaurant, tel. 01947/602-878, www.yha.org.uk, whitby@yha.org.uk).

Eating in Whitby

Fish-and-chips are on everybody's mind here. The **Magpie Café** is a local institution, generally marked by a line of loyal eaters waiting to get in; there's also a carry-out window to the right (£10–12 fish-and-chips, £10–18 fish dinners, daily 11:30–21:00, closed much of Jan, 14 Pier Road, tel. 01947/602-058). The **Dolphin Hotel** offers a scenic location with outdoor seating and serviceable food dead-center in the old town, right at the bridge. They serve £5–10 fish-and-chips and sandwiches for lunch, and an £8–16 grill menu for dinner (food served daily 12:00–14:30 & 18:00–21:00, from Oct–May Sat–Sun only, Bridge Street, tel. 01947/602-197).

Staithes

A ragamuffin village where the boy who became Captain James Cook got his first taste of the sea, Staithes (pronounced "staythz," just north of Whitby) is a salty jumble of cottages bunny-hopping down a ravine into a tiny harbor. About a tenth the size of its big sister down the coast, Staithes is the yang to Whitby's yin. This refreshingly unpretentious town is gloriously stubborn about not wooing tourists (www.staithes -town.info).

While dead as a doornail today, in 1816 Staithes was home to 70 boats and the busiest fishing station on the northeast coast of England. Ten years ago, the town supported 20 fishing boats—today, only three. But fishermen (who pronounce their town "steers" in the local dialect) still outnumber tourists in undiscovered Staithes. The town has changed little since Captain Cook's days. Lots of flies and seagulls seem to have picked the barren cliffs raw. There's nothing to do but stroll the beach and nurse a harborside beer or ice cream.

For a bit more activity, drop by the **lifeboat station,** operated by the Royal National Lifeboat Institution (RNLI)—Britain's entirely volunteer answer to the Coast Guard. Entering the big barn, notice the boards up on the eaves with not-quite-stirring accounts of the boats being called to duty. As this organization—England's sole method for responding to maritime emergencies—is entirely funded by donations, consider supporting the cause with a coin or two (typically open daily 10:00–16:00 in summer, most days in winter, shop tel. 01947/840-373, www.rnli.org.uk or www.staithes-lifeboat.co.uk).

Getting to Staithes

Staithes is an easy **drive** north of Whitby. Parking is tough—generally, you can drive in only to unload. Service trucks clog the windy main (and only) lane much of the day. There's a pay-and-display lot at the top of the town—an easy downhill walk to the action (but a more strenuous hike back up). While the **bus** #5/#5A connection from Whitby to Staithes is fairly straightforward, there's not much in low-key Staithes to justify the trip (1-2/hour, 30 minutes; 10-minute walk from bus stop into town, www.arriva bus.co.uk).

Sleeping and Eating in Staithes

There are no fancy rooms, and it's a cash-only town with no ATMs.

$$$ Endeavour House B&B is usually booked as a unit, but check with them at the last minute to see if one of their four rooms is available (Db-£65–80, free Wi-Fi, parking, 1 High Street, tel. 01947/841-735, www.endeavour-restaurant.co.uk, endeavour .restaurant@virgin.net, Brian Kay and Charlotte Willoughby).

A pair of lowbrow pubs serves lunch and dinner daily: **The Royal George** sits along the main drag (tel. 01947/841-432). **The Cod and Lobster,** overlooking the harbor, has scenic outdoor benches and a cozy living room warmed by a coal fire (tel. 01947/840-295). Drop in to see its old-time Staithes photos.

In nice weather, the best option is to enjoy a drink, snack, or light meal (i.e., fish-and-chips) sitting at an outdoor table fronting the harbor. Try the friendly **Seadrift Café,** which specializes in sweets, but also does basic grub (daily 10:00–17:00, tel. 01947/841-345).

DURHAM AND NORTHEAST ENGLAND

Northeast England harbors some of the country's best historical sights. Go for a Roman ramble at Hadrian's Wall, a reminder that Britain was an important Roman colony 2,000 years ago. Make a pilgrimage to Holy Island, where Christianity gained its first toehold in Britain. Marvel at England's greatest Norman church, Durham's cathedral, and enjoy an evensong service. At the Beamish Museum, travel back in time to the year 1913.

Planning Your Time

For train travelers, Durham is the most convenient overnight stop in this region. If you like Roman ruins, visit Hadrian's Wall (doable with transfers, easiest Easter–Oct). The Beamish Museum is an easy day trip from Durham (25 minutes by car, one hour by bus). If you're traveling by train, note that it's problematic to visit Durham en route to another destination, since there's no baggage storage in Durham. Either stay overnight or do Durham as a day trip from York.

By car, you can easily visit Beamish Museum, Hadrian's Wall, Bamburgh Castle, and Holy Island. Spend a night in Durham and a night near Hadrian's Wall.

For the best quick visit, arrive in Durham by mid-afternoon in time to tour the cathedral and enjoy the evensong service (Tue–Sat at 17:15, Sun at 15:30). Sleep in Durham. Visit Beamish the next morning before continuing on to your next destination.

Durham

Without its cathedral, Durham would hardly be noticed. But this magnificently situated cathedral is hard to miss (even if you're zooming by on the train). Seemingly happy to go nowhere, Durham sits along its river, and below its castle and famous cathedral. It has a medieval, cobbled atmosphere and a scraggly peasant's indoor market just off the main square. Durham is the home to England's third-oldest university, with a student vibe jostling against its lingering working-class mining-town feel. You'll see tattooed and pierced people in search of job security and a good karaoke bar. Yet Durham has a youthful liveliness and a small-town warmth that shines—especially on sunny days, when most everyone is licking ice-cream cones.

Orientation to Durham

(area code: 0191)
As it has for a thousand years, tidy little Durham clusters everything safely under its castle, within the protective hairpin bend of the River Wear. The longest walk you'll make will be a 30-minute uphill hike from the train station to the cathedral (also doable by bus).

Tourist Information
The TI books rooms and regional event tickets, and provides train times (Mon–Sat 9:30–17:30, Sun 11:00–16:00, WC, café; 1 block north of Market Place, past St. Nicholas Church, in Gala Theatre building; tel. 0191/384-3720, www.durhamtourism.co.uk, tourist info@durhamcity.gov.uk).

Arrival in Durham
From the **train station,** follow the walkway along the road downhill to the second pedestrian turnoff (within sight of railway bridge), which leads almost immediately over a bridge above the busy road called Alexander Crescent. Then take North Road into town or to the first couple of B&Bs (take Alexander Crescent to the other B&Bs). Or just hop on the convenient Cathedral Bus at the train station (described later, under "Getting Around Durham").

    Drivers simply surrender to the wonderful 400-space Prince Bishops Shopping Centre parking lot (at the roundabout at the base of the old town). It's perfectly safe, with 24-hour access, and an elevator deposits you right in the heart of Durham (£2/2 hours, £3.20/4 hours, £1.50 for overnight, a short block from Market Place, tel. 0191/383-9592, www.princebishops.co.uk).

Durham

P Parking

1. Farnley Tower B&B
2. Victorian Town House B&B
3. Castleview Guest House
4. Durham Castle Rooms
5. Durham Marriott Hotel Royal County
6. Kingslodge Hotel & Rest.
7. To Travelodge Durham
8. Melanzana Restaurant
9. Café Rouge & Bella Italia
10. Bimbi's Fish & Chips
11. Hide Café
12. Shaheen's Restaurant
13. The Court Inn Pub
14. To Bistro 21
15. Marks & Spencer

Helpful Hints

Internet Access: The library, across huge Millennium Place from the TI, has about 40 terminals with free Internet access (Mon–Fri 9:30–19:00, Sat 9:00–17:00, Sun 10:30–16:30, must join for free—bring ID, tel. 0191/386-4003).

Laundry: Durham has none within walking distance; ask at the TI for details if you're willing to drive or take a taxi.

Tours: The TI offers 1.5-hour **city walking tours** on summer weekends (£4, schedule varies but usually May–Sept Sat–Sun at 14:00—confirm with TI). **David Butler,** the town historian, gives excellent private tours (reasonable prices, tel. 0191/386-1500, david@dhent.fsnet.co.uk) as well as a Durham Ghost Tour on Mondays in summer (£5, meet at TI at 19:30, July–Sept only).

Harry Potter Sights: Durham Cathedral was used in the films, as were other nearby locations. For details, see page 714.

Getting Around Durham

While all my recommended hotels, eateries, and sights are easily walkable in Durham, taxis are available to zip tired tourists to their B&Bs or back to the station (about £4, wait on west side of Framwellgate Bridge on Silver Street).

If you don't feel like walking Durham's hills, hop on the convenient **Cathedral Bus** (#40), which runs between the train station and the cathedral, with stops near the North Road bus station, Millburngate, Market Place, and some car parks (£0.50 all-day ticket, daily 3/hour, leaves train station Mon–Fri 7:55–17:30, Sat 9:10–17:30, Sun 9:50–16:50; last bus leaves cathedral Mon–Sat at 17:40, Sun at 17:00; toll tel. 0871-200-2222, www.durham.gov.uk).

Self-Guided Walk

Welcome to Durham

• *Begin at Framwellgate Bridge (which connects the train station with the center).*

Framwellgate Bridge was a wonder when it was built in the 12th century—much longer than the river is wide and higher than seemingly necessary. It was well-designed to connect stretches of solid high ground, and to avoid steep descents toward the marshy river. Note how elegantly today's Silver Street (which leads toward town) slopes into the Framwellgate Bridge. (Imagine that as late as the 1970s, this people-friendly lane was congested with traffic and buses.)

• *Follow Silver Street up the hill to the town's main square.*

Durham's **Market Place** retains the same plotting the prince bishop gave it when he moved villagers here in about 1100. Each plot of land was the same width (about 8 yards). Find today's distinctly narrow buildings (Thomas Cook, Whittard, and the optician shop)—they still fit the 900-year-old plan. The widths of the other buildings fronting the square are multiples of that first shop width. Plots were long and skinny, maximizing the number of shops that could have a piece of the Market Place action.

Examine the square's **statues.** Coal has long been the basis of this region's economy. The statue of Neptune was part of an

ill-fated attempt by a coal baron to bribe the townsfolk into embracing a canal project that would make the shipment of his coal more efficient. The statue of the fancy guy on the horse is Charles Stewart Vane, the Third Marquess of Londonderry. He was an Irish aristocrat, and a general in Wellington's army, who married a local coal heiress. A clever and aggressive businessman, he managed to create a vast business empire controlling every link in the coal business chain—mines, railroads, boats, harbors, and so on.

In the 1850s throughout England, towns were moving their markets off squares and into Industrial Age iron-and-glass market halls. Durham was no exception, and today its **indoor market** (which faces Market Place) is a funky 19th-century delight to explore (Mon–Sat 9:00–17:00, closed Sun). There are also outdoor markets in Market Square (Sat retail market 9:00–16:30, farmers' market third Thu of each month, 9:00–15:30, tel. 0191/384-6153, www.durhammarkets.co.uk).

Do you enjoy the sparse traffic in Durham's old town? It was the first city in England to institute a "congestion fee." Look where traffic enters the old town on the downhill side of the square. The bollards (short posts) are up, blocking traffic Monday through Saturday from 10:00 to 16:00. Anyone can drive in...but it costs £2 to get out. This has cut downtown traffic by more than 50 percent. Locals brag that London (which now has a similar congestion fee) was inspired by their success.

• *Head up to the cathedral along Saddler Street. On the left, you'll see a bridge.*

A 12th-century construction, **Elvet Bridge** led to a town market over the river. Like Framwellgate, it's very long (17 arches) and designed to avoid river muck and steep inclines. Even today, Elvet Bridge leads to an unusually wide road—once swollen to accommodate the market action. Shops lined the right-hand side of Elvet Bridge in the 12th century, as they do today. An alley separated the bridge from the buildings on the left. When the bridge

Central Durham

TO TRAIN STN.

FRAMWELL

GALA THEATRE BLDG.

PROV. ROW

FREEMAN

MILL PL.

LIB.

CLAYPATH

GILESGATE

MILLBURNGATE BRIDGE

ST. NICH.

LEAZES RD.

A-690

TO BUS STN.

NORTH ROAD

INDOOR MKT.

MARKET PLACE

HIGH ST.

PRINCE BISHOP'S SHOPPING CENTRE

NEW

START

FRAMWELLGATE BRIDGE

SILVER

BOATS

ELVET BRIDGE

ELVET

CROSSGATE

Post

SADDLER

CASTLE

ST. MARG.

SOUTH STREET

PALACE GREEN

OWENGATE

NORTH BAILEY

100 YARDS

100 METERS

END

DUNCOW

BOW LANE

KINGSGATE BR.

CHURCH ST.

PIMLICO

OLD MILL

CATHEDRAL

SOUTH BAILEY

R I V E R   W E A R

WEIR

ST. OSWALD'S

PREBENDS BR.

DCH

QUARRYHEADS LANE

VIEW

- - - **FOOTPATH**

P PARKING

PEDESTRIAN ZONE

DURHAM AND NE ENGLAND

was widened, it met the upper stories of the buildings on the left, which became "street level."

The Scots, living just 50 miles from here, were on the rampage in the 14th century. After their victory at Bannockburn in 1314, they pushed farther south and actually burned part of Durham. Wary of this new threat, Durham built these **city walls.** As people settled within the walls, the population density soared. Soon, open lanes were covered by residences and became tunnels (called "vennels"). A classic vennel leads to Saddlers Yard, a fine little 16th-century courtyard (immediately opposite Elvet Bridge). While the vennels are cute today, centuries ago they were Dickensian nightmares—the filthiest of hovels.

• *Continue up Saddler Street. Between the two* Georgian Window *signs, go through the purple door to see a bit of the medieval wall incorporated into the brickwork of a newer building, and a turret from an earlier wall. Back on Saddler Street, you can see the ghost of the old wall. (It's exactly the width of the building now housing the Salvation Army.) Veer right at Owengate as you continue uphill, until you reach the Palace Green.*

The **Palace Green** was the site of the original 11th-century Saxon town, filling this green between the castle and an earlier church. Later, the town made way for 12th-century Durham's defenses, which now enclose the green. With the threat presented by the Vikings, it's no wonder people found comfort in a spot like this.

The **castle** still stands—as it has for a thousand years—on its motte (man-made mound). Like Oxford and Cambridge, Durham University is a collection of colleges scattered throughout the town, and even this castle is part of the school. Look into the old courtyard from the castle gate. It traces the very first and smallest bailey (protected area). As future bishops expanded the castle, they left their coats of arms as a way of "signing" the wing they built. Because the Norman kings appointed prince bishops here to rule this part of their realm, Durham was the seat of power for much of northern England. The bishops had their own army and even minted their own coins (castle entrance by 45-minute guided tour only, £5, call ahead for schedule, 24-hour info tel. 0191/334-3800, www.dur.ac.uk/university.college/tours).

• *This walk ends at Durham's stunning **cathedral**, described next.*

Sights in Durham

▲▲▲Durham's Cathedral

Built to house the much-venerated bones of St. Cuthbert from Lindisfarne, Durham's cathedral offers the best look at Norman architecture in England. ("Norman" is British for "Romanesque.") In addition to touring the cathedral and its attached sights, try to fit in an evensong service.

Cost and Hours: Entry to the cathedral itself is free, though a £4 donation is requested and you must pay to enter its several interior sights (described under

---

Durham's Early Years

Durham's location, tucked inside a tight bend in the River Wear, was ideal for easy fortifications. But it wasn't settled until A.D. 995, with the arrival of St. Cuthbert's body (buried in Durham Cathedral). Shortly after that, a small church and fortification were built upon the site of today's castle and church to house the relic. The castle was a classic "motte-and-bailey" design (with the "motte," or mound, providing a lookout tower for the stockade encircling the protected area, or "bailey"). By 1100, the prince bishop's bailey was filled with villagers—and he wanted everyone out. This was *his* place! He provided a wider protective wall, and had the town resettle below, around today's Market Place. But this displaced the townsfolk's cows, so the prince bishop constructed a fine stone bridge (today's Framwellgate) to connect the new town to grazing land he established across the river. The bridge had a defensive gate, with a wall circling the peninsula and the river serving as a moat.

"Other Cathedral Sights," later). The cathedral is open to visitors mid-July–Aug daily 9:30–20:00; Sept–mid-July Mon–Sat 9:30–18:00, Sun 12:30–17:30; opens daily at 7:15 for worship and prayer, tel. 0191/386-4266, www.durhamcathedral.co.uk. A bookshop, cafeteria, and WC are tucked away in the cloisters. No photos, videos, or mobile phones are allowed inside the cathedral.

Tours: The cathedral offers regular tours in summer. If one is already in session, you're welcome to join (£4; late July–late Sept Mon–Sat at 10:30, 11:00, and 14:30; tours also possible near Easter and during school vacations in May and Oct, call or check website to confirm schedule, tel. 0191/386-4266).

Evensong: For a thousand years, this cradle of English Christianity has been praising God. To really experience the cathedral, go for an evensong service. Arrive early and ask to be seated in the choir. It's a spiritual Oz, as the choristers (20 young-sters—now girls as well as boys—and 12 men) sing psalms—a red-and-white-robed pillow of praise, raised up by the powerful pipe organ. If you're lucky and the service goes well, the organist will run a spiritual musical victory lap as the congregation breaks up (Tue–Sat at 17:15, Sun at 15:30, 1 hour, sometimes sung on Mon; visiting choirs nearly always fill in when choir is off on school break mid-July–Aug; tel. 0191/386-4266).

Organ Recitals: On most Wednesday evenings in July and August you can catch a recital at the cathedral (£8, 19:30).

❷ Self-Guided Tour: Begin your visit outside the cathedral. From the Palace Green, notice how this fortress of God stands boldly opposite the Norman keep of Durham's fortress of man.

The **exterior** of this awe-inspiring cathedral—if you look closely—has a serious skin problem. In the 1770s, as the stone was crumbling, they crudely peeled it back a few inches. The scrape marks give the cathedral a bad complexion to this day. For proof of this odd "restoration," study the masonry 10 yards to the right of the door. The L-shaped stones in the corner would normally never be found in a church like this—they only became L-shaped when the surface was cut back.

At the cathedral **door,** the big, bronze, lion-faced knocker (a replica of the 12th-century original—now in the treasury) was used by criminals seeking sanctuary (read the explanation).

Immediately inside, at the **information desk,** church attendants are standing by to happily answer questions. Ideally, follow a church tour. The £1 pamphlet, *A Short Guide to Durham Cathedral,* is informative but dull.

Notice the **modern window** with the novel depiction of the Last Supper (above and to the left of the entry door). It was given to the church by a local department store in 1984. The shapes of the apostles represent worlds and persons of every kind, from the shadowy Judas to the brightness of Jesus. This window is a good reminder that the cathedral remains a living part of the community.

Near the info desk, the **black marble strip** on the floor was as close to the altar as women were allowed in the days when this was a Benedictine church (until 1540). Sit down (ignoring the black line) and let the fine proportions of England's best Norman nave—and arguably Europe's best Romanesque nave—stir you. All the frilly woodwork and stonework were added in later centuries.

The architecture of the **nave** is particularly harmonious because it was built in a mere 40 years (1093–1133). The round arches and zigzag carved decorations are textbook Norman. The church was also proto-Gothic, built by well-traveled French masons and architects who knew the latest innovations from Europe. Its stone and ribbed roof, pointed arches, and flying buttresses were revolutionary in England. Notice the clean lines and simplicity. It's not as cluttered as other churches for several reasons: Out of respect for St. Cuthbert, for centuries no one else was buried here (so it's not filled with tombs). During Reformation times, sumptuous Catholic decor was cleaned out. And subsequent fires and wars destroyed what Protestants didn't.

Enter the **Galilee Chapel** (late Norman, from 1175) in the back of the nave. The paintings of St. Cuthbert and St. Oswald (seventh-century king of Northumbria) on the side walls of the side altar niche are rare examples of Romanesque (Norman) paint-

Durham's Cathedral

TO CASTLE ↑ ⟨ PALACE ⟩ TO GREEN TOWN CENTER

ENTRY

← COLUMNS →

N A V E CHOIR HIGH ALTAR

4 **1** **2** **3** **6** **5**

9

THE **8** CLOISTER

10

PCH

30 YARDS
30 METERS

1 Information Desk
2 Modern Window
3 Black Marble Strip
4 Galilee Chapel &
   Tomb of the Venerable Bede
5 Chapel of the Nine Altars

6 Tomb of St. Cuthbert
7 Tower Entry
8 Cloisters
9 Treasury
10 Monks' Dormitory

DURHAM AND NE ENGLAND

ings. Facing this altar, look above to your right to see more faint paintings on the upper walls above the columns. Near the center of the chapel, the upraised tomb topped with a black slab contains the remains of the **Venerable Bede,** an eighth-century Christian scholar who wrote the first history of England. The Latin reads, "In this tomb are the bones of the Venerable Bede."

Back in the main church, stroll down the nave to the center, under the highest **bell tower** in Europe (218 feet). Gaze up. The ropes turn wheels upon which bells are mounted. If you're stirred by the cheery ringing of church bells, tune in to the cathedral on Sunday (9:15–10:00 & 14:30–15:30) or Thursday (19:30–21:00 practice, trained bell ringers welcome) when the resounding notes tumble merrily through the entire town.

Continuing east (all medieval churches faced east), you enter the **choir.** Monks worshipped many times a day, and the choir in the center of the church provided a cozy place to gather in this vast, dark, and chilly building. Mass has been said daily here in the heart of the cathedral for 900 years. The fancy wooden chairs are from the 17th century. Behind the altar is the delicately carved Neville Screen from 1380 (made of Normandy stone in London, shipped to Newcastle by sea, then brought here by wagon). Until the Reformation, the niches contained statues of 107 saints. Exit the choir from the far right side (south). Look for the stained-glass window (to your right) that commemorates the church's 1,000th anniversary in 1995. The colorful scenes depict England's history, from coal miners to cows to computers.

Step down behind the high altar into the east end of the church, which contains the 13th-century **Chapel of the Nine Altars.** Built later than the rest of the church, this is Gothic—taller, lighter, and relatively more extravagant than the Norman nave.

Climb a few steps to the **tomb of St. Cuthbert.** An inspirational leader of the early Christian Church in north England, St. Cuthbert lived in the Lindisfarne monastery on Holy Island (100 miles north of Durham). He died in 687. Eleven years later, his body was exhumed and found to be miraculously preserved. This stoked the popularity of his shrine, and pilgrims came in growing numbers. When Vikings raided Lindisfarne in 875, the monks fled with his body (and the famous illuminated *Lindisfarne Gospels,* now in the British Library in London). In 995, after 120 years of roaming, the monks settled in Durham on an easy-to-defend tight bend in the River Wear. This cathedral was built over Cuthbert's tomb.

Throughout the Middle Ages, a shrine stood here and was visited by countless pilgrims. In 1539, during the Reformation—whose proponents advocated focusing on God rather than saints—the shrine was destroyed. But pilgrims still come, especially on St. Cuthbert's feast day (March 20).

Other Cathedral Sights: The entry to the **tower** is in the south transept; the view from the tower will cost you 325 steps and £5 (Mon–Sat 10:00–16:00, closes at 15:00 in winter, closed Sun, last entry 20 minutes before closing; closed during events and in bad weather; must be at least 4'3" tall, no backless shoes). The following sights are within the **cloisters:** The **treasury,** filled with medieval bits and holy pieces (including Cuthbert's coffin, vestments, and cross), fleshes out this otherwise stark building. The actual relics from St. Cuthbert's tomb are at the far end (treasury well worth the £2.50 admission, Mon–Sat 10:00–16:30, Sun 14:00–16:30). The **Monks' Dormitory,** now a library with an original 14th-century timber roof filled with Anglo-Saxon stones, is worth its £1 admission (likely Mon–Sat 10:00–16:00, Sun 12:30–16:00). Skip the unexceptional **AV show** about St. Cuthbert in the unexceptional undercroft (£1, Mon–Sat 10:00–15:00, no showings Sun, off-season also no showings Fri, closed Nov–early Jan).

Near the treasury, you'll find the **WCs, bookshop** (in the old kitchen), and fine **Undercroft** cafeteria (daily 10:00–16:30, tel. 0191/386-3721).

Activities in Durham

Riverside Path—For a 20-minute woodsy escape, walk Durham's riverside path from busy Framwellgate Bridge to sleepy Prebends Bridge.

Boat Cruise and Rental—Hop on the *Prince Bishop* for a relaxing one-hour narrated cruise of the river that nearly surrounds Durham (£6, Easter–Oct, for schedule call 24-hour info line at 0191/386-9525, check at TI, or go down to dock at Brown's Boat House at Elvet Bridge, just east of old town, www.princebishoprc.co.uk). Sailings vary based on weather and tides. For some exercise with the same scenery, you can rent a rowboat at the same pier (£4/hour per person, £10 deposit, Easter–Sept daily 10:00–18:00, last boat rental one hour before dusk, tel. 0191/386-3779).

Sleeping in Durham

B&Bs

$$$ Farnley Tower, a luxurious B&B, has 13 large rooms with all the comforts. On a quiet street at the top of a hill, it's a 15-minute hike from the town center (Sb-£65, Db-£85, superior Db-£95, family room-£120, some rooms have cathedral views, paying with credit card costs 2 percent extra, free Wi-Fi, phones in rooms, easy free parking, inviting yard, The Avenue, tel. 0191/375-0011, fax 0191/383-9694, www.farnley-tower.co.uk, enquiries@farnley-tower.co.uk, Raj and Roopal Naik). The Naiks also run the adjacent, wildly inventive Gourmet Spot restaurant.

$$ Victorian Town House B&B offers three spacious, tastefully updated rooms in an 1853 townhouse in a nice residential area

Sleep Code

(£1 = about $1.60, country code: 44, area code: 0191)
S = Single, **D** = Double/Twin, **T** = Triple, **Q** = Quad, **b** = bathroom, **s** = shower only. You can assume credit cards are accepted, and breakfast is included, unless otherwise noted.

To help you sort easily through these listings, I've divided the rooms into three categories based on the price for a standard double room with bath (during high season):

$$$ Higher Priced—Most rooms £85 or more.
$$ Moderately Priced—Most rooms between £50-85.
$ Lower Priced—Most rooms £50 or less.

Prices can change without notice; verify the hotel's current rates online or by email. For other updates, see www.ricksteves.com/update.

just down the hill from the train station (Sb-£50–60, Db-£80–85, family room-£85–105, cash only, some view rooms, Wi-Fi, DVD library, 2 Victoria Terrace, 5-minute walk from train or bus station, tel. 05601/459-168, www.durhambedandbreakfast.com, stay @durhambedandbreakfast.com, friendly Jill and Andy).

$$ Castleview Guest House rents six airy, restful rooms in a well-located, 250-year-old guesthouse next door to a little church, close to Silver Street (Sb-£55–60, Db-£80–85, cash only, free Internet access and Wi-Fi, free street-parking permit, 4 Crossgate, tel. 0191/386-8852, www.castle-view.co.uk, castle_view@hotmail.com, Mike and Anne Williams).

$$ *Student Housing Open to Anyone:* Durham Castle, a student residence actually on the castle grounds facing the cathedral, rents rooms during the summer break (generally end of June–Sept only). Request a room in the stylish main building, or you may get one of the few bomb shelter–style modern dorm rooms (S-£28.50, Sb-£39, D-£51, Db-£70, fancier Db-£180, elegant breakfast hall, free parking down the hill at Prince Bishops Shopping Centre parking lot with voucher from reception, Palace Green, tel. 0191/334-4108 or 0191/334-4106, fax 0191/334-3801, www.dur.ac.uk/university .college, durham.castle@durham.ac.uk).

Hotels

$$$ Durham Marriott Hotel Royal County scatters its 150 posh, four-star rooms among several buildings sprawling across the river from the city center. The Leisure Club has a pool, sauna, Jacuzzi, and fitness equipment (Db-£150 is official rate—but check website for exact prices and deals, breakfast not included, elevator, 2 restaurants, bar, free parking, Old Elvet, tel. 0191/386-6821 or toll tel. 0870-400-7286, fax 0191/386-0704, www.marriott.co.uk).

$$ Kingslodge Hotel & Restaurant is a slightly worn but comfortable 21-room place with charming terraces, an attached restaurant, a pub, and a champagne-and-oyster bar. Located in a pleasantly woodsy setting, it's nevertheless convenient for train travelers (Sb-£60, Db-£75, family room-£95, breakfast-£7, free Wi-Fi, free parking, Waddington Street, Flass Vale, tel. 0191/370-9977, www.kingslodge.info, kingslodgehotel@yahoo.co.uk).

$$ Travelodge Durham's 57 simple rooms are in a converted 1844 train station, with the former waiting room now housing the reception desk (Db-£55–65 but check website for deals, cold breakfast delivered to room—not worth price, Wi-Fi, half-mile northeast of cathedral, off A690 at Station Lane, Gilesgate, toll tel. 0871-984-6136, fax 0191/386-5461, www.travelodge.co.uk).

Eating in Durham

Durham is a university town with plenty of lively, inexpensive eateries. Stroll down North Road, across Framwellgate Bridge, through Market Place, and up Saddler Street, and consider these places.

Melanzana, just over Elvet Bridge on the other side of town, is an Italian restaurant with £8–9 pizzas and pastas and £11–17 dinners in an inviting setting (daily 9:00-21:00, Fri-Sat until 22:00, even cheaper during happy hour, 96 Elvet Bridge, tel. 0191/384-0096).

Café Rouge, a chain restaurant with French-bistro food and decor, is just east of Framwellgate Bridge (Mon–Sat 9:00–23:00, Sun 10:00–22:00, 21 Silver Street, tel. 0191/384-3429). **Bella Italia,** next door and down the stairs, overlooks the river. Although it's another chain, it's popular and has surprisingly good food (Tue–Sat 10:00–23:00, Sun–Mon 10:00–22:30, reservations recommended, 20 Silver Street, tel. 0191/386-1060). **Bimbi's,** on Market Place, is a standby for fish-and-chips (generally Mon–Wed 11:00–17:00, Thu–Sat 11:00–19:00, Sun 12:00–17:00).

Saddler Street, leading from Market Place up to the cathedral, is lined with eateries. The hip **Hide Café,** with youthful, jazz-filled ambience, serves the best modern continental cuisine in the old town (£6–10 lunches, £8–14 meals, Mon–Sat 12:00–15:00 & 18:00–21:30, Sun 12:00–15:00, reservations smart, 39 Saddler Street, tel. 0191/384-1999).

Shaheen's is the place for good Indian cuisine (£6–10 meals, Tue–Sat 17:00–22:00, closed Sun–Mon, 48 North Bailey Street, just past turnoff to cathedral, tel. 0191/386-0960).

The Court Inn, on the outskirts of town, is a local favorite for traditional pub grub (£7–12 meals, tapas, daily 11:00–22:20, 10-minute walk east of old town over Elvet Bridge, Court Lane, tel. 0191/384-7350).

Bistro 21, with modern French/Mediterranean fare and good seafood, works well for drivers looking for a nontouristy splurge (£15–22 entrées, £15–18 two- or three-course dinner specials, Mon–Sat 12:00–14:00 & 18:00–22:00, closed Sun, 1.5 miles northwest of town, Aykley Heads, tel. 0191/384-4354).

Supermarket: **Marks & Spencer** is in the old town, just off the main square (Mon–Sat 9:00–18:00, Sun 11:00–17:00, 4 Silver Street, across from post office). You can **picnic** in Market Square, or on the benches and grass outside the cathedral entrance (but not on the Palace Green, unless the park police have gone home).

Durham Connections

From Durham by Train to: York (3–4/hour, 45 minutes), **Keswick/Lake District** (train to Penrith—hourly, 3 hours, change in Newcastle and Carlisle; then bus to Keswick—hourly Mon–Sat, Sun 8/day, 40 minutes), **London** (2/hour, 3 hours), **Hadrian's Wall** (take train to Newcastle—4/hour, 15 minutes, then a bus or a train/bus combination to near Hadrian's Wall), **Edinburgh** (2/hour, 2 hours, less frequent in winter). Train info: toll tel. 0845-748-4950, www.nationalrail.co.uk.

Near Durham: Beamish Museum

This huge 300-acre open-air museum, which re-creates the years 1825 and 1913 in northeast England, takes at least three hours to explore. Vintage trams and cool circa-1910 double-decker buses shuttle visitors to the four stations: Colliery Village, The Town, Pockerley Manor/Waggonway, and Home Farm. Tram routes are more plentiful than bus routes, but attendants on both are helpful and knowledgeable. Signs on the trams advertise a variety of 19th-century products, from "Borax, for washing everything" to "Murton's Reliable Travelling Trunks." This isn't a wax museum. If you touch the exhibits, they may smack you. Attendants at each stop happily explain everything. In fact, the place is only really interesting if you talk to the attendants. In 2008, the "Westoe netty"—a circa 1890 men's public WC—was acquired and rebuilt near the 1913 railway station. The loo became famous in 1972 as the subject in a painting by a local artist.

Cost and Hours: £16, £12 with bus receipt, £7.50 in winter, choose the Beamish Unlimited Pass at no extra charge for a 2-day visit; Easter–Oct open daily 10:00–17:00; in Nov–Easter only The Town, Colliery Village, and Tramway are open, Tue–Thu and Sat–Sun 10:00–16:00, closed Mon and Fri and mid-Nov–early Jan; check events schedule as you enter, last tickets sold at 15:00 year-round, tel. 0191/370-4000, www.beamish.org.uk, museum @beamish.org.uk.

Getting There: By **car,** the museum is five minutes off the A1/M1 motorway (one exit north of Durham at Chester-le-Street/Junction 63, well signposted, 12 miles and a 25-minute drive northwest of Durham).

Getting to Beamish from Durham by **bus** is a snap on peak-season weekends via the direct "Waggonway" bus #B1 (£3.70 day pass, 5/day, 30 minutes, runs April–Oct only, stops at Durham train and bus stations, tel. 0845/606-0260, www.simplygo.com).

Otherwise, catch **bus** #21 or #50/#50A from the Durham bus station (3–4/hour, 25 minutes, £3.70 day pass) and transfer

Near Durham

TO EDINBURGH

HOLY ISLAND

BERWICK

SCOTLAND

BAMBURGH CASTLE

JEDBURGH

BORDERS

A-68

NORTH SEA

HOUSESTEADS ROMAN FORT

HADRIAN'S WALL

B-6318

GREEN HEAD

A-69

NEWCASTLE

TO AMSTERDAM

TO CARLISLE & LAKE DISTRICT

A-69

VINDO-LANDA ROMAN FORT

HEXHAM

BEAMISH MUSEUM

HALTWHISTLE

A-693

DURHAM

A-691

SEE DETAIL MAP

ENGLAND

TO YORK & LONDON

DCH

20 MILES

20 KM

at Chester-le-Street to bus #X8, #28, or #28A (2/hour Mon-Sat, hourly Sun, 15 minutes, leaves from central bus kiosk a half-block away; get handy bus schedule at Durham TI, toll tel. 0871-200-2233, www.traveline.org.uk). When you get off the bus at Beamish, the museum is a five-minute walk down the hill. Show your bus receipt for a 25 percent museum discount. To catch the bus leaving Beamish, the bus stop for bus #X8 is on the side of the street near the pub; the stop for #28 and #28A is on the opposite side of the street.

 ❍ **Self-Guided Tour:** Start with the **Colliery Village** (company town around a coal mine), with a school, a church, miners' homes, and a fascinating—if claustrophobic—20-minute tour into the Mahogany drift mine. Your guide will tell you about beams collapsing, gas exploding, and flooding; after that cheerful speech, you'll don a hard hat as you're led into the mine.

The Town is a bustling street featuring a 1913 candy shop (the chocolate room in back is worth a stop for chocolate fans), a dentist's office, a Masonic hall, a garage, a working pub (The Sun Inn, Mon–Sat 11:00–16:30, Sun 12:00–16:30), Barclays Bank, and a hardware store featuring a variety of "toilet sets" (not what you think). For lunch, try the Tea Rooms cafeteria (upstairs, daily 10:00–16:30). If the weather is good, picnic in the grassy pavilion next to the tram stop.

Pockerley Manor and the Waggonway has an 1820s manor house whose attendants have plenty to explain. Enjoy the lovely view from the gardens behind the manor, then enter through the kitchen, where bread is baked several times a week. Ask for a sample if you have a taste for tough rye. Adjacent is the re-created first-ever passenger train from 1825, which takes modern-day visitors for a spin on 1825 tracks—a hit with railway buffs. **Home Farm** is the least interesting section.

Hadrian's Wall

This is one of England's most thought-provoking sights. In about A.D. 122, during the reign of Emperor Hadrian, the Romans built this great stone wall. Its actual purpose is still debated. While Rome ruled Britain for 400 years, it never quite ruled its people. The wall may have been used for any number of reasons: to define the northern edge of the empire, to protect Roman Britain from invading Pict tribes from the north (or at least cut down on pesky border raids), to monitor the movement of people, or to simply give an otherwise bored army something to do. (Emperors understood that nothing's more dangerous than a bored army.) Stretching 73 miles coast to coast across the narrowest stretch of northern England, it was built and defended by some 20,000 troops. Not just a wall, this was a military complex that included forts, ditches, settlements, and a road on the south side. At every mile of the wall, a castle guards a gate, and two turrets stand between each castle. The mile castles are numbered. (Eighty of them cover the 73 miles, because a Roman mile was slightly shorter than our mile.)

Today, several chunks of the wall, ruined forts, and museums thrill history buffs. About a dozen Roman sights cling along the wall's route; the best are Housesteads Roman Fort and Vindolanda. Housesteads shows you where the Romans lived; Vindolanda's

Hadrian's Wall

NOT TO SCALE

--- WALL HIKE

1. Once Brewed National Park Visitor Centre & Youth Hostel
2. To High Reins B&B
3. Montcoffer B&B
4. The Twice Brewed Inn
5. Vallum Lodge
6. Gibbs Hill Farm B&B & Hostel
7. Milecastle Inn
8. Ashcroft Guest House
9. To Bessiestown Farm Country Guest House

museum shows you how they lived.

The Hadrian's Wall National Trail runs 84 miles, following the wall's route from coast to coast (for details, see www.national trail.co.uk/HadriansWall).

Tourist Information

Portions of the wall are in Northumberland National Park. The **Once Brewed National Park Visitor Centre** is located along the Hadrian's Wall bus #AD122 route and has information on the area, including walking guides to the wall (Easter–Oct daily 9:30–17:00, Nov–Easter 10:00–15:00 Sat–Sun only, parking-£3, Military Road, Bardon Mill, tel. 01434/344-396, www.northumber landnationalpark.org.uk, tic.oncebrewed@nnpa.org.uk).

The helpful **TI** in Haltwhistle, right at the train station, has schedule information for Hadrian's Wall bus #AD122 (Easter–Oct Mon–Sat 9:30–13:00 & 14:00–17:00, Sun 13:00–17:00; Nov–Easter Mon–Sat 9:30–12:00 & 13:00–15:30, closed Sun; good selection of maps and guidebooks, tel. 01434/322-002, www.hadrians -wall.org).

Getting to Hadrian's Wall

Hadrian's Wall is anchored by Newcastle on the east and Carlisle on the west. Driving is the most convenient way to see Hadrian's Wall; if you're coming by train, consider renting a car for the day at either Newcastle or Carlisle; otherwise, you'll rely on a bus to connect the sights. If you're just passing through for the day using public transportation, it's impossible to stop and see all the sights—study the bus schedule carefully and prioritize. If you want to see everything—or even hike part of the wall—you'll need to stay at least one night along the bus route.

By Car

Take B6318; it parallels the wall and passes several viewpoints, minor sights, and "severe dips." (These road signs add a lot to a photo portrait.) Buy a good local map to help you explore this interesting area more easily and thoroughly.

By Train and Bus

To reach the Roman sights without a car, you'll take the made-for-tourists Hadrian's Wall **bus #AD122** (named for the year the wall was built; daily Easter–Oct only). Essential resources for navigating the wall by public transit include the *Hadrian's Wall Country Map,* the bus #AD122 schedule, and a local train timetable—all available at local visitor centers and train stations, or at www.hadrians-wall.org. If you arrive by train during the off-season (Nov–Easter), you'll need to take either a local bus or a taxi to visit the wall (explained later, under "Off-Season Options").

Bus Logistics: Bus #AD122 connects the Roman sights with the following train stations (west to east): **Carlisle, Haltwhistle, Hexham,** and **Newcastle** (£8 day pass, buy tickets on board or at any TI, tel. 01434/322-002, www.hadrians-wall.org). While the bus is handy for reaching the main sights (as well as several recommended accommodations), not every bus makes every stop; it's essential to get and study an up-to-date copy of the complete schedule. Two #AD122 buses a day have on-board guides (noted on the schedule).

Buses run most frequently between Haltwhistle and Hexham (6/day each way, plus 2 additional buses between the main sights). However, the bus runs less frequently from the end points: from Carlisle, five times a day; and from Newcastle, just once a day (at 9:00—if you miss this bus, take the train to Hexham and pick up the bus there).

From Newcastle by Train to: Hexham (Mon–Sat 2/hour, Sun hourly, 30 minutes), **Haltwhistle** (Mon–Sat hourly, Sun almost hourly, 1 hour); from either town, you can catch bus

#AD122. You can store your bags at the left-luggage office at the **Newcastle train station** (£5/bag per day, Mon–Sat 8:00–20:00, Sun 9:00–20:00, platform 12).

From Carlisle by Train to: Hexham (Mon–Sat hourly, Sun 11/day, 50 minutes), **Haltwhistle** (Mon–Sat hourly, Sun 11/day, 30 minutes)—bus #AD122 stops in both towns. In Carlisle, you can store your luggage across the street from the train station at **Bar Solo** (£2/bag per day, Mon–Wed 9:00–23:00, Thu–Sat 9:00–24:00, Sun 11:00–22:30, tel. 01228/631-600).

Taxi: If you're staying near the wall, your B&B host can arrange a taxi through Melvin's Taxi (tel. 01434/320-632, mobile 07903-760-230) or Turnbull Taxi (tel. 01434/320-105, mobile 07825-004-901; one-way about £11 from Haltwhistle to Housesteads Roman Fort, arrange for return pickup or have museum staff call a taxi).

Off-Season Options: Off-season (Nov–Easter), public transportation becomes trickier. For the train/bus option, take a train to Haltwhistle, then bus #681 to Housesteads Roman Fort (3/day). For local bus info, see www.traveline.info. To fill the gaps in the bus schedule, consider a taxi (described above).

Luggage: It's difficult to bring your luggage along with you. If you're side-tripping, store your luggage in Newcastle or Carlisle (see train information for each station, earlier). If you must travel with luggage, visit Housesteads Roman Fort, where you can ask to leave baggage at the entrance while exploring (Vindolanda may also agree to keep luggage, if asked nicely). Alternatively, if you want to walk the wall, **Hadrian's Haul** baggage-courier service will send your luggage ahead (£5/bag per pick-up, mobile 07967-564-823, www.hadrianshaul.com).

Sights at Hadrian's Wall

▲▲**Housesteads Roman Fort**—With its tiny museum, powerful scenery, and the best-preserved segment of the wall, this is your best single stop at Hadrian's Wall.

All Roman forts were the same rectangular shape and design, containing a commander's headquarters, barracks, and latrines (lower end); this fort even has a hospital. The fort was built right up to the wall, which is on the far side. From the parking lot and gift shop, it's a half-mile, mostly uphill walk to the entrance of the sprawling fort and minuscule museum.

At the car park are WCs, a snack bar, and a gift shop. Ask nicely if you want to leave your luggage at the gift shop (same hours as fort, tel. 01434/344-525).

Cost and Hours: £4.80 for sight and museum—pay up at fort, not at gift shop; daily April–Sept 10:00–18:00, Oct–March closes at 15:50 or dusk, parking-£3, tel. 01434/344-363, www.english-heritage.org.uk/housesteads).

▲▲Hiking the Wall—From Housesteads, hike west along the wall speaking Latin. For a good, craggy, three-mile walk along the wall, hike between Housesteads and Steel Rigg (free guides available at Once Brewed Visitor Centre). You'll pass a castle sitting in a nick in a crag (milecastle #39, called Castle Nick). There's a parking lot near Steel Rigg (take the little road up from the Twice Brewed Inn). East of Steel Rigg you'll see the "Robin Hood Tree," a large symmetrical tree (in a little roller-coaster gap) that was featured in the movie *Robin Hood: Prince of Thieves* (with Kevin Costner, 1991).

▲Vindolanda—This larger Roman fort (which actually predates the wall by 40 years) and museum are just south of the wall. Although Housesteads has better ruins and the wall, Vindolanda has the better museum, revealing intimate details of Roman life. It's an active dig—from Easter through September, you'll see the work in progress (usually daily, weather permitting).

Eight forts were built on this spot. The Romans, by carefully sealing the foundations from each successive fort, left modern-day archaeologists with seven yards of remarkably well-preserved artifacts to excavate: keys, coins, brooches, scales, pottery, glass, tools, leather shoes, bits of cloth, and even a wig. Impressive examples of early Roman writing were discovered here in 1973. While the actual letters—written on thin pieces of wood—are in London's British Museum, see the interesting video here and read the translations, including the first known example of a woman writing to a woman (an invitation to a birthday party). These varied letters, about parties held, money owed, and sympathy shared, bring Romans to life in a way that stones alone can't.

From the free parking lot, you'll pay at the entrance, then walk 500 yards of grassy parkland decorated by the foundation stones of the Roman fort and a full-size replica chunk of the wall. At the far side are the museum, gift shop, and cafeteria.

Cost and Hours: £5.90, £9 combo-ticket includes Roman Army Museum, daily April–Sept 10:00–18:00, mid-Feb–March and Oct 10:00–17:00, closed Nov–mid Feb, last entry 45 minutes before closing, free parking with entry, tel. 01434/344-277, www.vindolanda.com.

Roman Army Museum—This museum, a few miles farther west at Greenhead, is redundant if you've seen Vindolanda. Its film offers a good eagle-eye view of a portion of the wall (£4.50, or buy £9 combo-ticket that includes Vindolanda, same hours as Vindolanda, but closed Nov–early March, free parking with entry, tel. 016977/47485, www.vindolanda.com).

Sleeping and Eating near Hadrian's Wall

(£1 = about $1.60, country code: 44)

Near Hexham
(area code: 01434)
$$ High Reins offers four rooms in a stone house built by a shipping tycoon in the 1920s (Sb-£45, Db-£68, cash only, ground-floor bedrooms, lounge, 1 mile south of train station on the western outskirts of Hexham, Leazes Lane, tel. 01434/603-590, www.high reins.co.uk, pwalton@highreins.co.uk, Jan and Peter Walton).

In and near Bardon Mill
(area code: 01434)
The Twice Brewed Inn, Once Brewed Youth Hostel, Vallum Lodge, and Milecastle Inn are reachable with Hadrian's Wall bus (#AD122), which stops nearby several times a day.

$$ Montcoffer, a restored country home, is decorated with statues, old enameled advertising signs, and other artifacts collected by owner John McGrellis and his wife, Dehlia, whose textile art is displayed in the three guest rooms (Sb-£48, Db-£78, 2 ground-floor bedrooms, 200 yards from train station and 2 miles from Vindolanda, Bardon Mill, tel. 01434/344-138, mobile 07912-209-992, www.montcoffer.co.uk, john-dehlia@talk21.com).

$$ The Twice Brewed Inn, two miles west of Housesteads and a half-mile from the wall, rents 14 workable rooms and serves real ales and decent pub grub all day (pub open daily 11:00–23:00, food served daily 12:00–20:00, Fri–Sat until 20:30). It's a friendly pub that serves as the community gathering place (S-£33, D-£55, Db-£70–82, ask for a room away from the road, free Internet access for hotel guests, otherwise £1/30 minutes, Military Road, Bardon Mill, tel. 01434/344-534, www.twicebrewedinn.co.uk, info@twicebrewedinn.co.uk).

$ Once Brewed Youth Hostel is a comfortable place near the Twice Brewed Inn and right next door to the Once Brewed National Park Visitor Centre (£16–19/bed with sheets in 2- to 6-bed rooms, D-£30, £3 extra for non-members, breakfast-£4.65, packed lunch-£5, dinner-£9, reception open daily 8:00–10:00 & 16:00–22:00, closed Dec–Jan, laundry, Military Road, 2.5 miles north of Bardon Mill, tel. 01434/344-360, fax 01434/344-045, www.yha.org.uk, oncebrewed@yha.org.uk).

$$ Vallum Lodge is an almost-cushy, comfortable renovated base situated near the vallum (the ditch that forms part of the fortification a half-mile from the wall itself). The six cheery rooms are all on the ground floor, and it's near The Twice Brewed Inn—a handy dinner option, especially if you don't have a car (Sb-£65, Db-£80–85, closed late Oct–Easter, free Wi-Fi, lounge, Military Road, tel. 01434/344-248, www.vallum-lodge.co.uk, cheerful Ann).

$$ Gibbs Hill Farm B&B and Hostel is a friendly working sheep-and-cattle farm set on 700 acres in the stunning valley on the far side of the wall (works best for drivers). It offers four big, airy rooms in the main house, and three six-bed dorm rooms in a restored hay barn (hostel bed/bedding-£15, Sb-£45, Db-£70, laundry facilities, packed lunch-£5, bikes available for rent, 5-minute drive from Once Brewed National Park Visitor Centre, tel. 01434/344-030, www.gibbshillfarm.co.uk, val@gibbshillfarm .co.uk, warm Val). They also rent several cottages for two to six people by the week (£280–600).

Milecastle Inn cooks up all sorts of exotic game and offers the best dinner around, according to hungry national park rangers (daily 12:00–20:30, smart to reserve, North Road, tel. 01434/ 321-372).

In Haltwhistle
(area code: 01434)

$$ Ashcroft Guest House, a large Victorian and former vicarage in the middle of a cute village with several eating options and a launderette, is 400 yards from the Haltwhistle train station and 200 yards from a Hadrian's Wall bus #AD122 stop. The family-run B&B has nine rooms, huge terraced gardens, and views from the comfy lounge (Sb-£48, Db-£78, four-poster Db-£88, ask about family deals and two-bedroom suite, free Internet access and Wi-Fi, 1.5 miles from the wall, Lanty's Lonnen, tel. 01434/320-213, www.ashcroftguesthouse.co.uk, info@ashcroftguesthouse .co.uk, helpful Geoff and Christine James).

Near Carlisle
(area code: 01228)

$$$ Bessiestown Farm Country Guest House, located northwest of the Hadrian sights, is convenient for drivers connecting the Lake District and Scotland. It's a quiet and soothing stop in the middle of sheep pastures, with five bedrooms in the main house and two 2-bedroom apartments in the former stables (Sb-£57, Db-£90, Tb-£110, family room-£99–110, fancier suite-£130, discounts for 3-night stays, indoor pool; in Catlowdy, midway between Gretna

Green and Hadrian's Wall, a 20-minute drive north of Carlisle; tel. 01228/577-219, fax 01228/577-019, www.bessiestown.co.uk, info@bessiestown.co.uk, gracious Margaret Sisson).

Holy Island and Bamburgh Castle

This area is worthwhile only for those with a car.

▲Holy Island

Twelve hundred years ago, this "Holy Island" was Christianity's

toehold on England. It was the home and original burial ground of St. Cuthbert (he's now in Durham). We know it today for the *Lindisfarne Gospels,* decorated by monks in the seventh century with some of the finest art from Europe's "Dark Ages" (now in the British Museum). It's a pleasant visit—a quiet town with a strik-

ing castle (not worth touring) and an evocative priory that was founded in 635.

Lindisfarne Priory: The museum in the priory is tiny but instructive. It's adjacent to the ruined abbey (£4.50; April–Sept daily 9:30–17:00; Oct daily 9:30–16:00; Nov–Jan Sat–Mon 10:00–14:00, closed Tue–Fri; Feb–March daily 10:00–16:00; tel. 01289/389-200, www.english-heritage.org.uk/lindisfarne). You can wander the abbey grounds and graveyard and pop in to the church without paying.

Holy Island is reached by a two-mile causeway that's cut off twice a day by high tides. Safe crossing times are posted at each end of the causeway (and on the priory's website), warning you when this holy place becomes Holy Island—and you become stranded.

For tourist and tide information, check with the **Berwick TI** (generally May–Sept Mon–Sat 10:00–17:00, Sun 11:00–15:00; Oct–April Mon–Sat 10:00–16:00, closed Sun; tel. 01289/330-733, www.visitnorthumberland.com, berwick.tic@northumberland.gov.uk). Park at the pay-and-display lot and walk five minutes into the town.

▲▲Bamburgh Castle

About 10 miles south of Holy Island, this grand castle dominates the Northumbrian countryside, and overlooks Britain's loveliest beach. The place was bought and passionately refurbished by Lord Armstrong, a big industrialist in the 1890s. Its interior, lined with well-described history, feels lived-in because it still is—with Armstrong family portraits and aristocratic-yet-homey knickknacks hanging everywhere. Take advantage of the talkative guides posted throughout the castle. The included **Armstrong Museum** features the inventions of the family that has owned the castle through modern times (£8, daily mid-Feb–Oct 11:00–17:00, winter Sat–Sun only 11:00–16:30, last entry one hour before closing, parking-£2, tel. 01668/214-515, www.bamburghcastle.com). Crisscrossed by walking paths, rolling dunes lead to a vast sandy beach and lots of families on holiday.

BRITISH HISTORY AND CULTURE

Britain was created by force and held together by force. It's really a nation of the 19th century, when this rich Victorian-era empire reached its financial peak. Its traditional industry, buildings, and the popularity of the notion of "Great" Britain are a product of its past wealth.

To best understand the many fascinating guides you'll encounter in your travels, have a basic handle on the sweeping story of this land. (Generally speaking, the nice and bad stories are not true... and the boring ones are.)

What's So Great About Britain?

Regardless of the revolution we had 230-some years ago, many American travelers feel that they "go home" to Britain. This most popular tourist destination has a strange influence and power over us. The more you know of Britain's roots, the better you'll get in touch with your own.

Geographically, the Isle of Britain is small (about the size of Uganda or Idaho)—600 miles long and 300 miles at its widest point. England occupies the southeastern part of Britain (with about 60 percent of its land—similar in size to Louisiana—and 80 percent of its population). England's highest mountain (Scafell Pike in the Lake District) is 3,206 feet, a foothill by our standards. The population is a fifth that of the United States. At its peak in the mid-1800s, Britain owned one-fifth of the world and accounted for more than half the planet's industrial output. Today, the Empire is down to the Isle of Britain itself and a few token, troublesome scraps, such as the Falklands, Gibraltar, and Northern Ireland.

Economically, Great Britain's industrial production is about 5 percent of the world's total. After emerging from a recession in 1992, Britain's economy enjoyed its longest period of expansion on record. But in 2008, the global economic slowdown, tight credit, and falling home prices pushed Britain back into a recession.

Culturally, Britain is still a world leader. Her heritage, culture, and people cannot be measured in traditional units of power. London is a major exporter of actors, movies, and theater; of rock and classical music; and of writers, painters, and sculptors.

Ethnically, the British Isles are a mix of the descendants of the early Celtic natives (in Scotland, Ireland, Wales, and Cornwall), descendants of the invading Anglo-Saxons who took southeast England in the Dark Ages, and descendants of the conquering Normans of the 11th century...not to mention more recent immigrants from around the world. Cynics call the United Kingdom an English Empire ruled by London, whose dominant Anglo-Saxon English (50 million) far outnumber their Celtic brothers and sisters (10 million).

Politically, Britain is ruled by the House of Commons, with some guidance from the mostly figurehead Queen and House of Lords. Just as the United States Congress is dominated by Democrats and Republicans, Britain's Parliament is dominated by two parties: left-leaning Labour and right-leaning Conservative ("Tories"). Recently the center-left Liberal Democrats ("Lib Dems") have made some inroads, but still remain a distant third.

Strangely, Britain's "constitution" is not one single document; the government's structures and policies are based on centuries of tradition, statues, and doctrine, and much of it is not actually in writing. While this might seem potentially troublesome—if not dangerous—the British body politic takes pride in its ethos of civility and mutual respect, which has long made this arrangement work.

The prime minister is the chief executive. He or she is not elected directly by voters; rather, he or she assumes power as the head of the party that wins a majority in Parliamentary elections. (If no party wins a clear majority—as none did in the 2010 election—it's a "hung parliament," and is usually resolved by at least two parties forming a coalition that adds up to a majority.) In the interest of protocol, the Queen symbolically "invites" the winner to form a "government" (administration). Instead of imposing term limits, the Brits allow their prime ministers to choose when to leave office. The ruling party also gets to choose when to hold elections, as long as it's within five years of the previous one—so prime ministers carefully schedule elections for times that (they hope) their party will win. (Breaking with tradition, the current coalition government has already announced an election for May 7, 2015.) When an election is announced, the Queen dissolves the parliament so the parties can focus on a short-and-sweet, one-month campaign.

Prime Minister David Cameron

David Cameron succeeded Gordon Brown as prime minister in May of 2010, and lives at #10 Downing Street with his wife, Samantha, and their young children. At 44, Cameron is the youngest PM in two centuries. He heads the Conservative Party (the "Tories"), but he has never quite fit the stodgy Conservative image. In his college days at Oxford, there were rumors of wild parties and illicit drugs. He's known as "Dave" to his friends, and he developed a habit of riding his bike to work. Cameron rose quickly through the political ranks: He worked to re-elect Conservative PM John Major (1992), assisted the finance minister at #11 Downing Street (1992–1994), and was himself elected to Parliament in 2001, becoming head of the Conservative Party in 2005. By 2008, he was on the cover of *Time* magazine, which hailed him as the future of conservatism.

In 2010, Cameron's Conservative Party came to power. The prime minister is not elected directly by popular vote (the way the American president is), but rules as leader of the party that garners the most votes in Parliamentary elections. The 2010 elections were hardly a sweeping Conservative mandate: Three parties split the vote, forcing Cameron's Conservatives to form a coalition with the (more left-leaning) Liberal Democrat Party. The Labour Party, which had held power in Britain for 13 years under Gordon Brown and Tony Blair, is the coalition's chief opposition.

Politically, Cameron is a moderate Conservative who is more pragmatic than ideological. Socially, he's "liberal," advocating for personal freedoms—gay rights, decriminalization of drugs, allowing hunting and smoking, and ensuring citizens' privacy against government intrusion. Fiscally, he rails against big-government waste. In his early days as PM, he delivered a sober speech about a time of austerity looming on Britain's horizon, when belts would need to be tightened to get the budget under control. His most right-of-center stance is his support for distancing Britain from the euro and the European Union.

Despite his personal appeal, Cameron can't quite shake the Conservatives' image as the party of the upper class. Cameron was born rich, married rich, and has worked within the corporate culture. His colleagues form an old boys' network from his days at Eton, England's most exclusive prep school. The Mayor of London, Boris Johnson, is not only an old Oxford frat buddy but also a distant cousin. As the Conservatives try to unite the country to solve Britain's severe economic and cultural problems, it remains to be seen whether David Cameron has brought a fresh enough approach to #10.

In the 1980s, Conservatives were in charge under Prime Minister Margaret Thatcher and Prime Minister John Major. As proponents of traditional, Victorian values—community, family, hard work, thrift, and trickle-down economics—they took a Reaganesque approach to Britain's serious social and economic problems.

In 1997, a huge Labour victory brought Tony Blair to the prime ministership. Labour began shoring up a social-service system (health care, education, the minimum wage) undercut by years of Conservative rule. Blair started out as a respected and well-liked PM. But after he followed US President George W. Bush into war with Iraq, his popularity took a nosedive. In May of 2007, Blair announced that he would resign; a few weeks later, his Chancellor of the Exchequer and longtime colleague, Gordon Brown, was sworn in as Britain's new prime minister. Burdened with an economic crisis and lacking his predecessor's charisma, Brown never achieved a level of popularity anywhere near Blair's.

Elections in May of 2010 pitted Brown against a Conservative opponent, David Cameron, and a third-party Liberal Democrat challenger, Nick Clegg. Brown, Cameron, and Clegg participated in a series of three television debates—the first in UK history. Thanks to the economic crisis—and his own, characteristic stumbles (such as being caught on tape referring to a voter he'd just met as a "bigoted woman")—Brown failed to win a clear majority for his Labour Party. Clegg won acclaim for his performance in the debates, though ultimately his Lib Dems won barely more seats than in previous elections. Other smaller parties helped split the vote, and no party won the number of seats needed for a majority—resulting in the first "hung parliament" since 1974. After a few days of wrangling, the Conservatives and the Lib Dems formed a coalition government (the first since World War II), Gordon Brown stepped down, and David Cameron became the new prime minister.

Because of a huge—and growing—budget deficit, Cameron announced a program right after the election that would dramatically cut back spending and increase the VAT (Value-Added Tax—the national sales tax) from 17.5 to 20 percent. It remains to be seen whether these bold steps will return Britain to its previous prosperity, or douse the spark of economic recovery.

In the meantime, visitors to England might begin to notice the country's economic woes (locals grumbling about tax hikes or sudden closures of a tourist office or minor sight). However, Britain remains stronger, economically, than some of its fellow EU nations (such as Greece). And Brits are turning their attention to the summer of 2012, when the world's eyes will be on their capital city as London hosts the 30th Olympiad. As the city and country spiff up even more than usual for the Olympics, the Brits can look forward to an even brighter future.

Challenges Facing Today's Britain

Great as Britain is, the country has its share of challenges. You'll likely hear people talking about some of the following hot-button topics during your visit: the recession, the war in Afghanistan, terrorism, immigration, and binge-drinking.

From early 2008 to late 2009, the British economy shrank more than 6 percent—the largest decline since the Great Depression. While the country came out of its recession in early 2010, that summer it still suffered from a 7.8 percent unemployment rate. There's been talk of a "double-dip" downturn. In this era of uncertainty, British consumers don't seem to be spending much as they try to gauge the effects of Cameron's budget cuts.

While British forces ended combat operations in Iraq in April of 2009, its troops remain in Afghanistan, and every new casualty re-invigorates public debate about the merits and possible outcomes of this war.

Like the US, Britain has been coping with its own string of terrorist threats and attacks. On the morning of July 7, 2005, London's commuters were rocked by four different bombs that killed dozens across the city. In the summer of 2006, authorities foiled a plot to carry liquid bombs onto a plane (resulting in the liquid ban air travelers are still experiencing today). On June 29, 2007, two car bombs were discovered (and defused) near London's Piccadilly Circus, and the next day, a flaming car drove into the baggage-claim level at Glasgow Airport. Most Brits have accepted that they now live with the possibility of terrorism at home—and that life must go on.

Britain has taken aggressive measures to prevent future attacks, such as installing "CCTV" (closed-circuit) surveillance cameras everywhere, in both public and private places. (You'll frequently see signs warning you that you're being filmed.) These cameras have already proved helpful in piecing together the events leading up to an attack, but as Brits trade their privacy for security, many wonder if they've given up too much.

The terrorist threats have also highlighted issues relating to Britain's large immigrant population (nearly 4 million). Second-generation Muslims—born in Britain, but who strongly identify with other Muslims rather than their British neighbors—were responsible for the July 2005 bombs. Some Brits reacted to the event known as "7/7" as if all the country's Muslims were to blame. At the same time, a handful of radical Islamic clerics began to justify the bombers' violent actions. Unemployment and the economic downturn further stretch the already strained relations between communities within Britain.

The large Muslim population is just one thread in the tapestry of today's Britain. While nine out of ten Brits are white, the country has large minority groups, mainly from Britain's former overseas colonies: India, Pakistan, Bangladesh, Africa, the Caribbean, and many other places. But despite the tensions between some groups, for the most part Britain is well integrated, with minorities represented in most (if not all) walks of life.

Recently another wave of immigration has hit Britain. Throughout the British Isles, you'll see many Eastern Europeans (mostly Poles, Slovaks, and Lithuanians) working in restaurants, cafés, and B&Bs. These transplants—who started arriving after their home countries joined the EU in 2004—can make a lot more money working here than back home. British small-business owners have found these new arrivals to be polite, responsible, and affordable. While a few Brits complain that the new arrivals are taking jobs away from the natives, and others are frustrated that their English is often far from perfect, for the most part Britain has absorbed this new set of immigrants gracefully.

Over the last several years, Britain has seen an epidemic of binge-drinking among young people. A 2007 study revealed that one out of every three British men, and one out of every five British women, routinely drink to excess. It's become commonplace for young adults (typically from their mid-teens to mid-20s) to spend weekend nights drinking at pubs and carousing in the streets. (And they ratchet up the debauchery even more when celebrating a "stag night" or "hen night"—bachelor and bachelorette parties.) While sociologists and politicians scratch their heads about the causes and effects of this phenomenon, tourists are complaining about weekend noise and obnoxious (though generally harmless) young drunks on the streets.

Basic British History for the Traveler

When Julius Caesar landed on the misty and mysterious isle of Britain in 55 B.C., England entered the history books. The primitive Celtic tribes he conquered were themselves invaders (who had earlier conquered the even more mysterious people who built Stonehenge). The Romans built towns and roads, establishing their capital at Londinium. The Celtic natives in Scotland and Wales—consisting of Gaels, Picts, and Scots—were not easily subdued. The Romans built Hadrian's Wall near the Scottish border as protection against their troublesome northern neighbors. Even today, the Celtic language and influence are strongest in these far reaches of Britain.

As Rome fell, so fell Roman Britain, a victim of invaders and internal troubles. Barbarian tribes from Germany and

British Empire

GREAT BRITAIN

ASIA

EUROPE

NORTH AMERICA

AFRICA

EQUATOR

SOUTH AMERICA

THE BRITISH EMPIRE IN 1900

Denmark, called Angles and Saxons, swept through the southern part of the island, establishing Angle-land. These were the days of the real King Arthur, possibly a Christianized Roman general who fought valiantly against invading barbarians, but in vain. In 793, England was hit with the first of two centuries of savage invasions by barbarians from Norway, called the Vikings or Norsemen. The island was plunged into 500 years of Dark Ages—wars, plagues, and poverty—lit only by the dim candle of a few learned Christian monks and missionaries trying to convert the barbarians. The sightseer sees little from this Anglo-Saxon period.

Modern England began with yet another invasion. William the Conqueror and his Norman troops crossed the English Channel from France in 1066. William crowned himself king in Westminster Abbey (where all subsequent coronations would take place) and began building the Tower of London. French-speaking Norman kings ruled the country for two centuries. Then followed two centuries of civil wars, with various noble families vying for the crown. In one of the most bitter feuds, the York and Lancaster families fought the Wars of the Roses, so-called because of the white and red flowers the combatants chose as their symbols. Rife with battles, intrigues, and kings, nobles, and ladies imprisoned and executed in the Tower, it's a wonder the country survived its rulers.

England was finally united by the "third-party" Tudor family. Henry VIII, a Tudor, was England's Renaissance king. He was handsome, athletic, highly sexed, a poet, a scholar, and a musician. He was also arrogant, cruel, gluttonous, and paranoid. He went through six wives in 40 years, divorcing, imprisoning, or beheading them when they no longer suited his needs.

BRITISH HISTORY

Typical Castle Architecture

Castles were fortified residences for medieval nobles. Castles come in all shapes and sizes, but knowing a few general terms will help you understand them.

The Keep (or Donjon): A high, strong stone tower in the center of the castle complex that was the lord's home and refuge of last resort.

Great Hall: The largest room in the castle, serving as throne room, conference center, and dining hall.

The Yard (or Bailey or Ward): An open courtyard inside the castle walls.

Loopholes: Narrow slits in the walls (also called embrasures,

Henry "divorced" England from the Catholic Church, establishing the Protestant Church of England (the Anglican Church) and setting in motion years of religious squabbles. He also "dissolved" the monasteries (circa 1540), left just the shells of many formerly glorious abbeys dotting the countryside, and pocketed their land and wealth for the crown.

Henry's daughter, Queen Elizabeth I, who reigned for 45 years, made England a great trading and naval power (defeating the Spanish Armada) and presided over the Elizabethan era of great writers (such as William Shakespeare) and scientists (such as Francis Bacon).

The longstanding quarrel between England's divine-right kings and Parliament's nobles finally erupted into a civil war (1643). Parliament forces under the Protestant Puritan farmer Oliver Cromwell defeated—and beheaded—King Charles I. This civil war left its mark on much of what you'll see in Britain. Eventually, Parliament invited Charles' son to take the throne. This "restoration arrow slits, or arrow loops) through which soldiers could shoot arrows at the enemy.

Towers: Tall structures serving as lookouts, chapels, living quarters, or the dungeon. Towers could be square or round, with either crenellated tops or conical roofs.

Turret: A small lookout tower projecting up from the top of the wall.

Moat: A ditch encircling the wall, often filled with water.

Wall Walk (or Allure): A pathway atop the wall where guards could patrol and where soldiers stood to fire at the enemy.

Parapet: Outer railing of the wall walk.

Crenellation: A gap-toothed pattern of stones atop the parapet.

Hoardings (or Gallery or Brattice): Wooden huts built onto the upper parts of the stone walls. They served as watch towers, living quarters, and fighting platforms.

Machicolation: A stone ledge jutting out from the wall, fitted with holes in the bottom. If the enemy was scaling the walls, soldiers could drop rocks or boiling oil down through the holes and onto the enemy below.

Barbican: A fortified gatehouse, sometimes a stand-alone building located outside the main walls.

Drawbridge: A bridge that could be raised or lowered, using counterweights or a chain-and-winch.

Portcullis: A heavy iron grille that could be lowered across the entrance.

Postern Gate: A small, unfortified side or rear entrance used during peacetime. In wartime, it could become a "sally-port" used to launch surprise attacks, or as an escape route.

BRITISH HISTORY

of the monarchy" was accompanied by a great colonial expansion and the rebuilding of London (including Christopher Wren's St. Paul's Cathedral), which had been devastated by the Great Fire of 1666. Parliament gained ultimate authority over the throne when it deposed Catholic James II in 1688, guaranteeing a Protestant succession.

Britain grew as a naval superpower, colonizing and trading with all parts of the globe (although it lost its most important colony to ungrateful Americans in 1776). Admiral Horatio Nelson's victory over Napoleon's fleet at the Battle of Trafalgar secured her naval superiority ("Britannia rules the waves"), and 10 years later, the Duke of Wellington stomped Napoleon on land at Waterloo. Nelson and Wellington—both buried in London's St. Paul's Cathedral—are memorialized by many arches, columns, and squares throughout England.

Economically, Britain led the world into the Industrial Age with her mills, factories, coal mines, and trains. By the time of

Royal Families: Past and Present

Royal Lineage

802–1066	Saxon and Danish kings
1066–1154	Norman invasion (William the Conqueror), Norman kings
1154–1399	Plantagenet (kings with French roots)
1399–1461	Lancaster
1462–1485	York
1485–1603	Tudor (Henry VIII, Elizabeth I)
1603–1649	Stuart (civil war and beheading of Charles I)
1649–1653	Commonwealth, no royal head of state
1653–1659	Protectorate, with Cromwell as Lord Protector
1660–1714	Stuart (Parliament replaces James II with Protestant heirs)
1714–1901	Hanover (four Georges, Victoria)
1901–1910	Saxe-Coburg (Edward VII)
1910–present	Windsor (George V, Edward VIII, George VI, Elizabeth II)

The Royal Family Today

It seems you can't pick up a British newspaper without some mention of the latest scandal or oddity involving the royal family. Here is the cast of characters:

Queen Elizabeth II wears the traditional crown of her great-great grandmother Victoria. Her husband is Prince Philip, who's not considered king.

BRITISH HISTORY

Queen Victoria's reign (1837–1901), Britain was at its zenith of power, with a colonial empire that covered one-fifth of the world.

The 20th century was not kind to Britain. Two world wars devastated the population. The Nazi Blitz reduced much of London to rubble, although the freedom-loving world was inspired by Britain's determination to stand up to Hitler. After the war, the colonial empire dwindled to almost nothing, and Britain lost its superpower economic status.

One post-Empire hot spot—Northern Ireland, plagued by the "Troubles" between Catholics and Protestants—heated up, and then finally started cooling off. In the spring of 2007, the unthinkable happened when leaders of the ultra-nationalist party sat down with those of the ultra-unionist party. London returned control of Northern Ireland to the popularly elected Northern Ireland Assembly. Perhaps most important of all, after almost 40 years, the British Army withdrew from Northern Ireland that summer.

Their son, Prince Charles (the Prince of Wales), is next in line to become king. In 1981, Charles married Lady Diana Spencer (Princess Di) who, after their bitter divorce, died in a car crash in 1997. Their two sons, William and Harry, are next in line to the throne after their father. In 2005, Charles married his longtime girlfriend, Camilla Parker Bowles, who is trying to gain respectability with the Queen and the public. But she's doesn't call herself a princess—she uses the title "Duchess of Cornwall."

Prince Charles' siblings are occasionally in the news: Princess Anne, Prince Andrew (who married and divorced Sarah "Fergie" Ferguson), and Prince Edward (who married Di look-alike Sophie Rhys-Jones).

But it's Prince Charles' sons who generate the tabloid buzz these days. Handsome Prince William (b. 1982), a graduate of Scotland's St. Andrews University and an officer in both the Royal Air Force and Royal Navy, serves as the royal family's public face at many charity events. There's endless speculation about his romantic interests, especially about his long-time, on-again-off-again girlfriend, Kate Middleton (a commoner he met at university). Whomever he marries may eventually become Britain's queen.

Redheaded Prince Harry (b. 1984) made a media splash as a bad boy when he wore a Nazi armband (as an ill-advised joke) to a costume party. Since then, he's proved his mettle as a career soldier, serving two months in Afghanistan (early 2008). In 2008, he and his regiment did charity work in Africa, and since then he's been training to become a pilot with the Army Air Corps. Harry's love life, like his brother's, is a popular topic for the tabloids.

For more on the monarchy, see www.royal.gov.uk.

Three years later, the British government formally apologized for the 1972 shooting of 26 civilians in Derry by British soldiers—a day of infamy known as "Bloody Sunday."

The tradition (if not the substance) of greatness continues, presided over by Queen Elizabeth II, her husband, Prince Philip, and their son Prince Charles. With economic problems, the marital turmoil of Charles and the late Princess Diana, and a relentless popular press, the royal family has had a tough time. But the queen has stayed above it all, and most British people still jump at an opportunity to see royalty. With the 1997 death of Princess Diana and the historic outpouring of grief, it was clear that the concept of royalty is still alive and well as Britain entered the third millennium.

Queen Elizabeth, who turns 85 in 2011, marked her 58th year on the throne in 2010. While many wonder who will succeed her, the case is fairly straightforward: The queen sees her job as a lifelong position, and legally, Charles (who wants to be king) cannot be skipped over for his son, William. Given the longevity in the family (the queen's mum, born in August of 1900, made it to 101 before she died in 2002), Charles is in for a long wait.

Architecture in Britain

From Stonehenge to Big Ben, travelers are storming castle walls, climbing spiral staircases, and snapping the pictures of 5,000 years of architecture. Let's sort it out.

The oldest ruins—mysterious and prehistoric—date from before Roman times back to 3000 B.C. The earliest sites, such as Stonehenge and Avebury, were built during the Stone and Bronze ages. The remains from these periods are made of huge stones or mounds of earth, even man-made hills, and were created as celestial calendars and for worship or burial. Britain is crisscrossed with lines of these mysterious sights (ley lines). Iron Age people (600 B.C.–A.D. 50) left desolate stone forts. The Romans thrived in Britain from A.D. 50 to 400, building cities, walls, and roads. Evidence of Roman greatness can be seen in lavish villas with ornate mosaic floors, temples uncovered beneath great English churches, and Roman stones in medieval city walls. Roman roads sliced across the island in straight lines. Today, unusually straight rural roads are very likely laid directly on these ancient roads.

As Rome crumbled in the fifth century, so did Roman Britain. Little architecture survives from Dark Ages England, the Saxon period from 500 to 1000. Architecturally, the light was switched on with the Norman Conquest in 1066. As William earned his title "the Conqueror," his French architects built churches and castles in the European Romanesque style.

English Romanesque is called Norman (1066–1200). Norman churches had round arches, thick walls, and small windows; Durham Cathedral and the Chapel of St. John in the Tower of London are prime examples. The Tower of London, with its square keep, small windows, and spiral stone stairways, is a typical Norman castle. You'll see plenty of Norman castles—all built to

Typical Church Architecture

History comes to life when you visit a centuries-old church. Even if you wouldn't know your apse from a hole in the ground, learning a few simple terms will enrich your experience. Note that not every church has every feature, and that a "cathedral" isn't a type of church architecture, but rather a designation for a church that's a governing center for a local bishop.

Aisles: The long, generally low-ceilinged arcades that flank the nave.

Altar: The raised area with a ceremonial table (often adorned with candles or a crucifix), where the priest prepares and serves the bread and wine for Communion.

Apse: The space beyond the altar, often bordered with small chapels.

Choir: A cozy area, often screened off, located within the church nave and near the high altar where services are sung in a more intimate setting.

Cloister: A square-shaped series of hallways surrounding an open-air courtyard, traditionally where monks and nuns got fresh air.

Facade: The outer wall of the church's main (west) entrance, viewable from outside and usually highly decorated.

Groin Vault: An arched ceiling formed where two equal barrel vaults meet at right angles. Less common usage: term for a medieval jock strap.

Narthex: The area (portico or foyer) between the main entry and the nave.

Nave: The long, central section of the church (running west to east, from the entrance to the altar) where the congregation stood through the service.

Transept: The north–south part of the church, which crosses (perpendicularly) the east–west nave. In a traditional Latin cross-shaped floor plan, the transept forms the "arms" of the cross.

West Portal: The main entry to the church (on the west end, opposite the main altar).

secure the conquest of these invaders from Normandy.

Gothic architecture (1200–1600) replaced the heavy Norman style with light, vertical buildings, pointed arches, soaring spires, and bigger windows. English Gothic is divided into three stages. Early English (1200–1300) features tall, simple spires; beautifully carved capitals; and elaborate chapter houses (such as the Wells Cathedral). Decorated Gothic (1300–1400) gets fancier, with more elaborate tracery, bigger windows, and ornately carved pinnacles, as you'll see at Westminster Abbey. Finally, the Perpendicular Gothic style (1400–1600, also called "rectilinear") returns to square towers and emphasizes straight, uninterrupted vertical lines from ceiling to floor, with vast windows and exuberant decoration, including fan-vaulted ceilings (King's College Chapel at Cambridge). Through this evolution, the structural ribs (arches meeting at the top of the ceilings) became more and more decorative and fanciful (the most fancy being the star vaulting and fan vaulting of the Perpendicular style).

As you tour the great medieval churches of Britain, remember that almost everything is symbolic. For instance, on the tombs of knights, if the figure has crossed legs, he was a Crusader. If his feet rest on a dog, he died at home, but if the legs rest on a lion, he died in battle. Local guides and books help us modern pilgrims understand at least a little of what we see.

Gothic houses were a simple mix of woven strips of thin wood, rubble, and plaster called wattle and daub. The famous black-and-white Tudor (or "half-timbered") look came simply from filling in heavy oak frames with wattle and daub.

The Tudor period (1485–1560) was a time of relative peace (the Wars of the Roses were finally over), prosperity, and renaissance. Henry VIII broke with the Catholic Church and "dissolved" (destroyed) the monasteries, leaving scores of Britain's greatest churches as gutted shells. These hauntingly beautiful abbey ruins (Glastonbury, Tintern, Whitby, Rievaulx, Battle, St. Augustine's in Canterbury, St. Mary's in York, and lots more) surrounded by lush lawns are now pleasant city parks.

Although few churches were built during the Tudor period, this was a time of house and mansion construction. Heating a home was becoming popular and affordable, and Tudor buildings featured small square windows and many chimneys. In towns, where land was scarce, many Tudor houses grew up and out, getting wider with each overhanging floor.

The Elizabethan and Jacobean periods (1560–1620) were followed by the English Renaissance style (1620–1720). English architects mixed Gothic and classical styles, then Baroque and classical styles. Although the ornate Baroque never really grabbed Britain, the classical style of the Italian architect Andrea Palladio did. Inigo Jones (1573–1652), Christopher Wren (1632–1723), and those they inspired plastered Britain with enough columns, domes, and symmetry to please a Caesar. The Great Fire of London (1666) cleared the way for an ambitious young Wren to put his mark on London forever with a grand rebuilding scheme, including the great St. Paul's Cathedral and more than 50 other churches.

The celebrants of the Boston Tea Party remember Britain's Georgian period (1720–1840) for its lousy German kings. Georgian architecture was rich and showed off by being very classical. Grand ornamental doorways, fine cast-ironwork on balconies and railings, Chippendale furniture, and white-on-blue Wedgwood ceramics graced rich homes everywhere. John Wood Jr. and Sr. led the way, giving the trendsetting city of Bath its crescents and circles of aristocratic Georgian row houses. "Georgian" is English for "Neoclassical."

The Industrial Revolution shaped the Victorian period (1840–1890) with glass, steel, and iron. Britain had a huge new erector set (so did France's Mr. Eiffel). This was also a Romantic period, reviving the "more Christian" Gothic style. London's Houses of Parliament are Neo-Gothic—just 140 years old but looking 700, except for the telltale modern precision and craftsmanship. Whereas Gothic was stone or concrete, Neo-Gothic was often red brick. These were Britain's glory days, and there was more building in this period than in all previous ages combined.

The architecture of modern times obeys the formula "form follows function"—it worries more about your needs than your eyes. Britain treasures its heritage and takes great pains to build tastefully in historic districts and to preserve its many "listed" buildings. With a booming tourist trade, these quaint reminders of its past—and ours—are becoming a valuable part of the British economy.

British TV

Although it has its share of lowbrow reality programming, much British television is still so good—and so British—that it deserves a mention as a sightseeing treat. After a hard day of castle climbing, watch the telly over tea in the living room of your village B&B.

There are currently five free channels that any television can receive. BBC-1 and BBC-2 are government-regulated and commercial-free. Broadcasting of these two channels (and of the five BBC radio stations) is funded by a mandatory £145.50-per-year-per-household television and radio license (hmmm, 65 cents per day to escape commercials and public-broadcasting pledge drives). Channels 3, 4, and 5 are privately owned, are a little more lowbrow, and have commercials—but those commercials are often clever and sophisticated, providing a fun look at British life. In addition, about 85 percent of households now receive digital cable or satellite television, which offer dozens of specialty channels, similar to those available in North America.

Like the US, Britain is joining the Digital Age, gradually converting its TV signals to digital-only, which requires a digitally equipped set or a converter. By 2013, the old analog signals will be switched off and only digital signals will be broadcast.

Whereas California "accents" fill our airwaves 24 hours a day, homogenizing the way our country speaks, Britain protects and promotes its regional accents by its choice of TV and radio announcers. See if you can tell where each is from (or ask a local for help).

Commercial-free British TV, while looser than it used to be, is still careful about what it airs and when. But after the 21:00 "watershed" hour, when children are expected to be in bed, some nudity and profanity are allowed, and may cause you to spill your tea.

American programs (such as *Mad Men, CSI, Oprah,* and trash-talk shows) are very popular. The visiting viewer should be sure to tune the TV to a few typical British shows, including a dose of British situation- and political-comedy fun, and the top-notch BBC evening news. British comedies have tickled the American funny bone for years, from sketch comedy *(Monty Python's Flying Circus)* to sitcoms (such as *Are You Being Served?, Fawlty Towers,* and *Absolutely Fabulous*). A more recent cross-the-pond mega-hit, *The Office,* has made its star Ricky Gervais the top name in British comedy today, and has spawned successful adaptations in the US, Germany, France, French Canada, Chile, and Israel. Quiz shows and reality shows are taken very seriously here (*Who Wants to Be a Millionaire?, American Idol,* and *Dancing with the Stars* are all based on British shows). Jonathan Ross is the David Letterman of Britain for sometimes edgy late-night talk—he left the BBC in 2010, but watch for his return on a private channel in 2011. For a tear-filled, slice-of-life taste of British soaps dealing in all the controversial issues, see the popular *Emmerdale, Coronation Street,* or *EastEnders.*

APPENDIX

Contents

Tourist Information

Tourist Information Offices

The **Visit Britain** office in the US is a wealth of knowledge. Request free maps of London and Britain and any specific information you may want (such as regional information, a garden-tour map, urban cultural activities brochures, and so on). The phone line is mainly intended as a customer service number for their online shop and isn't staffed (but they do check their messages). For most questions, it's best to inquire by email (tel. 800-462-2748, www.visitbritain .com, travelinfo@visitbritain.org).

In England, your best first stop in every town is generally the tourist information office—abbreviated **TI** in this book. (The **Britain and London Visitors Centre** in London is particularly good—see page 50.) A TI is a great place to get a city map, advice on public transportation (including bus and train schedules), walking-tour schedules, information on special events, and recommendations for nightlife. For all the help TIs offer, steer clear of their room-finding services (bloated prices, booking fee up to £4, no opinions, and they take a 10 percent cut from your B&B host). Many TIs have information on the entire country or at least the region, so try to pick up maps for destinations that you'll be visiting later in your trip. If you're arriving in town after the TI closes, call ahead or pick up a map in a neighboring town.

Communicating

Telephones

Smart travelers use the telephone to book or reconfirm rooms, get tourist information, reserve restaurants, confirm tour times, or phone home. Generally, the cheapest way to go is to buy an international phone card in Britain and make your calls from hotel-room phones or mobile phones, but not pay phones. The handiest—though pricier—way to make calls is by using a mobile phone (brought from home or purchased in Britain). This section covers dialing instructions, phone cards, and types of phones (for more in-depth information, see www.ricksteves.com/phoning).

How to Dial

Calling from the US to Britain, or vice versa, is simple—once you break the code. The European calling chart in this chapter will walk you through it.

Dialing Domestically Within Britain

Britain, like much of the US, uses an area-code dialing system. To make local calls, if you're calling within an area code, just dial the local number to be connected; if you're calling outside your area code, you have to dial both the area code (which starts with a 0) and the local number.

Area codes are listed in this book and by city on phone-booth walls, and are available from directory assistance (dial 118-500, £0.64/minute). It's most expensive to call within Britain between 8:00 and 13:00, and cheapest between 17:00 and 8:00. Still, a short call across the country is inexpensive; don't hesitate to call long distance.

Dialing Internationally to or from Britain

If you want to make an international call, follow these steps:

1. Dial the international access code (00 if you're calling from Britain, 011 from the US or Canada).
2. Dial the country code of the country you're calling (44 for Britain, or 1 for the US or Canada).
3. Dial the area code (without the initial zero) and the local number.

The English Accent

In the olden days, an English person's accent indicated his or her social standing. Eliza Doolittle had the right idea—elocution could make or break you. Wealthier families would send their kids to fancy private schools to learn proper pronunciation. But these days, in a sort of reverse snobbery that has gripped the nation, accents are back. Politicians, newscasters, and movie stars have been favoring deep accents over the Queen's English. While it's hard for American ears to pick out all of the variations, most English can determine where a person is from based on his or her accent...not just the region, but often the village, and even the part of town.

Calling from the US to Britain: To call a London hotel from the US, dial 011 (the US international access code), 44 (Britain's country code), 20 (London's area code without its initial 0), then 7730-8191 (the hotel's number).

Calling from any European Country to the US: To call my office in Edmonds, Washington, from anywhere in Europe, I dial 00 (Europe's international access code), 1 (the US country code), 425 (Edmonds' area code), and 771-8303.

Note: You might see a + in front of a European number. When dialing the number, replace the + with the international access code of the country you're calling from (00 from Europe, 011 from the US or Canada).

Public Phones and Hotel-Room Phones

To make a call from a public pay phone, you'll need a lot of coins (Britain doesn't use insertable phone cards, and calls are pricey). Even prepaid international phone cards are prohibitively expensive on public phones.

International Phone Cards: These cards are the cheapest way to make international calls from Britain (less than $0.10 a minute to the US; they also work for local calls). But there's a catch: British Telecom levies a hefty surcharge for using international calling cards from a pay phone (so instead of 100 minutes for a £5 card, you'll get less than 10 minutes—a miserable deal). But they're still a good deal if you use them when calling from a mobile phone or fixed line (e.g., a hotel-room phone; ask at the front desk if they charge any fees for toll-free calls). The cards are sold all over; look for them at newsstand kiosks and hole-in-the-wall long-distance shops. Ask the clerk which of the various brands has the best rates for calls to the US. Because cards are occasionally duds, avoid the more expensive denominations. These cards usually work only in the country where they're

European Calling Chart

Just smile and dial, using this key:
AC = Area Code, LN = Local Number.

European Country	Calling long distance within ...	Calling from the US or Canada to ...	Calling from a European country to ...
Austria	AC + LN	011 + 43 + AC (without the initial zero) + LN	00 + 43 + AC (without the initial zero) + LN
Belgium	LN	011 + 32 + LN (without initial zero)	00 + 32 + LN (without initial zero)
Bosnia-Herzegovina	AC + LN	011 + 387 + AC (without initial zero) + LN	00 + 387 + AC (without initial zero) + LN
Britain	AC + LN	011 + 44 + AC (without initial zero) + LN	00 + 44 + AC (without initial zero) + LN
Croatia	AC + LN	011 + 385 + AC (without initial zero) + LN	00 + 385 + AC (without initial zero) + LN
Czech Republic	LN	011 + 420 + LN	00 + 420 + LN
Denmark	LN	011 + 45 + LN	00 + 45 + LN
Estonia	LN	011 + 372 + LN	00 + 372 + LN
Finland	AC + LN	011 + 358 + AC (without initial zero) + LN	999 (or other 900 number) + 358 + AC (without initial zero) + LN
France	LN	011 + 33 + LN (without initial zero)	00 + 33 + LN (without initial zero)
Germany	AC + LN	011 + 49 + AC (without initial zero) + LN	00 + 49 + AC (without initial zero) + LN
Gibraltar	LN	011 + 350 + LN	00 + 350 + LN
Greece	LN	011 + 30 + LN	00 + 30 + LN
Hungary	06 + AC + LN	011 + 36 + AC + LN	00 + 36 + AC + LN
Ireland	AC + LN	011 + 353 + AC (without initial zero) + LN	00 + 353 + AC (without initial zero) + LN

European Country	Calling long distance within ...	Calling from the US or Canada to ...	Calling from a European country to ...
Italy	LN	011 + 39 + LN	00 + 39 + LN
Montenegro	AC + LN	011 + 382 + AC (without initial zero) + LN	00 + 382 + AC (without initial zero) + LN
Morocco	LN	011 + 212 + LN (without initial zero)	00 + 212 + LN (without initial zero)
Netherlands	AC + LN	011 + 31 + AC (without initial zero) + LN	00 + 31 + AC (without initial zero) + LN
Norway	LN	011 + 47 + LN	00 + 47 + LN
Poland	LN	011 + 48 + LN (without initial zero)	00 + 48 + LN (without initial zero)
Portugal	LN	011 + 351 + LN	00 + 351 + LN
Slovakia	AC + LN	011 + 421 + AC (without initial zero) + LN	00 + 421 + AC (without initial zero) + LN
Slovenia	AC + LN	011 + 386 + AC (without initial zero) + LN	00 + 386 + AC (without initial zero) + LN
Spain	LN	011 + 34 + LN	00 + 34 + LN
Sweden	AC + LN	011 + 46 + AC (without initial zero) + LN	00 + 46 + AC (without initial zero) + LN
Switzerland	LN	011 + 41 + LN (without initial zero)	00 + 41 + LN (without initial zero)
Turkey	AC (if there's no initial zero, add one) + LN	011 + 90 + AC (without initial zero) + LN	00 + 90 + AC (without initial zero) + LN

- The instructions above apply whether you're calling a land line or mobile phone.
- The international access codes (the first numbers you dial when making an international call) are 011 if you're calling from the US or Canada, or 00 if you're calling from virtually anywhere in Europe (except Finland, where it's 999 or another 900 number, depending on the phone service you're using).
- To call the US or Canada from Europe, dial 00, then 1 (the country code for the US and Canada), then the area code and number. In short, 00 + 1 + AC + LN = Hi, Mom!

purchased (unless otherwise noted on the card).

Hotel-Room Phones: Phones are rare in B&Bs. If your room has a phone, it can be a cheap way to make local calls (ask for the rates at the front desk first), but is often a rip-off for long-distance calls, unless you use an international phone card. Incoming calls are free, making this an inexpensive way for friends and family to stay in touch (provided they have a good long-distance plan for calls to Europe—and a list of your hotels' phone numbers).

US Calling Cards: These cards, such as the ones offered by AT&T, Verizon, and Sprint, are the worst option. You'll nearly always save money by using a locally purchased phone card instead.

Mobile Phones

For most travelers in Britain, a mobile phone is the best option for making calls.

Using Your Mobile Phone: Your US mobile phone works in Britain if it's GSM-enabled, tri-band or quad-band, and on a calling plan that includes international calls. Phones from T-Mobile and AT&T, which use the same GSM technology that Europe does, are more likely to work overseas than Verizon or Sprint phones (if you're not sure, ask your service provider). Most US providers charge $1.29 per minute while roaming internationally to make or receive calls, and $0.20–0.50 to send or receive text messages.

You'll pay cheaper rates if your phone is electronically "unlocked" (ask your provider about this); then, in Britain, you can simply buy a tiny **SIM card,** which gives you a British phone number. SIM cards are available at mobile-phone stores and some newsstand kiosks. You might have to pay a nominal amount for these (around $5), but you'll often get one for free—they make their money selling you calling time, not the SIM card itself. When you buy a SIM card, you may need to show ID, such as your passport. Insert the SIM card in your phone (usually in a slot behind the battery), and it'll work like a British mobile phone. When buying a SIM card and calling credit, always ask about fees for domestic and international calls, roaming charges, and how to check your credit balance and buy more time. To call home, save money by using an international calling card (described earlier).

Many **smartphones,** such as the iPhone or BlackBerry, work in Europe—but beware of sky-high fees, especially for data down-loading (checking email, browsing the Internet, watching stream-ing videos, and so on). Ask your provider in advance how to avoid unwittingly roaming your way to a huge bill. Some applications allow for cheap or free smartphone calls over a Wi-Fi connection (see "Calling over the Internet," later).

Using a European Mobile Phone: Mobile-phone shops all over Europe sell basic phones. (For example, Britain's Carphone

Warehouse sells pay-as-you-go mobile phones for as little as £10 plus £10 for calling time.) You'll also need to get a SIM card and prepaid credit for making calls. If you remain in Britain, incoming calls are generally free, and outgoing domestic calls to a fixed line generally run about £0.15–0.20/minute—less than from a pay phone. (It's more expensive to call a mobile phone or a toll number.) You'll pay more if roaming in another country.

Calling over the Internet

Some things that seem too good to be true...actually are true. If you're traveling with a laptop, you can make calls using VoIP (Voice over Internet Protocol). With VoIP, two computers act as the phones, and the Internet-based calls are free (or you can pay a few cents to call from your computer to a telephone). If both computers have webcams, you can even see each other while you chat. The major providers are Skype (www.skype.com), followed by Google Talk (www.google.com/talk).

Useful Phone Numbers

Understand the various prefixes—numbers starting with 09 are telephone-sex–type expensive. Numbers that begin with 0800 are toll-free, but numbers with prefixes of 0844, 0845, 0870, and 0871 cost about £0.10 per minute from a fixed line (but can be much more expensive if you're calling from a mobile phone). If you have questions about a prefix, call 100 for free help.

Emergencies and Directory Assistance

Police and Ambulance: tel. 999
Operator Assistance: tel. 100 (free)
Directory Assistance: tel. 118-500 (£0.64/minute, plus £0.23/minute connection charge from fixed lines)
International Directory Assistance: tel. 118-505 (£1.99/minute, plus £0.69 connection charge)

Embassies and Consulates in London

US Consulate and Embassy: tel. 020/7499-9000, passport info tel. 020/7894-0563, passport services available Mon–Fri 8:30–11:30, Mon, Wed, Fri also 14:00–16:00 (24 Grosvenor Square, Tube: Bond Street, www.usembassy.org.uk)
Canadian High Commission: tel. 020/7258-6600, passport services available Mon–Fri 9:30–13:30 (Trafalgar Square, Tube: Charing Cross, www.unitedkingdom.gc.ca)

Travel Advisories

US Department of State: US tel. 202/647-5225 (www.travel.state.gov)

Canadian Department of Foreign Affairs: Canadian tel. 800-267-6788 (www.dfait-maeci.gc.ca)

US Centers for Disease Control and Prevention: US tel. 800-CDC-INFO (800-232-4636, www.cdc.gov/travel)

Trains and Buses

Train information for trips within England: toll tel. 0845-748-4950, overseas tel. 011-44-20-7278-5240 (www.nationalrail.co.uk)

Eurostar (Chunnel Info): toll tel. 0870-518-6186 (www.eurostar.com)

Trains to all points in Europe: toll tel. 0870-584-8848 (www.raileurope.com)

National Express Buses: toll tel. 0871-781-8181 (www.nationalexpress.com)

Airports

For online information on the first three airports, check www.baa.co.uk.

Heathrow (flight info): toll tel. 0870-000-0123

Gatwick (general info): toll tel. 0870-000-2468 for all airlines, except British Airways—toll tel. 0870-551-1155 (flights) or 0870-850-9850 (booking)

Stansted (general info): toll tel. 0870-000-0303

Luton (general info): tel. 01582/405-100 (www.london-luton.com)

London City Airport (general info): tel. 020/7646-0088 (www.londoncityairport.com)

Airlines

Aer Lingus: toll tel. 0870-876-5000, US tel. 800-474-7424 (www.aerlingus.com)

Air Canada: toll tel. 0871-220-1111 (www.aircanada.com)

Alitalia: toll tel. 0871-424-1424 (www.alitalia.com)

American: toll tel. 0845-778-9789 (www.aa.com)

bmi: reservations toll tel. 0870-607-0555, flight info tel. 020/8745-7321 (www.flybmi.com)

British Airways: reservations toll tel. 0844-493-0787, flight info toll tel. 0844-493-0777 (www.ba.com)

Brussels Airlines: toll tel. 0905-609-5609, US tel. 516/740 5200, 40p/minute (www.brusselsairlines.com)

Continental Airlines: toll tel. 0845-607-6760 (www.continental.com)

easyJet: toll tel. 0871-244-2366, 10p/minute (www.easyjet.com)

KLM Royal Dutch/Northwest Airlines: toll tel. 0870-507-4074 (www.klm.com)

Lufthansa: toll tel. 0871-945-9747 (www.lufthansa.com)

Ryanair: toll tel. 0871-246-0000 (www.ryanair.com)

Scandinavian Airlines (SAS): toll tel. 0871-521-2772 (www.flysas .com)
United Airlines: toll tel. 0845-844-4777 (www.unitedairlines .co.uk)
US Airways: toll tel. 0845-600-3300 (www.usair.com)

Heathrow Airport Car-Rental Agencies
Avis: toll tel. 0844-544-6000 (www.avis.co.uk)
Budget: toll tel. 0844-544-4600 (www.budget.co.uk)
Enterprise: tel. 020/8897-2100 (www.enterprise.co.uk)
Europcar: tel. 020/8564-3500 (www.europcar.co.uk)
Hertz: toll tel. 0870-846-0006 (www.hertz.co.uk)

Internet Access

It's useful to get online periodically as you travel—to confirm trip plans, check train or bus schedules, get weather forecasts, catch up

on email, blog or post photos from your trip, or call folks back home (explained earlier, in "Calling over the Internet").

Some hotels and B&Bs offer a computer in the lobby with Internet access for guests. If you ask politely, smaller places may sometimes let you sit at their desk

for a few minutes just to check your email. If your hotel doesn't have access, ask your hotelier to direct you to the nearest place to get online. Most of the towns where I've listed accommodations in this book also have Internet cafés. Many libraries offer free access, but they also tend to have limited opening hours, restrict your online time to 30 minutes, and may require reservations.

Traveling with a Laptop: With a laptop or netbook, it's easy to get online if your hotel has Wi-Fi (wireless Internet access) or a port in your room for plugging in a cable. Some hotels offer Wi-Fi for free; others charge by the minute or hour. A cellular modem—which lets your laptop access the Internet over a mobile phone network—provides more extensive coverage, but is much more expensive than Wi-Fi.

Mail

Get stamps at the neighborhood post office, newsstands within fancy hotels, and some mini-marts and card shops. You can arrange for mail delivery to your hotel (allow 10 days for a letter to arrive), but phoning and emailing are so easy that I've dispensed with mail stops altogether.

APPENDIX

Transportation

By Car or Public Transportation?

Cars are best for three or more traveling together (especially families with small kids), those packing heavy, and those scouring the countryside. Trains and buses are best for solo travelers, blitz tourists, and city-to-city travelers. While a car gives you the ultimate in mobility and freedom, enables you to search for hotels more easily, and carries your bags for you, the train zips you effortlessly from city to city, usually dropping you in the center and near the tourist office.

England's 100-mph train system is one of Europe's best. Buses pick you up when the trains let you down. Travelers who don't want (or can't afford) to drive a rental car can enjoy an excellent tour using public transportation.

In England, my choice is to connect big cities by train and to explore rural areas (Cornwall, Dartmoor, the Cotswolds, and the Lake District) footloose and fancy-free by rental car. The mix works quite efficiently (e.g., London, Bath, and York by train, with a rental car for the rest). You might consider a BritRail & Drive Pass, which gives you various combinations of rail days and car days to use within two months' time.

Trains

Regular tickets on England's great train system (15,000 departures from 2,400 stations daily) are the most expensive per mile in all of Europe. Those who save the biggest book in advance, leave after rush hour (after 9:30), or ride the bus. Now that Britain has privatized its railways, it can be tricky to track down all your options; a single bus or train route can be operated by several companies. However, one British website covers all train lines (www.national rail.co.uk), and another covers all bus and train routes in Britain (www.traveline.org.uk). Another good resource, which also has schedules for trains throughout Europe, is German Rail's timetable (http://bahn.hafas.de/bin/query.exe/en).

As with airline tickets, British train tickets can come at many different prices for the same journey. A clerk at any station can figure out the cheapest fare for your trip (or call the helpful National Rail folks at toll tel. 0845-748-4950, 24 hours daily). Savings can be significant. For a London–York round-trip (standard class), the full fare is more than £100; if you book the day of departure for travel after 9:30, it's around £84; and the cheapest fare, booked a couple of months in advance as two one-way tickets, can cost as little as £27.

While not required on English trains, reservations are free and a good idea for long journeys or any train travel on Sunday.

Sample Train Journey

Here is a typical example of a personalized train schedule printed out at England's train stations. At the Salisbury station, I told the clerk that I wanted to leave after 16:30 for Moreton-in-Marsh in the Cotswolds.

Stations	Arrive	Depart	Class
Salisbury	—	16:41	Standard
Bristol	17:48	18:28	1st/Standard
Cheltenham Spa	19:10	19:29	1st/Standard
Worcester	19:52	20:05	1st/Standard
Moreton-in-Marsh	20:42	—	

Even though the trip involved three transfers, this schedule allowed me to easily navigate the rails.

Train departures are listed on overhead boards at the station by their final destination (note that your destination could be an intermediate stop on this route, and therefore not listed on the overhead). It's helpful to ask at the info desk—or any conductor—for the final destination of your next train (such as Oxford), so you'll be able to figure out quickly which platform it's departing from. Upon arrival at Worcester, I looked for *Oxford* on the station's overhead train schedule to determine where to catch my train to Moreton-in-Marsh.

Often the conductor on your previous train can even tell you which platform your next train will depart from, but it's wise to confirm.

England's train system can experience delays, so don't schedule your connections too tight if you need to be at your destination at a specific time.

Make them at any train station before 18:00 on the day before you travel.

Buying Train Tickets in Advance: The best fares go to those who book their trips well in advance of their journey. (While only a 7-day minimum advance booking is officially required for the cheapest fares, these sell out fast—especially in summer—so a 6–8 week advance booking is often necessary.) Keep in mind that when booking in advance, "return" (round-trip) fares are not always cheaper than buying two "single" (one-way) tickets. Also note that cheap advance tickets often come with the toughest refund restrictions, so be sure to nail down your travel plans before you reserve. To book ahead, you can go in person to any station, book online at www.nationalrail.co.uk, or call 0845-748-4950 (from the US, call 011-44-20-7278-5240, phone answered 24 hours) to find out the schedule and best fare for your journey; then you'll be referred to

Public Transportation Routes in Britain

GROATS

MAP NOT TO SCALE

—ABERDEEN

LAND

ANDREWS
BURGH
WICK

— RAIL
— EUROSTAR
--- BUS
⋯ FERRY w/ CROSSING TIME
(6H)
✈ AIRPORT (NOT ALL SHOWN)

TO
AMST.
(15H)

DURHAM
YORK
HULL
GRIMSBY
LINCOLN

<u>London-Area Airports</u>
Ⓐ Heathrow
Ⓑ Gatwick
Ⓒ Luton
Ⓓ Stansted
Ⓔ London City

LAND

KING'S LYNN   NORWICH
PETER-
BOROUGH
ELY
CAMBRIDGE

NORTH
SEA

✈Ⓓ

TO
ESBJERG
(DENMARK)
(18H)

DON
✈
Ⓔ   HARWICH
EBBSFLEET
ASHFORD   CANTERBURY
NEW-
HAVEN   DOVER
FOLKE-
STONE   PARIS (2.5H)
CHUNNEL
TO
DIEPPE (4H)   TO
PARIS & BRUSSELS

→ TO HOEK VAN HOLLAND
(6H)

TO
CALAIS
(1.5H)
TO
BOUL.
(1.5H)

DCH

Railpasses

Prices listed are for 2010 and are subject to change. For the latest prices, details, and train schedules (and easy online ordering), see my comprehensive *Guide to Eurail Passes* at www.ricksteves.com/rail.

"Standard" is the polite British term for "second" class. "Senior" refers to those age 60 and up. No senior discounts for standard class. "Youth" means under age 26. For each adult or senior BritRail or BritRail England pass you buy, one child (5–15) can travel free with you (ask for the "**Family Pass**," not available with all passes). Additional kids pay the normal half-adult rate. Kids under 5 travel free.

Note: Overnight journeys begun on the final night of your pass can be completed the day after your pass expires—only BritRail allows this trick. A bunk in a twin sleeper costs $75.

BRITRAIL CONSECUTIVE PASS

	Adult 1st Class	Adult Standard	Senior 1st Class	Youth 1st Class	Youth Standard
3 consec. days	$289	$199	$249	$235	$159
4 consec. days	365	249	305	289	199
8 consec. days	509	359	435	405	285
15 consec. days	759	535	649	609	425
22 consec. days	965	645	819	769	515
1 month	1139	759	965	909	605

BRITRAIL FLEXIPASS

	Adult 1st Class	Adult Standard	Senior 1st Class	Youth 1st Class	Youth Standard
3 days in 2 months	$359	$255	$305	$285	$205
4 days in 2 months	445	315	379	359	249
8 days in 2 months	649	459	555	519	365
15 days in 2 months	975	689	829	779	555

BRITRAIL & DRIVE PASS

Any 4 rail days and 2 car days in 2 months.

	1st Class	Standard Class	Extra Car Day
Mini	$513	$374	$44
Economy	519	380	50
Compact	527	389	59
Compact Auto	556	418	88
Intermed. Auto	569	430	100
Minivan Auto	644	505	175

Prices are per person, two traveling together. Third and fourth persons sharing car buy a regular BritRail pass. To order a Rail & Drive pass, call Rail Europe at 800-438-7245. *Not sold by Europe Through the Back Door.*

Map key:

Approximate point-to-point one-way standard-class fares in US dollars by rail (solid line) and bus (dashed line). First class costs 50 percent more. Add up fares for your itinerary to see whether a railpass will save you money.

BRITRAIL ENGLAND CONSECUTIVE PASS

	Adult 1st Class	Adult Standard	Senior 1st Class	Youth 1st Class	Youth Standard
3 consec. days	$229	$159	$195	$189	$129
4 consec. days	$285	$199	$245	$229	$159
8 consec. days	$409	$285	$349	$329	$229
15 consec. days	$615	$429	$525	$489	$345
22 consec. days	$775	$519	$665	$619	$415
1 month	$915	$609	$775	$729	$489

Covers travel only in England, not Scotland, Wales, or Ireland.

BRITRAIL ENGLAND FLEXIPASS

Type of Pass	Adult 1st Class	Adult Standard	Senior 1st Class	Youth 1st Class	Youth Standard
3 days in 2 months	$289	$205	$249	$235	$165
4 days in 2 months	$365	$255	$305	$289	$205
8 days in 2 months	$525	$369	$445	$419	$295
15 days in 2 months	$779	$549	$665	$625	$439

Covers travel only in England, not Scotland, Wales, or Ireland.

BRITRAIL LONDON PLUS PASS

	Adult 1st Class	Adult Standard
2 out of 8 days	$199	$139
4 out of 8 days	275	225
7 out of 15 days	355	269

Covers much of SE England (see London Plus Coverage Map at www.ricksteves.com/rail).Includes vouchers to cover two trips on the Heathrow, Stansted, or Gatwick Express, separate from your counted travel days, which can be used up to 6 months from the date you validate the pass in Britain (but not before pass is validated for the 8- or 15-day travel window). Many trains are standard class only. The 7 p.m. rule for night trains does not apply. Kids 5–15 half price; under 5 free.

BRITRAIL SCOTTISH FREEDOM PASS

4 out of 8 days	$235
8 out of 15 days	315

Valid in Scotland only, standard class only. Not valid on trains that depart before 9:15 a.m. Mon–Fri. Covers Caledonian MacBrayne and Strathclyde ferry service to popular islands. Discounts on some P&O ferries, some Citylink buses & more. Kids 5–15 half fare; under 5 free.

BRITRAIL CENTRAL SCOTLAND PASS

3 out of 7 days	$79

Passes are prevalidated at the time of purchase for a specific, 7-day travel window and cannot be refunded after that planned travel date! Covers frequent service between Edinburgh and Glasgow's Queen St Station (not Glasgow Central), some nearby side-trips (see Central Scotland Coverage Map at www.ricksteves.com/rail), and the Glasgow Underground (on your three travel days). Standard class only. No highlands or islands. Not valid on trains that depart before 9:15 a.m. Mon–Fri, Glasgow Airport Coach Links, excursion trains, nor private railways. The 7 p.m. rule for night trains does not apply. No child discount; under 5 free.

BRITRAIL PASS PLUS IRELAND

	First Class	Standard Class
5 days in 1 month	$665	$469
10 days in 1 month	1185	839

Covers the entire British Isles (England, Wales, Scotland, Northern Ireland, and the Republic of Ireland). No longer covers ferries. Kids 5-15 pay half fare; under 5 free. No Family Pass, Party Pass, Eurail Discount, nor Off-Peak Special. Consider the cost of separate BritRail and Ireland passes.

the appropriate number to call—depending on the particular rail company—to book your ticket. If you order online, be sure you know what you want; it's tough to reach a person who can change your online reservation. You'll pick up your ticket at the station (unless your order was lost—this service still has some glitches). If you want your ticket mailed to you in the US, you need to allow a couple of weeks and cover the shipping costs. (BritRail passholders, however, cannot use the Web to make reservations.)

A company called **Megabus** (through their subsidiary Megatrain) sells some discounted train tickets well in advance on a few specific routes, though their focus is mainly on selling bus tickets (toll tel. 0871-266-3333, www.megatrain.com).

Buying Train Tickets as You Travel: If you'd rather have the flexibility of booking tickets as you go, you can save a few pounds by buying a round-trip ticket, called a "return ticket" (a same-day round-trip, called a "day return," is particularly cheap); buying before 18:00 the day before you depart; traveling after the morning rush hour (this usually means after 9:30 Mon–Fri); and going standard class instead of first class. Preview your options at www .nationalrail.co.uk or www.thetrainline.com.

Senior, Youth, and Family Deals: To get a third off the price of most point-to-point rail tickets, seniors can buy a Senior Railcard (for ages 60 and above), and younger travelers can buy a 16–25 Railcard (for ages 16–25, or for full-time students 26 and above with a valid ISIC card). A Family Railcard allows adults to travel about 33 percent cheaper while their kids ages 5 to 15 receive a 60 percent discount for most trips (maximum of 4 adults and 4 kids). Each Railcard costs £26; see www.railcard.co.uk. Any of these cards are valid for a year on almost all trains except special runs, such as the Heathrow Express or the Eurostar to Paris or Brussels (fill out application at station, brochures on racks in info center, need to show passport; passport-type photo needed for 16–25 Railcard).

Railpasses: Consider getting a railpass. The BritRail pass comes in "consecutive day" and "flexi" versions, with price breaks for youths, seniors, off-season travelers, and groups of three of more. Most allow one child under 16 to travel free with a paying adult. If you're exploring England's backcountry with a BritRail pass, standard class is a good choice since many of the smaller train lines don't even offer first-class cars. Choose between England-only BritRail passes and ones that cover Scotland and Wales as well.

More BritRail options include England/Ireland passes, "London Plus" passes (good for travel in most of southeast England but not in London itself), and BritRail & Drive passes (which offer you some rail days and some car-rental days). These BritRail passes, as well as Eurailpasses, get you a discount on the Eurostar train that zips you to continental Europe under the English Channel. These passes are sold outside of Europe only. For specifics, contact your travel agent or see www.ricksteves.com/rail.

Buses

Although buses are about a third slower than trains, they're also a lot cheaper. Most buses are operated by **National Express** (toll tel. 0871-781-8181, www.nationalexpress.com). Note that Brits distinguish between "buses" (for in-city travel with lots of stops) and "coaches" (long-distance cross-country runs)—though for simplicity in this book, I call both "buses."

Round-trip bus tickets usually cost less than two one-way fares (e.g., London–York one-way costs about £26; round-trip cost about £40). And buses go many places that trains don't. Budget travelers can save a wad with a bus pass. National Express sells **Brit Xplorer bus passes** for unlimited travel on consecutive days (£79/7 days, £139/14 days, £219/28 days, sold over the counter, non-UK passport required, toll tel. 0871-781-8181, www.nationalexpress.com). Check their website to learn about online Funfare deals; senior/youth/family cards and fares; and discounts for advance booking.

If you want to take a bus from your last destination to the nearest airport, you'll find that National Express often offers **airport buses.** Bus stations are normally at or near train stations (in London, the main bus station is a block southwest of Victoria Station).

Megabus sells very cheap promotional fares on certain routes, often beating National Express in price. While this can save you some money, you have to book far ahead for the best rates, and journey times tend to be longer than those on National Express (toll tel. 0900-160-0900, www.megabus.com). They also sell discounted train tickets on selected routes.

A couple of companies offer **backpackers' bus circuits.** These easy hop-on, hop-off bus circuits take mostly youth hostelers around the country for super-cheap fares, with the assumption that they'll be sleeping in the hostels along the way. For instance, **Backpacker Tours** offers 1–19-day excursions through England and other destinations in Great Britain (from about £65/1 day, £90/3 days, £266/5 days, toll tel. 0870-745-1046, www.backpacker tours.co.uk, sales@backpackertours.co.uk).

Renting a Car

To rent a car in England, you must be at least 23 years old and have a valid license. Drivers under the age of 25 may incur a young-driver surcharge, and some companies do not rent to anyone 75 and over. If you're considered too young or old, look into leasing, which

APPENDIX

has less-stringent age restrictions (see "Leasing," later). To drive in England, an International Driving Permit is recommended, but not required ($15 through your local AAA, plus two passport-type photos, www.aaa.com); I've frequently rented cars in Britain without having or being asked to show this permit.

Research car rentals before you go. It's cheaper to arrange most car rentals from the US. Call several companies and look online to compare rates, or arrange a rental through your hometown travel agent. Most of the major US rental agencies—such as Enterprise, Alamo, National, Avis/Budget, Dollar, Hertz, and Thrifty—have offices in England (although some subcontract to Europcar). It can be cheaper to use a consolidator, such as Auto Europe (www.autoeurope.com) or Europe by Car (www.ebctravel .com), but by using a middleman, you risk trading customer service for lower prices; if you have a problem with the rental company, you can't count on the consolidator to intervene on your behalf.

For the best deal, rent by the week with unlimited mileage. If you want to save money on gas, ask for a diesel car. I normally rent the smallest, least-expensive model with a stick-shift. Almost all rentals are manual by default, so if you need an automatic, you must request one in advance; beware that these cars are usually larger models (not as maneuverable on narrow, winding roads). An automatic transmission adds about 50 percent to the car-rental cost over a manual transmission. But weigh this against the fact that in England you'll be sitting on the right side of the car, and shifting with your left hand...while driving on the left side of the road. The floor pedals are in the same locations as in the US, and the gears are found in the same basic "H" pattern as at home (i.e., first gear, second, etc.).

Expect to pay about $900 per person (based on two people sharing) for a small economy car for three weeks with unlimited mileage, including gas, parking, and insurance. Consider leasing to save money on insurance and taxes.

Compare pick-up costs (downtown can be cheaper than the airport) and explore drop-off options. If you pick up the car in a smaller city, such as Bath, you'll more likely survive your first day on the English roads. Returning a car at a big-city train station can be tricky; get precise details on the car drop-off location and hours. Note that rental offices usually close from midday Saturday until Monday.

If you drop the car off early or keep it longer, you'll be credited or charged at a fair, prorated price. But keep your receipts in case any questions arise about your billing.

When you pick up the car, check it thoroughly and make sure any damage is noted on your rental agreement. Find out how your car's lights, turn signals, wipers, and gas cap function. Ask what type of fuel your car takes before you fill up. When you return the car, make sure the agent verifies its condition with you.

Car Insurance Options

When you rent a car, you are liable for a very high deductible, sometimes equal to the entire value of the car. Limit your financial risk by choosing one of these three options: Buy Collision Damage Waiver (CDW) coverage from the car-rental company, get coverage through your credit card (free, if your card automatically includes zero-deductible coverage), or buy coverage through Travel Guard.

CDW includes a very high deductible (typically $1,000–1,500). Though each rental company has its own variation, basic CDW costs $15–25 a day (figure roughly 25 percent extra) and reduces your liability, but does not eliminate it. When you pick up the car, you'll be offered the chance to "buy down" the basic deductible to zero (for an additional $15–30/day; this is sometimes called "super CDW").

If you opt for **credit-card coverage**, there's a catch. You'll technically have to decline all coverage offered by the car-rental company, which means they can place a hold on your card (which can be up to the full value of the car). In case of damage, it can be time-consuming to resolve the charges with your credit-card company. Before you decide on this option, quiz your credit-card company about how it works.

Finally, you can buy CDW insurance from **Travel Guard** ($9/day plus a one-time $3 service fee covers you for up to $35,000, $250 deductible, tel. 800-826-4919, www.travelguard.com). It's valid everywhere in Europe except the Republic of Ireland, and some Italian car-rental companies refuse to honor it. Oddly, residents of Washington state and Texas aren't allowed to buy this coverage.

For more on car-rental insurance, see www.ricksteves.com/cdw.

Leasing

For trips of 2.5 weeks or more, leasing (which automatically includes zero-deductible collision and theft insurance) is the best way to go. By technically buying and then selling back the car, you save lots of money on tax and insurance. Leasing provides you a brand-new car with unlimited mileage and a 24-hour emergency assistance program. You can lease for as little as 17 days to as long as six months. Car leases must be arranged from the US. One of many reliable companies offering affordable lease packages is Europe by Car (US tel. 800-223-1516, www.ebctravel.com).

Driving in England

Driving in England is basically wonderful—once you remember to stay on the left and after you've mastered the roundabouts. Every year, however, I get a few notes from traveling readers advising me that, for them, trying to drive in England was a nerve-racking and regrettable mistake. If you want to get a little slack on the roads, drop by a gas station or auto shop and buy a green *P* (probationary driver with license) sign to put in your car window (don't get the red *L* sign, which means you're a learner driver without a license and thus prohibited from driving on motorways).

Many Yankee drivers find the hardest part isn't driving on the left, but steering from the right. Your instinct is to put yourself on the left side of your lane, which means you may spend your first day or two constantly drifting off the road to the left. It can help to remember that the driver always stays close to the center line.

STOP AND LEARN THESE ROAD SIGNS

Speed Limit (mph) • Yield • No Passing • End of No Passing Zone • One Way • Intersection • Main Road • Freeway • Danger • No Entry • No Entry for cars • All Vehicle Prohibited • Parking • No Parking • Customs • Peace

Road Rules: Seat belts are mandatory for all, and kids under age 12 (or less than about 4.5 feet tall) must ride in an appropriate child-safety seat. It's illegal to use a mobile phone while driving—pull over if you need to chat or text. For more information about driving in Britain, read the Department for Transport's *Highway Code* (buy it in the UK or visit www.direct.gov.uk—click on "Motoring" and look for "The Highway Code" link).

Speed Limits: Speed limits are 30 mph in town, 70 mph on the motorways, and 50 or 60 mph elsewhere (though, as back home, many British drivers consider these limits advisory). The national sign for 60 mph is a white circle with a black slash. Motorways have electronic speed limit signs; posted speeds can change depending on traffic

How to Navigate a Roundabout

NOTE:

- TRAFFIC IN ROUNDABOUTS FLOWS IN A CLOCKWISE DIRECTION.

- VEHICLES ENTERING A ROUNDABOUT MUST YIELD TO VEHICLES IN THE ROUNDABOUT.

- LOOK TO YOUR RIGHT AS YOU MERGE!

or the weather. Follow them accordingly.

Note that road-surveillance cameras strictly enforce speed limits. Any driver (including foreigners renting cars) photographed speeding will get a nasty bill in the mail. (Cameras—you'll see the foreboding gray boxes—flash on your rear license plate in order not to invade the privacy of anyone sharing the front seat with someone he or she shouldn't be with.)

Roundabouts: Don't let a roundabout spook you. After all, you routinely merge into much faster traffic on American highways back home. Traffic in roundabouts has the right-of-way; entering traffic yields (look to your right as you merge). You'll probably encounter "double-roundabouts"—figure-eights where you'll slingshot from one roundabout directly into another. Just go with the flow and track signs carefully. When approaching an especially complex roundabout, you'll first pass a diagram showing the layout and the various exits. And in many cases, the pavement is painted with which lane you should be in for which road or town.

Freeways (Motorways): The shortest distance between any two points is usually the motorway (what we'd call a "freeway"). In Britain, the smaller the number, the bigger the road. For example, M4 is a freeway, while B4494 is a country road.

Motorway road signs can be confusing, too few, and too late. Miss a motorway exit and you can lose 30 minutes. Study your map before taking off. Know the cities you'll be lacing together, since road numbers are inconsistent. British road signs are never marked with compass directions (e.g., *A30 West*); instead, you need to know what major town or city you're heading for (*A30 Penzance*). The driving directions in this book are intended to be used with a good local map. An England road atlas, easily purchased at gas stations in England, is money well-spent (see "Maps," page 713).

Unless you're passing, always drive in the "slow" lane on motorways (this is the lane farthest to the left). The British are very disciplined about this; ignoring this rule could get you a ticket (or into a road-rage incident). Remember to pass on the right, not the left.

Rest areas are called "services" and often have a number of useful amenities, such as restaurants, cafeterias, gas stations, shops, and motels.

Fuel: Gas (petrol) costs about $9 per gallon and is self-serve. Diesel rental cars are common; make sure you know what your car takes before you fill up. Unleaded pumps are usually green. Note that your US credit and debit cards are unlikely to work at self-service gas pumps, as well as toll bridges and automated parking garages. It might help if you know your PIN, but just in case, be sure to carry sufficient cash.

Driving in Cities: Whenever possible, avoid driving in cities. Be warned that London assesses a congestion charge (see page 55). Most cities have modern ring roads to skirt the congestion. Follow signs to the parking lots outside the city core—most are a 5- to 10-minute walk to the center—and avoid what can be an unpleasant grid of one-way streets (as in Bath) or roads that are only available to public transportation during the day (as in Oxford).

Driving in Rural Areas: Outside of the big cities and the motorways, British roads tend to be narrow. In towns, you may have to cross over the center line just to get past parked cars. Adjust your perceptions of personal space: It's not "my side of the road" or "your side of the road," it's just "the road"—and it's shared as a cooperative adventure. If the road's wide enough, both directions

England by Car: Mileage and Time

of traffic can pass parked cars simultaneously, but frequently you'll have to take turns—follow the locals' lead and drive defensively. Some narrow country lanes are barely wide enough for one car. Go slowly, and if you encounter an oncoming car, look for the nearest pullout (or "passing place")—the driver who's closest to one is expected to use it, even if they have to back up to reach it. If another car pulls over and blinks its headlights, that means, "Go ahead; I'll wait to let you pass." British drivers are quick to offer a friendly wave to thank you for letting them pass (and they appreciate it if you reciprocate). Pull over frequently—to let faster locals pass and to check the map.

Parking: Parking can be confusing. One yellow line marked on the pavement means no parking Monday through Saturday during work hours. Double yellow lines mean no parking at any time. Broken yellow lines mean short stops are OK, but you should always look for explicit signs or ask a passerby. White lines mean you're free to park.

In towns, rather than look for street parking, I generally just pull into the most central and handy "pay and display" parking lot I can find. To "pay and display," feed change into a machine, receive a timed ticket, and display it on the dashboard or stick it to the driver's-side window. Rates are reasonable by US standards, and locals love to share stickers that have time remaining. If you stand by the machine, someone on their way out with time left on their sticker will probably give it to you. Keep a bag of coins in the ashtray or glove box for these machines and for parking meters.

Traffic Alerts: If you want to stay up-to-date on traffic conditions, ask your rental-car company about turning on automatic traffic alerts that play on the car radio. Once these are enabled (look for the letters *TA* or *TP* on the radio readout), traffic reports for the area you are driving in will periodically interrupt programming.

The AA: An Automobile Association membership for Britain comes with most rentals (www.theaa.com). Understand its towing and emergency road-service benefits.

Stock Up: Set your car up for a fun road trip. Establish a cardboard-box munchies pantry. Buy a rack of liter boxes of juice for the trunk, and some Windex and a roll of paper towels (called a "kitchen roll" in Britain) for cleaner sightseeing.

Cheap Flights

London is the hub for many cheap, no-frills airlines, which affordably connect the city with other destinations in the British Isles and throughout Europe. While trains are still the best way to connect places that are close together, a flight can save both time and money on long journeys.

One of the best websites for comparing inexpensive flights is www.skyscanner.net. Other comparison search engines include www.wegolo.com and www.whichbudget.com. Buy tickets in advance. Although you can usually book right up until the flight departs, the cheap seats will often have sold out long before, leaving the most expensive seats for latecomers.

Be aware of the potential drawbacks of flying on the cheap: nonrefundable and nonchangeable tickets, minimal or nonexistent customer service, additional charges for everything (with Ryanair being the worst offender), treks to airports far outside town, and pricey baggage fees. Read the small print—especially baggage policies—before you book.

With **bmi,** you can fly inexpensively from London to destinations in the UK and beyond. Fares start at about £45 one-way to

Edinburgh, Dublin, Brussels, or Amsterdam (toll tel. 0870-607-0555, US tel. 800-788-0555, www.flybmi.com).

Another low-cost airline, **easyJet,** flies from Gatwick, Luton, and Stansted. Prices are based on demand, so the least popular routes make for the cheapest fares, especially if you book early (toll tel. 0905-821-0905, calls £0.65/minute, www.easyjet.com).

Irish-owned **Ryanair** flies from London (mostly Stansted Airport, though also Gatwick and Luton) to often obscure airports near Dublin, Glasgow, Frankfurt, Stockholm, Oslo, Venice, Turin, and many others. Sample fares: London–Dublin—£50 round-trip (sometimes as low as £30), London–Frankfurt—£45 round-trip (Irish toll tel. 0818-303-030, British toll tel. 0871-246-0000, www.ryanair.com). However, be warned that Ryanair charges additional fees for nearly everything. The company requires a mandatory online-only check-in (£5 charge), from 15 days to four hours before your flight (no airport check-in). When checking in, you must also print out your boarding pass; if you show up without it, there's an additional £40 charge. You can carry on only a small day bag; you'll pay a fee for each checked bag (price depends on number of bags; up to three bags allowed per passenger).

Brussels Airlines (formerly Virgin Express) is a Brussels-based company with good rates and hubs in Bristol, Birmingham, Gatwick, Manchester, and Newcastle (book by phone and pick up ticket at airport an hour before your flight, US tel. 516/740-5200, British toll tel. 0905-609-5609—£0.40/minute, www.brusselsairlines.com).

Resources

Resources from Rick Steves

Rick Steves' England 2011 is one of many books in my series on European travel, which includes country guidebooks (such as *Rick Steves' Great Britain*, covering Scotland and Wales), city and regional guidebooks (including London), Snapshot guides (excerpted chapters from my country guides), Pocket guides (full-color little books on big cities), and my budget-travel skills handbook, *Rick Steves' Europe Through the Back Door*. My phrase books—for French, Italian, German, Spanish, and Portuguese—are practical and budget-oriented. My other books include *Europe 101* (a crash course on art and history) and *Travel as a Political Act* (a travelogue sprinkled with tips for bringing home a global perspective). For a list of my books, see the inside of the last page of this book.

APPENDIX

Begin Your Trip at www.ricksteves.com

At our travel website, you'll find a wealth of free information on European destinations, including fresh monthly news and helpful tips from thousands of fellow travelers. You'll also find my latest guidebook updates (www.ricksteves.com/update) and my travel blog.

Our **online Travel Store** offers travel bags and accessories specially designed by Rick Steves to help you travel smarter and lighter. These include Rick's popular carry-on bags (roll-aboard and rucksack versions), money belts, totes, toiletries kits, adapters, other accessories, and a wide selection of guidebooks, planning maps, and DVDs.

Choosing the right **railpass** for your trip—amidst hundreds of options—can drive you nutty. We'll help you choose the best pass for your needs, plus give you a bunch of free extras.

Rick Steves' Europe Through the Back Door travel company offers **tours** with more than three dozen itineraries and 400 departures reaching the best destinations in this book...and beyond. We offer a 14-day England tour, an 11-day Scotland tour, and a 7-day in-depth London city tour. You'll enjoy great guides, a fun bunch of travel partners (with small groups of around 28), and plenty of room to spread out in a big, comfy bus. You'll find European adventures to fit every vacation length. For all the details, and to get our Tour Catalog and a free Rick Steves Tour Experience DVD (filmed on location during an actual tour), visit www.ricksteves.com or call the Tour Department at 425/608-4217.

APPENDIX

Video: My public television series, *Rick Steves' Europe*, covers European destinations in 100 shows, with 10 episodes on Great Britain. To watch episodes, visit www.hulu.com/rick-steves -europe; for scripts and other details, see www.ricksteves.com/ audioeurope.

Audio: My weekly public radio show, *Travel with Rick Steves*,

features interviews with travel experts from around the world. I've also produced free self-guided audio tours of the top sights and neighborhoods in London. All of this audio content is available for free at Rick Steves Audio Europe, an extensive online library organized by destination. Choose whatever interests you, and download it for free to your iPod, smartphone, or computer at www.rick steves.com or iTunes.

Maps

The black-and-white maps in this book, drawn by Dave Hoerlein, are concise and simple. Dave, who is well-traveled in Britain, designed the maps to help you locate recommended places and get to local TIs, where you can pick up more in-depth maps of towns or regions (usually free). Better maps are sold at newsstands and bookstores. Before you buy a map, look at it to be sure it has the level of detail you want.

If you'll be lingering in London, buy a city map at a London newsstand; the red *Benson's London Street Map* (£2.75) is excellent. Even the vending-machine maps sold in Tube stations are good. The *Rough Guide* map to London is well-designed (£5, sold at London bookstores). The *Rick Steves' Britain, Ireland & London City Map* has a good map of London ($6, www.ricksteves.com). Many Londoners, along with obsessive-compulsive tourists, rely on the highly detailed *London A–Z* map book (generally £5–7, called "A to Zed" by locals, available at newsstands).

If you're driving, get a road atlas (1 inch equals 3 miles) covering all of England. Ordnance Survey, AA, and Bartholomew editions are all available for about £7 at tourist information offices, gas stations, and bookstores. Drivers, hikers, and cyclists may want more in-depth maps for the Cotswolds and the Lake District.

Other Guidebooks

If you're like most travelers, this book is all you need. But if you're heading beyond my recommended neighborhoods and destinations, $40 for extra maps and books is money well-spent. Especially for several people traveling by car, the extra weight and expense are negligible.

Harry Potter Sights

Harry Potter's story is set in a magical Britain. Except for those in London, all of the places mentioned in the books are fictional—though you can still visit many real film locations. So quicker than you can say "Lumos," let's shine a light on where to get your Harry Potter fix if you're a die-hard fan.

Spoiler Warning: The following information will ruin surprises for the three of you who haven't yet read or seen any of the Harry Potter books or movies.

London

In the first film, Harry first realizes his wizard powers when talking with a boa constrictor, filmed at the **London Zoo's Reptile House** in Regent's Park (Tube: Great Portland Street).

London bustles along oblivious to the parallel universe of wizards, hidden in the magical Diagon Alley (filmed, like many of the other fictional settings, on a set at Leavesden Studios, north of London). The goblin-run Gringotts Wizarding Bank, though, was filmed in the real-life marble-floored Exhibition Hall of **Australia House** (Tube: Temple), home of the Australian Embassy.

Harry catches the train to Hogwarts at **King's Cross Station.**

Inside the glass-roofed train station, on a **pedestrian sky bridge** over the tracks, Hagrid gives Harry a train ticket. Harry heads to platform 9¾. You'll find a fun re-creation—complete with a *Platform 9¾* sign and a luggage cart that appears to be disappearing into the wall—on the way to platform 9. (Walk toward the pedestrian bridge and make a left at the arch.)

In film #3, Harry careens through London's lamp-lit streets on a purple three-decker bus that dumps him at the Leaky Cauldron pub. The exterior was shot on rough-looking Stoney Street at the southeast edge of **Borough Street Market,** by The Market Porter pub (Tube: London Bridge).

In film #5, the Order of the Phoenix takes to the night sky on broomsticks over London, passing over plenty of identifiable landmarks, including the **London Eye, Big Ben,** and **Buckingham Palace.**

In film #6, the **Millennium Bridge** is attacked and collapses into the Thames.

Near Bath

The mysterious side of Hogwarts is often set in the elaborate, fan-vaulted corridors of the **Gloucester Cathedral** cloisters, 50 miles north of Bath. In film #1, when Harry and Ron set out to save Hermione, they look down a long, dark Gloucester hallway and spot a 20-foot troll at the far end.

Also in film #1, the scene showing Harry being chosen for Gryffindor's Quidditch team was shot in the halls of the 13th-century **Lacock Abbey,** 13 miles east of Bath. Harry attends Professor Snape's class in one of the Abbey's bare, peeling-plaster rooms—appropriate to Snape's temperament. (Mad Max tours include Lacock on its day-trip itinerary; for details, see page 348.)

Oxford

Hogwarts, Harry's prestigious wizarding prep school, is a composite of several locations, many of them real places in Oxford. (For information on Harry Potter tours in Oxford, see page 423.)

Christ Church College—with plenty of Harry-related sights—inspired two film sets familiar to Potter fans. In the first film, the kids are ferried to Hogwarts and then ascend a **stone staircase** that leads into the Great Hall. Christ Church's high-ceilinged **dining hall** was a model for the one seen throughout the films (with the weightless candles and flaming braziers).

Later in the first film, Harry sneaks into the restricted book section of Hogwarts Library under a cloak of invisibility. This scene was filmed inside Oxford's **Duke Humfrey's Library.** Hermione reads about the Sorcerer's Stone here, too.

At the end of the first film, Harry awakens from his dark battle into the golden light of the Hogwarts infirmary, filmed in the big-windowed **Divinity School,** on the ground floor of the Bodleian Library; Ron also recuperates here after being poisoned in film #6. In film #4, Mad-Eye Moody turns Draco into a ferret in the **New College cloister.**

Durham and Northeast England

In the first film, Harry walks with his white owl, Hedwig, through a snowy cloister courtyard located in **Durham's Cathedral** (see listing on page 652). The bird soars up and over the church's twin 13th-century towers.

Harry first learns to fly a broomstick on the green grass of Hogwarts school grounds, filmed inside the walls of **Alnwick Castle,** located 30 miles from Newcastle. In film #2, this is where the Weasleys' flying car crashes into the Whomping Willow.

The following books are worthwhile, though not updated annually; check the publication date before you buy. The *Lonely Planet* and *Let's Go* guidebooks on London and on Britain are fine budget-travel guides. *Lonely Planet's* guidebooks are more thorough and informative; *Let's Go* books are youth-oriented, with good coverage of nightlife, hostels, and cheap transportation deals. For cultural and sightseeing background, look into Michelin and Cadogan guides to London, England, and Britain. The readable Access guide for London is similarly well-researched. *Secret London* by Andrew Duncan leads the reader on unique walks through a less-touristy London.

If you'll be focusing on London or traveling elsewhere in Britain, consider *Rick Steves' London 2011* or *Rick Steves' Great Britain 2011*.

Recommended Books and Movies

To learn more about England past and present, check out a few of these books and films.

Nonfiction

For a serious historical overview, wade into *A History of Britain*, a three-volume collection by Simon Schama. *Literary Trails* (Hardyment) reunites famous authors with the environments that inspired them.

In *Notes from a Small Island,* American expat Bill Bryson records his witty notes about every British foible. For more good memoirs, pick up any of the books by Susan Allen Toth on her British travels. If you'll be spending time in the Cotswolds, try *Cider with Rosie,* Laurie Lee's boyhood memoir set just after World War I. Animal-lovers enjoy James Herriot's adventures as a Yorkshire vet, told in *All Creatures Great and Small* and its sequels. And the obsessive world of English soccer is illuminated in Nick Hornby's memoir, *Fever Pitch*.

Fiction

For the classics of British fiction, read anything—and everything—by Charles Dickens, Jane Austen, and the Brontës. Mystery fans can't miss with any of the books by Agatha Christie.

Pillars of the Earth (Follett) traces the building of a fictional 12th-century cathedral in southern England. For a big book on the era of King Richard III, try *The Sunne in Splendour,* one in a series by Sharon Kay Penman. *The Other Boleyn Girl* (Gregory) sets its intrigues in the court of Henry VIII, while *Restoration* (Tremain) returns readers to the time of King Charles II.

Set in the 19th-century Anglican church, *The Warden* (Trollope) dwells on moral dilemmas. *Brideshead Revisited* (Waugh) satirizes the British obsession with class and takes place between the World Wars. A rural village in the 1930s is the social battlefield for E. F. Benson's *Mapp and Lucia*. For evocative Cornish settings, try Daphne du Maurier's *Rebecca* or *The House on the Strand*.

For a more contemporary read, check out *Bridget Jones's Diary* (Fielding), *Behind the Scenes at the Museum* (Atkinson), *White Teeth* (Smith), *Saturday* (McEwan), or anything by Nick Hornby (*High Fidelity*, *About a Boy*, etc.).

Films

Goodbye, Mr. Chips (1939) is set in a boys' boarding school during Victorian England. If you're in the mood for something completely different, try *Monty Python and the Holy Grail* (1975), a surreal take on the Arthurian legend. *Chariots of Fire* (1981) ran away with the Academy Award for Best Picture. *Hope and Glory* (1987) is a semi-autobiographical story of a boy growing up during WWII's Blitz.

A Room with a View (1985) and *The Remains of the Day* (1993) include scenes filmed in rural England. *Shadowlands* (1993) tells a fictionalized account of author C. S. Lewis' relationship with his future wife. Among the many versions of *Pride and Prejudice*, the 1995 BBC miniseries starring Colin Firth is the winner. In *The Full Monty* (1997), some working-class Yorkshire lads take it all off to pay the bills. *Calendar Girls* (2003) has a similar setting and premise, if a slightly more noble cause.

For a taste of Tudor-era London, try *Shakespeare in Love* (1999), which is set in the original Globe Theatre. The all-star *Gosford Park* (2001) is part comedy, part murder mystery, and part critique of England's class stratification in the 1930s. In *The Queen* (2006), Helen Mirren expertly channels Elizabeth II during the days after Princess Diana's death. In *The Duchess* (2008), the 18th-century Duchess of Devonshire glides languidly through life in big skirts and even bigger wigs. *An Education* (2009), about a bright schoolgirl who falls for an older man, takes place in 1960s London.

Holidays and Festivals

This list includes many—but not all—big festivals in major cities, plus national holidays observed throughout Great Britain. Before planning a trip around a festival, make sure you verify its dates by checking the festival's website or contacting the Visit Britain office (tel. 800-462-2748, www.visitbritain.com). Many sights and banks close down on national holidays—keep this in mind when planning your itinerary.

Many British towns have holiday festivals in late November and early December, with markets, music, and entertainment in

2011

JANUARY
S	M	T	W	T	F	S
						1
2	3	4	5	6	7	8
9	10	11	12	13	14	15
16	17	18	19	20	21	22
23/30	24/31	25	26	27	28	29

FEBRUARY
S	M	T	W	T	F	S
		1	2	3	4	5
6	7	8	9	10	11	12
13	14	15	16	17	18	19
20	21	22	23	24	25	26
27	28					

MARCH
S	M	T	W	T	F	S
		1	2	3	4	5
6	7	8	9	10	11	12
13	14	15	16	17	18	19
20	21	22	23	24	25	26
27	28	29	30	31		

APRIL
S	M	T	W	T	F	S
					1	2
3	4	5	6	7	8	9
10	11	12	13	14	15	16
17	18	19	20	21	22	23
24	25	26	27	28	29	30

MAY
S	M	T	W	T	F	S
1	2	3	4	5	6	7
8	9	10	11	12	13	14
15	16	17	18	19	20	21
22	23	24	25	26	27	28
29	30	31				

JUNE
S	M	T	W	T	F	S
			1	2	3	4
5	6	7	8	9	10	11
12	13	14	15	16	17	18
19	20	21	22	23	24	25
26	27	28	29	30		

JULY
S	M	T	W	T	F	S
					1	2
3	4	5	6	7	8	9
10	11	12	13	14	15	16
17	18	19	20	21	22	23
24/31	25	26	27	28	29	30

AUGUST
S	M	T	W	T	F	S
	1	2	3	4	5	6
7	8	9	10	11	12	13
14	15	16	17	18	19	20
21	22	23	24	25	26	27
28	29	30	31			

SEPTEMBER
S	M	T	W	T	F	S
				1	2	3
4	5	6	7	8	9	10
11	12	13	14	15	16	17
18	19	20	21	22	23	24
25	26	27	28	29	30	

OCTOBER
S	M	T	W	T	F	S
						1
2	3	4	5	6	7	8
9	10	11	12	13	14	15
16	17	18	19	20	21	22
23/30	24/31	25	26	27	28	29

NOVEMBER
S	M	T	W	T	F	S
		1	2	3	4	5
6	7	8	9	10	11	12
13	14	15	16	17	18	19
20	21	22	23	24	25	26
27	28	29	30			

DECEMBER
S	M	T	W	T	F	S
				1	2	3
4	5	6	7	8	9	10
11	12	13	14	15	16	17
18	19	20	21	22	23	24
25	26	27	28	29	30	31

the Christmas spirit (for instance, Keswick's Victorian Fayre).
Here are some major holidays in 2011:

Jan 1	New Year's Day
Feb (one week)	London Fashion Week (www.london fashionweek.co.uk)
Mid-Feb	Jorvik Viking Festival, York (costumed warriors, battles; www.jorvik-viking -centre.co.uk)
Feb 26–March 6	Literature Festival, Bath (www.bath litfest.org.uk)
April 22	Good Friday
April 24–25	Easter Sunday and Monday
May 2	Early May Bank Holiday
Mid-May	Jazz Festival, Keswick (www.keswick jazzfestival.co.uk)
Late May	Chelsea Flower Show, London (book tickets in advance for this popular event

	at www.rhs.org.uk/chelsea)
May 25–June 5	International Music Festival, Bath (www.bathmusicfest.org.uk)
Late May–early June	Fringe Festival, Bath (alternative music, dance, and theater; www.bathfringe .co.uk)
May 30	Spring Bank Holiday (last Monday in May)
June 3–4	Beer Festival, Keswick (music, shows; www.keswickbeerfestival.co.uk)
Early–mid-June	Trooping the Colour, London (military bands and pageantry, Queen's birthday parade; www.trooping-the-colour .co.uk)
June 14–18	Royal Ascot Horse Race, Ascot (near Windsor; www.ascot.co.uk)
Mid-late June	Golowan (Midsummer) Festival, Penzance (www.golowan.com)
Late June–early July	Wimbledon Tennis Championship, London (www.wimbledon.org)
July 8–16	Early Music Festival, York (www.ncem .co.uk)
Late July–early Aug	Cambridge Folk Festival (buy tickets early at www.cambridgefolkfestival .co.uk)
Late Aug	Notting Hill Carnival, London (costumes, Caribbean music, www .thenottinghillcarnival.com)
Aug 29	Late Summer Bank Holiday (England and Wales only, not Scotland)
Sept–Nov	Illuminations, Blackpool (waterfront light festival, www.visitblackpool.com /illuminations)
Sept (one week)	London Fashion Week (www.london fashionweek.co.uk)
Mid-Sept	Jane Austen Festival, Bath (www .janeausten.co.uk)
Late Sept	York Festival of Food and Drink (www .yorkfoodfestival.com)
Nov 5	Bonfire Night, or Guy Fawkes Night, Britain (fireworks, bonfires, effigy-burning of 1605 traitor Guy Fawkes)
Dec 24–26	Christmas holidays

APPENDIX

Conversions and Climate

Numbers and Stumblers

- In Europe, dates appear as day/month/year, so Christmas is 25/12/11.
- What Americans call the second floor of a building is the first floor in Britain.
- On escalators and moving sidewalks, Brits keep the left "lane" open for passing. Keep to the right.
- When pointing, use your whole hand, palm down.
- When counting with fingers, start with your thumb. If you hold up your first finger to request one item, you'll probably get two.
- To avoid the British version of giving someone "the finger," don't hold up the first two fingers of your hand with your palm facing you. (It looks like a reversed victory sign.)
- And please...don't call your waist pack a "fanny pack."

Metric Conversions (approximate)

Britain uses the metric system for everything but driving measurements. Weight and volume are typically calculated in metric: A kilogram is 2.2 pounds, and a liter is about a quart. The weight of a person is measured by "stone" (one stone equals 14 pounds). Temperatures are generally given in both Celsius and Fahrenheit.

On the road, Britain uses miles and posts speed limits in miles per hour.

1 foot = 0.3 meter	1 square yard = 0.8 square meter
1 yard = 0.9 meter	1 square mile = 2.6 square kilometers
1 mile = 1.6 kilometers	1 ounce = 28 grams
1 centimeter = 0.4 inch	1 quart = 0.95 liter
1 meter = 39.4 inches	1 kilogram = 2.2 pounds
1 kilometer = 0.62 mile	32°F = 0°C

Weights and Measures

1 British pint = 1.2 US pints
1 imperial gallon = 1.2 US gallons or about 4.5 liters
1 stone = 14 pounds (a 168-pound person weighs 12 stone)

Clothing Sizes

When shopping for clothing, use these US-to as general guidelines (but note that no conve

- Women's dresses and blouses: Add 4
  (US women's size 10 = UK size 14)
- Men's suits and jackets: US and UK use the same sizing
- Men's shirts: US and UK use the same sizing
- Women's shoes: Subtract 2½
  (US size 8 = UK size 5½)
- Men's shoes: Subtract about ½
  (US size 9 = UK size 8½)

Climate

First line, average daily temperature; second line, average daily low; third line, average days without rain. For more detailed weather statistics for destinations in this book (as well as the rest of the world), check www.worldclimate.com.

	J	F	M	A	M	J	J	A	S	O	N	D
LONDON												
	43°	44°	50°	56°	62°	69°	71°	71°	65°	58°	50°	45°
	36°	36°	38°	42°	47°	53°	56°	56°	52°	46°	42°	38°
	16	15	20	18	19	19	19	20	17	18	15	16
YORK												
	43°	44°	49°	55°	61°	67°	70°	69°	64°	57°	49°	45°
	33°	34°	36°	40°	44°	50°	54°	53°	50°	44°	39°	36°
	14	13	18	17	18	16	16	17	16	16	13	14

Temperature Conversion:
Fahrenheit and Celsius

Britain uses both Celsius and Fahrenheit to take its temperature. For a rough conversion from Celsius to Fahrenheit, double the number and add 30. For weather, remember that 28°C is 82°F—perfect. For health, 37°C is just right.

Essential Packing Checklist

Whether you're traveling for five days or five weeks, here's what you'll need to bring. Remember to pack light to enjoy the sweet freedom of true mobility. Happy travels!

- ❏ 5 shirts
- ❏ 1 sweater or lightweight fleece jacket
- ❏ 2 pairs pants
- ❏ 1 pair shorts
- ❏ 1 swimsuit (women only—men can use shorts)
- ❏ 5 pairs underwear and socks
- ❏ 1 pair shoes
- ❏ 1 rain-proof jacket
- ❏ Tie or scarf
- ❏ Money belt
- ❏ Money—your mix of:
    - ❏ Debit card for ATM withdrawals
    - ❏ Credit card
    - ❏ Hard cash in US dollars (in $20 bills)
- ❏ Documents (and back-up photocopies):
    - ❏ Passport
    - ❏ Printout of airline e-ticket
    - ❏ Driver's license
    - ❏ Student ID and hostel card
    - ❏ Railpass/car rental voucher
    - ❏ Insurance details
- ❏ Daypack
- ❏ Sealable plastic baggies
- ❏ Camera and related gear
- ❏ Empty water bottle
- ❏ Wristwatch and alarm clock
- ❏ Earplugs
- ❏ First-aid kit
- ❏ Medicine (labeled)
- ❏ Extra glasses/contacts and prescriptions
- ❏ Sunscreen and sunglasses
- ❏ Toiletries kit
- ❏ Soap
- ❏ Laundry soap
- ❏ Clothesline
- ❏ Small towel
- ❏ Sewing kit
- ❏ Travel information
- ❏ Necessary map(s)
- ❏ Address list (email and mailing addresses)
- ❏ Postcards and photos from home
- ❏ Notepad and pen
- ❏ Journal

If you plan to carry on your luggage, note that all liquids must be in three-ounce or smaller containers and fit within a single quart-size baggie. For details, see www.tsa.gov/travelers.

Hotel Reservation

To: _____   _____
        hotel   email or fax

From: _____   _____
          name   email or fax

Today's date: _____ / _____ / _____
                day   month   year

Dear Hotel _____ ,
Please make this reservation for me:

Name: _____

Total # of people: _____   # of rooms: _____   # of nights: _____

Arriving: _____ / _____ / _____   My time of arrival (24-hr clock): _____
            day   month   year   (I will telephone if I will be late)

Departing: _____ / _____ / _____
             day   month   year

Room(s): Single____   Double ____   Twin ____   Triple ____   Quad____

With: Toilet ____   Shower ____ Bath ____   Sink only____

Special needs: View____ Quiet____ Cheapest ____ Ground Floor____

Please email or fax confirmation of my reservation, along with the type of
room reserved and the price. Please also inform me of your cancellation
policy. After I hear from you, I will quickly send my credit-card information
as a deposit to hold the room. Thank you.

_____
Name

_____
Address

_____
City   **State**   **Zip Code**   **Country**

*Before hoteliers can make your reservation, they want to know the informa-
tion listed above. You can use this form as the basis for your email, or you can
photocopy this page, fill in the information, and send it as a fax (also available
online at www.ricksteves.com/reservation).*

British–Yankee Vocabulary

For a longer list, plus a dry-witted primer on British culture, see *The Septic's Companion* (Chris Rae).

advert–advertisement

afters–dessert

anticlockwise–counter-clockwise

Antipodean–an Australian or New Zealander

aubergine–eggplant

banger–sausage

bangers and mash–sausage and mashed potatoes

Bank Holiday–legal holiday

bap–small roll

bespoke–custom-made

billion–a thousand of our billions (a million million)

biro–ballpoint pen

biscuit–cookie

black pudding–sausage made from dried blood

bloody–damn

blow off–fart

bobby–policeman ("the Bill" is more common)

Bob's your uncle–there you go (with a shrug), naturally

boffin–nerd, geek

bollocks–testicles; also used as an exclamation of strong disbelief or disagreement

bolshy–argumentative

bomb–success or failure

bonnet–car hood

boot–car trunk

braces–suspenders

bridle way–path for walkers, bikers, and horse riders

brilliant–cool

brolly–umbrella

bubble and squeak–cabbage and potatoes fried together

bum–butt

candy floss–cotton candy

caravan–trailer

car-boot sale–temporary flea market, often for charity

car park–parking lot

cashpoint–ATM

casualty–emergency room

cat's eyes–road reflectors

ceilidh (KAY-lee)–informal evening of song and folk fun (Scottish and Irish)

cheap and cheerful–budget but adequate

cheap and nasty–cheap and bad quality

cheers–good-bye or thanks; also a toast

chemist–pharmacist

chicory–endive

chippie–fish-and-chips shop; carpenter

chips–French fries

chock-a-block–jam-packed

chuffed–pleased

cider–alcoholic apple cider

clearway–road where you can't stop

coach–long-distance bus

concession–discounted admission

concs (pronounced "conks")–short for "concession"

cos–romaine lettuce

cotton buds–Q-tips

courgette–zucchini

craic (pronounced "crack")–fun, good conversation (Irish/Scottish and spreading to England)

crisps–potato chips

cuppa–cup of tea

dear–expensive

dicey–iffy, risky

digestives–round graham cookies

dinner–lunch or dinner
diversion–detour
donkey's years–ages, long time
draughts–checkers
draw–marijuana
dual carriageway–divided highway (four lanes)
dummy–pacifier
elevenses–coffee-and-biscuits break before lunch
elvers–baby eels
face flannel–washcloth
fag–cigarette
fagged–exhausted
faggot–sausage
fancy–to like, to be attracted to (a person)
fanny–vagina
fell–hill or high plain (Lake District)
first floor–second floor
fizzy drink–pop or soda
flutter–a bet
football–soccer
force–waterfall (Lake District)
fortnight–two weeks (shortened from "fourteen nights")
fringe–hair bangs
Frogs–French people
fruit machine–slot machine
full Monty–whole shebang, everything
gallery–balcony
gammon–ham
gangway–aisle
gaol–jail (same pronunciation)
gateau (or gateaux)–cake
gear lever–stick shift
geezer–"dude"
give way–yield
glen–narrow valley (Scotland)
goods wagon–freight truck
green fingers–green thumbs
half eight–8:30 (not 7:30)
heath–open treeless land

hen night–bachelorette party
holiday–vacation
homely–homey or cozy
hoover–vacuum cleaner
ice lolly–Popsicle
interval–intermission
ironmonger–hardware store
ish–more or less
jacket potato–baked potato
jelly–Jell-O
Joe Bloggs–John Q. Public
jumble sale–rummage sale
jumper–sweater
just a tick–just a second
kipper–smoked herring
knackered–exhausted (Cockney: cream crackered)
knickers–ladies' panties
knocking shop–brothel
knock up–wake up or visit (old-fashioned)
ladybird–ladybug
lady fingers–flat, spongy cookie
lady's finger–okra
lager–light, fizzy beer
left luggage–baggage check
lemonade–lemon-lime pop like 7-Up, fizzy
lemon squash–lemonade, not fizzy
let–rent
licenced–restaurant authorized to sell alcohol
lift–elevator
listed–protected historic building
loo–toilet or bathroom
lorry–truck
mac–mackintosh raincoat
mangetout–snow peas
marrow–summer squash
mate–buddy (boy or girl)
mean–stingy
mental–wild, memorable

mews–former stables converted to two-story rowhouses

mobile (MOH-bile)–cell phone

moggie–cat

motorway–freeway

naff–tacky or trashy

nappy–diaper

natter–talk on and on

neep–Scottish for turnip

newsagent–corner store

nought–zero

noughts & crosses–tic-tac-toe

off-licence–liquor store

on offer–for sale

panto, pantomime–fairy-tale play performed at Christmas (silly but fun)

pants–underwear, briefs

pasty (PASS-tee)–crusted savory (usually meat) pie from Cornwall

pavement–sidewalk

pear-shaped–messed up, gone wrong

petrol–gas

pillar box–mailbox

pissed (rude), **paralytic, bevvied, wellied, popped up, merry, trollied, ratted, rat-arsed, pissed as a newt**–drunk

pitch–playing field

plaster–Band-Aid

publican–pub owner

public school–private "prep" school (e.g., Eton)

pudding–dessert in general

pull, to be on the–on the prowl

punter–customer, especially in gambling

put a sock in it–shut up

queue–line

queue up–line up

quid–pound (£1)

randy–horny

rasher–slice of bacon

redundant, made–laid off

Remembrance Day–Veterans' Day

return ticket–round trip

revising; doing revisions–studying for exams

ring up–call (telephone)

roundabout–traffic circle

rubber–eraser

rubbish–bad

sausage roll–sausage wrapped in a flaky pastry

Scotch egg–hard-boiled egg wrapped in sausage meat

self-catering–accommodation with kitchen

Sellotape–Scotch tape

services–freeway rest area

serviette–napkin

setee–couch

shag–intercourse (cruder than in the US)

shandy–lager and 7-Up

silencer–car muffler

single ticket–one-way ticket

skip–Dumpster

sleeping policeman–speed bumps

smalls–underwear

snogging–kissing, making out

sod–mildly offensive insult

sod it, sod off–screw it, screw off

soda–soda water (not pop)

solicitor–lawyer

spanner–wrench

spend a penny–urinate

stag night–bachelor party

starkers–buck naked

starters–appetizers

state school–public school

sticking plaster–Band-Aid

sticky tape–Scotch tape

stone–14 pounds (weight)

stroppy–bad-tempered

subway–underground walkway

suet–fat from animal rendering (sometimes used in cooking)

sultanas–golden raisins

surgical spirit–rubbing alcohol

suspenders–garters

suss out–figure out

swede–rutabaga

ta–thank you

take the mickey/take the piss–tease

tatty–worn out or tacky

taxi rank–taxi stand

telly–TV

tenement–stone apartment house (not necessarily a slum)

tenner–£10 bill

theatre–live stage

tick–a check mark

tight as a fish's bum–cheapskate (watertight)

tights–panty hose

tin–can

tip–public dump

tipper lorry–dump truck

top hole–first rate

top up–refill (a drink, mobile-phone credit, petrol tank, etc.)

torch–flashlight

towel, press-on–panty liner

towpath–path along a river

trainers–sneakers

Tube–subway

twee–quaint, cutesy

twitcher–bird-watcher

Underground–subway

verge–grassy edge of road

verger–church official

way out–exit

wee (adj)–small (Scottish)

wee (verb)–urinate

Wellingtons, wellies–rubber boots

whacked–exhausted

whinge (rhymes with hinge)–whine

wind up–tease, irritate

witter on–gab and gab

yob–hooligan

zebra crossing–crosswalk

zed–the letter Z

INDEX

INDEX

MAP INDEX

Audio Europe

Free mobile app (and podcast)

With the **Rick Steves Audio Europe** app, your iPhone or smartphone becomes a powerful travel tool.

This exciting app organizes Rick's entire audio library by country—giving you a playlist of all his audio walking tours, radio interviews, and travel tips for wherever you're going in Europe.

Let the experts Rick interviews enrich your understanding. Let Rick's self-guided tours amplify your guidebook. With Rick in your ear, Europe gets even better.

Thanks Facebook fans for submitting photos while on location! From top: John Kuijper in Florence, Brenda Mamer with her mother in Rome, Angel Capobianco in London, and Alyssa Passey with her friend in Paris.

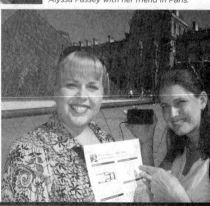

Find out more at ricksteves.com/audioeurope

Free information and great gear

▸ Plan Your Trip

Browse thousands of articles and a wealth of money-saving tips for planning your dream trip. You'll find up-to-date information on Europe's best destinations, packing smart, getting around, finding rooms, staying healthy, avoiding scams and more.

▸ Eurail Passes

Find out, step-by-step, if a railpass makes sense for your trip—and how to avoid buying more than you need. Get a bunch of free extras!

▸ Graffiti Wall & Travelers' Helpline

Learn, ask, share—our online community of savvy travelers is a great resource for first-time travelers to Europe, as well as seasoned pros.

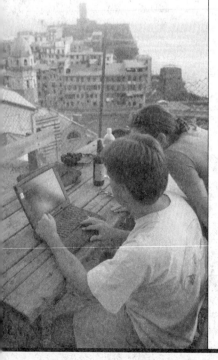

rn your travel dreams into affordable reality

Free Audio Tours & ravel Newsletter

et your nose out of this guide ok and focus on what you'll be eing with Rick's free audio tours the greatest sights in Paris, ondon, Rome, Florence and enice.

Subscribe to our free Travel ews e-newsletter, and get onthly articles from Rick on hat's happening in Europe.

▶ Great Gear from Rick's Travel Store

Pack light and right—on a budget—with Rick's custom-designed carry-on bags, roll-aboards, day packs, travel accessories, guidebooks, journals, maps and DVDs of his TV shows.

130 Fourth Avenue North, PO Box 2009 • Edmonds, WA 98020 USA
Phone: (425) 771-8303 • Fax: (425) 771-0833 • www.ricksteves.com

Rick Steves

EUROPE GUIDES

Best of Europe
Eastern Europe
Europe Through the Back Door

COUNTRY GUIDES

Croatia & Slovenia
England
France
Germany
Great Britain
Ireland
Italy
Portugal
Scandinavia
Spain
Switzerland

CITY & REGIONAL GUIDES

Amsterdam, Bruges & Brussels
Budapest
Florence & Tuscany
Greece: Athens & the Peloponnese
Istanbul
London
Paris
Prague & the Czech Republic
Provence & the French Riviera
Rome
Venice
Vienna, Salzburg & Tirol

SNAPSHOT GUIDES

Barcelona
Berlin
Bruges & Brussels
Copenhagen & the Best of
    Denmark
Dublin
Dubrovnik
Hill Towns of Central Italy
Italy's Cinque Terre
Krakow, Warsaw & Gdansk
Lisbon
Madrid & Toledo
Munich, Bavaria & Salzburg
Naples & the Amalfi Coast
Northern Ireland
Norway
Scotland
Sevilla, Granada & Southern Spain
Stockholm

POCKET GUIDES

London
Paris
Rome

TRAVEL CULTURE

Europe 101
European Christmas
Postcards from Europe
Travel as a Political Act

Rick Steves guidebooks are published by Avalon Travel,
a member of the Perseus Books Group.

NOW AVAILABLE: eBOOKS, APPS, DVDS, & BLU-RAY

eBOOKS

Most guides available as eBooks
from Amazon, Barnes & Noble,
Borders, Apple iBook and Sony
eReader, beginning January 2011

RICK STEVES' EUROPE DVDs

Austria & the Alps
Eastern Europe, Israel & Egypt
England & Wales
European Travel Skills & Specials
France
Germany, Benelux & More
Greece & Turkey
Iran
Ireland & Scotland
Italy's Cities
Italy's Countryside
Rick Steves' European Christmas
Scandinavia
Spain & Portugal

BLU-RAY

Celtic Charms
Eastern Europe Favorites
European Christmas
Italy Through the Back Door
Surprising Cities of Europe

PHRASE BOOKS & DICTIONARIES

French
French, Italian & German
German
Italian
Portuguese
Spanish

JOURNALS

Rick Steves' Pocket Travel Journal
Rick Steves' Travel Journal

APPS

Rick Steves' Ancient Rome Tour
Rick Steves' Historic Paris Walk
Rick Steves' Louvre Tour
Rick Steves' Orsay Museum Tour
Rick Steves' St. Peter's Basilica Tour
Rick Steves' Versailles

PLANNING MAPS

Britain, Ireland & London
Europe
France & Paris
Germany, Austria & Switzerland
Ireland
Italy
Spain & Portugal

Credits

Researchers
To help update this book, Rick relied on...

Lauren Mills

Lauren, a map editor and in-house search engine at Rick Steves, was an ardent Anglophile even before bringing home her British husband as a souvenir. They live in Seattle with their cat Annabel.

Cameron Hewitt

Cameron writes and edits guidebooks for Rick Steves, specializing in Eastern Europe. For this book, he spent a week swinging through the urban jungle of London, studied up on England's great university towns, and overdosed on quaint in the Cotswolds. When he's not traveling, Cameron lives in Seattle with his wife Shawna.

Cathy McDonald

Cathy, an editor and researcher for Rick Steves, enjoys England's natural history and how it affects its people. She lives in Seattle, where she has written about the Pacific Northwest for more than 15 years as a free-lancer for *The Seattle Times*.

Contributor
Gene Openshaw

Gene is the co-author of seven Rick Steves books. For this book, he wrote material on Europe's art, history, and contemporary culture. When not traveling, Gene enjoys composing music, recovering from his 1973 trip to Europe with Rick, and living everyday life with his daughter.

Images

Location	Photographer
Front color matter: British Museum	Rick Steves
Front color matter: York Minster	Rick Steves
Introduction: Whitby	Cameron Hewitt
England: Salisbury Cathedral	Cameron Hewitt
London: Houses of Parliament	Rick Steves
Greenwich, Windsor, and Cambridge: Windsor's Changing of the Guard	Lauren Mills
Canterbury: Canterbury	Sarah Murdoch
Dover: White Cliffs of Dover	David C. Hoerlein
Brighton: Brighton Pier	Sarah Murdoch
Portsmouth: View from the Spinnaker Tower	Cameron Hewitt
Dartmoor: Dartmoor Ponies	Cameron Hewitt
Cornwall: Mousehole	Sarah Murdoch
Bath: Pulteney Bridge	Lauren Mills
Near Bath: Avebury Stone Circle	David C. Hoerlein
Oxford: Spires of Old Souls	Melanie Jeschke
The Cotswolds: Typical Cotswold Scene	Dominic Bonuccelli
Stratford-Upon-Avon: Anne Hathaway's Cottage	Rick Steves
Ironbridge Gorge: The Iron Bridge	Lauren Mills
Blackpool and Liverpool: Blackpool	Rick Steves
Lake District: Derwentwater	Rick Steves
York: York Minster	Rick Steves
North Yorkshire: Whitby Abbey	Cameron Hewitt
Durham and Northeast England: Durham Cathedral	David C. Hoerlein

Acknowledgments

Thanks to Roy and Jodi Nicholls for their research help, to Sarah Murdoch for writing the original version of the southern England chapters, to Melanie Jeschke for the original version of the Oxford chapter, and to friends listed in this book, who put the "Great" in Great Britain.

Rick Steves' Guidebook Series

Country Guides

Rick Steves' Best of Europe
Rick Steves' Croatia &
   Slovenia
Rick Steves' Eastern Europe
Rick Steves' England
Rick Steves' France
Rick Steves' Germany

Rick Steves' Great Britain
Rick Steves' Ireland
Rick Steves' Italy
Rick Steves' Portugal
Rick Steves' Scandinavia
Rick Steves' Spain
Rick Steves' Switzerland

City and Regional Guides

Rick Steves' Amsterdam,
   Bruges & Brussels
Rick Steves' Athens &
   the Peloponnese
Rick Steves' Budapest
Rick Steves' Florence &
   Tuscany
Rick Steves' Istanbul
Rick Steves' London

Rick Steves' Paris
Rick Steves' Prague &
   the Czech Republic
Rick Steves' Provence &
   the French Riviera
Rick Steves' Rome
Rick Steves' Venice
Rick Steves' Vienna,
   Salzburg & Tirol

Rick Steves' Phrase Books

French
French/Italian/German
German
Italian
Portuguese
Spanish

Snapshot Guides

Excerpted chapters from country guides, such as *Rick Steves' Snapshot Barcelona, Rick Steves' Snapshot Scotland,* and *Rick Steves' Snapshot Hill Towns of Central Italy.*

Pocket Guides (new in 2011)

Condensed, pocket-size, full-color guides to Europe's top cities: Paris, London, and Rome.

Other Books

Rick Steves' Europe 101: History and Art for the Traveler
Rick Steves' Europe Through the Back Door
Rick Steves' European Christmas
Rick Steves' Postcards from Europe
Rick Steves' Travel as a Political Act

Avalon Travel
a member of the Perseus Books Group
1700 Fourth Street
Berkeley, CA 94710

Text © 2011 by Rick Steves
Portions of this book appeared in *Rick Steves' Great Britain* © 2010, 2009, 2008, 2007,
2006, 2005, 2004, 2003, 2002, 2001
Maps © 2011 by Europe Through the Back Door. All rights reserved.

Printed in the U.S.A. by Worzalla
First printing December 2010

ISBN 978-1-59880-666-3
ISSN 1930-4617

For the latest on Rick's lectures, guidebooks, tours, public radio show, and public television
series, contact Europe Through the Back Door, Box 2009, Edmonds, WA 98020, 425/771-
8303, fax 425/771-0833, www.ricksteves.com, rick@ricksteves.com.

Europe Through the Back Door Reviewing Editors: Cameron Hewitt, Jennifer Madison
 Davis
ETBD Editors: Cathy Lu, Tom Griffin, Cathy McDonald, Gretchen Strauch, Sarah
 McCormic
ETBD Managing Editor: Risa Laib
Research Assistance: Lauren Mills, Cameron Hewitt, Cathy McDonald
Avalon Travel Senior Editor and Series Manager: Madhu Prasher
Avalon Travel Project Editor: Kelly Lydick
Copy Editor: Naomi Adler-Dancis
Proofreader: Denise Silva
Indexer: Laura Welcome
Production and Layout: McGuire Barber Design
Cover Design: Kimberly Glyder Design
Graphic Content Director: Laura VanDeventer
Maps and Graphics: David C. Hoerlein, Laura VanDeventer, Brice Ticen, Lauren Mills,
 Barb Geisler, Pat O'Connor, Mike Morgenfeld
Front Matter Color Photos: British Museum, London © Rick Steves; York Minster, York
 © Rick Steves; London Eye © Dominic Bonuccelli; Bibury © Lauren Mills; Beachy
 Head © Cameron Hewitt; London Guards © Dominic Bonuccelli; Castlerigg © Rick
 Steves
Front Cover Photo: Dartmoor Ponies on Dartmoor © Penny Tweediel/Alamy
Additional Photography: Rick Steves, Cameron Hewitt, Sarah Murdoch, Gene
 Openshaw, Lauren Mills, Rich Earl, Bruce VanDeventer, Melanie Jeschke, David C.
 Hoerlein, Jennifer Hauseman, Darbi Macy, Patrick Luscri